Land Law

Visit the Land Law, eighth edition Companion Website at
www.mylawchamber.co.uk/chappelle to find valuable **student** learning material
including:

- Exam-style questions and answer guidance to independently test your ability
  to apply knowledge
- Links to relevant sites on the web
- An online glossary with definitions of key terms
- Regular updates on major legal changes affecting the book

Case Navigator

Visit www.pearsoned.co.uk/casenavigator to find unique
online support to help improve your case reading and
analysis skills. This resource can also be used as an
effective seminar preparation tool.

Please note that access to Case Navigator is free but you
must register with us for access. Full registration
instructions are provided at www.pearsoned.co.uk/casenavigator.

Case Navigator provides:

- **Short introductions** to a selection of core cases in Land Law, providing guidance on what to look out for while reading cases.
- **Direct deep links** to the core cases in Land Law.
- **Questions** to test knowledge and understanding. Answer guidance is provided
  after the test has been completed.
- **Summaries** outlining and contextualising the cases, pointing you towards
  further reading so that you are fully prepared for seminars and discussions.

For more information about Case Navigator please contact your local Pearson
Education sales representative or visit www.pearsoned.co.uk/casenavigator

Navigator is only available to those who
s Butterworths online. The Publishers are
igator fully available from early Summer 2007.

Eighth Edition

Land Law

DIANE CHAPPELLE

Senior Lecturer in Law
Liverpool John Moores University

PEARSON
Longman

Harlow, England • London • New York • Boston • San Francisco • Toronto • Sydney • Singapore • Hong Kong
Tokyo • Seoul • Taipei • New Delhi • Cape Town • Madrid • Mexico City • Amsterdam • Munich • Paris • Milan

Pearson Education Limited
Edinburgh Gate
Harlow
Essex CM20 2JE
England

and Associated Companies throughout the world

Visit us on the World Wide Web at:
www.pearsoned.co.uk

First published 1992
Second edition published 1995
Third edition published 1997
Fourth edition published 1999
Fifth edition published 2001
Sixth edition published 2004
Seventh edition published 2006
Eighth edition published 2008

ISBN 978-1-4058-5825-0

British Library Cataloguing-in-Publication Data
A catalogue record for this book is available from the British Library

10 9 8 7 6 5 4 3 2 1
11 10 09 08

Typeset in 9.5/12.5 pt Stone Serif by 3
Printed by Ashford Colour Press Ltd., Gosport

The publisher's policy is to use paper manufactured from sustainable forests.

For Tim

Brief contents

Contents

Part 1
Let's start at the very beginning – laying the foundations

9 Commonhold

Part 3
Interests in land - *The buyer beware*

10 Introduction to interests in land

11 Mortgages

Supporting resources

Visit www.mylawchamber.co.uk/chappelle to find valuable online resources
Companion Website for students

- Exam-style questions and answer guidance to independently test your ability to apply knowledge
- Links to relevant sites on the web
- An online glossary with definitions of key terms
- Regular updates on major legal changes affecting the book

For more information please contact your local Pearson Education sales representative or visit www.mylawchamber.co.uk/chappelle

Guided tour

Wayling v Jones (1995) 69 P&CR 170

In *Wayling* the parties had lived together in a homosexual relationship for 16 years until Jones died. Jones had owned a succession of businesses, the first being a café which Wayling, who was a qualified chef, helped to run. Jones promised to leave the property to Wayling and did in fact make a will in which he left him a house, a café and a flat. A couple of years later, Jones sold the flat and the café and bought a hotel in Aberystwyth. Again, Wayling helped Jones to run the business and also acted as his chauffeur. He was paid what amounted to pocket money and living expenses. Jones repeated his promise of leaving his property to Wayling and made a new will in which he left him a car and the hotel. Three years later the hotel was sold and two years after that Jones bought another in Barmouth. Again, Wayling helped, on the same terms as before. At one point Wayling did suggest to Jones that his work deserved more money, to which Jones replied, 'it'll all be yours one day', and promised to change his will, leaving the Barmouth Hotel to him. Jones never did change his will and when he died in 1987 all that Wayling got was a car worth £375 and some worthless furniture. Wayling's claim against Jones' estate failed at first instance, but the Court of Appeal found for him. Balcombe LJ stated that although there must be a sufficient link between the promises and the detriment, the promises do not have to be the sole inducement for the detriment - a point already well established. However, he went on to deal with what the judge at first instance had considered a fatal response to Wayling in cross-examination, where he had said that if Jones, having made the promise, had told him he did not intend to keep it, Wayling would have left. Had no promise been made, again, he would have left. However, given that the promise had been made, he, Wayling, would have acted very differently if he had known it was not going to be kept. In Balcombe LJ's view this was sufficient to prevent the defendant from showing that Wayling had not relied upon the promise.

Detriment

'There is no doubt that for proprietary estoppel to arise the person claiming must have incurred expenditure or otherwise have prejudiced himself or acted to his detriment' - Dunn LJ in *Greasley v Cooke*. The detriment may be the expenditure of money, but is not confined to it. However, as the Court of Appeal of Australia explained in *Territory Insurance Office v Adlington* [1993] ALMD 1475, although pecuniary loss is not necessary, the detriment must be material and real. It was also stated that the time for considering whether there has been any real detriment is the moment when the promisor or representor proposes to go back on his word.

However, as Robert Walker LJ emphasised in *Gillet v Holt*, the quality of the relevant assurances could influence the issue of reliance which is often intertwined with detriment. Detriment itself is not a narrow or technical concept, and it need not consist of the expenditure of money or other quantifiable financial detriment, provided that it is something substantial. It has to be approached as part of a broad enquiry as to whether repudiation of an assurance was or was not unconscionable in all the circumstances.

Thus, the detriment may consist of the giving up of one's job and going to live nearer to the promisor - *Jones v Jones* [1977] 1 WLR 438; by cohabiting with the owner's son and nursing his daughter - *Greasley v Cooke*; by relying upon the promise that 'the house is yours' - *Pascoe v Turner*; or by selling off part of your land without being able to reach land which you have retained except over the promisor's

Case Summaries - highlight the facts and key legal principles of essential cases that you need to be aware of in your study of Land Law

Chapter summaries – Chapter summaries - located at the end of each chapter, chapter summaries draw together the key points that you should be aware of following your reading, and provide a useful checklist for revision.

fundamental principle that equity is concerned to prevent unconscionable conduct permeates all the elements of the doctrine. In the end the court must look at the matter in the round'. Thus, said Walker LJ, a broad inquiry must be conducted as to whether, in all the circumstances, what was being sought to be done by the person having the legal rights was unconscionable. The importance of the doctrine of proprietary estoppel in modern land law can hardly be overstated. It can provide a 'right' or a 'remedy' where resulting and constructive trust principles will not; it has enabled a licence to evolve as a proprietary right (as we have already seen); it provides a possible 'replacement' for the doctrine of part performance in regard to contracts.

How to protect them

Ensuring the interest is binding on third parties

In unregistered land, rights by way of estoppel are protected by the doctrine of notice (see Chapter 3, Residual interests).

In registered land, the Land Registration Act 2002, s 116 confirms that, in registered land, an equity arising by estoppel is a proprietary right, capable of protection by entry of a notice. Alternatively, where the promise is in actual occupation of the land, his interest will automatically bind purchasers, without the need for registration, as an overriding interest (providing no enquiry was made) - LRA 2002, Sched 3, para 2.

Summary

FORMAL ACQUISITION
Here we looked at:

- the statutory requirements for a valid contract for the creation or disposition of legal interests in land;
- the statutory requirements for valid deeds for the creation of interests in land and for conveyances/transfers thereof;
- the advent of electronic conveyancing;
- the statutory requirements for the creation or disposition of equitable interests in land.

INFORMAL ACQUISITION
We considered the following:

ADVERSE POSSESSION

- the nature and characteristics of adverse possession – possession, which must be adverse; *animus possidendi*; the time period and the running of time; the effect of not bringing an action; the nature of the title acquired; adverse possession of leasehold title;

References

Cooke, E, 'Cohabitants, Common Intention and Contributions (Again)' [2005] Conv 555.
Dixon, M, 'A Classic of our Time: Co-ownership and its Consequences' [2006] Conv 577.
Gray, K. and Gray S.F., *Elements of Land Law*, 4th edition, Oxford University Press, 2005.
Gray, K, *Elements of Land Law*, 2nd edition, London: Butterworths, 1993.
Gray, K.J., and Symes, P.D., *Real Property and Real People*, London: Butterworths, 1981.
Law Commission, *Sharing Homes* (Cm 5666) (Law Com No 278, July 2002).
Oakley, J.A., *Megarry's Manual of the Law of Real Property*, 8th edition, London: Sweet and Maxwell, 2002.
O'Hagan, P, 'Indirect Contributions to the Purchase of Property' [1991] 56 MLR 224.
Pascoe, S, 'Section 15 of the Trusts of Land and Appointment of Trustees Act 1996: A Change in the Law?' [2000] Conv 315.
Ruoff and Roper, *The Law and Practice of Registered Conveyancing*, London: Sweet and Maxwell, 1991.

Further reading

Trusts of Land and Appointment of Trustees Act 1996, s 15

Pascoe, S, 'Section 15 of the Trusts of Land and Appointment of Trustees Act 1996: A Change in the Law?' [2000] Conv 315.
Probert, R, 'Creditors and section 15 of the Trusts of Land and Appointment of Trustees Act 1996: first among equals?' [2002] Conv 61.

The right to occupy

Barnsley, D G, 'Co-owners' Rights to Occupy Trust Land' [1998] 57 CLJ 123.
Ross Martyn, J G, 'Co-owners And Their Entitlement To Occupy Their Land . . .' [1997] Conv 254.

Resulting and constructive trusts

Dixon, M, 'Resulting and Constructive Trusts: The Mist Descends and Rises' [2005] Conv 79.

Express common intention

Dixon, M, 'A Classic of our Time: Co-ownership and its Consequences' [2006] Conv 577.
Lawson, A, 'The things we do for love: detrimental reliance in the family home' (1996) *Legal Studies* 218.

Implied common intention

Bottomley, A, 'Women and Trust(s): Portraying the Family in the Gallery', *Land Law Themes and Perspectives*, eds Susan Bright and John Dewar, Oxford University Press, 1998 (p 206).
Cooke, E, 'Cohabitants, Common Intention and Contributions list (Again)' [2005] Conv 555.
Dewar, J, 'Land, Law and the Family Home', *Land Law Themes and Perspectives*, eds Susan Bright and John Dewar, Oxford University Press, 1998 (p 327).

Further Reading - at the end of each chapter, use the further reading section to delve deeper into the topic, and read those articles which will help you to gain higher marks in both exams and assessments!

Glossary

Land law has a language of its own which frequently creates difficulty for students. Not only are many of the expressions technical, but also even apparently familiar words are given a different meaning. Obviously, if you cannot understand its language, you cannot hope to understand land law. Therefore, this glossary aims to explain the meanings of words and phrases which commonly arise in land law. As well as the technical terms appearing in this book, those which you may encounter in your lectures and in your other reading are also included. Although the most frequently used expressions are explained here, this glossary does not provide an exhaustive list and you should, whenever you come across a term which is not contained in it, immediately ascertain its meaning, noting also the context in which it is used, and add it to the glossary.

abatement the removal of an obstruction to the exercise of an easement by the dominant tenement owner.

absolute an interest which is neither conditional nor determinable by some specified event.

abstract of title a summary of all matters which affect the title offered by the vendor, including the various dispositions, eg sales of the property and deaths of interest holders.

acquiescence failure to take steps to prevent some act, such as the exercise of a right which has not been granted, or an obstruction to the exercise of a right which is in the course of being acquired.

administrators persons appointed by the court to administer the estate of a person who died intestate, ie without leaving a will.

adverse possession a means by which an adverse possessor can acquire the title to land, thus dispossessing the previous 'paper-title' owner.

alienation the transfer of interests in property from one owner to another. This can be by way of sale, gift or some other transaction.

animus possidendi the intention to (adversely) possess the land of another.

annexation the attaching of the benefit of a restrictive covenant to the dominant tenement so that it will run with the land.

ante-nuptial prior to marriage.

appendant a right which is attached to the land by operation of law.

appurtenant (1) a right which is attached to the land by agreement between the parties. (2) A profit *à prendre* which benefits a piece of land, and not merely the owner of it.

assent the means by which personal representatives vest the deceased's property in those entitled under his will or intestacy. An assent need not be by deed.

476

Glossary - forgotten the meaning of a word? Turn to the glossary at the back of the book to remind yourself of its meaning and to revise key terminology before an exam.

Companion Website - sample exam-style questions and answer guidelines help you practice applying the law to practical scenarios, whilst web links point you to relevant sites where you can find out more about land law and an online glossary aids your understanding of complex legal terms. Regular updates allow you to stay up to date with all the latest developments in law.

Preface to eighth edition

I love land law. I have always loved it, from my early days in conveyancing to the 'real thing' in my LLB. After 20 years of trying to pass on my enthusiasm for this wonderful subject (and I have actually succeeded in a handful of cases!), I have seen many changes – in students, in conveyancing practice and in land law itself – but I remain as besotted as ever with this very special area of law and the teaching of it. I hope that comes across in this book and that I can inspire at least one more student!

With its lovely language – *cestui que trust, en ventre sa mere,* profits *a prendre* etc; its sources – equity, common law and statute; its rules and principles that seem like twisting country lanes, dual carriageways and motorways (with even a canal thrown in); its wonderful scenery – rivers, parks, gardens, fields; its buildings – barns, cottages, bungalows, houses, flats, office blocks, stately homes; its characters – spouses (including the spectral spouse!), civil partners, cohabitees, trustees and beneficiaries, landlords and tenants, lenders and borrowers, neighbours and local authorities – all in conflict with each other (for, as George Herbert said back in 1639, 'he that hath land, hath quarrels'), you'll not find another subject with so much breadth and depth, all of it evolving constantly so as to meet the current needs, both social and economic, of our ever changing society.

Don't believe anyone who tells you land law is boring and irrelevant – it is neither! Yet it is a challenge, but one well worth the effort (as Beverly Sills once remarked, 'there are no shortcuts to anywhere that's worth going to'). So, go on, start your journey here. Enjoy it and be prepared to become fascinated as you take to the skies on an aeroplane, travel along a canal, cross a railway line, drive across someone else's land and, finally, park your car – if land law allows!

Writing a Land Law book, especially one for students, is a challenge too. Luckily, I have had much help in my endeavours from the following: Zoe Botterill and Beth Rix at Pearson HQ for commissioning this 8th edition and steering it through its passage to publication; Heather Palomino for copyediting the manuscript and Jenny Kallin for editing it, both in such a short space of time. Then there are those who supported me on a personal level through what has been a difficult period – Susan George, who, as ever, was always there and knew exactly what was needed when I didn't; Lorie Charlesworth for dealing with those people whom I couldn't; all those who emailed, 'phoned, visited and had me to stay, reminding me of just how lucky I am to have so many true friends and, most of all, my wonderful son, Tim, without whom I would not have made it back from the brink. To all of these and to you for buying my book, a huge 'thank you'.

Di Chappelle
Liverpool
July 2007

List of journals

Journals

(with abbreviations where applicable)

Australian Legal Monthly Digest	ALMD
Cambridge Law Journal	CLJ
Conveyancer	Conv
Current Legal Problems	—
Family Law	FL
Gazette	Gaz
Law Notes	—
Law Quarterly Review	LQR
The Law Society's Gazette	Law Soc Gaz
Legal Action	—
The Legal Executive Journal	Legal Exec Jo
Legal Studies	—
Liverpool Law Review	—
Modern Law Review	MLR
New Law Journal	NLJ
Oxford Journal of Legal Studies	OJLS
Solicitor's Journal	Sol Jo
Student Law Review	—

Acknowledgements

We are grateful to the following for permission to reproduce copyright material:

Susan George for extracts from *Liverpool Park Estates* by Susan George, published by Liverpool University Press; Oxford University Press for extracts from *Elements of Land Law* by Gray, K, 2004; LexisNexis Butterworths for extracts from *Real Property and Real People* by Gray and Symes; Elizabeth Cooke for extracts from *The New Law of Land Registration 2003* by Elizabeth Cooke, published by Hart Publishing Limited; and Methuen Publishing Limited for an extract from *The Stately Homes of England* by Noël Coward © The Estate of Noël Coward.

In some instances we have been unable to trace owners of copyright material, and we would appreciate any information that would enable us to do so.

Table of cases

Table of statutes and statutory material

Statutory instruments

Table of EC legislation

PART 1

Let's start at the very beginning
Laying the foundations

1 The who, how, why and what of land law - *An introduction to this book and to the subject*

2 How can you acquire them? - *The rules, principles and formalities governing the acquisition of interests in land*

3 How can you protect them? - *Methods of protection afforded to all interests in land*

4 How can you lose them? - *Matters which may subsequently defeat an estate or interest*

1 The who, how, why and what of land law

An introduction to this book and to the subject

A About this book

With so many land law texts on the shelves of bookshops, you may well be wondering why you are being offered yet another.

It has to be said that many of the texts already on offer are excellent, but a view commonly held by students is that they were written for the lecturers and not for them. Indeed, some do seem to presuppose a level of understanding which is unlikely to exist unless – and even when – the subject has been studied.

This book has been written for you – the student – in an attempt to enable you to understand your lectures, and then, hopefully, land law.

Every lecturer accepts, sooner or later, that very few people will ever actually understand land law, and therefore even fewer enjoy it. Still, it is a 'core' subject and has to be passed, though, rather like the driving test, you always admire the person who not only passes, but does so with distinction, first time!

'What's it got to do with me?' This is a question students ask all the time in regard to land law, complaining that it has no relevance to their lives. In each chapter, in the section 'Who Cares?', I hope to show you that, more than any other area of law, land law affects every single one of us throughout our lives. After all, everyone has to live somewhere and, unless you are a recluse, you will have to live in close proximity to other people. As Susan George (2000) explains in the introduction to her book, *Liverpool Park Estates*:

> A recurring urge of human nature is a desire to have a stake in society and roots in a particular place, which in many cultures is manifested in a yearning to own immovable property, land or a house, or both – p 1.

Land is the most important commodity there is and in the United Kingdom it is something of a scarce resource. As Will Rogers, an American comedian, said, buy land now because no more of it is being made! Clearly, the more heavily populated the land (and in the UK 90 per cent of home owners live on less than 10 per cent of the land – source: BBC, 'Whose Britain Is It Anyway?', 10 January 2006), the greater the possibility for conflict between people over the various uses each wishes to make of it. Current government regulations specify a maximum of 14 houses per acre for building, making the average family house one-third smaller than a generation ago – (BBC 'Whose Britain'). Recent years have seen increasing protest at the use of 'greenbelt' land for building houses on: we need new houses for people to live in, but we do not want to lose the countryside. On the other hand, 'townies' moving into commutable rural areas can cause much discord by their objections to country ways. The United Kingdom is very heavily populated.

As we shall see, on one piece of land may live several people, and others, though they do not live on the land, may have rights over it. It is quite possible for someone who owns the title to the land to let others live there instead of himself: he may live there not knowing that others are also living on his land at the same time. The continual question is who is entitled to what and when? In deciding these matters the question is how can any entitlement come into being and continue not merely to exist but to defeat the claimed rights of others, especially of those who come to the land subsequently? Of course, being lawyers, in explaining how to come to your conclusion, you must always answer the question 'Why?' Thus, in order to solve the seemingly endless problems that can arise in relation to the land and people's use and enjoyment of it, a series of questions has to be asked.

We all know that Jack and Jill went up the hill to fetch a pail of water, but what we do not know is who owns the land from which they took the water. If it is not them, has the owner granted them any right over his land? Has he merely given them a personal permission? Are they trespassing? What if the owner sells the land to someone else? Must the new owner let Jack and Jill take the water? Before we can answer these questions, even more will have to be asked!

In Part I we shall be looking at fundamental issues which apply to all interests in land, but in Parts II and III each chapter will deal with a particular interest in land.

What's the Problem?
Putting land law into context

Under this heading (with which most chapters will begin) one or more examples of problems which can and do arise in connection with the matter or interest under discussion will be given, providing a context and showing how land and people's needs have been inseparable for centuries. We shall then proceed to answer a series of questions. These questions, and the order in which they are asked, give you the correct approach to dealing with legal problems.

Who cares?
The many and varied people who can be affected by the ownership of and dealings with interests in land

People's lives are complicated, their needs complex, their relationship with the land changing all the time. Thus, this is the first question to be asked, as it deals with all the people who may be affected by the existence of a particular interest in the land, and you may be surprised to realise just how many people may care about the same piece of land! This section is designed to show that land law is people law and just how important land is to people. The land in question may be only a small plot, but to most people their land is their most valuable asset. As Gerald O'Hara said to his daughter, Scarlett, in Margaret Mitchell's *Gone with the Wind*, 'Do you mean to tell me . . . the land doesn't mean anything to you? Why, land is the only thing in the world worth working for, worth fighting for, worth dying for, because it is the only thing that lasts.'

After you have studied each area fully, go back to this section and see if you can answer everyone's questions.

Courts in the United Kingdom have always taken the view that every bit of land is unique, irreplaceable, and, as Mr O'Hara said, it lasts – for ever. In the UK we cannot own the land itself, but there are different interests in land which we can own. The next question, then, is:

What are they?

Estates and interests in land

Students often say that part of the problem with land law is its preoccupation with history. To be fair, it is not land law itself which is so preoccupied but writers and teachers of it. As one who finds land law fascinating, I enjoy digging back into history for its roots and connections with the social and economic changes wrought over the centuries. However, I do appreciate that students wrestling with the complexities and intricacies of this difficult subject do not share my enthusiasm! Indeed, I believe it is quite possible to learn and understand land law as it applies today (which really means after 1925) with a limited knowledge of its history and in this book I shall endeavour to keep the historical aspect of land law to a minimum. Having said that, however, we must go back for a moment to 1066!

As everyone knows, 1066 was the year of the Battle of Hastings. As a result of his victory, William declared himself King and owner of all land. To this day all land belongs ultimately to the Crown. Thus, if a person dies intestate (without leaving a will) and with no relatives to inherit under the intestacy rules, his property goes back – *bona vacantia* – to the Crown (or Duchy of Lancaster or Duke of Cornwall, as appropriate). In fact, the property, or its value, goes to the Treasury but, glad though the Treasury is to receive such bounty, it does make strenuous efforts to trace any person who may have a valid claim to the property.

Example

An example was provided in an article in the *Daily Telegraph* (31 July 1991) regarding the estate of a widowed millionairess, Dorothea Allen. Mrs Allen died in 1965, she and her husband having had no children. Mrs Allen left no will and upon her death it was discovered that she had destroyed anything from which her origins could be traced – she had even mutilated her passport. She did, though, leave a fortune in the form of a house, its contents, jewellery, clothes and so on. Despite making enquiries in Britain, Europe and the United States of America, the Treasury could find no heir to this fortune and the Treasury received £1,000,000. However, the Treasury was not the only beneficiary for, as the article explained, 'The story spawned television documentaries and a confidence trick in Australia, New Zealand and South Africa. A bogus research company took money from people named Allen, promising them substantial reward in return for "one-off" fees.'

The Law Commission intends to begin a project on *bona vacantia* ('ownerless land') and the Royal Duchies before the end of 2007 – www.lawcom.gov.uk/feudal.htm

If, then, the Crown owns all the land, what, if anything, can anyone else own? The answer is one or more estates or interests in or over the land. This, of course, raises the question, 'What are estates and interests?' and we could find no better, nor more poetic, definition of an estate than that provided in *Walsingham*'s case in the sixteenth century where it was explained that:

> the land itself is one thing, and the estate in the land is another thing, for an estate in the land is a time in the land, or land for a time . . .

Thus, an estate in land has a fourth dimension beyond the purely physical – it can be divided into amounts of time. An estate owner can, in turn, grant lesser estates – lesser amounts of time – or interests to someone else. Interests are rights over someone else's land and, though they do not entitle you to occupy the land itself, they do entitle you to restrict the estate owner in his occupation and use of it. Therefore, an estate entitles the holder to the management and enjoyment of the land itself, whilst an interest entitles someone else to a specific right over that land which may reduce the estate owner's enjoyment of it. By way of example, a restrictive covenant can be granted by an estate owner to his neighbour, the terms of which may well prevent the estate owner building on his land, or using his land for any purpose other than a domestic dwelling.

Land law has a language of its own and it is essential to learn it in order to understand this subject. We have just come across two terms which must be distinguished from their ordinary, everyday meaning, and from each other. First, we now know that the word 'estate' in land law has a very particular meaning – it is not the same as a housing estate, for instance. It does not refer to an area of land, but to the time during which one can enjoy the land. Secondly, the word 'interest' has the meaning explained above, but it is also used as a generic term embracing all rights in land, that is, estates and interests. The context in which it is used will show its meaning. However, it is important to remember the wider meaning when an examination question asks you to discuss 'interests in land' – you must be sure to interpret the word correctly.

It is essential to appreciate that interests in land attach to the land itself and not to the owner thereof, just as barnacles attach to the hull of the ship and not to the captain! Thus, as the barnacles go wherever the ship goes regardless of who is steering, only being removed by being chiselled off in dry dock, so too do interests remain attached to the land regardless of who holds the legal estate in it unless and until they are extinguished. Thus, a purchaser will only take the land – or, rather, the legal estate in it – free of those interests which have been removed in the appropriate way. This introduces a third word which has a meaning much wider than in everyday use – 'purchaser'. The Law of Property Act 1925, s 205(1)(xxi), defines this as:

> a purchaser in good faith for valuable consideration and includes a lessee, mortgagee or other person who for valuable consideration acquires an interest in property . . . and where the context so requires 'purchaser' includes an intending purchaser . . .

'Purchaser' has the same meaning in the Law of Property (Miscellaneous Provisions) Act 1989, s 1(6) and in the Trusts of Land Act 1996, s 23(1).

For the purposes of the Settled Land Act 1925, s 117(1)(xxi):

> 'Purchaser' means a purchaser in good faith for value, and includes a lessee, mortgagee or other person who in good faith acquires an interest in settled land for value; and in reference to a legal estate includes a chargee by way of legal mortgage.

So far, then, 'purchaser' has more or less the same meaning in each Act. However, for the purposes of the Land Charges Act 1972, s 17(1):

> 'purchaser' means any person (including a mortgagee or lessee) who, for valuable consideration, takes any interest in land or in a charge on land.

Thus, the Land Charges Act does not require a purchaser to be bona fide. In *Midland Bank Trust Co Ltd* v *Green* [1981] AC 513 the respondents asked the court (the House of Lords) to imply a requirement of good faith into the definition. However, Lord Wilberforce would have none of it:

> All the Acts of 1925, and their precursors, were drafted with the utmost care, and their wording, certainly where this is apparently clear, has to be accorded firm respect … As to the requirement of 'good faith' … the expression … appears in the Law of Property Act 1925 definition of 'purchaser' … in the Settled Land Act 1925; in the Administration of Estates Act 1925 and in the Land Registration Act 1925 … So there is certainly some indication of an intention to carry the concept of 'good faith' into much of the 1925 code … So far as concerns the Land Charges Act 1925, the definition of 'purchaser' … does not mention 'good faith' at all. The expression 'good faith' appears nowhere in its antecedents … If canons of construction have any validity at all, they must lead to the conclusion that the omission in [the Land Charges Act] was deliberate.

In its Consultation Document, *Land Registration for the Twenty-First Century* (Law Com 254 (1998)), the Law Commission recommended that 'purchaser' should be defined to mean 'any person (including a mortgagee or lessee) who, for valuable consideration takes an interest in land or in a charge on land', 'valuable consideration' should be defined to mean 'money or money's worth, but should not include marriage or a nominal consideration of money'. A transfer for marriage consideration should take effect as a gift – whether registered or unregistered land. The Land Registration Act 2002, s 132 adopts the recommended definition of 'valuable consideration', but is silent in regard to 'purchaser'.

How can they exist?

Classification of interests

Land law is governed by equity, common law and statute. The interests in land may be legal or equitable: which it is will depend to a large extent upon certain statutory provisions.

This brings us to what is probably the single most important section of any of the property statutes. The section is s 1. The statute is the Law of Property Act 1925. (However, you must not think that this Act alone constitutes 'the 1925 legislation', for in fact the phrase incorporates five other statutes as well – the Settled Land Act, the Trustee Act, the Administration of Estates Act, the Land Registration Act and the Land Charges Act. The Land Registration Act 1925 has been repealed and replaced by the Land Registration Act 2002.)

Section 1 tells us how each of the interests in land can exist – whether as legal rights or equitable rights. The distinction is crucial because of the impact upon a purchaser of the land to which the interests relate.

Section 1(1) reduces the number of legal estates to two, so that after 1925 there are only two 'estates in land which are capable of subsisting or of being conveyed or created at law' – the fee simple absolute in possession and the term of years absolute. 'Legal estate' has the same meaning in the Land Registration Act 2002 (s 132); s 1(2) provides that there are only five 'interests or charges in or over land which are capable of subsisting or of being conveyed or created at law' – easements, rentcharges, profits *à prendre*, rights of entry, charge by way of legal mortgage ('and any other similar charge on land which is not created by an instrument'). Thus these are the only legal interests in land that can exist today. There can be no other estates at law, and no equitable estates at all.

It must be understood, however, that the two legal estates and the five legal interests are only '*capable of* subsisting or of being conveyed or created at law'. In order so to exist, the estate or interest must satisfy every aspect of its statutory definition; for example, a fee simple, though absolute, will only be legal if it is 'in possession'. Here is another word which has a special meaning in land law; indeed, it has more than one meaning. First, it means that the estate (or an interest) takes effect immediately, not in the future and not, therefore, subject to a prior interest.

Example

Thus, if the fee simple absolute in possession in a house is left by will (which will only take effect upon the death of the Testator or Testatrix - the person who made it) 'to Tim for life and then to his children absolutely'; Tim's interest is in possession because it comes first (his children's interest is 'in remainder').

The second meaning is provided by the defining section of the Law of Property Act 1925 – section 205(1): 'Possession' includes receipt of rent and profits or the right to receive the same, if any' – s 205(1)(xix). Thus it is far wider than mere occupation.

In addition, the estate or interest, though 'capable' of being legal, will only be so if it is created or conveyed in the appropriate manner. The legal interests must, in addition, equate in time to one or other of the two legal estates, that is, they must be either perpetual or for a definite term. They may also need to be protected by registration to become legal.

Section 1(3) confirms that 'all other estates, interests, and charges in or over land take effect as equitable interests'. Therefore, any estate, interest or charge which does not appear within s 1(1) or s 1(2), or which fails to satisfy the relevant requirements of time and form must, by definition, be only equitable. Thus, all the estates which existed prior to 1926 and which do not fall within s 1(1) are now equitable interests. As Gray (1993) explains:

[t]he rights referred to in section 1(1) and (2) are alike in that they are all potentially *legal* in character. The distinction between estates, interests and charges consists in the fact that an 'estate' is a right in land owned or occupied by oneself, while an 'interest' or 'charge' tends to be a right acquired in or over property owned or occupied by someone else – p 68.

Although a legal right is a right '*in rem*', that is, a right in the thing itself, and an equitable right is a right '*in personam*' – against the person – a right in land which is capable of binding a third party is a 'proprietary', and not merely a personal right. **Therefore, a right or interest is only proprietary if it can bind a third party**. It is crucial to appreciate that an interest does not bind the third party because it is proprietary: it is proprietary *because* it binds.

Whether or not each interest is capable of binding, or indeed does bind a third party, depends upon its nature and the relevant protection afforded it by statute, at law and in equity. This in turn depends upon whether the title to the land in question is registered or not. These matters will be dealt with shortly, but it is perhaps useful to mention here that land in England and Wales can fall within one of two systems – the 'registered land' system or the 'unregistered land' system. (In fact it is the title to the land which is or is not registered.) The distinction between the two is relevant to conveyancing practices and the methods of protection for the various interests in or over the land and, in registered land, the 'creation' of interests.

As from December 1990 all land in England and Wales became compulsorily registrable 'upon sale', that is, title to it must be registered at HM Land Registry. The Land Registration Act 1997, s 1 extended the requirement further, so that it is not only dealings 'for sale' which must be registered, but also any disposition by way of gift and any made by personal representatives in administering a dead person's estate. A court order may also be made. Even if land is unregistered land and the owner is not actually transferring his estate in it, if the owner grants over it a first legal mortgage protected by the deposit of the title deeds, his legal estate will become registrable. Although these changes are intended to quicken the pace of registration of title to land in England and Wales, it will be many years before some titles are registered. Indeed, unless and until this ceases to be so, there will never be a time when title to all land will be registered because large areas are never likely to be sold, given away, left by will or mortgaged, for example Crown lands, church lands, old university colleges, land held by the National Trust, English Heritage, Cadw and so on. (Eventually, no doubt, all titles still unregistered will be required to be registered. Indeed, the Law Commission foresees that its proposals in the afore-mentioned *Land Registration in the Twenty-First Century* (Law Com 254 (1998)) will make registration of title so attractive and the benefits so obvious that most title owners will want to register voluntarily.)

How can you hold them?

The various ways in which the legal estates can be held

This question arises only in connection with the legal estates: the fee simple absolute in possession and the term of years absolute (the freehold and the leasehold estates). How they can be held brings us to the greatest invention of equity: the trust. The trust, as we shall see in Part II, enables title to land to be split between those who **hold** the legal title (the trustees) and those who **own** the equitable or beneficial interests (the beneficiaries, also known as the *cestuis que trust*). **The beneficiaries are the true owners**, even when they do not hold the legal title. The trustees have what is known as a mere 'paper title', an empty shell. There are many types of trust. Indeed, there is a trust to meet every situation in regard to property, real or personal, or, to put it another way, there is no problem which cannot be solved by the use of a trust, if equity so decides. However, where the same individual both holds the legal title and owns the whole of the beneficial interest in land, there is no need for a trust: he is the absolute owner. It is only where more than one person holds title to or owns the beneficial interest in the land, either at the same time or one after the other, or where a trustee and his beneficiary are different people, that the equitable interests separate from the legal estate and a trust arises.

Who does what?

The respective roles of trustees and beneficial owners, and of landlords and tenants

Like the last question, this one arises in regard to the legal estates only. As a trust arises upon the separation of the legal estate from the beneficial interests, we need to know what responsibilities and privileges the people involved have. In any trust there is the relationship between the trustees and the beneficiaries, but with a term of years absolute there is the added relationship of landlord and tenant.

In each case there will be leading players, cameo roles and bit parts. Frequently the same person will have to play more than one part and wear more than one costume! For instance, the same person could be trustee, beneficiary and landlord all at the same time.

We shall look at the roles played by the various players and the duties which each owes to the other.

How can you acquire them?

The rules, principles and formalities governing the acquisition of interests in land

Obviously, interests and estates have to be acquired somehow. Less obvious at this stage is that the way in which they are acquired will dictate whether they are legal or equitable. There are general rules governing the acquisition of estates and interests but, as your studies in law so far will already have shown, there are exceptions to the general rules. Many of the interests in land have individual requirements in regard to their acquisition and these will be looked at in each chapter in Parts II and III. A chapter on the general rules follows shortly.

When and for how long?

The points in time at which a holder acquires and loses his interest in land

Here we look at the points in time at which an interest is acquired and lost. Again, different rules can apply depending upon the interest, but we need to note that there are two systems operating in land law (the registered and the unregistered) and that in the registered system the point in time at which an estate or interest can vest in – pass to – the purchaser differs from that in unregistered land.

In unregistered land, the interest vests upon completion of the relevant formalities; thus the fee simple absolute in possession in the land or even a term of years thereof, will vest in the purchaser as soon as the conveyance to him has been completed, all the relevant formalities having been observed. We shall see, however, that it is possible to acquire an equitable interest, under the rule in *Walsh* v *Lonsdale* (1882) or by way of a resulting or constructive trust or estoppel, where such legal formalities are not complied with. In such cases the equitable interest thus acquired comes into existence at the time when the necessary requirements for the relevant equitable rule or principle are complied with, though, of course, such interests are only truly recognised when the court decides in favour of the equitable interest holder.

In the registered land system, on the other hand, even though the transaction has been completed, the legal estate or interest will not pass until the relevant rules as to its protection have been complied with, and this usually means upon registration of the interest. We shall see shortly how this has to be done; we need only note here that it must be done. Therefore, until registered, all proprietary rights in registered land remain equitable, notwithstanding that they would have become legal in unregistered land upon completion.

Thus, a mortgagee acquires a legal mortgage of unregistered land as soon as a valid mortgage deed has been executed and the transaction has been completed, but a mortgagee will not acquire a legal interest in registered land until the validly executed deed and completed transaction have been registered at HM Land Registry. The time lapse between completion and registration will, of course, depend primarily upon the workload at the local land registry, and this should be shortened as each local registry becomes computerised. However, all applications are date-stamped upon arrival and are registered as at that date. Therefore, the effective date of registration is the stamp date, i.e. the date the application arrived at the Land Registry.

These, then, are the general rules as to acquisition of interests. However, we need also to know when interests terminate or expire. Needless to say, there are individual rules for each interest! So, the next question will be: when and for how long? Followed by:

How can you protect them?

Methods of protection afforded to all interests in land after 1925

The benefit of each interest in land must be protected if the burden of it is to be enforceable against purchasers. In this section we consider different ways of protecting the benefit in both registered and unregistered land.

If the benefit of an interest has not been protected in the correct way, the burden is unlikely to be binding upon a purchaser of the burdened land. Effectively, then, this causes the interest to end.

Example

Say that George sells part of his land to Francis but subject to a restriction on Francis' use of the land he is buying. Francis subsequently sells the land to Ross. Is Ross bound by the restriction too? This will depend upon several things, such as whether the restriction is an interest in land and whether it is capable of binding Ross, who was not a party to the original agreement. Only then can we consider whether the burden actually does bind him.

Those of you who have studied contract law will be familiar with the concept of privity of contract, under which only those who were party to an agreement can benefit or be bound by its terms. As you can see from what has just been said, in land law third parties can, and frequently are, bound or benefited by agreements made by others. Therefore, in land law you must always watch out for the third-party purchaser!

We shall look at the systems of registered and unregistered land and the methods provided by each for protecting interests generally in Part I. In Parts II and III we shall see how each individual interest needs to be protected.

Human rights

The Human Rights Act 1998 (HRA), which came into force on 2 October 2000 and applies to all cases coming before the courts after that date irrespective of when the activities which form the subject matter of the case took place, provides that:

> so far as it is possible to do so, primary legislation and subordinate legislation must be read and given effect in a way which is compatible with Convention rights – s 3(1).

The Convention referred to is, of course, the European Convention on Human Rights (ECHR). Now, although

> the suggestion that the Human Rights Act may have relevance to property in land is one that is invariably greeted with surprise . . . it is clear that in a society which admits of private property rights in land, protection from interference with those rights is an important principle. For most people, their home is the most important possession they have, almost certainly in economic terms and also in social terms: many have a strong emotional attachment to their home. Even if a citizen has no rights to private property he must have some sort of right, however loosely defined, to a place to live: there is no human activity which does not require, at the very least, access to land. Equally, property rights, whether in the form of freehold or leasehold ownership . . . are a vital aspect to any commercial enterprise. Protection of property rights is thus of paramount importance – Jean Howell (1999).

This being so, the question is, does the Convention (and thus the HRA) protect rights in land? The answer is yes: Articles 1 (Protocol 1) and 8 of the Convention provide this. Under Article 1,

> Every natural or legal person is entitled to the peaceful enjoyment of his possessions. No one shall be deprived of his possessions except in the public interest and subject to the conditions provided for by law and by the general principles of international law.
>
> The preceding provisions shall not, however, in any way impair the right of a State to enforce such laws as it deems necessary to control the use of property in accordance with the general interest or to secure the payment of taxes or other contributions or penalties.

As Deborah Rook (2002) explains:

> Article 1 . . . does not, in principle, guarantee a right to the peaceful enjoyment of possessions in a pleasant environment. It protects against interference with the economic value of property, but it does not extend to purely aesthetic qualities relating to the greater peace, comfort or enjoyment of the property.

However, if, for example, excessive noise substantially reduces the value of the property, it can, in principle, amount to confiscation of property – *Powell* v *UK* (App No

9310/81), ECtHR. *Powell* concerned property affected by noise from Heathrow airport, but, on the facts, the Commission decided the value of Powell's property had not been seriously affected. In *Marcic v Thames Water Utilities Limited* [2001] 3 All ER 698, Marcic's claim for compensation for nuisance caused by the flooding of his home was the first example of a breach of Article 1, arising from a reduction in the value of a person's home due to nuisance.

Under Article 8,

1. Everyone has the right to respect for his private and family life, his home and his correspondence.

2. There shall be no interference by a public authority with the exercise of this right except such as is in accordance with the law and is necessary in a democratic society in the interests of national security, public safety or the economic well-being of the country, for the prevention of disorder or crime, for the protection of health or morals, or for the protection of the rights and freedoms of others.

Article 8 clearly provides protection for the home, but Article 1 refers only to 'possessions'. However, '"possessions" is a "concept which clearly includes land ..."' – Jean Howell.

In addition to this protection, 'In determination of his civil rights and obligations ... everyone is entitled to a fair public hearing' – Article 6. (Public Authorities includes courts – HRA, s 6(3).)

Cases which have been brought under the HRA in connection with specific points of property law will appear in the relevant chapters, but there are cases which are of more general effect, such as *Godin-Mendoza v Ghaidan* (2002) 46 EG 197 (CS), where it was held that, in general terms, Article 14 provides that sexual orientation is no longer a permissible ground for discrimination. (We shall see later, in Chapter 7, that equity has never made any distinction on this ground.)

It was thought that Convention rights were only enforceable vertically, that is against states, but it is now well established that rights are also enforceable horizontally, that is against private individuals.

It was also thought that the HRA would have little, if any, direct effect upon property law. Again, this has proved not to be so; 'property law has not escaped the influence of a new era of human rights protection' – Deborah Rook, and, with the clearly established principle

> that deprivation of possessions is not to be tolerated apart from in those circumstances where it can be justified in the public interest, and then only subject to conditions unequivocally provided for by domestic and international law ... For the property lawyer, as for civil rights and other practitioners, the bringing home of the Convention has led to much more interesting times – Peter Halstead (2002).

As well as the right to remain in your home, the right to exclude others from land is protected – *Ward v London Borough of Hillingdon* [2002] EWHC Admin 91, but there is no guaranteed right under the Convention to be able to acquire possessions or to inherit property on intestacy – *Marckz v Belgium* (1979) EHRR 330 ECtHR.

Reform

Proposals regarding certain aspects of land law

> Teaching land law is becoming increasingly difficult ... the introduction of recent legisla-
> tive reforms and judicial reinterpretation of existing principles adds to the complexity of
> the core content of the subject. The need for further reform is unquestioned, and the
> central problem is that a legislative framework introduced in 1925, building on earlier
> reforms of the late nineteenth century, has to be constantly reinterpreted in the light of
> changing social and commercial concerns to meet the modern needs of conveyancers, land
> owners, occupiers and mortgagees – John Stevens (1997).

Throughout this book we shall see how the court of equity has 'reformed' several
areas of land law, for example, the use of the resulting trust, what has been called
'the new model' constructive trust and the doctrine of notice in unregistered land,
to protect those persons left with no remedy under the 1925 legislation owing to the
fact that overreaching requires at least two trustees. Cases like *Kingsnorth Finance Co
Ltd* v *Tizard* [1986] 1 WLR 783 and *Williams & Glyn's Bank* v *Boland* [1981] AC 487
have turned the 1925 legislation's preference for the purchaser into a preference for
the occupier. The seemingly unstoppable march of proprietary estoppel not only
provides an equitable solution, but has actually been relied on by reformers, for
instance the Law Commission and the Law of Property (Miscellaneous Provisions)
Act 1989, s 2. However, property law generally, and land law in particular needs
forever to evolve and change to meet current social and political needs and, as we
shall see, in several areas huge changes have been brought about through recent
legislation in an attempt to do just that – the Landlord and Tenant (Covenants) Act
1995, which improved the lot of an original tenant following assignment of his
interest; the Housing Act 1996, addressing yet again the relative positions of landlord and tenant in the area of domestic property; the Trusts of Land and
Appointment of Trustees Act 1996, making radical changes to the way in which the
legal estate in land can be held and administered; the Treasure Act 1996, altering the
rules of treasure trove with the intention of protecting cultural, historical and
archaeological treasures for the nation; the introduction of commonhold, enabling
flats to be held on 'freeholds'. All in all, a great deal of reform has, then, already
taken place. However, the Law Commission still has several consultation documents
and reports underway.

The Law Commission produces a quarterly bulletin of law reform projects entitled
'Law Under Review'. Your law library should carry these. Where relevant, the more
important proposals for change in regard to the various interests in land will be considered throughout this book.

How to apply it all

Too often land law is seen by students as merely a series of sets of rules. Though there
are many rules, land law is the way in which they are applied to the facts in question. Two sets of facts will never be exactly the same. Therefore, the outcomes for
the people involved will vary from case to case. There will seldom be a specific
answer. Indeed, to go looking for *the* answer is to court disaster.

Of course, you must know the rules, but you will be assessed – by your examiner, your client or the court – upon your ability to *apply* them to the case in hand. When you go to consult your doctor, you do not wish to know everything he knows about medicine, nor do you wish to have to make your own diagnosis: you expect him to tell you what is wrong and to suggest a cure. It is the same with law. *You* are expected to know the rules: the client does not need to know them (though you must, of course, convince an examiner that *you* know them!). What the client wants, and what he will press you for is *an answer* but, as one of my lecturer's told me, you will know you are on the right road when you answer by saying, 'It will all depend . . .', and he groans! Yet, it *will* all depend upon the facts of the question and the other side's case. You must have a full understanding of the rules, but your success will depend upon how you apply them to all the facts, that is to both sides. In effect, if you have done the job properly you will have advised all parties.

It is very much like driving a car: understanding how the engine works is of no use unless you can apply that understanding in actually making the vehicle go. Even that is not enough. You may be an excellent driver, but what of the other drivers on the road? You must always be alert to what they do and react accordingly. The Highway Code is all well and good, but once you are on the road things happen which require you to sum up the situation and, based on what you know and using your common sense, make the right decision in the circumstances. Even on an uneventful journey, you have to know the route to take. You need to get on the right motorway and know when and where to get off it. You need to know which signs to follow and which are not relevant to your journey, and all the time you need to be aware of how what you do can affect everyone else on the road. When you set off in your car you never know what may be waiting for you. That is partly what makes driving so enjoyable.

It is the same with land law, except that it can be more than merely enjoyable: it can be fascinating! Operating in the world of equity, it offers kaleidoscopic possibilities: the slightest movement of the lens and the whole pattern changes completely! Always remember, land is precious. It usually represents the largest financial investment you will ever make. People will fight very hard to keep their land or any interest they have over someone else's land. Equally, the person with the burdened land will fight to be free of the burden. So, *the* answer will, as often as not, be 'on the one hand . . . but on the other hand . . .', and, sometimes, 'and then again . . .'.

'What is the use of a book', thought Alice, 'without pictures or conversation?' – Lewis Carroll's *Alice's Adventures in Wonderland*. What indeed? In this book you will find diagrams, charts and tables, each intended to put you in the picture. I have tried to write it so that it reads something like a conversation: treat this book as your friend! You will find between its covers an explanation of all the principles of land law – statutory, legal (that is, at common law) and equitable – together with the relevant authority, be it statutory provisions, the leading cases or useful and important quotations from judgments and leading writers. A note of caution: all law books quickly become out of date in certain areas. However, your lecturers should always be bang up to the minute on the current law, so take your lead from them.

Of course, text books are only a secondary source of law. The primary sources are the cases (via the law reports) and statutes. In regard to cases, the references given in this book have been chosen 'at random' in that they do not necessarily follow the orthodox order. This is intentional and is meant to encourage you to use as varied a selection of law reports as possible. The law library is an Aladdin's cave: get in there, explore, discover its gems. Legal research can be an exciting treasure hunt. All leading cases should be read *in full*, that is *all the judgments* – including dissenting judgments – and not merely the headnotes! Every student of land law should have an up-to-date copy of *Property Statutes*.

At the end of each chapter you will find recommended further reading, most of which provide you with relevant articles. It may be that the article gives a clear explanation of the matters under discussion or that it takes the discussion further: it could do both. Do try to find the time to read at least one article from each section: a good article can be worth several chapters of any book. If your library does not hold any of the law reports, texts or journals mentioned (in hard copy, on disc or via its intranet), ask about inter-library loans.

You will already have found that you certainly do read for a law degree. This is even more true of the study of land law. The very best approach to studying this subject is to **read ahead of your lectures** so that they will not seem like so much gobbledegook. You must get to grips with the language of land law. At the back of this book I have provided a glossary to start you off. This is not an exhaustive list of every term of art in land law, but it is quite comprehensive. As you come across a word or phrase that you are not familiar with, or which has a special meaning in land law, turn to the glossary and learn the meaning of it **and** the context in which it is to be used. If you cannot find what you are looking for in the glossary, go to another source – law dictionaries, other texts, your lecturer – and add the item to your list. The more familiar you become with its language, the more comfortable you will become with land law. On the next page is a wordsearch to whet your appetite! It is impossible to over-emphasise the need for precision in your use of language in land law: imprecision leads to ambiguity or inaccuracy. In *Joyce* v *Rigolli* [2004] EWCA Civ 79, Arden LJ agreed that the judge at first instance 'was rightly critical of what he also termed "sloppy conveyancing" '. I agree with his comment that this case

> illustrates the time and trouble which can be wasted and the trouble which can be caused by sloppy conveyancing. It would have been far more satisfactory to the vendor . . . if the boundary had been fixed in a proper manner before she sold . . . This case is an object lesson for conveyancers. Boundary disputes are costly in terms of the money, court resources and the strain they impose on the parties individually and in their relations as neighbours. It is in the interests of consumers of legal services and the public generally that conveyancers should take careful note of the warnings about imprecise boundaries given and now repeated by this court in several cases.

Sadly, as Neuberger J stated in *Purbrick* v *Hackney London Borough* [2004] 1 P&CR 34, '. . . almost any judgment, if subjected to very detailed scrutiny, can be shown to have some defect in terms of unhappy expression . . .', but this should not deter us from striving to avoid it!

Like Alice, you may well ask yourself, 'Where shall I begin?' As the King said, 'Begin at the beginning and go on till you come to the end: then stop.' 'The beginning' is your first lecture – that is where your preparation for your examination starts! You 'go on' by reading ahead of the lectures, reading around the lectures, making notes on your further reading, consolidating those notes with your lecture notes, and preparing fully for tutorials or seminars (which does not mean merely regurgitating your notes!). Tutorials and seminars are your opportunity to test your ability to **apply** what you have learnt to a given set of facts or proposition. From this you will discover what you do not understand. If, after further study on the point, you are still struggling, then ask your tutor. From the questions you ask, your tutor will be able to tell how much effort you have made and what it is that is hampering your understanding. You need to take an active part in tutorial discussion, incorporating your final tutorial notes into your file (which is, of course, not the same thing as merely filing them!). It

```
T  K  E  G  R  A  H  C  D  E  E  D  U  E  E  S  S  E  L
N  D  M  K  V  F  E  E  S  I  M  P  L  E  I  C  T  Y  A
A  I  L  Q  Y  I  G  A  A  B  X  V  E  A  U  T  R  E  N
N  D  A  U  V  N  E  S  B  L  E  J  S  T  N  T  I  M  O
E  C  N  E  C  I  L  E  S  I  P  B  T  E  E  Y  C  I  I
V  R  D  E  T  E  R  M  O  F  Y  E  A  R  S  A  T  N  T
O  E  L  S  X  F  C  E  L  E  T  N  T  Q  T  W  S  O  I
C  N  O  T  A  Z  N  N  U  P  L  E  E  S  O  E  E  R  D
E  T  R  A  E  I  L  T  T  O  A  F  C  E  P  L  T  E  N
V  E  D  T  F  L  L  N  E  S  N  I  O  L  P  A  T  E  O
I  N  T  E  R  V  I  V  O  S  O  C  N  A  E  S  L  G  C
T  A  E  G  E  L  W  T  R  E  S  I  T  S  L  R  E  A  E
C  N  T  L  S  E  Q  R  J  S  R  A  R  F  E  O  M  G  R
I  T  U  E  P  A  M  R  F  S  E  R  A  O  T  F  E  T  U
R  R  L  S  R  S  T  E  W  I  P  Y  C  R  U  T  N  R  T
T  L  O  S  O  E  S  D  I  O  V  A  T  E  T  S  T  O  X
S  P  S  O  F  Z  U  E  O  N  P  U  R  W  A  U  A  M  I
E  H  B  R  I  P  R  E  Q  U  I  T  Y  O  T  R  I  B  F
R  E  A  L  T  Y  T  M  L  A  G  E  L  P  S  T  L  H  O
```

Key to wordsearch

ABSOLUTE *AUTRE* BENEFICIARY CHARGE CONDITIONAL DEED EASEMENT ENTAIL EQUITY ESTATE ESTATE CONTRACT ESTOPPEL FEE SIMPLE FINE FIXTURE *INTER VIVOS* LANDLORD LEASE LEGAL LICENCE LIFE LESSEE LESSOR MINOR MORTGAGEE PERSONALTY POSSESSION POWER OF SALE PROFIT PUR REALTY REDEEM RENT RESTRICTIVE COVENANT RULE STATUTE STRICT SETTLEMENT TENANT TERM OF YEARS TRUST TYA VIE VOID WAY WILL

will seem a long time before you come 'to the end': for most students the end is the examination. You can stop when you have passed it!

You will find examples of how to apply the relevant authority, principles and 'rules' on the companion website. When attempting questions set (whether in tutorials, exams or practice!), remember to ask those posed by the headings throughout this book – Who cares?, What is it?, etc – in the order they appear. Finally, you must provide support for your arguments by way of case law, statutory provisions and academic comment, **all of which must be fully and correctly referenced**.

B What is land law?

Oliver Cromwell said that land law is 'an ungodly jumble' – a description which, sad to say, can be applied to a large number of land law scripts marked by examiners each year. Hardly surprising, then, that most legal practitioners admit to never having understood it. Yet, though it is admittedly a challenging, not to say, difficult subject it is 'logical and orderly, its concepts are perfectly defined and they stand in well recognised relations to one another' – Professor F H Lawson (1951, p 79).

By now you will be wanting to know exactly what is the problem with land law. What indeed! First of all, it is unlike any other area of law, whether in the United Kingdom or elsewhere. It is unique. It has a language all of its own – 'double Dutch', according to the bewildered student! It is exceptionally technical and never seems to deal with anything solid at all, let alone land. Its concepts can be difficult to grasp and 'new combinations are constantly worked out', according to Professor Lawson, who explains the problem like this:

> above all, this part of the law is intensely abstract and has become a calculus remarkably similar to mathematics. The various concepts ... seem to move among themselves according to the rules of a game which exists for its own purpose. So extreme are these various characteristics that they make of this part of the law something more logical and more abstract than anything that to my knowledge can be found in any other law in the world. (p 79)

Still, forewarned is forearmed, so do not be surprised, not to say disheartened, if you do not grasp a point straightaway. Above all, do not – as so many students do – simply give up. Remember Robert the Bruce! Better still, imagine you are on a motorway, travelling at 70 mph, when suddenly you run into dense fog. You cannot simply stop the car and get out; you must slow down – to a crawl if need be – and struggle on until the sunshine breaks through. More than with any other subject, you may find that you will need to go over each point repeatedly if you are to see daylight.

Professor Lawson says that this lack of solidity, this feeling of being lost in the fog, is one of 'moving in a world of pure ideas from which everything physical or material is entirely excluded'. Yet we can make an analogy between land law and a bridge – a very solid, everyday thing which provides a pathway from one place to another. The aim of this book is to provide you with a pathway – from chariness to challenge, from confusion to comprehension, and from infuriation to fascination; but, just as a bridge needs a firm foundation, so too does land law. This foundation in its turn depends upon well prepared earthworks. From these a solid structure, created from bricks, can be built – building from both sides at the same time towards the keystone. This point is very important, because in studying land law you must adopt lateral thinking, for there are two streams running under our bridge – law and equity – and there are two systems in land law – registered and unregistered. Similarly, any new legislation in this area tends not to be retrospective, so that with each enactment a new lane must be added to our bridge.

The bricks represent all the legal estates and equitable interests which it is possible to have in land. As you cannot own the land itself, the legal estates provide the main bricks (the springers) from which the arch rises towards the keystone.

Having identified and acquired an interest in land, we must protect it against third-party purchasers, who would, naturally, prefer to take the land without, say, a restrictive covenant which would prevent them from building on the land. The bridgehead provides this protection.

Finally, we must have mortar to hold everything together – hopefully it will help you achieve a mortarboard!

In order to build any bridge, the apprentice needs a master – someone to guide him in the selection of materials and the way in which to put them all together. Each stage must be well planned and supervised, for faulty earthworks, a rocky foundation, poor quality bricks or badly mixed mortar will cause the whole structure to collapse into Cromwell's 'ungodly jumble'. So too with land law. Understanding must be built up – stage by stage, brick by brick. No part can be left out for it is an integrated whole made up of history (though we shall keep this to a minimum), statutory provisions, legal principles, equitable doctrines and technical rules – all of which seem to be expressed in an alien tongue.

We shall see that land law is, above all else, a study of relationships – the relationship between the land and the rights which can exist in or over it, and the relationship between the various persons who own, wish to own or wish to defeat these competing interests. As Professor Bruce Ackerman (1977, pp 26ff) pointed out:

> it is all too easy to start thinking that 'the' property owner, by virtue of being 'the' property owner, must *necessarily* own a particular bundle of rights over a thing. And this is to commit the error that separates layman from lawyer. For the fact (or is it the law?) of the matter is that property is not a thing, but a set of legal relations between persons governing the use of things.

This is particularly true of land law, which is concerned with the various rights over and interests in land, which of those a person can enjoy over 'his own' land, which can be enjoyed over that land by his neighbour, and which he can enjoy over his 'neighbour's land'.

We shall see that frequently the court will have to decide such issues between two 'innocent' parties, the problem having been caused by a third. It is always necessary, therefore, to consider **both sides** of any claim to a right in or over land.

In short, as Lawson and Rudden (2002, p 3) put it:

> A person may acquire something by making it, but is more likely to get it from someone else and have to pay for it. Buyers want to be sure that they get what they are paying for

... The buyer may prefer to pay for the goods or the house by instalments, and in such cases no one would provide credit without security ... Having got the thing, its owner may keep and use it, or keep and forget about it, or may want to sell it or give it away ... Furthermore – especially if the thing is of a fairly permanent nature like a house or shares – the owner may want to distribute it among others either commercially by charging a rent or by way of gift or bequest to family and friends.

All these, and similar, transactions are entirely normal, peaceful and useful. The law of property underlies them ... In general ... the function of the law relating to private property is to provide us with a bag of tools with which to achieve our wishes.

Land law is, then, a heady, even intoxicating mix of equity, common law and statute. The totally discretionary nature of equitable remedies ensures always an individual decision depending upon the facts of a given case. This operates to produce a field of law which, more than any other, reacts to its social setting and attempts to meet the needs of people, no matter what the time or place. Seldom does property law in general, and land law in particular, impose rules which society must adopt. Rather, the courts, by developing principles in a flexible and equitable manner, hone the law so that it meets current needs by addressing current problems. While you are studying land law, look out for the various needs which have arisen over time and the ways in which they have been met: if a need arises, the courts will find a solution (even if it takes some time before a fully formed principle evolves). It is said by the unenlightened non-believer that this leads to uncertainty in the law! Not so. The principles are developed and refined case by case. If decisions appear always to be different, that has more to do with the fact that they arise directly from the facts of individual cases than from uncertainty in the law. Surely it is better to have an equitable result than a certain forecast?

Much of land law is governed by the great property legislation of 1925 – probably the greatest legislative achievement ever – but this addressed mainly administrative matters, such as how a legal estate in land should be held and by whom, and how interests in land should be conveyed and protected. In almost every instance, property legislation acts retrospectively. This frequently means that we have to deal with two sets of rules, one which existed before the new legislation, the other provided for in that legislation. In addition, new legislation does not always improve the situation. Unfortunately, some more recent statutory forays have not been of the same high standard as the 1925 legislation, being, in some instances, poorly drafted. It may be that the old practice, no matter how unsatisfactory, is so entrenched and familiar that it is best to leave well alone. We shall see that even the most apparently clear provision can give rise to a stream of cases as guidance is sought from the court on interpretation of the new law. Far better to stick with the old, where the cases have already created fairly settled principles: better the devil you know. Certain other new legislation and proposed reform would benefit from the 'if it ain't broke, don't fix it' approach.

The Law Commission and legislators alike would do well to heed this warning from Jean Howells in her paper, 'The Dangers of Reform' delivered at the SPTL Property Group Seminar in Manchester, May 1996:

> Reform of land law requires a deftness of touch which may not be as necessary in other areas of law and there are numerous examples of land reform with good intent which has had either disastrous or at least unexpected consequences ... It is particularly difficult to

change land law. Land law is like a jigsaw, where most of the pieces fit together. The problems of modern land law are where the pieces do not fit. Changes in land law tend to have long-term effects which may not become apparent for a considerable length of time. It follows that, so far as possible, political expediency and 'short termism' should be avoided. ... Legislative reform that attempts to correct a single perceived defect within the law itself is often difficult. Any reform is bound to bring a crop of cases but if the amendment is in the long term desirable, one must live with a period of turbulence. However one must be sure that the tweak given to straighten out one problem does not leave other areas in a badly crumpled state. The best safeguard against this must be that the reform be of the minimum to achieve the desired effect and be done with a consciousness of the whole ... no reform in land law is ever complete or watertight. It [is] therefore vital that, so far as possible, eventualities are foreseen and that after the invariable period of settlement, the system is fundamentally better than it was before ... the whole question of legislative reform should be approached with extreme caution.

C   What types of property are there?

Land is, for the most part, real property, as distinct from personal property. This distinction arose from the different forms of action which could be brought in order to recover various types of property.

Personal property could not always be recovered, in which case the true owner would have to be satisfied with payment of its value by way of compensation for his loss. An action against the dispossessor (the person who has taken your property) is an action 'in personam' – an action against the person. Personal property is recoverable by such an action, 'personal property' – or 'choses' – being any property other than land. Tangible things are 'choses in possession', for example cars, books, paintings, clothes or furniture. Intangible things, such as debts, copyright, patents, trademarks, stocks and shares, are 'choses in action'.

Real property is, for the most part, land, but quite often the words 'realty' and 'land' are used as if they were the same thing, which is not the case. This is because some interests, whilst they may be interests in land, are not 'real' property. Leaseholds are personalty, not realty. The reason for this lies again in the old forms of action. Until 1500 a tenant who was ousted from 'his land' could only recover damages in an action *in personam*, because leases were considered to be no more than a form of commercial contract. However, after 1500 an ousted tenant could recover the land itself in a 'real' action – an action *in rem* – that is, an action against the thing – the land (or the interest therein) – itself. From then on leaseholds became known as 'chattels real'.

The distinction is of more than mere historic interest, however, for if a person (the testator) who only 'owned' leasehold land leaves, in his will, 'all my real property to my son, Albert, and all my personal property to my great-nephew, Bertrand', Albert would get nothing!

Unfortunately, whether a right is proprietary or personal is not always clear-cut. In trusts, as we shall see, the legal 'owner' is the trustee, but in equity it is the cestui que trust, or beneficiary, who is the true owner. Is the cestui's interest a right *in rem* or *in personam*? The traditional view is that it is merely *in personam*, but if 'equity looks to the substance, not the form', and as a cestui que trust can enforce his rights against almost the whole world (that is, except 'Equity's Darling'), then, surely, his right is *in rem*? Indeed, the crucial characteristic of proprietary rights is that they are capable of binding third parties: rights which are not so capable are merely personal. As Lord Wilberforce explained in *National Provincial Bank Ltd* v *Ainsworth* [1965] AC 1175, if a right is to fall within 'the category of property, or of a right affecting property' it must be: 'definable, identifiable by third parties, capable in its nature of assumption by third parties, and have some degree of permanence or stability'.

The nature of a cestui que trust's interest is paramount in cases of trusts of a family home but, as Professor Gray (1993) pointed out, the courts were slow to recognise that: at least in the area of residential security, proprietary rights and personal rights are not distinct but interactive – p 927.

However, Lord Denning was one judge who did recognise this. In *Davis* v *Johnson* [1979] AC 264 he noted that the personal rights of the deserted wife in *Ainsworth* were: 'not allowed to override the proprietary rights of the husband'. In Lord Denning's view this concept of 'rights of property' was:

> quite out of date . . . It is true that in the nineteenth century the law paid high regard to right of property. But this gave rise to such misgivings that in modern times the law has changed course. Social justice requires that personal rights should, in a proper case, be given priority over rights in property.

We shall see later, when looking at trusts of land, that Lord Denning went further and held a beneficiary's rights to be proprietary rights which could take priority over third parties.

Some other rights which, traditionally, have been classified as *in personam* have evolved and become rights *in rem*. We shall see that the freehold restrictive covenant is an illustration of this and that, until more recently, the same seemed to be occurring in the case of contractual licences.

However, the case of *Webb* v *Webb*, Case C-294/92 *The Times*, 24 June [1994] shows that the distinction has a wider significance, the Court of the European Communities finding that for the purposes of art 16(1) of the Brussels Convention a right *in rem* in immovable property is essential: any action under the article has to be based upon a right *in rem* and not upon a right *in personam*.

The interests of beneficiaries behind trusts for sale (now trusts of land) existed, not in the land but in the proceeds of sale, that is, in money and thus personalty. This was the result of the doctrine of conversion under which a beneficiary had only an interest in the proceeds of sale of the land. This was due to the equitable maxim, 'Equity deems to be done that which ought to be done': in a trust for sale, equity deemed the sale to have already taken place. The doctrine of conversion was abolished for trusts of land (which have replaced trusts for sale) by the Trusts of Land and Appointment of Trustees Act 1996. Then again, we shall see that personalty can become realty, when it is held to be a fixture.

The property legislation of 1925, upon which modern land law is founded, assimilated real and personal property to a large extent. However it did not create a completely new law of land, rather:

the effect of these Acts was more akin to the restoration of an old building than the construction of a new one. Although many cobwebby attics and passages were cut away, much of the building still stands although refaced and modernized in many places. In fact, much of the modernization carried out in 1925 was aimed at the kitchen where the conveyancing is done. The reforms here were radical. Over much of the house, however, the structure is old and you must not be surprised to find the motor car in the stable – Patrick J Dalton (1996, p 3).

As Lawson and Rudden rightly said, however, 'Even now, when it has been greatly simplified, [land law] is still something of a mystery'. Indeed, 'In spite of the streamlining the law of property underwent in the 1925 legislation, it remains very complicated and not entirely free of confusion' (Lawson and Rudden, 1982, p 224). Though the law relating to real and personal property has been greatly assimilated, the distinction is still important. We have already seen the importance of specifying correctly which type of property you wish to leave by will, but it is just as important to note the difference when dealing with the property 'inter vivos' – during your lifetime – because any disposition of land must comply with the formal requirements laid down, whereas there are generally no such requirements for disposing of personalty.

D   What is land?

'Land' includes land of any tenure, and mines and minerals ... buildings or any parts of buildings ... and other corporeal hereditaments, also ... a rent and other incorporeal hereditaments, and an easement, right, privilege, or benefit in, over or derived from land – Law of Property Act 1925, s 205(1)(ix).

'Land' includes:
(a) buildings and other structures,
(b) land covered with water, and
(c) mines and minerals, whether or not held with the surface – Land Registration Act 2002, s 132(1).

'Land' is, therefore, far more than merely the physical soil – the 'corporeal hereditament' – more than 'the physical clods of earth which make up the surface layer of land, mines and minerals beneath the surface, and buildings or parts of buildings erected on the surface' – Gray and Symes (1981, p 51). It is also the 'incorporeal hereditaments' – the intangible rights over the land, such as an easement.

Land is unique, 'it is permanent, almost indestructible, has an income value and is capable of almost infinite division and subdivision' – Lawson and Rudden (2002), p 22.

In order to be so capable, land must be more than merely three-dimensional, and the doctrine of estates introduced into land the fourth dimension of time.

In addition, two maxims – *cuius est solum eius est usque ad coelum et ad inferos* (he who owns the land owns everything extending to the heavens and the depths of the earth), and *quicquid plantatur solo, solo cedit* (whatever is attached to the ground becomes a part of it) – helped to achieve the extra dimension required. However, certain restraints and limitations have been placed upon these maxims.

To the heavens above

It can no longer be said that he who owns the land owns everything extending to the heavens and to the depths of the earth, for a combination of common law and statute has redrawn these apparently limitless entitlements. It was held in *Bernstein v Skyviews & General Ltd* [1978] QB 479 that 'to the heavens' had to be restricted in order:

> to balance the rights of an owner to enjoy the use of his land against the rights of the general public to take advantage of all that science now offers in the use of airspace. This balance is in my judgment best struck in our present society by restricting the rights of an owner in the airspace above his land to such a height as is necessary for the ordinary use and enjoyment of his land and the structures upon it: and declaring that above that height he has no greater rights in the airspace than any other member of the public. (Griffith J)

The Civil Aviation Act 1982, s 76, imposes a restriction upon an owner's right to sue in trespass or nuisance by providing that no action shall lie where an aircraft flies over property at a reasonable height.

To the depths of the earth

Treasure trove

Coming down to earth, literally, it was held in *Duppa* v *Mayo* (1669) 1 Saund 282 that though '*fructus naturales*' (the natural produce of the soil which grows without human labour, such as grass) may be 'land', '*fructus industriales*' (that which does require human endeavour, such as annual crops) are not. However, the restrictions imposed by the common-law rule with regard to 'treasure trove' went even deeper, for treasure trove belongs to the Crown alone. It has been said that, 'buried treasure glitters even in the dull pages of a law report' – [1980] CLJ 281. In order for items to qualify as treasure trove, certain requirements had to be satisfied: the items had to be gold or silver, they must have been deliberately hidden in the soil or in a building, with the intention of being retrieved later, and the real owner must have been unknown or untraced. For an item to satisfy the requirement of being gold or silver, there must have been a substantial proportion of either of those elements present. It could, therefore, in the case of coins, come down to the date of the coins, as happened in the leading case of *Attorney General of the Duchy of Lancaster* v *G E Overton (Farms) Ltd* [1980] 3 WLR 869, where it was also explained that 'if the coins are not treasure trove, they are the property of the owner of the soil, and not the finder' – Dillon J. Of course, it was not only coins which could be treasure trove – any article which satisfied the requirements would belong to the Crown. Whether or not an item was treasure trove was decided by a coroner's jury, and it is a criminal offence under the Theft Act 1968 not to produce any potential treasure trove (now called treasure) for examination.

Not only did the common law uphold the Crown's right to treasure trove, but it also grants a general right of all gold and silver lying underground to the Crown – *Case of Mines* (1568) 1 Plowd 310. Statute also grants certain precious minerals to the Crown – coal, oil and natural gas, and the Water Resources Act 1963, s 23(1), provides that a landowner has no property in water, though he may draw it from any source which flows or percolates over or on to his land. He also has the sole right to fish from such water, so long as it is not tidal. (For the purposes of the Land Registration Act 2002, '"mines and minerals" includes any strata or seam or minerals or substances in or under any land, and powers of working and getting any such minerals or substances' – s 132.)

The law of treasure trove – and now treasure – provides a good example of how land law is concerned with the relationship between persons in regard to things. Several 'persons' are involved: the Crown, the 'landowner' (that is the holder of the legal estate in the land), the finder and the nation.

If the article was found to be treasure trove, then it belonged to the Crown. However, where finds were declared to be treasure trove, the Treasury customarily made an *ex-gratia* payment to the finder. There was no legal obligation to do so, but the Treasury made such payments as 'compensation' or 'reward' to finders who declared their finds promptly – even, in some cases, where the finder was trespassing at the time of making the discovery. This practice caused dissatisfaction, not least amongst the landowners who received nothing: only if the article was found not to be treasure trove would a non-finder landowner receive anything (unless, in granting a licence to the treasure seeker, he made some arrangement in regard to the find or value thereof). The Treasury justified the *ex-gratia* payments on the basis that they encouraged finders to come forward. Were they, then, a reward? If so, this in itself causes problems: under the common law rule, a finder must be aware of any reward on offer if he is to be entitled to it (*R* v *Clarke* (1927) 40 CLR 227). However, *ex-gratia* payments may be large or small. Indeed, if no museum wished to have the article, it was returned to the finder without payment. Therefore, a finder could not know what the 'reward' was to be. Indeed, if the article was not treasure trove, he would not be entitled to anything (subject to any agreement with the landowner in regard to anything the seeker does find). The likelihood of high payments could encourage trespassing by treasure seekers who may well, in their eagerness to make a discovery, ruin an archaeological site. Where the payment was likely to be small, finders may be discouraged from coming forward and this may result in important archaeological sites remaining undiscovered. These problems arose from the value of any *ex-gratia* payment made to the finder, but the true worth of the articles was often incalculable and rested not merely on its monetary value: the value of many finds did not lie in their being substantially gold or silver.

Where an object was found in or attached to land and it was not treasure trove, the owner or lawful possessor of the land had a better title to the object than the finder, but where the object was unattached on land, the owner or lawful possessor only has a better title than the finder where he has exercised such manifest control over the land as to indicate an intention to control it and everything found on it – see *Waverley Borough Council* v *Fletcher* [1995] QB 334, where the Court of Appeal applied the leading cases of *Parker* v *British Airways Board* [1982] QB 1004 and *Elwes* v *Brigg Gas Co* (1886) 33 Ch D 562.

Items that were not treasure trove, and those that were but which were returned to the finder were lost to the nation as a whole, notwithstanding they represented the heritage of us all. This concern has been addressed to a large extent by the Treasure Act 1996. The intention of the Act is to improve the legal protection of archaeological objects of historical value. Treasure trove is abolished and fresh provision is made 'in relation to treasure'.

'Treasure' is defined in s 1 as:

(a) any object at least 300 years old when found which –
    (i) is not a coin but has metallic content of which at least 10 per cent by weight is precious metal;
    (ii) when found, is one of at least two coins in the same find which are at least 300 years old at that time and have that percentage of precious metal; or
    (iii) when found, is one of at least ten coins in the same find which are at least 300 years old at that time;

(b) any object at least 200 years old when found which belongs to a class designated under section 2(1);

(c) any object which would have been treasure trove if found before the commencement of section 4;

(d) any object which, when found, is part of the same find as –
    (i) an object within paragraph (a), (b) or (c) found at the same time or earlier; or
    (ii) an object found earlier which would be within paragraph (a) or (b) if it had been found at the same time.

(2) Treasure does not include objects which are –
    (a) unworked natural objects, or
    (b) minerals as extracted from a natural deposit,

or which belong to a class designated under section 2(2) [Treasure Act 1996, s 1].

Section 2(1) provides the Secretary of State with the power to alter the meaning of 'treasure' under which he may 'designate any class of object which he considers to be of outstanding historical, archaeological or cultural importance'. Section 2(2) provides that for the purposes of s 2(1) the Secretary of State may 'designate any class of object which ... would be treasure'. The power under s 2 must be used by way of an order made by statutory instrument.

Concern was expressed during the passage of the Bill that whole categories of items of archaeological, historical and national importance are excluded by s 1 which defines treasure according to its metal content, not its importance or intrinsic worth. At first glance, s 2 would appear to redress this: however, as was pointed out in Standing Committee during the passage of the Bill, many finds will not be covered by the Act because they fall outside the s 1 definition: the Secretary of State will, therefore, not be aware of them, nor of the nature of the items found. The duty of a finder to notify the coroner relates only to 'an object which he [the finder] believes or has reasonable grounds for believing is treasure' – s 8, that is 'treasure' as defined by s 1. Therefore, the power under s 2 is not a safety net by which items of national and archaeological importance are likely to be saved.

Section 1(1)(c) refers to s 4. This relates to the ownership of treasure which vests, subject to prior interests and rights, in '(a) the franchisee, if there is one; (b) otherwise in the Crown.' 'Franchisees' are defined in s 5 and include, for example, the Duchies of Cornwall and Lancaster. Section 4 applies 'whatever the nature of the place where the treasure was found, and whatever the circumstances in which it was left (including being lost or being left with no intention of recovery) – s 4(4).

Rewards are still to be considered in favour of the finder of treasure; however any other person involved in the find, the occupier of the land at the time of the find, and any person who has an interest in the land at that time, or has had such an interest at any time since then may also be considered – s 10(5). The total reward must not exceed the treasure's market value, and the Secretary of State will also determine whether a reward is to be paid, and, if so, to whom and the amount – s 10(3).

The Secretary of State is required to prepare a code of practice relating to treasure, following consultation with 'such persons appearing to him to be interested as he thinks appropriate' – s 11. The code of practice was duly published, and the Act came into force on 24 September 1997. The code is not only informative, but also very interesting. Apart from the Act itself and a clear explanation of it and as to how treasure will be disposed of, the code of practice contains lots of fascinating facts – a list of the various bodies that deal with treasure and from which further advice can be sought; a list of coins commonly found in England and Wales that contain less than 10 per cent of gold or silver (now capable of being treasure); advice on the care of finds and a list of further sources of conservation advice.

Early indications are that many more ancient treasures have been reported under the new Act than under the old common law rules of treasure trove. Before the Act, reported finds averaged 25 in a year; in the first eight months after it, there were 90. The government puts this down to the clearer reward system and more responsible metal detector users. Indeed, almost all the reported finds were made by metal detector users, one of whom, Mr Fisher, was appointed to the Treasure Valuation Committee. In acknowledging the contribution made by responsible detector users, he stated that the Committee is 'keen to ensure that finders have confidence that they will receive a fair reward'.

The code of practice contains a government announcement on pilot schemes for the voluntary recording of archaeological finds and the government, together with the British Museum, are funding six liaison officers to work around the country to promote this. The Home Office has produced guidelines and procedures to be followed by coroners in regard to finds.

We shall see that land may also be subject to rights of others, so that a man may, on the one hand, have to allow his neighbour to cross his land freely, whilst, on the other, be restrained from building on it. Liability can arise at common law under the torts of nuisance, trespass and negligence, as well as under the Occupiers' Liability Acts 1957 and 1984.

These restrictions, together with those imposed under statutes such as the Town and Country Planning Acts, the Rent Act, the Housing Acts and the Leasehold Reform, Housing and Urban Development Act 1993, all ensure that an Englishman's home is no longer his castle, to do with as he pleases.

Whatever is attached to the ground

While the first maxim imposes restrictions, the second has the effect of granting extended rights, so that in *Rogers (Inspector of Taxes)* v *Longsdon* [1967] Ch 93 an artificial heap of waste was held to have become part of the land once trees and grass started growing on it, and in *Southern Centre of Theosophy Inc* v *State of South Australia*

[1982] 1 All ER 283 land was held to have been added by gradual accretion from the sea.

It is not only case law that extends the meaning of 'land' in this way. The Interpretation Act 1978, Sch 1 provides that '"land" includes buildings and other structures, land covered with water, and any estate, interest, easement, servitude or right in or over land', and, as we have seen, the Law of Property Act 1925, s 205(1)(ix), states that 'land' includes 'buildings or parts of buildings (whether the division is horizontal, vertical or made in any other way) and other corporeal hereditaments', and, under the Land Registration Act 2002, s 132, 'buildings and other structures'.

It is not only actual 'buildings or parts of buildings' either, but also, under common law, anything which attaches to them in such a way as to become a 'fixture'.

Fixtures and fittings

Though fixtures become part of the land, fittings do not and it is, therefore, imperative to distinguish between the two. Two tests have evolved for this purpose – the degree of annexation test, and the purpose of annexation test.

The degree of annexation

Under this test, an object which has been firmly attached to the land is a fixture, while one which is merely resting on its own weight is not.

Berkley v *Poulett* (1976) 242 EG 39

A marble statue which was merely standing on a plinth by virtue of its own weight, albeit half a ton, was only a fitting. So long as the object is attached, however, it can be a fixture no matter how light. However, whilst this test does establish a *prima facie* case and, therefore, where the burden of proof lies, it is no longer the predominant test: the purpose of annexation test is, so that:

> articles not otherwise attached to the land than by their own weight are not to be considered as part of the land unless the circumstances are such as to show that they were intended to be part of the land ... and that on the contrary, an article which is affixed to the land even slightly is to be considered as part of the land, unless the circumstances are such as to show that it was intended all along to continue a chattel - Blackburn J in *Holland* v *Hodgson* [1872] LR 7 CP 328.

The purpose of annexation

The question here is whether the object has been fixed for the more convenient use of the land or building rather than for the enjoyment of the thing itself. It is not surprising, then, that similar objects may be held to be a fitting in one case, but a fixture in another. Thus, tapestries which had been tacked to a wooden frame which, in turn, had been nailed to a wall, were held to be only fittings in *Leigh* v *Taylor* [1902] AC 157, while tapestries which had been hung to create a beautiful room were held in *Re Whaley* [1908] 1 Ch 615 to be fixtures. Similarly, figures, statues and vases were held in *D'Eyncourt* v *Gregory* (1866) LR 3 Eq 382 to be fixtures because they formed part of an overall architectural design, whilst in *Berkley* v *Poulett* (1976) 242 EG 39, a very heavy statue was held to be a fitting, notwithstanding the difficulty of removing it.

If an item is held to be a fixture, it may only be removed by a vendor if the contract excludes it from the sale. On the other hand, any fittings can be removed, though the purchaser can, of course, negotiate to purchase them separately. It has for many years been common for vendors and purchasers to agree to sell and buy items such as carpets, curtains, gas or electric fires, bathroom 'fittings', kitchen appliances such as cookers and washing machines, light fittings etc, 'privately', so that the purchaser pays the vendor cash at an agreed price: the cost of these items was not, therefore, included in the mortgage loan. All were, until recently, considered to be fittings – until, that is:

TSB Bank plc v *Botham* (1996) 73 P&CR D1 (also noted at [1998] Conv 137)

Here the bank, the mortgagee (lender), had taken possession of the mortgaged property which was a purpose-built flat. Items such as those listed above were contained inside the flat and the bank sought a declaration that they were fixtures. If they were declared fixtures, the bank could include them in the sale of the flat, thereby increasing its value - an important consideration in times of negative equity. Needless to say, Mr Botham claimed the items were fittings and that he was therefore entitled to remove them. Jacob J held that the fitted carpets, even though they were easily removable, were fixtures, as were the light fittings. The gas fires were so fitted and placed as to be enjoyed as part of the room, not as chattels, and so they too were fixtures. The pelmets, curtains and blinds had been specifically designed for the windows and so were fixtures. The bathroom fittings and mirrors were attached to the walls; the kitchen units and sink were attached; the white goods were all physically fixed by being plumbed or wired in and formed part of the overall design of the kitchen: all were, therefore, fixtures.

Mr Botham appealed. The Court of Appeal stated that it was misleading to apply tests formulated for machinery in factories or those designed for ornamental items too literally to domestic dwellings. If an item, viewed objectively, was intended to be permanent and to provide a lasting improvement, it will be a fixture. However, many factors, including the utility and removability of an item, would affect the outcome. On the facts of this case, the bathroom 'fittings' were fixtures, as were the kitchen units, work surfaces and fitted sink. Though the recessed light fittings were fixtures, the other light fittings were not as they had not been shown to be part of the electrical installation of the flat. Decorative gas fires, which were to be treated on the evidence like plug-in electric fires, were fittings as were the fitted carpets, curtains and blinds. On what were described as the 'slender' facts of the case, the white goods in the kitchen were also fittings. This case shows the importance of excluding even everyday items from any sale; the distinction between a coordinated room and an overall design has become very fine indeed. Whether items are held to be fixtures or fittings will, it seems, continue to depend very much upon the facts of individual cases.

Elitestone Ltd v *Morris* [1997] 2 All ER 512

The House of Lords held that where a house was constructed in such a way that it could not be removed, save by destruction, it could not have been intended to remain a chattel and must have been intended to form part of the realty, but where it was constructed in such a way as to be removable, whether as a unit or in sections, it might remain a chattel, even though it was connected temporarily to mains services such as water and electricity. Accordingly, if a structure could only be enjoyed *in situ*, and could not be removed in whole or in sections to another site, there was a strong inference that the purpose of placing the structure on the original site was that it should form part of the realty at that site and should, therefore, cease to be a chattel. The case concerned a bungalow or chalet which rested on concrete foundation blocks in the ground. It had a living room, two bedrooms, a kitchen and bathroom and was connected to mains supplies. Overruling the Court of Appeal, the House of Lords held that a common-sense approach must be applied and, taking such a view, the bungalow had become part and parcel of the land and the absence of any physical attachment to the land was irrelevant. It was stated *per curiam* that the traditional twofold distinction between chattels and fixtures can be confusing and it is better to adopt the three-fold classification that an object brought on to land is either: (i) a chattel, (ii) a fixture or (iii) part and parcel of the land itself, with objects in categories (ii) and (iii) being treated as being part of the land.

Elitestone was applied in *Wessex Reserve Forces and Cadets Association* v *White* [2006] 1 P&CR 22, where it was held, on the basis of 'common sense and authority' that firmly attached huts and a stone shed were part of the land, but easily removable sheds and a Portakabin were not.

Does that mean that, when selling his land, a vendor must leave all fixtures and objects which have become part and parcel of the land behind? No. If he wishes to remove them he can do so, provided that the contract makes provision for this. If the contract is silent, the purchaser will take the land plus all fixtures and objects which have become part of the land. 'In everyday house purchases people are entitled to be confident that, unless some different agreement is reached and recorded, the property which is to pass includes its fixtures.' – Sedley LJ in *Taylor* v *Hamer* [2002] EWCA Civ 1130. However, there are one or two exceptions: a tenant for life (see strict settlements) can remove trade, ornamental and domestic fixtures at common law. So too can a tenant for years (a lessee), who can also take agricultural fixtures under statute (Agricultural Holdings Act 1986, s 10). The Court of Appeal held in *Chelsea Yacht & Boat Club Ltd* v *Pope* (2000) *The Times*, 7 June, that a boat, albeit one used as a home, was not of the same genus as real property. Before a houseboat, being a mere chattel, could qualify as a dwellinghouse, it had to be so annexed to land as to make it part of that land. However, in *Cinderella Rockerfellas Ltd* v *Rudd* [2003] EWCA Civ 529, the Court of Appeal held that the principle that a chattel attached to land could become part of the land applied equally to a floating vessel placed upon land covered with water – in this case a nightclub aboard a floating vessel which was moored and berthed (under licence) on a river – so that 'a permanently moored vessel, moored in position over part of a river bed licensed to the owner for that purpose, even without such a physical connection, could in appropriate circumstances be enjoyed with the riverbed and enhance its value'. On the facts, the vessel was a fixture, and thus rateable.

It may not be the vendor who takes a fancy to removing old fireplaces and panelling from the house, and statues and valuable plants from the garden, however. In recent years these items have become very marketable and theft of them is rife. Many of these items are of historic interest and important to the national heritage. If a building is listed, the Planning (Listed Buildings and Conservation Areas) Act 1990 prohibits the removal of its fixtures, but where a building has no such status there is no special protection. Even where a building is covered by the Act, problems can arise. The owner of Leighton Hall, a 'Tudorbethan Gothic' house in Powys, Wales, had let this listed property fall into dilapidation. He was charged under s 9 of the 1990 Act for failing to repair and reinstate a statue of Icarus which had been a feature of the garden design. To this charge he pleaded guilty but then went on to sell three of the chandeliers from the Great Hall and a unique carillon clock. The removal of the clock had a disastrous effect upon the panelling and cornice work of the room in which it had stood and the room below. The local authority contended that all three items were covered by the Act; the owner said not. Even if he were charged again, the items had been sold – 'Conveyancers Notebook' [1994] Conv 1.

All land belongs to the Crown

Even though these things may attach to the land, we can never own the land itself, for all land belongs to the Crown. This has been so since the Norman Conquest.

E   Licences

What's the problem?

Licences in context

Vera Duckworth (as she was always reminding Jack and Alec) held the licence to run the Rover's Return in Coronation Street: she was the licensee. From time to time, you may call in to see your local licensee. Instead of walking to the pub, you may decide to drive to the off-licence for your drink, take it home and enjoy it in front of the television: you will need a driving licence and a television licence. Following the opening of Scottish commercial television, Lord Thomson of Fleet remarked, 'It's just like having a licence to print your own money'. However, the ultimate licence belongs to James Bond – he has a licence to kill!

Who cares?

Those who will be affected

All the above licences entitle the holder to do legally something which without the licence would be illegal. Therefore, the holding of a valid licence represents a permission to do something.

If you have already studied public law, you will know of the doctrine of legitimate expectation under which, as between the same parties – licensor and licensee – the holder of a current licence is entitled to have it renewed if he has not infringed the terms of it. Who will ever forget Harry Hook, The Barnsley market-stall holder? – see *R v Barnsley Metropolitan Borough Council, ex parte Hook* [1976] 1 WLR 1052.

However, licences are not transferable: they are personal to the holder only. When Alec took over the running of the 'Rover's Return', he had to get his own licence; he could not continue under Vera's. If Vera had taken on the running of another pub outside Weatherfield, she would have had to get a new licence from the magistrates' court.

What, though, if the permission relates to acts over someone else's land, say to use a path across that person's field as a shortcut to the village? To do so without the owner's permission would clearly be a trespass, but does the permission amount to anything more than a merely personal favour: can it be an interest in land? The difference is crucial, because not only the benefit, but also the burden, of a proprietary right – an interest in land – can pass on to the next owner of the land affected.

Example

If Vera, as owner of the Rover's Return, gave Ken permission to store his old school books in a shed in her back yard, could any purchaser of Ken's house do so? If all Ken has is a mere licence, the answer is generally no. However, if he has an interest in land - which, if anything, would be an easement - the answer could be yes. Would Alec, upon his purchase from Vera, have to allow Ken, or his purchaser, to use the shed? Again, if Ken had been granted an easement, yes, but if Vera had only given a licence, no.

What are they?

The nature and characteristics of licences

We have seen that since 1925 only two legal estates can exist in land and five legal interests – Law of Property Act 1925, s 1(1) and (2). All other interests in land can only be equitable – s 1(3). However, some rights may have regard to or affect land and not be an interest in land at all, not proprietary. If an interest is not proprietary, it can only be personal. Personal rights do not bind purchasers, or third parties.

Licences *per se* or 'mere' licences, cannot bind third parties. They are merely personal rights. They apply only to the parties to the licence – the licensor and the licensee. Neither the benefit nor the burden of the licence can be transferred to another. However, a licence *by estoppel* is capable of binding third parties and, if it relates to land, can be a proprietary right.

A licence is a permission given by the occupier of land (the licensor) to another (the licensee) to do something on that land which, without the permission, would otherwise be a trespass. The licensee does not have to have any interest in any other land.

Thomas v Sorrell (1673) 2 Keb 372

'A ... licence properly passeth no interest, nor alters or transfers property in anything, but only makes an action lawful which without it had been unlawful'. - Vaughan CJ. As we shall see, recent developments have changed the picture - slightly.

There are four main classes of licence: bare, contractual, coupled with an interest and licences by estoppel (three of which are personal rights only, creating no proprietary interest in or over land). If the permission relates to some use of land, it will not survive the conveyance of land by the licensor, or by the licensee.

> ### Example
>
> Say that Lorie lets Bill fly his kite in her field. What if she later changes her mind? Whether she can put an end to Bill's kite flying will depend, as we shall see, upon the type of licence he has. However, as it has nothing to do with land, it is purely a personal right. Thus, if Lorie sells her land, Bill cannot force her purchaser to let him fly his kite. Neither can Bill claim that the flying of his kite is a benefit to his own land, even if he lives nearby. So, if he sells his land, his purchaser cannot claim the benefit of the licence.

We need to look at each type of licence, remembering that in the context of land law, each is a permission to do something on another's land which, without the licence, would be a trespass.

Bare licences

These are gratuitous, that is, granted for no consideration from the licensee for the permission. They may be express, for example permission to hold a pop concert on a field, or implied, such as permission for the postman to deliver your mail to your house.

A bare licence terminates upon the licensor requesting the licensee to cease the previously permitted act; for example, by asking an invitee to leave, that is, they can be revoked by the licensor at will – see *Wood* v *Leadbitter* (1845) 13 M&W 838.

Contractual licences

These are granted for consideration, for instance a licence to enter a cinema and watch the film upon purchase of a ticket. This would be a very short licence, but others last longer. A member of, say, a golf club, having paid his annual subscription, has a licence during that period to enjoy the facilities and privileges of the club. We shall see in Chapter 8 that lodgers and service occupiers can only be licensees, not tenants. However, their licences can, potentially, last many years.

Traditionally treated as purely personal rights, as in bare licences, contractual licences were later treated like contracts, in that, if the licensor revoked the licence before its agreed termination date, or, if no period had been specified, without giving reasonable notice, he would be in breach of contract and the licensee could apply for an injunction or damages, for example in *Hurst* v *Picture Theatres Ltd* [1915] 1 KB 1.

A contractual licence is acquired upon completion of the contract which creates it and continues for the period agreed in the contract, such as the duration of a football match. However, as in any contract, either party may act in breach of its terms, in which case the other is entitled to sue him. Where the contract provides for termination of the licence upon notice, such notice must be reasonable – *Winter Garden Theatre (London) Ltd* v *Millennium Products Ltd* [1948] AC 173. It will depend upon the circumstances of the case as to what is reasonable: in *Millennium* one month was upheld; in *Chandler* v *Kersey* [1978] 1 WLR 693 the Court of Appeal held 12 months was reasonable in the circumstances.

The nature of the contractual licence was brought into question in 1952. The traditional view was as expressed by the House of Lords in *King*.

King v *David Allen & Sons, Billposting Ltd* [1916] 2 AC 54

The parties had an agreement under which Allen had the exclusive right to fix posters and advertisements on the walls of a cinema to be built on King's land, Allen paying £12 per annum for four years for the right. King then leased the cinema and the tenant refused to allow Allen to exercise the right. Allen sued for breach of the agreement. The House of Lords held that Allen could claim against King for the breach, but not against the tenant: a contractual licence is merely a personal obligation and does not bind third parties.

However, Lord Denning caused something of an upset with his revolutionary decision in the following case.

Errington v *Errington & Woods* [1952] 1 KB 290

The case concerned a father, his son, the son's wife and the son's mother. The father purchased a house in his own name, paying £250 of the £750 purchase price, the balance being raised by way of mortgage. The house was bought for the son and daughter-in-law to live in and the father told the daughter-in-law that the £250 was a gift but that she and her husband had to pay the mortgage instalments. The father promised that when the mortgage had been paid off he would transfer the house into the names of his son and daughter-in-law, who went into occupation of the house and paid the mortgage instalments as they fell due. Nine years later the father died, leaving the property to his wife by his will. The son left his wife and went to live with his mother. His wife stayed in the property and continued making the mortgage repayments. The mother sought possession against the daughter-in-law. In all this, of course, the mother was a third party. Lord Denning held that the son and his wife were contractual licensees under a unilateral contract created by the father's promise. This contract could not be revoked once the son and daughter-in-law had begun to rely upon that promise and made the mortgage repayments. Upon the mortgage being paid off the son and daughter-in-law would be entitled to have the property transferred to them. Furthermore, as the couple had 'acted upon the promise ... neither the father **nor his widow** ... can eject them in disregard of it'. Thus the widow/mother, a third party, became bound by a contractual licence which became, effectively, an interest in land! (Given the promise and the detrimental reliance upon it, the case should, surely, have been decided upon the basis of an estoppel.)

A string of cases (and academic articles) followed *Errington*, but the matter was more or less resolved by a *per curiam* statement by the Court of Appeal as follows:

Ashburn Anstalt v *Arnold & Co* [1989] Ch 1

'A contractual licence does not create a property interest'. With this *obiter*, Millett J declared in *Camden LBC* v *Shortlife Community Housing* (1992) 90 LGR 358 that the Court of Appeal had 'finally repudiated the heretical view that a contractual licence creates an interest in land capable of binding third parties'.

Whilst it will take a House of Lords decision specifically on this point to clear the matter up completely, the *obiter* in *Ashburn Anstalt* provides very strong authority. Much of the ratio and decision in *Ashburn Anstalt* has since been overruled by the House of Lords in *Prudential Assurance Co Ltd* v *London Residuary Body* [1992] 2 AC 386, but the *per curiam* statement remains intact, further strengthening its authority. Indeed, in *Habermann* v *Kochler* (1996) 72 P & CR DIO it was stated that *Ashburn Anstalt* now 'governs contractual licences'.

A licence coupled with an interest

The interest to which the licence is coupled must be an interest in the land, usually a profit *à prendre*. A profit to pick apples from an orchard is of no use whatsoever if you would be trespassing by entering into the orchard, therefore a licence to enter is implied which will exist so long as the interest to which it is attached continues to exist. Easements of drainage provide another example of a licence coupled with an interest, that is a licence implied in order to give effect to the proprietary right.

A licence of this type is acquired by implication as soon as the right to which it attaches and gives effect is created. It continues whilst the interest, for instance a profit *à prendre*, exists. It is collateral to the interest and owes its entire existence to it. They rise and fall together.

Licences by estoppel

As we shall see in Chapter 2 'Proprietary estoppel' arises where one party, A, makes a representation or promise to another, B, that B will acquire an interest in the land and B acts to his or her detriment in reliance upon A's representation or promise. A, the licensor, will be estopped from denying his or her representation or promise.

Inwards v *Baker* [1965] 2 QB 29

Where a son built a bungalow on his father's land at his father's suggestion and in the belief that he would be able to stay there for his lifetime, the son was held to have a licence by estoppel under which he could remain on the land for as long as he wanted following the death of his father (under whose will the legal estate in the land had been left to others).

Two other cases – *Greasley* v *Cooke* [1980] 3 All ER 710 and *Re Sharpe (a Bankrupt)* [1980] 1 WLR 219 – resulted in the grant of licences which were binding upon third parties.

Greasley v *Cooke*

Miss Cooke was a maid servant to Mr Greasley, and had been since she was 16. She was paid 10 shillings (50p) a week. Some eight years later Miss Cooke began to cohabit with Mr Greasley's son, Kenneth, and she continued to do so until he died 29 years after that. Mr Greasley had died two years after Miss Cooke began cohabiting with Kenneth, and after that time she was not paid any wages although she continued to look after the house and the family, including caring for a daughter of the family who was mentally ill. Miss Cooke, being led by the family to believe that she would have a home for life, did not ask for wages. When Kenneth died, his interest in the house (which had been inherited from his father) had passed to his brother. Lord Denning held that Miss Cooke could stay in the house, rent-free, for as long as she wished, because the statements made by the family:

> were calculated to influence her – so as to put her mind at rest – so that she should not worry about being turned out.... So, instead of looking for another job, [Miss Cooke] stayed on in the house looking after Kenneth and Clarice [the daughter]. There is a presumption that she did so, relying on the assurances given to her ... The burden is not on her, but on them, to prove that she did not rely on their assurances. They did not prove it, nor did their representatives. So she is presumed to have relied on them.
>
> The second point [regarding estoppel] is about the need for some expenditure of money – some detriment – before a person can acquire any interest in a house or any right to stay in it as long as he wishes. It so happens that in many of these cases of proprietary estoppel there has been expenditure of money. But that is not a necessary element ... It is sufficient if the party, to whom the assurance is given, acts on the faith of it – in such circumstances that it would be unjust and inequitable for the party making the assurance to go back on it.

Re Sharpe (a Bankrupt)

On the understanding that she could live in her nephew's house and be cared for by him and his wife, an aunt lent the nephew £12,000 to enable him to buy the house (which cost £17,000). In addition, she spent some £2,000 in decorating it. She also paid off some of her nephew's debts in an attempt to prevent him from becoming bankrupt (but as you can see from the title of the case, she was not successful). The aunt moved into her nephew's house but, when her nephew went bankrupt, the trustee in bankruptcy sought vacant possession of it. Browne-Wilkinson J held that she could stay until the loan was repaid, explaining that:

> In a strict case of proprietary estoppel the plaintiff has expended his own money on the defendant's property in an expectation encouraged by or known to the defendant that the plaintiff either owns the property or is to have some interest conferred on him. Recent authorities have extended this doctrine and, in my judgment, it is now established that, if the parties have proceeded on a common assumption that the plaintiff is to enjoy a right to reside in a particular property and in reliance on that assumption the plaintiff has expended money or otherwise acted to his detriment, the defendant will not be allowed to go back on that common assumption and the court will imply an irrevocable licence on trust which will give effect to that common presumption.

A licence by estoppel is the only type of licence that is capable of being a proprietary right, because it is the only one that is capable of binding a third party (see Chapter 2IIB). It will arise upon the conditions for proprietary estoppel being satisfied. However, it is vital to understand that the interest arises **from the estoppel, not from the licence**: without a finding of estoppel the licence would remain just that – a mere permsision and a personal 'right' only. The next case provides a good example of the need to distinguish a licence from an interest in land, and how estoppel can have the effect of turning a mere licence into an interest in land, making it proprietary and not merely personal.

E R Ives Investments Ltd v High [1967] 2 QB 379

High, in 1949, began to build a house on a piece of land and soon after his neighbour, Westgate, started to build a block of flats. The foundations of the flats encroached upon H's land to a distance of about one foot, or approximately 30 centimetres. H agreed that the foundations could remain as laid upon a promise by W that he (H) could have a right of way for his car over W's yard. H never registered the agreement in regard to this right of way. In 1959, H built a garage, access to which could only be had via W's yard, and in 1960 H contributed to the surfacing of the yard. W sold the block of flats to Flt Lt and Mrs Wright, who knew all about the agreement for the right of way and the fact that H had erected a garage in reliance upon it. The Wrights sold the block in 1962, the purchasers taking expressly subject to H's right of way but later seeking a declaration that the right of way, which was only equitable, was void for lack of registration. The Court of Appeal found for High, Lord Denning explaining that:

> The right arises out of the expense incurred by Mr High in building his garage, as it is now, with access only over the yard: and the Wrights standing by and acquiescing in it, knowing that he believed he had a right of way over the yard. By so doing the Wrights created in Mr High's mind reasonable expectation that his access over the yard would not be disturbed. That gives rise to an 'equity arising out of acquiescence'. It is available not only against the Wrights but also their successors in title. The court will not allow that expectation to be defeated when it would be inequitable to do so.

Alternatively, Lord Denning was willing to hold for Mr High under the mutual benefit and burden doctrine, as in *Halsall* v *Brizell* [1957] Ch 169, being of the opinion that:

> [that] principle clearly applies in the present case. The owners of the block of flats have the benefit of having their foundations in Mr High's land. So long as they take that benefit, they must shoulder the burden. They must observe the condition on which the benefit was granted, namely, they must allow Mr High and his successors to have access across their yard ... Conversely, so long as Mr High takes the benefit of the access, he must permit the block of flats to keep their foundations on his land.

Thus, because licences by estoppel can bind third parties, they are capable of becoming interests in land – the only type of licence which is so capable. As Cheshire and Burn (2000, p. 649) so rightly say, 'The development of the doctrine of estoppel in the context of licences over the past 50 years has been remarkable'. **It must be understood, however, that not all rights 'acquired' by way of estoppel are merely licences.** In *Pascoe* v *Turner* [1979] 1 WLR 431, where a man had repeatedly told his cohabitee that 'the house is yours and everything in it', he was ordered to convey the fee simple absolute to her when he left her for another woman, as she had relied to her detriment upon his representations. Though it provides an excellent example of the application of proprietary estoppel, *Pascoe* v *Turner* obviously gave rise to far more than a mere licence!

Licences by estoppel do not appear in the Law of Property Act 1925, s 1(1) or (2), and can, therefore, never be legal. It is only natural, as they arise under the doctrine of estoppel, that they can only be equitable. In registered land, estoppel licences are treated as minor interests.

The length of a licence by estoppel depends upon the original representation or promise which gave rise to it and what the court deems necessary to satisfy the equity. Two cases, both concerning fathers and sons, illustrate this point.

Dillwyn v *Llewellyn* (1862) 4 De GF&J 517

A father gave his son possession of his land and permission to build a house thereon. The father also thought he had conveyed the land to his son, but he had only effected a memorandum in writing. The son duly entered on the land and built a house upon it. When the father died it was found that he had left his son only a life interest in the land. It was held that the son was entitled to the fee simple, notwithstanding the maxim 'there is no equity to perfect an imperfect gift'. Lord Westbury LC explained why:

> if A puts B into possession of a piece of land and tells him: 'I give it to you that you may build a house on it' and B, on the strength of that promise, with the knowledge of A, spends a large sum of money in building a house accordingly, I cannot doubt that the donee acquires a right from the subsequent transaction to call on the donor to perform that contract and complete the imperfect donation which was made ... The equity of the donee and the estate to be claimed by virtue of it depend on the transaction, that is, on the acts done ... the subsequent expenditure by the son with the approbation of the father, supplied a valuable consideration originally wanting.

The facts of *Inwards* v *Baker* are very similar.

Inwards v *Baker* [1965] 2 QB 29

A father suggested to his son that he (the son) build a bungalow on the father's land rather than purchase a plot elsewhere. The son duly did so, his father providing some financial assistance, which the son had repaid in part. The son lived in the bungalow, believing he could remain there for the rest of his life, or for as long as he wished. When his father died, the trustees of his will claimed possession of the bungalow saying that the son was a mere licensee. The Court of Appeal held that the son was entitled to remain in the bungalow for as long as he wished. Danckwerts LJ expressed the view that:

> this is one of the cases of equity created by estoppel, or equitable estoppel, as it is sometimes called, by which the person who has made the expenditure is induced by the expectation of obtaining protection and equity protects him so that an injustice may not be perpetrated.

Lord Denning explained that it was not only the father who was bound:

> the plaintiffs, the successors in title of the father, are clearly themselves bound by this equity. It is an equity well recognised in law. It arises from the expenditure of money by a person in actual occupation of land when he is led to believe that, as a result of that expenditure, he will be allowed to remain there. It is for the court to say in what way the equity can be satisfied by holding that the defendant can remain there as long as he desires to use it as his home.

These two cases show the different ways in which the equity was held to be satisfied – one son attained the fee simple, the other a right to possession for life – where, on the face of it, both sons had done the same thing, that is, built a dwelling. Also, the fact that the successors in title of the father in *Inwards* v *Baker*, namely, third parties, were bound, made the estoppel licence an interest in land – it is an interest in land because it binds: it does not bind a third party because it is an interest.

Pascoe v Turner [1979] 1 WLR 431

Mrs Turner moved in with Mr Pascoe, originally as a housekeeper and later as cohabitee. Later on Mr Pascoe bought another house and the couple, still living as man and wife, moved in. Later still, Mr Pascoe began an affair with another woman, but assured Mrs Turner on several occasions that 'the house is yours and everything in it'. In reliance on this promise, Mrs Turner redecorated the house, carried out some repairs and improvements and had carpets fitted. Mr Pascoe then gave Mrs Turner two months' notice to 'determine her licence to occupy' the house. The Court of Appeal ordered Mr Pascoe to convey the fee simple to Mrs Turner, in order to perfect the imperfect gift of the house (there being no problem with the contents, as no formality is required to pass title to them).

It may seem unfair that Mrs Turner, for her relatively small outlay, attains the fee simple, whilst the son in *Inwards* v *Baker* has a mere right of occupation for life. However, to think in that way is to miss the point because, as Cummins-Bruce LJ explained in *Pascoe*:

> the principle to be applied is that the court should consider all the circumstances ... decide what is the minimum equity to do justice to her, having regard to the way in which she changed her position for the worse by reason of the acquiescence and encouragement of the legal owner ... the equity to which the facts in this case give rise can only be satisfied by compelling the plaintiff to give effect to his promise and her expectations.

Thus, it is the promise or representation in reliance upon which it was made that decides the matter: in *Pascoe* a fee simple absolute was promised, in *Baker* a mere licence to remain.

It was held in *Greasley* v *Cooke* that it is for the promisor to prove that the promisee did not rely on the promise or representation made, and that expenditure is not a necessary element of detriment, as Lord Denning explained:

> The second point is about the need for some expenditure of money, some detriment, before a person can acquire any interest in a house or any right to stay in it as long as he wishes. It so happens that in many of these cases of proprietary estoppel there has been expenditure of money. But that is not a necessary element ... It is sufficient if the party, to whom the assurance is given, acts on the faith of it, in such circumstances that it would be unjust and inequitable for the party making the assurance to go back on it.

Therefore, a licence by estoppel arises upon a promisee acting to his detriment in reliance upon some promise, assurance or representation made to him by the promisor. (In addition, acquiescence by the licensor in the detrimental reliance of the licensee may suffice.) How long the licence will continue will depend upon the nature of the promise and the nature of the equity required to give effect to it. It is the expectation, not the expenditure, which dictates the outcome.

So, only licences arising from estoppel are even capable of being interests in land.

We shall return to proprietary estoppel in Chapter 2, section II B.

With regard to unregistered land, it was held in *E R Ives* v *High* [1967] 2 QB 379 that such an interest cannot be registered as a land charge, nor can those arising under the doctrine of mutual benefit and burden. They are, therefore, subject to the doctrine of notice.

In registered land 'an equity by estoppel ... has effect from the time the equity arises as an interest capable of binding successors in title ...' – Land Registration Act 2002, s 116. Consequently, they are minor interests (see Chapter 3, section C).

Licences affecting land were held to fall within the protection of Article 1 of the ECHR in *JS* v *Netherlands* (1995) 20 EHRR CD 89, ECtHR.

Summary

In this introductory chapter we discover the foundations of land law:

- The various matters to be considered when addressing any problem in land law – the people who will be affected by the finding or otherwise of an interest in land; the nature of the interest claimed or challenged; the classification of interests as legal or equitable; the different relationships that may be involved in the holding of the legal estate – trustee and beneficiary, landlord and tenant; the methods by which interests in land can be acquired and their duration; the existence of third parties and the need to protect interests; the relevance of the Human Rights Act 1998 in land law; the role of reform.
- How to apply land law.
- The importance of the correct use of language in land law.
- The nature of land law – the types of property, realty and personalty.
- The meaning of 'land' – treasure; fixtures and fittings; licences.

References

Ackerman, B, *Private Property and the Constitution*, New Haven and London: Yale University Press, 1977.

Burn, E H, *Cheshire and Burn's Modern Law of Real Property*, 16th edition, London: Butterworths, 2000.

Dalton, P J, *Land Law*, 4th edition, London: Financial Times Pitman Publishing, 1996.

George, S, *Liverpool Park Estates*, Liverpool: Liverpool University Press, 2000.

Gray, K, *Elements of Land Law*, 2nd edition, London: Butterworths, 1993.

Gray, K.J. and Symes, P.D., *Real Property and Real People*, London: Butterworths, 1981.

Halstead, P, 'Human Property Rights' [2002] Conv 153.

Howell, J, 'The Protection of Rights in Property in Land under the Human Rights Act', *The Human Rights Act 1998: What It Means*, ed Lammy Betten, Kluwer Law International, 1999.

Law Commission, *Land Registration for the Twenty-First Century* (Law Com No 254, 1998).

Lawson, F H, *The Rational Strength of the English Law*, London: Stevens, 1951.

Lawson, F H and Rudden, B, *The Law of Property*, 3rd edition, Oxford University Press, 2002.

Rook, D, 'Property Law and the Human Rights Act 1998: A Review of the First Year' [2002] Conv 316.

Stevens, 'Land Law: Old Complexities, New Reform?' *Sweet & Maxwell's Academic News*, Winter 1997.

Yale, D E C, 'Treasure Trove - Old Law and New Needs' [1980] CLJ 281.

Further reading

ABOUT THIS BOOK

Allen, T, 'Transactions at an undervalue, purchases and the impact of the Human Rights Act 1998' [2004] JLB 1.

Bright, S, 'Of Estates and Interests: A Tale of Ownership and Property Rights', *Land Law Themes and Perspectives*, eds Susan Bright and John Dewar, Oxford University Press, 1998 (p 529).

Cretney, S M, 'The Law Commission: True Dawns and False Dawns' (1996) 59 MLR 631.

Grear, A, 'A tale of the land, the insider, the outsider and human rights' (2003) 23(1) *Legal Studies* 33.

Halstead, P, 'Human Property Rights' [2002] Conv 153.

Harpum, C, 'The Law Commission and the Reform of Land Law', *Land Law Themes and Perspectives*, eds Susan Bright and John Dewar, Oxford University Press, 1998 (p 151).

Howell, J, 'Land and Human Rights' [1999] Conv 287.

Howell, J, 'The Protection of Rights of Property in Land under the Human Rights Act', *The Human Rights Act 1998: What It Means*, ed Lammy Betten, Kluwer Law International, 1999.

Rook, D, 'Property Law and the Human Rights Act 1998: A Review of the First Year' [2002] Conv 316.

WHAT IS LAND LAW?

Alexander, G, 'Critical Land Law', *Land Law Themes and Perspectives*, eds Susan Bright and John Dewar, Oxford University Press, 1998 (p 52).

Garner, Prof., 'Land law 1900–1992', NLJ, 5 June 1992.

Greed, J A, 'Land law 2000–2092', NLJ, 30 April 1993.

WHAT IS LAND?

Anderson, S, 'Of Licences and Similar Mysteries', 42 MLR 203.

Baughan, S, 'Estoppels over land and third parties. An open question?' (1994) 14 *Legal Studies* 147.

Bridge, S, 'Part and Parcel: Fixtures in the House of Lords' (1997) CLJ 498.

Gray, K and S F, 'The Idea of Property in Land', *Land Law Themes and Perspectives*, eds Susan Bright and John Dewar, Oxford University Press, 1998 (p 15).

Haley, M, 'The Law of Fixtures: An Unprincipled Metamorphosis?' (1998) Conv 137.

Lawson, F H and Rudden, B *The Law of Property*, 3rd edition, Oxford University Press, 2002, Chapters I and II.

Luther, P, 'Fixtures and Chattels – A Question of More or Less . . .' 24 DJLS 597.

Marston, J and Ross, L, 'Treasure and Portable Antiquities in the 1990s still chained to the ghosts of the past: The Treasure Act 1996' [1997] Conv 273.

Marston, J and Ross, L, 'The Treasure Act 1996, Code of Practice and Home Office Circular on Treasure Inquests' [1998] Conv 252.

Stevens, J, 'Finders Weepers – Landowners Keepers' [1996] Conv 216.

2 How can you acquire them?

The rules, principles and formalities governing the acquisition of interests in land

I FORMAL ACQUISITION

What's the problem?
Formalities in context

For what seems like an eternity (especially for Richard), Hyacinth and Richard, an elderly married couple, have been looking for a new home. At last they have found just what they (or at least, Hyacinth) want: a bungalow with room for a Mercedes and a pony. They agreed the price with the owners, Violet and Bruce. They paid for a private survey as well as for one on behalf of the building society, from whom they were to borrow the purchase price. Hyacinth began to make up cushions and matching lampshades in chintz. Richard paid £750 for a set of plans for the garden. Just before they were due to 'exchange contracts', Bruce rang to say 'It's all off. I've had a better offer from a Mr Emmett. You've been gazumped, mate.'

Sybil and Basil, a middle-aged couple, have, for some months, been negotiating to buy a hotel in Torquay from Manuel. With Manuel's permission, they have had a new central heating system installed and replaced all the windows and doors with UPVC double glazed units. In all, they have laid out £50,000. They recently heard something which has decided them not to go ahead with the purchase. Sybil has just rung their solicitor to inform him of their decision, but he told her that they cannot pull out of the deal now because of the work they have done on the hotel.

Years ago, Billy agreed in writing to grant a lease of a radio station to Wally for 25 years. It was agreed that a deed would be executed and that it would contain a provision that rent should be paid annually in advance. Wally took possession of the studio and has been paying £1,000 monthly in arrears. No deed has ever been executed. Wally has not paid any rent for the last three months. Billy has demanded £15,000 – the arrears and a year's rent in advance. Billy has told Wally that he will take all the radio equipment 'by way of distress' if Wally does not pay up. Wally is certainly distressed!

Who cares?

Those who will be affected

The property owner. Can Violet and Bruce go ahead at the higher offer? If so, do they owe anything to Hyacinth and Richard by way of compensation for the money they have spent? Can Manuel force Sybil and Basil to go through with the purchase? If not, must he pay them for the work they have had carried out? Can Billy lawfully carry out his threat?

The intended purchasers. Can Hyacinth and Richard force Violet and Bruce to sell to them? If not, can they get from them any of the money they have spent? Can Sybil and Basil pull out from the purchase of the hotel? If so, can they get back the money they have spent improving Manuel's property? Can Wally simply pay the arrears of rent and carry on paying a month in arrears? If not, as Wally has not got £15,000, can Billy take all his equipment?

Any prospective purchasers. Will Hyacinth and Richard have any interest which may be binding on Mr Emmett? If Manuel cannot enforce the agreement with Sybil and Basil, and he does not pay them anything for the central heating and double glazing, will any purchaser of the hotel be liable to them in his stead? If Billy decides to grant a lease of the studio to someone else, will they be able to take possession of it, or will they have to let Wally stay in occupation?

In each case, the answer to one party will, as often happens, be the answer to all. What that answer may be will depend upon several things. Was there a valid contract? Was there any 'exchange of contracts'? What was the date of any agreement? Has the plaintiff in each case acted 'bona fide', in good faith? Did the vendor have title to sell? In each case the claimant would probably ask how, if at all, it would have been different had a deed been executed in his, her or their favour.

What is it?

The rules, principles and formalities governing the acquisition of interests in land

In this chapter we shall consider the rules, principles and formalities which govern the acquisition of proprietary interests, whether they are acquired as legal or equitable rights. We know, of course, that there are only two estates and five interests that are even capable of being legal, and if they are to be legal, they must, as a general rule, be created by deed because 'All conveyances of land or of any interest therein are void for the purpose of conveying or creating a legal estate unless made by deed' – Law of Property Act 1925, s 52(1). However, the Act itself provides an exception: legal leases of less than three years can be created without a deed – s 54(2). (However, any assignment of a lease, that is any transfer of all of the time left in the lease, must be by deed – even leases governed by s 54(2)). In regard to interests in land, easements can be legal even where there is no deed of grant (Chapter 12). Remember the wide meaning of 'land' which includes, for example, the buildings on land and fixtures in them – Law of Property Act 1925, s 205(1)(ix).

Unless a contrary intention appears in a conveyance of freehold land, it will 'pass to the grantee the fee simple or other the whole interest which the grantor had power to convey in such land' – Law of Property Act, s 60. Therefore, unless expressly stated otherwise in a conveyance, it will pass to the purchaser the whole of the fee simple in the land. However, s 60 cannot convert non-proprietary rights into proprietary rights:

> ... if on the true construction of the document it creates personal interests only and not rights of the nature of property rights, then a contrary intention does not appear. The Law of Property Act 1925, section 60, does not convert what would under the general law be a personal right into a freehold – property right – Sir Nicholas Browne-Wilkinson VC in *IDC Group Ltd* v *Clark* (1992) 08 EG 108.

Remember also that 'purchaser' has a far wider meaning for the purposes of land law than it has in everyday language, for:

> 'Purchaser' means a purchaser in good faith for valuable consideration and includes a lessee, mortgagee or other person who for valuable consideration acquires an interest in property ... and in reference to the legal estate includes a chargee by way of legal mortgage; and where the context so requires 'purchaser' includes an intending purchaser; 'purchase' has a meaning corresponding with that of 'purchaser' and 'valuable consideration' includes marriage but does not include a nominal consideration in money – Law of Property Act 1925, s 205(1)(xxi).

Deeds

Section 52, then, requires all conveyances of land or of interests therein to be by deed. Needless to say, the deed must be valid and this depends upon the date of it. If created before 30 July 1990, the conveyance must be signed, sealed and delivered; if after 31 July 1990, it must comply with the requirements of the Law of Property (Miscellaneous Provisions) Act 1989, s 1 of which provides that:

(1) Any rule of law which –
    (a) restricts the substances on which a deed may be written;
    (b) requires a seal for the valid execution of an instrument as a deed by an individual; or
    (c) requires authority by one person to another to deliver an instrument as a deed on his behalf to be given by deed, is abolished.

(2) An instrument shall not be a deed unless –
    (a) it makes it clear on its face that it is intended to be a deed by the person making it or, as the case may be, by the parties to it (whether by describing itself as a deed or expressing itself to be executed or signed as a deed or otherwise);
    (b) it is validly executed as a deed by that person or, as the case may be, one or more of those parties.

(3) An instrument is validly executed as a deed by an individual if, and only if –
    (a) it is signed –
        (i) by him in the presence of a witness who attests the signature; or
        (ii) at his direction and in his presence and the presence of two witnesses who each attest the signature; and
    (b) it is delivered as a deed by him or a person authorised to do so on his behalf.

If the relevant formality is not complied with, the conveyance will be void and thus the legal estate will not have passed to the purchaser, but will remain with the vendor.

Shah v Shah [2001] 3 WLR 31

The Court of Appeal held that what was fundamental to the public interest for the perceived need for formality in s 1 was the requirement for a signature, not that the person attesting it should be present when the document was signed. Thus, failure to comply with the additional formality of attestation should not permit a party to escape the consequences of an apparently valid deed by claiming that the attesting witness was not present at the time of the signature.

However, even a valid deed can only convey (that is, transfer or pass) what the vendor has. So, if the right claimed is not an interest in land, it will not become one simply because the purported creation or transfer of it was by deed.

We have already seen (in Chapter 1, section E) that a contractual licence is not an interest in land, but it can look very like a lease. As we shall see shortly, the Court of Appeal in *Pitt v PHH Asset Management Ltd* [1994] 1 WLR 327 held that a 'lock-out' agreement, though it relates to the sale of land, is not an interest in land.

It may be that the transferor does not own the interest which he claims to be transferring. You can only grant that which you have, thus the purported grant of something you do not possess – albeit by deed – will not pass the interest to the transferee. (However, the agreement may be held to operate as between the transferor and the transferee personally by estoppel. If the transferor later acquires the interest in question, this is said to 'feed the estoppel' and the transfer of the interest is then validated (see II B).)

It is not possible to convey a legal estate to a minor (anyone under 18): Law of Property Act 1925, s 1(6). See *Hector v Lyons* (1989) 58 P&CR 156.

A deed to convey land or any interest in land will specify the parties, the land or interest to be conveyed, the price and any special terms. If the price is below £60,000 (£150,000 for property which is wholly or partly non-residential), the deed will certify that fact and that no stamp duty land tax is payable.

Deeds usually begin with the words 'This Conveyance', 'This Transfer', 'This Lease', 'This Assignment' or 'This Deed'. You may even come across older deeds which begin with the words 'This Indenture'. 'This Deed' will probably satisfy s 1(2), but if any of the other terms are used it must be made clear somewhere else in the document that it is executed **as a deed**. If not, it will be void (of no effect), as if it were never made. The most convenient place to include the necessary words would be in 'the testimonium' which is required by s 1(3): witnesses now attest, rather than merely sign, a deed. So, whereas before August 1990 parties would sign, seal and deliver the deed, witnesses signing it also, deeds after July 1990 must comply with s 1.

In unregistered land we deal with title deeds. In registered land we do not see these again once the Land Registrar has investigated them one last time. In registered land a Land Certificate is produced for each title and any conveyances take effect by way of transfers. Mortgages are known as charges.

As I R Storey (1990, p 226) explains: 'Delivery is a rather strange concept. It does not mean the handing over of the deed to the other party, for example handing over to the buyer on completion, although this would certainly amount to delivery'. What, then, does it mean? '... delivery ... means an act done so as to evince an intention to be bound. Even though the deed remains in the possession of the maker, or of his solicitor, he is bound by it if he has done some act evincing an intention to be bound' – Court of Appeal in *Vincent v Premo Enterprises (Voucher Sales) Ltd* [1969] 2 QB 609. The date on the deed is the date of delivery.

'Completion' will not take place until there has been effective execution and delivery of the deed and the purchase price has been paid. In unregistered land title then passes to the buyer, but in registered land title will not pass until the buyer is registered as the new registered proprietor.

E-conveyancing

The Land Registration Act 2002 introduces electronic conveyancing. It is this concept which encapsulates the new principle of *title by registration*, which will replace registration *of* title.

The introduction of electronic documents will necessitate new formalities and these are set down in s 91. Whether the document is to have the effect of a deed or a contract, s 91(3) lays down uniform requirements that –

(a) the document makes provision for the time and date when it is to take effect,

(b) the document has the electronic signature of each person by whom it purports to be authenticated,

(c) each electronic signature is certified, and

(d) such other conditions as rules may provide are met.

A document which satisfies these requirements is to be regarded as being in writing and properly executed – s 91(4), and as a deed – s 91(5).

Section 91(6) provides for authentication of a document by the electronic signature of an agent (which will be regarded as authentication under the written authority of the agent's principal). As yet the exact nature of the electronic signature is not known. Indeed there is much about the new electronic system which has yet to be explained. Given that one government prediction is that it will be anything up to ten years before the system becomes fully operational, and the speed with which computer technology evolves, all will not become clear until the system actually comes on line.

However, e-conveyancing is far more than a means of creating documents online. It is an entire process by which title to land is transferred, for,

A disposition to which this section applies, or a contract to make such a disposition, only has effect if it is made by means of a document in electronic form and if, when the document purports to take effect –
(a) it is electronically communicated to the registrar, and
(b) the relevant registration requirements are met – s 93(2).
Relevant dispositions for this purpose are of registered estates or charges, or of interests which are the subject of a notice in the register – s 93(1).

Thus the need for 'exchange' and 'delivery' is eliminated. With the click of a mouse both creation or transfer of the estate or interest and its registration take place. No more deeds, no more paper. Some of us, especially those who were brought up on unregistered conveyancing, still miss real deeds with their lovely language, on vellum with crimson seals and green silk ribbon: it was never the same in registered conveyancing (or in unregistered after the Law of Property (Miscellaneous Provisions) Act 1989)! Yet, quite apart from the beauty of a properly engrossed conveyance, the language, with its lack of any punctuation, had an important role to play in guarding against fraud. One has one's doubts as to the security of a totally paperless conveyancing world. For example, it is likely that electronic signatures will be protected by private 'keys' – a bit like pin numbers. The instance of fraud on the use of bankers' cards and cash machines is extremely high. Computer hackers have broken into systems in Fort Knox and Buckingham Palace. What is to prevent a hacker from breaking into the new Land Registry system and creating interests (such as mortgages) or estates (by replacing the name of the registered proprietor) himself? The Land Registry assures us that its system will be secure. As with so much else here, we shall have to wait and see.

Under the Land Registration Act 2002 there will be no estate except by registration, thus, where registration is required, it will not only protect the estate, but create it.

Contracts

However, between the negotiations for purchase and the completed conveyance of the legal estate or interest, there is a contract stage. The contract is usually in a standard form produced by the Law Society. It contains the Standard Conditions of Sale which can be altered by the parties by agreement, but in contracts for the sale of dwellinghouses alteration is rare.

As with the general rules of contract, contracts for the sale or other disposition of land or any interest in land must contain all the essential terms of the agreement – parties, property, interest to be granted, consideration (price) and any special terms.

Until contracts are 'exchanged', that is each party holds the duly signed part of the other, and the agreed deposit has passed to the vendor, there is no binding contract. Until exchange, the agreement is usually made 'subject to contract', which means that, as yet, there is no contract and either party can withdraw from negotiations with impunity. It is generally believed that, following the Law of Property (Miscellaneous Provisions) Act 1989, s 2, under which there can be no contract unless it is in writing and signed by or on behalf of both parties, there is no longer any need for negotiations to be labelled 'subject to contract'.

Contracts made before 27 September 1989

There are separate formal requirements for the creation of a valid contract. Here again, the relevant requirements depend upon the date of the agreement. If it is before 27 September 1989, the Law of Property Act 1925, s 40 applies. This provides that:

(1) No action may be brought upon any contract for the sale or other disposition of land or any interest in land, unless the agreement upon which such action is brought, or

some memorandum or note thereof, is in writing, and signed by the party to be charged or by some other person thereunto by him lawfully authorised.

(2) This section ... does not affect the law relating to part performance ...

Thus, a contract made prior to 27 September 1989 must be either *in writing* and signed by the party to be charged (ie the defendant in any action upon the contract), or evidenced by some written memorandum or note thereof similarly signed, or by some act of part performance. Any memorandum or note should set out all the terms of the agreement – the names of the parties, a description of the property, the consideration (purchase price), any special terms which have been agreed and show or imply an intention to create legal relations. If no such memorandum exists, it is possible for a parol (oral) contract to be evidenced by acts of part performance, that is acts which by their nature evidence the existence of a contract between the parties and which were done in part performance of it. Whilst the taking of possession of the property by the purchaser would be an act of part performance, such acts need not necessarily, as that would, constitute the performance of an agreed obligation or right under the contract. However, they must 'be such that by themselves they suggest that it is more likely than not that the parties have entered into some contract of the kind alleged' – *Steadman* v *Steadman* [1976] AC 536, and they must be the acts of the claimant (whereas it is the defendant who must have signed any written contract).

Lloyds Bank plc v *Carrick* [1996] 4 All ER 630

There was an oral agreement between a widow and her brother-in-law (B). The widow sold her house, giving the proceeds of £19,000 to B on an oral understanding that it would be payment for a maisonette, the lease of which was owned by B. The Court of Appeal held that at the time the agreement was made there was a valid contract but it was not enforceable because it did not comply with s 40 (the agreement pre-dated the 1989 Act), in that there was no writing and no part performance. However, it became enforceable when Mrs Carrick paid the purchase money to B and went into possession, thereby providing part performance. See the judgment of Evans-Lombe J in *Bankers Trust Co* v *Namdar* [1995] NPC 139, which provides a survey of the cases on part performance. *Carrick* could well be the swan song for s 40.

Failure to comply with the requirements of s 40 renders the contract unenforceable by action, but not void. Therefore you could, for example, claim for the return of your deposit, but not for an order of the court compelling the vendor to go ahead with the sale.

Contracts made after 26 September 1989

Barnsley (1988, p 105) describes s 40 as a 'familiar provision engraved on the hearts of all real property students'. However, as from 26 September 1989, another provision must become equally engraved – Law of Property (Miscellaneous Provisions) Act 1989, s 2. This provides that:

(1) A contract for the sale or other disposition of an interest in land can only be made in writing and only by incorporating all the terms which the parties have expressly agreed in one document or, where contracts are exchanged, in each ...

(3) The document incorporating the terms or, where contracts are exchanged, one of the documents incorporating them (but not necessarily the same one) must be signed by or on behalf of each party to the contract.

Thus, contracts entered into after 26 September 1989 must be actually *in writing* and signed by *both* parties. (Normally there are two copies of the contract, each being signed by one of the parties and then exchanged. Until this exchange of contracts there is no binding contract.) Nothing less than this will create a valid contract and it would seem, therefore, that there can be no role for part performance – either the agreement complies with the requirements of s 2, in which case it creates a valid and binding contract, or it does not so comply and there is no contract to be part performed. Failure to comply with the requirements of s 2 renders the 'contract' void. In *Spiro* v *Glencrown Properties Ltd* [1991] 1 All ER 600, Hoffmann J explained that, 'Section 2 . . . was intended to prevent disputes over whether the parties had entered into a binding agreement or over what terms they had agreed. It prescribes the formalities for recording their mutual consent'. Thus, Hoffmann J took a purposive approach in his interpretation of s 2, as did Peter Gibson LJ in *Firstpost Homes Ltd* v *Johnson* [1995] 4 All ER 355: he was also clear about the purpose behind the Act, which he stated to be the making of a 'new provision with respect to contracts for the sale or other disposition of interests in land . . . intended to make radical changes to such contracts in a way that was intended to simplify the law and to avoid disputes'. Given this purpose, Peter Gibson LJ refused 'to encumber the Act with . . . ancient baggage' by applying cases on the interpretation of s 40 to questions arising in connection with s 2.

Unfortunately, though the aim to simplify the law and avoid disputes may have been a good one, the number of cases which have fallen to be decided upon the meaning of s 2 prove that many a rocky road is paved with good intentions.

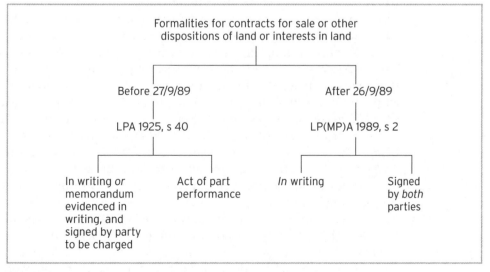

Figure 2.1

Contracts must contain all expressly agreed terms

The requirement that a s 2 contract must contain all the expressly agreed terms gave rise to one of the earliest cases – *Record* v *Bell* [1991] 1 WLR 853. The contract here was for the sale and purchase of a very expensive property in London, title to which was registered. Contracts in duplicate had been prepared and signed by or on behalf of the parties, but exchange was made conditional by the purchaser's solicitor upon office copy entries confirming the vendor's solicitor's statement of the facts. The fact that exchange was conditional was mentioned by the vendor's solicitor in the letter which accompanied his client's signed part of the contract. When sending the purchaser's part, his solicitor attached to it a signed note setting out the agreed condition. When eventually the office copy entries were to hand, they upheld the vendor's solicitor's version of the facts.

Come the date of completion the purchaser was not in a position to go through with the purchase due to financial losses sustained during the Gulf War. Naturally, the vendor sought specific performance of the contract, but the purchaser contended that there was no valid contract under s 2 on the basis that the condition agreed to by both solicitors was one which should have been incorporated into or referred to in the written contracts, which it was not. The court held that there had in fact been two contracts – one for the sale of the land, the other a collateral contract based upon the agreed condition. As the collateral agreement related only to production of proof of the legal title to the property, it was not itself a contract for the sale of an estate or interest in land. Therefore, it was not subject to s 2 and could be validly created orally. The principal contract, that for the transfer of title, satisfied s 2 and was, therefore, enforceable also.

Although this transaction was held not to be one involving a later variation of the contract, the court stated that a letter of variation of a contract, or one containing additional terms, could be enforced if both parties had signed it. A case which did concern the variation of a contract was *McCausland* v *Duncan Lawrie* [1997] 1 WLR 38. The contract in question, as originally written, satisfied all the requirements of s 2. However, subsequently the date for completion contained in the contract was varied by agreement contained in correspondence between the parties. The purchaser failed to complete on the new date and also failed to comply with the vendor's notice to complete. As a result, the vendor sought rescission of the contract, but the purchaser counterclaimed for specific performance of it. Relying upon s 2, the purchaser argued that the variation was ineffective. The Court of Appeal agreed with him. It held that this was a variation of a material term in the contract and as such had to comply with s 2 if either party was to be able to enforce the varied term.

This approach to satisfying s 2 is stricter than that taken in *Record* v *Bell* and *Tootal Clothing Ltd* v *Guinea Properties Management Ltd* [1992] EGCS 80, the next case we are going to look at. Taken together, all three cases show how the apparently simple requirement that a contract contain all the terms in writing is not as easy to interpret as it would seem.

As we have just seen, the purchaser in *Record* v *Bell* was unsuccessful in his attempt to avoid liability by relying upon the requirements of s 2; so too was the tenant in *Tootal Clothing*. Here again there were two contracts – one for the grant of a lease, the other an agreement under which the tenant would carry out work on the premises upon completion of which the landlord would pay £30,000. The grant of the lease duly went ahead and the tenant carried out the necessary works, but the landlord refused to pay up. The question arose as to whether both agreements had to comply with s 2. The Court of Appeal held that upon completion of the grant of the lease, s 2 ceased to apply. This left the agreement for the works and payment of them as a separate contract. Not being a contract for the sale of land, s 2 did not apply to it: as Scott LJ said, 'If parties choose to hive off parts of the terms of their composite bargain into a separate contract distinct from the written land contract that incorporates the rest of the terms, I can see nothing in s 2 that provides an answer to an action for enforcement of the land contract, on the one hand, or of the separate contract on the other hand. Each has become, by the choice of the parties, a separate contract'.

The claimant building contractor in *Godden* v *Merthyr Tydfil Housing Association* (1997) 76 P&CR, D1, sought to rely upon *Tootal Clothing*. He claimed that an oral contract to purchase land from the housing association and develop it, though it failed to satisfy s 2, was 'validated' by the second contract, the contract for the actual purchase, which did satisfy s 2. The Court of Appeal held the contract was void. There was no 'composite bargain' in which the first contract merely provided consideration for the second and it was not, therefore, a land contract. In the words of Simon Brown LJ:

> ... there was in this case but one single unified agreement – an agreement under which the defendants undertook to purchase from the plaintiff land which in the first place he was to acquire, prepare and develop to their order. It seems to me entirely unreal to attempt to separate that out into two discrete, or even distinct, agreements – one involving the disposition of land, the other not. Rather, all the obligations between the parties were integral to each other, part and parcel of a single scheme.

The Court of Appeal had to look at this sort of problem again in *Wright* v *Robert Leonard (Developments) Ltd* [1994] NPC 49, but in doing so took a slightly different tack. The contract in question was for the sale and purchase of a show flat and its furnishings. The written contract made no mention of the furnishings and, upon moving in after completion, the purchaser found the furnishings had been removed. He claimed damages for breach of contract, but the vendors argued there was no contract in regard to the furnishings. Were there, in fact, two contracts here, as in *Record* v *Bell*? No: there was only one contract, though there were two elements to it, and, if the contract is all one arrangement, there is no collateral contract, and all the terms in it must be in writing, even those which do not refer to the land.

Again, this case shows a stricter approach to the requirement under s 2 for written terms. (However, the purchaser still won back the furnishings – or at least the value of them: the court used its power under s 2(4) to rectify the agreement and grant damages for breach of it.)

Contracts must be signed by both parties

Surely there can be no difficulty with the need for contracts to be signed by both parties? Not so.

Firstpost Homes Ltd v *Johnson* [1995] 4 All ER 355

The Court of Appeal held that for the purposes of s 2 a letter purporting to constitute a contract for the sale of land, which contained a reference to the plan enclosed with it, was a separate document from the plan itself. The letter was one document and the plan was another. The terms of the agreement were incorporated in the letter. It followed that the letter, and not the plan, was the document which was required to be signed for the purposes of s 2, so that the purchaser's signature on the plan alone did not suffice to create a contract where that party had prepared the document and had caused his name merely to be printed or typed at the head of the document: this did not amount to a sufficient signature of the contract for the purposes of s 2, which requires each party to the agreement to write his name on the document in his own handwriting. In this case, the purchaser had prepared a letter for the vendor to sign: the purchaser's name was typed at the top of the letter. The purchaser had signed the plan to which the letter referred but not the letter itself. There was no valid contract.

Contracts must be in writing

Even the apparently straightforward requirement that a contract be in writing has not been free from doubt, as two cases show.

Hooper v *Sherman* [1994] NPC 153

An unmarried couple agreed that the man be freed from his obligation to repay the mortgage loan on their family home if he transferred his interest in it to the woman. Their respective solicitors confirmed the agreement by letter. Due to the fault of the mortgagees there was some delay in completing the arrangement and in the interim the man had changed his mind and refused to complete. Could the agreement be enforced against him? The majority of the Court of Appeal held that it could, based upon a bilateral contract which came into being with the exchange of letters. However, Morritt LJ dissented on the ground that the letters merely represented confirmation of an oral agreement: they were not, in themselves, sufficient to satisfy the requirement of writing for the purposes of s 2 (though they would have satisfied s 40).

This dissenting view is reflected in the decision in the following case.

Commission for the New Towns v *Cooper (Great Britain) Ltd* [1995] 2 WLR 677

Another case involving letters between vendor and purchaser: again, the letters purported to record an oral agreement between the parties and the question was whether this correspondence amounted to a contract for the purposes of s 2. The Court of Appeal held that it did not, stating that s 2 required 'a greater degree of formality in relation to contracts for sale or other disposition of interests in land' and also exchange of those contracts. If a contract is to be capable of exchange, the parties must have concluded all the terms of it and have put these in writing and signed their respective copies of it. Being merely the process by which such an agreement is reached, a written offer and acceptance can no longer create a written contract.

Contracts which do not need to satisfy s 2

Though the requirements we have been looking at are required for most contracts of land, s 2(5) provides three which are exempt:

(a) a contract to grant a lease of less than three years. (As we know, the actual grant of such a lease does not have to be by deed – LPA 1925, s 54(2));

(b) a contract made in the course of a public auction; and

(c) a contract regulated under the Financial Services Act 1986.

In addition, 'nothing in this section affects the creation or operation of resulting, implied or constructive trusts'. Also, it was held by the Court of Appeal in *Joyce* v *Rigolli* [2004] EWCA Civ 79, that, in a case concerning the demarcation of a boundary 'it can . . . properly be concluded that s 2 does not apply to trivial dispositions of land consciously made pursuant to an informal boundary agreement of the "demarcating" kind'. – Aiden LJ (at para 34).

s 2 and part performance

As M P Thompson (1994) points out in his case note on *Morritt* v *Wonham* [1993] NPC 2:

> under the law of part performance, it was generally the case that the oral contract agreed between the parties was enforced. Under the new law, however, it seems that the court can make any order it chooses in order to do justice between the parties. In this writer's view, the certainties of the past were preferable to the uncertainties of the new. It will be unfortunate if there is a plethora of litigation to determine the rights of parties to an oral agreement concerning land, which has been partly implemented: a process which may involve recasting their agreement.

That case concerned an agreement made prior to 27 September 1989 which was, therefore, governed by s 40, under which the defendant's part performance was sufficient. However, the judge went on to state that if the defendant had failed on this point, he would have succeeded under proprietary estoppel on the facts. Yet, although s 2 replaces s 40 and s 2 appears to leave no room for part performance, does this mean that the doctrine has been completely abolished? All that the relevant part of s 40 said in relation to part performance was that '[t]his section . . . does not affect the law relating to part performance . . .' – s 40(2). The 'law' referred to originated in equity which evolved into the doctrine under which a party to a contract who had acted to his detriment upon it, would have it enforced in his favour even if it had not been in writing nor could any written evidence of it be produced. If s 40 had no effect upon the doctrine then, surely, neither does the repeal of s 40? Peter Gibson LJ in *Firstpost Homes Ltd* v *Johnson* said that part performance 'now has no application', but Neill LJ in *Singh* v *Beggs* (1996) 71 P&CR 120, doubting the doctrine had been abolished by s 2, said, 'it may be that in certain circumstances the doctrine could be relied upon'. Phillips LJ in *United Bank of Kuwait* v *Sahib* [1997] Ch 107, agreed with Peter Gibson LJ, explaining that the doctrine of part performance depended upon the old theory that an oral contract was not void, but merely unenforceable, and for that reason does not survive s 2, the clear intention of which 'is to introduce certainty in relation to contracts for the disposition of interest in land where uncertainty existed before'. Although each view was expressed *obiter*, it appears that that of Peter Gibson LJ is now accepted as correct.

s 2 and proprietary estoppel

Obviously, then, the date of the agreement is crucial. However, although it appears that part performance cannot be relied upon for contracts created after 26 September 1989, the doctrine of proprietary estoppel may well apply on the facts. We shall be looking at proprietary estoppel in more detail shortly, but for now it is sufficient that you understand that it is an equitable doctrine under which, if A promises B an interest in land, and B relies upon that promise to his detriment, the court will 'estop', that is prevent, A from relying upon his strict legal rights in order to avoid complying with his promise.

The point here is whether a contract, which is void by reason of a failure to satisfy s 2, can be enforced against a party to it by way of estoppel. Indeed, the Law Commission (Law Com No 164) always intended that the one doctrine – proprietary estoppel – should replace the other – part performance.

In *Walton* v *Walton* (1994) Lexis, Hoffmann LJ remarked 'Ordinarily the law does not enforce promises unless they have been made formally under seal or as part of a contract'. An exception to this general rule was made by the Privy Council in *Lim Teng Huan* v *Ang Swee Chuan* [1992] 1 WLR 113 where an agreement for the transfer of land which did not satisfy s 2 was upheld by way of proprietary estoppel. However, is it right that estoppel be used to give effect to agreements which were simply not made properly? Is this not part performance in disguise?

Godden v *Merthyr Tydfil Housing Association* (1997) 76 P&CR D1

Mr Godden had sought enforcement of the contract by way of estoppel, but the Court of Appeal denied his claim, stating that it is a 'cardinal rule that the doctrine of estoppel may not be invoked to render valid a transaction which the legislature has enacted to be invalid'. However, in the Court of Appeal in *Yaxley* v *Gotts* [2000] 1 All ER 711, Robert Walker LJ had:

> no hesitation in agreeing with what I take to be the views of Peter Gibson [in *Bankers Trust Co* v *Namdar* [1997] EGCS 20], Neill and Morritt LJJ [in *McCausland* v *Duncan Lawrie Ltd*] that the doctrine of estoppel may operate to modify (and sometimes perhaps even counteract) the effect of s 2 of the 1989 Act. The circumstances in which s 2 has to be complied with are so various, and the scope of the doctrine of estoppel is so flexible, that any general assertion of s 2 as a 'no-go area' for estoppel would be unsustainable. Nevertheless, [the 'cardinal rule'] does call for serious consideration . . . If an estoppel would have the effect of enforcing a void contract and subverting Parliament's purpose, it may have to yield to the statutory law which confronts it, except so far as the statute's saving for a constructive trust provides a means of reconciliation of the apparent conflict.

Section 2(5) of the 1989 Act provides that 'nothing in this section affects the creation or operation of resulting, implied or constructive trusts'. The Court of Appeal in *Yaxley* – neatly sidestepping the s 2/estoppel policy debate – held the contract valid by virtue of a constructive trust of the 'express common intention' type (see Chapter 7), suggesting, apparently, that the principles of this and those of proprietary estoppel are identical. *Yaxley* was applied by the Court of Appeal in *Shah* v *Shah* [2001] 3 WLR 31, where it was stated that general social policy does not require the exclusion of estoppel in all circumstances when the validity of a deed is in issue, either before or after the 1989 Act, and in *Kinane* v *Mackie-Conteh* [2005] EWCA Civ 45, where it held that an agreement for a charge over property to secure a loan (which complied with neither s 2(2) LP(M)A 1989 nor s 53(1)(c) of the LPA 1925) would be enforceable by way of a constructive trust and therefore fall within s 2(5) of the 1989 Act.

It is a fine line between validating a contract which fails for want of the necessary formalities and estopping one party from going back on his bargain. However, Arden LJ stated in *Ottey* v *Grundy* [2003] EWCA Civ 1176 that 'the purpose of proprietary estoppel is not to enforce an obligation which does not amount to a contract nor yet to reverse a detriment which the claimant has suffered, but to grant an appropriate remedy in respect of unconscionable conduct', an approach which would take proprietary estoppel outside of the s 2 formalities (and, as in *Ottey*, the testamentary gift debate – see later in Section II B). In *Cobbe* v *Yeoman's Row Management Ltd (No 1)* [2006] EWCA Civ 1139, the Court of Appeal dismissed an appeal against Etherton J's approach (at [2005] 2 P&CR DG1) which looked not at the relationship between compliance with s 2, constructive trusts and s 2(5), but rather at the role of estoppel in preventing unconscionability. Framing the question in terms of s 2 concentrates upon the existence of and/or need for a valid contract, whereas framing it in terms of unconscionability treats contracts for land cases in exactly the same way as any other claims for proprietary estoppel, thus obviating the need for a constructive trust. With such an approach, a claimant may succeed by way of (a) a contract that complies with s 2; (b) facts which give rise to a constructive trust (thus bringing it within s 2(5)); or (c) facts that give rise to unconscionability that can be addressed by proprietary estoppel. In practice, (b) and (c) may well arise on the same facts but, where they do not, why should (c) not apply on its own merits? Why should the unconscionability be allowed to go unredressed in this situation? We shall see later (in Proprietary estoppel and wills) that this has already been the approach taken to promises to leave property by will: 'The inherent revocability of testamentary dispositions (even if well understood by the parties) is irrelevant to a promise or assurance that "all this will be yours"' – Robert Walker LJ in *Gillet* v *Holt* [1998] 3 All ER 917.

Of course, if there is no valid contract under s 2, no constructive trust and no unconscionability, the claim to the contract will fail – see *Representative Body for the Church in Wales* v *Newton* [2005] EGCS 145.

Another situation which has been held to enable a claim based upon proprietary estoppel is 'subject to contract' correspondence. Such correspondence, even if contained in written form, is not contractually binding unless and until its terms are incorporated in a formal contract of sale signed and exchanged by the parties. In advance of a formal contract, the parties have merely a 'gentleman's agreement', which in reality incorporates little more than a mutual hope that 'the other will act like a gentleman' in circumstances where neither 'intends so to act if it is against his material interests' – Sacks J in *Goding* v *Frazer* [1967] 1 WLR 286 at 293 B. There being no valid contract, there is nothing for a party to sue upon, even when he has incurred expense or other detriment. Can a claim be made in estoppel? The effect of 'subject to contract' is that either party can withdraw from the agreement at any time prior to a formal contract being signed and exchanged, thus this understanding, under which 'everybody knows that there is a risk that, at the end of the day, either side may back out of negotiations, up to the point where [contracts] are exchanged' – Oliver J *Derby & Co Ltd* v *ITC Pension Trust Ltd* [1977] 2 All ER 890 at p 896, must be shown to have been displaced by one encouraged by the other party that he would not withdraw. As Gray and Gray state, 'there must also be evidence that the purchaser relied, at least implicitly, on this expectation' (2005, p 1167 at 12.20). The most recent case on this point is *Gonthier* v *Orange Contract Scaffolding Ltd* [2003] EWCA Civ 873 where the judgment of Lindsay J bears reading.

One final point – for now – is the fact that there has been no policy debate of the s 2 kind in regard to s 52 of the Law of Property Act 1925. Section 52 requires all legal estates to be created or transferred by a valid deed. However, we shall see (in Chapter 2IIB) that a legal estate can be awarded by proprietary estoppel, eg *Pascoe* v *Turner* [1979] 1 WLR 431. Section 53(2) of the LPA 1925, like s 2(5), also excludes the need for formality in the case of resulting, constructive and implied trusts, yet there has been no argument here of estoppel going against Parliament's intention.

Estate contracts

There are three types of estate contract – contracts to convey, options to purchase and rights of pre-emption.

Contracts to convey

We have just been discussing this type of estate contract, that which exists following the exchange of a valid contract for the creation or sale of interests in land. As this contract arises in every conveyance of title, there are many thousands each year. Under the contract the buyer can require the seller to convey the estate or interest to him in accordance with the terms of the contract and the seller can require the buyer to complete the purchase. If either party fails to honour their part of the agreement, an order for specific performance can be sought.

Options to purchase

Under an option to purchase a landowner, A, grants an option to another, B, for B to purchase the land at an agreed price at some future time. Once granted, A has to wait and see if B will exercise his option and it is up to B (who is commonly a builder who wishes to ensure a steady supply of development land) whether to go ahead with the purchase. If B does exercise it, then A must sell the land to B at the agreed price, even if the land is now worth much more. In the leading case of *Midland Bank Trust Co Ltd* v *Green* [1981] AC 513 a father granted his son an option to purchase a 300-acre farm for £75 an acre within ten years. Within six years of the agreement the value of the farm had increased from £22,500 to £40,000. Today, land values are rising even faster. As with contracts to convey, the terms of the option must be certain; any uncertainty will render the option void – see *Hillreed Land* v *Beautridge* [1994] EGCS 55.

Thus, there are two stages with an option to purchase: one under which A grants the option, the other by which B exercises his option. Is the latter stage a land contract which must satisfy s 2? In *Spiro* v *Glencrown Properties Ltd* [1991] 1 All ER 600, the notice of exercise was, as usual, signed by the option holder only. He then failed to complete the purchase and claimed he was not liable in damages to Glencrown because the notice of exercise was void under s 2. Hoffmann J (taking a purposive approach to s 2) held that an option to purchase constitutes a single contract, albeit one in two stages. Of the two stages, only the first – the grant of the option – was held to be a contract for the sale or other disposition of an interest in land: only this had to comply with s 2. The exercise of the option is a unilateral act by the option holder and does not need to comply with s 2. Though Hoffmann J's judgment was not without its critics, it has been accepted and followed in spirit in *Trustees of the Chippenham Gold Club* v *North Wiltshire District Council* (1992) 64 P&CR 527 and in *Armstrong & Holmes Ltd* v *Holmes* [1994] 1 All ER 826 (*Sherlock* v *Mycroft* perhaps?!)

A tenant's option for renewal of his (long) lease of a house is an estate contract, as is his right to purchase the freehold from his landlord or to acquire an enlarged lease under the Leasehold Reform Act 1967, s 5(5). (Whether this right will be extended to cover commonhold unit flats is not certain, though it is clear that it will not apply in relation to the common parts of a commonhold.)

Once an option has been registered, additional registration of the contract of sale is not necessary – *Armstrong & Holmes Ltd* v *Holmes* [1994] 1 All ER 826.

Rights of pre-emption

Whereas the holder of an option can require the conveyance to him of the interest in land at any time during the continuance of the option, the holder of a right of pre-emption has merely a right of first refusal and even that only arises if and when the grantor of the right decides to sell. Thus, if the grantor, X, never decides to sell, the grantee, Y, acquires no interest in the land, whereas B, the grantee of an option, has the right to require sale to himself from the date of the grant. The Court of Appeal in *Pritchard* v *Briggs* [1979] 3 WLR 868 held that, until X decides to sell, Y acquires no interest in the land: only when X does decide to sell does such an interest actually arise. This was a case of unregistered land concerning the priority of an option to purchase and a right of pre-emption under the Land Charges Act. However, in registered land, under the Land Registration Act 2002, s 115(1), 'a right of pre-emption in relation to registered land has effect from the time of creation as an interest capable of binding successors in title (subject to the rules about the effect of dispositions on priority)'.

The priority of dispositions for all estate contracts is decided by the relevant systems: in unregistered land, estate contracts (which, not being included in LPA 1925, s 1(1) or (2), can only be equitable) must be protected by registration as Class C(iv) land charges. If not so registered, they will be void for non-registration only against purchasers for value. In registered land, they are minor interests and should be protected by entry of a notice. If they are not entered as a minor interest but the holder is in actual occupation, the right may also be an overriding interest under LRA 2002, Sched 3, para 2.

It can be seen, then, that only the contract to convey land provides a contract which can be enforced by either party to it, one against the other. With an option to purchase, it is the option holder only who has the right to enforce the agreement: he cannot be compelled to buy. With a right of pre-emption, on the other hand, the holder of the right can do nothing to enforce it against a landowner who does not wish to sell.

LP(MP)A 1989, s 2 governs all three estate contracts, but not everyone was a fan of s 2! 'Section 2 is a nightmare. The Statute of Frauds was enacted in 1677 and the courts worked out ways of getting round if for the next 200 years. If s 2 remains in force it may take the courts another 200 years to get back to the sensible situation which obtained before the section came into force. 'It should be repealed and the old law restored' (Victor Gersten, 1993, p 2). It is hard to argue with this especially in the light of the continuing uncertainty whether the court will apply proprietary estoppel in place of part performance. In addition, the major problem under s 40 was 'gazumping' (remember poor Hyacinth and Richard?), and s 2 has done nothing to address this. When the property market is buoyant and rising, a landowner may 'accept' as many offers as he likes, leaving the would-be buyers – each of whom will be involved in the great expense of surveys and search fees, at least – to bid against each other, the seller taking the highest price. (Sometimes the race is one against time, the first to exchange contracts being the winner. It would seem that a gentleman's word is not necessarily his bond nowadays.) The unlucky contestants cannot claim their outlay from the vendor. Of course, when the market is falling, purchasers can play a similar game – gazundering – against vendors.

However, though s 2 will not protect you from gazundering, we all have a hero in Mr Pitt!

Pitt v *PHH Asset Management Ltd* [1993] 4 All ER 961

Mr Pitt had been gazumped twice by the same lady on the same house. He then threatened the vendors that he would tell the lady that he was withdrawing. She could then lower her offer. At this, the vendors entered into an agreement not to consider any further offers for the property provided Mr Pitt exchanged contracts within two weeks of receipt of the contract. If this deadline was not met, they would be free to take offers from elsewhere. This is known as a 'lock-out' agreement. The vendors went back on this agreement and sold to the lady at a higher price. Mr Pitt sued for damages. The vendors claimed there was no binding contract because the arrangement, which had originally been oral, had only been contained in letters, each signed by one party only. The Court of Appeal held the lock-out agreement was not itself a contract for the sale of an interest in land. Therefore, it was not subject to s 2. So, a lock-out agreement can provide a device for avoiding gazumping – or gazundering – and, what's more, it does not have to comply with s 2. In a judgment which is well worth reading in full, Sir Thomas Bingham MR recognised that:

> [For] very many people, their first and closest contact with the law is when they come to buy or sell a house. They frequently find it a profoundly depressing and frustrating experience. The vendor puts his house on the market. He receives an offer which is probably less than his asking price. He agonises over whether to accept or hold out for more. He decides to accept, perhaps after negotiating some increase. A deal is struck. Hands are shaken. The vendor celebrates, relaxes, makes plans for his own move and takes his house off the market. Then he hears that the purchaser who was formerly pleading with him to accept his offer has decided not to proceed. No explanation is given, no apology made. The vendor has to embark on the whole dreary process of putting his house on the market all over again.
>
> For the purchaser the process is, if anything, worse. After a series of futile visits to unsuitable houses he eventually finds the house of his dreams. He makes an offer, perhaps at the asking price, perhaps at what the agent tells him the vendor is likely to accept. The offer is accepted. A deal is done. The purchaser instructs solicitors to act. He perhaps commissions an architect to plan alterations. He makes arrangements to borrow money. He puts his own house on the market. He makes arrangements to move. He then learns that the vendor has decided to sell to someone else, perhaps for the price already offered and accepted or an increased price achieved by a covert, unofficial auction. Again, no explanation, no apology. The vendor is able to indulge his self-interest, even his whims, without exposing himself to any legal penalty . . .

However, as Sir George Jessell MR declared in *Lysaght* v *Edwards* (1876) 2 Ch D 499, it

> Has been settled for more than two centuries, [that] the moment you have a valid contract for sale the vendor becomes in equity a trustee for the purchaser of the estate sold, and the beneficial ownership passes to the purchaser, the vendor having a right to the purchase money, a charge or lien on the estate for the security of that purchase money, and a right to retain possession of the estate until the purchase money is paid, in the absence of express contract as to the time of delivering possession.

Another problem with s 2 is the age in which we live – the age of the computer. Although Philip and Ann Kenny (1989) in their article feel that, 'the path to fraud would be too obvious' for courts to accept deeds on disk, and that, in any event, a 'deed on disk would not comply with the definition of "signature"' for the purposes of s 2, 'computers are now able to "talk" to one another without human control, and computer memories can be altered without trace. The very flexibility which makes these machines attractive provides a danger to a profession which relies on unalterable evidence' – Hilary Lim and Kate Green (1995, p 51).

We have seen that the Land Registry is moving towards 'electronic conveyancing', that is 'paperless conveyancing'. As the Law Commission explains in its Consultation Document, *Land Registration for the Twenty-First Century* (Law Com No 254):

> To facilitate the introduction of paperless conveyancing, it will be necessary to disapply the existing formal requirements for the transfer and creation of estates, rights and interests in land. There are many provisions in the property legislation which apply only to transactions made by deed. These will also have to be amended to enable electronic conveyancing to be introduced. Even in advance of the introduction of paperless conveyancing, it is likely to be desirable to move towards the conduct of conveyancing according to standardised formats and computer generated documents.

So, a client will be able to sit beside his solicitor or licensed conveyancer as he types in the relevant information on to a 'form' on the computer screen. This 'form' and its content will be electronically transmitted to the Land Registry. Hey presto! The interest in land is transferred or created. However, as Lim and Green so rightly say, computers can be tampered with. Hackers can gain access and alter information. A registered proprietor's name could be removed and another substituted. With no 'paperwork' to prove the original valid entry, will the opportunities for fraud be greater than at any time past? (What's more, if a fraud is perpetrated, will the true owner be entitled to any compensation? See Chapter 3, Indemnity.)

Whilst the current formal requirements are of general application, there are, as always, certain exceptions and we shall consider each of these specifically as they arise.

Remedies

Where a contract is valid for the purposes of s 2 and has been exchanged, but the agreement does not proceed to completion, what can the parties do?

Sue for damages at common law for breach of the contract. Ordinary principles of contract damages apply – Law of Property (Miscellaneous Provisions) Act 1989, s 3.

Apply for an order of specific performance of the contract. This is an equitable remedy and is, therefore, entirely discretionary. All maxims and principles of equity apply, so the mere fact that the contract is valid may not be enough. As equity considers all land to be special and every bit of it unique, damages are not considered an adequate remedy for the loss. Specific performance is, therefore, awardable, but 'he who seeks equity, must do equity' and 'he who seeks equity must come with clean hands'. So, if the party seeking the order has not acted bona fide, no order will be made, notwithstanding the validity of the contract. See *Coatsworth* v *Johnson* (1886) 54 LT 520. Either party can seek specific performance.

If the court will make an order, under the rule in *Walsh* v *Lonsdale* (1882) 21 Ch D 9 the specifically performable agreement to convey the interest in land takes effect in equity on the same terms as agreed. Thus, interests under the rule, for example a specifically performable agreement for a lease, are known as equitable – an equitable lease, for instance. The rule applies also to mortgages, easements and profits. For more detailed explanation of the rule, see Chapter 8, Leases.

Apply for an injunction to restrain a threatened breach of the contract. Again, this is an equitable remedy.

Rescission. Either party can rescind, but the remedy is only available if it is possible for the parties to be returned to their original positions. If this is not possible, the aggrieved party could confirm the contract and sue for damages for breach of it.

Seek a declaration from the court. The court can be asked to decide the exact meaning of any term of the contract which is in dispute.

Ask for rectification of the contract. This is the correction of an inaccurate written record of a contract by parol (an oral contract). Courts are not keen to comply with such a request, however. See *Wright* v *Robert Leonard Developments Ltd* [1994] NPC 49.

Under the Contracts (Rights of Third Parties) Act 1999

It may be possible under s 1(5) of this Act for a third party to sue for breach of a benefit under the contract as if he had been an actual party to the contract, but 'the third party must be expressly identified in the contract by name, as a member of a class or as answering a particular description but need not be in existence when the contract is entered into' – s 1(3).

Equitable interests

The above formal requirements relate to the legal estates and interests in land, but what if the intended transfer relates to an equitable interest? The Law of Property Act 1925, s 53(1) provides that:

Subject to the provisions . . . with respect to the creation of interests by parol –

(a) no interest in land can be created or disposed of except by writing signed by the person creating or conveying the same, or by his agent thereunto lawfully authorised in writing, or by will, or by operation of law;

(b) a declaration of trust respecting any land or any interest therein must be manifested and proved by some writing signed by the person who is able to declare such trust or by his will;

(c) a disposition of an equitable interest or trust subsisting at the time of the disposition, must be in writing signed by the person disposing of the same, or by his agent . . . or by will.

However, these requirements do 'not affect the creation or operation of resulting, implied or constructive trusts' – s 53(2).

II INFORMAL ACQUISITION

A Adverse possession

What's the problem?

Adverse possession in context

Sir Arthur Conan Doyle, creator of Sherlock Holmes (who, I know, would have loved land law), believed there were fairies at the bottom of his garden. Alan Bennett, another writer, really did have a lady living in his! Her name was Miss Shepherd and she lived – first in an old van and then in a lean-to shed – in his garden for some 15 years, until she died. (See Alan Bennett's *The Lady in the Van*, Profile Books, 1999, for the full story.) Not only had Mr Bennett given Miss Shepherd permission to live on his land, he actually pushed her van into the garden from the road. But what if he had not invited her, and she had asked no permission but merely taken up occupation on Mr Bennett's land? Could he, after so long, have forced her to leave?

Who cares?

Those who will be affected

The landowner: the paper-title holder. He may want to regain possession of his land – after all, a squatter could take up occupation of the whole of it. The owner may not have minded whilst he did not wish to use the land himself. What if, later, he decides to go ahead with plans which he had shelved, or to sell the land? Can he evict the squatter? Has the squatter gained any interest in the land? If so, what?

The occupier or squatter. Clearly, the land, if he or she has been there for some years, may feel like 'home' now. If so, the squatter will not want to leave. Even if he or she is not too attached sentimentally to the land, it would cost a lot more to move away and pay for somewhere else to live. A lot of time, effort and money may have been put into the land – renovations and repairs, building, landscaping. Has any interest in the land been acquired? If so, what is it and who will it bind?

Any purchaser from the landowner. Can the purchaser get vacant possession of the land or must he allow the squatter to continue his or her occupation and use of the land? Can the squatter claim to have better title to the land than the purchaser?

A subsequent squatter. Can the original squatter force a second squatter to move off the land? If the first squatter has left, can the time he occupied the land be of any assistance to the latercomer?

What is it?

The nature and characteristics of adverse possession

The layman would call 'adverse possession' by another name – 'squatters' rights'. This description is not so very far from the truth, but it is not every squatter who satisfies the requirements for adverse possession. Indeed, the layman will not look upon the squatter as a person who can lay claim to any right, let alone consider the possibility that he may even acquire the legal title to the land upon which he is squatting.

Adverse possession of unregistered land

However, as title is based on a form of possession (known as 'seisin'), disputes as to ownership are decided on the basis of a hierarchy of possession of the property. (This physical possession is not technically the same as seisin, but today possession is always seen as clear evidence of seisin and so the difference is seldom an issue.) Also, as Neuberger J stated in *Purbrick* v *Hackney London Borough* [2004] 1 P&CR 34,

> it is to some extent implicit in the present law of adverse possession, that an owner of property who makes no use of it, whatever, should be expected to keep an eye on the property to ensure that adverse possession rights are not being clocked up.

Any possession must be exclusive, in that it gives the possessor the right to recover the land from any subsequent possessor. Say A is the present owner of the legal estate in a piece of land. If B takes possession of it, A can sue B for recovery of the land. If C later takes possession of the same land, B can sue to recover it from C, and A can sue both B and C, and so on. It would be no defence to C to claim that B was not the true owner.

Robert Walker LJ, in *Simpson* v *Fergus* (2000) 79 P&CR D16, explained that:

> Possession is a legal concept which depends on the performance of overt acts, and not on intention (although intention is no doubt a necessary ingredient in the concept of adverse possession). It may or may not be sufficient in international law to annex an uninhabited and uninhabitable place by placing a flag on it ... But to establish exclusive possession under English law requires much more than a declaration of intention, however plain that declaration is. Actual occupation and enclosure by fencing is the clearest, and perhaps the most classic, way of establishing exclusive possession ... it is not correct, and would indeed be a serious heresy, to say that because it is difficult or even impossible actually to take physical possession of part of a reasonably busy service road, that simply for that reason some lower test should be imposed in deciding the issue of exclusive possession.

In this case the sweeping of the road in question, the cutting of tree branches overhanging it, the erection of 'no parking' signs and the putting of notices on any cars which parked 'unauthorised' in marked out spaces were held not to amount to exclusive possession and thus there had been no adverse possession of the road.

Adverse possession rests on entitlement due to relativity of possession. If two people claim entitlement to a piece of land, the one who was in possession first would have the better claim.

Although land law in the United Kingdom is different from that in other countries, as Cheshire and Burn (2000) point out:

> Most systems of law have realized the necessity of fixing some definite period of time within which persons who have been unlawfully dispossessed of their land must pursue their claims. It is, no doubt, an injustice that after this period has elapsed the wrongdoer should be allowed to retain the land against the person whom he has ousted, but it would be an even greater injustice to the world at large if the latter were allowed after any interval of time, however long, to commence proceedings for recovery of possession – p 961.

As recently as 2001, the government of Venezuela gave peasants the right to expropriate land that was not being used productively, in order to redistribute wealth (5 per cent of the population owns 80 per cent of the land) – *The Week*, 15 January 2005.

It may seem strange that a person can take another's title to land, his legal estate, his time in the land, without payment and without any documentation at all. Indeed, '[m]isunderstandings have sometimes arisen from an unwarrantable belief that title deeds are sacrosanct documents, whereas the truth is that neither a conveyance nor a land certification retains its value if the landowner is so indifferent as to lose physical control of his land' – Ruoff and Roper (1991) in the practitioners' 'bible', *The Law and Practice of Registered Conveyancing*.

The Limitation Act 1980 specifies the periods after which no civil action may be brought, and in regard to land states: 'No action shall be brought by any person to recover any land after the expiration of 12 years from the date on which the right of action accrued to him or, if it first accrued to some person through whom he claims, to that person' – s 15(1). As Neuberger J said in *Purbrick*, 'A period of 12 years is a long period during which to neglect a property completely'. (As we shall see shortly, the period of 12 years is replaced by one of 10 years in registered land under the Land Registration Act 2002. However, this is still a long period!)

As Streatfield J explained in *R B Policies at Lloyd's* v *Butler* [1950] 1 KB 76, the policy behind this is 'that those who go to sleep upon their claims should not be assisted by the courts recovering their property, but another, and I think equal policy behind the Acts, is that there shall be an end to litigation'. However, the Crown is allowed to 'sleep upon [its] claims' a little longer than the rest of us, for it can bring an action to recover Crown land within 30 years – Limitation Act 1980, s 15(7), but a claim against the Crown to recover land must be brought within 12 years.

Time is crucial.

> I can say that truth, friendship and the statute of limitations have a common root in time. The true explanation of title by [adverse possession] ... seems to me to be that man, like a tree in a cleft rock, gradually shapes his roots to his surroundings, and when the roots have grown to a certain size, can't be displaced without cutting at his life. The law used to look with disfavour on the statute of limitations, but I have been in the habit of saying that it is one of the most sacred and indubitable principles that we have – Oliver Wendell Holmes, quoted by H Lim and K Green (1995, p 62).

Powell v *McFarlane* (1979) 38 P&CR 452

The relevant principles of adverse possession were laid down in this case: they are, first, that no action can be brought by a person to recover land more than 12 years from the date on which the right accrued. (However, this is now different for registered land - see later.) Secondly, that the land must be in adverse possession of some person in whose favour the period of limitation can run before a right of action can be said to accrue. Thirdly, that adverse possession includes a loss of possession by the owner (whether by subsequent discontinuance of use or dispossession) and a taking of possession by the adverse possessor. Fourthly, that the adverse possessor must take factual possession and have the plain and unequivocal intention to exclude the world at large (the *animus possidendi*). Finally, that possession is never adverse when it is taken by agreement or consent (or, as in *Lambeth London Borough Council* v *Archangel* [2002] 1 P&CR 18, where the adverse possessor acknowledges that the paper owner has a better title).

Peter Gibson LJ, in the Court of Appeal in *Bolton Metropolitan Borough Council* v *Musa Ali Qasmi* (1999) 77 P&CR D36, affirmed these principles and also that it is for the person claiming adverse possession to prove that the user amounted to factual possession and the relevant intention to exclude all others, and the House of Lords affirmed the requirements laid down in *Powell*, in *J A Pye (Oxford) Ltd* v *Graham* [2003] 1 AC 419. In particular, Lord Browne-Wilkinson emphasised the need for not only factual possession but also the intention to possess (*animus possidendi*).

Possession

We are, of course, looking at the possession of AP, the adverse possessor, of land belonging to someone else, PO, the true, or paper, owner.

As we have already seen, PO must bring any claim for recovery of his land from AP within 12 years from the beginning of the adverse possession – Limitation Act 1980, s 15(1) in unregistered land; in registered land PO will be given a 'wake up call' at 10 years – see later. There must not only be somebody for PO to claim against, but PO must be in a position to know that he needs to claim! Thus, adverse possession must be unconcealed, thereby giving PO the opportunity to take action to prevent AP acquiring his title. However, 'unconcealed' does not necessarily mean blatantly obvious: in *Rains* v *Buxton* (1880) 14 Ch D 537 a claim to adverse possession of an underground cellar was upheld, because the door to the cellar was 'quite visible to anybody' and there had been no deliberate concealment of the user. It was merely 'from its very nature . . . not perhaps a thing at all times necessarily seen' – Fry J.

Mulcahy v *Curramore Property Limited* [1974] 2 NSWLR 464

Possession must be 'open, not secret; peaceful, not by force; adverse, not by consent of the true owners'.

In effect, then, adverse possession must be possession of the land by AP as if it were already his. Some cases are clear – such as in *Mount Carmel Investments Ltd* v *Peter Thurlow Ltd* [1988] 1 WLR 1078 where AP built on land belonging to PO, and both occupied and used the building. Again, in *Seddon* v *Smith* (1877) 36 LT 168, possession was clear from incorporation of PO's land into AP's farm, from which time AP used that land in exactly the same way as he used his own land.

Of course, each case will be considered on its own facts, and a relevant fact would be the nature of the land in question and the use to which it is usually put. Thus, what amounts to possession will differ according to whether the land in question is a dwellinghouse, uncultivated land or agricultural land – *Lord Advocate* v *Lord Lovat* (1880) 5 App Cas 273. Although occasional acts of trespass will not amount to adverse possession, if the land in question is normally used at certain times of the year only, then possession of it by AP during these periods should suffice – *Bligh* v *Martin* [1968] 1 WLR 804.

Possession must be adverse

For a squatter to acquire the title, there must have been adverse possession, that is, possession which is inconsistent with that of the true owner: it need not be hostile, however. Adverse possession is a question of fact, but 'there must be something of an ouster of the true owner by the wrongful possessor' – Lord Denning in *Wallis's Cayton Holiday Camp Ltd* v *Shell Mex & BP Ltd* [1975] QB 94. However, it is not always an easy matter to decide.

Lord Advocate v *Lord Lovat* (1880) 5 App Cas 273

As to possession, it must be considered in every case with reference to the peculiar circumstances. The acts, implying possession in one case, may be wholly inadequate to prove it in another. The character and value of the property, the suitable and natural mode of using it, the course of conduct which the proprietor might reasonably be expected to follow with a due regard to his own interests - all these things, greatly varying as they must, under various conditions, are to be taken into account in determining the sufficiency of a possession - Lord O'Hagan.

Wallis was one of several cases where the paper-title holder claimed that he had not abandoned his land, but was holding it in readiness for proposed future plans. In *Wallis*, Shell-Mex had acquired a piece of land in the middle of a field with the intention of building a new filling station. The field belonged to Wallis who farmed it. The land which adjoined that bought by Shell-Mex was the site of a proposed new road but after several years the local authority dropped this scheme. In the meantime, for some eleven-and-a-half years, Wallis had farmed the land sold to Shell-Mex. Upon hearing of the local authority's abandonment of its road scheme, Shell-Mex wrote to Wallis offering to sell the land back to him. Wallis did not reply, but carried on farming the land for a further eight months, after which time Wallis claimed to have acquired title to it by adverse possession. [Had Wallis acknowledged Shell-Mex's letter, Wallis would, of course, have lost any such claim.] The Court of Appeal held that Wallis could show only a few months' adverse possession, representing the time since Shell-Mex abandoned its plans for the land. In the earlier cases of *Leigh* v *Jack* (1879) 5 Ex D 264 and *Williams Brothers Ltd* v *Raferty* [1957] 3 All ER 593 it had also been held that where the paper-title holder retained plans for the land and where they had done nothing to render such plans impossible, no adverse possession of the land was possible. However, in *Buckinghamshire*

County Council v *Moran* [1989] 3 WLR 152 the Court of Appeal held that this principle had been overruled by the Limitation Act 1980, Sched 1, para 8(4), so that even if the paper-title holder does still have plans for the disputed land, adverse possession will be possible (provided of course the squatter can satisfy all the other requirements of adverse possession). In addition, the Court of Appeal held in *Moran* that both factual possession and a requisite intention to possess – *animus possidendi* – must be shown if a person is to acquire the title by adverse possession. As Nourse LJ noted, if *Leigh* v *Jack* was followed rigidly, any owner may resist claims of adverse possession merely by claiming to have plans to develop the land at some time in the future. The approach taken in *Moran* was confirmed and its correctness stressed by the Court of Appeal in *The Mayor and Burgesses of London Borough of Hounslow* v *Minchinton* (1997) 74 P&CR 221.

However, an intention actually to acquire the title is not necessary: intention to possess is sufficient (although adverse possession can, apparently, be acquired where the possessor occupies the land in the mistaken belief that he already owns the legal estate – *Hughes* v *Cook* (1994) *The Independent*, 21 March and *Lodge* v *Wakefield City Council* (1995) 38 EG 136). Such an intention to possess must be such that it is clear to the world – the Court of Appeal in *Wilson* v *Marton's Executors* (1993) 24 EG 119: but in *Powell* v *McFarlane* (1979) 38 P&CR 452, Slade J recognised that it is normally impracticable to exercise absolute physical control over open land, 'if only because it is generally impossible to secure every part of a boundary so as to prevent intrusion'. (In *Powell* the AP grazed his cow, made hay and repaired fences on PO's land, but this was held to be insufficient. AP later used the land for his business and erected a noticeboard relating to it; this later use would have been sufficient, but it had not lasted for 12 years.)

Though not actually necessary for possession to be adverse, Cockburn CJ stated in *Seddon* v *Smith* (1877) 36 LT 168 that '[e]nclosure is the strongest possible evidence of adverse possession'. However, the erection of fencing which was removed 24 hours later, with no attempt at re-erection, was held to be insufficient in *Marsden* v *Miller* (1992) 64 P&CR 239.

In *Boosey* v *Davis* (1998) 55 P&CR 83, the Court of Appeal held that adverse possession is dependent upon dispossession of the owner and that the grazing of goats and erection of a fence are insufficient for this. The adverse possessor had also cleared scrub but this was still not enough to constitute dispossession of the owner. The absence of fencing does not, of itself, defeat a claim to adverse possession, but the maintenance of a fence may be sufficient – *Bligh* v *Martin* [1968] 1 All ER 1157. In *Wilson* v *Marton's Executors* (1993) 24 EG 119 fence repairs, cutting and selling wood and clearance of the land were not sufficient acts of control to amount to adverse possession, but it was held in *Marshall* v *Taylor* [1895] 1 Ch 641 that cultivation of the land may be enough. In *Treloar* v *Nute* [1976] 1 WLR 1295 development works, such as building a house on the land, were held to give adverse possession and in *Bligh* v *Martin*, leasing the property to a third party was held to be a clear example of adverse possession.

However, as Lord Hagan said in *Lord Advocate* v *Lord Lovat* (1880) 5 Ap Cas 273, 'Acts implying possession in one case may be totally inadequate in another.' Thus in *Fruin* v *Fruin* (1983) Court of Appeal Bound Transcript 448, where a fence had been erected to keep a senile member of the squatter's family in, rather than to keep everyone else out, this was held not to provide evidence of the necessary *animus pos-sidendi*.

The Mayor and Burgesses of the London Borough of Hounslow v Minchinton
(1997) 74 P&CR 221

Here the Court of Appeal held that the important thing is the motive behind enclosing land. In that case the squatters had enclosed land in order to keep their dogs in, rather than to keep other people out. Holding this to be irrelevant, the Court of Appeal explained that what was relevant was the intention by the squatters that their dogs be able to make full use of what the squatters plainly regarded as their land. The enclosure was inconsistent with any continuance of possession by the true owner and, in the absence of him of any use of the land at all, adverse possession had been constituted.

Obviously, if adverse possession has to be inconsistent with the title of the true owner, it cannot arise if the 'dispossessor' is there by consent. (Thus, where the title is to a leasehold, time can only begin to run against the reversioner – the landlord – when the lease expires.) In *Morrice* v *Evans* (1989) *The Times*, 27 February, a claim to the ownership of a plot of land used as a garden based on 12 years' adverse possession failed because of the claimant's acceptance of an assertion by the paper-title holder of a right to restrict the claimant's activities on the land. As Balcolme LJ explained, 'Mr Evans's evidence had been that "if Mr Morrice told me not to do something I accepted that I was not to do it". That evidence together with the facts of the case, showed that ... Mr Evans did not have the necessary *animus possidendi* to establish relevant adverse possession of the plot'.

However, the Court of Appeal held in *Mount Carmel Investments Ltd* v *Peter Thurlow Ltd* [1988] 1 WLR 1078 that the mere assertion of a claim to possession made to a squatter by a true owner in a letter was not sufficient to prevent the acquisition of title by the squatter by adverse possession. On the other hand, in *R* v *Secretary of State for the Environment, ex parte Davies* (1990) 59 P&CR 306, the Court of Appeal held that an offer to pay rent, and a claim by the 'dispossessor' to be a gypsy, were factors which tended to suggest that the claimant did not have the necessary intention of possessing the land. In *Pulleyn* v *Hall Aggregates (Thames Valley)* (1992) 65 P&CR 276, the Court of Appeal held that as well as factual possession and the intention to possess, acts relied on to prove dispossession of the true owner will be less likely to succeed where they are in accordance with the purpose of the true owner. On the facts, as the acts relied upon by Pulleyn, the would-be owner, were fully in accordance with the true owner's, Hall's, purposes for the disputed land, there was no adverse possession.

In *Colchester Borough Council* v *Smith and Others* [1991] 1 All ER 29 the Court of Appeal held that, the occupier having entered into an agreement under which the plaintiff granted him a tenancy of the land in question on the express ground that the occupier had no title to the land, except for the tenancy granted to him under the terms of the agreement, the claimant would be estopped from going back on that contractual stipulation and asserting he had gained title to the land by adverse possession. (This decision is not without its critics – see A H Brierley (1991) and Martin Dixon (1992). In *Trustees of Grantham Christian Fellowship* v *The Scouts*

Association Trust Corpn [2005] EWHC 209 (Ch), a claim to title by an AP failed because for many years he had been in negotiations with PO for the purchase of the property. 'It is natural to draw an inference of permission where a person is in possession pending negotiation for the grant of an interest in that land. Where that inference is drawn the possession cannot be adverse.' Similarly, in *Colin Dawson Windows Limited* v *Howard* [2005] EWCA Civ 9, it was held that the fact that a licence continued for many years did not mean that it ceased to be a licence merely because there had been no contact between the licensor and licensee: 'in this respect the licence is in marked contrast to the grazing agreement [in *Pye* v *Graham*] which was for a fixed term which expired and which the landowner refused to renew'.

Beaulane Properties Ltd v Palmer [2006] Ch 79 (Ch D)

Mr Palmer, the AP, claimed that, following termination of his licence from Beaulane in 1986, he was in possession of land near Heathrow Airport by virtue of his use of it for grazing, the general repair of fencing and for securing access to his own adjacent land (which he let to certain village residents for the grazing of horses and livestock). We shall return to this case shortly in regard to other matters arising out of it, but on this point it was held that Mr Palmer had shown possession that was adverse, plus the necessary *animus possidendi*.

We shall be coming shortly to the changes rendered by the Land Registration Act 2002 to claims for adverse possession of registered land. That Act came into force on 13 October 2003, but it can affect any claim where the period of adverse possession starts to run after 2 October 1988, as did Mr Palmer's. Indeed, the 2002 Act creates two sets of principles – the 'old', applying to cases where time runs before 3 October 1988, the 'new' to those after. Following *Beaulane* the Land Registry has introduced the following additional practice note to Practice Guide 5 –

> 'Note that in the light of Beaulane Properties and Palmer [*sic*] . . . where an application is made under paragraph 18 of Schedule 12 of the Land Registration Act 2002, and the necessary period of adverse possession started after 2nd October 1988, the applicant must show an arguable case for the possession being inconsistent with the use or intended use of the land of the registered proprietor, and not merely that possession was without the registered proprietor's consent.

However, this does not affect unregistered land.

In *Rimmer* v *Pearson* (2000) 79 P&CR D22, the claim was to adverse possession of 'a tiny sliver of land'. The hearing in the County Court had lasted 22 days and Swinton Thomas LJ lamented that it was 'a tragedy that so much money should have been spent by private individuals on a dispute such as this'. Robert Walker LJ explained that:

> There is to my mind an obvious difficulty in proving adverse possession of such a tiny sliver of land, and it would require exceptionally strong evidence of acts amounting to adverse possession by one owner and of dispossession of the other owner in relation to a piece of land of that size and shape. That is partly a matter of the practicalities of the situation, but it can also be supported as a matter of public policy. Neighbours should not be encouraged to conduct themselves in such a way that it is necessary for adjoining owners to defend every last inch of territory or to lose it'.

However, it is possible to have adverse possession of one face of a divided wall – *Prudential Assurance Co Ltd* v *Waterloo Real Estate Inc* [1998] EGCS 51.

Animus possidendi

As we have seen, possession on its own is not sufficient for adverse possession: AP must also have *animus possidendi*, the intention to possess. Further, as Browne-Wilkinson LJ explained in *Pye*, an adverse possessor must have 'a sufficient degree of physical custody and control [and] an intention to exercise such custody and control on one's own behalf, and for one's own benefit'. However, his lordship, approving *Buckinghamshire County Council* v *Moran*, confirmed that the adverse possessor need only show an intention to use the property for his own benefit, not to acquire ownership of it. From this it follows that,

> Once it is accepted that the necessary intent is an intent to possess, not to own, and an intention to exclude the paper owner only so far as is reasonably possible, there is no inconsistency between a squatter being willing to pay the paper owner if asked and his being in the meantime in possession. An admission of title by the squatter is not inconsistent with the squatter being in possession in the meantime. – *J A Pye (Oxford) Ltd* v *Graham* [2003] 1 AC 419.

This being so, the Court of Appeal's decision was reversed and the adverse possessors were entitled to be registered as owners of the land in question. Thus, even where there is factual occupation by AP, if the necessary intention is not present there can be no adverse possession – see *Batt* v *Adams* (2001) 82 P&CR 406, where AP had maintained a fence, used the land for pasture and taking hay, and given contractors permission to store pipes.

Further, 'clear and affirmative evidence that the trespasser ... not only had the requisite intention to possess, but made such intention clear to the world' is what is required: thus the need for AP to possess the land openly, not in secret. As Peter Gibson LJ stated in *Prudential Assurance Co Ltd* v *Waterloo Real Estate Inc* [1999] 2 EGLR 85, if it were otherwise, it would be unjust to deprive PO of his rights. AP must 'at least make his intentions sufficiently clear so that [PO], if present on the land, would clearly appreciate that [AP] is not merely a persistent trespasser, but is actually seeking to dispossess him' – *Powell*. Generally, *animus* has to be inferred from the acts themselves' – Sachs LJ in *Tecbild Ltd* v *Chamberlain* (1969) 20 P&CR 633. However

Bucks CC v Moran [1990] Ch 623

Where a trespasser's use of land does not by itself clearly show his intention to possess the land to the exclusion of PO, so that his acts are

> open to more than one interpretation and he has not made it perfectly plain to the world at large by his actions or words that he has intended to exclude the owner as best he can, the courts will treat him as not having had the requisite *animus possidendi* and consequently as not having dispossessed the owner: AP must show 'compelling evidence' of his *animus* - Slade J.

Though AP must show an intention to exclude PO, he does not have to have the intention 'to exclude the owner of the paper title in all future circumstances'; it is sufficient to show 'an intention for the time being to possess the land to the exclusion of all others, including the owner of the paper title' – Slade LJ in *Moran*. On the facts of *Moran*, AP intended to possess the land only until PO exercised its plans to build a by-pass over it, but, having possessed the land adversely for more than 12 years with the necessary *animus possidendi* during that period, AP had successfully acquired PO's title.

See also *London Borough of Lambeth* v *Blackburn* (2001) 82 P&CR 494, where intention to possess until evicted was sufficient.

Purbrick v *Hackney London Borough* [2004] 1 P&CR 34

The PO claimed that, as the AP could have done more than he had to evidence his intention, the claim for adverse possession must fail. However, Neuberger J was clear on this point'... the simple contention that the fact that the squatter could have done more on the land should defeat his claim for adverse possession, would fall foul of the reasoning of Slade J in *Powell* and of Lord Wilkinson in *Pye*. ... the question is not what the squatter could have done, but what he did, and whether he did sufficient to amount to physical possession. In addition, the fact that Purbrick knew that he was liable to be dispossessed as a right did not prevent him being in possession.

It is this 'intention to possess' – to exclude the world, including (or especially) PO – that is essential: merely intending to acquire a benefit from PO's land is not enough (for example, in *Riley* v *Penttila* [1974] VR 547, AP had built a tennis court on PO's land. AP showed merely an intention to acquire a benefit, not an intention to possess the land to the exclusion of all others). However, it has been made clear in *Powell* and *Moran* and *Pye* that AP need only intend to possess, not own, PO's land.

London Borough of Lambeth v *Blackburn* [2001] EWCA Civ 912

The Court of Appeal added that AP does not have to regard himself as being entitled to exclude the lawful owner from the premises – it is sufficient if he intends to keep the true owner out for the time being and until AP is evicted. AP's intention to maintain possession against the whole world, including PO, must be manifested so that, if PO were present at the property, he would be aware that AP had taken possession of it and intended to keep others out. AP's acts must be unequivocal, sufficient to make it clear to PO, if he were present on the land, that AP intended to exclude him as best he could. There is no need for AP to intend to possess indefinitely rather than temporarily, nor to intend to exclude the paper owner in all future circumstances. It is sufficient that AP have a present manifested intention to possess the property to the exclusion of all others, including PO, throughout the 12 years when he has the necessary factual possession. There is no distinction between a trespasser who actively seems to dispossess and one who merely passively occupies the land. Further, although a willingness on the part of AP to pay rent to PO (if that was necessary for AP to stay in the property) may, in some circumstances, negate an intention to possess, in general it will not. On the facts, Blackburn had broken the council's lock on a flat and replaced it with one of his own, after which he lived in the flat. Even though he expected to be evicted at any time, and, had the Council approached him, he would have 'leapt at the chance to pay rent in order to be able to remain in the flat', he had the necessary intention to possess and factual possession.

Though AP must possess openly so that PO, if present on his land, would be aware of AP's presence, it is generally irrelevant that PO is, nonetheless, ignorant of the fact that he is being dispossessed – *Rains* v *Buxton* (1880) 14 Ch D 537. An exception would, of course, be where AP is acting in bad faith: AP knowing that he is not the true owner is not a bar here, for 'one of the more surprising features of the law of adverse possession is perhaps that the doctrine of long possession operates even in favour of the opportunist or consciously wilful trespasser who is perfectly aware that the land he occupies is not his own' – Gray and Gray (2000, p 277). Dean Ames stated (in *The Nature of Ownership: Lectures on Legal History*, 1913, p 197), 'English lawyers regard not the merit of the possessor, but the detriment of the one out of possession.'

However, where AP does know that he is trespassing on someone else's land (as opposed to believing that he is actually the owner of that land), 'the courts are much less inclined to lean in [AP's] favour: [AP] can be treated as a land thief, not deserving to benefit by adverse possession' – Roger J Smith (2003), citing by way of example the result in *London Borough of Lambeth* v *Bigden* (2000) 33 HLR 478 under which 'millions of pounds worth of public housing stock in one of the poorest boroughs in the country has passed gratis into private ownership'. Is such an outcome not a breach of PO's rights under Article 1 of the European Convention on Human Rights?

J A Pye (Oxford) Ltd v *Graham* (2001) 83 P&CR 23

Here, Mummery LJ concluded that, as limitation periods are not in principle incompatible with the European Convention, there was no reason to conclude that s 15 of the Limitation Act 1980 was incompatible with Article 1, as the s 15 provisions, 'do not deprive a person of his possessions or interfere with his peaceful enjoyment of them. They deprive a person of his right of access to the Courts for the purpose of recovering property, if he has delayed the institution of his legal proceedings for 12 years or more after he has been dispossessed of it for at least that period. The extinction of the title of the claimant in those circumstances is not a deprivation of possessions or a confiscatory measure for which the payment of compensation would be appropriate: it is simply a logical and pragmatic consequence of the barring of his right to bring an action after the expiration of the limitation period.'

As the Limitation Act 1980 was the culmination of almost a thousand years of development on the limitation of actions in England and Wales and as every legal system requires such a policy (indeed, the limitation periods in European Law are not nearly so generous), s 15 falls within 'the public interest' for the purposes of Article 1 and the provision is not disproportionate.

On this view, the same principle would apply to the ten-year period under the Land Registration Act 2002.

Park J in *Family Housing Association* v *Donnellan* [2002] 1 P&CR 449, held expressly that s 15 of the Limitation Act was not a breach of the ECHR.

Pye went to the House of Lords – [2002] 3 All ER 865 – but, accepting that the Human Rights Act does not have retrospective effect, their lordships did not pursue this issue (though they did overrule the Court of Appeal's decision as to adverse possession).

However, a first instance case that we have already come across has set the cat amongst the pigeons.

Beaulane Properties Limited v *Palmer* [2006] Ch 79 (Ch D)

As Martin Dixon (2005) explains, 'there are some judicial decisions that make a real differ-ence, and some that simply melt away like snow at Easter. The judgment of Nicholas Strauss QC, sitting as a deputy judge in *Beaulane* ... could follow either path. This apparently simple case of adverse possession, turning on disputed factual evidence, may prove to be one of the most important property cases of recent years, both for its impact on the substantive law of adverse possession and as an example of the impact of human rights in real property dis-putes. Or it may slip into a footnote of Megarry and Wade having been overtaken by decisions in Strasbourg or overturned on appeal.' In fact, *Pye* is currently before the EU Grand Chamber – now, who said land law wasn't exciting?!

We have already noted the impact of *Beaulane* on the substantive law, as well as the great significance of the date on which Mr Palmer's adverse possession was com-pleted (the end of June 2003). As we know, this not only fulfilled the statutory period of 12 years, it also kept Mr Palmer's claim within the 'old' rules. So far, so good for Mr Palmer. However, not so good was the fact that it also meant that – unlike in *Pye* – his case was brought within the ambit of the Human Rights Act 1998, which was by then in force. It is not surprising, then, that Beaulane argued that the 'old' law of adverse possession in registered land , ie prior to the Land Registration Act 2002, was inconsistent with Article 1 of Protocol 1 of the ECHR and that the loss by a PO of its title was disproportionate to any public interest consideration. This being so, they argued, the court was under a duty under s 3(1) of the HRA 1998 to interpret the UK law of adverse possession 'so far as it is possible to do so . . . in a way which is compatible with Convention rights'.

Now, Mr Palmer's original licence had been granted by a predecessor in title to Beaulane, who sold the land to CTN, who in turn sold it to a series of companies (all of which were owned or controlled by members of a large family) – 'the interim owners' – before it was bought by Beaulane. When that licence terminated in 1986, Mr Palmer gave the false impression to one of the interim owners that he still had a licence to occupy the land, thereby concealing his trespass. (The irony of this is that, had Mr Palmer not concealed his trespass, he would have clocked up his 12 years of adverse possession by 1988 – before the HRA came into force! As it was, however, Mr Palmer 'found himself deep in the human rights jungle' – Martin Dixon.)

Despite the view of the Court of Appeal in *Pye*, Deputy Judge Strauss agreed with Beaulane's argument and held that the limitation principles in adverse possession amount not merely to a restriction on access to a remedy for the recovery of land, but to a deprivation of the land itself. In so finding, he anticipated correctly the European Court of Human Rights' decision in *Pye* that the application of the pro-visions of the Limitation Act 1980 are inconsistent with Article 1, Protocol 1. However, *Beaulane* unpicks *the actual common law* upon which **all** claims for adverse possession – in registered (both before and after LRA 2002) and unregistered land – depend.

In Deputy Judge Strauss's opinion, the procedural changes introduced by the LRA 2002 will make it compatible with Article 1 and a PO will only lose his title by his own inaction or because of some unfairness (see LRA 2002, Sched 6); but does this alter the fact that the PO has lost his title for no compensation? Is the situation substantially different to that pre-LRA 2002? The Deputy Judge's view on this, and his reinterpretation of the substantive law of adverse possession, is debatable. Yet will it be the final nail in the coffin of adverse possession? If so, that would be a great shame for, as Kevin Gray (1987, p 285) said, without it, 'every transfer of real property would be jeopardised by the encroachment of ancient or increasingly stale claims in derogation of the transferor's rights ... The law of adverse possession has the merit of ensuring that *de facto* possession does not diverge too markedly from *de Jure* title'.

We now await the outcome of the European Grand Chamber's deliberations and any appeal by Mr Palmer.

The time period

In all cases, time will only begin to run if there is someone in adverse possession of the land: it does not run simply because the land is unoccupied – *M'Donnell* v *M'Kinty* (1847) 10 ILR 514. In other words, the true owner must be absent and the adverse possessor must be present: there has to be somebody for the true owner to claim against! Therefore if a person, having dispossessed the true owner, abandons the land before the end of the 12-year period, the true owner loses nothing more than the time during which the adverse possessor was in occupation. As Lord MacNaghtan said in *Trustees, Executors and Agency Co Ltd* v *Short* (1888) 13 App Cas 793, the idea is not to enable 'some casual interloper or lucky vagrant' to dispossess the true owner. Thus:

> Where a right of action to recover land has accrued and after its accrual, before the right is barred, the land ceases to be in adverse possession, the right of action shall no longer be treated as having accrued and no fresh right of action shall be treated as accruing unless and until the land is again taken into adverse possession – Limitation Act 1980, s 15(6).

If the land is 'again taken into adverse possession', it need not necessarily be so taken by the same adverse possessor. If, between one adverse possessor, A, and another, T, the true owner, O, has regained possession, T cannot rely on the time during which A had ousted O. T's time will begin to run from the moment he went into possession.

Example

Thus, if:

A goes into adverse possession against O in 1990
O regains possession in 1995
T goes into adverse possession against O in 2000

T cannot claim to have acquired O's title by claiming adverse possession since 1990, only from 2000. O retains his title.

On the other hand, if T were to go into possession immediately after A, T could, upon being sued by O, add A's period of adverse possession to his own. However, T could not, in order to defeat A, claim that O was the true owner, because the court will only decide between the competing claims of T and O. Thus, suppose that:

A goes into adverse possession against O in 1990

T goes into adverse possession against A in 1995

If the year is now 2003, T can acquire O's title. By adding both his own and A's periods together he has 13 years.

Here the limitation period has been attained by adding together two periods of adverse possession. Any number of periods can be used in this way, provided that they follow one immediately after the other – see *Mount Carmel Investments Ltd* v *Peter Thurlow Ltd* [1988] 1 WLR 1078.

Even if T took over possession because of, or following A's death, the years that A was in adverse possession can be used by T – they do not die with A.

When does the time start to run?

Difficulties could arise in identifying 'the date on which the right of action accrued', but the Limitation Act 1980 forestalls such difficulties by making specific provisions in regard not only to present interests, but to future interests, settled land, land held subject to a trust of land, forfeiture or breach of covenant, and tenancies – s 15(6), Sched 1. We shall look at the first two only.

(a) Present interests. Time only starts to run when the land is in the possession of some other person, thus:

> Where the person bringing an action to recover land, or some person through whom he claims, has been in possession of the land, and has while entitled to the land been dispossessed or discontinued his possession, the right of action shall be treated as having accrued on the date of the dispossession or discontinuance – s 15(6).

As Cheshire and Burn (2000, p 967) point out, the wording of the statute is 'not altogether happy, for it might be thought that a mere abandonment of possession is sufficient to set time running. This is not so, however, for the factor common to dispossession and discontinuance is entry upon the land by a stranger'.

Thus, as Sir John Pennycuick explained in the following case:

Treloar v *Nute* [1976] 1 WLR 1295

The person claiming by possession must show either (1) discontinuance by the paper owner followed by possession or (2) dispossession (or as it is sometimes called "ouster") of the paper owner. Clearly, possession concurrent with the paper owner is insufficient.

(b) Future interests. We shall be looking at future interests when we consider the rule against perpetuities. A trust of land arising from successive interests is a nice example of a future interest, for example

> **Example**
>
> 'Inchcape House to Ann for life and then to Helen absolutely'. What happens if Helen does not take up possession immediately upon Ann's death? It depends upon whether Ann was in possession of the disputed land at her death or not. If she was, then Helen must sue any adverse possessor within 12 years of Ann's death: Limitation Act 1980, s 15(6), Sched 1, para 4; if she was not, then Helen can sue within either 12 years from when Ann could have sued, or six years from Ann's death: s 15(2).

If the true owner is a minor or a patient under the Mental Health Acts at the time of dispossession, the running of the time can be postponed until six years after the disability ceases or the owner's death, whichever happens first. This could, obviously, occur after the usual limitation period has expired, but there is a limit: no action can be brought to recover the land after 30 years from the date when the right accrued. If the disability arises only after the right accrued, time will continue to run in the usual way – Limitation Act 1980, s 28.

If the action is based upon the fraud of the defendant (i.e. the dispossessor), or the defendant has deliberately concealed any relevant fact from the plaintiff, time will not begin to run until the plaintiff is aware, or would have been aware, had he made reasonable efforts, of the fraud or concealment – Limitation Act 1980, s 32(1)(b). However, no such recovery can be made against a bona fide purchaser for value. 'Deliberate concealment' was said by Lord Denning in *Applegate* v *Moss* [1971] 1 QB 406 to mean 'conduct by the defendant or his agent such that it would be "against conscience" for him to avail himself of the lapse of time'; for example, the intentional concealment by the defendant of a voluntary conveyance to the plaintiff in *Re McCallum* [1901] 1 Ch 143. Though there is no general rule to prevent the running of time where a mistake has occurred, 'where the mistake is an essential ingredient of the cause of action' the situation is similar to that for fraud. As we noted earlier, in *Beaulane* evidence was brought by one of the interim owners that Mr Palmer had concealed his trespass by giving the impression that his terminated licence was still in existence. Would that debar his claim to adverse possession under the Limitation Act 1980, s 32(1)(b)? Yes, it would have – had he not been given seven days' notice to quit in June 1991 – a notice which he ignored. Also ignored was his continuing occupation of the land, which meant that, by June 2003, Mr Palmer had completed the statutory 12 years without the period of concealed trespass.

Topplan Estates Ltd v *Townley* [2004] EWCA Civ 1369

On its facts, this case was similar to *Pye* v *Graham* in that a farmer held over after the end of a grazing agreement, in 1982, for more than 12 years. Though the licensee farmer was granted adverse possession of most of the claimed land, the grant did not include land which, before the 12 years had elapsed, had been sold by the PO: in regard to this part of the land, possession had been interrupted by the sale. (However, in *Generay Ltd* v *Containerised Storage Co Ltd* (2005) unreported, the Court of Appeal held that a period of three months' interruption of possession caused by the erection of a temporary fence was insufficient to defeat AP's claim.)

The time may start to run afresh by a signed acknowledgement in writing of the paper owner's title or part payment of principal or interest. Either the acknowledgement or the payment must be signed or made by the person in whose favour the time is running, or by his agent, and must be made to the paper-title owner, or his agent – Limitation Act, ss 29 and 30.

In unregistered land the effect of adverse possession is negative, not positive and thus adverse possession does not transfer any title to the adverse possessor but rather it merely extinguishes the title of the paper owner. Lapse of time may successively bar different persons with claims to the land until eventually the adverse possessor's fee simple is free of rival claims. However, 'even if a squatter acquires title to an estate in fee simple, he may not be able to take a clean title; for burdens which bound the land will continue to bind it in the hands of the squatter' – Megarry's *Manual of the Law of Real Property* (2002, p 560). The Court of Appeal in *Smith* v *Lawson* [1997] EGCS 85 stated that the Limitation Act period did not run when the person entitled to occupy the property had no right of entry. (On the facts, the plaintiff would have been estopped from recovering the property.)

The effect of not bringing an action

If an owner fails to bring an action for repossession within the stipulated period, his ability to seek to recover the land by legal proceedings is barred by the Limitation Act, and his title is extinguished. However, where the land is settled land or land subject to a trust of land, the legal estate is only extinguished when all the beneficiaries have been barred.

The adverse possessor, once the relevant period has expired, is immune from action by the dispossessed owner, but not from any third party who has rights which run with the land and which have not been extinguished.

Therefore, PO can stop AP's time running, that is prevent AP from acquiring the necessary 12 years, simply by bringing an action against him before then. Clearly, the sooner PO takes action, the better; the nearer AP is to acquiring his 12 years, action against him would be PO's best course (if PO did take action against AP and was granted an order against him but failed to act upon it, a new period of 12 years would begin to run in favour of AP).

How else can PO stop AP's time running? It is clear from *Mount Carmel Investments Ltd* v *Peter Thurlow Ltd* [1988] 1 WLR 1078 that a simple demand by PO that AP should leave will not suffice. As adverse possession must not be possession by permission, could PO stop the clock by giving AP permission to remain? It was held by the Court of Appeal in *BP Properties* v *Buckler* (1987) 55 P&CR 337 that the permission would have to amount to a licence (on the facts, a licence to remain for life), and, *if accepted by AP*, this would prevent AP – though PO would be bound to let him remain under the terms and nature of the licence. AP could, of course, reject the licence (his silence would not amount to rejection).

As AP has to be treating the land very much as if it were already his, any acknowledgement by him that PO has a better title or the right to claim possession will stop time running – Limitation Act 1980, s 29. It was held in *Lambeth London Borough Council* v *Bigden* (2000) 33 HLR 478 that a request by AP that PO not sell the land fell within this principle. It would seem obvious, then, that an offer by AP to pay rent to PO would have the same result and, in *R v Secretary of State for the Environment, ex parte Davies* (1990) 61 P&CR 487, it was held that such an act would be fatal to a claim by AP. However, as we have already seen in *Pye*, where AP had made a written offer to pay rent, this may not be so. Indeed, Browne-Wilkinson LJ, in the House of Lords in *Pye*, disapproved of the decision in *ex parte Davies*. This seems odd, given that s 29 of the Limitation Act provides that any written acknowledgement of PO's title will stop AP's time running, with AP needing 12 years in possession from the date of his acknowledgement of PO's title (which, in *Davies*, he did not). In *Pye*, AP made several written requests for a new tenancy, each of which should have started time running afresh. Of course, if AP had already acquired 12 years' adverse possession before his written acknowledgement of PO's better title, the acknowledgement would be of no effect as AP had already acquired PO's title! (See, however, *Colchester Borough Council v Smith* [1992] Ch 421.) Of course, 12 years' possession on its own will not suffice – AP must show an intention to possess the land throughout that period (any intention on the part of PO normally being irrelevant).

The nature of the title acquired

The effect, then, is that the adverse possessor extinguishes the title of the paper owner. Thus there is nothing for the adverse possessor to 'take over': he takes an entirely new title. See *Fairweather v St Marylebone Property Co* [1962] 2 All ER 288 below, also *Colchester Borough Council v Smith* [1991] 1 All ER 29, and Martin Dixon's note on that case: 'Adverse Possession – Compromises and Estoppel', [1992] CLJ 420. At least, this is the case in unregistered land, where the adverse possessor is able to claim a new title of his own. However, the effect of the Limitation Act is not to grant a 'statutory' or 'parliamentary' conveyance, the paper owner's title having been completely wiped out.

Merely proving adverse possession does not give a good title, no matter how long the period. To establish good title by operation of the Limitation Act it must be shown (a) who was the true owner of the interest in land in question, and (b) that he has been barred by lapse of time from asserting his title. Where an adverse possessor can show this, the court will force even an unwilling purchaser to accept the title from him. See *Re Atkinson's & Horsell's Contract* [1912] 2 Ch 1 and *George Wimpey & Co Ltd v Sohn* [1967] Ch 487.

Leasehold land

Where the land that is being adversely possessed is leasehold, which title is being adversely possessed – the landlord's or the tenant's? It is the tenant's. This situation illustrates the true nature of adverse possession, in that there is no 'transfer' of the title from the paper-title holder to the adverse possessor: rather, the paper title is extinguished and the adverse possessor acquires an entirely new title – a fee simple – based upon his adverse possession – *Tichborne v Weir* (1892) 67 LT 735. However,

> although he takes a fee simple, the adverse possessor is bound by all proprietary rights other than those of the tenant whom he has adversely possessed. Thus the landlord can recover the property at the end of the leasehold term. Although the adverse possessor is not liable on the covenants in the lease, he will be well advised to comply with the covenants. Any breach will normally entitle [the landlord] to forfeit the lease; [the landlord] will thereby

gain a right to immediate possession which can be enforced against [the adverse possessor]. Furthermore, [the adverse possessor] cannot assert [the tenant's] rights to relief of forfeiture – *Tickner* v *Buzzacott* [1965] Ch 426 – Roger J Smith (2003, p 82).

Where the title is a lease, then the claim of the adverse possessor will not normally exceed the term left in the leasehold title.

Once the title (whether leasehold or freehold) has been acquired by adverse possession, the paper-title holder holds simply that – a piece of paper! Thus, 'We all have heard the phrase "Possession is nine-tenths of the law". In the context of land law, this cliche is correct! A person in possession of land, though he has no title to it, can nevertheless defend that possession by legal proceedings against **anyone but the true owner**. . . . The practical effect of [Limitation Act 1980, s 15(1)] is to declare that in appropriate circumstances possession shall be ten-tenths of the law!' – Roger Sexton in his book *Land Law* (1996, p 270). Once this has happened, the adverse possessor can take proceedings against anyone, including the previous paper-title holder.

Fairweather v *St Marylebone Property Co* [1962] 2 All ER 288

This is the leading case on adverse possession of leasehold title. Here the land in question was a house and adjoining shed. It was unregistered land. In 1893, the fee simple owner, L, granted a 99-year lease of the house and shed to T, but T left the shed derelict. In 1920, a neighbour, N, took possession of it. Fairweather acquired N's land and continued with the adverse possession of the shed. In 1959, St Marylebone bought L's fee simple absolute in the house and shed, and by agreement T surrendered the remainder of his lease to it, thereby giving St Marylebone the right to immediate occupation. St Marylebone claimed possession of the shed against Fairweather, who, of course, claimed that he had acquired title to the rest of T's term by adverse possession so that St Marylebone could not have occupation until 1992. The House of Lords held that it could go into occupation immediately. Why? Although a tenant has the right to occupy land under his lease, this right is lost after 12 years' adverse possession against him. (In this case, then, T lost possession of the shed from 1932 owing to first N's and then Fairweather's adverse possession.) Because adverse possession 'creates' an entirely new estate for the adverse possessor, Fairweather could not claim to have 'acquired' T's leasehold estate. Their lordships explained that, in fact, where a tenant loses his right to occupy to an adverse possessor, the lease itself is not totally destroyed: it continues to have a 'notional' existence between the landlord and the tenant – here L and T. If this 'notional' lease is terminated by agreement between the landlord and the tenant (as it was here), the landlord has an immediate right to possession of the land – not only as against the former tenant, but also against that tenant's adverse possessor. Not until 12 years' adverse possession has elapsed following termination of the 'notional' lease with no proceedings being brought by the landlord against the adverse possessor will the landlord be barred under the Limitation Act from claiming possession of the land.

So, an adverse possessor against a tenant is in a much less secure position than someone in adverse possession of freehold land: should the 'notional' lease be terminated, the landlord can take proceedings within 12 years of the termination to evict the adverse possessor: the likelihood being that such proceedings would be brought immediately upon termination! One method of termination would be merger of the lease with the reversion, so a tenant who has been adversely possessed could try to buy his landlord's reversion, thereby becoming the fee simple absolute owner, and evict the adverse possessor. Alternatively, the tenant could ask his landlord to agree to terminate the notional lease, thus allowing the landlord to evict the adverse possessor: thereafter, the tenant could seek a new lease (though this could be costly, especially if a large premium had already been paid for the original lease).

Title acquired by adverse possession by a tenant is presumed to accrue to the benefit of his landlord. Laddie J in *Batt* v *Adams* (2001) 82 P&CR 406 held that this presumption applies equally whether the land acquired belongs to the landlord or to a third party, and to registered as well as unregistered land.

Adverse possession of registered land

As Elizabeth Cooke (2003) says,

> the law relating to adverse possession has been changed fundamentally by the Land Registration Act 2002, and accordingly its position in the structure of land law has shifted. Formerly it was among the fundamental principles, because possession was the basis of title. Now it is relegated to two peripheral roles, functioning both as a way of making abandoned land marketable and also as an element in procedures for resolving boundary disputes – p 133,

and at p 138,

> since 1925 considerable thought has been given to the purpose of the law of limitations of actions to recover land. In a very general way it is summarised in the twenty-first report of the Law Reform Committee as follows:
> (a) to protect defendants from stale claims;
> (b) to encourage plaintiffs to institute proceedings without unreasonable delay and thus enable actions to be tried when the recollection of the witnesses is still clear;
> (c) to enable a person to feel more confident, after the lapse of a given period of time, that an incident which might have given rise to a claim against him is finally closed.

Martin Dixon (2005) is more forthright: the LRA 2002 'effectively emasculates adverse possession'.

So, new Act, new philosophy and, as we are about to discover, a new scheme. **However, the rules with regard to what can amount to adverse possession, possession that is adverse, and *animus possidendi* remain the same as in unregistered land** – LRA 2002, Sched 6, para 11. Thus, again the time period will only begin to run if there is someone in adverse possession of the land; it does not run simply because the land is unoccupied.

The time period

LRA 2002, s 96(1) provides that 'no period of limitation under section 15 of the Limitation Act 1980 ... shall run against any person, other than a chargee, in relation to an estate in land or rentcharge the title to which is registered'. Instead, 10 years is the starting point, for, after 10 years an adverse possessor (AP) can 'apply to the Registrar to be registered as the proprietor of a registered estate in land...' – Sched 6, para 1. AP will normally need to show 10 years' adverse possession up to the date of application (but it is possible that an AP who had completed 10 years' adverse possession before being evicted by the registered owner (RO), *may* be able to apply under para 1(2) and (3), if he applies within six months of the eviction, and the eviction was not due to a court order. It is still possible for an AP (AP2) to rely on time clocked up by a previous AP (AP1) under LRA 2002, Sched 6, para 11(2) (provided, of course, that AP2 takes possession immediately after AP1). Having received AP's application, the Registrar must inform RO and certain other interested people, mainly a mortgagee or a landlord – para 2(1).

If, following such notification, the recipients neither respond or object to the application, the AP is registered as proprietor of the estate – para 4. However, if there is some response or opposition, the AP's application will be rejected, except in the circumstances laid down in Sched 6, para 5:

(2) The first condition is that –
(a) it would be unconscionable because of an equity by estoppel for the registered proprietor to seek to dispossess the applicant, and
(b) the circumstances are such that the applicant ought to be registered as the proprietor.

(We have already seen – in licences – that proprietary estoppel is based upon a promise or representation, thus it will be difficult for AP to show adverse possession during the period of such an assurance. As Elizabeth Cooke says, '... the use of adverse possession to give an extra string to the bow of someone who has an equity by estoppel is odd, to say the least, and cases arising under this head will be read with great interest' – p 143.

(3) The second condition if that the applicant is for some other reason entitled to be registered as the proprietor of the estate.

(According to the Law Commission (Rep 271 at 14 and 43), this would cover cases where AP has already got an entitlement to the land, say under a will or intestacy. If this is so, why does he need the possibility of a claim in adverse possession?)

(4) The third condition is that –
(a) the land to which the application relates is adjacent to land belonging to the applicant,
(b) the exact line of the boundary between the two has not been determined under rules under s 60,
(c) for at least ten years of the period of adverse possession ending on the date of the application, the applicant (or any predecessor in title) reasonably believed that the land to which the application related belonged to him, and
(d) the estate to which the application relates was registered more than one year prior to the date of application.

In such cases, the parties will be encouraged to reach some kind of agreement, but if this is not possible, then the application will be referred to the Adjudicator, who has a judicial function in this respect.

Example

So, if there is no response or objection to his application, or if any of the three exceptions in para 5 apply, AP will gain title after only ten years. On the other hand, if there has been an objection by RO (a mortgagee or a landlord), and the exceptional cases under para 5 do not exist, AP's application will be rejected, no matter how long he has been in adverse possession. However, it will then be up to RO (or another person interested in the land) to recover the land by legal proceedings. If he/they do not do so, and AP continues in adverse possession for two more years from the date of his application, AP can reapply (this time under para 6) to be registered as proprietor - para 7 provides that he would be entitled to do this.

If, instead of applying for registration, AP is defending an action against him by RO for possession, AP can rely in his defence upon the matters in Sched 6 and s 98(5) that he could have relied upon for an application. If AP succeeds in his defence, the court must order the Registrar to register AP as proprietor.

The nature of title acquired

Schedule 6 provides that, following a successful application (or defence), AP will be registered as proprietor of the estate of which he has been in adverse possession – paras 5 and 7 – a leasehold if he was adversely possessing against a tenant, a freehold if against the freeholder. Thus, AP takes the title of RO, not a new freehold title:

> Thus when the squatter is registered as proprietor of the land he has taken ... he steps into the shoes of the previous registered proprietor [Sched 6, para 4] and he takes the land as he finds it, subject to all estates and rights that bound the previous proprietor. He takes it free of any registered charge, because the chargee had his own opportunity to object to the squatter's registration, *unless* he succeeded because of a paragraph 5 factor. – Elizabeth Cooke, p 146 (original emphasis).

Under the LRA 1925, s 70(1)(a), AP had an overriding interest even before he had clocked up 12 years, as that provision included 'rights ... in the course of being acquired under the Limitation Acts'. However, under the 2002 Act, the only way that AP could claim an overriding interest would be if he could satisfy the requirements of Sched 3, para 2 – an interest of a person in actual occupation, though rights which had already been acquired by adverse possession before the 2002 Act came into force – ie under the Limitation Acts – will continue against RO and for three years the right to be registered will have overriding status, so that AP can protect his pre-existing rights by applying for registration within three years from 13 October 2003 (when the Act came into force) – Sched 12, paras 11 and 18. You will recall that by June 2003 Mr Palmer had been in adverse possession against Beaulane for 12 years. Not only did this satisfy the statutory period under s 18 of the Limitation Act, being before 13 October 2003 it also kept his claim within the 'old' system under the Land Registration Act 1925. Thus Mr Palmer's right would continue to enjoy overriding status until June 2006 (by which time he should have applied to be registered as the registered proprietor). If, after that three-year period, AP has not been registered as proprietor, and RO sells to P, P will only be bound by AP if AP remains in actual occupation of the land. (AP could, in any case, still apply under Sched 6, but is unlikely to succeed.)

In conclusion, then,

> the approach to adverse possession seen in the Land Registration Act 2002 works very much in favour of the registered proprietor and of the integrity of the register. On the one hand,

it represents an about-turn – the principle that possession is the basis of title has simply gone. Adverse possession *by itself* can never deprive a registered proprietor of his land. On the other hand, adverse possession still has limited effect in combination with other factors. It can be used to enable a squatter to acquire title to land that the registered proprietor has abandoned or shown no interest in, and it remains a tool in the resolution of boundary disputes. Registered land has therefore been rendered virtually squatter-proof – Elizabeth Cooke (2003, p 139) (original emphasis).

Trusts

In unregistered land, adverse possession of trust property does not bar the trustees' title until the interests of all beneficiaries are barred.

In registered land, 'a person is not to be regarded as being in adverse possession . . . at any time when the estate is subject to a trust, unless the interests of each of the beneficiaries in the estate is an interest in possession' – Sched 6, para 12. Therefore, if the land being adversely possessed is registered land, and it is held in trust for successive, not concurrent, interests, there can be no registration of AP as proprietor – Sched 6, para 12.

Remedies

The paper-title owner can, of course, defeat a would-be adverse possessor simply by removing him or defeating his *animus possidendi* at any time before the statutory period expires. If a paper owner uses force against the squatter, such force must be such as is reasonably necessary for the purpose. In regard to its self-help remedy, the Criminal Law Act 1977, s 6(1) provides that it is a criminal offence for any person without lawful authority to use or to threaten violence for the purpose of securing

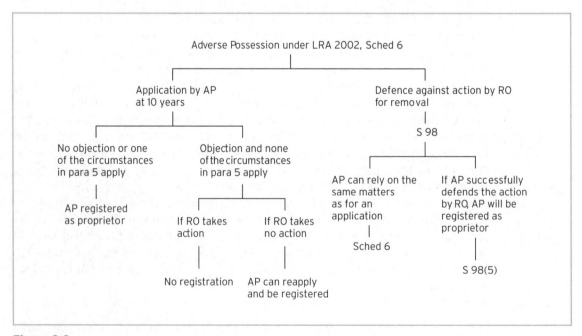

Figure 2.2

entry into any premises if, to his knowledge, there is someone present on those premises who is opposed to his entry. However, the Act provides a defence to any charge of violent entry for any person who is kept out of his own living accommodation by trespassers. See also the effect of the Public Order Act 1986. Clearly, once the squatter has acquired title, the self-help remedy is lost.

B Proprietary estoppel

What's the problem?

Proprietary estoppel in context

Mrs Walton was left a small farm by her husband in 1962. The plaintiff, her son Alfred, had worked on that farm since leaving school in 1960 at the age of 15. When he married he built a bungalow there where he lived with his wife and two children. Until 1970 he worked up to 70 hours a week, for which his mother paid him a wage considerably lower than a hired agricultural worker. In 1977 she was persuaded to hand the day-to-day management of the farm business over to him and he used the profits from the farm to invest in new buildings and make improvements.

'Relations between them gradually deteriorated: in 1988 she contracted to sell the farm to a neighbouring landowner. Before completion could take place, her son went to court to stop it. The old lady subsequently died, leaving money to her niece and her grandchildren' – *Walton* v *Walton and Others* (1994) Lexis: Transcript by John Larking.

Who cares?

Those who will be affected

Alfred. Encouraged by his mother:

> to believe that one day the farm would be his . . . he worked for years for low wages and put work and money into improving the land and buildings. These acts were irrevocable. He cannot have his life over again. If he does not get the farm, he will have to start again at the age of nearly 50, whereas if Mrs Walton had never promised him the farm, he might by now have established himself in some other way – Hoffmann LJ.

Can Alfred stay? Is the farm his?

The niece and grandchildren. They are expecting money from Mrs Walton's will, but the only way in which it can be paid is by selling the farm and freeing up the capital. If Alfred wins, what will be left for them?

Any purchaser of the farm. What if the proposed sale of the farm had not been stopped? Could the intending purchaser have forced the sale, or would any right which Alfred has against his mother be binding on the purchaser too?

What is it?

The nature and characteristics of proprietary estoppel

Walton v Walton and Others (1994) Lexis

As Hoffmann LJ explained in the Court of Appeal in *Walton*, the son's claim:

> is based upon equitable estoppel. That sounds very technical but the principle is quite simple. Ordinarily the law does not enforce promises unless they have been made formally under seal or as part of a contract. Mrs Walton's promise was not, of course, made under seal and . . . I do not think it was part of a contract. So if there was nothing more than the promise, she would have been free to change her mind. It would have been a matter for her conscience and not the law. But the position is different if the person who has been promised some interest in property has, in reliance upon it, incurred expense or made sacrifices which he would not otherwise have made. In such a case the law will provide a remedy . . . The choice of the remedy is flexible. The principle on which the remedy is given is equitable estoppel.

As Oliver J put it in *Taylors Fashions Ltd v Liverpool Trustees Co Ltd* [1982] 1 QB 133 . . . the question is:

> 'whether, in particular individual circumstances, it would be unconscionable for a party to be permitted to deny that which, knowingly or unknowingly, he has allowed or encouraged another to assume to his detriment'.

You may well have come across estoppel in your common law studies. However, proprietary estoppel is stronger than common law as it can be used to found a claim, as well as to defend one: it can be used 'as a sword as well as a shield'. You may, therefore, find it easier to think of the parties as promisor and promisee, rather than plaintiff (or claimant) and defendant (with non-proprietary estoppel, of course, the promisee is always the defendant). Thus, if a beneficial interest in land cannot be acquired by way of a resulting or constructive trust (see later in Chapter 7), it may be possible on the facts to claim estoppel.

Baker v Baker (1993) 25 HLR 408

Here, for instance, the plaintiff father gave up his secure tenancy and moved in with his son and daughter-in-law. The property in which they all lived had been purchased by the son and daughter-in-law with a substantial contribution from the father, on the understanding that the father was to live there rent free for the rest of his life. Shortly after they all moved in together there was a 'family dispute' and the plaintiff father left, moving, eventually, into council accommodation which provided him once again with security of tenure, this time rent free as he was granted housing benefit. The father claimed a beneficial interest in his son's house by way of resulting trust. On the facts this failed but he did succeed by way of equitable estoppel.

Voyce v Voyce (1991) 62 P&CR 290

A mother gave one of her sons a cottage and some land as a gift on condition that he 'do it up'. This he did, incurring considerable expense in so doing. There was no deed in regard to this gift, but several years later the mother executed a deed of gift in regard to the same cottage in favour of her younger son: he provided no consideration for the gift. Much later the elder son began to build an extension to the property, the younger brother claiming that this interfered with the light to his property. The Court of Appeal held that as the elder son had spent substantial sums on the cottage in reliance upon his mother's promise, she was estopped from denying the gift and, as the younger brother could not be in any better position than his mother, the elder son was the owner of the property. This being so, the younger son could claim against his brother in regard to the interference with light (although on the facts no action could lie).

We have already seen the effect that estoppel can have in regard to licences, enabling a purely personal right to become an interest in land – a proprietary right. However, as the question in regard to estoppel is 'How should the equity be satisfied?', and the answer, 'By enforcing the promise ...', the nature of or entitlement granted will depend entirely upon what the plaintiff was led to expect. It does not depend so much upon what he did, so long as that represents reliance upon the promise and detriment as a result of that reliance. Thus, it may be that the one who relied to his detriment (the promisee) is held to be entitled to have back the money he has laid out; it may be that he is entitled to remain in occupation of the land for a specified period, or for as long as he desires, or for life; it may be that he is entitled to the entire fee simple absolute in possession.

In *Walton*, counsel for those who would have taken under the will argued that because the promise was made in a family context and related to what would happen many years later, it could not be taken seriously. However, as Hoffmann LJ said, 'Many cases on proprietary estoppel concern promises made in a family or other intimate relationship. Even within a family it may not be unreasonable to expect that promises will be kept.' In fact, we shall see (in Chapter 7) that estoppel may be the only 'remedy' a person can turn to in order to remain in his home. The fact that it may also bind a third party, such as a mortgagee, is, of course, vital. As Gray says, then,

> One of the most significant movements occurring in the contemporary law of real property is the emergence of a new 'equity' based on the concept of 'estoppel' ... It is increasingly clear that the doctrine of estoppel, although first adumbrated by the courts over a century ago, is beginning to play a substantial role in the ordering of rights in property ... The central concern of the doctrine of proprietary estoppel is the notion of conscientious dealing in relation to land – Gray (1993, p 312).

As Lord Denning explained in *Crabb* v *Arun DC* [1976] Ch 179, the doctrine seeks to:

> prevent a person from insisting on his strict legal rights – whether arising under a contract, or on his title deeds, or by statute – when it would be inequitable for him to do so having regard to the dealings which have taken place between the parties:

its purpose is to:

> afford protection against the detriment which would flow from a party's change of position if the assumption that led to it were deserted – Mason CJ in *Commonwealth* v *Verwayen* (1990) 170 CLR 394.

Thus, in one way, estoppel could ('should', some would say) come under the heading of 'How can you lose them?', in that the holder of a legal right is denied the enjoyment of it. On the other hand, however, the party favoured by the doctrine, in effect, 'acquires' an interest in equity. The debate as to whether proprietary estoppel gives rise to a right or a remedy is a hot one!

We have already seen, in regard to licences, that the essential ingredients for any claim of proprietary estoppel are a promise or assurance or declaration, reliance upon it being to the detriment of the person so relying. These three are interdependent. The detriment must flow from reliance upon the promise and, in its turn, the promise must have been intended to be relied upon: there must be what common lawyers would call 'a causal link'. In the case of *Matharu v Matharu* (1994) 26 HLR 648, Roch LJ restated the elements which have to be established by the person claiming proprietary estoppel as laid down in *Willmott v Barber* (1880) 15 Ch D 96:

1   that that person had made a mistake as to his or her legal rights;
2   that he had expended some money or done some act on the faith of that mistaken belief;
3   that the possessor of the legal right knew of the existence of his legal right which was inconsistent with the equity, if it existed;
4   that the possessor of the legal right knew of the other person's mistaken belief;
5   that the possessor of the legal right had encouraged the other person in the expenditure of money or in doing other acts on which that person relied.

In *Matharu* the Court of Appeal held the wife of the plaintiff's son was entitled to a licence to occupy the property for the rest of her life, or such shorter period as she might decide. The plaintiff's claim for possession was, therefore, refused.

Unconscionability

In *Commonwealth of Australia v Verwayen* (1990) 95 ALR 321, Mason CJ stated, 'unconscionability is the driving force behind equitable estoppel', and in *Crabb v Arun*, Scarman LJ explained that, by insisting on his strict legal rights, the promisor must be taking advantage of the promisee 'in a way which is unconscionable, inequitable or unjust. In the watershed case of *Taylors Fashions* Oliver J stated that proprietary estoppel requires a broader approach than that in *Willmott v Barber*, an approach 'directed rather at ascertaining whether ... it would be unconscionable for a party to be permitted to deny that which, knowingly or unknowingly, he has allowed or encouraged another to assume to his detriment'. Indeed, it is this more relaxed approach that is followed today: 'it now seems to be accepted that "the real question comes down simply to whether or not the assertion of strict legal rights would be unconscionable, without any detailed conditions or criteria being specified"' – Megarry VC in *Appleby v Cowley* (1982) *The Times*, 14 April.

The Privy Council applied *Taylors Fashions* in *Lim Teng Huan v Ang Swee Chuan* [1992] 1 WLR 113, holding that if, in all the circumstances, it was unconscionable for the promisor to go back on the assumption which he permitted the promisee to make, that was sufficient for estoppel. Thus, there is no need for any unconscionable conduct *per se* by the promisor, merely that it would be unconscionable for one party to go back on his promise.

Taken with other cases, such as *Gillett v Holt* [1998] 3 All ER 917 and *Ottey v Grundy* [2003] EWCA Civ 1176 (both of which concerned wills), it is clear that all elements of the doctrine of proprietary estoppel are permeated by the fundamental principle that equity is concerned to prevent unconscionable conduct; the court must, therefore, look at the matter in the round. As we saw earlier, the Court of Appeal in *Cobbe v Yeoman's Row Management Ltd (No 1)* [2006] EWCA Civ 1139, endorsed the 'unconscionability' approach to cases concerning contracts invalid under s 2 of the Law of Property (Miscellaneous Provisions) Act 1989, which echoes the statement in *Jennings v Rice* [2003] 1 P&CR 8 that the essence of the doctrine is to do what is necessary to avoid an unconscionable result.

Whilst the court, naturally, looks at the claim of the promisee, it was stated in *Dodsworth v Dodsworth* (1973) 228 EG 1115 that the court must also consider the contributions and expectations of the promisor. This was followed by the Court of Appeal in *Price v Hartwell* [1996] EGCS 98 – a case involving a joint tenancy.

Encouragement

The promisee must have been encouraged in his belief by the promisor. The encouragement can be active or passive. In *Inwards v Baker* [1965] 2 QB 29 and in *Dillwyn v Llewellyn* (1862) 4 De GF&J 517 the fathers actively persuaded their sons to build on the fathers' land, and in *Pascoe v Turner* [1979] 1 WLR 431 the man assured the woman that the house they lived in was as much hers as his.

In regard to passive encouragement, Lord Eldon LC said in *Dann v Spurrier* (1802) 7 Ves 231 that 'the circumstance of looking on is in many cases as strong as using terms of encouragment'. Thus, in *Steed v Whitaker* (1740) Barn Ch 220, where a mortgagee stood silently by while a purchaser, who knew nothing of the mortgage, built on the secured land.

It was said in both *Greasley v Cooke* [1980] 3 All ER 710 and *Grant v Edwards* [1986] 1 Ch 638 that once a promisee has shown that she did something to her detriment, the burden of proof lies with the promisor to show that such acts were not done in reliance upon the promise.

Reliance

So, if detrimental reliance is established, a rebuttable presumption arises that the conduct was performed in reliance on the assurance. Once a claimant has shown 'that a promise had been made, and that his conduct was such that inducement could be inferred, the burden of proof shifted to the maker of the promise to show that the claimant had not, in fact, relied on it' – Court of Appeal in *Ottey v Grundy* [2003] EWCA Civ 1176. In that case, as the defendant had not disproved any causal connection with the promise, the claimant's case was successful. This point was the central issue in *Wayling v Jones* (1995) 69 P&CR 170, the decision in which 'shows that when a promise has been made, one does not test reliance by asking what the plaintiff would have done if it had never been made. One asks what he would have done if, the promise having been made, he had been told it would not be kept . . .' – Hoffmann LJ in *Walton v Walton* (1994).

Wayling v *Jones* (1995) 69 P&CR 170

In *Wayling* the parties had lived together in a homosexual relationship for 16 years until Jones died. Jones had owned a succession of businesses, the first being a café which Wayling, who was a qualified chef, helped to run. Jones promised to leave the property to Wayling and did in fact make a will in which he left him a house, a café and a flat. A couple of years later, Jones sold the flat and the café and bought a hotel in Aberystwyth. Again, Wayling helped Jones to run the business and also acted as his chauffeur. He was paid what amounted to pocket money and living expenses. Jones repeated his promise of leaving his property to Wayling and made a new will in which he left him a car and the hotel. Three years later the hotel was sold and two years after that Jones bought another in Barmouth. Again, Wayling helped, on the same terms as before. At one point Wayling did suggest to Jones that his work deserved more money, to which Jones replied, 'It'll all be yours one day', and promised to change his will, leaving the Barmouth Hotel to him. Jones never did change his will and when he died in 1987 all that Wayling got was a car worth £375 and some worthless furniture. Wayling's claim against Jones' estate failed at first instance, but the Court of Appeal found for him. Balcolmbe LJ stated that although there must be a sufficient link between the promises and the detriment, the promises do not have to be the sole inducement for the detriment – a point already well established. However, he went on to deal with what the judge at first instance had considered a fatal response by Wayling in cross-examination, where he had said that if Jones, having made the promise, had told him he did not intend to keep it, Wayling would have left. Had no promise been made, again, he would have left. However, given that the promise had been made, he, Wayling, would have acted very differently if he had known it was not going to be kept. In Balcolmbe LJ's view this was sufficient to prevent the defendant from showing that Wayling had not relied upon the promise.

Detriment

'There is no doubt that for proprietary estoppel to arise the person claiming must have incurred expenditure or otherwise have prejudiced himself or acted to his detriment' – Dunn LJ in *Greasley* v *Cooke*. The detriment may be the expenditure of money, but is not confined to it. However, as the Court of Appeal of Australia explained in *Territory Insurance Office* v *Adlington* [1993] ALMD 1475, although pecuniary loss is not necessary, the detriment must be material and real. It was also stated that the time for considering whether there has been any real detriment is the moment when the promisor or representor proposes to go back on his word.

However, as Robert Walker LJ emphasised in *Gillet* v *Holt*, the quality of the relevant assurances could influence the issue of reliance which is often intertwined with detriment. Detriment itself is not a narrow or technical concept, and it need not consist of the expenditure of money or other quantifiable financial detriment, provided that it is something substantial. It has to be approached as part of a broad enquiry as to whether repudiation of an assurance was or was not unconscionable in all the circumstances.

Thus, the detriment may consist of the giving up of one's job and going to live nearer to the promisor – *Jones* v *Jones* [1977] 1 WLR 438; by cohabiting with the owner's son and nursing his daughter – *Greasley* v *Cooke*; by relying upon the promise that 'the house is yours' – *Pascoe* v *Turner*; or by selling off part of your land without being able to reach land which you have retained except over the promisor's land – *Crabb* v *Arun District Council* [1976] Ch 179 and *E R Ives Investment Ltd* v *High* [1967] 2 QB 379.

All elements must be certain for, as Auld J explained in *Willis* v *Hoare* (1999) 77 P&CR D42:

> There may be uncertainties in transactions which go to the question whether uncon-scionable behaviour has in fact given rise to any detriment to the party seeking to rely on an equity. There may be uncertainties in transactions in which unconscionable behaviour may have produced such detriment but its nature and extent are so uncertain that even equity may not be able to devise an appropriate remedy for it. There are parts that some-times even equity cannot reach; and, sometimes, as here, the two aspects of uncertainty may overlap.

Orgee v *Orgee* [1997] EGCS 152 provides an example of the difficulty. There the son of a freeholder claimed that his father, by virtue of his conduct, was obliged to grant him a tenancy of a farm. Due to the 'potentially insuperable problems as to terms left in the air', the Court of Appeal found against the son. As Chadwick LJ con-cluded, 'I am unable to recognise an equitable estoppel based on a representation which is so uncertain ... To fetter [the father's] legal right by reference to some obli-gation which cannot be spelt out seems to me to be thoroughly inequitable'. It would also be inequitable to uphold a claim for estoppel based upon unconscionable actions by the claimant:

> When a party comes to the court and seeks to obtain from it equitable relief, it is accepted ... that he must come with clean hands. I accept also ... that not every item of misconduct can possibly be sufficient to deprive a party who seeks equity from being granted the relief he seeks. Some misconduct may be trivial. But when a party acts as these have done ... it seems to be impossible for this court to do other than to take the most serious view of it and to decline to grant equitable relief even if ... they would otherwise have been so entitled. – Lindsay J in the Court of Appeal in *Gonthier* v *Orange Contract Scaffolding* [2003] EWCA Civ 873.

All human life is here! However, no detriment, no estoppel.

Proportionality

We have seen that the need to prevent unconscionable conduct is the touchstone of proprietary estoppel. In addition, the need for proportionality pervades each aspect of the doctrine.

In *Jennings* v *Rice* the Court of Appeal stated that the most essential requirement is that there should be proportionality between the expectation and the detriment, and that any remedy must be proportionate to the degree of reliance. In *Evans* v *HSBC Trust Co (UK) Ltd* [2005] WTLR 1289 the need for proportionality between the detriment and the remedy was made clear.

Proprietary estoppel and wills

We saw earlier that the correctness of allowing proprietary estoppel to give effect to a contract which is void by virtue of s 2 of the Law of Property (Miscellaneous Provisions) Act 1989 has been questioned on the ground of policy. Although not based on statutory formality, a similar question mark was raised against the use of proprietary estoppel to give effect to promises in regard to wills. This is based upon the very nature of a will, which is 'ambulatory', that is, the testator (the maker of the will) is entitled to revoke it – partly or wholly – at any time up to his death.

As Carnworth J stated in *Gillett* v *Holt & another* [1998] 3 All ER 917, 'the right to decide and change one's mind as to the devolution of one's estate is a basic and well understood feature of English law'. This being so, is it possible to succeed in a claim for proprietary estoppel where a promise to leave property by will was detrimentally relied on, but no such provision was made in the will that was effective at the promisor's death?

Taylor v *Dickens* [1998] 1 FLR 806; *Gillett* v *Holt & another* [2000] 2 All ER 289

In both these cases the claimants had worked for no or low wages due to a promise by their employer that he/she would leave them property in his/her will. In each case the employer made a will benefitting his employee but later changed the will, thereby revoking the promised benefit. In *Taylor*, the promise to leave property by will was held to be an inadequate representation upon which to rely because it is well known that a testator or testatrix (the maker of a will) is entitled to revoke his or her will at any time up to his or her death.

The court in *Taylor* distinguished two successful claims based on estoppel of promises to make a will in *Re Basham deceased* [1987] 1 All ER 405 and *Wayling* v *Jones* (1995) 69 P&CR 170. In each of those cases no will was ever made, and there was no evidence that the promisors had changed their minds.

However, the Court of Appeal in *Gillett* criticised *Taylor*:

[whilst t]he actual result in the case may be justified on the other ground on which it was put ... the inherent revocability of testamentary dispositions ... is irrelevant to a promise or assurance that 'all this will be yours' ... Even when the promise or assurance is in terms limited to the making of a will ... the circumstances make it clear that the assurance is more than a mere statement of present (revocable) intention, and is tantamount to a promise ... In the generality of cases [it] is no doubt correct [that one should not count his chickens before they were hatched], and it is notorious that some elderly persons of means derive enjoyment from the possession of a testamentary power, and from dropping hints as to their intentions, without any question of an estoppel arising. But in this case [*Gillett*] Mr Holt's assurances were repeated over a long period, usually before the assembled company on special family occasions, and some of them (such as 'it was all going to be yours anyway ...') were completely unambiguous. ... Plainly the assurances given ... were intended to be relied on, and were in fact relied on. In any event, reliance would be presumed [see *Greasley* v *Cooke* [1980] 3 All ER 710] – Robert Walker LJ.

Ottey v *Grundy* [2003] EWCA Civ 1176

The testator and the claimant had lived together as a couple for a number of years. During their time together the testator (T) had promised the claimant (C) that, upon T's death, C would inherit a life interest in the Chelsea houseboat that they had lived on, and a flat in Jamaica outright. T had sent a letter confirming this to his solicitor in Jamaica. T was a chronic alcoholic and, at his request, C gave up her 'job as an aspiring actress and model' in order to care for him. The couple parted in October 1999, and T died in July 2000, naming C as his executor but making no provision for her in his will. The Court of Appeal upheld both the finding of estoppel and the award made at first instance – £50,000, plus a further £50,000 if the defendant could not secure a transfer of the Jamaican flat to C.

Another case concerning a claim against a will is *Uglow* v *Uglow* [2004] EWCA Civ 987. It is also an example of how the courts use their discretion based on the facts of the individual case, Mummery LJ explaining that,

> the scope of the court's enquiry is not limited to what it would be unconscionable for [the testator – T] to have done in 1976, but should take account of subsequent events affecting the conscience [of T] who ... was not committing himself to leaving [the property] to [the claimant – C] come what may.

On the facts, the arrangement made in his lifetime by T in favour of C satisfied equity, and 'the court should not use the flexible principles of proprietary estoppel to secure greater benefits for [C] than he had already derived from [T] in his lifetime'.

Citing *Gillett* v *Holt*, Lawrence Collins J stated in *Edwin Shirley Productions Ltd* v *Workspace Management Ltd* [2001] 2 EGLR 16, at p 21,

> ... the importance of the decision [in *Gillett*] is that it confirms that the promise or assurance relied upon by the claimant need not be binding or irrevocable (for otherwise there would be no need for an estoppel doctrine), that the element of detriment is not a narrow or technical concept, and the requirement of detriment must be approached as part of a broad inquiry as to whether repudiation of an assurance is, or is not, unconscionable in all the circumstances'. – Quoted by Lindsay J in *Gonthier*,

who went on to say '*Gillett* thus suggests that where the facts are strong enough, a right to revoke an unbinding assurance can be lost even where the recipient of the assurance accepts that he has actual knowledge of its revocability'.

In *Ottey* v *Grundy*, the Court of Appeal reiterated that the rationale underlying proprietary estoppel is that it would be unconscionable for the maker of the assurance not to give effect to his promise. Not a wills case but on a related point, the Consistory Court in *Re West Norwood Cemetery* [2005] 1 WLR 2176 granted proprietary estoppel of the right to burial in a family grave.

How to satisfy the equity

Having conferred a right by way of equitable estoppel, the court has to decide how best to satisfy the equity. This, of course, will depend entirely upon the facts of the instant case. Thus, the woman in *Pascoe* v *Turner* [1979] 1 WLR 431 who was promised 'the house is yours and everything in it', was granted the entire fee simple absolute in possession, whilst the father in *Baker* v *Baker* (1993) 25 HLR 408 and the daughter-in-law in *Matharu* were granted only licences to occupy for life.

E R Ives Investments Ltd v *High* [1967] 2 QB 379 shows how an estoppel can arise 'out of acquiescence' and, more importantly, how it is a right which is capable of binding third parties and, therefore, of being a proprietary right (see Chapter 3B). Like *Soames-Forsythe Properties Ltd* v *Tesco Stores Ltd* [1991] EGCS 22, it was held to be an estoppel in the nature of an easement. However, as we have just seen, the courts do not have an unfettered discretion as to how the equity should be satisfied – there must be proportionality between expectation and detriment, detriment and remedy and remedy and reliance. Thus the claimant may not get all he expected – as in *Jennings*. See also *Parker* v *Parker* [2003] All ER(D) 421. Whatever, the court is not bound to satisfy the equity in the way the parties intended – *Voyce* v *Voyce* (1991) 62 P&CR 290.

Thus, as Gray and Gray (2000) state,

> few other doctrines of modern property law demonstrate so clearly the flexibility and potency of the courts' jurisdiction to arrive at broadly 'just' or 'equitable' solutions to the property difficulties of opposed parties ... The sheer flexibility of estoppel doctrine has proved uniquely suitable for translating into comprehensible legal form the more nebulous and confused aspects of lay persons' informal arrangements with regard to land – p 755.

Quantification

In some cases of equitable estoppel, such as *Dodsworth* v *Dodsworth* (1973) 228 EG 1115 and *Baker* v *Baker* [1993] 2 FLR 247, the course taken by the court to satisfy the equity has been to order the defendant to repay the plaintiff's expenditure.

The Court of Appeal in *Sledmore* v *Dalby* (1996) 72 P&CR 196 stated that the court's function in determining the extent of the equity created by a proprietary estoppel is especially important as its effect is permanent: the extent of the equity has to make good, so far as may fairly be done between the parties, the expectations which were encouraged. The court should ask itself whether it is still inequitable for the expectation to be defeated, bearing in mind the effect of the continuing estoppel upon the legal owner. On the facts it was held that the effect had long since been exhausted and no injustice had been done by permitting the enforcement of the legal owner's rights. This being so, it was held that the plaintiff had lost merely the right to rent-free accommodation for the rest of his life and that was the basis for quantifying his right. (see also *Clark* v *Clark* [2006] 2 P&CR DG 10.)

This shows how essential it is in assessing entitlement under proprietary estoppel to **go back to the beginning, to the promise or representation**. The detrimental reliance merely brings proprietary estoppel into operation: it is the promise relied upon which lays down the entitlement though, as already noted, the 'remedy' must be proportionate to the degree of reliance. It was stated by the Court of Appeal in *Ottey* v *Grundy* [2003] EWCA Civ 1176 that the remedy should be no more than necessary on the facts to protect against unconscionable conduct. Needless to say, it should never be greater than the expectation.

Sledmore v *Dalby* represents, perhaps, the broadest approach yet to quantifying the equity in proprietary estoppel. The Court of Appeal stated in *Jennings* v *Rice* [2003] 1 P&CR 8 that an equity arising from a proprietary estoppel would depend on all the circumstances of the case, the most essential requirement being that there should be proportionality between the expectation and the detriment.

Of course, like adverse possession, estoppel works in a negative way in that it estops the promisor from going back on his promise. An important question is, how long does the estoppel last? How long is a piece of string?! It is only possible to say that the estoppel will continue until the detriment suffered has been recompensed. In *Beale* v *Harvey* [2004] 2 P&CR 18, the Court of Appeal held that, as the detriment suffered had lasted only a matter of months, it was too insubstantial to make it unconscionable for the defendant to seek rectification of its mistake at its own expense. If Sarah has been promised a home for as long as she wants it, once she decides to leave she has had her entitlement: she cannot claim for the house too, even if she built it herself. Thus, in *Inwards* v *Baker*, if the son decided to move away, he would have to leave behind the bungalow which he had built: he could not claim ownership of it under any other principle. He had been promised merely the right to live there as long as he wished. On the other hand, the son in *Dillwyn* v *Llewellyn*, who had been promised the fee simple could move away, selling the house and keeping the capital monies (after paying off any mortgage loan).

Proprietary estoppel, then, gives nothing new. It merely prevents the removal of what already exists, that which was promised and relied upon.

The right arises after the promisee has acted to his detriment but before the court can make an order declaring it to be a proprietary, and not merely a personal, right. This is called an 'inchoate equity'.

Categories of estoppel

Gray and Gray (2000, pp 763–8) placed the estoppel cases into three categories: first, the 'imperfect gift' cases, such as *Pascoe* v *Turner* and *Dillwyn* v *Llewellyn*; second, the 'common expectation' cases – for example, *Ramsden* v *Dyson* (1866) LR 1 HL 129 and *Taylors Fashions Ltd* v *Liverpool Victoria Trustee Co Ltd*. In the latter case, Oliver J stated that this type of proprietary estoppel presupposes:

> ... the fostering of an expectation in the minds of *both* parties at the time but from which, since it has been acted upon, it would be unconscionable to permit the landlord to depart.

This is another example of estoppel by acquiescence, or encouragement, like *E R Ives* v *High*. Lord Kingsdown in *Ramsden* gave a good explanation of the circumstances which would give rise to this type of proprietary estoppel:

> If a man, under a verbal agreement with a landlord for a certain interest in land, or, what amounts to the same thing, under an expectation, created or encouraged by the landlord, that he shall have a certain interest, takes possession of such land, with the consent of the landlord, and upon the faith of such promise or expectation, with the knowledge of the landlord, and without objection by him, lays out money upon the land, a Court of Equity will compel the landlord to give effect to such promise or expectation. (See also *Crabb* v *Arun DC*.)

The Grays' third and final category is the 'unilateral mistake cases'. The basis of this category was explained by Lord Cranworth LC in *Ramsden* as follows:

> If a stranger begins to build on my land supposing it to be his own, and I, perceiving his mistake, abstain from setting him right, and leave him to persevere in his error, a Court of Equity will not allow me afterwards to assert my title to the land on which he had expended money on the supposition that the land was his own. It considers that, when I saw the mistake into which he had fallen, it was my duty to be active and to state my adverse title, and that it would be dishonest in me to remain wilfully passive on such an occasion, in order afterwards to profit by the mistake which I might have prevented.

This last category, the unilateral mistake, is:

> remarkable in that [the cases] exemplify some of the very few instances in English law where the courts have recognised a right to payment or other compensation for services rendered gratuitously . . . . True 'unilateral mistake' cases are fairly rare – Gray (1993, p 321).

However, as Robert Walker LJ emphasised in *Gillett* v *Holt* [2000] 2 All ER 289, proprietary estoppel must not be divided into 'watertight compartments', '. . . the fundamental principle that equity is concerned to prevent unconscionable conduct permeates all the elements of the doctrine. In the end the court must look at the matter in the round'. Thus, said Walker LJ, 'a broad inquiry must be conducted as to whether, in all the circumstances, what was being sought to be done by the person having the legal rights was unconscionable'. The importance of the doctrine of proprietary estoppel in modern land law can hardly be overstated. It can provide a 'right' or a 'remedy' where resulting and constructive trust principles will not; it has enabled a licence to evolve as a proprietary right (as we have already seen); it provides a possible 'replacement' for the doctrine of part performance in regard to contracts.

How to protect them

Ensuring the interest is binding on third parties

In unregistered land, rights by way of estoppel are protected by the doctrine of notice (see Chapter 3, Residual interests).

In registered land, the Land Registration Act 2002, s 116 confirms that, in registered land, an equity arising by estoppel is a proprietary right, capable of protection by entry of a notice. Alternatively, where the promisee is in actual occupation of the land, his interest will automatically bind purchasers, without the need for registration, as an overriding interest (providing no enquiry was made) – LRA 2002, Sched 3, para 2.

Summary

FORMAL ACQUISITION
Here we looked at:

- the statutory requirements for a valid contract for the creation or dispostion of legal interests in land;
- the statutory requirements for valid deeds for the creation of interests in land and for conveyances/transfers thereof;
- the advent of electronic conveyancing;
- the statutory requirements for the creation or disposition of equitable interests in land.

INFORMAL ACQUISITION
We considered the following:

ADVERSE POSSESSION

- the nature and characteristics of adverse possession – possession, which must be adverse; *animus possidendi*; the time period and the running of time; the effect of not bringing an action; the nature of the title acquired; adverse possession of leasehold title;

- adverse possession and human rights;
- adverse possession of registered land;
- adverse possession and trusts;
- remedies.

PROPRIETARY ESTOPPEL

- the nature and characteristics of proprietary estoppel – the need for a promise or representation; unconscionability in allowing the promisor to go back on his promise; encouragement of the belief of the promisee; reliance on the promise; detriment of the promisee; proportionality between all elements;
- proprietary estoppel and wills;
- how to satisfy the equity;
- quantification;
- categories of estoppel;
- methods for protecting the equity arising from proprietary estoppel.

References

Ames, Dean J.B., *The Nature of Ownership: Lectures on Legal History*, Cambridge, Mass: Harvard Law Review, 1913.

Barnsley, D.G., *Conveyancing Law and Practice*, 3rd edition, London: Butterworths, 1988.

Bennett, A, *The Lady in the Van*, London: Profile Books, 1999.

Brierley, A H, 'Adverse Possession – A Case of Death and Regrettable Resurrection' [1991] Conv 397.

Burn, E H, *Cheshire and Burn's Modern Law of Real Property*, 16th edition, London: Butterworths, 2000.

Cooke, E, *The New Law of Land Registration*, Oxford: Hart Publishing, 2003.

Dixon, M, 'Adverse Possession – Compromises and Estoppel' [1992] CLJ 420.

Dixon, M, 'Adverse Possession and Human Rights' [2005] Conv 345.

Gersten, V, 'Nightmare on Main Street', Law Soc Gaz, 1 September 1993, p 2.

Gray, K, *Elements of Land Law*, 1st edition, London: Butterworths, 1987.

Gray, K, *Elements of Land Law*, 2nd edition, London: Butterworths, 1993.

Gray, K and Gray, S F, *Elements of Land Law*, 3rd edition, London: Butterworths, 2000.

Gray, K and Gray, S F, *Elements of Land Law*, 4th edition, Oxford: Oxford University Press, 2005.

Kenny, P and Kenny, A, 'The Law of Property (Miscellaneous Provisions) Act 1989', Law Soc Gaz, 1 November 1989, p 15.

Law Commission, *Formalities for Contracts for Sale of Land* (Law Com No 164, 1987).

Law Commission, *Land Registration for the Twenty First Century: A Conveyancing Revolution* (Law Com No 271, 1988).

Law Commission, *Land Registration for the Twenty-First Century: A Consultative Document* (Law Com No 254, 1998).

Lim, H and Green, K, *Cases and Materials in Land Law*, 2nd edition, London: Pitman Publishing, 1995.

Oakley, J.A., *Megarry's Manual of the Law of Real Property*, 8th edition, London: Sweet and Maxwell, 2002.

Ruoff and Roper, *The Law and Practice of Registered Conveyancing*, London: Sweet and Maxwell, 1991.

Sexton, R, *Land Law*, London: Blackstone, 1996.

Smith, R J, *Property Law*, 4th edition, London: Longman, 2003.

Storey, I R, *Conveyancing*, 3rd edition, London: Butterworths, 1990.

Thompson, M P, 'New Wine from Old Bottles', Case Note on *Morritt* v *Wonham* [1993] NPC 2; [1994] Conv 233.

Further reading

FORMAL ACQUISITION

Critchley, P, 'Taking Formalities Seriously', *Land Law Themes and Perspectives*, eds Susan Bright and John Dewar, Oxford: Oxford University Press, 1998.

DEEDS

Capps, D, 'Conveyancing in the 21st Century: An outline of electronic conveyancing and electronic signatures' [2002] Conv 443.

Hopkins, N, 'Acquiring Property Rights from Uncompleted Sales of Land' [1998] 61 MLR 486.

CONTRACTS

Dixon, M, 'Invalid Contracts, Estoppel and Constructive Trusts' [2005] Conv 247.

Griffiths, G Ll H, 'Part Performance: Still Trying to Replace the Irreplaceable?' [2002] Conv 216.

Hopkins, N, 'Conscience, Discretion and the Creation of Property Rights' (2006) 26(4) *Legal Studies* 475.

INFORMAL ACQUISITION

ADVERSE POSSESSION

Advisory Service for Squatters, 'Land Registration for the Twenty-First Century: A Response', www.squat.freeserve.co.uk/lawcomm.htm

Cooke, E, *The New Law of Land Registration*, Oxford: Hart Publishing, 2003.

Cooke, E, 'The Land Registration Bill 2001' [2002] Conv 11.

Dixon, M, 'Adverse Possession – Compromises and Estoppel' [1992] CLJ 420.

Dixon, M, 'Adverse Possession & Human Rights' [2005] Conv 345.

Green, K, 'Citizens and Squatters: Under the Surfaces of Land Law', *Land Law Themes and Perspectives*, eds Susan Bright and John Dewar, Oxford University Press 1998 (p 229).

Land Registry, 'Land Registration Act 2002, Legislation Update 5: Adverse Possession'.

Nield, S, 'Adverse Possession and Estoppel' [2004] Conv 123.

Rhys, O, 'Adverse Possession, Human Rights and Judicial Heresy' [2002] Conv 470.

PROPRIETARY ESTOPPEL

Battersby, G, 'Informally Created Interests in Land', *Land Law Themes and Perspectives*, eds Susan Bright and John Dewar, Oxford University Press, 1998 (p 487).

Cooke, E, 'Reliance and Estoppel' (1995) 111 LQR 389.

Davis, C J, 'Proprietary Estoppel: Future Interests and Future Property' [1996] Conv 193.

Davis, C J, 'Informal acquisition and loss of rights in land: what justifies the doctrines?' (2000) 20 *Legal Studies* 198.

Gardner, S, 'The Remedial Discretion in Proprietary Estoppel' (1999) 115 LQR 438.

Robertson, A, 'Reliance and expectation in estoppel remedies' (1998) 18 *Legal Studies* 360.

Thompson, M P, 'Estoppel and Proportionality' [2004] Conv 137.

Wells, R, 'The Element of Detriment in Proprietary Estoppel' [2001] Conv 13.

How can you protect them?

Methods of protection afforded to all interests in land

What's the problem?

The need to protect interests in context

First, go over the facts of *Lloyds Bank plc* v *Carrick* [1996] 4 All ER 630 – we met Mrs Carrick in the previous chapter. Now consider the facts of *Barclays Bank plc* v *Zaroovabli* [1997] 2 WLR 729. In May 1988 the Zaroovablis mortgaged their freehold property to the bank. The property was registered land. For some reason best known to itself, the bank did not register the mortgage at HM Land Registry until August 1994. In registered land, the legal interest does not pass until registration: pending registration, it takes effect in equity only. In July 1988 the Zaroovablis granted to a Mrs P a six-month tenancy of the house by written agreement. Under the terms of the mortgage, the bank's consent was needed for such a grant, but none was obtained. The bank was unaware of Mrs P's tenancy. The Zaroovablis having fallen behind with repayments on the mortgage loan, the bank, in October 1995, sought possession of the house. By this time, Mrs P's contractual tenancy had become a statutory one. Did her statutory tenancy bind the bank?

Who cares?

Those who will be affected

The grantors. The legal estate will be affected by any incumbrance (burden) granted on it. It may limit the legal owner's use and enjoyment of the land, as with the lease granted to Mrs P by the Zaroovablis: during the term of her lease, they cannot have occupation of the house. It will certainly have the potential to affect third parties. Depending upon who the third party is, this could prove to be either a blessing or a curse: a blessing in that it may actually protect the legal owner's own right to remain in occupation, a curse in that it may make sale of the house virtually impossible.

The grantees. Have they acquired any interest in the land? More importantly, will it bind a third party, for example Lloyds or Barclays Bank? If so, Mrs Carrick and Mrs P could remain in occupation and defeat the banks because, unless the banks can gain vacant possession (that is, without anyone being entitled to remain in the house), there is no point in them exercising their power of sale. Purchasers will not pay anything like the market price for a property without vacant possession. Even if Mrs C or Mrs P have acquired an interest, unless it is binding upon the bank, she will have to go.

Third parties. Here, it is the banks. Are they bound by Mrs Carrick's beneficial interest and consequent right of occupation, or Mrs P's lease? Clearly, they would prefer not to be.

In order to advise any or all of these people, we need to know whether the land in question is registered or unregistered land. Only then will we know the relevant methods of protection affecting the interests of each. Only if the correct method has been fully complied with will the interest be binding on the third party.

Both these cases show that a different result can arise depending upon which system – registered or unregistered – operates. In *Carrick* the land was unregistered. Under that system Mrs Carrick's interest was not binding on Lloyds Bank, but had it been registered land her interest would have bound them. In *Zaroovabli* the land was registered. Under that system, because the Bank had not registered its mortgage, Mrs P's lease, being first in time, took priority, but had it been unregistered land, the bank's mortgage would have prevailed over her lease.

So, we must look at both systems to see the different ways in which each provides for the conveyance or transfer of interests in land and the protection of them.

As with most land law books, this area is being dealt with early on and, indeed, in practical conveyancing it may well be the starting point, for an interest can only bind a third party if it has been protected in the proper way. The person with the benefit of the interest is the one who needs to protect it, in order to impose the burden of it on others.

Example

Say, your client, Bill, is buying a house from Ben (who bought it from Edie) but is rather put off by the fact that Ben says he cannot extend the house or erect any other buildings on the land. As his solicitor, the first thing you would do would be to check the relevant register - Land Charges in unregistered land, Land Register in registered - to see if the benefit of such a right (which, if it exists, would be a restrictive covenant) has been registered. If it has, then (and only then) would you go on to consider whether the right claimed is capable of existing as an interest in land. If it is, you must check to see that the benefit of it has 'run' to your client's vendor - Ben. If it has, you will need finally to consider whether the covenant could be modified or discharged.

However, as a student of land law – that is, the law not merely conveyancing – you will need to leave all thoughts of protection until after you have considered all other matters. It may well be that the 'answer' will be that Bill takes the land free of the covenant (which, presumably, was imposed upon Ben by Edie) simply because Edie failed to register the benefit of it. Unfortunately, such an 'answer', though correct, would gain you precious few marks from an examiner! The whole of your land law course is designed to help you to understand land law, surprisingly enough. Any examiner or assessor does not want 'the answer'. As with case law and the system of binding judicial precedent, what is required is the reasoning behind your suggested solution – the '**why**', not merely the what. It is the difference between the decision and the *ratio decidendi*. Therefore, you must first consider whether the right claimed is capable of existing as an interest in land and, if so, which one. Then you must see if it has been acquired by the person claiming the benefit of it. Now you can think about protection! To do this you will need to know whether the land is registered or unregistered (if unregistered, you will need to know whether the interest is legal or equitable).

As we know, since 1926 only two estates and five interests in land can be legal (though the introduction of the commonhold will, in effect, create a third legal estate, and land obligations a sixth legal interest) – Law of Property Act 1925, s 1. Everything else must, therefore, be equitable, as will be any potential legal estate or interest which fails to satisfy the relevant requirements of formality and time.

Whether an interest is legal or equitable is relevant, for the most part, with regard to the mode of its protection.

Prior to the 1925 legislation, when virtually all land fell into the 'unregistered' system, that is, title to the land was not registrable, it would be said that whilst all legal estates and interests bound the whole world, so that any third-party purchaser would take the land subject to them, equitable interests bound the whole world except Equity's Darling. However, unless we understand the situation prior to 1926, this is meaningless!

A   Before 1926

It has been mentioned already that there are two systems operating in land law – the system under which title to land is registered at HM Land Registry ('registered land') and the unregistered system. Whilst it was possible to register title to land before 1926, it was not until the Land Registration Act 1925 that it became compulsory to do so. Therefore, prior to the Land Registration Act most land in England and Wales fell within the unregistered system, and it is to this system that the maxims mentioned above truly apply, for in unregistered land the issue of whether an interest is legal or equitable is crucial.

As the great Maitland said (1936, p 158):

> An agreement for a lease is not equal to a lease. An equitable right is not equivalent to a legal right; between the contracting parties an agreement for a lease may be as good as a lease; just so between the contracting parties an agreement for the sale of land may serve as well as a completed sale and conveyance. But introduce the third party and then you will see the difference. I take a lease; my lessor then sells the land to X; notice or no notice my lease is good against X. I take a mere agreement for a lease, and the person who has agreed to grant the lease then sells and conveys to Y, who has no notice of my merely equitable right. Y is not bound to grant me a lease.

(The 'notice' which Maitland refers to is the doctrine of notice which governed equitable interests in land prior to 1926. After 1925, statutory notice operates, that is, registration of the benefit in the correct manner. The 'agreement for a lease' and 'agreement for the sale of land' are estate contracts.)

Legal interests

Because all legal interests – including legal estates – bind the world, every purchaser of land takes subject to all legal interests attached to unregistered land. It is crucial to understand that interests attach to the land and not to the owner thereof. The Law of Property Act 1925, s 62 implies into every conveyance of land 'all . . . privileges, easements, rights and advantages whatsoever', unless a contrary intention is expressed in the conveyance. Therefore, if you do not wish to convey all your land or all of the interests you have in it, you must make it clear in the conveyance otherwise everything will be conveyed by virtue of s 62.

Remember also that 'purchaser' has a wide definition, being 'a purchaser in good faith for valuable consideration . . . a lessee, mortgagee or other person who for valuable consideration acquires an interest in property', and that, except for ss 1 to 39, '"purchaser" means a person who acquires an interest in or charge on property for money or money's worth; and in reference to a legal estate includes a chargee by way of legal mortgage' – Law of Property Act 1925, s 205(1)(xxi).

Thus, a mortgagee, for example a building society or a bank, is a purchaser, and, like everyone else, will be bound by a legal interest in or over unregistered land held by someone else.

Example

Therefore, if Alan granted a legal mortgage to Priority Building Society, secured with the deposit of title deeds to Blackacre, and later granted a second mortgage to Second City Bank, the bank's mortgage would be subject to that of the building society. So, if Alan becomes bankrupt and both mortgagees seek to regain their security, the bank must wait until the building society's outstanding debt has been satisfied before it can be paid out, and, of course, there may not be sufficient funds from the proceeds of sale to satisfy the bank's indebtedness in full or, indeed, at all.

Equitable interests

Equitable interests bind the whole world **except** Equity's Darling. If a purchaser should prove to be Equity's Darling, the interest holder would lose his interest, as in *Pilcher* v *Rawlins* (1872) 7 Ch App 259. Furthermore, it could not be revived by a purchaser with notice who took from a purchaser without – *Wilkes* v *Spooner* [1911] 2 KB 473. Who, then, is Equity's Darling? Equity's Darling is the bona fide purchaser for value of the legal estate without notice. Again, we need to understand the terminology here.

'Bona fide' means 'in good faith'.

Midland Bank Trust Co Ltd v *Green* [1981] AC 513

As Lord Wilberforce explained: The character in the law known as the bona fide (good faith) purchaser for value without notice was the creation of equity. In order to affect a purchaser for value of a legal estate with some equity or equitable interest, equity fastened upon his conscience and the composite expression was used to epitomise the circumstances in which equity would or rather would not do so. I think that it would generally be true to say that the words 'in good faith' related to the existence of notice. Equity, in other words, required not only absence of notice, but genuine and honest absence of notice ... But it would be a mistake to suppose that the requirement of good faith extended only to the matter of notice, or that when notice came to be regulated by statute, the requirement of good faith became obsolete. Equity still retained its interest and power over the purchaser's conscience ...

However, a purchaser must also be a 'purchaser for value'. This is because a purchaser can acquire the property otherwise than by buying it: he may acquire it under a will or the intestacy rules, or by way of trust or gift. However, equity will not assist a volunteer, that is, someone who gave no consideration in equity, thus the requirement of 'value'. 'Value', or consideration, has a different meaning in equity to that which it has at common law: in equity 'value' means money, money's worth or marriage. Whilst value need not, in equity, be adequate – indeed the money or money's worth may be purely nominal – 'marriage' requires a future marriage based upon a promise, that is a promise made in consideration of a particular future marriage.

The purchase must be of the legal estate, not merely of an equitable interest, and the purchaser must be 'without notice'. There are three types of notice – actual, constructive and imputed – the absence of all three being fatal to the interest holder, who will lose out against the purchaser, who will take the land free of the interest. This is the doctrine of notice.

The doctrine of notice

'Actual notice' is actual knowledge; thus a purchaser has actual notice of all matters of which he actually knows, no matter how he came to know of them. However, actual notice does not extend to matters of hearsay, so that a purchaser who hears a rumour about the existence of an interest will not have actual notice, though he will have constructive notice of it. This is because 'constructive notice' is knowledge which a purchaser would have had, had he made all relevant enquiries and inspections which ought reasonably to have been made in order to discover any interests on the land.

Therefore, a purchaser must inspect the title deeds for the relevant period, for he will be deemed to have notice of all the matters which he would have discovered had he done so. The 'relevant period' used to be at least 60 years, but it is now at least 15 years – 'at least' because a purchaser must go back as far as needs to produce a good 'root of title', that is, a document dealing with the whole of the legal estate and all interests in the land which casts no doubt upon the title.

A purchaser must also inspect the land itself for anything which could throw doubt upon the title, so he must look, for example, for unexplained tracks which may be the result of the exercise of an easement, or for a doubtful boundary. Enquiries must also be made of all occupiers of the land under the rule in *Hunt* v *Luck*.

Hunt v Luck [1902] 1 Ch 428

Provided a purchaser enquires of an occupier and is told by him that he has no interest in the land, the purchaser will take free of any interest which the occupier may have had. However, if the occupier informs the purchaser of any interest he has, the purchaser will be bound by it, as he will if he fails to enquire at all.

An occupier may be a tenant, in which case the purchaser could find himself bound to allow him to remain in occupation for the remainder of what could be a long term. As we saw in Chapter 2IIA, the occupier may actually have acquired the legal estate by way of adverse possession, leaving the purchaser with nothing. It may be that the occupier has an equitable interest in the land. In this case, the legal estate owner, especially when negotiating a mortgage, may well try to hide the fact of the occupier and his equitable interest but, because of the nature and extent of constructive notice, a purchaser may yet be bound if there is anything on the land which should have put him on notice, such as the presence of children, or children's clothes and toys, or a woman's personal belongings where the vendor appears to be a single man.

Kingsnorth Finance Co Ltd v Tizard [1986] 1 WLR 783

Here the finance company was held to have constructive notice of the estranged wife's equitable interest in the former matrimonial home, notwithstanding that it had called to inspect the house when she was not living there, because, as Judge John Finlay QC explained:

> The fact that the husband was married at the time of the valuation was material. When the surveyor was told that the husband was married, but separated, the surveyor was under a duty to look for signs of occupation by anyone other than the husband and the children ... Also the reference in the report to a 'son and daughter' should have put the plaintiffs on further inquiry which would have led to the discovery of the wife's beneficial interest in the matrimonial home ... the presence of the vendor, with occupation, does not exclude the possibility of occupation of others.

The judge held that 'This information should have been communicated to [the surveyor's] principals. Thus his knowledge that there was a wife was deemed to be knowledge in the plaintiffs'. This is 'imputed notice' - the actual or constructive notice of an agent. Therefore, the actual or constructive notice of a solicitor will be imputed to his client purchaser.

In *Strover* v *Harrington* [1998] 09 EG 61, Browne-Wilkinson VC held that knowledge of a purchaser's solicitor that a representation was false was imputed to the purchaser notwithstanding the purchaser's lack of negligence. The cause of any loss suffered by the purchaser was not his reliance upon the vendor's misrepresentation, but the failure of his own solicitors to pass on to him the relevant information.

It can be seen, therefore, that it was very difficult for a purchaser to be without notice of any kind. However, the doctrine, which evolved to protect the holder of the equitable interest, also proved insecure for the interest holder, for, once Equity's Darling arrives upon the scene, the interest is lost forever. Furthermore, a purchaser from Equity's Darling – even though he has actual notice of the interest – will take free of it. This was illustrated in *Wilkes* v *Spooner*.

Wilkes v *Spooner* [1911] 2 KB 473

Spooner, who was the lessee of two properties, assigned the lease of one of them to Wilkes, covenanting in the assignment not to compete with Wilkes's business – he was a general butcher. Later, Spooner surrendered his own lease to his landlord, who knew nothing of the covenant with Wilkes. The landlord then granted a lease of the surrendered premises to Spooner's son, who promptly opened up in direct competition with Wilkes. Obviously, Spooner's son knew all about the covenant, but because the landlord did not, and was therefore Equity's Darling, Wilkes could not revive the covenant.

B   After 1925: Unregistered land

We saw in the previous chapter that, in unregistered land, we deal with title deeds. If the interest is capable of existing as an interest in land, and it is capable of being legal (it is included in the Law of Property Act 1925, s 1(2)), and it is equivalent in time to one or other of the two legal estates, and it is created by deed, it will be legal. Legal interests in unregistered land, with the exception of one (the puisne mortgage) continue to bind the whole world.

A purchaser traces back through the title deeds to a good 'root of title', that is a clear and continuous line of ownership from his vendor to his vendor and so on for at least 15 years. Whilst tracing the root of title, a purchaser (or his solicitor) will also be on the look out for any incumbrances – the burden of any interests – affecting the land. If there are any and they are legal interests, the purchaser will be bound by them. If they are equitable interests, the purchaser will only be bound by them if he has notice of them.

The doctrine of notice created insecurity for both the interest-holder (whom the doctrine aimed to protect) and the purchaser: the purchaser could find himself bound by the burden of all sorts of equitable interests, whilst the interest-holder could lose his interest at the hands of Equity's Darling. This was why one of the main aims of the 1925 legislation was to render the doctrine redundant. To this end two alternative methods of protecting equitable interests were introduced into the unregistered land system: one for the 'family' beneficial interests behind trusts, the other for the more 'commercial' equitable interests.

Overreaching

This is the protection provided for the family interests, the beneficial interests which arise behind a trust of land or a strict settlement (Part II). Under a trust, the legal estate is separated from the beneficial – equitable – interests of the beneficiaries. The legal estate is held on behalf of the beneficiaries by the 'tenant for life' in a strict settlement, by the trustees in a trust of land. The purchaser must take the conveyance from all of the trustees, of which there must be a minimum of two and a maximum of four. However, the real ownership lies not with the legal estate holders but with the beneficiaries, in the beneficial interests. How can a purchaser be sure that he takes the land free of all these beneficial interests (which give rights of occupation)? By ensuring that they are *overreached*.

Overreaching can only occur upon the signing of the receipt for the capital monies (for example, the purchase price) by **all of the trustees**, up to the maximum of four. Both the Law of Property Act 1925 and the Trusts of Land and Appointment of Trustees Act 1996 require there to be at least two trustees of the legal estate in order to facilitate the machinery of overreaching. The Court of Appeal held in *Birmingham Midshires Mortgage Services Limited* v *Sabherwal* (2000) 80 P&CR 256 that the overreaching provision in s 2(1)(ii) of the 1925 Act had not been excluded in any way by the 1996 Act. Therefore the position remains the same: there must be a minimum of two trustees and a maximum of four and, no matter how many there are, **all of them**, be it two, three or four, must sign the receipts (and execute all the necessary documentation).

When the receipt is so signed, the beneficial interests behind the trust are over-reached, that is, they are swept off the land and into the proceeds of sale, thus converting the interest from realty into personalty. By this machinery the purchaser takes the land free of the interests of the beneficiaries, and the beneficiaries themselves receive, in exchange for their interest in the land, the equivalent proportionate interest in the proceeds of sale.

Example

So, if the legal estate in Blackacre is held by A, B, C and D as joint tenants and trustees for sale for themselves and E and F as equitable joint tenants, then, upon the sale by A, B, C and D of the legal estate to X for £120,000, and upon A, B, C and D signing the receipt for the purchase monies, the equitable interests of A, B, C, D, E and F will be converted into interests in the money. Being joint tenants, they each held a one-sixth interest in the land: upon signature of the receipt by the four trustees, these interests exist in the proceeds of sale, each joint tenant having £20,000.

It is essential to understand that though a minimum of two trustees can bring the overreaching mechanism into operation, it will only actually operate when **all** trustees (up to the maximum of four) sign the receipt. Therefore, there must be as many signatures on the receipt as there are trustees, up to a maximum of four.

The situation is slightly different where the interests are successive:

Example

If Ted leaves Blackacre, a large rambling Victorian mansion, to Ann, his wife, for life, and then to his four grown-up children absolutely, but leaves no money, it is likely that Ann, faced with huge maintenance costs and no means of meeting them, will sell the house and purchase something smaller – perhaps a thatched cottage called 'Hathaway' in Shakespeare country! The difference between the sale price of Blackacre and the purchase price of the cottage (if there is any) can be invested to provide Ann with an income, thus enabling her to enjoy her remaining years in comfort and security. Upon her death, the four children will be entitled, not to the original house, Blackacre, nor to the proceeds from the sale of it, but to the cottage and the capital as now invested. It may well be that they would all rather have inherited their family home but their wishes are not taken into account: because of overreaching, their interests are protected. This is due to the fact that Ann had only an equitable life interest so that, upon sale, she would be entitled only to the income from the proceeds of sale for life, not the capital sum.

Williams & Glyn's Bank Ltd v *Boland* [1981] AC 487; *City of London Building Society* v *Flegg* [1988] AC 54

These two cases provide classic examples of the overreaching machinery.

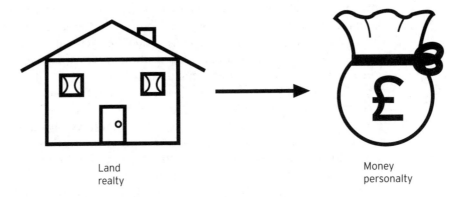

Land
realty

Money
personalty

In *Boland* the situation was:

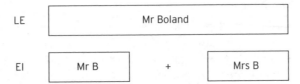

Therefore, Mrs Boland's interest was not overreached. There was only one trustee. On the other hand, in *Flegg*, the situation was:

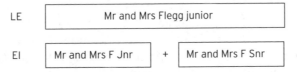

Here the older Fleggs' interests were overreached by the signatures on the mortgage of the two younger Fleggs.

Of the family interests, only those which arise behind a trust with at least two trustees can be overreached. Thus, the beneficial interests behind a bare trust – where all the legal estate is held by A and all the equitable interests by B – cannot be overreached, as there is only one trustee. A bare trust arose in *Lloyds Bank plc* v *Carrick* [1996] 4 All ER 630. When Mrs Carrick paid the whole of the purchase price to her brother-in-law, as vendor he became a bare trustee on her behalf. (However, as the source and origin of this trust arose from the contract, and the contract was itself void against the bank because she had not registered it, Mrs Carrick could not rely upon the bare trust, and the consequent lack of overreaching.) Similarly, in cases like Mrs Boland's, where there is only one holder of the legal estate, but more than one person interested in the beneficial interests, there can be no overreaching. What happens in cases like these, where the interest is neither overreachable nor registrable as a land charge? Where the 'new' law does not provide for a situation, we must fall back upon the old. Therefore, in these situations the doctrine of notice still applies as the form of protection afforded to the equitable interest in unregistered land.

For overreaching to be effective, the persons signing the receipt for capital monies must actually be trustees for sale. Thus, when a trustee husband acquired a mortgage on the matrimonial home by passing off another woman's signature as that of his wife, it was held that he had merely mortgaged his own beneficial interest: *First National Securities Ltd* v *Hegerty* [1984] 3 WLR 769.

State Bank of India v Sood [1997] Ch 276

Property was held on a trust of land by two members of the Sood family as trustees for themselves and five other members of their family as beneficiaries. All of them occupied the house. The trustees executed a legal charge (mortgage) in favour of the bank. They subsequently defaulted and the bank sought possession. However, the beneficiaries claimed that their beneficial interests had not been overreached because there had been no capital advance at the time of the mortgage. The Court of Appeal held that the interests had been overreached, though Peter Gibson LJ stated that the law as it applied to the facts of the case was not satisfactory. He also noted the fact that the Law Commission (Law Com No 188) has recommended that a conveyance should not overreach the interests of beneficiaries in occupation without their consent. However, this recommendation has yet to be implemented.

The Court of Appeal in *Birmingham Midshires Mortgage Services Ltd* v *Sabherwal* (2000) 80 P&CR 256 held that an interest by way of equitable or proprietary estoppel is subject to overreaching in the same way as an interest under a trust. The only interests which ought not to be overreached are interests of a commercial, rather than a family, nature.

In *National Westminster Bank plc* v *Malhan* [2004] EWHC 847 (Ch), the court had to consider whether overreaching is discriminatory under Article 8 (and/or Article 1 of the First Protocol) in conjunction with Article 14 – prohibition against discrimination – of the ECHR. The argument was that the overreaching provision in s 24(1) of the Law of Property Act 1925 is discriminatory because a sole trustee cannot effect overreaching but more than one can (an issue which had previously been addressed by both the Law Commission (Report 188), and Peter Gibson LJ in *State Bank of India* v *Sood* [1997] Ch 276 at 290). On the facts in *Malhan*, Sir Andrew Morritt VC held that the point did not arise as the Human Rights Act 1998 did not apply (not being retrospective). However, it is an interesting argument and may well be raised again in a future case. If upheld, it would have important ramifications.

The doctrine of conversion

The provision in the Law of Property Act 1925 for overreaching in trusts for sale (now trusts of land) was something of a mystery, however, because under the doctrine of conversion, interests behind a trust for sale lay in the proceeds of sale from the moment the trust arose. This was based on the maxim: 'equity deems to be done that which ought to be done', under which, the trust being for sale, the sale was deemed to have already taken place – leaving the interests in the proceeds thereof.

Thus, under this doctrine the interests were always in the money, whereas with over-reaching they are assumed to be in the land **until** sale.

However, by virtue of a series of cases – such as *Cooper* v *Critchley* [1955] Ch 431, *Irani Finance Ltd* v *Singh* [1971] Ch 59, *Elias* v *Mitchell* [1972] Ch 652 and *Cedar Holdings Ltd* v *Green* [1979] 3 WLR 31 – culminating in *Boland*, it was settled that the doctrine was not appropriate in the situation of a family home trust for sale, where the parties had no choice as to how they held their respective beneficial interests. When considering the nature of Mrs Boland's interest, Lord Denning asked:

> What is the nature of this interest? It was suggested to us that it was not a trust of the house itself, but only a trust in the proceeds of sale. That cannot be right. When a married man and his wife buy a house, they do so to live in it – so that it should be a home for them both and their children – for the foreseeable future. They do not intend to sell it – at any rate not for many years hence. In determining what the nature of the trust is, the court must give effect to the intention of the parties – to be inferred from their words and conduct. . . In nearly all these cases the inexorable inference is that the husband is to hold the legal estate in the house in trust for them both – for both to live in for the foreseeable future. The couple do not have in mind a sale – nor a division of the proceeds of sale – except in the far distance.

Lord Ormrod agreed, saying that beneficial interests like those of Mrs Boland:

> are not accurately described as an interest in a sum of money, simpliciter . . . In the instant cases the object of the trust was to provide a joint home and the last thing the parties con-templated was that the house would be sold and the cash divided between them. In converting such a relationship into a trust for sale the legislation of 1925 created, in effect, a legal fiction . . . This may have been an inescapable consequence of the method adopted to achieve its primary objective, that is, the simplification of conveyancing. But to press this legal fiction to its logical conclusion and beyond the point which is necessary to achieve the primary objective is not justifiable, particularly when it involves the sacrifice of the interests of a class or classes of person. The consequence is that the interests of persons in the position of the [appellant] wives ought not to be dismissed as a mere interest in the proceeds of sale except where it is essential to the working of the scheme to do so.

When *Boland* went to the House of Lords, Lord Wilberforce reinforced the views of Lords Denning and Ormrod, noting that 'to describe the interests of spouses in a house jointly bought to be lived in as a matrimonial home as merely an interest in the proceeds of sale, or rents and profits until sale, is just a little unreal'. The doc-trine has now been abolished – Trusts of Land and Appointment of Trustees Act 1996, s 3 – but remains important in other areas of property law.

Registrable interests

The Land Charges Act 1925, now 1972, introduced a system of land charges by which the commercial equitable interests, such as easements, could be protected. The system is based on the Land Charges Register upon which interest holders reg-ister their interests as land charges.

Land charges fall into six classes – A to F, and if a charge on or an obligation affecting land falls into one of these classes, it must be registered as a land charge of the relevant class at the Land Charges Registry.

The Law of Property Act 1925, s 198(1), provides that: 'registration of any instrument or matter ... shall be deemed to constitute actual notice of such instrument or matter, and of the fact of such registration, to all persons for all purposes connected with the land affected as from the date of registration or other prescribed date and so long as the registration continues in force'. However, it must be noted that though registration 'shall be deemed to constitute actual notice', this is **not** the same as the doctrine of notice.

Midland Bank Trust Co Ltd v *Green* [1981] AC 513

This case, as we know, concerned an option to purchase granted by a father to his son. The father later sold the land to his wife (and the son's mother) for a purely nominal sum. (By the time the mother bought the farm it was worth £50,000, but she paid only £500. Under the terms of the option the son would have been able to buy the farm for £22,500.) Notwithstanding that all the parties – including the wife – knew of the existence of the option, the son lost it for failure to register it as a land charge. His mother took the land free of it.

Had it been the doctrine of notice, the mother, having actual notice, would have been bound by the interest. In finding for the mother, Oliver J expressed his regret:

> because it seems to me [the son] had a clear legal right which was deliberately frustrated by his parents in breach of the contract created by the option. Nevertheless, I cannot, with the best will in the world, allow my subjective moral judgment to stand in the way of what I apprehend to be the clear meaning of the statutory provision.

The House of Lords agreed:

> The case is plain: the Act is clear and definite. Intended as it was to provide a simple and understandable system for the protection of title to land, it should not be read down or glossed: to do so would destroy the usefulness of the Act. Any temptation to remould the Act to meet the facts of the present case, on the supposition that it is a hard one, and that justice requires it, is ... removed by the consideration that the Act itself provides a simple and effective protection for persons in [the son's] position – viz – by registration.

(Following his failure in land law, the son sued his father for damages in contract and tort (conspiracy), the property then being worth £400,000. The son obtained judgment against his (by then deceased) father's estate in the sum of £100,000 on the conspiracy ground – *Midland Bank Trust Co Ltd* v *Green (No 3)* [1982] Ch 529.)

Classes of land charge

Of the six classes of land charge, three – Classes A, B and E – arise so rarely that we shall concentrate on Classes C, D and F only.

Class C. This class is subdivided into four.
A Class C(i) land charge is a puisne mortgage. This is unique within the land charges system, being a legal interest. However, whereas a legal mortgage which has been protected by the deposit of title deeds is secure, because the purchaser must acquire the deeds from the mortgagee, a mortgage which is not so protected is insecure – in that a purchaser may be unaware of its existence. The purchaser would then fail to require the mortgage to be paid off by his vendor out of the proceeds of sale, and would thus take the land subject to it. Therefore, in order to afford protection to the purchaser, who would be bound by the mortgage, and the mortgagee, whose

security may be insecure against the new owner of the legal estate, puisne mortgages must be registered in this way.

Being part of the system, they operate just like all other land charges – they receive no preferential treatment merely because they are legal. Thus, priority between competing registrable mortgages – which will usually be all mortgages created subsequent to the first legal mortgage with deposit of title deeds – will be determined purely by reference to the dates of registration, not the dates of creation.

A Class C(ii) land charge is 'a limited owner's charge', as, for example, where a tenant for life under a strict settlement charges inheritance tax due on the estate to the settled land, rather than pay them out of his own pocket.

A Class C(iii) land charge is 'a general equitable charge', which is defined in s 2(4) of the Land Charges Act as:

any equitable charge which

(a) is not secured by a deposit of documents relating to the legal estate affected; and

(b) does not arise or affect an interest arising under a trust of land or a settlement; and

(c) is not a charge given by way of indemnity against rents equitably apportioned or charged exclusively on land in exoneration of other land and against the breach or non-observance of covenants or conditions; and

(d) is not included in any other class of land charge.

By virtue of paragraph (a) quoted above, therefore, any mortgage in unregistered land – whether legal or equitable – which is accompanied by the deposit of the title deeds is incapable of registration.

A Class C(iv) land charge is an estate contract.

Class D. Class D is subdivided into three.

A Class D(i) land charge is 'an Inland Revenue Charge'. These arise, for example, where inheritance tax payable on land has not been paid.

A Class D(ii) land charge is a restrictive covenant which was created after 1 January 1926, and which is not contained in a lease.

A Class D(iii) land charge is an equitable easement created after 1 January 1926.

Class F. A Class F land charge is the matrimonial home right originally provided by the Matrimonial Homes Act 1983, and now by the Family Law Act 1996. It is unique in the land charges system because it is not an interest in the land: as Megarry J explained '[t]he right is in essence a personal and non-assignable statutory right not to be evicted from the matrimonial home in question during marriage or until the court otherwise orders' – *Wroth* v *Tyler* [1974] Ch 30. (See this case for the possible consequences of a Class F registration for the spouses and a purchaser.) The charge ends upon the death of either spouse, or on the termination of the marriage (unless the court makes an order to the contrary during the marriage). The matrimonial home right is a right not to be evicted or excluded from the home if already in occupation, and a right, with leave of the court, to enter and occupy if not already in occupation. The right is available to spouses (s 30), to cohabitants (s 36), and now also to civil partnerships following the Civil Partnerships Act 2004.

Residual interests

In looking at the more important changes made by the 1925 legislation, one of its chief draughtsmen – Sir Benjamin Cherry – remarked that: 'In a subject so vast there are bound to be mistakes which will occupy the attention of the legislature at a later date'. However, it is not only the legislature which has been called upon to amend or rectify the legislation; the courts too have had to lend a hand.

Once the two methods of protecting equitable interests in unregistered land had been provided – overreaching and the registration of land charges – it was thought that the doctrine of notice had been successfully relegated to history. However, it became clear very early on that lacunae (gaps) in the legislation meant that certain interests were incapable of being either overreached or registered as land charges, as the case may be.

We have seen that only restrictive covenants and equitable easements created after 1 January 1925 can be registered as Class D(ii) or D(iii) land charges, not those created before that date. Neither can an equitable mortgage created by deposit of title deeds be registered as a land charge. The Act itself provides these exceptions. Yet they are not the only exceptions.

In *E R Ives Investment Ltd* v *High* [1967] 2 QB 379 it was held that licences by estoppel cannot be registered as land charges, nor can interests arising under the doctrine of mutual benefit and burden – see *Halsall* v *Brizell* [1957] Ch 169; and in *Shiloh Spinners Ltd* v *Harding* [1973] AC 691, it was held that an equitable right of entry cannot be registered either, nor can a tenant's right to enter and remove fixtures at the end of a lease – *Poster* v *Slough Estates* [1968] 1 WLR 1515. All of these interests are still subject to the old doctrine of notice.

(Two other interests are not registrable: leasehold covenants and equitable mortgages of equitable interests. However, these are not subject to the doctrine of notice. The lease itself provides the relevant 'protection' for the covenants in it by being itself appropriately protected. An equitable mortgage or an equitable interest would arise, for example, where a beneficiary behind a trust of land granted a mortgage upon his beneficial interest: this type of mortgage is protected under the rule in *Dearle* v *Hall* (1823) 3 Russ 1 which requires the trustees of the legal estate to be notified of the granting of the mortgage upon the equitable interest.)

Where an interest is capable of registration but has not been registered, the holder of the benefit cannot claim assistance from the doctrine of notice. The doctrine only applies to interests not provided for by the land charges system.

The effect of registration and non-registration

Interests must be registered 'in the name of the estate owner whose estate is intended to be affected' – s 3(1), and it is vital to register land charges against the correct name. This may not be as simple as it would appear.

Diligent Finance Ltd v *Alleyne* (1972) 23 P&CR 346

Mrs Alleyne registered a Class F land charge against 'Erskine Alleyne' – her husband. However, his full name, unbeknownst to her, was Erskine Owen Alleyne. Her registration was void. See also *Oak Co-operative Building Society* v *Blackburn* [1967] Ch 1169.

In practice, it is as well to search against the name of every estate owner since 1925. This safety measure is necessary because of two characteristics of the unregistered system: the need to trace back to a good root of title and the fact that registration is against the name of the owner, not the property.

As already mentioned, the root of title is a valid document of title, and to find it, you must search all title deeds at least 15 years old – Law of Property Act 1925, s 23. Unfortunately, however, a purchaser is not entitled to have access to the actual deeds until after contracts have been exchanged, by which time he is legally bound to go through with the purchase. Only by examining the title deeds can the names of all previous estate owners be discovered. A proper search cannot be made unless all relevant names are known. What is more, the purchaser's right of access to the deeds only extends to the 15-year period (unless otherwise agreed).

Example

So, if A conveys land to B in 1928, in 1957 B conveys it to C subject to a restrictive covenant in favour of B, C conveys the land to D in 1982 and D conveys it to E this year, E's investigation of the title deeds would not reveal the restrictive covenant in the 1958 conveyance. If it has been duly registered as a Class D(ii), the burden of it would be binding on E even though he will not have searched against B or C. A clear search against D does not help E at all. The Law of Property Act 1969, s 25(1) went some way towards alleviating this problem. Under it, any purchaser of an estate or interest in unregistered land who finds himself subject to a 'hidden' registered interest, despite making a proper search to a good root of title, and who suffers loss can seek compensation from a fund set up for this purpose. Thus, the burden of the restrictive covenant remains binding on E, but he is compensated for the loss caused thereby. (The fact that the covenant remains in existence and binding, however, may well affect E's chances of selling his land, or the price he can ask for it.)

The effective date for all interests is the date of registration at the land charges registry.

Where interests are registrable as land charges but are not so registered, Class A, B, C(i), C(ii), C(iii), E and F land charges are void 'as against a purchaser of the land charged with it, or of any interest in such land' – s 4(2), (5) and (8). However, Class C(iv) and D land charges, if not registered as such, are only void 'as against a purchaser for money or money's worth of a legal estate in the land charged with it' – s 4(6).

Example

Therefore, if Tom leaves Blackacre to Jerry in his will, though Jerry will only be bound by any Class A, B, C(i), C(ii), C(iii), E or F land charges which are registered, he will be bound by all Class C(iv) and D land charges - whether registered or not.

Where an interest is void under the Act for want of registration, it is completely irrelevant that the purchaser had notice under the doctrine:

[he] shall not be prejudicially affected by notice of . . . any instrument or matter capable of

registration under the Land Charges Act [1972] ... which is void or not enforceable as against him under that Act ... by reason of the non-registration thereof – Law of Property Act 1925, s 199(1)(i).

See *Midland Bank Trust Co Ltd* v *Green* [1981] AC 513, which also held that, 'money or money's worth' need not be adequate.

Thus, where the Act provides for registration of a land charge, the only 'notice' which is relevant is notice provided by the register: any 'notice' acquired outside of the register is irrelevant. As Gray (1993) explains, this illustrates the preference of certainty over justice in the field of property rights:

> The major objective of the 1925 legislation was the simplification of conveyancing, and in the context of land charges this objective is more effectively ensured if the consequences of registration and non-registration are absolutely clear-cut and conclusive: ... it is for this reason that the traditional doctrine of notice is displaced or, more accurately, is drastically adapted by the land charges system ... the orthodox concept of notice suffered modification to the extent that registration of a land charge became the *only* recognised form of notice to third parties in respect of wide categories of commercial equitable interests. The law of land charges thus conforms to the general tendency in English property law to facilitate certainty as to outcome rather than justice as between parties – p 121.

C After 1925: Registered land

The system of registration by title

'Registered land' means a registered estate or registered charge' – LRA 2002, s 132(1).

The Land Registration Act 2002 (LRA 2002) came into force on 13 October 2003. It was heralded by the then Law Commissioner, Charles Harpum as the 'most fundamental reform in property law since 1925', and, indeed, the new Act does make several important changes – some of which will be effective immediately, others not for some time to come. The most fundamental change is that from registration *of* title to *by* registration title –

> One of the objectives of the Law Commission and Land Registry's report is that registration alone should confer title – 'Explanatory Notes to Land Registration Act 2002', HMSO, 2002, para 17 (ISBN 010 560 902 1).

This means, then, that legal estates in registered land will be *created* by registration. What's more, registration is to be effected electronically, with 'completion' – the transfer of title – taking place

> at the click of a mouse ... triggering the transfer to the buyer; immediate registration of the change of ownership at the Land Registry; automatic payment of the purchase price and the discharge of any mortgage on the property; automatic payment of stamp duty ... Thus, E-conveyancing is the whole process by which land transfers can take place electronically. It encompasses due diligence, exchange, completion and registration – www.egi.co.uk/properte_info.asp?propertepage=faq.

The person named as registered proprietor will, therefore, be the title holder, no matter how he or she came to be registered (eg by fraud).

As already noted, in registered land we do not deal with title deeds. Instead transfers, filed plans and office copies became the order of the day. Holders of the legal estate became known as registered proprietors. Now, the LRA 2002 heralds the totally paperless age! Land Certificates and Charge Certificates will no longer be issued automatically. (Sir Beesley Scott, if he were commenting today, might well consider this to be 'revolution, not evolution'!) The paperless system will be brought into being by the introduction of e-conveyancing, which will itself be introduced gradually. According to one government prediction, it will be anything up to ten years before the whole system of title by registration will be covered. However, parties will be able to print off hard copies of the 'e-documents' and, under the proposed Law of Property (Electronic Communications) Order, valid e-contracts and e-deeds will be as effective as paper ones.

In its public information leaflet 'HM Land Registry: A part of the landscape', the Land Registry states its main purpose to be: 'to register title to land in England and Wales and to record dealings once the land is registered'. It goes on:

> There are a number of important advantages for everybody: it provides a safe, simple and economic system for the transfer and mortgage of land. Once a piece of land is registered: a legal title is guaranteed; an accurate plan is provided; there is an up-to-date and authoritative public record of ownership, rights, covenants and mortgages; dealings can take place with confidence; the risk of fraud is reduced; simple forms replace complicated documents; disputes can be resolved more easily; repeated and lengthy examinations of the title deeds can be dispensed with.

It also dispenses with the need to trace to a good root of title. Information on some 18 million properties in England and Wales is now registered at HM Land Registry (which represents around 80% of freehold titles).

The system of registration 'by' title to land takes all the interests in land – legal, equitable, family, commercial and residual – and recategorises them as 'registrable', 'overriding' or 'minor'. Therefore, the distinction between legal and equitable became less in registered land. However, the distinction is still important nonetheless.

The aim behind the Land Registration Act was to create a register of title which would, at any given time, act as a mirror which accurately reflects all the interests existing in or over any piece of land. Therefore, all that a purchaser would have to do was check at the Land Registry for any entries on the register, because a purchaser would take the land subject only to all entries on the register and any overriding interests existing at the time. This is the 'mirror principle'. There are two other principles – the curtain principle, behind which the details of trusts affecting registered land are kept off the title (the purchaser, being protected by overreaching, has no need to know); and the insurance principle under which the state guarantees the accuracy of the registered titles and provides an indemnity fund to compensate registered proprietors who have been adversely affected by the operation of the system. These principles are retained by LRA 2002.

The problem which Mrs Alleyne encountered in unregistered land does not arise in registered land because here entries are made against the property, not the property owner, by way of a title number. (If the title number is not known, a search of

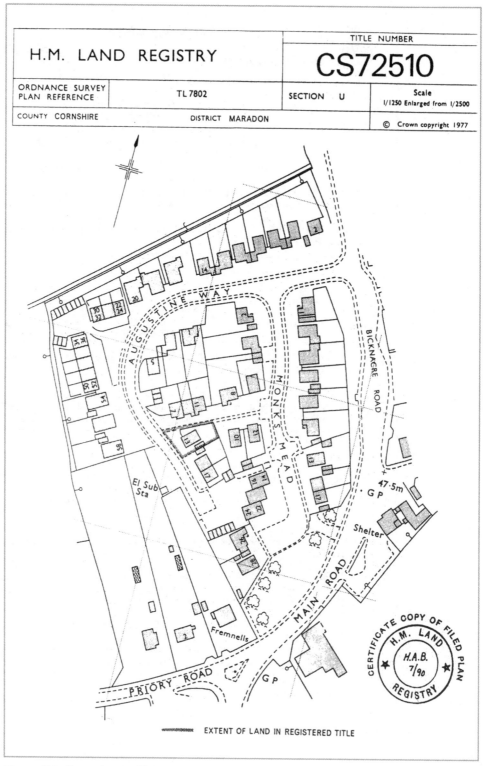

Figure 3.1 Example of a filed plan

Specimen Register

HM Land Registry

TITLE NUMBER: CS72510

Edition date: 31 August 1990

Entry No.	A. PROPERTY REGISTER containing the description of the registered land and the estate comprised in the Title
	COUNTY DISTRICT CORNSHIRE MARADON
1.	(19 December 1989) The Freehold land shown edged with red on the plan of the above Title filed at the Registry and being 13 Augustine Way, Kerwick.
2.	(19 December 1989) The land has the benefit of a right of way on foot only over the passageway at the rear leading into Monks Mead.

Entry No.	B. PROPRIETORSHIP REGISTER stating nature of the Title, name, address and description of the proprietor of the land and any entries affecting the right of disposing thereof **TITLE ABSOLUTE**
1.	(31 August 1990) Proprietor(s): PAUL JOHN DAWKINS and ANGELA MARY DAWKINS both of 13 Augustine Way, Kerwick, Maradon, Cornshire.
2.	(31 August 1990) RESTRICTION: Except under an order of the registrar no disposition by the proprietor(s) of the land is to be registered without the consent of the proprietor(s) of the Charge dated 29 July 1990 in favour of Weyford Building Society referred to in the Charges Register.

Entry No.	C. CHARGES REGISTER containing charges, incumbrances etc. adversely affecting the land and registered dealings therewith
1.	(19 December 1989) A Conveyance of the land in this title and other land dated 19 May 1924 made between (1) Allen Ansell (Vendor) and (2) Frances Amelia Moss (Purchaser) contains the following covenants:- "And the purchaser for herself her heirs executors administrators and assigns hereby covenants with the Vendor his heirs and assigns that she will perform and observe the stipulations set out in the First Schedule hereto so far as they relate to the hereditaments hereby assured THE FIRST SCHEDULE above referred to (a) No caravan shall be allowed upon the premises and the Vendor or owner or owners of adjoining premises may remove and dispose of any such caravan and for that purpose may forcibly enter upon

Continued on the next page

Figure 3.2 Specimen register

Specimen Register

HM Land Registry

TITLE NUMBER: CS72510

Entry No.	C. CHARGES REGISTER (continued)
	any land upon which a breach of this stipulation shall occur and shall not be responsible for the safe keeping of any such caravan or for the loss thereof or any damage thereto or to any fence or wall
	(b) No earth gravel or sand shall at any time be excavated or dug out of the land except for the purpose of excavations in connection with the buildings errected on the land and no bricks or tiles shall at any time be burnt or made nor any clay or lime be burnt on the land."
2.	(19 December 1989) The passageway at the side included in the title is subject to rights of way on foot only.
3.	(31 August 1990) A Transfer of the land in this title dated 29 July 1990 made between (1) JOHN EDWARD CHARLES BROWN and (2) PAUL JOHN DAWKINS and ANGELA MARY DAWKINS contains restrictive covenants. *NOTE:- Copy in Certificate*
4.	(31 August 1990) REGISTERED CHARGE dated 29 July 1990 to secure the moneys including the further advances therein mentioned.
5.	(31 August 1990) Proprietor(s): WEYFORD BUILDING SOCIETY of Society House, The Avenue, Weymouth, Cornshire.

* * * * * END OF REGISTER * * * * *

NOTE A: A date at the beginning of an entry is the date on which the entry was made in the Register.

NOTE B: This certificate was officially examined with the register on **31 August 1990.**
This date should be stated on any application for an official search based on this certificate.

Figure 3.2 Continued

the Index Map should be requested: this will provide the title number or the information that title to the land has not yet been registered.)

The problem of searching through numerous deeds to find a good root of title is also solved in that the title deeds would only have to be checked once – by the Land Registrar. This would reduce repetition, time and cost. As a result, you never see title deeds in registered land, until, possibly, after completion of a first registration.

All land in England and Wales is compulsorily registrable upon sale, transfer by gift, pursuant to a court order, the grant of a lease or the creation of a protected first legal mortgage out of or upon 'a qualifying estate'. 'A qualifying estate' is an unregistered legal estate which is (a) a freehold estate in land, or (b) a leasehold estate in land for a term which, at the time of transfer, grant or creation, has more than seven years to run – s 4(1). A mortgagee can ask for first registration with or without the mortgagor's consent – s 6(6) and Land Registration Rules.

> There is a possibility that estate owners will regard these provisions as a nuisance. I can see cases where a property company wishes to remortgage its assets being a source of needless expense and work. The boxes of titles to be considered will range around the walls of some solicitor's office – thousands of individual titles – and in every one which is presently unregistered a requirement for first registration to be effected if there is to be an effective first legal charge over the title . . . It is doubtful if the lender will seriously consider restructuring the security in order to reduce a cost which is to be borne by the borrower – Conveyancer's Notebook, 'To Assent or Not to Assent' [1997] Conv 245.

This extension of the classes of registrable titles, coupled with the computerisation of HM Land Registry's records and electronic conveyancing, puts the future of title deeds in jeopardy. They are private, not public, documents and will either be returned to their owners (by HM Land Registry, the registered proprietor's solicitors or the mortgagee, even if only after the mortgage has been paid off) or, presumably, destroyed. These documents contain our heritage – not merely the history of the physical land, but more especially of the people who lived on it, their communities, how they managed their greatest asset, etc. These documents must be preserved – a (central) registry should be created to hold them. Obviously, the cost of this storage would be high – but not so high as the loss of our history. It is not only academics who would bemoan the loss of this archive material, so important to research. In her article 'Old deeds – a plea for their preservation', Elizabeth Rothey (1992) emphasises their value to people tracing their family history, or the history of family homes, or of communities. In this pursuit she found:

> the most useful and important source – the title deeds – are often missing, some, because they were not passed on, or were lost, when they were not required to establish the root of title, or, others, with increasing frequency, because they were not passed on when the title was registered.
>
> When the title to the property had been registered, the Land Registry returns the deeds to the solicitors who should retain them and pass them to the next owner. Some solicitors do this – but not all. It seems that some are sold and others are destroyed . . . The absence of title deeds sometimes results in being unable to trace the history of a property.

As Susan George explains in her book, *Liverpool Park Estates* (2000, p 2):

> Most unfortunately and ironically, when the Land Registry recently moved over to computerisation, the contents of the land certificate publicly available were significantly abbreviated (and much of the old card index system was then destroyed), so that only current ownership appears on the Register. The history of a piece of land is therefore in general still not traceable without access to the deeds in the possession of the householder, his lawyer or the mortgagee; hence research into a series of pieces of land now individually owned is not practical.

Ms Rothey echoes my plea, asking conveyancers:

> to ensure that old deeds are not left to gather dust. Either pass them to the new owner along with the land certificate or lodge them with the local record office. . . . This also applies to building societies and banks who hold deeds.

To this I would add the Land Registry. Please bear this in mind when you go into practice!

Each register of title is, in fact, made up of three registers – the property register, which contains a description of the property by reference to a filed plan and any interests which benefit the land registered; the proprietorship register, which sets out the name and address of the person or persons who own the legal estate in the land, the type of title held and any inhibitions or restrictions affecting his or their right to deal with the land; and the charges register, which details all encumbrances or charges affecting the land, that is, any interests which burden it. Thus, in the case of a restrictive covenant, if the land the title to which was registered was the servient tenement, the burden of the covenant would appear in the charges register – the benefit being noted in the property register of the dominant tenement. All mortgages affecting the land will appear in the charges register, as will any leases over seven years granted on the land. See Figures 3.1 and 3.2 for an example of a filed plan and entries on the register.

Since January 1991 any person can, on payment of a fee, obtain office copies of the entries upon the register, or inspect any registered title and any documents referred to in the register (other than mortgages and leases).

Title must be registered by the 'responsible estate owner, or his successor in title' within two months of the date of the transaction – LRA 2002, s 6(4). Even if the estate transferred or granted has a negative value, it is a transfer or grant for valuable or other consideration. Compulsory registration is triggered by the events set out in s 4(1). Failure to register where necessary will result in the transfer, grant or creation becoming void.

The compulsory registration triggers are:

(a) the transfer of a qualifying estate [an unregistered freehold or leasehold with seven or more years left to run]
   (i) for valuable or other consideration, by way of gift or in pursuance of an order of any court, or
   (ii) by means of an assent (including a vesting assent);

(c) the grant out of a qualifying estate in land –
   (i) for a term of years absolute of more than seven years from the date of grant, and
   (ii) for valuable or other consideration, by way of gift or in pursuance of an order of any court;

(d) the grant out of a qualifying estate in land for a term of years absolute to take effect in possession after the end of a period of three months beginning with the date of the grant;

(e) the grant of a lease in pursuance of Part 5 of the Housing Act 1985 (the right to buy) out of an unregistered legal estate in land [see Chapter 8];

(g) the creation of a protected first legal mortgage of a qualifying estate.

Paragraphs (b) and (f) relate to circumstances under the Housing Act 1985 under which disposal by a landlord leads to a person no longer being a secure tenant. Even if the estate transferred or granted has a negative value, it is a transfer or grant for 'valuable' or other consideration – s 1(6).

However, this leaves several types of transfer which are not subject to compulsory registration – transfers by operation of law, for example where a deceased's estate vests in his Personal Representatives – s 4(3); on the assignment of a mortgage term – s 4(4); on the assignment or surrender of a lease which results in the merger of that lease with the immediate reversion – s 4(4).

In addition to compulsory registration under s 4, s 3 provides for voluntary registration of unregistered fees simple, leases of more than seven years, rentcharges (see Chapter 5), profits *à prendre* in gross (see Chapter 13), and franchises (grants by the Crown under the Royal Prerogative, such as a right to treasure).

As noted above, failure to register where necessary will result in the transfer, grant or creation becoming void, and title to the legal estate falling within s 4(1)(a) or (b) reverting to the transferor, to be held by him on a bare trust for the transferee – s 7(2)(a), and those falling within s 4(1)(c) and (g) will take effect as a contract made for valuable consideration to grant or create the legal estate concerned – s 7(2)(b). In other words, they will take effect in equity only (however, once e-conveyancing comes in, registration and creation will be simultaneous).

The effect of dispositions on priority between competing interests is set out in ss 28–30. The basic rule is that

(1) Except as provided in sections 29 and 30, the priority of an interest affecting a registered estate or charge is not affected by a disposition of the estate or charge.

(2) It makes no difference for the purposes of this section whether the interest or disposition is registered – s 28.

Thus, under s 28, priority of interests in registered land depends upon the time they are created, whether or not they have been registered.

Example

Michael owns freehold land in Shropshire and decides to give it to his friend, Di. The transfer must be registered under s 4(1)(a). However, before the transfer, Michael entered into a contract to sell some of the land to his neighbour, John, and then to his brother, Trevor. Even though Di has been registered as proprietor, she will take subject to the pre-existing claims of John and Trevor.

So, the maxim 'the first in time prevails' applies. As Professor Kenny explains in his annotations to the Act, 'The purpose of the Act is to make this principle even clearer and more absolute than was the case under the Land Registration Act 1925'. To put it another way, where no valuable consideration has been given by the transferee, registration is subject to any prior interests, whether they were registered or not; registration only protects against subsequent dispositions.

However, under ss 29 and 30, if the disposition (of estates under s 29 and charges under s 30) is for valuable consideration (which does not include marriage consideration or a nominal consideration in money), then the new proprietor takes subject only to interests which are registered or protected by notice on the register, or which are overriding.

> **Example**
>
> Thus if Michael had sold the land to Di, she would take it free of the interests of John and Trevor. (If Michael had granted Di a lease of less than seven years for valuable consideration, although the lease itself would not be registrable, it would be subject to the same interests as under s 29.)

The three categories of interest for the purposes of registered land – registrable, overriding (or 'interests which override') and minor – will remain, as will the general aims and principles, though these are, ultimately, to be achieved through e-conveyancing.

The register of title will continue to be made up of three registers – the property register, the proprietorship register and the charges register.

As already noted, first registration by the 'responsible estate owner, or his successor in title' must take effect within two months of the date of the transaction – LRA 2002, s 6 (subject to extension). The legal estate will pass immediately on registration. Failure to apply for registration in time will result in the legal estate reverting to the vendor or former owner – s 7. Once title has been registered, all subsequent dealings with it are called 'registered dispositions' (we shall be coming shortly to situations where a distinction has to be made between first registration and registered dispositions).

Rectification

Schedule 4 provides for 'alterations of the Register' including rectification. Under LRA 1925, 'rectification' covered all alterations to the register, but under LRA 2002 'rectification' applies only to alterations which involve 'the correction of a mistake, and which prejudicially affect the title of a registered proprietor' – para 1.

Thus 'rectification' under the new rules is available only to make changes to the legal position immediately prior to the alteration. It can therefore have a negative effect upon the current registered proprietor's title; clearly, great caution must be taken in relying on cases under the LRA 1925.

All other possible alterations are administrative in nature, that is they merely amend the register so that it represents existing legal rights accurately.

There are two categories of alterations – 'alterations pursuant to a court order' (paras 2–4), and 'alterations otherwise than pursuant to a court order' (paras 5–7). Under para 2(1):

the court may make an order for alteration of the register for the purpose of
(a) correcting a mistake [for example, where the original entry was obtained by fraud],
(b) bringing the register up to date, [for example, where a rentcharge has been terminated by right of re-entry], or
(c) giving effect to any estate, right or interest excepted from the effect of registration [for example, an overriding interest].

Paragraph 3 sets out the circumstances in which an alteration can be made against the title of a proprietor in possession. These are the same as under LRA 1925, s 82, and thus case law on s 82, can still be relied on.

They are:

(a) to give effect to an overriding interest,

(b) to give effect to an order of court,

(c) because he, through fraud or lack of proper care, caused, or substantially contributed to, the error in or omission from the register, or

(d) if it would for any other reason be unjust not to rectify the register against him.

The case law on this aspect of LRA 1925, s 82 began with *Chowood v Lyall (No 2)* [1930] 2 Ch 156, where the register was rectified in favour of a squatter who had acquired title to part of the land by adverse possession, providing an example of type (a) rectification.

For an illustration of rectification of type (b) see *Hayes v Nwajiaku* [1994] EGCS 106 (where it was held that 'proprietor' means proprietor of land, not of charges).

Examples of type (c) are provided by two cases. First, *Re Sea View Gardens* [1967] 1 WLR 134, where rectification was ordered by Pennycuick J who felt that he had the discretion to rectify, notwithstanding that the registered proprietor was in possession, because he had substantially contributed to the Land Registrar's mistake in registering him as the proprietor of a plot of disputed land, even though he had not known that inclusion of the disputed plot in the transfer was an error. Secondly, in *Re Leighton's Conveyance* [1937] Ch 149, where rectification of the proprietorship register was made against a daughter in favour of her mother, whom she had tricked into transferring the property to her. (However, no rectification was made in the charges register in regard to the mortgagees to whom the daughter had mortgaged the property, they having had no knowledge of the fraud against the mother.)

In *Epps v Esso Petroleum Co Ltd* [1973] 1 WLR 1071, an application for rectification of type (d) was refused because it would not be unjust not to order rectification. The fact that such refusal meant the defendants would not be entitled to be indemnified was irrelevant. In *Horrill v Cooper* (1999) 78 P&CR 336, rectification under this head was ordered to give effect to the benefit of restrictive covenants restricting building operations on the registered land, the court holding this to be 'one of those rare cases where the register should be disturbed'. In this case compensation, ie indemnity, was available.

The Court of Appeal in *Norwich & Peterborough Building Society v Steed* [1992] 3 WLR 669 had to consider whether s 82 gave the court power to rectify in circumstances which would not have been available before 1926, and held it could not: s 82 had created no new substantial powers to challenge proprietary rights. On its true construction, s 82 is not a general discretion to grant rectification merely because it might be just so to do. Section 82 provides a power to order rectification only on the grounds specified in s 82(1). The Court of Appeal, in *Malory Enterprises Ltd v Cheshire Homes (UK) Ltd* [2002] EWCA Civ 151, held that the statutory right to rectify could constitute an overriding interest. The question was raised whether rectification could be backdated: Arden LJ, following a full consideration of the issue, decided that there could not be, but Clarke and Scheiman LLJ left the matter open (as it was not necessary to decide the issue on the facts of the case). However, it was held that there can be no disposition where there has been a forgery, and therefore nothing to be rectified.

Alterations which can be made 'otherwise than pursuant to a court order' are, in fact, the same as those which the court can order under para 2, but with one addition – the removal of a superfluous entry – para 5.

Indemnity

Schedule 8, para 1(1) sets out the situations where a person is entitled to be indemnified –

(a) rectification of the register,

(b) a mistake whose correction would involve rectification of the register,

(c) a mistake in an official search,

(d) a mistake in an official copy,

(e) a mistake in a document kept by the registrar which is not an original and is referred to in the register,

(f) the loss or destruction of a document lodged at the registry for inspection or custody,

(g) a mistake in the cautions register, or

(h) failure by the registrar to perform his duty under s 50.

However, a person will only be entitled to be indemnified if he suffers loss *by reason of* the situations set out in para 1(1). Thus there is no indemnity for alterations giving effect to overriding interests; as a purchaser of registered land takes subject to all overriding interests anyway, there is no loss incurred by the alteration (though para 1(2)(b) provides one possible exception). Where the loss has been caused by the claimant's own fraud there will, of course, be no indemnity – para 5. Similarly, if the loss was due solely to the claimant's lack of proper care there will be no indemnity (if he was merely contributory, then a pro rata reduction in the indemnity will be made – para 5(2)).

All dealings after first registration of the title take effect under LRA 2002, under which title will not pass until registration of the purchaser as proprietor.

The interests

As mentioned above, the 2002 Act retains the three categories of interest in registered land – registrable, overriding ('interests which override') and minor. However, there are several important changes to the interests contained in each category.

Registrable interests

These are the substantively registrable interests, those which are capable of being registered in their own right.

All fees simple absolute in possession are registrable interests, but only terms of years over seven years. It cannot, therefore, be said that the registrable interests equate to the legal estates of LPA 1925, s 1(1).

Upon substantive registration, a title number is allocated which is unique to the title registered. Thus, where there is a term of years absolute of more than seven years, there will be two separate titles registered: one for the term of years, the other for the fee simple out of which it was granted. Similarly, if there is a sublease there will be three titles: any term of years will be noted on the register relating to the fee simple out of which it was granted. Any sublease will be noted on the register of the term of years out of which it was granted, and so on. A legal mortgage is also registrable in its own right as a registered charge. A legal rentcharge is registrable in this way too.

As this is the category of registrable interest, it is confusing to speak in terms of 'registering' other interests; 'entered', or 'noted' is clearer.

Transfer of title to registered land does not take effect until the title is registered in the names of the new registered proprietors. Upon first registration after land has become compulsorily registrable, the final conveyance is carried out as for unregistered land and within two months of completion the title must be registered in the names of the purchasers. Failure to so register renders the transaction 'void so far as regards the transfer, grant or creation of a legal estate' – LRA 2002, s 7(1), and therefore the legal estate remains with the vendor, who will hold on trust for the purchasers, or the grant or creation will take effect only as a contract for valuable consideration to grant or create the legal estate concerned – ss 7(2) and 4(1).

The dangers of not applying promptly for registration of a registrable interest were highlighted in *Mortgage Corporation Ltd* v *Nationwide Credit Corporation Ltd* [1993] 4 All ER 623 and *Barclays Bank plc* v *Zaroovabli* [1997] 2 WLR 729. Both cases concerned the non-registration of mortgages. A case concerning registration of legal title was *Pinkerry* v *Needs (Contractors)* (1992) 64 P&CR 245, where the Court of Appeal stated that in an area of compulsory registration a vendor cannot require his purchaser to complete until he, the vendor, is registered as proprietor of the legal estate: until that time, the vendor has no legal estate to transfer, merely an equitable interest. Presumably, the same will apply under LRA 2002.

Obviously, every subsequent transfer of the legal estate must be registered: until it is, the title remains with the vendor, the purchaser having only an equitable interest. However, from the date of completion of the transfer, pending registration, the purchaser is entitled to receive mesne profits from the land.

The LRA 2002 provides that 'legal estate' includes 'estates, interests and charges' – s 132. Therefore, a 'legal estate' is much wider than merely the freehold and leasehold – but it is also narrower, in that not all leaseholds are registrable.

Section 2 provides the 'Scope of title registration' and provides for registration of –

(a) unregistered legal estates which are interests of any of the following kinds –
    (i)   an estate in land,
    (ii) a rentcharge,
    (iii) a franchise,
    (iv) a profit *à prendre* in gross, and
    (v)   any other interest or charge which subsists for the benefit of, or is a charge on, an interest the title to which is registered; and

(b) interests capable of subsisting at law which are created by a disposition of an interest the title to which is registered.

However, as Elizabeth Cooke says (at p 36), 'the drafting of section 2 is
as s 2(a)(i) . . . refers simply to the legal estates of section 1(1) of the Law
Act of 1925, our old friends the freehold and the lease' (and not all leases)
ficult to understand, given the meaning of 'legal estate' in the 2002 Ac
inclusion in s 2(a) of the words 'which are interests' after 'legal estates'!

The Act provides for titles which *may* be registered – s 3, and those which *must* be
registered – s 4.

Those that **must** be registered are all freeholds; leases **with over seven years to
run**; commonholds; legal mortgages (including any granted on registered land after
the Act came into force – but not assignments); express legal easements and profits
à prendre, and legal rentcharges. Unless registered, these will take effect in equity
only (as minor interests). Under s 3, legal profits *à prendre* in gross, and franchises
may be registered.

The effects of first registration of a person as proprietor of an estate in land are
laid down in ss 11 and 12. Section 11 deals with freehold estates, s 12 with leaseholds. Under s 11, an absolute freehold is vested in the proprietor together with all
interests subsisting for the benefit of the estate – s 11(3). The estate is vested in the
proprietor subject only to interests which are the subject of an entry on the register
of that estate or to overriding interests under Schedule 1 (that is, interests which
override first registration) and to any interests acquired by adverse possession of
which the proprietor has notice – s 11(4).

Likewise, under s 12, first registration of a person with an absolute leasehold title
vests in the proprietor of the estate with all interests subsisting for the benefit of the
estate – s 12(1). A leasehold estate is vested subject only to the same interests as
affect a freehold estate at the time of registration, plus implied and express
covenants, obligations and liabilities incident to the estate – s 12(4).

Finally, where the proprietor is a trustee, he is bound by all beneficial interests of
which he has notice – s 11(5).

Until registration, there can be no legal interest (unless it falls within the overriding interests): an unregistered interest can, therefore, only take effect in equity,
that is as a minor interest.

Voluntary registration of title of a registrable estate is not only possible at any
time, but is positively encouraged by statutory inducements (in order to hasten the
complete transfer of all titles from the unregistered to the registered system).

We have already seen that the effect of registration will differ according to
whether a disposition was for value or not.

'Overriding' interests

The 2002 Act refers to 'interests which override', but such a clumsy phrase is unlikely
to supplant the familiar 'overriding interests'. The curious characteristic of overriding interests is that, in a system which is based upon the mirror principle, they
are not capable of being entered on the register, yet they are binding on all purchasers. Thus they create a large crack in the mirror.

Indeed, the overriding interests cause, as Agatha Christie would say (not to
mention Lord Alfred Tennyson!), the mirror to crack from side to side. This is
because they bind a purchaser even though they cannot be entered on the register.
Therefore, the purchaser takes the land subject not only to all the interests reflected

by the register, but also to the overriding interests which, not being on the register, cannot be reflected.

The list of overriding interests includes some of the most important interests in land, making it essential for a purchaser to satisfy himself as to the existence or absence of them. However, it is clear, from the Royal Commission Report 1857, that they did not arise by accident:

> The register will be a substitute for the documentary or parchment title. But the registered ownership ... will remain subject, as the fee simple now is ... to such other rights as are not usually included in the abstract of title ... These are rights which are commonly evidenced by known usage or continued enjoyment or may be ascertained on the spot by inspection or inquiry; and the title to them is generally so independent of the documentary title to the property that they will necessarily form a partial exception to that which will constitute the registered ownership.

The consequence of the overriding interests is, therefore, that 'persons dealing with registered land must obtain information outside the register in the same manner and from the same sources as people dealing with unregistered land would obtain it' – Cross J in *National Provincial Bank Ltd* v *Hastings Car Mart Ltd* [1965] AC 1175.

Under the Land Registration Act 1925, s 70(1) there were 12 overriding interests; the LRA 2002 reduces them in number and, in some cases, in scope. Their importance can be reduced by entering them on the register by way of a notice: such entry will reduce them to minor interests. Peter Collis, in the Land Registry's 'Legislative Update Number 6' on the Act, says that 'this is in keeping with the overall objective of making the register as complete a record of title as possible'. (However, it is difficult to see how an action which reduces the importance of an overriding interest is likely to encourage the owners of them to enter notices!)

Something which is entirely new is the provision of two sets of 'interests which override' – those which will override first registration of title (Schedule 1), and those which will override registered dispositions (Schedule 3). The reason for the distinction is because

> the two situations are different. On first registration, we need to preserve any rights that bind the owner, who already has the legal estate, and who is not necessarily a recent purchaser. On registered dispositions, the legal estate does not pass until registration takes place, and there is greater scope to prevent a purchaser being bound by interests that could not easily be discovered – Peter Collis.

With regard to interests which override first registration, there is a new duty upon a person applying for first registration to disclose any such interests of which he knows – s 71. So, we need here to consider Schedules 1 and 3, and also Schedule 12 which provides for transitional arrangements.

Under both Schedules 1 and 3, several interests (contained mainly in LRA 1925, s 70(1)(d), (e) and (j)) will cease to be overriding after ten years, that is by 13 October 2013. A notice will need to be entered before this date in order to provide continuing protection of these interests.

However, under both Schedules, customary and public rights (paras 4 and 5, Sched 1); local land charges (para 6, Sched 1); certain mineral rights (paras 7–9, Sched 1), and rights in coal and coal mines will continue to be overriding indefinitely.

The new Land Registration Rules will provide for the disclosure of certain overriding interests upon application for first registration and for registration of a registrable disposition.

Interests which will override first registration are set out in Schedule 1, and they are:

Para 1 – a legal leasehold estate granted for a term not exceeding seven years from the date of grant (except leases under s 4(1)(d), (e) or (f)). Schedule 12, para 12 provides that this includes any lease which, when the provision came into force, was an overriding interest under LRA 1925, s 70(1)(k), a lease not exceeding 21 years. This, and paras 2 (and 3), show how important it is for a purchaser to inquire of any person on the land other than the registered proprietor/s. However, there is no provision in para 1 such as there is in para 2, so that any inquiry here is merely to inform the purchaser. All he can do then is to decide whether to purchase or not – he will be bound by any such lease, regardless, if he goes ahead. An agreement for a lease will not give rise to a claim under para 1.

Para 2 – 'an interest belonging to a person in actual occupation, so far as relating to land of which he is in actual occupation, except for an interest under a settlement under the Settled Land Act'. **This is not the same as LRA 1925, s 70(1)(g)**. Under s 70(1)(g) not only rights of persons in actual occupation, but those in receipt of rents and profits were protected. Here it is only those in actual occupation. Another important difference is that Schedule 1 does protect a person who has been asked by the purchaser about any interest which they may have and who has not disclosed it, where s 70(1)(g) did not and Schedule 3 does not. As we shall see shortly, this provision is an example of the importance of distinguishing between Schedule 1 – the interests which override first registration, and Schedule 3 – interests which override registered dispositions.

Para 3 – legal easements or profits *à prendre*. Does the use of the word *or* rather than *and* here mean that all profits, legal or equitable, are overriding for the purposes of Schedule 1? We shall have to wait and see! What is clear is that all equitable easements must be protected as minor interests. *Celsteel Ltd* v *Alton House Holdings* has gone.

Para 4 – customary rights.

Para 5 – public rights.

Para 6 – local land charges. The local land charges registry deals with such matters as planning permissions, demolition orders and listed buildings – all of which a purchaser will wish to be aware of. A local land charges search must, therefore, be made in addition to the search of the land register. Schedule 12, para 13 provides that any interest which, immediately before the coming into force of Schedule 1, was an overriding interest under LRA 1925, s 70(1)(i), is included in para 6.

Paras 7–9 – 'an interest in any coal or coal mine, the rights attached to any such interest and the right of any person under section 38, 49 or 51 of the Coal Industry Act 1994' – para 7; 'in the case of land to which title was registered before 1898, rights to mines and minerals (and incidental rights) created before 1898' – para 8; 'in the case of land to which title was registered between 1898 and 1925 inclusive, rights to mines and minerals (and incidental rights) created before the date of registration of the title' – para 9.

Paras 10–14 – five miscellaneous rights (which shall cease to have effect ten years after Schedule 1 comes into force – s 117. They should, therefore, be protected before then as minor interests by entry of a notice).

Schedule 3 sets out those interests which will override registered dispositions – 'a disposition which is required to be completed by registration' – s 132. They are:

Para 1 – a leasehold estate in land granted for a term not exceeding seven years from the date of the grant, except for

(a) a lease the grant of which falls within s 4(1)(d), (e) or (f);

(b) a lease the grant of which constitutes a registrable disposition. Sub-para (b) is an addition to the equivalent provision in Schedule 1.

As with Schedule 1, any lease which was an overriding interest under LRA 1925, s 70(1)(k) when the 2002 Act comes into force will be included. Again, for the purposes of para 1, the lease must be legal.

Para 2 – an interest belonging at the time of the disposition to a person in actual occupation, so far as relating to land of which he is in actual occupation, except for:

(a) an interest under a settlement under the Settled Land Act 1925;

(b) an interest of a person of whom inquiry was made before the disposition and who failed to disclose the right when he could reasonably have been expected to do so;

(c) an interest –
   (i) which belongs to a person whose occupation would not have been obvious on a reasonably careful inspection of the land at the time of the disposition, and
   (ii) of which the person to whom the disposition is made does not have actual knowledge at that time;

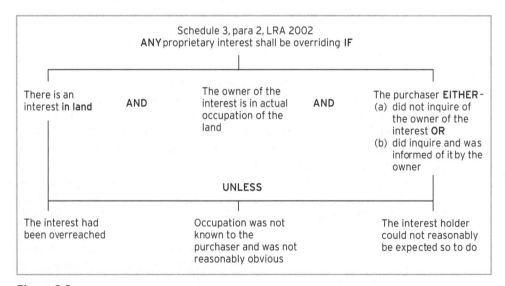

Figure 3.3

(d) a leasehold estate in land granted to take effect in possession after the end of the period of three months beginning with the date of the grant and which has not taken effect in possession at the time of the disposition.

Paragraph 2 is the successor to s 70(1)(g) of the 1925 Act, and it continues to create by far the greatest danger to a purchaser. Paragraph 2 differs from s 70(1)(g) in that the interest holder must now be 'in actual occupation'. Under s 70(1)(g), being in receipt of rents and profits also qualified, but no longer. Another change is that, under s 70(1)(g), a purchaser who enquired of the interest holder took free of the interest if the holder of it denied it. Here, the purchaser will only take free of the interest if the holder of it could reasonably be expected to disclose it. This is more generous to the interest holder, then. Not so the provision in sub-para (c), however, for this favours the purchaser: only if the interest holder's occupation 'would have been obvious on a reasonably careful inspection of the land' and the purchaser had actual knowledge of the interest at the time of the disposition, will the purchaser be bound by it. This raises another interesting possibility – is this the doctrine of notice by any other name? Section 70(1)(g) gave rise to many cases, the vast majority of which will remain good law under the new Act. (Indeed, it is likely that both paras 1 and 2 of Schedule 3 will also lead to much litigation.) As with the old s 70(1)(g), para 2 has hidden depths and we need, therefore, to take it apart and look at each aspect of it. It is **vital** that each aspect be taken in the order in which it appears in the statutory provision – interest, occupation, inquiry. It is also vital to understand that it can apply to **any** *interest in land* which is not excluded by para 2.

First then, *'the rights of every person in actual occupation'* is often read to mean 'occupational rights', but nothing could be further from the truth. We must separate 'the rights' from 'every person ...'. 'The rights' must be rights **in the land**. Therefore, any such right is (as we shall see) first and foremost a **minor** interest, which should have been entered in the appropriate manner. However, where it has not been so entered, and the holder of it is in actual occupation the unprotected minor interest may be transformed into an overriding interest which will bind everyone, but needs no protection. The Court of Appeal in *Wallcite Ltd* v *Ferrishurst Ltd* [1999] 1 All ER 977 held that a person in actual occupation of a part of land comprised in a registered title can enforce against the new registered proprietor any overriding interest which he has in the land, or part of the land, occupied by him or in the remainder (or part of the remainder) of the registered land in question.

Another common failing is to ignore the exception in para 2(b), under which a purchaser who inquires of a person with an interest in the land and who is in actual occupation of it, etc whether he or she has an interest in the land will take free of such interest if the holder of it 'failed to disclose the right when he could reasonably have been expected to do so'.

Example

Say Helen and Steve, a married couple, live together at 26, Something Lane, Somewhere, and the title is registered in the name of Steve alone. Unknown to Helen, Steve grants a mortgage on 26, Something Lane in favour of Liverpool Lenders Ltd (LLL), to secure a loan for his business: he then fails to meet the repayments. The first Helen knows of this is when a letter arrives from LLL informing Steve that they are going to repossess and sell the house in order to get their money back – what can Helen do?

Well, just like anyone else in a dispute over land, she must first prove she has an interest in it. If she can do this, she must then show that her interest is binding on LLL. As Helen is in actual occupation of the house, then, so long as she has an interest in it, she will be safe against LLL *unless* they asked her about any interest she may have, and she denied any interest 'when she could reasonably have been expected to do so'. Therefore, if LLL had not asked Helen at all, or if they had asked her and she had told them of her interest, LLL would have been bound by it – unless her interest had been overreached. However, as Steve was the sole trustee, his signature could not overreach Helen's interest. This was the situation in the leading case under s 70(1)(g) – *Williams & Glyn's Bank Ltd* v *Boland* [1981] AC 487 – which would be decided the same way today under Sched 3, para 2.

With regard to a purchaser's inquiry, the person who must be inquired of is the person who holds the interest. It is not enough to inquire of the registered proprietor – he is the very person who is least likely to disclose any such rights!

Williams & Glyn's Bank Ltd v *Boland* [1981] AC 487

This is the leading case on s 70(1)(g). As Mrs Boland had been held to have an equitable interest in the land, the question was whether her interest was binding on the bank. This was not a problem for Lord Denning who said:

> Once it is held that the wife has an equitable interest in the land ... it is easy to apply the provisions of the Land Registration Act 1925. Her interest is then a 'minor interest' because it is capable of being overridden by a sale by the trustees for sale ... But it may also be an 'overriding interest' if it comes within section 70(1)(g). Being an equitable interest in the land, it is clearly an interest 'subsisting in reference' to the land ... The crucial question therefore is whether it can be shown to be an 'overriding interest' within section 70(1)(g) ... The wife clearly has rights. The only question is whether she is herself a person 'in actual occupation of the land' ... 'actual occupation' is a matter of fact, not a matter of law ... Once it is found that a wife is in actual occupation, then it is clear that in the case of registered land, a purchaser or lender would be well advised to make inquiry of the wife. If she then discloses her rights, he takes subject to them. If she does not disclose them, he takes free of them.

As Mrs Boland had been held to have an overriding interest, the only way in which the bank could defeat her would be by overreaching, for even an overriding interest can be overreached, as was shown in *Flegg*, if there are sufficient trustees' signatures on the receipt for the capital monies, for, as Lord Oliver stated:

> Once the beneficiary's rights have shifted from the land to capital monies in the hands of the trustees there is no longer an interest in the land to which the occupation could be referred or which it could protect. The charge created in favour of the society accordingly overreached the beneficial interests of the [parents] and nothing in Section 70(1)(g) or in *Boland* had the effect of preserving against the society any rights to occupy the land by virtue of the [parents'] beneficial interests in the equity of redemption.

Several points which emerge from the decisions cited above must be stressed:

1 'Actual occupation' in this context is merely a further protection provided for the unprotected minor interest. Occupation on its own is of no use whatsoever, its only purpose being to protect an interest.

2 As the Court of Appeal in *Skipton Building Society* v *Clayton* (1993) 25 HLR 596 stated plainly, the interest must be an interest in land, so that a licence was held to be incapable of constituting an overriding interest (though, on the facts, the licence was held to be a sham, being, in reality, a term of years). An interest in the proceeds of sale will not suffice either, and a right under the Family Law Act 1996 can never become an overriding interest – it is merely a right of occupation.

3 The interest must be in existence at the date of the disposition.

The House of Lords in *Abbey National Building Society* v *Cann* held that though occupation must exist at execution of the instrument, the right would not become an overriding interest until registration of the transaction. If this will also apply to para 2, then the need for occupation at execution will limit most claims to cases of second or later mortgages (eg *Boland* and *Flegg*), as it is rare for purchasers to be in occupation before completion. Thus, again, the purchaser must inquire of every person on the land: failure to do so could well see him bound by such person's interests, like the Bank in *Boland*.

Lloyds Bank plc v *Carrick* [1996] 4 All ER 630

This case shows how para 2 can protect the interest of a beneficial owner in registered land, where a similar owner in unregistered land would be defeated. As we have seen, Mrs Carrick, a widow, sold her house for £19,000 and gave this money to her brother-in-law, B, on an oral agreement that it would be payment for a maisonette, the lease of which B owned. The land was unregistered. The agreement was subject to the Law of Property Act 1925, s 40 and, being oral, needed to be evidenced by some act of part performance. Though there was no part performance at the time of the agreement, once Mrs Carrick paid the money to B and went into possession the deficiency was satisfied. Thus, there was now an estate contract which, if it were to bind the bank, needed to be registered as a Class C(iv) land charge. This had not been done. Therefore, it was void against the bank - a purchaser for value.

The £19,000 represented the whole of the purchase price of the maisonette and when Mrs Carrick paid it over she acquired the whole of the beneficial interest, though not the legal estate: this remained with B, making him a bare trustee on her behalf. However, it was held that Mrs Carrick could not rely upon the fact that her interest behind a bare trust could not be overreached by B, the sole trustee: as that trust relied upon the contract, and the contract was void against the bank, the bank was not bound by the trust.

However, had title to the maisonette been registered, the contract would have been a minor interest. This should, in registered land, have been entered by way of a notice. However, as she would have been in actual occupation of the land - and occupying it before B granted the legal charge on it to the bank - and as the bank had made no inquiry of her, Mrs Carrick would have succeeded under para 2, attaining an overriding interest which would have been binding on the bank because it could not be overreached.

Always remember that the starting point for any claim under para 2 is an interest in land. Therefore, the matrimonial home right under the Family Law Act 1996 cannot become an overriding interest, nor can a mere licence: *Skipton Building Society v Clayton* (1993) 25 HLR 596. See also *Gracegrove Estates Ltd v Boateng* [1997] EGCS 103.

It was held in *Hypo-Mortgage Services Ltd v Robinson* [1997] 2 FLR 71 that minor children of the legal owner are not 'in actual occupation' for the purposes of a claim under s 70(1)(g), and presumably para 2.

Remember, interests in a matrimonial home are not the only 'rights in land' capable of falling under para 2: see also *London & Cheshire Insurance Co Ltd v Laplagrene Property Co Ltd* [1971] Ch 499 – an unpaid vendor's lieu; *Webb v Pollmount* [1966] Ch 584 – an option to purchase land; *Grace Rymer Investments Ltd v Waite* [1958] Ch 831 – an equitable lease; *Re Sharpe* [1980] 1 WLR 219 – the equitable rights of a licensee by way of proprietary estoppel, but not a mere licensee (ie one without estoppel); *Strand Securities Ltd v Caswell* [1965]. The Family Law Act matrimonial homes right of occupation can not become an overriding interest – Family Law Act 1996, s 31(10)(b).

Strand Securities Ltd v Caswell [1965] Ch 958

This is an important case in which Lord Denning described s 70(1)(g) as:

> an important provision. Fortunately its object is to protect a person in actual occupation of the land from having his rights lost in the welter of registration. He can stay there and do nothing. Yet he will be protected. No one can buy the land over his head and thereby take away or diminish his rights. It is up to every purchaser before he buys to enquire on the premises. If he fails to do so it is at his own risk.

In *Caswell*, a sublessee of a flat, who had not registered his interest, allowed his stepdaughter to live in the flat rent free. Upon the landlord selling the flat, subject to the sublease, Mr Caswell, the sublessee, applied for registration of the sublease. A short while after, the plaintiffs applied for registration of the transfer to them, claiming that they took the flat free from the sublease. They based their claim on two grounds: that the application for registration of the sublease was void for failure to comply with the relevant formalities, and that Mr Caswell had no overriding interest under s 70(1)(g). On the latter point, Lord Denning held that:

> In this case, it is clear that [the stepdaughter] was in actual occupation of the flat. The plaintiff, there-fore, took subject to her rights, whatever they were. She was not a tenant, but only a licensee. She had no contractual right to stay there. Her licence would be determined at any time and she would have to go in a reasonable time thereafter. So, the plaintiffs could get her out provided always that they could get rid of Mr Caswell's sub-lease . . .
>
> I would like to hold that Mr Caswell was sharing the occupation of the flat with [his stepdaughter]. But I cannot bring myself to this conclusion. The truth is that he allowed her to be in actual occu-pation and that is all there is to it. She was a licensee rent free. And I fear that it does not give him protection. It seems to be a very rare case – a case which the legislature did not think of. For, it is quite clear that if [the stepdaughter] had paid a token sum as rent, or for use and occupation, to Mr Caswell, he would be 'in receipt of rents and profits' and his rights would be protected under s 70(1)(g) . . . It is odd that Mr Caswell is not protected simply because he let his stepdaughter in, rent free. Odd as it is however, I fear the words of the statute do not cover this case.

It was a rare case indeed, with Mr Caswell having 'the right' and his stepdaughter the 'actual occupation'. Unfortunately for them, neither had both 'right' and 'occupation'.

In *Caswell*, Lord Denning said that 'if Mr Caswell put his servant or caretaker into the flat, rent free, he would be protected because his agent would have actual occupation on his behalf', and this point was picked up in the following case.

Lloyds Bank plc v Rosset and Another [1988] 3 All ER 915

The Court of Appeal held that 'occupation' for the purposes of s 70(1)(g) must exist at the time of execution of the relevant transaction, in this case a mortgage. Their Lordships then went on to decide that Mrs Rosset was in actual occupation by virtue of the presence of her builders on the property at the relevant time. The House of Lords, reversing the earlier decision, found that Mrs Rosset had no equitable interest in the property. They agreed with the time at which occupation must exist – as did a differently constituted House of Lords in *Abbey National Building Society* v *Cann* [1990] WLR 832 - but the matter of being in occupation through an agent was not raised.

Following *Cann*, it was held in *Malory Enterprises Ltd* v *Cheshire Homes (UK) Ltd* [2002] Ch 216 that the requirement of occupation for the purposes of s 70(1)(g) – and presumably for para 2 also – 'is a concept which may have different connotations according to the nature and purpose of the property' over which the interest is claimed.

As in Schedule 1, the leases in para 2, subpara (d) – which were overriding under s 70(1)(k) – must now be protected by registration.

(However, Schedule 12, para 8, provides that 'an interest which, immediately before the coming into force of this Schedule, was an overriding interest under s 70(1)(g) of the Land Registration Act 1925 by virtue of a person's receipt of rents and profits, except for an interest of a person of whom enquiry was made before the disposition and who failed to disclose the right when he could reasonably have been expected to do so' will continue to be overriding.)

Para 3 – (1) a legal easement or profit *à prendre*, except for an easement, or a profit *à prendre* which is not registered under the Commons Registration Act 1965, which at the time of the disposition:

(a) is not within the actual knowledge of the person to whom the disposition is made, and

(b) would not have been obvious on a reasonably careful inspection of the land over which the easement or profit is exercisable.

(2) the exception in sub-paragraph (1) does not apply if the person entitled to the easement or profit proves that it has been exercised in the period of one year ending with the day of the disposition.

Thus, though easements and profits *à prendre* continue to be overriding interests, the protection is reduced. As with Schedule 1, only legal interests are covered, and not all of those: as we have seen already, *express* legal easements are registrable. Therefore only **implied** legal easements are capable of being overriding (see Chapter 12). As for profits *à prendre*, the same applies, provided they are not registered under the Commons Registration Act 1965. (However, all easements and profits which were overriding interests under s 70(1)(a) of the LRA 1925 immediately before Schedule 3

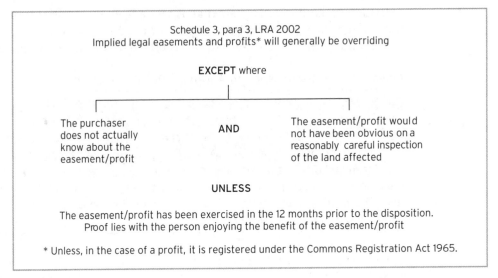

Figure 3.4

came into force are included in Schedule 3, regardless – including any equitable ease-ments!)

Para 4 – a customary right.

Para 5 – a public right.

Para 6 – a local land charge. As with Schedule 1, any such interest which was an overriding interest under s 70(1)(i) immediately before Schedule 3 came into force will be included in Schedule 3.

Paras 7–9 – an interest in any coal or coal mine as for Schedule 1.

Paras 10–14 – miscellaneous rights as for Schedule 1. As with Schedule 1, these rights will cease to have effect ten years after the day on which they came into force – s 117.

The glaring omission from Schedule 3 is rights by way of adverse possession, which were overriding under LRA 1925, s 70(1)(f).

As we have already seen, the possibility of acquisition of title by way of adverse possession has been radically curtailed by the LRA 2002. Furthermore, it is no longer an overriding interest. However, para 7 of Schedule 12 provides that a right acquired by adverse possession before the coming into force of Schedule 1 shall, for a period of three years beginning with the day on which the Schedule comes into force, be included therein. Schedule 12, para 11 provides that for the period of three years beginning with the day on which Schedule 3 comes into force, Schedule 3 should be read as if there were a paragraph 15, and that it should read, 'a right under paragraph 18(1) of Schedule 12'. Para 18(1) provides that:

> where a registered estate in land is held in trust for a person by virtue of s 75(1) of the Land Registration Act 1925 immediately before the coming into force of section 97, he is entitled to be registered as the proprietor of the estate.

Paragraph 15 would have the effect of including the right of an adverse possessor to be registered as proprietor of the estate in Schedule 3. (Paragraph 18(5) makes a similar provision in regard to rentcharges.)

Finally, remember that effective overreaching continues to override overriding interests.

Minor interests

As under the LRA 1925, any interests which are neither registrable nor overriding are minor interests. This category now encompasses some 'new' interests in registered land – rights of pre-emption, rights by way of proprietary estoppel and mere equities. Taking each in turn:

Rights of pre-emption

We have seen that in unregistered land rights of pre-emption are not 'interests in land' – *Pritchard* v *Briggs* [1979] 3 WLR 868. However, under the 2002 Act they are interests in registered land – s 115(1); but only in the future, only those created on or after the day that s 115 comes into force.

Rights by way of proprietary estoppel, or mere equities

it is hereby declared for the avoidance of doubt that, in relation to registered land, each of the following –

(a) an equity by estoppel, and
(b) a mere equity,

has effect from the time the equity arises as an interest capable of binding successors in title (subject to the rules about the effect of dispositions on priority) – s 116.

Of course, it will still be for the court to decide what interest has arisen, and when the necessary circumstances have been satisfied.

In regard to sub-para (b), a 'mere equity'

> refers to a right which that person has in equity to claim relief in respect of a potential interest in registered land. It may be a possibility to have a document rectified. It may be a right to have a document set aside for fraud; may be a right of a party who has entered into a charge or other instrument because of undue influence to have that set aside – Professor Philip Kenny in his annotation note to s 116.

The effect of s 116 is to give retrospective effect to rights by way of proprietary estoppel and mere equities which, by their nature, cannot be known for certain to exist until the court so determines. This should protect them under the general rule of 'first in time prevails' under s 28.

Under the LRA 1925, there were four ways in which to protect minor interests. However, the 2002 Act has reduced these to two – entry of notices, or entry of restrictions. (Though the Act uses the word 'register' to cover both substantive registration of registrable interests and entry of minor interests, it is much less confusing to refer to *entry* of minor interests.)

Notices

A notice is an entry in the register in respect of the burden of an interest affecting a registered estate or charge – s 32(1),

but

> the fact that an interest is the subject of a notice does not necessarily mean that the interest is valid, but does mean that the priority of the interest, if valid, is protected – s 32(3).

Subsection (3) makes it clear that you can only protect what you have: you cannot 'create' an interest merely by entering a notice. Thus, if a notice is entered to protect the priority of an option to purchase and the option is, in fact, invalid, the entry of the notice cannot give it validity.

Although there is no definition in the Act of what is a minor interest, nor of the interests which can be protected by entry of a notice, s 33 provides a list of interests for which no notice may be entered:

(a) an interest under a trust of land, or a settlement under the Settled Land Act 1925,

(b) a leasehold estate in land which is granted for a term of three years or less from the date of the grant, and is not required to be registered,

(c) a restrictive covenant made between a lessor and lessee, so far as relating to the demised premises,

(d) an interest which is capable of being registered under the Commons Registration Act 1965, and

(e) an interest in any coal or coal mine, the rights attached to any such interest and the rights of any person under section 38, 49 or 51 of the Coal Industry Act 1994.

In regard to the interests under para (a), these should be protected by entry of a restriction.

There are, in fact, two types of notice – an agreed notice and a unilateral notice – s 34.

> The registrar may only approve an application for an agreed notice if –
> (a) the applicant is the relevant registered proprietor, or a person entitled to be registered as such proprietor,
> (b) the relevant registered proprietor, or a person entitled to be registered as such proprietor, consents to the entry of the notice, or
> (c) the registrar is satisfied as to the validity of the applicant's claim.

Of course, 'the fact that an interest is the subject of a notice does not necessarily mean that the interest is valid, but does mean that the priority of the interest, if valid, is protected for the purposes of s 29 and 30' – s 32(3), and this is so even if the registrar was satisfied as to the validity of the applicant's claim.

Unilateral notices are covered by s 35, under which, if the registrar is to enter a unilateral notice, he

> must give notice of the entry to –
> (a) the proprietor of the registered estate or charge to which it relates, and
> (b) such other persons as rules may provide – s 35(1).

Under s 35(3) 'the person shown in the register and the beneficiary of a unilateral notice, or such other person as rules may provide, may apply to the registrar for removal of the notice from the register'. Section 36 provides that the registered proprietor of the estate or charge to which a unilateral notice relates, or a person entitled to be registered as proprietor of it, may apply to the registrar for cancellation of a unilateral notice. If such application is made, the registrar must give notice of the application to the beneficiary of the notice and of the effect of subsection (3), which provides that 'if the beneficiary of the notice does not exercise his right to object to the application before the end of such period as rules may provide, the registrar must cancel the notice'.

Presumably, rights under the Family Law Act 1996, will be entered by way of an agreed notice (the equivalent of protecting such rights under LRA 1925)?

Though leasehold covenants binding on a tenant are automatically protected on transfer of the leased land without anything else – s 29(2)(b), a covenant binding land other than the leased land (generally landlord covenants) must be entered by way of a notice. This is a new requirement.

Restrictions

Section 40 provides that:

(1) A restriction is an entry in the register regulating the circumstances in which a disposition of a registered estate or charge may be the subject of an entry in the register.
(2) A restriction may, in particular –
  (a) prohibit the making of an entry in respect of any disposition, or a disposition of a kind specified in the restriction;
  (b) prohibit the making of an entry –
    (i) indefinitely,
    (ii) for a period specified in the restriction, or
    (iii) until the occurrence of an event so specified.

The purpose of entering a restriction is to have specific requirements which must be complied with before there is a registrable disposition noted on the register, for example the need for two or more trustees in order to overreach beneficial interests.

The effect of entering a restriction is explained in s 41:

(1) Where a restriction is entered in the register, no entry in respect of a disposition to which the restriction applies may be made in the register otherwise than in accordance with the terms of the restriction, subject to any order under subsection (2).
(2) The registrar may by order–
  (a) disapply a restriction in relation to a disposition specified in the order or disposition of a kind so specified, or
  (b) provide that a restriction has effect, in relation to a disposition specified in the order or dispositions of a kind so specified with modifications so specified.
(3) The power under subsection (2) is exercisable only on the application of a person who appears to the registrar to have a sufficient interest in the restriction.

All pre-existing cautions and inhibitions become notices under the 2002 Act.

 **The doctrine of notice and registered land**

We now know that a purchaser under a registered disposition in registered land takes subject to all interests on the register and all overriding interests. He takes free, therefore, of all other interests. Thus, 'One of the essential features of registration of title is to substitute a system of registration of rights for the doctrine of notice' – Plowman J in *Parkash* v *Irani Finance Ltd* [1970] Ch 101.

Lord Wilberforce was emphatic in *Boland*:

> to have regard . . . to the doctrine of notice . . . would run counter to the whole purpose of the Act. The purpose, in each system, is . . . to safeguard the rights of persons in occupation . . . In the case of unregistered land, the purchaser's obligation depends on what he has notice of, notice actual or constructive. In the case of registered land, it is the fact of occupation that matters. If there is actual occupation, and the occupier has rights, the purchaser takes subject to them. If not he does not. No further element is material . . . the doctrine of notice has no application to registered conveyancing.

Walton J in *Freer* v *Unwins Ltd* [1976] Ch 288 explained that: 'The general scheme of the Act is that one obtains priority according to the date of registration, and one is subject or not to matters appearing on the register according to whether they were there before one took one's interest or after one took one's interest'. This being so, 'The registered land "Registrar's Darling" equivalent of "Equity's Darling" is thus a purchaser acquiring title under a registered disposition for value without there being any entry on the register' – David J Hayton (1981, p 132).

That having been said, there have been attempts to introduce the doctrine of notice into registered land. In both *Peffer* v *Rigg* [1977] 1 WLR 431 and *Lyus* v *Prowsa Developments Ltd* [1982] 1 WLR 1044, a constructive trust was used to avoid a statute being used as an instrument of fraud. Dillon J, in *Lyus*, explained that the trust was not imposed simply because Prowsa had notice of Lyus's rights – for that would be an application of the old doctrine of notice – but because they had notice of the fraudulent nature of the transaction. Similarly, in *Peffer*, the trust arose from notice of the fraud, not of the interest itself. (In *Lyus* the minor interest could, indeed should, have been entered by way of a notice or caution, and in *Peffer* by a restriction.)

In *Howell* v *Montey* (1990) 61 P&CR 18, however, there was no fraud involved. There had simply been a failure by Montey to deliver the transfer to him of title to the Land Registry within the priority period. However, the Court of Appeal held that Montey took free from an earlier charging order which was not entered on the register because he was an innocent purchaser with no knowledge of the order – an application of the old doctrine of notice, pure and simple.

Will the 2002 Act be entirely free of the old doctrine of notice? We shall, of course, have to wait and see, when, if at all, the court retains case law under the LRA 1925, and how it interprets the new Act. One area which is ripe for the issue to be raised upon interpretation is contained in Schedule 3, para 2 – the overriding interests of a person in actual occupation. As we have seen, this has been reduced in scope from s 70(1)(g) of the LRA 1925, and one of the new exceptions from this overriding interest occurs where the interest holder's occupation 'would not have been obvious on a reasonably careful inspection of the land at the time of the disposition', of which the purchaser of the estate did not have 'actual knowledge at that time'. The Explanatory Notes to the Act (at 227) state that 'to fail the test as formulated in the Act, it is the occupation that has to be obvious, not the interest'. Will this be sufficient to finally nail down the lid on the coffin of the old doctrine of notice? Gray and Gray (2005) state categorically that the doctrine *never* applies in relation to titles which have already been registered under the Land Registration Act 2002' – at p 195, para 2.191, fn2 (original emphasis). Nevertheless, it will be interesting to watch this.

The effect of registration

It is worth repeating that the mere fact of registering a land charge in unregistered land, or title to or registrable interest in registered land or entry of any minor interest, **cannot, of itself, alter the nature or validity of the interest:** you can only protect what you actually have. If you have no right to land, mere registration of some purported proprietary right will not give you anything. Take a basket of dirty washing: whether you wash the items in a washing machine in the kitchen, or in the bath upstairs, the articles to be washed do not alter: the sheets are still sheets, the towels still towels, whether they are washed or not, whether they are washed in the bath or in the machine. It is the same with interests in land. An equitable easement is protectable in unregistered land by entering a Class D(iii) land charge; in registered land it is protected as an overriding interest. However, the right must be an easement: it must have satisfied all the requirements of *Re Ellenborough Park* [1956] Ch 131 (see Chapter 12) and have been acquired. Simply registering a land charge, or relying on *Celsteel Ltd* v *Alton House Holdings* cannot turn it into something which it is not.

Example

In the attic of my house there are two large boxes: one containing the Christmas decorations, the other the summer holiday things. As it is not the custom here in Liverpool to hang buckets and spades on the Christmas tree, nor to wear tinsel to the beach, the two boxes are mutually exclusive. Therefore, if it is Christmas, I do not bring the summer box down from the loft. It is the same with the protecting of interests in land. If title to the land is registered, any estates and interests in that land must be protected under the registered land system; if title to the land is unregistered, the unregistered land system operates. **It must be one or the other; it cannot be both** (though an exam question may well require you to discuss, explain or apply each of the two).

A box for unregistered land would have four compartments, one each for the methods of protection available – legal, registrable under the Land Charges Act, overreachable and those still subject to the doctrine of notice.

A box for registered land would have three main compartments and one subsidiary one. The three main ones would accommodate the registrable, minor and overriding interests; the subsidiary compartment would hold those (minor) interests which are overreachable – the beneficial interests behind trusts of land which ought to be entered as minor interests by way of a restriction, but which may also become overriding under Sched 3 to LRA 2002. [Of course, it is not only these minor interests upon which Sched 3 can work its magic, so you should save some room in this compartment for any others.]

So, identify the interest in land and the system in which it exists. Take down the relevant box and place the interest in the relevant compartment. **Provided it is an interest in land,** and the correct method of protection has been adopted, it is protected to the extent provided by the system which operates upon it.

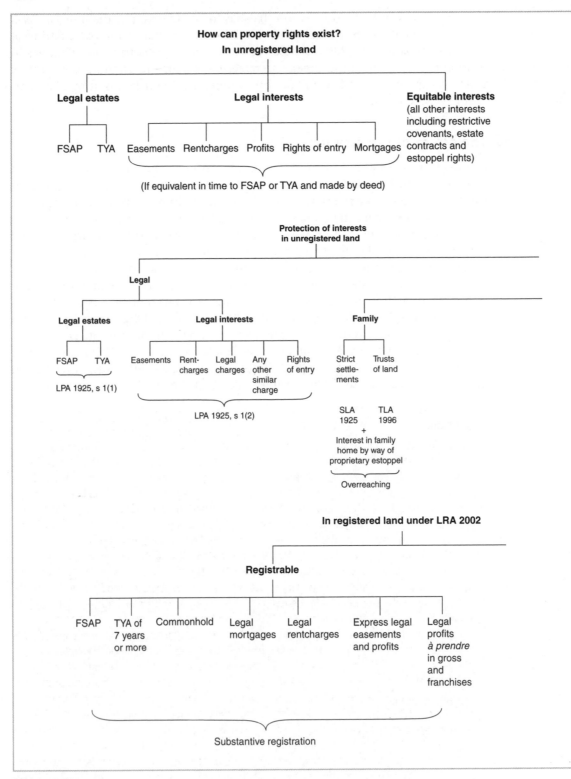

Figure 3.5

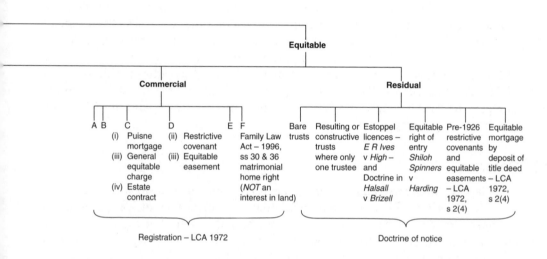

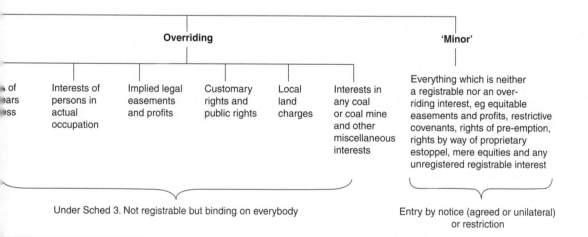

'Free Land'

In 1995 Simon J Hill produced a pamphlet, 'How to Claim Free Land & Property' in which he advertised his book, *The Layman's Guide to Claiming Free Land & Property*, priced £20. The guide was written to show 'ANYONE how to go about claiming future ownership of all the land and property they could ever wish for FREE'. Very tempting! Indeed, Mr Hill was himself, 'as you would expect, starting to claim such property and land for myself, in my own area. Over the last few weeks alone, I have already laid claim to 5 plots of land AND to 4 properties. *ALL within a 4 mile radius of my own home!* ... I shall continue to build up my personal portfolio of land and property. It is my intention to carry on with my Claim Program [is Mr H American?] until my personal portfolio reaches an estimated maturity value of not less than ONE MILLION POUNDS STERLING'. Unfortunately for Mr Hill, he is doomed to disappointment – unless, of course, he makes the money from the sale of his book. In March 1995, the Customer Services Manager of the Birkenhead District Land Registry produced a newsletter in which he explained that Mr Hill's advertisement was 'seriously misleading' and sought 'to leave an impression that because titles are unregistered they are "unowned", whereas all land is owned by someone'. Indeed: ultimately, by the Crown. A Public Information Leaflet was published shortly after by HM Land Registry – '"Free land and property" – advertisements about claiming unregistered land in England and Wales'. The only way to get land 'for free' is by way of adverse possession!

Reform

In its report, *Transfer of Land – Overreaching: Beneficiaries in Occupation* (Law Com No 188), the Law Commission recommends that, 'A conveyance of a legal estate in property should not have the effect of overreaching the interest of anyone of full age and capacity who is entitled to a beneficial interest in the property and who has a right to occupy it and is in actual occupation of it at the time of the conveyance, unless that person consents'. Further, the Commission recommends that there be no particular fomality requirement for the giving of such consent and that the court should, where it thinks fit, have the discretion to waive the need for consent. As we saw earlier, Peter Gibson LJ in *State of India Bank* v *Sood* [1997] Ch 276 referred to this proposal, but the recommendation has still not been implemented.

Summary

In this chapter we looked at the following:

- third parties;
- protecting legal and equitable interests in land –

    (a) before 1926 –
        - legal interests bind the world
        - the doctrine of notice and equitable interests

(b) unregistered land after 1925 –
- overreaching
- doctrine of conversion
- the system of registration under LCA 1972
- residual interests (which remain subject to the doctrine of notice)
- the effect of registration and non-registration

(c) registered land after 1925 –
- system of registration by title
- the register
- compulsory registration
- priority of interests
- rectification
- indemnity
- the interests – registrable, 'overriding', minor
- notices and restrictions
- the doctrine of notice and registered land
- the effect of registration
- reform.

References

George, S, *Liverpool Park Estates*, Liverpool: Liverpool University Press, 2000.

Gray, K, *Elements of Land Law*, 2nd edition, London: Butterworths, 1993.

Gray, K and Gray, S F, *Elements of Land Law*, 4th edition, Oxford: Oxford University Press, 2005.

Hayton, D J, *Registered Land*, 3rd edition, London: Sweet & Maxwell, 1981.

Law Commission, *Transfer of Land - Overreaching: Beneficiaries in Occupation* (Law Com No 188, 1989).

Maitland, F.W., *Equity*, 2nd edition, Cambridge: Cambridge University Press, 1936.

Rothey, E, 'Old deeds - a plea for their preservation', *The Legal Executive Journal*, December 1992, p 51.

Further reading

OVERREACHING

Dixon, M, Case note on *Birmingham Midshires Mortgage Services Ltd* v *Sabherwal* (2000) 80 P&CR 256, [2000] Conv 267.

Ferris, G and Battersby, G, 'Overreaching and the Trusts of Land and Appointment of Trustees Act 1996 - A Reply to Mr Dixon' [2001] Conv 221.

Ferris, G and Battersby, G, 'The General Principles of Overreaching and the Modern Legislative Reforms, 1996-2002' (2003) 119 LQR 94.

Harpum, C, 'Overreaching, Trusts of Land and Proprietary Estoppel' (2000) 116 LQR 341.

Thompson, M P, 'Overreaching Without Payment' [1997] Conv 134.

UNREGISTERED LAND

Law reports: *Midland Bank Trust Co Ltd* v *Green* [1980] Ch 5903, judgment of Lord Denning MR in the Court of Appeal. See also the judgment of Lord Wilberforce in the House of Lords, [1981] AC 513.

Crane, F R, 'Equitable Interests in Land: Some Problems of Priority' [1956] Conv 455.

Ferguson, P, 'Estate Contracts, Constructive Trusts and the Land Charges Act' [1996] 112 LQR 549.

Howell, J, 'Notice: A Broad View and a Narrow View' [1996] Conv 34.

Howell, J, 'The Doctrine of Notice: An Historical Perspective' [1997] Conv 431.

Howell, J, 'Deeds Registration in England: A Complete Failure?' [1999] 58 CLJ 366.

Tayleur, T, 'For how long must one search?' Sol Jo, 25 July 1997, p 724.

Wade, H W R, 'Land Charges Registration Reviewed' [1956] CLJ 216.

REGISTERED LAND

Baughan, S, 'Some Lessons of Cann' [1990] Conv 117.

Cooke, E and O'Connor, P, 'Purchase Liability to Third Parties in the English Land Registration System – A Comparative Perspective' [2004] LQR 640.

Dixon, M, 'Proprietary Rights and Rectifying the Effect of Non-registration' [2005] Conv 447.

Ferris, G and Battersby, G, 'The Impact of the Trusts of Land and Appointment of Trustees Act 1996 on Purchases of Registered Land' [1998] Conv 168.

Howell, J, 'Land Law in an E-conveyancing World' [2006] Conv 553.

Sheehan, D, 'Rights to Rectify the Land Register as Interests in Land' (2003) 119 LQR 31.

Smith, R J, 'Overriding Interests and Wives' (1997) 95 LQR 501.

4 How can you lose them?

Matters which may subsequently defeat an estate or interest

'The house of every one is to him as his castle and fortress'.
> – Edward Coke in *Semayne's* Case (1604) 5 Co Rep 91a at 91b.

'In London ... a man's house is truly his castle, in which he can be in perfect safety from intrusion'.
> – Boswell (1791), Life of Johnson II, 284, as quoted in the Concise Oxford Dictionary of Proverbs (1982), London Book Club Associates.

Is an Englishman's home still his castle, safe against intrusion? In *Parker* v *Parker* [2003] All ER(D) 421, the 9th Earl of Macclesfield went to court to try to maintain his right to live in the ancestral family home since 1715, Shirburn Castle.

We have seen already that unless the relevant formalities are complied with, you cannot acquire a legal estate or legal interest, though you may acquire the interest in equity under the rule in *Walsh* v *Lonsdale* (1882) 21 Ch D 9.

Even if you have acquired an interest, be it legal or equitable, you may yet lose it. The most obvious way in which you would lose your interest, or at least its effectiveness against third-party purchasers, would be if you failed to protect it in the relevant manner.

It may be that the parties would wish to terminate or extinguish an interest prior to the end of its specified lifespan. This can usually be achieved by agreement (with the relevant formalities).

In Parts II and III we shall come across specific instances of how an estate or interest will end other than by agreement, the benefit of it being lost.

Although we considered adverse possession in relation to the acquisition of the legal estate, the effect on the paper-title holder is, of course, that he loses it. In addition, there are two other general ways in which estates and interests can be lost. We shall look at them now.

A   Compulsory purchase

It is not only private land law which can deprive an individual of his legal title, for public law abounds in the areas of planning and control of land. However, whereas public planning law, in the form of planning permission, can be defeated by the Lands Tribunal refusing to modify or discharge a restrictive covenant, a compulsory purchase order will always prevail. Various Acts provide public bodies, particularly local authorities, with powers of acquisition under which they can compulsorily acquire land under a compulsory purchase order. Provided the local authority does not act *ultra vires* its powers, a confirmed order cannot be challenged. However, every order must be given prior publicity in the press, and in every case the owners and occupiers of the land which is to be compulsorily acquired must be notified in advance. Any objections must be heard by an inspector from the ministry or department which constitutes the 'confirming authority', to which all proposals must be submitted.

As Gray and Gray (2000) say, compulsory purchase is 'without doubt, the most far-reaching form of social intervention in the property relations of individual citizens' – p 1203.

Here, unlike his counterpart in adverse possession, the dispossessed owner must be compensated for his loss. Compensation must not only represent a purchase price (which must be the current 'market price', that is, the price which could reasonably have been expected if the property were to have been sold voluntarily in normal market conditions), but also compensation for any depreciation in the value of any land retained by the owner. He is also entitled to 'all damage directly consequent on the taking' – Denning LJ in *Harvey* v *Crawley Development Corpn* [1957] 1 QB 485. Should the retained land of the owner actually increase in value as a result of the compulsory purchase, such increase must be set off against any compensation payable.

If the buildings on the land have no 'market value', by virtue of being derelict, the compensation paid will be based on the site value alone. If the land itself is incapable of an assessable 'market value', being, say, a graveyard, then the Lands Tribunal has the power under the Lands Compensation Act 1961, s 5, to order compensation to 'be assessed on the basis of the reasonable cost of equivalent reinstatement', provided it is 'satisfied that reinstatement in some other place is bona fide intended'.

The aim of the compensation is to place the owner, as far as possible, in the position he would have been in had the order not been made and he had sold privately.

Having made a compulsory purchase order, an authority must enforce it within three years, or else it will lapse. Once the authority decides to enforce its order, it must serve a notice to treat upon the owner, upon receipt of which the owner must submit details of his interest in the land and a claim for compensation. Cases of dispute are referable to the Lands Tribunal, as are those where no claim has been submitted within 21 days of service of the notice to treat.

The local land charges register contains details of planning matters generally, such as enforcement notices, conditional planning permissions, tree preservation orders, listed buildings and certain compulsory purchase orders. Even if a compulsory purchase order on the specific property which you intend to buy does not appear on the register, roadway schemes or other local authority proposals for the future in the vicinity which may well lead to compulsory purchases of nearby property may show up. Watch out particularly for any proposed motorway building or extension.

Therefore, a local land charge search must be made on every purchase of land, be it unregistered or registered (local land charges are overriding interests under LRA 2002, Sched 3). In December 2002, the Law Commission published a consultation paper (No 169) looking at procedural issues relating to compulsory purchase.

We have seen (in Chapter 1, Section A) that the European Convention on Human Rights guarantees individuals 'peaceful enjoyment of possessions, but subject to the 'public interest and the right of the state' to enforce such laws as it deems necessary to control the use of property in accordance with the general interest ...' – Article 1, Protocol 1. However, the courts take the view, as expressed by Upjohn J in *Simpsons Motor Sales (London) Ltd* v *Hendon Corpn* [1963] Ch 57, that Parliament assumes that an authority acquiring land under the Compulsory Purchase Act 1965 will 'act reasonably in the public interest – but with due regard to the interests of the person being dispossessed' – at p 83.

Reform

The Law Commission published two consultation papers in regard to Compulsory Purchases – *Towards a Compulsory Purchase Code: (1) Compensation* (December 2003) and *(2) Procedure* (December 2004).

B The rule against perpetuities

We can put this off no longer! Again, forewarned is forearmed and, as Paul Todd (1989, p 122) says, 'Of all the topics ... the Rule against Perpetuities is one of the most disliked (even feared) by students'. Indeed, 'The mysteries of this rule have bemused and irritated whole generations of law students' – Gray and Symes (1981, p 185).

It is not only law students who find it mysterious. Gibson CJ of the Supreme Court of California in *Lucas* v *Hamm* 15 Cal Rptr 821, having warned of the danger of the 'net which the Rule spreads for the unwary', refused to find a lawyer negligent when he drafted an instrument in such a way as to cause the gift to fail for breach of the rule, because the lawyer could not be said to have 'failed to use such skill, prudence and diligence as lawyers of ordinary skill and capacity commonly exercise'. However, as Gray and Symes (p 185) point out, 'Such indulgence, although commending itself to the Supreme Court of California, is unlikely to be extended to the law student by his examiners in land law'!

What, then, is the rule?

Under the rule against perpetuities a gift must vest, if it ever does, within 21 years of a life or lives in being at the relevant date of grant.

The rule applies only to contingent interests – see Chapter 5.

'If it ever does'

It is irrelevant that the gift may never vest, but 'if it ever does' it must do so within the perpetuity period of a life plus 21 years. Any possibility that the contingency will not be satisfied until after the perpetuity period will render it void. As we shall see, the common law was concerned only with 'possibilities', no matter how remote. 'Probabilities' are irrelevant as, indeed, are actual events sometimes.

Re Wood [1894] 2 Ch 310

Here a gift was void for being in breach of the rule even though it had vested well within the perpetuity period. A testator had directed his trustees to continue working certain gravel pits until they, the pits, that is, were exhausted, at which time the trustees could sell them and divide the proceeds of such sale amongst nominated beneficiaries. In actual fact the pits were worked out well within the perpetuity period, but the court had to ignore this fact and apply the rule as at the testator's death. Applying it then, there was the possibility that the pits would not be exhausted until after the perpetuity period.

'Relevant date of grant'

It is essential to identify the relevant date of grant at the outset, because, at common law, everything has to be decided as at that date – the life or lives in being, the possibility of the gift vesting too late and whether there is anyone who can 'close the class'.

The relevant date of grant depends upon the method used to create the gift. If it is created by will, then the relevant date is that of the death of the testator. If it is created *inter vivos*, the relevant date is the date of the instrument of grant. You must always remember that this is the starting point.

'A life or lives in being'

This is something of a misnomer, for all we are actually interested in is the date when the last of 'the lives in being' dies!

When they have all died, the 21 years start to run. However, we cannot sit back and wait for any of these things to happen for, remember, everything must be decided at the relevant date of grant.

One of the main difficulties associated with the rule is the identification of the lives in being. In theory, every person ('lives' must be human lives) in the world who is alive at the relevant date of grant could be a life in being, but it would be impossible to identify every single life, which would have to be done in order to decide whether the gift could vest more than 21 years after the last of them died. Thus, in *Re Moore* [1901] 1 Ch 936 a gift was held void for uncertainty where vesting was to be postponed 'for the longest period allowed by law, that is to say, until the period of 21 years from the death of the last survivor of all persons who shall be living at my death'.

The common law requires lives in being to be 'relevant'. A 'relevant life' is either one which has been nominated for the purpose, or one which is relevant to the vesting of the gift (or rather the one, or more, whose death will affect the vesting of the gift). It is important to distinguish between a death which will affect the vesting of the gift, and one which will merely affect the size of the gift.

'Nominated lives'

In order to avoid the difficulties encountered with the rule, a testator or settlor (the 'donor') can nominate someone to be the 'measuring life'. Naturally, he would be well advised to select a young and healthy life for this purpose, for, as we shall see, the younger and healthier the life, the better the chance of the gift succeeding.

'Royal lives clauses' are the most commonly adopted form of nominating lives, if for no other reason than that they guarantee the gift's validity. This is because such a clause stipulates that the gift is to vest within the perpetuity period, that is within 21 years of the death of the last of the lives in being. Also, the monarchy tended to have larger families than the average, and tended also to live longer. Needless to say, Queen Victoria was the favourite choice for a royal lives clause!

Re Villar [1928] Ch 471

Here, a testator left property upon trust which provided that interests should not vest until 'the period ending at the expiration of 20 years from the day of the death of the last survivor of all the lineal descendants of Her late Majesty Queen Victoria who shall be living at the time of my death'. Though this clause, and the trust, was held to be valid, doubts were expressed about the advisability of it, for as Astbury J explained:

> the testator has in 1921 used an old form of precedent, restraining the distribution of his estate to a period expiring twenty years from the death of the last survivor of all the lineal descendants of the late Queen Victoria living on 6 September 1926. That must postpone the vesting for a very long period, but having regard to the character of this class, I have come to the conclusion that I cannot say it will be impracticable, having regard to the legal testimony probably available, to ascertain the period when the capital becomes distributable twenty one years after the survivor's death. The expense involved will probably be very great. The trust operates very hardly upon the testator's five children. If I could have seen my way to hold this tying up invalid, I would gladly have done so, but in my opinion I am not at liberty to do so.

Notwithstanding the doubts expressed, a very similar clause was upheld as recently as 1961, in *Re Warren's Will Trusts* (1961) 105 SJ 511. However, it was accepted that it would be better to use the descendants of George V, and today the choice of Queen Elizabeth II would probably be advised. (It is not only royalty that can live long lives, producing many descendants. Lizzie Bolden, the daughter of a freed slave in America, died in 2006, aged 116. She had seven children (outliving five of them) and left 40 grandchildren, 75 great-grandchildren, 150 great-great-grandchildren, 220 great-great-great-grandchildren and 75 great-great-great-great-grandchildren – Source: *The Week*, 23 December 2006)

When a donor nominates his own measuring life or lives, there is no need for them to have any connection with the gift.

What if there are no nominated lives?

If no lives are nominated, then the 'relevant' lives must be identified. This is not always easy! However, we can say with certainty that a gift must vest, if it ever does, within 21 years of a life in being if either the donee is specifically named, or the contingency concerns a named life.

> ### Example
>
> Thus, 'to Jim when he becomes a classical guitarist' is bound to vest, as is a gift 'to the first of my grandchildren to meet Madonna'. Why? If Jim is ever to become a classical guitarist, he must do so within his lifetime. Therefore, he is the relevant life in being, and he must satisfy the contingency, if he ever does, during his life, which is well within 21 years of his death. With the other gift, Madonna is the relevant life in being, as the contingency must be satisfied, if it ever is, within her lifetime. Therefore, if any grandchild of the donor is to meet her, it must be within her lifetime – again, well within the perpetuity period of 21 years after her death.

Remember, it does not matter that Jim may never become a classical guitarist, nor that none of the grandchildren meets Madonna. All that matters is that if they ever do, they must do so within the perpetuity period, and this, in the above examples, they are bound to do. Beyond this, very little is certain.

It must not be assumed that every person implicated in a gift is a life in being, for frequently the death of the actual donee will not affect the vesting of the gift.

> ### Example
>
> Thus, in a gift 'to the first child of Sue to reach the age of 18', only Sue is a relevant life, even if she already has living children. This is because if any child of Sue is ever going to reach 18, it must be within 21 years of Sue's death, for she cannot produce any more children once she is dead. The deaths of any of Sue's children – whether alive at the date of grant or not – can have no effect upon any other child of hers attaining 18. Had the contingent age been greater than 21, say, 25, the gift would be void, because it is possible that the first child of Sue will not become 25 until more than 21 years after her (Sue's) death. Obviously, any child alive and at least five years of age at the date of grant would be bound to attain the age of 25 within 21 years of Sue's death, but any child less than five at the date of grant, or any child born after that date, could possibly not attain the specified age until later than 21 years after Sue's death: after all, Sue could die tomorrow.

Therefore, any contingent age of greater than 21 years must be looked upon with suspicion.

Matters become even more complicated when another generation is added.

> ### Example
>
> If the gift above had been 'to the first of Sue's grandchildren to reach 21', then two situations would have to be considered. If the gift had been made by David, either by will or by *inter vivos* deed, Sue and her children who were alive at the date of grant would be the relevant lives in being, but not any grandchildren who were born at that date. This is because Sue's death will affect the gift, because after her death she can no longer produce children. It is her children who will produce the grandchildren, therefore, their

deaths will affect the vesting of the gift. However, only those alive at the relevant date of grant can be lives in being, as can any child *en ventre sa mère* - a child in the womb. The deaths of the grandchildren cannot affect whether or not any of the others reaches 21, and therefore they are not relevant lives. The gift would, in fact, be void at common law. This is because it is possible that all of Sue's children, including the child *en ventre sa mère* (ie if Sue were pregnant), could be killed, but she could have another child (which would not, of course, be a life in being as it could not be alive at the date of grant). It is immaterial how old Sue is, for at common law no one is either too old or too young to produce children - *Jee v Audley* (1787) 1 Cox Eq Cas 324 and *Re Gaite's Will Trusts* [1949] 1 All ER 459. The older Sue is, the less likely it is that her late-born child will produce a grandchild who will reach 21 within 21 years of *Sue's* death - Sue being the last surviving life in being. Indeed, the shock of a pregnancy in old age could well hasten her death! It is possible, then, that Sue could have a child and die the next day. That child could not possibly produce a child of her own (ie a grandchild of Sue) who will reach 21 within 21 years of Sue's death.

It would be different, however, if Sue had been the donor, and she had made the gift by will. The relevant date would be the date of Sue's death. Sue cannot, therefore, be a life in being! The relevant lives must, then, be her children and if any of the grandchildren are to reach 21 it must be within 21 years of the death of their parents, that is, Sue's children. Thus, the gift would be valid. Had the donor been Sue's husband, and the donees his children, or the first of them to reach 21, any child which Sue was carrying *en ventre sa mère* at the date of her husband's death would be a life in being. (Had Sue made the gift by *inter vivos* settlement, however, the result would be void, as before.)

The problem that arises with grandchildren can arise also with gifts to nephews and nieces. Thus, in a gift 'to such of my nephews and nieces as reach the age of 21' the relevant lives would again be those of the grandparents and potential parents of the donees, in other words the parents and siblings of the donor. Even if this gift were made by will, however, it would be void because, here, the fact that the testator cannot be a life in being is irrelevant – he could not produce his nephews or nieces, nor the brothers or sisters who could produce them for him – *Ward v Van der Loeff* [1924] AC 653.

Another difficulty encountered at common law is the possibility of an unborn, or 'spectral' spouse.

Re Frost (1889) 43 Ch D 246

Here the gift was to Emma for life, remainder to any husband she might marry who survived her for life, remainder to such of their children as were alive at the death of the survivor of Emma or her husband. Obviously the gift to Emma is vested. Less obviously, perhaps, the gift to the husband is valid, for even if he is not yet born, he must marry Emma, if he ever does, within her lifetime, Emma being, of course, the life in being. The problem arises with the children. It is more than possible that Emma's husband will not die until at least 21 years after her death, and the children's interest cannot vest until he dies.

What if there are no relevant lives either?

If there are no relevant lives in being, for instance 'to Matthew when Manchester United beats Liverpool' (Matthew's death will have no effect on the vesting of the gift), a straight perpetuity period of 21 years in gross applies.

Class gifts

Re Frost also provides us with an example of a 'class gift', for the ultimate beneficiaries were 'such of their children', rather than 'the first'. Class gifts create another problematical situation, for until the class can be 'closed', that is, until we can ascertain the final number of class members, the contingency cannot be satisfied. Gifts to 'such of ...', 'all those ...', 'the children of ...' or 'the grandchildren of ...', and so on are class gifts, as is any gift which is to be shared amongst an as yet unascertained number of people.

Where the only contingency is the fact that the size of the interest cannot be identified, the problem is not too great.

Example

Thus, a gift 'to Grace's daughters' will be valid, because Grace is the life in being and upon her death the number of daughters will be known. A gift 'to Grace for life, and then to her daughters' would produce a vested life interest for Grace, and a valid future interest for her daughters. (If the gift were 'to Grace's three daughters', we would not even have to wait for her death.) However, a gift 'to Grace for life, and then to Audrey's sons' would give a different result. Grace would still have a life interest vested in possession, but it is not certain that all Audrey's sons will be born within 21 years of Grace's death, Grace being the life in being. Therefore, the boys' gift would be void.

Quite often a condition will attach to a class gift, creating a double contingency:

Example

'To all of John's children who become doctors'. John is the life in being. It is quite possible that one or more of John's children will qualify as doctors more than 21 years after his death. (Remember, it is irrelevant that none of them may actually become doctors.) The gift is void. However, had at least one of John's children already become a doctor *at the relevant date of grant*, such child could close the class at that date.

This is the rule in *Andrews* v *Partington* (1791) 3 Bro CC 401. In fact, it is a rule of general application which evolved to aid the administration of trusts. When applied in **any other context than perpetuities**, the rule closes a class when the first member becomes entitled in possession. However, as we now know, with perpetuities at common law everything has to be decided **at the relevant date of grant**. Therefore, application of *Andrews* v *Partington* to the rule of perpetuities is crucially different. Though it may not save the gift for every potential class member it will – if there is a member who satisfies the condition as at the relevant date of grant – save the gift for that child and any other already born or *en ventre sa mère*. Any children born later, however, would not get anything – even if they became doctors. Once the class has been closed the size of the interests can be calculated. Browne-Wilkinson VC in *Re Tom's Settlement* [1987] 1 WLR 1021 stated that, although one object of the rule is to permit as many beneficiaries as possible to take, the overriding consideration is to allow the beneficiaries to enjoy their share as soon as possible. The child who closed the class takes his share immediately, having satisfied the contingency. The others will take theirs as and when they, too, satisfy the contingency. If any of them should die before doing so, his share will be divided amongst the surviving members of the class. This rule can be excluded by a contrary intention – see, eg, *Re Edmondson's Will Trusts* [1972] 1 WLR 183, where, in a gift to children 'whenever born', these words were held to exclude the rule.

A gift cannot be part good, part bad

At common law a gift could not be part good, part bad.

> **Example**
>
> In a gift 'to the first of Timothy's children to qualify as a solicitor, but if Timothy has no children, to Neil and Louise absolutely', the gift to Timothy's child is void, for he may not qualify as a solicitor until more than 21 years after Timothy's death. Neil and Louise's gift is void also, because it is dependent upon the child's void gift. However, if the subsequent gift is not dependent upon the prior void gift, but merely follows it, it will be valid. Thus, in a gift 'to Timothy for life, remainder to his first child to qualify as a solicitor for life, remainder to such of Timothy's grandchildren as reach 21', Timothy's gift vests in possession, but the gift to his child will be void, as it is possible that it will not vest until more than 21 years after Timothy's death. However, the grandchildren's gift is not dependent upon the child's and is, therefore, valid.

That, then, is the rule at common law with its fascinating (or infuriating) cast of characters – the 'octogenarian parent', the 'precocious toddler', and the 'spectral spouse', not forgetting the 'magic gravel pits'!

The rule was supposed only to prevent gifts which tied up property for unacceptably long periods during which it could not be sold or used, ie the owner was unknown, but, applied as it was with remorseless logic, it resulted in many perfectly acceptable gifts failing.

Statutory modifications to the rule

The Law of Property Act 1925, s 163

One of the main causes of failure was the imposition of an age greater than 21. In order to save such gifts, the Law of Property Act 1925, s 163, provided that if that was the only cause of failure, the contingent age could be reduced to 21 and thus save the gift.

The Perpetuities and Accumulations Act 1964

The preamble to this Act states that it is 'An Act to modify the law of England and Wales relating to the avoidance of future interests in property on grounds of remoteness ...'. The word 'modify' is important, for the Act does not supplant the common-law rule, it merely supplements it. There are two important limitations upon the use of the Act:

1 The Act can only be used where a gift is void at common law. Therefore, the rule at common law must first be applied and only if it causes the gift to fail can the Act be applied.

2 Even where a gift fails at common law, the Act can only be applied to gifts made after 15 July 1964.

If a gift which came into effect after 15 July 1964 fails at common law, then we can apply the Act.

Section 1 – of lives there are none. Section 1 of the Act enables a donor to do away with lives in being altogether. Under s 1 the donor can specify a perpetuity period of not more than 80 years. However, this must be done expressly; such a term will not be implied. If s 1 is utilised, the period is as expressed by the donor, up to 80 years. In *Re Tom's Settlement*, for example, the vesting day for the purposes of the class gift was expressly stated to be 60 years from the date of grant (1955), or 25 years from the date of any appointment made under the settlement. (Due to this clear period the rule in *Andrews* v *Partington* was held not to apply: the class would remain open until the closing day.)

Section 2 – no can do. Section 2 tackles the problems caused by the octogenarian parent and the precocious toddler, by providing 'statutory sterile lives'. Section 2 introduces presumptions with regard to the ages at which parents can produce offspring. It is presumed that a girl is not capable of producing a child before the age of 12, nor a woman after the age of 55. A boy is presumed not to be able to father a child until he is over 14. These presumptions are rebuttable, for example if a woman of 35 has had a hysterectomy. An article in the *Daily Telegraph*, 19 July 1994, provided another example: 'Italian aged 63 becomes oldest mother after birth of 7 lb boy!' In addition, as Phillip Kenny (2005) says, '... it now seems that in the generality of cases the statutory presumption as to female capacity is made a nonsense by the perverse developments of medical science'. For example, in 2007 a Spanish woman gave birth, following IVF treatment, to twins at the age of 67, making her the oldest mother in the world. Frozen embryos create another possibility for long-delayed child bearing: in 2006 another Spanish woman gave birth to a child 13 years after the embryo had been fertilised by another couple, creating the world's oldest in-vitro child to date. Finally, for now, a woman whose frozen embryos were rescued from the floods of Hurricane Katrina in 2006, gave birth to a son in January 2007, naming him Noah. (Source: *The Week*, 18 November 2006, 6 and 20 January 2007.)

Section 3 – wait and see. This has been heralded as the greatest contribution made by the Perpetuities and Accumulations Act. We have seen the problems caused by the need at common law for everything to be decided at the relevant date of grant. Under s 3 we can sit back and wait until the death of the last of the lives in being (or any alternative period provided by the donor under s 1), and only when it becomes obvious that the gift cannot possibly vest within the 21 years which remain, will it be declared void. (It must be appreciated that though the Act saves many gifts which would otherwise have failed, it may itself fail to save some.)

Section 3 – who a life can be. Another major problem with the common law was the difficulty of identifying the relevant lives. Section 3 provides 'statutory lives' and, usually, there will be more statutory lives than there were relevant lives, especially in cases of class gifts. Under s 3 the following are statutory lives:

(a) the donor,

(b) the donees, including potential donees,

(c) the parent or grandparent of a donee or potential donee, and

(d) any prior interest holder.

Section 4 – close the door. This addresses the problem of class closing. The 'wait and see' provision under s 3 is applied first, as is any necessary age reduction. After a wait of as long as is possible (that is, as near to the end of the period of 21 years after the death of the last of the statutory lives, or their reaching the relevant age of statutory sterility, or the end of any period provided for under s 1), it may still be that some of the class members have not satisfied the contingency. If this is the case, the class can be closed for those who have satisfied it, the rest being excluded.

> ## Example
>
> Thus, in a gift 'to Steven for life, and then to such of his nephews and nieces as qualify as skiing instructors', the donor, the parents and grandparents who can produce the nieces and nephews and any nieces and nephews who are alive at the date of grant are the lives in being. We can wait until all those who can produce class members have become statutorily sterile, or, if needs be, until 21 years after all the lives in being have died before closing the class in favour of those nephews and nieces who have already become skiing instructors.

(Of course, such a gift would have been void at common law, unless there was, at the relevant date of grant, a nephew or niece who had already qualified as a skiing instructor.) However, if the rule in *Andrews v Partington* validates the gift at common law, s 4 cannot be applied, even if it would have saved the gift for a larger class.

Section 4 – key to the door. Section 4 deals with the problem of age reduction. The Act repealed the method provided by the Law of Property Act 1925, s 163 (which, therefore, only applies to gifts between 1 January 1926 and 15 July 1964). However, s 4 is not as easy to apply as s 163.

Again, the 'wait and see' provision is applied first, then if a gift would still fail because the donee has not reached the contingent age, that age can be reduced in order to save the gift. However, under s 4 it is not reduced automatically to 21 (though it can be reduced as far as that, but no further, if needs be), but only so far as is necessary to save the gift. This enables the donor's wishes to be complied with as closely as possible.

Example

Thus, in a gift 'to Jenny when she reaches 30', we wait until the last possible moment under s 3 and if Jenny has still not reached 30, we reduce her age to whichever age between 21 and 30 will save the gift. If the age would have to be reduced below 21, the gift fails.

With a class gift the age should be reduced so as to save it for the greatest number of class members. Therefore, calculate the reduction on the age of the youngest class member.

Example

In a gift 'to such of Linda's children as reach 30', if some cannot do so within 21 years of the death of the last life in being, we take the age of Linda's youngest child, say Kirsty who is six, and reduce the age to 27, i.e. 21 + 6. Once reduced, the new age applies to all class members who will, therefore, take their share as and when they reach 27. Had Kirsty been any older than nine, however, we would not have had to reduce the age at all.

It should be noted that had the gift been to 'Jenny provided she survives her mother by five years', age reduction could not operate: it operates only upon specified ages, not upon survival beyond a named event by a specified number of years.

Students often ask what happens when a class member satisfies his individual contingency, such as reaching a certain age: can he claim his share? The problem is that the general contingency – the size of the class – has still to be satisfied. Until it is, the size of individual shares cannot be ascertained. Does he have to wait until the class is closed – possibly for several years? Unless he can persuade the trustees to settle something on him, the answer is yes: his interest is, after all, still contingent. The dangers for trustees is obvious in that if they allocate too large a share they may be held to be in breach of trust to the rest of the class. If the claimant is under 18, the trustees could consider using their power of maintenance under the Trustee Act 1925, s 31. (However, being unable to identify his share, advancement under s 32 would not be possible.)

Section 5 – spouse alive. Section 5 deals with the unborn, or spectral spouse. We saw that this problem arises where the ultimate gift to children of a marriage where one of the spouses is not yet known, or even born, is bound to fail. Section 5 creates a presumption that the disposition must be construed as referring to a date immediately before the end of the perpetuity period, and not to the death of the surviving spouse.

Example

Thus, in a gift 'to Martin for life, then to his widow for life, then to such of his children as shall be living at the death of the survivor of them both', we first wait and see (which will not help if Martin's widow survives him for more than 21 years), and if the gift could still fail we apply s 5, so that the gift will vest 21 years after Martin's death if his widow is still alive. All children then living will take their interest, even if it is possible that some of them will die before the widow. If one does die, then such deceased's share will form part of that deceased child's estate.

Section 6 – do the splits. This solves the problem of gifts failing for being dependent upon void gifts. However, if the ultimate gift is dependent upon a contingency, that contingency must, of course, still be satisfied before the gift can vest.

Non-application of the rule

The effect of breaching the rule is to render the entire trust void, thereby defeating all the beneficial interests under it.

The rule against perpetuities does not apply to vested interests, to interests which follow an entailed interest, to certain gifts to charities, to covenants to renew leases, to administrative powers under settlements, to certain rights of entry or to any postponement of the right to redeem a mortgage. The Law Commission has recommended that the rule cease to apply to any situations, that is, it should be scrapped!

Reform

H W Wilkinson (1994) says that '[t]here was a time when law students could be divided readily into two categories – those who thought they understood the Rules Against Perpetuities . . . and those who were sure they did not. They divided in proportions of about 10 to 90' ([1994] Conv 92). Nothing has changed, then! To the 90 of the future will come the glad tidings that the Law Commission, in its consultation paper *The Rules Against Perpetuities and Excessive Accumulations* (Law Com No 251), published in March 1998, proposes the abolition of the rule as one option for change. Other proposals include:

- The restriction of the rule to interests arising under wills and trusts only – 'The rule should not apply to rights over property such as options, rights of first refusal or future easements created after legislation was brought into force';
- The replacement of the existing rules with, for example, a fixed period of 125 years '(which is about the most that can possibly be achieved under the present law). A future interest or right would be void for perpetuity only when it became clear that it would not take effect within 125 years from the date on which the instrument creating it took effect';
- Most welcome is the proposal that the 'circumstances in which the rule should apply would be set out in clear, statutory form to make it much easier for practitioners to advise their clients on the applicability [of the] rule'. And lecturers to explain it to their students?

Summary

In this chapter we have looked at the following:

- compulsory purchase;
- the rule against perpetuities –
  - the perpetuity period;
  - relevant date of grant;
  - 'lives in being';
  - class gifts;
- the Perpetuities Act 1964 –
  - the wait and see rule;
  - statutory lives;
  - class closing rule;
  - statutory ages;
  - spectral spouses;
- the effect of not complying with the rule;
- reform.

References

Gray, K and Gray, S F, *Elements of Land Law*, 3rd edition, London: Butterworths, 2000.

Gray, K.J. and Symes, P.D., *Real Property and Real People*, London: Butterworths, 1981.

Kenny, P, 'Conveyancer's Notebook' [2005] Conv 103.

Law Commission, *The Rules Against Perpetuities and Excessive Accumulations* (Law Com No 251, Mar 1998).

Law Commission, *Towards a Compulsory Purchase Code: (1) Compensation* (Cm 6071) (Law Com No 286, Dec 2003).

Law Commission, *Towards a Compulsory Purchase Code: (2) Procedure* (Cm 6406) (Law Com No 291, Dec 2004).

Todd, P, *SWOT, Equity & Trusts*, 2nd edition, London: Blackstone, 1989.

Wilkinson, H W, 'Your Money or Your Life or Lives in Being?' [1994] Conv 92.

Further reading

Harris, D, 'En ventre sa mère', NLJ, 15 July 1994, p 980.

Kenny, P, 'Conveyancer's Notebook' [2005] Conv 103.

Sparkes, P, 'How to Simplify Perpetuities' [1995] Conv 212.

Sparkes, P and Snape, R, 'Class Closing and the Wait and See Rule' [1988] Conv 339.

Wilkinson, H W, 'Your Money or Your Life or Lives in Being?' [1994] Conv 92.

PART 2

The legal estates
A time in the land

5 Introduction to legal estates

As we now know, since 1926 there are only two legal estates in land: the fee simple absolute in possession and the term of years absolute – Law of Property Act 1925, s 1(1).

The fee simple absolute in possession is the greater of the two for it gives the holder of it an infinite amount of time in the land: it can last forever. On the other hand, a term of years absolute is of finite duration; it is merely a piece of the fee simple absolute in possession (or a piece of another term of years absolute).

Either way, an estate in land is time in the land – the period during which the holder of the legal estate enjoys the land, its possession, occupation, use and

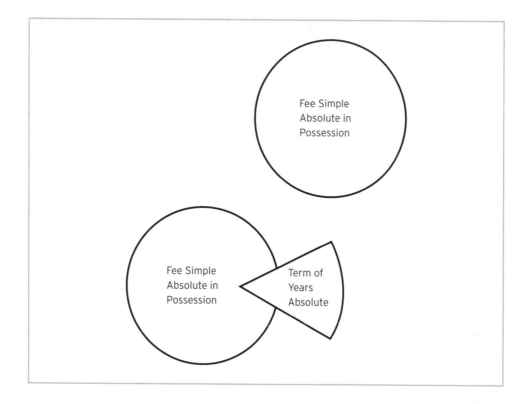

management. There is no limit to the number of legal estates which can exist on the same piece of land all at the same time: LPA 1925, s 1(5).

How can you hold them?

Holding of legal title and equitable interests

There are various ways in which the legal estates can be held and though we shall look at the principles of each in connection with the fee simple absolute (freehold title), they apply equally to the term of years absolute (leasehold).

> **Example**
>
> If A and B purchase a house together, whether the land be freehold or leasehold, they will hold the legal title upon a trust of land.

In order to understand who can hold what and how, we must look at the equitable invention known as the 'trust'. As Maitland (1936, p 23), one of the greatest lawyers, explained:

> Of all the exploits of equity the largest and the most important is the invention and development of the trust. It is an 'institute' of great elasticity and generality; as elastic, as general as contract. This perhaps forms the most distinctive achievement of English lawyers. It seems to us almost essential to civilisation, and yet there is nothing quite like it in foreign law.

The trust developed from the 'use', by which a person was enabled to enjoy property which he was not allowed to hold. For example, under the Statute of Mortmain, conveyance of land to the church was prohibited, but enjoyment of the land could be had if it were conveyed to someone else for the church's use, for example, 'I hereby convey Blackfriars to James Pope for the use of the Franciscan friars of Holyhead'. Although the common law would not uphold the use against the legal owner – James Pope – the Chancellor would. Thus equity created a division of ownership by separating the legal title from the beneficial interests.

The use was also used to get around the fact that a holder of land could not leave his land by will, and more widely to avoid feudal dues and death dues. It is easy to see, then, why the use was unpopular with the King, who passed the Statute of Uses in 1535 to counter the then widespread use of uses. However, by about 1700 the trust had arisen as a replacement for the use, with a 'trustee' holding the legal estate, and the 'cestuis que trust' or 'beneficiaries' owning the equitable interest in the land.

Given its 'elasticity and generality', precise definition of the trust is difficult, but the essential feature of all trusts is that the real owner of the property which is the subject of the trust is the *cestui* or beneficiary – not the trustee, who merely holds the paper (albeit legal) title.

Usually a trust is created for a specific purpose, the purpose being achieved by placing an obligation upon the trustee, to whom the legal title will be conveyed, on the understanding that he will only deal with the property in such a way as will satisfy the creator's intention. It is crucial to understand that, unless he made himself a beneficiary, the settlor, having set up the trust, no longer owns any interest in the property. Indeed, unless he himself is to be the trustee, he will have no further part to play.

The trustee, having the legal title vested in him, is duty bound to administer and manage the trust property in accordance with the terms of the trust, and always in the best interests of the beneficiaries. This is not always easy, as different beneficiaries have different needs. A person holding a life interest is never entitled to the property itself (as opposed to enjoyment of it) or its capital value, only to income from it for life; but the interest of the person absolutely entitled in remainder does lie in the capital sum. Therefore, a trustee investing trust funds must perform a difficult balancing act, for the interests of the two beneficiaries are diametrically opposed – one needs income, the other capital accumulation. All the benefit, whichever form it takes – money, enjoyment of the land and so on – must go to the beneficiaries, for a trustee is never allowed to make a profit from his trusteeship. This is one of the cardinal principles of trust law. The trustee's task is:

> simply one of decision making in the performance of the administrative duties connected with the trust. He manages the trust property and ultimately exercises the power of disposition over that property. However, even the latter function is purely administrative, since a disposition of trust property simply converts that property into cash which is still governed by the terms of the trust and which therefore requires to be reinvested in another form for the benefit of the person or persons entitled in equity – Gray and Symes (1981, p 22).

There are many types of trust, but in this book we shall be interested in only some of them – trusts of land, resulting trusts and constructive trusts. However, whenever one of these arises, it is essential always to separate the equitable interests from the legal estate and to treat each according to its own rules and principles. In separating the legal estate from the equitable interests we must also identify the trustee or trustees and the beneficiary or beneficiaries.

Where the same person owns all of the legal estate and the equitable interests, he is the absolute owner and no trust arises. However, where more than one person is interested in the property, either at the same time (concurrently) or in succession (consecutively), a trust situation arises.

Under the 1925 legislation there were two forms of statutory trust behind which the equitable interests could be held – the strict settlement, governed by the Settled Land Act 1925, and the trust for sale, governed by the Law of Property Act 1925 ('LPA 1925'). **Now there is just one statutory trust – the trust of land**, governed by the LPA 1925 and the Trusts of Land and Appointment of Trustees Act 1996. This latter Act came into force on 1 January 1997 and from that date no new strict settlements can be created (though those already in existence continue under the SLA), and all trusts for sale – whether made before or after the new Act – become trusts of land. Therefore, all references in older cases, textbooks etc to trusts for sale must now be read and interpreted in the light of the new Act.

Though similar in some ways to a trust for sale, the trust of land is different in several important respects and, whilst we shall concentrate upon the law as it now is, rather than what it was, we shall, occasionally, have to look at the pre-1997 law relating to the trust for sale.

However, all three of the statutory trusts – past and present – share one characteristic: in none is a minor – any person under 18 years of age – able to hold the legal estate, for '[a] legal estate is not capable of ... being held by an infant' – LPA 1925, s 1(6).

As already mentioned, interests may exist concurrently or successively. Concurrent interests are held by two or more people at the same time, for instance, where A and B buy a house together. Successive interests occur where the same piece of land is left to two or more people, but here those interests are not enjoyed at the same time.

Example

Where the land is left to A for life and then to B absolutely, B has a future interest, one which has yet to fall into possession. As we know, 'possession' does not have the ordinary meaning of everyday language: a person holds an interest in land 'in possession' where he is entitled immediately to that interest. Thus, a person who will not acquire his fee simple until the end of a life interest ahead of him cannot hold in possession. In fact, he would hold 'in remainder'. So, B above has the fee simple absolute in remainder, whilst A has a life interest in possession.

'In possession' does not necessarily mean 'in occupation' either, for '"Possession" includes receipts of rents and profits or the right to receive the same, if any' – Law of Property Act 1925, s 205(1)(xix). Therefore, you can be in possession whilst not being in physical occupation.

Example

Say L, the fee simple absolute owner in possession, granted a term of years to T subject to T paying rent to L. T would be in physical occupation, but L would still be in possession because he is entitled to receive the rent. Indeed, in this situation, L holds not only the fee simple absolute in possession, but also the 'reversion' of the lease for, at the end of the term of years, the rights of T will revert back to L so that he is then entitled once more to take up occupation, as well as possession, of the premises if he so wishes. L can, during the continuance of the term of years absolute, sell his reversion by selling his fee simple absolute in possession subject to the lease. Of course, as time goes on and the remainder of the term of years gets less, the value of the reversion increases.

An interest – whether in possession or future – can be vested or contingent. A vested interest is one which gives its owner an immediate right of present or future enjoyment of the land.

Example

In a devise of Blackacre 'to Gloria for life, and then to Louise and Neil absolutely', all the interests are vested - Gloria's in possession, and Louise and Neil's 'in interest'. Even though it will not take effect until after Gloria's death, Louise and Neil's entitlement is guaranteed.

It is rather like a bus queue when there is only one place available on the bus. The person who is at the head of the queue takes his place immediately, but the rest of the queue must wait their turn. However, anyone who is on the other side of the road, held up by traffic, cannot even join the queue: it is the same where an interest has vested neither in possession nor in interest. Such an interest is called 'a contingent interest'. A contingent interest cannot be vested until the contingency has been satisfied.

Contingent interests arise in three situations: where the person or persons entitled to the interest cannot be ascertained at the date of the grant; where the size of the beneficiaries' interests cannot be ascertained at the date of the grant; and where the interest is dependent upon some specified event. It is crucial to be able to identify such interests, because the rule against perpetuities only applies to contingent interests.

Where the person or persons entitled cannot be ascertained

Example

If, instead of Blackacre being devised ultimately to Louise and Neil absolutely, it had been devised to 'Louise and Neil for their joint lives, and then to the survivor of them absolutely', we should not be able to tell, at the date of grant, which of them is entitled to the legal estate. All we do know is that they will both die eventually and that, in all probability, one will predecease the other. Until we know which of them is the survivor, the gift cannot vest. Until then it is contingent.

Where the size of the interest cannot be ascertained

This problem usually arises in connection with class gifts.

Example

'Blackacre to Helen for life and then to her children equally', or 'Whiteacre to Timothy for life and then to such of his children as shall survive me'. Both Helen's and Timothy's interests are vested in possession, but in neither case can we say, at the date of grant, how many other beneficiaries there will be. Until we can determine the number of beneficiaries in a class we cannot calculate the size of each individual interest. Until we can do so the interests are contingent.

However, it is possible with gifts such as these, called 'class gifts', for even a vested interest to be caught by the rule against perpetuities.

Example

A gift 'to Diane for life, remainder to all her children who become accountants': Diane has a son, Timothy, who has already qualified as an accountant at the date of grant. Diane's interest is vested in possession, and, as Timothy has satisfied the condition, his interest is also vested (in interest); but, the gift was not to Timothy alone, it was to 'all' of Diane's children who become accountants. Therefore, upon other children of Diane becoming accountants, Timothy's interest is reduced. Until we know how many of the children have qualified as accountants, we cannot calculate the size of the interests. It may be that Timothy proves the only one so to qualify, but we cannot say that that will be the case at the date of grant. (Timothy could, of course, sell, mortgage, or make a gift of his interest, or leave it under his will, but the recipient of it will be liable to have the interest reduced in the same way.)

Where the interest is dependent upon some specified event

Even if we can identify the beneficiary and the size of the interest, it will still be contingent if some condition has been attached to it.

> **Example**
>
> 'Redacre to Graeme when Liverpool Football Club wins the European Cup' is contingent, even though we know that Graeme is the beneficiary, and Redacre the interest. However, it is more usual to specify a contingent age, such as 'to Laura when she reaches 21'.

Until the contingency is satisfied, the person for whom the interest was intended has no interest in it at all – merely the possibility of acquiring one. However, as we saw above, a contingent interest can be disposed of by its intended recipient *inter vivos*. Any interest which is subject to a contingency which relates to the intended recipient personally, as with Laura who must reach a certain age and Timothy who must qualify for a certain profession, or to anyone else upon their marrying, for example, can only be left *inter vivos*. However, any interest which is subject, like Graeme's, to a contingency which does not relate to him personally, can be left by will – though it will remain contingent, of course, until the condition is satisfied.

How can they exist?

Classification: legal or equitable?

Provided the fee simple absolute in possession or term of years absolute is created or conveyed properly it will be legal. In registered land, all fees simple absolute in possession are registrable interests which will, of course, not be legal until substantively registered at the Land Registry. The lesser fees, not being absolute, cannot be legal and are all, therefore, equitable interests. However, there is one minor exception to this: 'A fee simple subject to a legal or equitable right of entry or re-entry is for the purposes of this Act a fee simple absolute' – LPA 1925, s 7(1). Therefore, if in possession, such a fee would be legal. An example would be a fee simple subject to a rentcharge.

Rentcharges

The Rentcharges Act 1977, s 1(1), defines a rentcharge as, 'any annual or other periodic sum charged on or issuing out of land except (a) rent reserved by a lease or tenancy, or (b) any sum by way of interest'. In other words, a rentcharge is a right to the periodical payment of money secured upon land, other than rent or a mortgage.

As Lord Wilberforce said in *Shiloh Spinners Ltd* v *Harding* [1973] AC 691, a rentcharge is not merely 'a right to use or draw profit from another man's land' but a means 'to take his land altogether away'. Any such right of entry is a separate right in the land to the rentcharge itself. Like the rentcharge, the right of entry can be legal – s 1(2)(b) and (e) respectively.

Under the Act, no new rentcharges can be created after 1977 – with two exceptions, one of which is the 'family' rentcharge.

Example

By his will, Bill left his land in Portland to his son, Ben, but subject to 'the annual payment of £30,000 to my dear wife, Celia, so long as she shall live. She is also to have the right of entry should my said son, Ben, fail to respect my wishes'. This is a 'family' rentcharge, by way of which Bill has provided for both his spouse and his son.

Though Ben will, upon his father's death, hold the legal estate and beneficial interest in Portland, he must pay Celia £30,000 every year during her lifetime. These sums are payable 'off the land', but if the land produces no income or profit (say it is purely a dwellinghouse) then Ben must pay out of his own pocket. If he fails to do so he will forfeit Portland when Celia exercises her right of entry and takes possession.

If Ben were to sell Portland to Jack, Jack would be bound by Celia's equitable (being only for life) rentcharge, provided Celia had protected it (by registering a C(iii) land charge in unregistered land or entering a notice to protect it as a minor interest in registered land. Had it been legal, in unregistered land it would bind the world. In registered land, unless it was created for 'an interest equivalent to a term of years absolute not exceeding seven years from the date of creation', it must be entered against the burdened land by a notice and Celia (the grantee), or her successor in title must be entered in the register as proprietor of the rentcharge - Land Registration Act 2002, Sched 2, para 6.

Celia's equitable right of entry would be protected in the same way as her rentcharge, as it would if it were legal (LRA 2002, s 27(1) and (2)(e)).

In registered land, lesser fees are minor interests. Not all legal leases in registered land are registrable interests, only those over seven years. Leases less than seven years are overriding interests – Land Registration Act 2002, Sched 3. In registered land the interest only becomes legal upon registration, of course.

Who does what?

The roles of the parties

Where land, whether freehold or leasehold, is held upon one of the statutory trusts, we need to know the respective roles of the trustees and beneficiaries: in the case of leasehold land, we also have to consider the relationship between the landlord and his tenant.

In both strict settlements and trusts of land the legal estate and the equitable interests are separated, the legal estate being held by the tenant for life in a strict settlement and by the trustees in a trust of land: the equitable interests in both are held by the beneficiaries (or cestuis que trust). In trusts of land the trustees may also be – and usually are – beneficiaries. In strict settlements, the tenant for life is usually the person with the life interest in possession. She has a beneficial interest which is quite separate from the holding of the legal estate. She will have to act like a trustee in regard to any other beneficial interests, such as those of the remaindermen, but she will rarely be a trustee, that role being held by others. Thus, the principal players in either of the statutory trusts may have to wear several hats and we need to look at the roles played by the various players. In leases, of course, the parties concerned – the landlord and the tenant – both hold a legal estate. In regard to them, then, we shall look at the duties which each owes to the other.

Summary

This chapter introduces the two legal estates – the fee simple absolute in possession and the term of years absolute – by looking briefly at the following:

- The concept of the trust –
  - the separation of legal estates from beneficial/equitable interests;
  - the parties – trustees and beneficiaries;
  - minors cannot hold a legal estate;
  - successive and concurrent interests.
- The ways in which interests can be held –
  - in possession;
  - in remainder;
  - vested; and
  - contingent.
- The roles of trustees and their relationship with beneficiaries.
- The roles of and relationship between landlords and tenants.

References

Gray, K.J. and Symes, P.D., *Real Property and Real People*, London: Butterworths, 1981.

Maitland, F.W., *Equity*, 2nd edition, Cambridge: Cambridge University Press, 1936.

6 The fee simple absolute in possession

There are several types of fee simple.

The fee simple prior to 1926

The fee simple was, prior to 1926, an estate in land. Moreover, it was (and still can be) the greatest estate in land in that it lasts the longest – potentially forever. Indeed, a fee simple absolute in possession is tantamount today to absolute ownership in that it entitles the holder of it to unrestricted use and enjoyment of the land (subject, of course, to any restriction which he himself has created by granting interests over the land to others, or to which the land was subject when he took title, and to anything arising under the law of tort – for example nuisance or occupier's liability).

'Fee' means an estate capable of being inherited, so a fee simple can be passed down by the owner of it to future generations. 'Simple' means that there are no conditions upon the potential inheritors of the fee, thus, '. . . he who has a fee simple in land has a time in the land without end, or the land for time without end . . .' – *Walsingham's Case* (1573) 2 Plowd 547.

The fee simple absolute

This is the best fee of all because not only can it exist forever and be inherited by or transferred to anyone, but it is also free of other conditions, unlike a conditional or a determinable fee.

Where a fee simple absolute has been granted to more than one person – either consecutively or concurrently – when its holders' interests terminate depends upon the way in which the legal estate is held, that is, behind a strict settlement or under a trust of land.

A conditional fee simple

This is a fee to which the grantor has attached some condition upon which the fee depends either for its existence (condition precedent) or its determination (condition subsequent).

Example

If A were to grant an estate in land, called, say, Blackfriars, to B, provided that B qualifies as a solicitor, A would have created a conditional fee by way of a condition precedent, because B will only take the legal estate in Blackfriars if and when he so qualifies. Had A granted Blackfriars to B provided that he does not become a solicitor, he would have created a conditional fee by way of a condition subsequent, whereby if B did so qualify, A would have to take some action. In the event of the condition being satisfied, A, the grantor (or the person deriving title under him, namely, his successor in title) has the right to enter on to the land and determine the estate. Until he does so, however, the fee continues. A could, of course, provide for the necessary action in the event of B qualifying as a solicitor by creating a 'gift over' thus, 'Blackfriars to B but if he becomes a solicitor, then to C absolutely'.

Conditional fees are created with words which refer to the conditioning event, such as 'provided that', 'but if', 'if it should happen that', 'on condition that', and so on. Conditional fees terminate as soon as the conditioning event occurs. However, if the condition amounts to a total ban on alienation, such as 'to W, provided she never sells or otherwise disposes of the land', it is void, though one which amounts to a partial restraint only, such as 'to W, provided she never sells to an estate agent', may be held to be valid. If the condition is unlawful or against public policy, for example 'to W, provided she never marries', it is void, making the conditional fee an ordinary fee simple.

Where there is a condition precedent, the fee will come into being upon compliance with that condition; for example, 'to B when he passes his law degree' or 'to C when she becomes of age'.

A determinable fee simple

This is a fee which will determine upon the happening of some specified event. Thus, whereas a conditional fee can end in mid-flight, a determinable fee has its time limit set from the beginning in that it will end automatically and revert back to the grantor when and if the specified event occurs. Determinable fees are created by words which refer to the timescale, such as 'until', 'during', 'while', 'so long as', and so on.

It can sometimes be difficult to distinguish between a determinable fee and a fee subject to a condition subsequent, but the words used should decide the matter.

Example

The words 'to B until he becomes a solicitor' would create a determinable fee, whilst 'to B provided that he does not become a solicitor' would create a conditional fee. In the first example, upon B becoming a solicitor the fee will revert to the grantor, but in the second B can continue to occupy and enjoy the land until the grantor enters upon it and determines the estate.

Determinable fees come to an end automatically upon the happening of the specified event, the interest's time limit having been set from the moment of its creation. However, where a right of re-entry has been reserved in the event of a breach of the condition, exercise of the re-entry will defeat the interest even before its allotted time runs out. Upon breach of the condition the interest becomes voidable; upon re-entry it becomes void.

Even a total restraint upon alienation, such as 'to W in fee simple until she sells the land', is valid in a determinable fee, but if the condition is unlawful or against public policy, or if it is too uncertain, then the whole gift – not merely the condition attached to it – is void.

Conditional and determinable fees (unless the former are caught by the Law of Property Act 1925, s 7(1)) must, prior to 1 January 1997, take effect behind a strict settlement and will, therefore, be governed by the Settled Land Act which provides the additional limitation in s 106 which renders void any attempt by a settlor to persuade or prohibit the tenant for life from using his powers.

Middlemas v Stevens [1901] 1 Ch 574

A widow was entitled under her late husband's will to the enjoyment of a house so long as she resided there and remained a widow. The court held her attempt to grant a 21-year lease to her intended future husband invalid, as not being a bona fide exercise of her powers. The remaindermen had been much opposed to the intended lease – a fact which held great sway in Joyce J's mind:

> A tenant for life in exercising any of the powers conferred by the Settled Land Act must have regard to the interests of all parties entitled under the settlement. Here is a lady who is tenant for life during widowhood. Apart from any question as to her relationship with the gentleman who is the intended lessee, if I found a person, whose interest in the settled property would come to an end tomorrow, persisting in granting a lease which was objected to by all those entitled in remainder, I should regard the case with considerable suspicion. But this case goes beyond suspicion. It is clear from the correspondence that the real object of the lady in granting the lease is that she may herself continue in occupation of the premises. That, in my opinion, is not a bona fide exercise of her powers as tenant for life. But it does not rest there, because it is admitted by the correspondence that she has no intention of granting the lease in the event of her not marrying the gentleman in question. I think the plaintiffs are entitled to an injunction restraining the defendant from granting the lease without their consent or the sanction of the court.

That last thought of Joyce J's is particularly interesting in that it gives the beneficiaries a voice, whereas the Settled Land Act does not. There is no duty under the Act for a tenant for life to consult with the beneficiaries. It is, thus, often said that a tenant for life can act in total disregard of the beneficiaries' wishes, but this case proves the exception to the rule.

A fee tail

The fee tail, being a fee, is inheritable but, unlike the fee simple which can be inherited by anyone, inheritance under a fee tail is restricted. A fee tail is also referred to as an entailed interest and 'he who has the land in tail has a time in the land or the land for time as long as he has issue of his body ...' – *Walsingham's Case*.

Thus, whereas a fee simple can last indefinitely and be passed on to anyone, a fee tail can only be left to specified descendants of the original grantee, and will therefore only last as long as there continue to be such descendants. Where the inheritance is limited to male issue of the line, it is called a fee tail male; similarly, if the limitation is in favour of females, it is a fee tail female. A fee tail general arises where inheritance, though limited to lineal descendants of the original grantee, can be to either gender. If the line runs out because of the lack of issue of the relevant gender, the estate reverts back to the grantor or the person deriving title under him.

Historically, and to a lesser extent today, the fee tail was used to keep estates in land within the family from one generation to the next. However, as we have seen, it will only keep it within the family by direct descent so that if a tail male had been created and there were no sons, the fee simple would end even if there was a brother of the last holder still living. Of course, had a fee simple been created instead, the brother might well have inherited by virtue of either having been left the estate under a will or being the sole surviving relative of the fee simple owner. This alternative was not used in the settlement of 'Longbourn' in Jane Austen's *Pride and Prejudice*: Mr Bennett, husband of Mrs Bennett and father of five daughters, '[a]fter amusing himself some time with their curiosity' explained to his family that '[a]bout a month ago I received this letter, and about a fortnight ago I answered it, for I thought it a case of some delicacy, and requiring early attention. It is from my cousin, Mr Collins who, when I am dead, may turn you all out of this house as soon as he pleases'.

'Oh! my dear', cried his wife, 'I cannot bear to hear that mentioned. Pray do not talk of that odious man. I do think it is the hardest thing in the world, that your estate should be entailed away from your own children; and I am sure if I had been you, I should have tried long ago to do something or other about it'.

What, if anything, could Mr Bennett have done? After all, he did not set up the settlement. As long ago as 1472 it was decided in *Taltarum's Case, re* (1472) YB 12 Edw 4 Ed 19, that an entail could be 'barred', that is, cut off, with the result that the tenant in tail could dispose of the entire fee simple and thereby defeat the heirs of his body. Where this was done, a 'fee simple' would arise.

A base fee arose upon the barring of an entail when a tenant in tail (and for this purpose we shall use as our example a tail male), whose interest was still in remainder, barred his entail without the consent of his father (ie the tenant for life). The entail was only partially barred because the effect of the son's disentailment was only to set up a base fee which, though it would defeat his own issue, would not defeat the interests of any persons entitled after them.

Example

If T had left Home Farm 'to H for life with remainder to S's eldest son in tail, remainder to GS's son in tail etc', and S's son disentailed during H's life, but without his consent, S acquired a fee simple which could not be defeated by his own issue but which would devolve to GS's issue when S's issue failed.

It will not be possible to create an entailed interest after 1 January 1997 – Trusts of Land and Appointment of Trustees Act 1996, Sched 1, para 5.

The life interest

A life interest is not inheritable and is, therefore, not a fee. It ends with the death either of the life interest holder (where the grant was 'to W for life') or of the person during whose life it was to continue (where the gift was 'to W during S's life'; this is known as an interest *'pur autre vie'*, ie for the life of another). Thus, 'he who has an estate for life has no time in it longer than for his own life, and so of him who has an estate in land for the life of another . . .' – *Walsingham's Case* (1573) 2 Plowd 547. Therefore, in the first example the interest will end upon W's death, but in the second upon S's death. However, although W can, in neither case, leave the interest by will, she can alienate (give away, sell, lease, mortgage and so on) the land *inter vivos* (during her lifetime), but she can, of course, only alienate what she has and that is merely an interest for her (or someone else's) life.

> **Example**
>
> In a gift of Paradise 'to Adam for life, and then to Eve absolutely', Eve takes the fee simple absolute immediately upon Adam's death. If Adam sold Paradise during his lifetime to Miss Leaf, then Miss Leaf's interest in the land would cease upon Adam's death, as she only acquired an interest *pur autre vie*, that is, Adam's *vie*! Similarly, had the gift been of Paradise 'to Adam for the lifetime of Sir Pent', Adam's interest, being only *pur autre vie*, would cease upon Sir Pent's death.

It is, then, not a good idea to buy a life interest attached to a frail old person! Of course, even if the life tenant is young and healthy, there would be no knowing what tragedy might occur to strike down the interest early. Either way, you could end up paying a lot for a little.

In France they have a system known as *'en viager'* under which the purchaser buys property and pays the vendor a fixed sum every month until his death, when the purchaser may then take possession of the property – a bit like the arrangement now offered by some insurance companies and banks here.

> **Example**
>
> One case in France illustrates how a purchase under this system is, like that of a life interest, fraught with risk: Madame Jeanne Calment, when 77, entered into an *en viager* arrangement with Monsieur André-François Raffray under which M. Raffray was to pay Mme Calment about £350 per month until her death. Unfortunately for M. Raffray, Mme Calment lived on to become the world's oldest living person (120 years old) at which point the arrangement had cost him £126,000 for a first floor flat in Arles. Whilst M. Raffray could be one of the world's unluckiest property speculators, Mme Calment merely said of his gamble: 'In life, one makes bad deals.' Of course, it could have gone the other way with Mme Calment dying a mere two or three months after entering into the arrangement, in which case M. Raffray would have had the property for merely £700 or just over £1,000. Madame Calment had outlived all her relatives, including her only child. Had she left any family, they could not have inherited the property, of course, even if M. Raffray had only paid for a few months.

The owner of a life interest is entitled to occupation and use of the property and all income arising from it during the course of his life. A life tenant is never entitled to the capital, however, as this belongs to the remaindermen. If the life tenant remains in the property for life, then the remaindermen's interest vests in the land, but if the life tenant sold the property, or mortgaged it, he or she could not use the capital raised to, say, buy a car or go on a world cruise. If a car or a cruise is what the life tenant wants, he or she must pay for it out of income produced by the capital monies (which would usually mean waiting at least a year). Life tenants are subject to the doctrine of waste, which evolved to avoid the sort of situation described by Patrick Dalton (*Land Law*, 3rd edition, p 55):

> If land is settled on A for life with remainder in fee simple to B, and that land holds a fine house, an oak forest and a seam of unnationalized mineral, it would be unjust if A, unless specifically authorized by the settlor, cut down and sold the trees, won and sold the minerals and misused the house, so that on his death all that passed to B was a shack in a blasted landscape.

In Wilkie Collins's *Basil,* Basil himself was the 'second son of an English gentleman of large fortune', whose family was

> one of the most ancient in this country. On my father's side, it dates back beyond the Conquest; on my mother's, it is not so old, but the pedigree is nobler. Besides my elder brother, I have one sister, younger than myself. My mother died shortly after giving birth to her last child.

Clearly rather bitter, he states that:

> When a family is possessed of large landed property, the individual of that family who shows least interest in its welfare; who is least fond of home, least connected by his own sympathies with his relatives, least ready to learn his duties or admit his responsibilities, is often that very individual who is to succeed to the family inheritance – the eldest son. My brother Ralph was no exception to this remark.

Ralph could be Dalton's 'A'!

'Waste' is anything which alters the nature of the land – whether to its detriment or not. The doctrine provides four types of waste – ameliorating, equitable, permissive and voluntary – and the remaindermen can seek an injunction or damages for all or any of them. However, in regard to ameliorating waste, an action would fail because such waste actually enhances the land, and

> the Court of Equity ought not to interfere to prevent it . . . the waste with which a Court of Equity . . . ought to interfere, be not ameliorating waste, nor trivial waste. It must be waste of a substantially injurious character – Lord O'Hagan in *Doherty* v *Allman* (1877) 3 App Cas 709.

Equitable waste is 'that which a prudent man would not do in the management of his own property' – Lord Campbell in *Turner* v *Wright* (1860) 2 De GF&J 234, and permissive waste is that which occurs when the tenant for life fails to do something which ought to have been done to prevent it.

Voluntary waste arises where a positive act harms the land, such as cutting of timber. If the grant exempts the tenant for life from liability, he is 'unimpeachable for waste'. However, as the definition of 'timber' varies from one area to another (though oak, ash and elm of 20 years' growth are usually 'timber' everywhere), what may be waste in Oxfordshire may not be in Buckinghamshire, though it has been held that larch trees are not timber anywhere – *Re Harker's Will Trusts* [1938] Ch 323.

Under the Settled Land Act 1925, a tenant for life is empowered to cut and sell ripe timber, even though impeachable for waste – s 66. This would seem to enable the tenant for life to commit limitless waste. However, under the Law of Property Act 1925:

> An equitable interest for life without impeachment of waste does not confer upon the tenant for life any right to commit waste of the description known as equitable waste, unless an intention to confer such right expressly appears by the instrument creating such equitable interest – s 135.

The fee simple after 1925

As we know, only one fee simple is capable of being a legal estate today: the fee simple absolute in possession – LPA 1925, s 1(1). All the lesser fees can, therefore, be equitable interests only – s 1(3), and must take effect behind a trust. Before 1997, they took effect behind a strict settlement; after 1996 they take effect behind a trust of land. Of course, where there is a life interest or entail, there will be successive interests in the land. However, a fee simple absolute in possession which is subject to a rentcharge (and which is, therefore, conditional) can be legal – LPA 1925, s 7(1).

Where the interests are concurrent, not successive, a trust of land will come into existence. Trusts of land only came into being in 1997, under the Trusts of Land and Appointment of Trustees Act 1996: they replaced trusts for sale and any trust for sale – whether created before or after the Act – is now a trust of land. To this extent, the Act is retrospective.

This is not so in the case of successive interests. Prior to the Act, successive interests could exist behind a strict settlement or a trust for sale. Which had been created depended upon the words used in the trust instrument – unless it expressly stated that the land was to be held on trust for sale, the successive interests took effect behind a strict settlement. Since 1996, no new strict settlements can be created, but those which were already in existence and effective at that date continue and any later resettlement creates a new settlement. Not until there is no longer any land or heirlooms subject to the settlement will it come to an end. As pointed out in Maudsley and Burn, though '[t]he strict settlement is being phased out. . . . it will be a long time before it finally disappears. It is therefore essential to know whether a pre-1997 instrument has created a strict settlement' – *Land Law Cases and Materials* (2004, p 325).

Summary

In this chapter we have considered the meanings of the following:

■ Early types of fees simple – fees simple absolute, conditional fees, determinable fees, fees tail.

- A life interest.
- The doctrine of waste.
- The fee simple absolute in possession.

References

Burn, E H, *Maudsley & Burn's Land Law Cases and Materials*, 8th edition, London: Butterworths, 2004.

Dalton, P J, *Land Law*, 3rd edition, London: Financial Times Pitman Publishing, 1983.

7 Trusts of land

What's the problem?

Trusts of land in context

When couples set up home today they do not normally intend that one of them should enjoy the property for a time and then the other: they want to live in it together – at the same time! A simple enough wish, you may think, but it can become one fraught with difficulties, if, for example, the relationship between the couple breaks down. Much will depend upon whether they took the legal title to their house in joint names or in the name of one of them only. In the latter case, their reasons for such a decision may prove crucial.

Say Sarah and John, a young couple as yet unmarried, buy a new house together with the aid of a loan from the bank secured on the house – a mortgage. A 10 per cent deposit was paid at the outset, the parents of both John and Sarah providing this as a gift. As yet, their future life together is something of a mystery for in today's world many things may happen to disturb this happy scenario. They may fall behind with the repayments on the loan and the bank may seek possession of the house so that it can be sold to pay off the debt. If this happens, what, if anything, can either or both of them do to stay in the house? If nothing, who is entitled to what from the sale?

Sarah and John may decide to split up. If so, again the question is, who gets what? Can either of them stay in the house and exclude the other? If so, must the one who had to leave be compensated, for example by receiving rent from the one who stays? If not, how will the proceeds of a sale of the house be divided?

Any one of the four parents, say, Sarah's mother, may become widowed and decide to sell her house and use most of the purchase monies to pay for a loft extension in Sarah and John's house, thus providing the mother with a self-contained flat. Sarah and her mother later fall out and declare that they 'cannot live under the same roof a moment longer'. What happens then?

Sarah and John (or just one of them, unbeknown to the other) may grant a second mortgage on the house.

Either Sarah or John die. Who takes that share in the house?

In each of these cases several questions will need to be answered: Who holds the legal estate? Was anything expressly provided for in the conveyance? Who paid what? When were the various contributions made? What form did they take? What was the 'common intention' of the parties? Was this expressed in some way? If not, can the court imply or infer a common intention to their subsequent acts? Have Sarah and John had any children? Has either of them been declared bankrupt? Were Sarah and John married? What, if any, difference would that make? Is there enough 'equity' in the house to pay all debts and interests?

All of these facts have a bearing upon what, if any, interest each has in the house; the extent of such interest; whether the house must be sold in order to 'pay out' all interests; whether any of the interests are capable of binding a third party, the mortgagee for example, or creditors; how much will be paid to settle various debts, especially those of mortgagees (who, having taken the house as security for their loans, are secured creditors) – if there is negative equity there will not be enough to pay off all the loans in full.

Who cares?

Those who will be affected

The original co-owners, Sarah and John. If all goes well and they live happily ever after, pay off the bank (and any subsequent mortgagee), there will usually be no problem. What, though, if one dies before the other? What happens to the house then? Will it automatically go to the survivor? Both of them need to know: indeed, it is something which should be considered from the very beginning. Also, their parents may wish to know what happens to the 'gift' they made. If our young couple split up (probably due to the stress of considering all these questions), each will need to know what they are entitled to. It may be that they simply wish to 'call it quits', sell the house and share out any proceeds of sale left after paying off the bank. However, especially if they have since had children, one of them may wish to stay in the house. Will the other be willing to leave? If not, can he or she be made to go? If so, what, if any, compensation will have to be made?

Any subsequent co-owner (or claimant), Sarah's mother. Is she a co-owner? Has she gained any interest in the house? If she is held to have an interest, how can she 'get it out'? If John and Sarah are still together (despite the atmosphere!), it will be them against Sarah's mother, but if they are splitting up, it will be each against the others: worst case scenario for all concerned? Not necessarily, from Sarah's mother's point of view it could be the best chance of having the house sold and thereby freeing up the capital. However, if the problem is that mortgage repayments have fallen into arrears, it will be Sarah, John and Sarah's mother against the bank (and/or subsequent mortgagee): has any of them got an interest which will be binding upon the lender and thus prevent repossession?

The mortgagee(s), the lender. Here the bank lent the money so that the house could be bought in the first place and, so long as the loan is paid off as agreed, the bank will be happy. What, though, if repayments fall into arrears? Can the bank gain vacant possession of the house or does someone – Sarah, John or Sarah's mother – have an interest which is binding upon the bank and thus would prevent it from selling the house? (There is little point selling without vacant possession.)

Have there been any fraudulent dealings between the co-owners, for example did John, unknown to Sarah (and her mother), grant a second mortgage on the property? (If he and Sarah both held the legal title, he would have had to have got someone else to pretend to be her and sign Sarah's signature on the mortgage deed.) Have all the co-owners defrauded the bank (or any subsequent mortgagee), for example by obtaining a loan, secured on the house, supposedly for work which would increase the value of the house but which, in fact, was always intended to pay for an extended trip for them all to Disneyland?

Can any of the co-owners claim that they were the victim of 'undue influence' – either by the other co-owners or the bank? If by a co-owner, will the bank also be bound by the undue influence? (See Chapter 11.)

Was any other mortgage granted on the house? If so, will this affect the bank's chances of gaining possession, or of being paid in full? If such a mortgage was only granted by, say, John, what is the position in regard to Sarah's interest, or that of her mother? Would it be different if both Sarah and John had executed the mortgage?

Is there negative equity?

What is the position of any subsequent mortgagee in all of this?

You are beginning to see the minefield which mortgagees face today.

Any children of the co-owners. Does a child have any interest in his parents' house merely by being their child? If not, how can a child have an interest in the land? If no interest exists, can the child's occupation of the house be of any significance, especially against any mortgagee? Would it make any difference if the parent or parents were declared bankrupt? When one parent survives the other, will any share come to the child from his deceased parent? (This question is of greatest significance when there has been a second marriage and the surviving parent is the step-parent.)

Purchasers, that is anyone who buys the house. If the purchaser is buying the house from the co-owners, she will need to know who they are, who can execute a valid conveyance of the title and who should sign the receipt for the purchase monies – just John? John and Sarah? What of Sarah's mother? How, if at all, can the purchaser be sure that she is free of all interests in the house – including that of any mortgagee?

Of course, it could be that it is the mortgagee that is selling the house. The purchaser must be sure that there are no interests binding upon the bank, such as any interest Sarah's mother may have or a prior mortgage which has not been paid off: almost certainly, any such interest will also bind the purchaser.

What are they?

The nature and characteristics of trusts of land

Trusts of land operate on both concurrent and successive interests, therefore, not just on the situations we have seen in relation to Sarah's and John's house (which concern concurrent interests), but also anything which previously would have given rise to a strict settlement, for example to John and Sarah for life and then to their children absolutely. We already know that even before the Trusts of Land and Appointment of Trustees Act 1996 (TOLATA), successive interests in land could be the subject of a trust for sale, if expressly stated. Since the Act came into force on

1 January 1997, however, *all* concurrent and successive interests take effect behind a trust of land (except those successive interests which arose under a strict settlement created before 31 December 1996, that is created *inter vivos* by that day, or coming into effect under a will where the testator died on or before that date).

A trust of land is 'any trust of property which consists of or includes land' – Trusts of Land Act 1996, s 1(1)(a), but it 'does not include land which . . . is settled land' – s 1(3). Section 1(2) provides that:

The reference in subsection (1)(a) to a trust –

(a) is to any description of trust (whether express, implied, resulting or constructive), including a trust for sale and a bare trust, and
(b) includes a trust created, or arising, before the commencement of this Act.

As we have seen, s 2 goes on to prohibit the creation of any new strict settlements.

We shall see shortly that trusts of land may be created expressly, arise automatically under the new Act or be implied in equity. In all trusts it is the trustees who hold the legal estate, the equitable interests – the real ownership – belonging to the beneficiaries. There are two ways of holding interests behind a trust of land: as tenants in common or as joint tenants.

Tenants in common

Tenants in common each have 'an undivided share in land'. This phrase, rather confusingly, means that each tenant in common can, in fact, identify his own individual (or divided) share! However, the land itself remains undivided, each tenant having a specific, but undivided, share in the land.

Section 34 of the Law of Property Act 1925 provides that:

(1) an undivided share in land shall not be capable of being created except as provided by the Settled Land Act 1925 or as hereinafter mentioned;
(2) where, after the commencement of this Act, land is expressed to be conveyed to any persons in undivided shares and those persons are of full age, the conveyance shall . . . operate as if the land had been expressed to be conveyed to the grantees, or, if there are more than four grantees, to the four first named in the conveyance, as joint tenants in trust for the persons interested in the land.

Therefore, only the equitable interests, those of beneficiaries, can be held as tenants in common.

Joint tenants

Unlike tenants in common, joint tenants cannot identify a specific share, for they together own the whole of the interest in the land, each and every joint tenant being wholly entitled to the whole. It has therefore been said that each joint tenant 'holds everything and yet holds nothing'.

Example

If six friends held the beneficial interests in a holiday home, all six together would own the whole, but none of them individually could identify an individual share. On the other hand, had they held it as tenants in common, each would have a one-sixth share, or such other share as had been stipulated.

The major characteristic of a joint tenancy is 'the right of survivorship', by which, when any joint tenant dies, the surviving joint tenants take the whole interest.

Example

If one of the six friends died, the remaining five, as joint tenants, would now own the whole. This redistribution of interest occurs upon the death of each of the joint tenants until, finally, only one remains and he owns the whole.

As we have seen, s 34 provides that the legal estate can only be held as a joint tenancy, so that the death of each joint tenant will reduce the number of trustees, of which the maximum is four.

The right of survivorship does not operate upon a tenancy in common, where, if one of the tenants dies, the individual share of the deceased tenant passes under his will or intestacy.

Whilst the legal estate can only be held as a joint tenancy, the equitable interests may be held as either a joint tenancy or a tenancy in common. The right of survivorship operates upon both legal and equitable joint tenancies, but equity dislikes joint tenancies and requires the presence of 'the four unities' if a joint tenancy of the equitable interests is to exist.

The four unities

These are the unities of possession, interest, time and title. (As the legal estate can only be held as a joint tenancy, there is no point in considering the presence or absence of the four unities in regard to it.)

(a) *Unity of possession* Under this unity each joint tenant is as entitled to possession of the whole as the others. Therefore every joint tenant can occupy every part of the land. None of them can point to, say, a room in a house and declare it to be his to the exclusion of the others. As Lord Denning explained in *Bull* v *Bull* [1955] 1 QB 234:

> The son is, of course, the legal owner of the house, but the mother and son are, I think, equitable tenants in common. Each is entitled in equity to an undivided share in the house, the share of each being in proportion to his or her respective contribution ... until the place is sold, each of them is entitled to the possession of the land and to the use and enjoyment of it in a proper manner. Neither can turn out the other; but, if one of them should take more than his proper share, the injured party can bring an action for an account. If one of them should go so far as to oust the other, he is guilty of trespass ...

This is the only unity required for a tenancy in common, where each tenant in common is likewise entitled to possession of the whole of the property and can occupy each and every part of it – not merely a proportionate part.

Example

If Jack and Jill are tenants in common of 'Hill Top', Jack having paid ¼ of the purchase price and Jill ¾, Jack is entitled to possession of all of 'Hill Top', not merely ¼ of it. Their individual 'shares' have relevance to the proceeds of sale of 'Hill Top', not to the occupation of the land.

(b) Unity of interest As each joint tenant is wholly entitled to the whole, the interest of each of them in the land must be the same extent, nature and duration. Therefore, a joint tenancy cannot exist where, say, one tenant holds the freehold and the other a lease, or where one has the fee simple absolute but the other only a life interest.

The advantage to a purchaser from joint tenants is that he only has to investigate one title. However, as all the joint tenants together own the whole, the purchaser must ensure that all surviving joint tenants join in the conveyance to him. Having sold to the purchaser, the joint tenants must divide the purchase price equally amongst themselves, or, rather, the trustees must so divide the monies.

(c) Unity of time This means that the interest of each joint tenant must vest at the same time.

> ### Example
>
> If the land was left 'to Gloria and Barry in fee simple', there would be unity of time, but if the land were left instead 'to Gloria, and to Barry when he retires', there would be no unity of time because the two interests would not vest together.

(d) Unity of title Under this head all the joint tenants must acquire their title in the same way, usually by taking under the same conveyance.

The four unities and the need for them were reiterated by Lord Oliver in *A G Securities* v *Vaughan* [1988] 3 WLR 1025, where the House of Lords had to decide whether the four occupants of a large flat were joint tenants or mere licensees. For a joint tenancy all four unities must be present: the absence of any of them will mean there can only be a tenancy in common (or, as in *Vaughan*, a licence).

All four unities must, then, be present if there is to be a joint tenancy in equity. However, even in the presence of all four unities, equity may, by way of the equitable presumptions, still refuse to recognise a joint tenancy.

Equitable presumptions

Of the several such presumptions, four are most important.

(1) Where two or more persons purchase property together, but they contribute towards the purchase price in unequal shares, they are presumed to take as tenants in common, the share of each being proportionate to the contribution made – see *Bull* v *Bull* [1995] 1 QB 234.

(2) Where two or more persons lend money on mortgage each of them holds his interest under the mortgage as a tenant in common, even if each advanced the same amounts – see *Petty* v *Styward* (1631) 1 Eq Cas Abr 290.

(3) When two or more persons enter into a joint undertaking aimed at making a profit, they hold as tenants in common: the maxim is 'the right of survivorship has no place among merchants'. This presumption can be rebutted by express words to the effect that the tenants take under a joint tenancy – see, for example, *Barton* v *Morris* [1985] 2 All ER 1032 and *Lake* v *Craddock* (1732) 3 P Wms 158. *Bathurst* v *Scarborow* [2005] 1 P&CR 58 provides a rare example of a rebuttal of the presump-

tion of a tenancy in common of land owned by a business partnership. The Court of Appeal had to consider whether the property in question was partnership property, and, if so, whether 'the partners had wished to take the beneficial interest in a joint tenancy and that in doing so they knew the effect of the rule of survivorship' – Rix LJ at p 73. On the facts, both questions were answered in the affirmative. The consequence of this was, of course, that the right of survivorship operated upon the death of one of the partners.

(4) The fourth presumption was established by the Privy Council in *Malayan Credit Ltd* v *Jack Chia–Mph Ltd* [1986] AC 549 when it held that where owners hold premises for several business purposes, they will be presumed to hold as tenants in common.

Example

If Mr Marks and Mr Spencer together enter into a lease of a large unit but set up two trading enterprises therein, they will hold as tenants in common based on the relative sizes of their undertakings, say, 60 per cent and 40 per cent.

The proportions will also dictate their liability for service charges and so on. The Privy Council stated that the list of equitable presumptions in favour of tenancies in common is not exhaustive. (This case also shows that the same principles apply to leasehold as well as freehold land.)

Words of severance

A major cause of a joint tenancy failing in equity is the presence of 'words of severance', that is, any word or words in the conveyance which refer to a proportionate interest or share. Obviously, 'half to Timothy and a quarter each to Neil and Louise' would be words of severance, but so too would 'equally' or 'share and share alike', notwithstanding that they create the same proportionate share for each tenant.

In conclusion, therefore, for a joint tenancy to exist in equity there must be all four unities, no words of severance and none of the presumptions must apply. Even then, if the conveyance states that the grantees take as tenants in common, they will so take. Similarly, if the conveyance states that they take as joint tenants in equity, they will do so regardless.

Even when a joint tenancy arises in equity, it may be severed, that is, split up into a tenancy in common but **the legal estate can never be severed** because 'a legal estate is not capable of subsisting or of being created in an undivided share in land' – Law of Property Act 1925, s 1(6), and '[n]o severance of a joint tenancy of a legal estate, so as to create a tenancy in common in land, shall be permissible – s 36(2).

Sections 1(6), 34 and 36 thus combine to provide that where the legal estate is held under a trust of land it can only ever be held as a joint tenancy by a maximum of four trustees, and that the joint tenancy can never be severed. Therefore, the only event which can alter the holding of the legal estate is the death of one of the joint tenant trustees (apart from the execution of a deed of retirement or appointment as trustee).

However, the equitable interests can be created as either a joint tenancy or a tenancy in common and, even if created as a joint tenancy, the equitable interests can be severed and produce a tenancy in common – in whole or in part – but only *inter vivos*, that is, only by an act during the tenant's lifetime. You cannot, therefore, sever an equitable joint tenancy by an attempted disposition of your equitable interest by will.

No doubt this all seems very confusing, but if you think of a trust of land as a sandwich cake, with the legal estate (LE) forming the top layer, and the equitable interests (EI) the bottom, thus:

LE   [   ]

EI   [   ]

it may become clearer.

The top layer – the legal estate – will never change its shape. Only the names within it will alter, and then only by reduction upon the death of one of the joint tenant trustees.

However, the bottom layer – the equitable interests – can alter its shape, because it can be cut into individual pieces, the size of each piece being proportionate to the severed equitable interest. Say A, B, C, D and E purchase Blackacre together, it being conveyed to them as joint tenants (JT) at law and in equity, the effect will be:

LE   [A + B + C + D   ]   JT

EI   [A + B + C + D + E   ]   JT

If A dies, the right of survivorship will operate, thus:

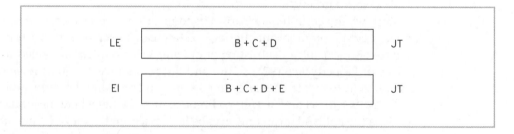

LE   [B + C + D   ]   JT

EI   [B + C + D + E   ]   JT

However, if, instead of dying, A had sold his equitable interest to X, the result would be:

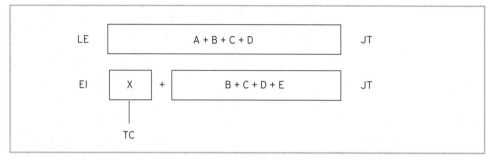

X could, of course, only be a tenant in common (TC) because he cannot satisfy the four unities, but the rest remain as joint tenants. As A has not died he remains a trustee of the legal estate, but he has severed his equitable interest.

If A, instead of selling to X (a stranger) had sold to one of his co-joint tenants, say, D, the result would have been rather different. The legal estate will remain with A, B, C and D as before, but D will now hold his equitable interest in two capacities. He will hold the one-fifth share which he bought from A as a tenant in common, and, together with B, C and E, he will hold the remaining four-fifths share as a joint tenant, thus:

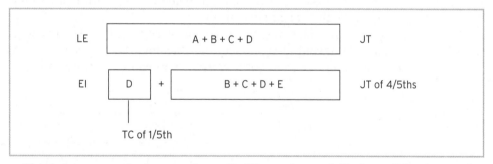

This is because only A severed, not D. D's purchase of A's share did not sever his joint tenancy with the others.

Should D die, his one-fifth share, being held as a tenant in common, will go as laid down in his will or by his intestacy. However, in regard to the four-fifths share, of which he is still a joint tenant, his interest here would, of course, go by right of survivorship upon his death.

If, however, Blackacre had been conveyed to 'A, B, C, D and E for life with remainder to A in fee simple', and D acquired A's fee simple in remainder, then D's life interest would merge in the fee simple and sever D's joint tenancy for life, thus:

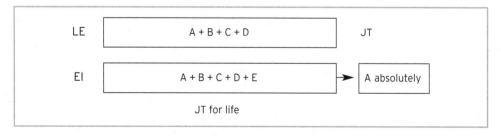

Then,

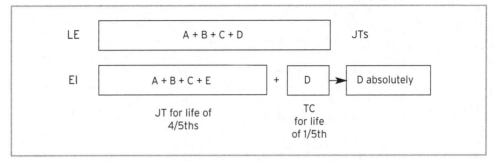

Wiscot's Case (1599) 2 Co Rep 60b.

The difference arises, of course, from the fact that A is transferring an estate in the land, not merely an interest. By acquiring an additional estate in the land, therefore, D has severed his tenancy for life. As Megarry (2002) explains:

> Although it was not fatal to a joint tenancy that one of the tenants was initially given some further estate in the land than his joint tenants, the subsequent acquisition of an additional estate in land destroyed the unity of interest and severed the joint tenancy – p 300.

However, as Gray says (p 510), it is odd that 'the dual nature of A's initial entitlements seems not to connote any merger of interests which would precipitate severance'. However, it is doubtful 'whether a modern court would adhere to the logic (or illogic) of this ancient rule'.

Say, though, Blackacre had been conveyed to A, B, C, D and E 'equally'. The word 'equally' is a word of severance, and therefore the equitable interests would not be held as a joint tenancy, but as a tenancy in common, thus:

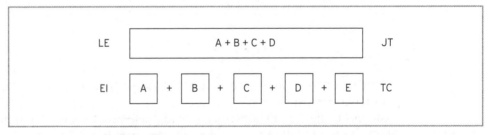

There would be no right of survivorship operating on the equitable interests now, so that if A died the result would be:

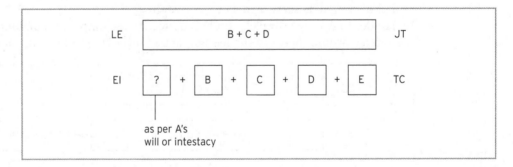

Had A sold to X, the result would be:

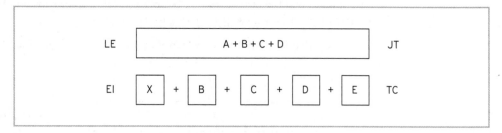

Had X then died, the result would have been:

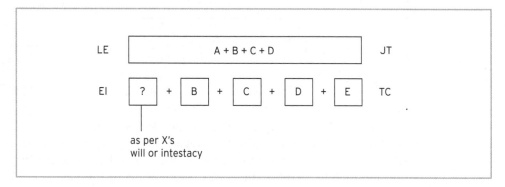

The Law of Property Act 1925, s 1(6) provides that: 'A legal estate is not capable of … being held by an infant'. We have already seen that a conveyance of a legal estate to an infant alone, if created before 1 January 1997, resulted in a strict settlement under the Settled Land Act, s 1(1)(ii)(d). However, where, in any conveyance after 31 December 1996:

> a person purports to convey a legal estate in land to a minor, or to two or more minors, alone, the conveyance –
>
> (a) is not effective to pass the legal estate, but
> (b) operates as a declaration that the land is held in trust for the minor or minors (or if he purports to convey it to the minor or minors in trust for any persons, for those persons) – Trusts of Land Act 1996, Sched 1, para 1(1).

Hector v Lyons (1989) 58 P&CR 156

The plaintiff entered into negotiations for the purchase of a house. He then instructed his solicitor that it should be bought in the name of his son, who was a minor. It was held that the plaintiff could not enforce the contract as he was not a contracting party to it. His son could not enforce it either as he could not hold the legal estate – s 1(6).

However:

> Where after the commencement of this Act a person purports to convey the legal estate in land to –
>
> (a) a minor or two or more minors, and
> (b) another person who is, or other persons who are, of full age,

the conveyance operates to vest the land in the other person or persons in trust for the minor or minors and the other person or persons (or if he purports to convey it to them on trust for any persons, for those persons) – para 1(2).

Thus, a conveyance to A, B and C, where C is only 15, will produce the following result:

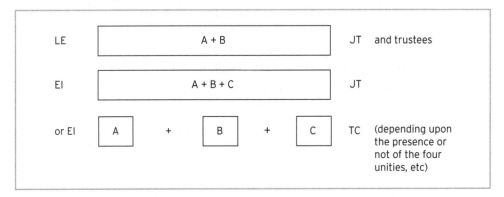

All of the above examples are based upon interests held concurrently. However, as we know, any successive interests created after 31 December 1996 must also take effect behind a trust of land – TOLATA 1996, s 2. Where land has been left to W for life, and then to S for life and then to GC absolutely, the 'cake' would look like this:

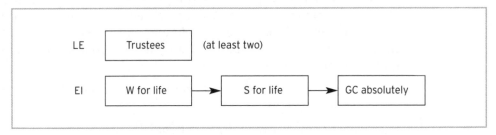

Note the difference between this and an equitable tenancy in common. Here, each beneficiary takes the whole layer of cake for a specified time, whereas tenants in common each take only a piece of the cake but for the whole time.

It is perfectly possible to create joint tenancies here too.

Example

To W and S for life, then to D and C for life, and then to GC absolutely. As between W and S, and D and C, the right of survivorship would operate, so that D and C's interest would not fall into possession (currently in remainder, of course) until both W and S have died. Likewise, GC's interest will not fall into possession until all four - W, S, D and C - have died.

See 'When and for how long' (p. 229), for a detailed explanation of the ways in which severance can be effected.

Party walls

Finally, a matter which causes perhaps more problems in practice than any other is party walls, the client's question being not so much who owns them, but who is responsible for them!

Fry J in *Watson* v *Gray* (1880) 14 Ch D 192 defined 'party walls' as:

(a) a wall of which two adjoining owners are tenants in common; or
(b) a wall divided vertically into two strips, one half of the thickness belonging to each of the neighbouring owners; or
(c) a wall belonging entirely to one owner, but subject to an easement in the other to have it maintained as a dividing wall; or
(d) a wall divided vertically into two equal strips, each strip being subject to a cross-easement in favour of the owner of the other.

Given that the vast majority of party walls in this country fall within category (a), that is, being held under a tenancy in common, an imposition by the 1925 legislation of a joint tenancy, with its associated right of survivorship, would have been ludicrous. Thus,

> Where, immediately before the commencement of this Act, a party wall or other party structure is held in undivided shares, the ownership thereof shall be deemed to be severed vertically as between the respective owners, and the owner of each part shall have such rights to support and of user over the rest of the structure as may be requisite for conferring rights corresponding to those subsisting at the commencement of this Act – Law of Property Act 1925, s 38, sched 1, Pt V.

This, of course, has the effect of bringing most party walls within category (d).

The Party Wall etc Act 1996 makes provision 'in respect of party walls, and excavation and construction in proximity to certain buildings or structures; and for connected purposes'. Under the Act,

> where lands of different owners adjoin and –

> (a) are not built on at the line of junction; or
> (b) are built on at the line of junction only to the extent of a boundary wall (not being a party fence wall or the external wall of a building)

and either owner is about to build on any part of the line of junction,

> [i]f a building owner desires to build a party wall or party fence wall on the line of junction, he shall, at least one month before he intends the building work to start, serve on any adjoining owner a notice which indicates his desire to build and describes the intended wall – s 1.

A 'party wall fence' is defined as:

> a wall (not being part of a building) which stands on land of different owners and is used or constructed to be used for separating such adjoining lands, but does not include a wall constructed on the land of one owner the artificially formed support of which projects into the land of another owner – s 20.

The Act makes provisions for new building on the line of junction, repairs of party walls and the rights of owners, disputes arising under any party structure notices served or counter notices, adjacent excavation and construction, compensation for any loss or damage caused, rights of entry, resolution of disputes and expenses.

In *Dean* v *Walker* (1996) 73 P&CR 366, the Court of Appeal held that the definition of land in the Access to Neighbouring Land Act 1992 was wide enough to include a party wall deemed by LPA, s 38 to be divided vertically (see Chapter 12).

Though not a case brought under the 1996 Act, *Louis & Louis* v *Sadiq* (1997) 74 P&CR 325, shows just how serious a situation may become in regard to party walls. The parties were neighbours whose properties were divided by a party wall. In 1988 Mr S told Mrs L that he wanted to build a small further extension to the rear of his property and Mrs L said she had no objection. Mr S subsequently began what turned out to be works of demolition and reconstruction involving the entire house. The work interfered with the party wall to such an extent that damage was caused to Mr and Mrs L's house, including cracks in their front wall. When they put their house on the market, the Ls were unable to sell, due in no small part to the structural damage. Mr S was held liable for private nuisance. (He should have obtained statutory authority, which had to be in writing, under the London Building Acts (Amendment) Act 1939.) Obviously, where the party wall is actually part of neighbouring houses, as in semi-detached and terraced houses, and not merely a boundary wall, any consequences for all concerned are far greater.

At the other end of the spectrum is what may seem a somewhat frivolous action. *Jones* v *Stones* (1999) 78 P&CR 293 concerned a stone wall which separated two adjacent properties. Jones sued Stones for trespass of the wall by placing an oil tank on and across it and placing and maintaining flowerpots on the wall. Stones claimed that the wall was a party wall, or, alternatively, that Jones should be estopped due to acquiescence over 10 years in the alleged acts of trespass.

The Court of Appeal held that the wall was not a party one but that it belonged to Jones. In regard to the claim to estoppel, it was held that none of the essential elements of the doctrine had been satisfied! (However, in *Prudential Assurance Co Ltd* v *Waterloo Real Estate Inc* [1998] EGCS 51, a claim to adverse possession of the south side of a party wall was upheld.) See also *Beale* v *Harvey* [2004] 2 P&CR 18.

Hedge and ditch presumption

Where two plots of land are divided by a hedge and an adjacent ditch, it is presumed that the boundary of the land runs along the edge of the ditch furthest from the hedge – *Vowles* v *Miller* (1810) 3 Taunt. 137. In *Alan Wibberley Building Ltd* v *Insley* (1999) 78 P&CR 327, the House of Lords had to consider whether the presumption applied where, although the deeds to the respondent's land were silent on the point, the appellant's deeds identified the land by reference to an Ordnance Survey field plan. According to that plan, the boundary in dispute lay along the centre line of the hedge. Their lordships held that the presumption in *Vowles* v *Miller* had not been displaced. In such cases, it is for the party not in possession of the relevant land to show he has a better title than his neighbour.

Another problem caused by hedges is their tendency to grow – some higher (and faster) than others! Indeed, certain plants, such as the leylandii, have become a positive menace to neighbours. For them, the provision of a remedy in the Anti-Social

Behaviour Act 2003 (which came into force on 1 June 2006) will come as a great relief. The relevant regulations are to be found in the High Hedges (Appeals) (England [or Wales]) Regulations 2005 (SI 2005/711). The Office of the Deputy Prime Minister's website explains that, 'The complainant must show that they have tried to resolve the matter with the hedge owner. Complaints will only be considered when the hedge is evergreen, over two metres high and blocking out light, access or reasonable enjoyment of the neighbour's property. If this is the case, local authorities will take a range of factors into account to come to a balanced decision on whether the high hedge is a problem.'

It is well worth taking on board the following extract from a letter to *The Times* (reported in *The Week*, 4 November 2006):

> All good lawyers . . . caution their clients at every stage against the danger of incurring large legal bills and the desirability of reaching a settlement' with the expense of a dispute of 'a few inches of garden' likely to be more than the cost of 'building a swimming pool or constructing a conservatory!

Who does what?

The roles of the trustees and beneficiaries

The role of the trustees under a trust of land is far more dynamic than that of trustees of a strict settlement for the simple reason that they, and not the tenant for life, hold the legal estate. Indeed, '[f]or the purposes of exercising their functions as trustees, the trustees of land have in relation to the land subject to the trust all the powers of an absolute owner' – Trusts of Land Act 1996, s 6(1). As we shall see, the position of trustees is an onerous one under which the relative positions and needs of all beneficiaries must be constantly considered, for example the needs or wishes of the holder of a life interest in possession as against those of the remaindermen. Obviously, minor beneficiaries need particular protection; however,

> [w]here in the case of any land subject to a trust of land each of the beneficiaries interested in the land is a person of full age and capacity who is absolutely entitled to the land, the powers conferred on the trustees by subsection (1) include the power to convey the land to the beneficiaries even though they have not required the trustees to do so – s 6(2).

It is crucial to note the meaning of 'beneficiary' for the purposes of the Trusts of Land Act: confusingly, '[i]n this Act "beneficiary", in relation to a trust, means any person who under the trust has an interest in property subject to the trust (including a person who has such an interest as a trustee or a personal representative)' – s 22(1); but, '[i]n this Act references to a beneficiary who is beneficially entitled do not include a beneficiary who has an interest in property subject to the trust only by reason of being a trustee or personal representative' – s 22(2)! What does this mean?

Example

Well, if Tony conveys Toxteth Towers to Diane and Susan on trust for Cindy, Diane and Susan will be trustees and 'beneficiaries' by virtue of s 22(1), but only Cindy is a 'beneficiary beneficially entitled'. Had the conveyance been to Diane and Susan on trust for themselves and Cindy, all three would have been beneficiaries and beneficiaries beneficially entitled!

Hopefully the distinction will become clearer as we work our way through the provisions of the Act and see how they apply to given situations.

Sale, postponement and purchase

Under the old trust for sale the trustees were under a duty to sell coupled with a power to postpone sale. As there is no such duty to sell in a trust of land, trustees do not require a power of postponement. As we know, all trusts for sale became trusts of land on 1 January 1997, but what is the position where under an old trust for sale the power to postpone was expressly excluded (as was possible)? Section 4(1) of the Trusts of Land Act 1996 covers this situation:

> [i]n the case of every trust for sale of land created by a disposition there is to be implied, despite any provision to the contrary made by the disposition, a power for the trustees to postpone sale of the land: and the trustees shall not be liable in any way for postponing sale of the land, in the exercise of their discretion, for an indefinite period.

Thus the trustees of a trust of land have the power to either sell or retain the land. Under s 6(3) they also have the power to purchase 'a legal estate in any land in England or Wales', and they may use this power to buy land 'by way of investment, . . . for occupation by any beneficiary, or . . . for any other reason' – s 6(4).

Consents

The person creating the trust of land – settlor or testator – can, if he so wishes, make any disposition of the land subject to consents being obtained from named persons. If the number of consents to be obtained exceeds two, then so far as any purchaser is concerned, the consent of any two of those named will be enough – s 10(1). If a person named as one whose consent must be obtained is a minor, then his consent is not required in favour of a purchaser but the trustees shall instead obtain the consent of that minor's parent or guardian – s 10(3).

Example

If Tom leaves his property to Tessa and Ted on a trust of land, but subject to their obtaining the consent of Charles and Camilla, when Tess and Ted sell to Peter, Peter must ensure that both Charles and Camilla give their consent to the sale. However, if Diana's consent had also been required, Charles's and Camilla's consents would still have been enough in favour of Peter. If either Charles or Camilla are under 18, of course, the consent of the parent or guardian of the minor must be obtained, or that of Diana. Although two out of the three consents will be enough for Peter, all three consents must be obtained if Tessa and Ted are not to be liable to the beneficiaries for breach of trust.

Consultation

Section 11 imposes a duty of consultation upon the trustees under which they:

> shall in the exercise of their function relating to land subject to the trust –
>
> (a) so far as practicable, consult the beneficiaries of full age and beneficially entitled to an interest in possession in the land, and

(b) so far as consistent with the general interest of the trust, give effect to the wishes of those beneficiaries, or (in case of dispute) to the majority (according to the value of their combined interests) – s 11(1).

The settlor or testator can, however, exclude this duty expressly – s 11(2)(a), and s 11(2)(b) provides that the duty shall not apply 'in relation to a trust created or arising under a will made before the commencement of this Act', though in this case a retrospective inclusion of the power can be made by deed – s 11(3).

Example

Anne and Jeanette hold land for Bill, Ben and Babs, all three of whom are over 18. If Anne and Jeanette wish to sell the land, they must consult Bill, Ben and Babs. If Bill and Ben were against the sale, although they would be the majority of the 'voting' beneficiaries – that is, the beneficiaries beneficially entitled – they may not necessarily hold the majority 'shares' in the land. Say that Babs was entitled to two-thirds and Bill and Ben only to a third between them, then Babs's wishes would prevail: it is the weight of the beneficial interests, not the number of beneficiaries, that counts.

Challenges

What can Bill and Ben do if Babs's wishes do prevail? Like '[a]ny person who is a trustee in land or has an interest in property subject to a trust of land' they could make an application to the court for an order under s 14. 'Any person who ... has an interest ... in land' is not limited to just the trustees and beneficiaries beneficially entitled: it includes, for example, a mortgagee, as in *Mortgage Corporation Ltd* v *Shaire* [2001] 3 WLR 639.

The court may make any order:

(a) relating to the exercise by the trustees of any of their functions (including an order relieving them of any obligation to obtain the consent of, or to consult, any person in connection with the exercise of any of their functions), or
(b) declaring the nature or extent of a person's interest in property subject to the trust

as it thinks fit – s 14(2), though the power does not extend to any order as to the appointment or removal of trustees – s 14(3).

Section 15(1) sets out the matters which the court must take into consideration when deciding upon an application. These include (a) the intentions of the person or persons who created the trust, (b) the purpose for which the property subject to the trust is held, (c) the welfare of any minor who occupies or might reasonably be expected to occupy any land subject to the trust as his home, and (d) the interests of any secured creditor of any beneficiary (for example, a mortgagee, though, according to *Shaire*, s 15 gives no priority to a mortgagee over other creditors). Consideration (a) appears to give the creator of the trust – the person who 'gave' the land – a voice. This could be crucial to the person with a life interest in possession where the trust was created by will and under which the remaindermen wish to force or prevent a sale of the land against the wishes of the life tenant. Under a strict settlement, of course, the tenant for life rarely had to worry about the wishes of the remaindermen, but s 14 enables them to challenge any dealings with the land. Therefore, the intention of the testator could prove to be vital.

> **Example**
>
> Thomas, in his will, leaves the 'family' home to his wife, Penelope, for life and then to their children absolutely, the house being very large and old and Thomas leaving no money. Penelope, under a strict settlement, could have sold the house, bought a small, convenient flat and directed the trustees to invest the balance of the purchase monies from the house, living off the income from it. She need not have consulted the children nor would she have been required to gain any consents. The children's entitlement would lie in the capital value of the house (now the flat and investments) after their mother's death - as Thomas had intended. However, under a trust of land it is the trustees who have the power of sale, not Penelope. She could ask them to do as she wishes and they may agree, but the children can challenge this under s 14. In deciding the matter the court must take Thomas's intentions into account - but it is only one of the factors to be considered.

Some cases under the old s 30 of the Law of Property Act 1925, which ss 14 and 15 of the 1996 Act replace, provide examples of consideration (b).

Re Buchanan-Wollaston's Conveyance [1939] Ch 217

Four people, each the owner of separate neighbouring properties, together purchased a strip of land in front of their houses in order to retain a sea view. As all four purchased the strip together, a trust for sale (now it would be a trust of land) arose under which they were all trustees and beneficiaries. In addition to the conveyance, all four entered into a covenant not to deal with or part with the land unless all were unanimous in that desire, or at least a majority of them. Some time later one of the four sold his own house and wanted also, against the wishes of the other three, to force a sale of the strip of land in order to recoup his financial contribution to it. The court refused his application for an order for sale because of the true purpose of the trust - to retain the land. In addition, the court would not grant an order which would enable the applicant to avoid his contractual obligations to the others. As Farwell J said at first instance, the applicant was 'putting forward a claim to equitable assistance merely to enable him thereby to escape from his contractual obligations' and if the court were to grant his request this 'would be to disregard the well established rule of equity that he who seeks equity must do equity'.

In regard to (c), the presence of children in a house was always a consideration in s 30 applications, their continuing occupation evidencing the continuing purpose of the land as a family home. However, (c) seems to raise the child's occupation above a mere consideration: it seems to raise the child to the position of a quasi-beneficiary. It is vital to understand that merely being a child of property-owning parents does not give any interest in that land. As Buckley LJ said in *Burke* v *Burke* [1974] 1 WLR 1063, 'it is not, I think, right to treat this case as though the husband was obliged to make provision for his children by agreeing to retain the property unsold. To do so is . . . to confuse with a problem relating to property considerations which are relevant to maintenance'. Whichever way the court interprets (c), where any of the true beneficiaries is bankrupt, the occupation of children of the family in the family home will not keep the roof over their heads.

Re Citro [1991] Ch 142

The husband was declared bankrupt, his beneficial interest in the matrimonial home vesting in his trustee in bankruptcy. Thus, the conflicting interests were those of the husband's creditors and the husband and the wife. Their lordships held that the interests of the creditors should prevail and ordered sale, stating that only in exceptional circumstances would the other spouse (here, the wife) prevail, even though the consequences for the non-bankrupt spouse and children of the marriage may be 'distressing':

> Where a spouse who has a beneficial interest in the matrimonial home has become bankrupt under debts which cannot be paid without the realisation of that interest, the voice of the creditors will usually prevail over the voice of the other spouse and a sale of the property ordered within a short period. The voice of the other spouse will only prevail in exceptional circumstances. No distinction is to be made between a case where the property is still being enjoyed as the matrimonial home and one where it is not - Nourse LJ.

Abbey National plc v Moss (1993) 26 HLR 249

Here the Court of Appeal distinguished Re Citro [1990] 3 All ER 952. In Moss, Mrs Moss had originally owned the property outright but, at the suggestion of her daughter, Mrs Leto, transferred it into their joint names. The transfer was on condition that the house would never be sold during Mrs Moss's lifetime. Subsequently, Mrs Leto borrowed £30,000 from the plaintiff upon security of the property. The mortgage documents appeared to have been signed by Mrs Leto and Mrs Moss but it was found that Mrs Moss, who had not known of the mortgage until some time after the advance was made, had not signed. Mrs Moss and Mrs Leto fell out in 1988 and Mrs Leto left the country, making no further repayments on the mortgage. The plaintiff sought payment of the monies due and possession. At first instance the judge held that the decision in Re Citro was authority for the proposition that the court would not normally take the existence of a collateral purpose into account where one of the joint owners has parted with his ownership of the share. In so doing the judge, according to Peter Gibson LJ:

> plainly erred ... On the contrary Re Citro only establishes that the collateral advantage will not be treated as subsisting when that purpose is to provide a matrimonial home and one of the parties ceased through bankruptcy or the like to own his share. It does not purport to apply where a different collateral purpose is not affected by the alienation by a party to that purpose of his share. The judge also erred in holding that the collateral purpose established by the agreement of Mrs Moss and Mrs Leto was not a factor to inhibit him from ordering a sale and that by reason of Re Citro it was for Mrs Moss to show that there were no exceptional circumstances present. Again I fear he has not appreciated the distinction between Re Citro and the present case, nor taken account of the fact that in every reported case where a collateral purpose has been held to continue (and I, therefore, exclude cases like that of Carmine Citro) the court has not allowed the trust for sale to prevail ... The consequence of that error is that the court must exercise the discretion under section 30 afresh ... I am left in no doubt that the court's discretion should be exercised against ordering a sale. To order a sale seems to me not to be right and proper but to be grossly inequitable'.

Hirst and Ralph Gibson LLJ agreed. In his judgment Peter Gibson LJ provides an excellent review of the case law on the exercise of the court's discretion in s 30 proceedings when consent was refused.

As already mentioned, although these cases predate the Trusts of Land Act 1996, they are likely still to be considered good law by the court in regard to any s 14 applications.

Just as the presence of children in the family home can be taken as evidence of the true purpose of the trust under which it is held, so can their departure prove the opposite.

Jones v *Challenger* [1961] 1 QB 176

A married couple bought a house as a matrimonial home for themselves. Upon their divorce, the wife asked the court to order sale of the house and, as the purpose for which the property had been bought had ended, sale was ordered. Had there been young children living with the husband in the house, the purpose of a family home would have prevailed, but had such children grown up and left home the outcome would have been the same as in *Challenger*. Devlin LJ explained the court's approach:

> the house was acquired as the matrimonial home. That was the purpose of the joint tenancy and, for as long as that purpose was still alive, I think that the right test to be applied would be that in *Re Buchanan-Wollaston's Conveyance* ... But with the end of the marriage, that purpose was dissolved ... there is no way in which the discretion can properly be exercised except by an order to sell because since they cannot now both enjoy occupation of the property, that is the only way whereby the beneficiaries can derive equal benefit from their investment which is the primary object of the trust.
>
> The test is not what is reasonable. It is reasonable for the husband to want to go on living in the house and reasonable for the wife to want her share of the trust property in cash. The true question is whether it is inequitable for the wife, once the matrimonial home has gone, to want to realise her investment.
>
> The Court is not concerned with the reasons for, or the rights or wrongs of, the termination of the joint purpose, but only the feasibility of its continuance.

Bank of Baroda v *Dhillon & Anor* (1997) *The Times*, 4 November

This case can be considered alongside *Moss*. Here the Court of Appeal found that the defendant husband held the property on trust for himself and his wife in equal shares, that the wife had an overriding interest under the Land Registration Act 1925, s 70(1)(g), and that the bank's legal charge took subject to that interest. Mrs Dhillon knew nothing of the second charge in favour of the bank. The bank made application under s 14 for an order for sale. Roch LJ felt that the bank was in the same position as a trustee in bankruptcy and, after balancing the various considerations, concluded that there was no prospect of the debt being paid in the foreseeable future unless the property was sold. An order for sale was made: following sale Mrs Dhillon would have a resource which should enable her to reaccommodate herself. Mrs Dhillon's counsel had sought to rely on *Moss* and had asked the court to distinguish *Re Citro*, but it seems clear that *Moss* is something of an exceptional case in that it concerned the occupation of only one of the co-owners; *Citro* and *Dhillon* concerned the occupation of both.

Mortgage Corporation v *Shaire* [2001] 3 WLR 639

Here Neuberger J provides an important judgment in regard to s 15. He held that, although prior to the Trusts of Land and Appointment of Trustees Act 1996 the court generally ordered the sale of a family home at the suit of a chargee (mortgagee), Parliament intended, by s 15 of the Act, to give the court a wider discretion when determining applications for sale of a home. Under s 14 of the Act, the court is required to consider s 15(1) and s 15(3), under which the interest of the chargee is just one of the factors to be taken into account: there is no suggestion that it should be given any more importance than the interests of the family residing in the property. Neuberger J went on to state *per curiam* that, whilst it would be wrong to reject the wealth of learning in the old authorities dealing with opposed applications for the sale of jointly owned property, given the change in the law introduced by s 15, pre-1996 cases should be treated with caution. Was s 15 intended to create a change in the law, however? As Susan Pascoe (2000) comments,

> only time will tell if judges are prepared to implement the consequences of [this] judgment and let a fresh wind blow away the remnants of the harshness for families of section 30 of the Law of Property Act 1925 when faced with applications by secured creditors.

The decision of the Court of Appeal in *Bank of Ireland Home Mortgages* v *Bell* [2001] 2 FLR 809 would suggest not. This case looks at the application of s 15 in detail and you are advised to read it in full. Rebecca Probert provides a good discussion in her note on the case, 'Creditors and section 15 of the Trusts of Land and Appointment of Trustees Act 1996: first among equals?' [2002] Conv 61. This may well prove to be merely a Pyrrhic victory for the mortgagor, however, because if a mortgagee (or other creditor) fails under its application under sections 14 and 15, it may well found a successful claim against the mortgagor (debtor) in bankruptcy. This almost always leads to sale of the property. See *Alliance and Leicester plc* v *Slayford* (2000) 33 HLR 743.

It was held in *Telecom Plus plc* v *Hatch* [2005] EWHC 1523 (Ch) that an application can be made under s 14 for an order relating to the exercise by the trustees of any of their functions or powers under s 6.

Right to occupy

Generally, however,

> [a] beneficiary who is beneficially entitled to an interest in possession in land subject to a trust of land is entitled by reason of his interest to occupy the land at any time if at that time –
>
> (a) the purposes of the trust include making the land available for his occupation (or for the occupation of beneficiaries of a class of which he is a member or of beneficiaries in general), or
> (b) the land is held by the trustees so as to be so available – Trusts of Land Act 1996, s 12(1);

but this 'does not confer on a beneficiary a right to occupy land if it is either unavailable or unsuitable for occupation by him' – s 12(2).

Of course, even where s 12(2) is not applicable it may still be unwise to have all the beneficiaries who are entitled to possession in occupation at the same time! Section 13 addresses this situation:

(1) Where two or more beneficiaries are (or apart from this subsection would be) entitled under section 12 to occupy land, the trustees of land may exclude or restrict the entitlement of any one or more (but not all) of them;

however, they may not . . .

(a) unreasonably exclude any beneficiary's entitlement to occupy land, or
(b) restrict any such entitlement to an unreasonable extent – s 13(2).

Where a beneficiary's right to occupy is excluded the trustees may make conditions upon any of the other beneficiaries under s 13(6), for example making them make payments to the excluded beneficiary by way of compensation, or by forgoing any payment or other benefit to which the included beneficiaries are entitled under the trust, in favour of the excluded beneficiary.

Under s 13(3) the trustees 'may from time to time impose reasonable conditions on any beneficiary in relation to his occupation of land', and s 13(5) provides examples of conditions which trustees could impose – the payment by the beneficiary of any outgoings or expenses in respect of the land, or the assumption by him of any other obligation in relation to the land or to any activity which is or is proposed to be conducted there.

In exercising any of the powers conferred by s 13 the trustees must have regard to:

(a) the intentions of the person or persons (if any) who created the trust,
(b) the purposes for which the land is held, and
(c) the circumstances and wishes of each of the beneficiaries who is (or apart from any previous exercise by the trustees of these powers would be) entitled to occupy under section 12 – s 13(4)

and they must not exercise them:

(a) so as [to] prevent any person who is in occupation . . . from continuing to occupy the land, or
(b) in a manner likely to result in any such person ceasing to occupy the land,

unless he consents or the court has given approval – s 13(7).

In *Rodway* v *Landy* [2001] 2 WLR 1775, the Court of Appeal addressed s 13, holding that on a proper construction of the section, trustees were entitled, in relation to a single building which lent itself to physical partition, to exclude or restrict one beneficiary's entitlement to occupy one part and at the same time exclude or restrict the other beneficiaries entitled to occupy the other part. Trustees were also entitled (under s 13(3)) to impose a condition requiring a beneficiary to contribute to the cost of adapting the property to make it suitable for his occupation.

Delegation

Section 9 of the Trusts of Land Act 1996 gives trustees the power to delegate 'any of their functions as trustees which relate to the land [to] any beneficiary or beneficiaries of full age and beneficially entitled to an interest in possession in land subject to the trust' – s 9(1). The delegation must be made by a power of attorney given by all the trustees jointly but it will, in most cases, be revocable by any one of them –

s 9(3). Where a delegation to a beneficiary is made under s 9(1), the trustees remain 'jointly and severally liable for any act or default of the beneficiary ... in the exercise of the function', but 'if, and only if, the trustees did not exercise reasonable care in deciding to delegate the function to the beneficiary' – s 9(8). However, it is unlikely that trustees who delegate will be able to escape liability for failing to monitor the delegated beneficiary's use of the powers merely by showing that the delegation itself was reasonable: after all, the trustees, like trustees of any trust, owe an overriding duty to all the beneficiaries to look after their rights.

Would delegation by trustees to the beneficiary with a life interest in possession not put him in the same position as the tenant for life under a strict settlement, then? No: the delegation (unless expressed to be irrevocable and to be given by way of security) is revocable. It is revocable by any one of the trustees (though the delegation can only be granted by all of them), and any such delegation is automatically revoked upon the appointment of a new trustee – s 9(3). The powers under s 14 also make any dealings, or proposed dealings, challengeable.

Appointment and retirement of trustees

Section 19(2) of the Trusts of Land and Appointment of Trustees Act 1996 provides that:

> [t]he beneficiaries may give a direction or directions of either or both of the following descriptions –
>
> (a) a written direction to a trustee or trustees to retire from the trust, and
> (b) a written direction to the trustees or trustee for the time being ... to appoint by writing to be a trustee or trustees the person or persons specified in that direction.

As we have just seen, a direction under s 19(2)(b) revokes a delegation made under s 9.

Section 19(1) lays down the circumstances in which s 19(2) will apply, and they are where:

> (a) there is no person nominated for the purpose of appointing new trustees by the instrument, if any, creating the trust, and
> (b) the beneficiaries under the trust are of full age and capacity and (taken together) are absolutely entitled to the property subject to the trust.

Thus, s 19(1), which provides the only two situations in which a direction can be made, refers only to beneficiaries beneficially entitled, whereas s 19(2), which sets out the requirements of any such direction, refers to 'the beneficiaries', which includes also the trustees – s 22(1). This could prove problematic, as s 21 requires a direction to be 'a single direction' if given jointly by all the beneficiaries, or a direction given by each of them. In either case, a withdrawal of it in writing given by any beneficiary before the direction has been complied with will revoke the direction. If the direction has to be given by 'the beneficiaries' – that is, including the trustees – and it has to be unanimous, it will be difficult, if not impossible, to remove a trustee against his wishes: it is not possible to make any application under s 14 in regard to the appointment or removal of trustees – s 14(3).

Where 'a trustee is incapable by reason of mental disorder of exercising his functions as trustee', or 'there is no person who is both entitled and willing and able to appoint a trustee in place of him', and 'the beneficiaries under the trust are of full age and capacity and (taken together) are absolutely entitled to the property subject to the trust', the beneficiaries may give a written direction to a receiver of the trustee or to an attorney or a person authorised under the Mental Health Act 1983 to act for him to replace such trustee by another – s 20. Note, however, that here again 'the beneficiaries' are not expressed to be limited to those beneficially entitled.

Protection of purchasers

As we know, a purchaser must make sure that all the trustees of a trust of land sign the receipt for the capital monies if the purchaser is to take the land free of the beneficiaries' rights: overreaching has the effect of taking these rights off the land and placing them in the capital monies, so that a beneficiary who was entitled before overreaching to a quarter share in the land becomes entitled instead to a quarter of the purchase price.

Even where a beneficiary has had the functions of the trustees delegated to him under s 9, the purchaser must still obtain his receipt for the capital monies from the trustees: this function cannot be delegated – s 9(7).

Other protections for the purchaser are set out in s 16(1), which provides that a purchaser need not concern himself as to whether or not the trustees have complied with any requirements imposed upon them under s 6(5) (which imposes a general duty to have regard to the rights of the beneficiaries when exercising any of the trustees' powers); s 7(3) (under which the trustees must obtain the consent of each beneficiary in favour of whom partition is effected (we shall come to partition shortly)); or s 11(1) (duty to consult the beneficiaries).

Section 9(2) includes similar protection for a purchaser who had no knowledge at the time of the transaction that a wrongful delegation had been made.

Section 6(6) and (8) restrict the trustees' powers in the light of 'any other enactment or any rule of law or equity' and any statutory powers 'subject to any restriction, limitation or condition'. In regard to these any disposition is effective in favour of a purchaser who has 'no actual notice of [any] contravention' – s 16(2). (As against the beneficiaries, such contravention will, of course, amount to a breach of trust.)

The protection under s 16 applies to unregistered land only, the assumption being that in registered land the register will warn a purchaser of any restrictions with which he needs to comply: it is to be hoped such confidence is justified.

Powers of trustees

Trustees under a trust of land have the power to postpone sale – TOLATA 1996, s 4 but, as we have seen, they may be bound both to consult the beneficiaries (s 11) and to obtain consents (s 10).

Trusts of land are governed not only by TOLATA, but also by the Law of Property Act 1925, the LPA dealing with the setting up of the framework of the trust – the cake – and TOLATA with the relationship between the trustees, beneficiaries and purchasers. It is the trustees who hold the legal estate and it is they who not only execute the conveyance but also sign the receipt for the capital monies:

> [N]otwithstanding anything to the contrary in the instrument (if any) creating a trust or in

any trust affecting the net proceeds of sale of the land if it is sold, the proceeds of sale or other capital money shall not be paid to or applied by the direction of fewer than two persons as trustees except where the trustee is a trust corporation – s 27(2).

There can be no more than four trustees of a legal estate held on trust of land, and s 27(2) provides that no fewer than two shall sign the receipt for the capital monies. However, where there are more than two trustees, **then all of them – up to the maximum of four** – must sign the receipt (as well as execute the conveyance in a trust of land).

The Trusts of Land Act provides for limitations upon the powers of trustees of a trust of land in s 10. Section 6, which sets out the functions of trustees of land, specifies that '[t]he powers conferred by this section shall not be exercised in contravention of, or of any order made in pursuance of, any other enactment or any rule of law or equity' – s 6(6), and '[w]here any enactment other than this section confers on trustees authority to act subject to any restriction, limitation or condition, trustees of land may not exercise the powers conferred by this section to do any act which they are prevented from doing under the other enactment by reason of the restriction, limitation or condition'. Apart from these statutory restrictions, however, it would seem that the powers of trustees of land cannot be reduced further by those setting up the trust. The fact that the provision in s 27(2) of the LPA as to payment of capital monies applies 'notwithstanding anything to the contrary in the instrument (if any)', supports this view.

Needless to say, minors, being unable to hold the legal estate, are not capable of being trustees and thus, '[t]he appointment of an infant to be a trustee in relation to any settlement or trust shall be void' – Law of Property Act 1925, s 20.

Where a trust of land arises automatically under statute, the trustees and the beneficiaries are usually the same people, for example a married couple purchasing the matrimonial home:

LE	H + W
EI	H + W

In a *Buchanan-Wollaston*-type situation, or in a business partnership it may be that there will be more beneficiaries than trustees:

LE	A + B + C + D
EI	A + B + C + D + E

(though, under the presumption of equity, in a business partnership situation the equitable interests may well be held as tenants in common). Here, E is not a trustee and, though he must be consulted if over 18, his wishes may well be defeated by the majority holding of the four trustee beneficiaries.

As we have seen, where a trust of land exists, the beneficiaries are able to have a say in the disposition of the land because of the duty to consult imposed upon the trustees by s 11, which requires that, 'so far as practicable', the trustees must 'consult the beneficiaries of full age and beneficially entitled to an interest in possession in the land'. Where the interests are concurrent, **all** the beneficial interests – whether held as joint tenants or tenants in common – are concurrent. However, where the beneficial interests are successive, only those of the life tenant are in possession (the rest, of course, being in remainder).

Example

Where land is held for W for life and then S absolutely, only W's interest is in possession and, therefore, W is the only beneficiary whom the trustees must consult under s 11.

Whether created as an express trust for sale or as a trust of land, the settlor could have specified the need for certain consents to any disposition of the property. If he did so, they must be obtained – s 10 of the Trusts of Land Act 1996. These provisions, and the fact that the settlor can appoint the trustees himself, and therefore appoint non-beneficially entitled beneficiaries as trustees – that is, persons who have no beneficial interest in the land and who are, therefore, only influenced by the duties imposed upon them by the trust and the needs of all the beneficiaries beneficially entitled – make the trust of land a more effective method of retaining land within the family than a strict settlement.

Example

Say, David leaves the family home, 'Formby Folly', to Jean and Geoff to hold for Barbara for life and then to Paul and Brian absolutely. 'Formby Folly' is a very large Victorian villa, very difficult and costly to maintain. Paul and Brian are grown up and, by the time David dies, have left home. Unfortunately, the house is all that David left; there is no money. Therefore, Barbara has only her state pension to live off. The Folly is too large for her now, all alone and in failing health. In addition, it has fallen into a serious state of disrepair. Barbara would like to sell it, buy a pretty cottage in Cornwall and invest the balance of the sale price, thereby providing herself with some additional income during her lifetime. The boys object; they want to see 'generations of our family growing up in Formby Folly'. Though he probably does not realise it, David has set up a trust of land under which Jean and Geoff are the trustees. It is they who would have to execute the conveyance or transfer of the legal title. As Barbara is the only beneficiary with a beneficial interest in possession, Jean and Geoff do not need to consult the boys, but David may have named persons whose consent to sale must be acquired and they may refuse, taking the boys' point of view. Indeed David may name the boys themselves as consentors: he could provide that they alone, and not Barbara, be consulted. It could well be, then, that Barbara would not be able to sell Formby Folly and would have to remain there, possibly incurring liability for waste.

Re Inns [1947] Ch 576

This case shows not only that a trust of land can be used to keep land within the family, but also that, by using one, it is easier to prevent the land being sold. The widow in this case was in a similar position to that of Barbara: her husband had left a luxurious mansion, 'Springfield', but, according to the widow, insufficient financial provision had been made to enable her to remain there. It was a very expensive house to run. The house was left on a trust for sale under which it could only be sold with the consent of both the widow and the Stevenage Urban District Council (to whom it was to be offered upon the widow's death or remarriage). Wynn-Parry J felt that:

> ... if I had been sitting in the testator's armchair, I might well have ... provided a somewhat larger fund ... From the plaintiff's point of view the provisions regarding 'Springfield' are unfortunate in that neither she nor the trustees can bring about a sale during her lifetime.

Re Herklott's Will Trusts [1964] 1 WLR 583 provides another illustration on this point.

In such cases, the main advantage of the trust of land is said to be that it provides a 'level playing field' for all the beneficiaries. It would seem that David's intention, which was clearly the opposite, is to be overriden: had he intended the boys to have the influence, and thus the power to defeat Barbara's wishes in regard to the disposition of the property, he would have been better advised to transfer the property direct to the boys subject to an annual rentcharge in favour of the person granted the life interest.

Does the provision of a level playing field necessarily make for simplicity, or will it turn certain situations into a scrum? Let us return to Barbara: as a tenant for life she can ask the trustees to sell Formby Folly. Though she will need their agreement to the sale in as much as it is they, not she, who will have to convey or transfer title, as David has made no provision for consents, Barbara does not need Jean and Geoff's consent, nor that of the boys or indeed of anyone. (Moreover, the boys may object and seek a court order preventing sale under s 14.) So long as she complies with all provisions in the Act in regard to such a sale – for example obtaining the best price – there is no opportunity for any litigation.

Of course, under s 9 the powers of the trustees could be delegated to Barbara but, again, she must still obtain their 'agreement' because delegation cannot be made of the ability to overreach all the beneficial interests: the trustees themselves must sign the receipt for the capital monies – s 9(7). In addition, the power of attorney, under which the delegation is exercised, may be revoked by **any one** of the trustees (unless expressly made irrevocable) – s 9(3).

Would the answer be to make Barbara the sole trustee? In regard to her having a free hand, probably yes, but under a trust of land in which there is only one trustee, and that Barbara, the person with the life interest, who will look out for the boys?

It will be interesting to see how the courts will interpret the new Act and how the judges will use their discretion under it – for example, under s 14. Hopefully, particular attention will be paid to the intention of the person who created the trust, especially in cases of successive interests. It will become, then, as important for those drafting wills and *inter vivos* trusts to specify the testator's or settlor's true intentions in the documents as it is for parties to an implied trust to prove their common intention.

Most trusts of land arise automatically.

How can you acquire them?

Rules, principles and formalities of acquisition

As already mentioned, trusts of land can arise expressly, automatically under statute or impliedly.

Express trusts of land

If a settlor wishes to vest the fee simple absolute in possession (or, indeed, a term of years absolute) by way of a trust of land, he must convey the legal estate to named trustees expressly 'upon trust of land' – for themselves, for others or for themselves and others.

> **Example**
>
> 'Blackacre to Tom and Jerry upon trust to sell the same and hold the net rents and profits until sale and the proceeds of sale upon trust for themselves', or '. . . upon trust for Jack and Jill', or '. . . upon trust for themselves and Jack and Jill', or even '. . . upon trust for Wilma for life and then to Pebbles absolutely'.

If the settlor specifies the shares to which the beneficiaries will be entitled, even if he specifies that they are to take 'equally', then, as we have seen, Tom and Jerry will hold the legal estate as trustees and joint tenants, but the equitable interests will be held by the beneficiaries as tenants in common.

What if, instead of declaring a joint tenancy, a declaration is made in the following terms: 'the purchasers declare that the survivor of them is entitled to give a valid receipt for capital money arising from a disposition of all or part of the property'? Is this a reference to the right of survivorship and proof of an intended joint tenancy – at law and in equity? Sadly not – *Huntingford* v *Hobbs* [1993] 1 FLR 736.

Stack v *Dowden* [2006] 1 FLR 254 (CA, Civ Div)

This is the latest authority on this point. Had Miss Dowden and Mr Stack created a joint tenancy, all that followed would have been straightforward. As it was, the Court had to decide (a) whether there was a joint tenancy in equity or a tenancy in common; (b) the effect of subsequent events; and (c) the proportions of the respective beneficial shares.

The property was a dwellinghouse in London which Miss Dowden and Mr Stack had cohabited for ten years, during which time they had had four children. The house was bought for £190,000 in 1993, of which Miss Dowden had provided £58,000 from her Halifax Building Society account and £67,000 from the proceeds of the sale of a house of which she was the sole legal owner. The remaining £65,000 was provided by way of a mortgage loan from Barclays Bank.

Clearly, then, the parties had contributed to the purchase price in unequal shares which, coupled with the fact that there was no express declaration of trust, meant that Miss Dowden and Mr Stack held as tenants in common from the outset. Therefore a notice of severance served by Miss Dowden in November 2002 was irrelevant.

As regards the proportionate shares, we shall return to this shortly (in Quantification).

Statutory trusts of land

There are several situations in which a trust of land will be imposed by statute, for example where the estate owner dies intestate (without leaving a will) – Administration of Estates Act 1925, s 33(1), and we have already seen the effect of conveying a legal estate to a minor jointly with one or more other persons of full age – Trusts of Land Act 1996, Sched 1, para 1, but the situations in which a trust of land is most commonly imposed are under the Law of Property Act 1925, ss 36(1) and 34(2), that is:

> Where a legal estate (not being settled land) is beneficially limited to or held in trust for any persons as joint tenants, the same shall be held in trust . . . – s 36(1), and

> Where . . . land is expressed to be conveyed to any persons in undivided shares and those persons are of full age, the conveyance shall . . . operate as if the land had been expressed to be conveyed to the grantees, or, if there are more than four grantees, to the four first named in the conveyance, as joint tenants in trust for the persons interested in the land . . . . – s 34(2).

Thus, whenever the legal estate is held by more than one person, it must be held upon a trust of land (except where it is a strict settlement under which the tenant for life is comprised of two or more persons as joint tenants – Settled Land Act 1925, s 19(2)).

Implied trusts of land

It may be that, though there is only one holder of the legal estate, more than one person owns the equitable interests. In such cases a trust of land will be implied. The existence of the additional beneficiary will not always be specified in the conveyance of the legal estate, and, in the absence of anything to the contrary, the presumption is that the owner of the legal estate is also the sole beneficial owner – *Gissing* v *Gissing* [1971] AC 886. However, a beneficial interest can be established for someone other than the legal estate owner by the imposition of an implied, resulting or a constructive trust: but, which one?

Hussey v *Palmer* [1972] 1 WLR 1286

It is more a matter of words than anything else. The two run together. By whatever name it is described, it is a trust imposed by law whenever justice and good conscience require it. It is a liberal process founded upon large principles of equity to be applied in cases where the legal owner cannot conscientiously keep the property for himself alone, but ought to allow another to have the property or the benefit of it or a share in it . . . - Lord Denning.

What is clear, though, is that: 'The trust of a legal estate . . . whether taken in the names of the purchasers and others jointly, or in the names of others without that of the purchaser, whether in one name or several, whether jointly or successive, results to the man who advances the purchase money' – Eyre CB in *Dyer* v *Dyer* [1788] 2 Cox Eq Cas 92.

In addition,

Gissing v *Gissing* [1971] AC 886

A resulting, implied or constructive trust - and it is unnecessary for present purposes to distinguish between these three classes of trusts - is created by a transaction between the trustee and the cestui que trust in connection with the aquisition by the trustee of a legal estate in the land, whenever the trustee has so conducted himself that it would be inequitable to allow him to deny the cestui que trust a beneficial interest in the land acquired. And he will be held so to have conducted himself if by his words or conduct he has induced the cestui que trust to act to his own detriment in the reasonable belief that by so acting he was acquiring a beneficial interest in the land - Lord Diplock.

However, as Peter Gibson LJ stated in *Drake* v *Whipp* [1996] 1 FLR 826, 'a potent source of confusion' was caused by suggestions that it matters not 'whether the terminology used was that of the constructive trust . . . or that of the resulting trust'.

There are no formal requirements for implied, resulting or constructive trusts – LPA, s 53(2).

Resulting trusts

The essential ingredient of both resulting and constructive trusts is common intention, that is an intention common to both parties, the legal estate holder and the claimant to a beneficial interest, that the claimant acquire an *interest in the land* (as opposed to an intention merely to share the occupation of it). However, a crucial distinction between resulting and constructive trusts is that in resulting trusts this common intention is **presumed** from the situations which give rise to the resulting trust. Whenever the legal title to land is purchased in the name of one (or more) person, but is actually paid for – in whole or in part – by another (or others), the title holder will hold on trust for himself and the other contributor in proportions reflecting their contributions.

Example

If David buys 'Teddy Bears' but pays for it with money provided solely by June, David will hold the legal estate on trust for June absolutely. As legal estate holder and trustee, David here has nothing more than a 'paper title': all the true ownership lies with June. (In this situation, where David holds the legal estate but June has the whole of the beneficial interest, a bare(!) trust comes into existence under which David can only deal with Teddy Bears as directed or authorised by June. Should David purport to sell to Bernard, Bernard will only acquire that which David had - a paper title!)

On the other hand, if David buys as above, but pays with money provided as to three-quarters by himself and one-quarter by June, then he would hold the legal estate on trust for himself and June in those proportions. Thus, a 'trust of a legal estate . . . results to the man who advances the purchase-money' - Eyre CB in *Dyer* v *Dyer*, and thereby recognises 'the solid tug of money' - Woodhouse J in *Hofman* v *Hofman* [1965] NZLR 795. If, instead of buying Teddy Bears, David was already the original sole legal and beneficial owner, and he transferred the legal title to June, June would take as sole legal and beneficial owner.

As a general principle in this difficult area of resulting and constructive trusts, the money, for the purpose of resulting trusts, or at least the common intention which lies behind it, must exist **at the time of acquisition of the legal estate**. Payment of the deposit by someone other than the holder of the legal estate would, obviously, raise the presumption of a resulting trust.

Williams & Glyn's Bank Ltd v Boland [1981] AC 487

In this leading case, Mr Boland was the sole legal owner but Mrs Boland claimed that she was entitled to a beneficial interest by virtue of her substantial contributions to the purchase of the matrimonial home. In fact, both Mr and Mrs Boland had been on the legal title of their first home but, on the purchase of their second house, only Mr Boland's name was used. However, Mrs Boland's interest in the first house was transferred to the second, thereby providing her contribution towards the purchase of it at the time of acquisition, and giving rise to a resulting trust in it.

Resulting trusts are founded on contributions of money towards acquisition of the legal title to property: any other forms of contribution should, therefore, fall under constructive trusts. As Peter Gibson LJ stated in *Curley v Parkes* [2004] EWCA Civ 1515, '... a resulting trust crystallises on the date that the property is acquired ... [mortgage] payments commencing a month after the completion of the purchase are not payments of the purchase price'. Thus, if the intention does not arise until after the acquisition of the legal title, there should be no resulting trust: we would then have to consider a constructive trust. Beware, however, because, in *Gissing*, for example, the court accepted a retrospective common intention, implied from *subsequent* conduct: though the interest could not be quantified until later, the common intention was inferred as at the date of acquisition.

The clear distinction which used to exist between resulting and constructive trusts has become blurred as the courts show a:

> new realism ... [in] the increasing judicial acceptance that intentions may not crystallise, either in fact or by retrospective inference, at the point of acquisition of title. Particularly where the process of acquisition is elongated by a mortgage-assisted purchase, the classic theory of resulting trusts that relevant intentions are formulated around the isolated moment of purchase has substantially broken down. It is now widely believed to be artificial – if not indeed untenable – to fashion such phantoms of intention in order to resolve property issues which arise perhaps many years later – Gray (1993, p 387).

Example

Purchase in the name of David, where June paid the deposit, creates a clear resulting trust in favour of June to the extent of the deposit; similarly, if June makes mortgage repayments from the outset. In both these situations the presumption will be that June's contribution was made to give effect to a common intention between David and June that June acquire such an interest in the land. However, if David can show that this was not the case, the presumption will be rebutted.

In *Re Sharpe (a Bankrupt)* [1980] 1 WLR 219, where the 'contribution' was shown to be a loan, there was no resulting trust. It would be the same if the money were proved to have been given by way of a gift – *Cowcher* v *Cowcher* [1972] 1 WLR 425. (However, apparently a loan can *become* a contribution! – see *Risch* v *McFee* (1990) 61 P&CR 42.)

Although a resulting trust is founded in money contributions, this does not always require the handing over of actual 'cash'. For example, under the right to buy under the Housing Act 1985, a local authority tenant may purchase his home at a price which represents a large discount as against the market value. In such cases, the proportion which the discount bears to the value of the property 'results' to the purchasing tenant.

Example

If John, a long-term tenant of a council house, exercises his right to buy, the purchase money being provided by Tom and Sue, his son and daughter-in-law (money which they raised by way of mortgage, the mortgage and the title to the house being in their names), subject to John's right to stay there for the rest of his life, what happens if the relations between them subsequently break down? What interest does John have? This will depend upon the market value of the house at the time of purchase and the price paid for it at that time. Say the house was purchased for £40,000 but it was at the time of acquisition worth £60,000 on the open market. John's interest would be one-third, that of Tom and Sue, two-thirds. Therefore, if the house is now worth £90,000, John would be entitled to £30,000 upon sale, Tom and Sue to £60,000 - *Costello* v *Costello* [1994] EGCS 40.

Tom and Sue raised the £40,000 purchase money by way of mortgage, repayment of which entails payment of interest. However, mortgage monies are treated as having been raised from cash that was available at the time of acquisition: no consideration is given to the interest payments attaching to the mortgage monies.

What would be the situation if Sue had been the council tenant, and she and Tom had purchased the house as joint tenants with a joint mortgage, and the relationship broke down? In *Evans (formerly Newton)* v *Hayward* [1992] NPC 85, the Court of Appeal (following *Springette* v *Defoe* [1992] NPC 34) held that as the Housing Act 1985 is only concerned with the position between the landlord and the tenant, and not to that between Tom and Sue, Tom and Sue are to be treated as having contributed half each to the mortgage. However, the whole of the discount (£14,000) would be credited to Sue as part of her contribution (see also *Kelly* v *Hammersmith LBC* [2004] EWHC 435 (Admin)). The fact that the conveyance was to joint tenants would not alter this.

However, as in all trusts, the beneficiaries can – as between themselves – vary the interests.

Savill v *Goodall* [1992] NPC 153

Cohabitees both claimed to exercise the right to buy under the Housing Act 1980, notwithstanding the fact that it was the woman who was the secure tenant (and could, therefore, have exercised the right for herself). The discount represented 42 per cent of the market value, but, upon the breakdown of the relationship, it was held that both parties had a half share based on contributions. The woman appealed, claiming that the whole of the discount should be credited to her alone, but the Court of Appeal held that when they bought the house the common intention communicated between them was that they should share the beneficial interest equally: where the actual intention of the parties was apparent there was no need to ascertain beneficial interests by reference to contributions.

Whatever 'form' the contribution takes, it must be equivalent to payment towards the acquisition of the property. Therefore, merely paying for things which, though they make the house habitable (such as fuel bills, decoration, gardening), do not go towards acquisition of the legal title, will not give rise to a resulting trust: but it may, as we shall see, very rarely, give rise to a constructive trust. In *Carlton* v *Goodman* [2002] EWCA Civ 545, the Court of Appeal held that although Ms Goodman had facilitated the purchase of the house by entering into a joint mortgage with Carlton, there was no resulting trust in her favour. Why? Because she had made no payments under the mortgage, nor had she made a contribution to the purchase price of the house.

Needless to say, in the area of trusts, we are in the realms of equity, where all equitable maxims apply. One of the most fundamental of all maxims is 'he who comes to equity must come with clean hands'; that is, the claimant must have acted fairly.

Tinsley v Milligan [1994] AC 340

The House of Lords had to consider whether or not to grant an equitable interest in land in light of an illegal transaction by the claimant. Their lordships held (by a bare majority – Lords Keith and Goff dissenting) that where property interests were acquired as a result of an illegal transaction, a party to the illegality could recover by virtue of a legal or equitable proprietary interest if, but only if, he could establish his title without relying upon his own illegality even if it emerged that the title upon which he relied was acquired in the course of carrying through an illegal transaction. Here a cohabiting couple, T and M, jointly purchased a house. In order to enable M (with the knowledge and assent of T) to make false claims for state benefits, the house was registered in the name of T alone. The house was used as a lodging house, run as a joint business venture. It provided most of T and M's income. The benefits obtained by M were shared with T, though they did not form a substantial part of their income. Subsequently, M owned up to the benefit office and they allowed her to continue drawing benefit, this time legally. Some time later T and M had a quarrel and T moved out, leaving M in occupation of the house. T sought possession; M claimed that she was entitled to a half share in the house and sought an order for sale. One of T's grounds was that, applying the maxim 'he who comes to equity must come with clean hands', the court ought to leave the estate to lie where it fell, namely with T! On the facts, the court found M had established a resulting trust by showing she had contributed to the purchase price of the house and that there was a common understanding between her and T that they owned the house equally. *Tinsley* v *Milligan* was considered by the Court of Appeal in *Tribe* v *Tribe* [1995] 3 WLR 913, and applied by the Court of Appeal in *Lowson* v *Coombes* (1999) 77 P&CR D25.

See also Millett LJ's judgment in *Twinsectra Limited* v *Yardley* [2002] 2 WLR 802, which provides 'a valuable debate on the true nature of resulting trusts, on their proper classification and on their role in reversing unjust enrichment' – Mummery LJ in *Carlton* v *Goodman*.

The presumption of advancement

Where equity imposes a moral duty upon one party to provide for the other, for example a husband to support his wife (though not a wife to support her husband), or a father his child, the doctrine of advancement raises a presumption of a gift so that the equitable interests follow the legal title. Thus, even a voluntary conveyance (one for no consideration) of the legal estate will pass the whole of the beneficial interest: no resulting trust will arise in favour of the husband or father who provided the purchase money. The same presumption would arise had H purchased the property in the joint names of himself and W – they would hold the equitable interests equally and jointly. The presumption does not apply to unmarried couples.

The presumption of advancement can be rebutted by evidence to the contrary.

Sekhon v *Alissa* [1989] 2 FLR 94

A house was conveyed into the sole name of a daughter, notwithstanding the fact that her mother had provided the majority of the purchase price. Evidence was brought showing that the mother's contribution was made in order to gain her a tax advantage, which led Hoffmann J to hold that there was no intention by the mother to pass the whole beneficial interest to her daughter. There was, therefore, no advancement.

Today, it is rare for the presumption of a resulting trust to be rebutted by the presumption of advancement. However, if there is no such presumption, a resulting trust must arise unless some other intent is proved.

Tribe v *Tribe* [1995] 3 WLR 913

This case did, however, raise the issue of presumption of advancement. The case concerned a voluntary transfer of shares for an illegal purpose. Since the transfer had been made between a father and his son for no consideration, the presumption of advancement applied unless the transferee (the defendant son) could rebut it. It was held that in a case where no presumption of advancement arose a transferor could recover property transferred without consideration if he could do so without reliance on an illegality and could show an intention to retain a beneficial interest in the property, and that that exception applied where the presumption of advancement arose but the illegal purpose which the transferor had to rely on in order to rebut the presumption had not been carried into effect in any way. On the facts, as the illegal purpose had never been carried into effect the plaintiff father was entitled to lead evidence to rebut the presumption of advancement. He succeeded: the son held the shares on trust for the father.

Constructive trusts

It used to be said that whilst resulting trusts arose by operation of law, irrespective of the parties' intentions, constructive trusts were imposed whenever good conscience required it, but, in fact, in *both* types of trust the crucial element is the intention of the parties – whether expressed or implied. Indeed, in the case of constructive trusts, the issue of whether the intention is express or implied is vital as each gives rise to a different situation.

Lloyds Bank plc v Rosset [1990] 1 All ER 1111

After much difficulty and uncertainty in this area, the House of Lords attempted to provide some clarity. Lord Bridge explained that,

> The first and fundamental question which must always be resolved is whether, independently of any inference to be drawn from the conduct of the parties in the course of sharing the house as their home and managing their affairs, there has at any time prior to acquisition, or exceptionally at some later date, been any agreement, arrangement or understanding reached between them that the property is to be shared beneficially. The finding of an agreement or arrangements to share in this sense can only, I think, be based on evidence of express discussions between the partners, however imperfectly remembered and however imprecise their terms may have been. Once a finding to this effect is made it will only be necessary for the partner asserting a claim to a beneficial interest against the partner entitled to the legal estate to show that he or she has acted to his or her detriment or significantly altered his or her position in reliance on the agreement in order to give rise to a constructive trust or proprietary estoppel.
>
> In sharp contrast with this situation is the very different one where there is no evidence to support a finding of an agreement or arrangement to share, however reasonable it might have been for the parties to reach such an arrangement if they had applied their minds to the question, and where the court must rely entirely on the conduct of the parties both as the basis from which to infer a common intention to share the property beneficially and as the conduct relied on to give rise to a constructive trust. In this situation direct contributions to the purchase price by the partner who is not the legal owner, whether initially or by payment of mortgage instalments, will readily justify the inference necessary to the creation of a constructive trust. But, as I read the authorities, it is at least extremely doubtful whether anything less will do.

Therefore, as Nourse LJ explained in *Grant v Edwards* [1986] 1 Ch 638:

> In most of these cases the fundamental, and invariably the most difficult, question is to decide whether there was the necessary common intention, being something which can only be inferred from the conduct of the parties, almost always from the expenditure incurred by them respectively. In this regard the court has to look for expenditure which is referable to the acquisition of the house . . . If it is found to have been incurred, such expenditure will perform the twofold function of establishing the common intention and showing that the claimant has acted upon it.
>
> There is another and rarer class of case, of which the present may be one, where, although there has been no writing, the parties have orally declared themselves in such a way as to make their common intention plain. Here the court does not have to look for conduct from which the intention can be inferred, but only for conduct which amounts to an acting upon it by the claimaint. And although that conduct can undoubtedly be the incurring of expenditure which is referable to the acquisition of the house, it need not necessarily be so.

Drake v Whipp [1996] 1 FLR 826

Here, Peter Gibson LJ pointed out that whether 'the terminology used is that of the constructive trust to which the intention, actual or imputed, of the parties is crucial, or that of the resulting trust which operates as a presumed intention of the contributing party in the absence of rebutting evidence of actual intention', is of great importance. His lordship went on to state that all that is required for the creation of a constructive trust is that there should be a common intention that the party who was not the legal owner should have a beneficial interest and that that party should act to his or her detriment in reliance thereon. Given the clear view that their lordships had formed that this was a case of constructive trust, 'it would be artificial in the extreme to proceed to decide the appeal on the false footing that the parties' shares were to be determined in accordance with the law of resulting trusts'. His lordship accepted the plaintiff's counsel's view that in constructive trust cases, the court could adopt a broad brush approach to determining the respective shares. Returning to this point in *Curley v Parkes*, Peter Gibson LJ explained that, 'In a constructive trust case one looks at the entire conduct of the parties and a broader approach as to what constitutes contributions is appropriate. Thus it is clear that payments of mortgage instalments would constitute relevant contributions to be taken into account.' On the facts, Ms Drake could have argued for a constructive trust and a 50 per cent share: however, she opted to rely solely on a resulting trust. On all the facts she was held to be entitled to one third of the proceeds of sale.

In *Curley v Parkes*, Peter Gibson LJ stated that '[with] the modern reliance on mortgage finance the importance of the resulting trust has diminished, and instead reliance is generally placed on a constructive trust where an agreement or common intention can be found or inferred from all the circumstances . . .' This illustrates just how important it is not only to get the terminology right, but also to found a claim under the correct form of trust.

However, the Court of Appeal, in *Oxley v Hiscock* [2004] 3 WLR 715, stated *per curiam* that,

> once it is recognised that what the court is doing . . . is to supply or impute a common intention as to the parties' respective shares (in circumstances in which there was, in fact, no common intention) on the basis of that which, in the light of all the material circumstances (including the acts and conduct of the parties after the acquisition), is shown to be fair, it seems to me very difficult to avoid the conclusion that an analysis in terms of proprietary estoppel will, necessarily, lead to the same result; and that it may be more satisfactory to accept that there is no difference between constructive trust and proprietary estoppel – Chadwick LJ at p 748.

Here we go again!

Express common intention

It is this type of constructive trust that Lord Bridge referred to in the first paragraph quoted above from *Rosset*.

The Court of Appeal, in *Eves v Eves* [1975] 1 WLR 1338, inferred an express common intention where, at the time of purchase, the defendant told the plaintiff that the house was to be their joint home and that it would have been conveyed into their joint names had she been of age (which she was not).

Grant v *Edwards* [1986] 1 Ch 638

Here, again, an express intention was inferred from the defendant telling the plaintiff that 'her name was not going onto the title because it would cause some prejudice in the matrimonial proceedings between her and her husband', from which 'it is clear that there was a common intention that the plaintiff was to have some sort of proprietary interest in [the house]' – Nourse LJ. However his Lordship went on:

> The more difficult question is whether there was conduct on her part which amounted to an acting upon that intention or, to put it more precisely, conduct on which she could not reasonably have been expected to embark unless she was to have an interest in the house. . . . it is in my view an inevitable inference that the very substantial contribution which the plaintiff made out of her earnings . . . to the housekeeping and to the feeding and to the bringing up of the children enabled the defendant to keep down the instalments payable under both mortgages out of his own income and, moreover, that he could not have done that if he had had to bear the whole of the other expenses as well. For example, in 1973, when he and the plaintiff were earning about £1,200 each, the defendant had to find a total of about £643 between the two mortgages. I do not see how he would have been able to do that had it not been for the plaintiff's very substantial contribution to the other expenses.

The woman in *Eves* was awarded a one-quarter share, Ms Grant one-half. We must contrast the situation of the woman in *Grant* v *Edwards* with that of Mrs Burns.

Burns v *Burns* [1984] Ch 371

Mrs Burns's 'contribution' amounted to making gifts of clothing and other things to the defendant and the children; paying for the housekeeping, the rates and the telephone bills; buying a dishwasher, a washing machine, a tumble dryer and 'either a drawing room suite or three armchairs and a bed', and providing doorknobs and door furnishings. Fox LJ found that 'None of this expenditure . . . indicates the existence of the common intention which the plaintiff has to prove. What is needed, I think, is evidence of a payment or payments by the plaintiff that can be inferred was referable to the acquisition of the house'. Mrs Burns, unlike Mrs Grant, could not show anything from which the court could infer an express common intention that she have an interest in the house. Her 'contribution' was not 'bricks and mortar' – it did not relate directly to the acquisition or improvement of the house, so there could be no implied common intention. Nothing on the facts raised an estoppel. Despite her name, Mrs Burns was not married to Mr Burns – a fact which caused May LJ to remark, 'When one compares this ultimate result with what it would have been had she been married to the defendant, and taken appropriate steps under the Matrimonial Causes Act 1973, I think that she can justifiably say that fate has not been kind to her'.

These cases also illustrate the fact that, unlike the presumption of advancement, these equitable principles apply regardless of the relationship between the parties – as do those governing resulting trusts. Indeed, the case of *Hammond* v *Mitchell* [1992] 2 All ER 109 concerned a mistress's claim to an interest in the house in which she lived with her cohabitee. Legal title had been conveyed to the man only: he had given several reasons for this and had assured his mistress that she need not 'fear for the future because when we are married [the house] will be half yours anyway . . .'. As in *Eves* v *Eves* and *Grant* v *Edwards*, the man's excuses for not putting the woman's name on the title were held to be an express common intention that she have a proprietary interest in the house. This having been established, the woman had only to show detrimental reliance which freed the man up to make the mortgage repayments. This the court found by virtue of the fact that she:

> gave her full support on two occasions to speculative ventures which, had they turned out unfavourably, might have involved the entire bungalow property being sold up to repay the bank an indebtedness to which the house and land were all committed up to the hilt.

In postponing any right she may have had in the property to the interest of the bank she had acted to her detriment. She was awarded a one-half share (though in regard to another property she got nothing, no excuse having been given in regard to it). The difficulty with this case is, however, that at the time of acting to her detriment, the woman appears to have had no interest in the land – she was not then married to the man. She seems to have been merely a licensee and the decision of Waite J to grant her a half share in the property sits uneasily with Lord Bridge's statement in *Rosset*. As Patrick O'Hagan (1993) says:

> ... by agreeing to risk a bare licence, [the woman] obtained a proprietary interest.

(See also *Clough* v *Killey*, 7 March 1996, unreported, Lexis transcript, where, again, the woman was awarded a half share.)

In *Mollo* v *Mollo* [1999] EGCS 117, an actual, as opposed to an inferred, express common intention was found. The claimant, having established the necessary agreement, the court 'was free to look at all his contributions, direct or otherwise, when determining the size of his share'. Part-payment of the deposit (which did not create a resulting trust, due to the fact that the house was being purchased 'for the boys', ie the claimant's sons by the claimant and his ex-wife), physical labour in renovating the house and spending £20,000 of his own money for that purpose provided the contribution.

It has been said that, post *Grant* v *Edwards*, there is no difference between a constructive trust arising from an express common intention and proprietary estoppel. However, this is not so: see *Jones* v *Jones* [1977] 1WLR 438, but the line is now a very fine one. In *Mollo*, though his interest was upheld by way of an express common intention constructive trust, the court held the father's claim could alternatively be founded on the doctrine of proprietary estoppel, and in *Birmingham Midshires Mortgage Services Ltd* v *Sabherwal* (2000) 80 P&CR 256, the Court of Appeal held that in the context of the family home the concepts of constructive or resulting trusts, however labelled, were almost interchangeable with equitable estoppel. However, it was also held that the creation of a constructive or resulting trust leaves no room for a separate interest by way of equitable estoppel.

As we saw in Chapter 2I, it was held in *Yaxley* v *Gotts* [2000] 1 All ER 711 that a written agreement which was unenforceable under the Law of Property (Miscellaneous Provisions) Act 1989 was enforceable by way of this type of constructive trust. Indeed, a valid written agreement would avoid the necessity of 'the tortuous complications' of this area of the law – Ward LJ in *Carlton* v *Goodman*. In the same case Ward LJ made the following heartfelt plea:

> I ask in despair how often this court has to remind conveyancers that they would save their clients a great deal of later difficulty if only they would sit the purchasers down, explain the difference between a joint tenancy and a tenancy in common, ascertain what they want

and then expressly declare in the conveyance or transfer how the beneficial interest is to be held because that will be conclusive and save all argument. When are conveyancers going to do this as a matter of invariable standard practice? This court has urged that time after time. Perhaps conveyancers do not read the law reports. I will try one more time: ALWAYS TRY TO AGREE ON AND THEN RECORD HOW THE BENEFICIAL INTEREST IS TO BE HELD [sic]. It is not very difficult to do.

Hear! Hear!

Implied common intention

As we have seen, if there is an express common intention, as in *Eves* v *Eves* and *Grant* v *Edwards*, the person seeking an interest must show detrimental reliance. Such cases are rare. If the court is to imply a common intention it must look to the party's conduct, which usually means contribution. If it is to raise the presumption of a common intention, such contribution must be towards the 'bricks and mortar' of the house.

Passee v *Passee* (1988) 18 Fam Law 132

This is a good case to illustrate the necessary kind of contribution. A house was purchased in the sole name of the plaintiff. The defendant and her (by then deceased) daughter had both contributed to the mortgage repayments, and other relatives had paid the running costs of the house. It was held that though the relatives' 'contributions' created no beneficial interest in the house, those of the defendant and her daughter did, the daughter's estate being entitled to 10 per cent, the defendant to 30 per cent and the plaintiff to 60 per cent.

However, the mere fact that A spends money or labour on B's property does not, in the absence of express agreement or a common intention inferred from the circumstances, entitle A to an interest in the property.

Thomas v *Fuller-Brown* [1988] 1 FLR 237

Here, A had carried out work which

> was obviously quite substantial ... he designed and constructed a two-storey extension, created a through lounge, carried out minor electrical and plumbing works, replastered and redecorated the property throughout, landscaped and reorganised the garden, laid a driveway, carried out repairs to the chimney and the roof and repointed the gable end of the property, constructed an internal entry hall at the property, rebuilt the kitchen and installed a new stairway – Slade LJ.

The house had been purchased in B's sole name, A having made no contribution to the household expenses. When B obtained a home improvement grant, A carried out the above work in return for his keep. The Court of Appeal, being of the view that what A had done was no more than any man would do about the house, held he had acquired no interest! Similarly, in *Burns* v *Burns*, the traditional 'wifely' role of looking after the house, having and raising children was held not to suffice either. (Contrast this outcome with that in *Mollo*, where an express common intention was shown.)

Perhaps the best explanation of what will amount to acceptable contribution for the purpose of establishing the necessary common intention is given to us by May LJ in *Burns* v *Burns*.

Burns v Burns [1984] Ch 317

Here

> [t]here was no express trust of an interest in the property for the benefit of the plaintiff; and there was no express agreement to create such an interest. And the plaintiff made no direct contribution to the purchase price. Her case, therefore, must depend upon showing a common intention that she should have a beneficial interest in the property – Fox LJ.

May LJ explains:

> I think the approach which the courts should follow, be the couples married or unmarried, is now clear. What is difficult, however, is to apply it to the facts and circumstances of any given case ... The inquiry becomes even more difficult when the home is taken in only one of the two names. For present purposes I will assume that it is the man, although the same approach will be followed if it is taken in the name of the woman. Where a matrimonial or family home is bought in the man's name alone on mortgage by the mechanism of deposit and instalments, then if the woman pays or contributes to the initial deposit this points to a common intention that she should have *some* beneficial interest in the house. If thereafter she makes direct contributions to the instalments, then the case is *a fortiori* and her rightful share is likely to be greater. If the woman, having contributed to the deposit, but although not making direct contributions to the instalments, nonetheless uses her own money for other joint household expenses so as to enable the man the more easily to pay the mortgage instalments out of his money, then her position is the same. Where a woman has made no contribution to the initial deposit, but makes regular and substantial contributions to the mortgage instalments, it may still be reasonable to infer a common intention that she should share the beneficial interest from the outset or a fresh agreement after the original conveyance that she should acquire such a share. It is only when there is no evidence upon which a court can reasonably show an inference about the extent of the share of the contributing woman, that it should fall back on the maxim 'equity is equality'. Finally, when the house is taken in the man's name alone, if the woman makes no 'real' or 'substantial' financial contribution towards either the purchase price, deposit or mortgage instalments by means of which the family home was acquired, then she is not entitled to any share in the beneficial interest in that home even though over a very substantial number of years she may have worked just as hard as the man in maintaining the family in the sense of keeping the house, giving birth to and looking after and helping to bring up the children of the union.

In other words, only contributions to acquisition of the property will do: mere contributions to the relationship and to the children thereof will not suffice. On the facts May LJ found, regretfully, that 'it is clear the plaintiff falls into the last of the categories'.

Notwithstanding Lord Bridge's apparent limitation purely to monetary contributions (in the second paragraph quoted from *Rosset* earlier), constructive trusts are imposed whenever it would be inequitable to allow a legal owner to defeat or deny an equitable interest. Thus, a claim based on another form of contribution *may* be possible. Of course, an alternative basis for the claim could be proprietary estoppel on the facts of the case. Whilst it accords with the modern view of resulting trusts, Lord Bridge's *obiter* remark in *Rosset* that 'it is at least extremely doubtful whether anything less [than direct contribution to the purchase price] will do', it is **not** supported by implied common intention constructive trust authority.

Contribution is relevant not only for raising the presumption of a common intention, and thus a resulting or constructive trust under which the legal owner holds the property on trust for himself and the contributor, but also to quantify the beneficial interest. Once contribution is established, the proportion which the contributor's interest bears to that of the legal owner is calculated by reference to the common intention and contribution, each of the parties being 'entitled in equity to an undivided share in the house, the share being in proportion to his or her respective contribution' – Lord Denning in *Bull* v *Bull*. However, as the Court of Appeal made clear in *Lightfoot* v *Lightfoot-Brown* [2005] EWCA Civ 201, the mere fact of payment towards property can not give rise to an equitable interest in it unless there is some understanding or arrangement to that effect between the parties. As Arden LJ explained, Chadwick LJ (in *Hiscock* v *Oxley*)

> did not dispense with the requirement for communication of the common intention when determining whether a constructive trust had arisen. Indeed, the concept of communication of common intention has much in common with the manifestation of intention. An intention to share a beneficial interest in property has to be manifested to give rise to a rival obligation ... [t]he need for communication was only held to be unnecessary in the *Oxley* case in respect of the size of the parties' beneficial interest.

In *Re Gorman (a Bankrupt)* [1990] 1 WLR 616, an equitable joint tenancy was implied, but not by way of a resulting or a constructive trust! A husband and wife bought a house as their matrimonial home, a third of the purchase price having been provided by the wife's father as a gift to her. The balance of the purchase price was raised on mortgage granted to a building society by both H and W. The transfer which conveyed the property to them declared that they were entitled to the beneficial interest in the property but it did not specify whether they were to hold as beneficial joint tenants or tenants in common. It did, however, state that 'the survivor of them can give a valid receipt for capital moneys arising on a disposition of the land'. The court held that this declaration was consistent only with a joint tenancy and that H and W were, therefore, beneficial joint tenants (though the husband's subsequent bankruptcy severed their interest, making them tenants in common). See, however, *Huntingford* v *Hobbs* [1993] IFLR 736.

The cash value of the interest is calculated at the date of sale or other realisation of the property – *Turton* v *Turton* [1987] 3 WLR 622. This is crucial, for in a falling property market the value of an interest may well have fallen below the amount of the contributions. See *Cheese* v *Thomas* [1944] 1 All ER 35.

Remember, constructive and resulting trusts are exempt from the formal requirements of the Law of Property Act 1925, s 53, and can, therefore, arise from merely oral declarations, as we have seen in the above cases.

In registered land, interests acquired in this way are minor interests.

Beneficiaries in any trust of land can plead the equitable doctrine of *laches* as a defence in an action against their trustees, as the Court of Appeal made clear in *Patel* v *Shah* [2005] 08 EG 190. Under the doctrine, the statutory limitation periods for actions may be lengthened or shortened where it would be inequitable to apply them (indeed, per Limitation Act 1980, s 21(1), there is no limitation period on claims by beneficiaries to recover trust property from a fraudulent trustee). However,

> mere delay alone will almost never suffice, ... the court has to look at all the circumstances ... and then decide whether the balance of justice or injustice is in favour of granting the remedy or withholding it. If substantial prejudice will be suffered by the defendant, it is not necessary for the defendant to prove that it was caused by the delay. On the other hand,

the plaintiff's knowledge that the delay will cause such prejudice is a factor to be taken into account – Laddie J in *Nelson* v *Rye* [1996] 1 WLR 1378.

The LA 1980, s 36(2) actually preserves the doctrine of *laches*.

Quantification

Having found an equitable interest in the property, the court must then quantify it.

As Peter Gibson LJ made clear in *Drake* v *Whipp* [1996] 1 FLR 826, whilst helpful (not to say desirable!), it is not necessary for the parties to have any common intention as to their proportionate shares in the property: indeed, the court should not impute such an intention from one party to the other. We have already seen, in *Midland Bank plc* v *Cooke* [1995] 4 All ER 562, where no such common intention is evident (but a resulting trust is presumed), that the court can take a 'broad brush approach' to quantifying the interests, taking all the circumstances into account – direct and indirect contributions, including non-monetary contributions such as labour or household duties, any intention of the parties, the length of their relationship, the conduct of the parties, etc.

However, as Peter Gibson LJ explained in *Clough* v *Killey*, 7 March 1996, CA, unreported (Lexis transcript), where such a common intention **does exist**, for example where the parties had actually formulated a common intention as to their respective beneficial interests, the court is **not** permitted to take an 'unscientific' approach to quantifying the beneficial interests. Therefore, the *Cooke* and *Whipp* approach is only to be adopted where the parties had not agreed a formula for quantifying their respective shares.

In *Baker* v *Baker*, as we saw, the father claimed an equitable interest by way of a resulting trust. At first instance, the judge had ordered the full repayment of the money provided by the father, but the Court of Appeal stated that the correct basis for assessing the sum to be paid was to calculate the value of the father's right to occupy rent-free accommodation for the rest of his life. As Dillon LJ explained:

> In some cases of equitable estoppel, the course taken by the court to satisfy the equity had been to order the defendant to repay the plaintiff's expenditure. That was the course the judge followed in this present case.
>
> However, the gift in the present case was directed to achieving two aims: the provision of a family home as well as rent-free accommodation for his life for the plaintiff.

The Court of Appeal in *Sledmore* v *Dalby* (1996) 72 P&CR 196 stated that the court's function in determining the extent of the equity created by a proprietary estoppel is especially important as its effect is permanent: the extent of the equity has to make good, so far as may fairly be done between the parties, the expectations which were encouraged. The court should ask itself whether it is still inequitable for the expectation to be defeated, bearing in mind the effect of the continuing estoppel upon the legal owner. On the facts it was held that the effect of any equity had long since been exhausted and no injustice had been done by permitting the enforcement of the legal owner's rights.

This being so, it was held that the plaintiff had lost merely the right to rent-free accommodation for the rest of his life and that was the basis for quantifying his right. This shows how essential it is in assessing entitlement under proprietary estoppel to **go back to the beginning, to the promise or representation**. The detrimental reliance merely brings proprietary estoppel into operation: it is the promise relied upon which lays down the entitlement.

Similarly, with constructive trusts, we must go back to the common intention as expressed, or as evidenced by substantial bricks and mortar contribution which gave rise to the implied common intention. However, as with proprietary estoppel, the courts will always use their discretion in the way that best results in an equitable outcome for all concerned.

Pritchard Englefield v *Steinberg* [2005] 1 P&CR DG 2

PE was claiming possession of a house, lived in by Mrs Steinberg (S), Jonathan's (JS) mother. S claimed that she had a lease or a licence under which she could live, rent free, in the house for life, or, alternatively, that JS held the property on constructive trust to allow her to occupy rent free until she died (and, if the latter claim was correct, it would provide an overriding interest which would be binding on PE). Peter Smith J held that, on the facts, there was no lease and 'a mere licence would not be sufficient to bind a third party': but the claim to constructive trust was upheld, and it would have been binding on PE. However, on the facts, the judge held that the most equitable outcome to all concerned would be achieved by ordering sale of the house, and the priorities for payment from the net proceeds of sale would be as follows: the Bank (mortgagee), S's life interest (to be valued actuarially and capitalised accordingly), PE's costs and charges, and the service arrears. Any remaining amount would be payable to JS (who was liable to pay the costs of the proceedings).

With a resulting trust the common intention is presumed, based upon the contributions made. If not rebutted, the contribution defines the interest. Of course, this is rather simplistic! The further reading detailed below provides excellent in-depth discussion of this area.

Midland Bank plc v *Cooke* [1995] 4 All ER 562

Here the Court of Appeal had to consider the correct approach to be taken on the facts to Mrs Cooke's beneficial interest. Mr and Mrs Cooke married in 1971 and moved into a house purchased in his sole name for £8,500. The purchase price was financed by a mortgage of £6,450, a wedding gift from Mr Cooke's parents of £1,000 and Mr Cooke's savings. At first instance, the judge held that Mrs Cooke's beneficial interest rested solely upon her monetary contributions to the purchase price, namely her half share of the £1,000 wedding gift: her proportionate share in the property was, on this basis, 6.74 per cent. Mrs Cooke appealed and the Court of Appeal held that she was entitled to a beneficial half interest in the matrimonial home: on the proper facts of the case, and considering the whole course of dealings between Mr and Mrs Cooke, it was clear that the couple's presumed intention was to share the beneficial interest in the property in equal shares (an intention reinforced by other proceedings). Waite LJ stated that,

> the duty of the judge is to undertake a survey of the whole course of dealings between the parties relevant to their ownership and occupation of the property and their sharing of its burdens and advantages. That scrutiny will not confine itself to the limited range of acts of direct contribution of the sort that are needed to found a beneficial interest in the first place. It will take into consideration all conduct which throws light on the question what shares were intended.

Of course, here the parties were married to each other and therefore it is unsurprising that any wedding gifts were deemed to be given to both parties equally, or that the court presumed the intention between them that it did. What this case does show is the importance of fully considering **all** of the facts of a case – the various kinds of contribution, the relationship between the contributors, any agreements or declarations made by them, any course of dealing between them, any collateral or subsequent matters which may reflect back upon the presumed intention of the parties, etc.

It is important to appreciate the effect of negative equity, which can leave an interestholder with a share of the debt rather than of profit, that is a share of the liability rather than an asset.

Cheese v *Thomas* [1994] 1 All ER 35

Mr Cheese, aged 85, put nearly all his savings towards the purchase of a house which was to be held in the sole name of Mr Thomas, his great nephew, Mr Cheese being promised a home for life. Mr Thomas borrowed £40,000 for the balance of the purchase price and granted a mortgage to the lender. Mr Thomas defaulted on the mortgage and the mortgagees sold the house for just £55,400. Although he succeeded in a claim of undue influence against his relative, Mr Cheese had to bear the loss in proportion of his contribution of £43,000. In these situations, the larger your contribution to the cost of the house, the larger your share of the debt. If advising a client like Mr Cheese, therefore, you would do best by him to argue against any interest in the house at all!

As Collins J explained in *Re Byford* [2004] 1 P&CR 12, the guiding principle when quantifying an equitable interest is that neither party can take the benefit of an increase in the value of the property without making an allowance for what has been expended by the other. On the facts, the appellant, having paid half of the mortgage interest repayments, was entitled to credit for that. In its endeavour to do broad justice or equity between co-owners, an occupation rent against the spouse in residence was payable to the excluded spouse.

Finally, do not forget that quantification arises only once a beneficial interest has been found under a resulting and/or constructive trust. As the outcome can vary enormously depending on whether a resulting or a constructive trust is used as the basis for quantification, it is essential to base a claim on the correct one. Nowhere is this illustrated more clearly than in *Drake* v *Whipp*.

Drake v *Whipp* [1996] 1 FLR 826

In 1988, Mrs Drake and Mr Whipp, a cohabiting but unmarried couple, bought a barn which they intended to convert into a dwellinghouse. Mrs Drake contributed 40 per cent and Mr Whipp 60 per cent to the purchase price, but only Mr Whipp's name appeared on the title. As well as the 40 per cent input, Mrs Drake also paid some £13,000 towards the cost of the conversion and contributed a further estimated 30 per cent of the total labour. She also bought their food and paid for all the household expenses, the household accounts and tax and insurance on her car, which Mr Whipp paid for. Their salaries were paid into a joint account.

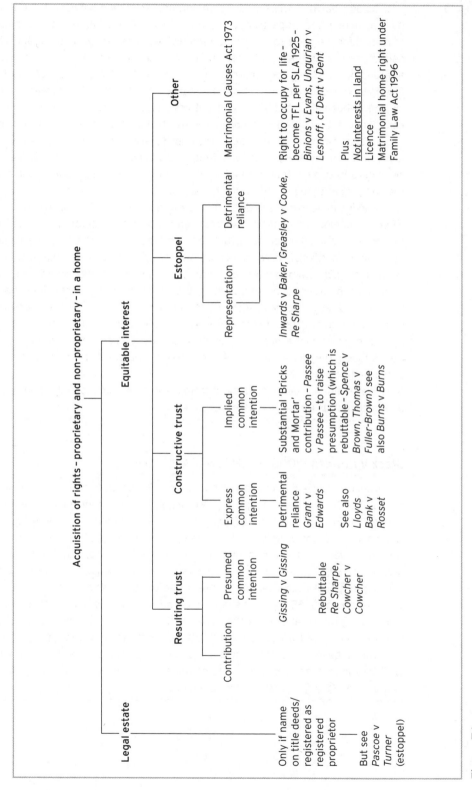

Figure 7.1

It being clear that there was a common understanding between them that each was to have a share in the property, but as the actual size of the shares had not been discussed, it remained for the court to quantify their individual interests. At first instance, Mrs Drake was held to have a 19.4 per cent share under a resulting trust. However, the Court of Appeal awarded her a 33 per cent share under a constructive trust. In the Court of Appeal, Peter Gibson LJ found it 'remarkable' in the first place that Mrs Drake had pleaded a resulting trust, which had been accepted by the court at first instance notwithstanding there was an agreed common intention between the parties in reliance upon which Mrs Drake had made substantial direct and indirect contributions. His lordship also pointed out the confusion made by the judge between constructive and resulting trusts, caused 'in part' by the judge's failure to consider Lord Bridge's categories in *Rosset* - the first as a constructive trust, the second as a resulting trust (though Lord Bridge himself seems to have confused the two).

In making it clear that the distinction between resulting and constructive trusts is crucial when calculating the beneficial shares, Peter Gibson LJ reiterated the requirements for an express common intention constructive trust - the finding of an express common intention between the parties of shared beneficial ownership in the property, plus an act of detrimental reliance on that common intention by the party not on the title. Only where such a common intention can **not** be found should the court infer a resulting trust from initial financial contributions towards the acquisition of the property: no finding of a common intention, no constructive trust. Once a common intention, and thus a constructive trust, is found, the court can ascertain the individual beneficial shares at its discretion. Where no common intention is found, the shares are quantified solely on the basis of the initial contribution to the purchase price.

However, not all claims will benefit from the express common intention constructive trust approach. Let us return to a case we saw earlier.

Stack v *Dowden* [2006] 1 FLR 254 (CA, Civ Div)

To recap, the house in question was bought in 1993 for £190,000, of which Miss Dowden had paid £125,000, the remaining £65,000 being met by a mortgage advance. As Elizabeth Cooke (2005) says, 'A resulting trust would have suited Miss Dowden nicely', as under that she would have got exactly what she had paid in. However, 'the reasoning of the Court of Appeal ... was that there was, of course, a trust in this case; and it must be a constructive trust. Chadwick LJ therefore moves straight to the consideration of quantum, without pausing to actually consider the nature of the trust'. Another mystery is why Miss Dowden was seeking only a 65 per cent share - less than she had actually contributed.

Following the breakdown of their relationship, Mr Stack had moved out of the house and Miss Dowden undertook to pay him £900 per month for nine months by way of compensation. The judge at first instance held that she must continue to pay this sum after that period until the house was sold. The Court of Appeal reversed this order and Miss Dowden was awarded the 65 per cent share she asked for.

Statutory rights

Whilst anyone can acquire an interest in land by virtue of the equitable principles, regardless of the relationship between them, additional rights are provided by various statutes for spouses, fiancés and civil partners.

Under the Matrimonial Proceedings and Property Act 1970, s 37:

> where a husband or wife contributes any money or money's worth to the improvement of real or personal property in which or in the proceeds of sale of which either or both of them has or have a beneficial interest, the husband or wife so contributing shall, if the contribution is of a substantial nature and subject to any agreement between them to the contrary expressed or implied, be treated as having then acquired by virtue of his or her contribution a share or an enlarged share in that beneficial interest . . .

Thus, under s 37 a spouse may acquire an actual interest in the land or in the proceeds of sale. If the spouse already has an interest, that may be enlarged. It is not only married couples who can benefit under s 37, however, for the Law Reform (Miscellaneous Provisions) Act 1970, s 2, provides that:

> where an agreement to marry is terminated, any rule of law relating to the rights of husbands and wives in relation to property in which either or both has or have a beneficial interest, including any such rule as explained by section 37 of the Matrimonial Proceedings and Property Act 1970, shall apply, in relation to any property in which either or both of the parties to the agreement had a beneficial interest while the agreement was in force, as it applies in relation to property in which a husband or wife has a beneficial interest.

Where a marriage, rather than an engagement, has ended, that is, upon divorce, the Matrimonial Causes Act 1973, s 24 provides the court with the discretion to rearrange the respective rights in the property of the spouses so as to preserve, so far as it possibly can, the spouses' rights prior to the divorce. As Lord Denning said in *Hanlon* v *Law Society* [1981] AC 124:

> In the property adjustment order (under ss 23 and 24 of the Matrimonial Causes Act 1973) we have a new concept altogether. The court takes the rights and obligations of the parties all together, and puts the pieces into a mixed bag. Such pieces are the right to occupy the matrimonial home or have a share in it, the obligations to maintain the wife and children, and so forth. The court then takes out the pieces and hands them to the two parties, some to one party and some to the other, so that each can provide for the future with the pieces allotted to him or to her. The court hands them out without paying any too nice a regard to their legal or equitable rights but simply according to what is the fairest provision for the future, for mother and father and the children.

In exercising its power under s 24, the court 'notionally pools all the assets and redistributes them in such a way as to produce as little change in real terms as possible' – Donaldson LJ in the same case.

Section 77 of and Schedule 5 to the Civil Partnership Act 2004 make provision for financial relief, in connection with civil partnerships, that corresponds to provision made for financial relief in connection with marriages in Part 2 of the Matrimonial Causes Act 1973, and application on dissolution or death.

Any order made by the court under the Matrimonial Proceedings and Property Act 1970, s 37, actually affects beneficial interests in the land itself, acting as a charge on the other spouse's estate or interest therein.

In registered land, either statutory right exists as a minor interest only.

While a marriage is subsisting there is not, either at law or in equity, any prefer-ential treatment of the spouses with regard to the acquisition of their interest, if any, in the matrimonial home. Any claim to such will, therefore, be based on the same principles as for anyone else. Thus a spouse, if not a holder of the legal estate, can only acquire an interest in equity by way of a resulting or constructive trust, or by estoppel. However, as between themselves, as Gray and Symes (1981) point out, such principles do place the male spouse in an advantageous position because:

> any law which recognises financial contribution as the basis of beneficial entitlement must inevitably generate injustice in the family context. The doctrine of resulting trust (even in its refined form in *Gissing* v *Gissing*) has the effect of working discrimination against wives, for the married woman's financial contributions towards the acquisition of property are usually restricted not only by reason of the sexual imbalance of the labour market, but also because of her fluctuation between periods of gainful employment and active motherhood. Her purely domestic contribution (in looking after the home and caring for children) are not cognisable within the strictures of our law of property. Ironically, it is only when a mar-riage terminates in divorce or death that such contributions become relevant in determining proprietary rights in the matrimonial assets. In the normal case, the spouses never think in terms of beneficial ownership when using indiscriminately mixed family funds in the purchase of real property during the course of a happy marriage. Their benefi-cial entitlements are left to be determined later (if at all) according to the unsympathetic principles of the law of property and the law of trusts – p 249.

Once a marriage breaks down it is possible for the courts, under the Matrimonial Causes Act 1973, s 26, to order a property adjustment between the divorced or divorcing spouses. The court has a wide discretion and in deciding whether to make an order and – if so – in what form, it will look at all the circumstances of each case, including the parties' earning power, their conduct and their needs. In regard to the latter the Court of Appeal stated in *Watchell* v *Watchell* [1973] Fam 72 that the court should concentrate on the parties' needs and not upon their existing shares in the property as arrived at by the application of principles of land law. Thus the court can look at a 'contribution' which would fail to suffice for the establishment of a resulting or constructive trust, because:

> Parliament recognised that the wife who looks after the home and family contributes as much to the family assets as the wife who goes out to work. The one contributes in kind. The other in money or money's worth. If the court comes to the conclusion that the home has been acquired and maintained by the joint efforts of both, when the marriage breaks down, it should be regarded as the joint property of both of them, no matter in whose name it stands. Just as the wife who makes substantial money contributions usually gets a share, so should the wife who looks after the home and cares for the family for 20 years or more.

However, what the court cannot do is assist an unmarried claimant under this pro-vision, as in *Burns* v *Burns* where 'there was no express trust of an interest in the property for the benefit of the plaintiff, no express agreement to create such an interest and the plaintiff had made no direct contribution to the purchase price ... the powers conferred by the Matrimonial Causes Act 1973 in relation to the prop-erty of married persons did not apply' and therefore, notwithstanding that the plaintiff had lived with the defendant 'for 19 years as man and wife and, at the end of it, had no rights against him ... the unfairness ... was not a matter which the courts could control. It was a matter for Parliament' – Fox LJ. Had Mrs Burns been the wife of Mr Burns in fact, and not merely in name, the court would have granted her an interest. As we shall see shortly, the Civil Partnerships Act 2004 can assist those who fall within its scope, that is, those who are in a relationship between two people of the same sex (civil partners), 'which is formed when they register as civil partners of each other' – s 1. A civil partnership ends only on death, dissolution or annulment – s 1(3). Thus the Act applies to single sex couples within a legal partnership, the partnership only becoming legal upon registration. Section 2 deals with registration. Anyone under 18 wishing to enter into a civil partnership must have parental consent – s 4.

By way of contrast, the Family Law Act 1996 makes provision not merely for spouses, but also for cohabitants who have 'lived together as husband and wife' or who intended so to occupy a home. However, the right provided here is merely a personal one – it is not a proprietary right. It is a 'matrimonial home right', which creates no right *in* the matrimonial home itself. What it does confer is a *personal* right of occupation only.

As between spouses, s 30(2) defines 'matrimonial home rights' as:

(a) if in occupation, a right not to be evicted or excluded from the dwellinghouse or any part of it by the other spouse except with the leave of the court given by an order;

(b) if not in occupation, a right with leave of the court so given to enter into and occupy the dwellinghouse.

The section applies if:

(a) one spouse is entitled to occupy a dwellinghouse by virtue of:
  (i) a beneficial estate or interest or contract; or
  (ii) any enactment giving that spouse the right to remain in occupation; and

(b) the other spouse is not so entitled.

(In respect of a commonhold unit, reference to a tenant includes 'a reference to a person who has matrimonial rights within the meaning of s 30(2) of the Family Law Act 1996' – Commonhold and Leasehold Reform Act 2002, s 61.)

Section 33 provides that a court order may be made to:

(a) enforce the applicant's entitlement to remain in occupation as against the other person (the respondent);

(b) require the respondent to permit the applicant to enter and remain in the dwellinghouse or part of the dwellinghouse;

(c) regulate the occupation of the dwellinghouse by either or both parties.

(d) (if the respondent is entitled to occupy the dwellinghouse by virtue of a beneficial estate or interest or contract or by virtue of any enactment giving him the right to remain in occupation) prohibit, suspend or restrict the exercise by the respondent of his right to occupy the dwellinghouse;

(e) to restrict or terminate any matrimonial home rights the respondent may have in the dwellinghouse;

(f) require the respondent to leave the dwellinghouse or part of the dwellinghouse; or

(g) exclude the respondent from a defined area in which the dwellinghouse is included – s 33(3).

Section 33(4) provides that an order may be made declaring that the applicant is entitled to occupy the dwellinghouse by nature of the right referred to in (d) above or has matrimonial home rights.

Cohabitees are covered by s 36, which applies if:

(1) (a) one cohabitant or former cohabitant is entitled to occupy a dwellinghouse by virtue of any beneficial estate or interest or contract or by virtue of any enactment giving him the right to remain in occupation;

(b) the other cohabitant or former cohabitant is not so entitled; and

(c) that dwellinghouse is the home in which they live together as husband and wife or a home in which they at any time so lived together or intended so to live together.

Section 36(2) provides that:

The cohabitant or former cohabitant not so entitled may apply to the court for an order under this section against the other cohabitant or former cohabitant ('the respondent').

If the applicant is in occupation, an order under s 36 must contain provision:

(a) giving the applicant the right not to be evicted or excluded from the dwellinghouse or any part of it by the respondent for the period specified in the order; and

(b) prohibiting the respondent from evicting or excluding the applicant during that period – s 36(3).

If the applicant is not in occupation, an order under s 36 must contain provision:

(a) giving the applicant the right to enter into and occupy the dwellinghouse for the specified period; and

(b) requiring the respondent to permit the exercise of that right – s 36(4).

In addition, an order under s 36 may:

(a) regulate the occupation of the dwellinghouse by either or both of the parties;

(b) prohibit, suspend or restrict the exercise by the respondent of his rights to occupy the dwellinghouse;

(c) require the respondent to leave the dwellinghouse or part of the dwellinghouse; or

(d) exclude the respondent from a defined area in which the dwellinghouse is included – s 36(5).

Therefore, ss 30 and 36 assist spouses or cohabitees who, although not holders of the legal estate, have an equitable interest in the matrimonial home, as well as those who have no interest at all, **but** *it must always be remembered that the right so conferred is **not** an interest in the property itself.*

It should be noted that 'cohabitants' include heterosexual couples only. (Of course, a claim to a beneficial interest by way of resulting or constructive trust, or seeking to enforce a claim by estoppel, is not limited to any specific relationship: equity applies to all.)

As between spouses, the matrimonial home right continues only so long as:

(a) the marriage subsists; and

(b) the other spouse is entitled to occupy the dwellinghouse – s 30(8).

However, an order may be made under s 33(5) extending the right beyond the death of the other spouse or the termination of the marriage (but such an order can only be made during the subsistence of the marriage).

In unregistered land, the matrimonial home right of occupation of a non-legally-owning spouse must be registered as a Class F land charge.

In registered land, such an interest is a minor interest and must be entered by way of a notice. As this is not an interest in land, it cannot be saved by the provisions of the Land Registration Act 2002, Sched 3, para 2, if the spouse fails to enter the notice – FLA 1996, s 31(10)(b).

Lord Denning, in *Boland*, pointed out the difficulties facing a spouse with regard to this right:

> the Matrimonial Homes Act 1967 ... gave ... a charge on the house; but it was subject to this severe restriction: it had to be registered as a Class F charge, and not all of the deserted wives had sufficient knowledge or advice to do this. That Act (as it was passed in 1967) did not apply to a wife who was entitled to a share in the house. Her position was remedied to a slight extent in 1970 by s 38 of the Matrimonial Proceedings and Property Act 1970. It enables a wife, who has a share, to register a Class F charge. But that amendment was of precious little use to her, at any rate when she was still living at home in peace with her husband. She would never have heard of a Class F charge; and she would not have understood it if she had.

(The Family Law Act 1996 replaced the Matrimonial Homes Act.)

Needless to say, Lord Denning's comments apply equally to the need to enter a notice in registered land.

Although the matrimonial home right is extinguished by the death of either spouse or divorce (subject to s 33(5)), it continues during the subsistence of the marriage notwithstanding a separation. It is easy to see that this can cause difficulties for the spouse who has to leave the home, but it also causes problems for anybody seeking to purchase the house. Indeed, a prospective purchaser may well lose his purchase altogether.

One case which illustrates the problems encountered by all parties – the husband, the wife, the purchaser and the court is *Wroth* v *Tyler* [1974] Ch 30. A husband agreed to sell the family home with vacant possession to the purchaser. Though the wife never specifically stated her agreement, it was assumed by both her husband and the purchaser that she would not oppose the sale. However, the day following the exchange of contracts (at which point there was, of course, a specifically enforceable contract) the wife registered a Matrimonial Homes Act right of occupation (Class F land charge), having decided she did not wish to move away from the area. (The situation that arises would have been the same had the land been registered except, of course, that the wife would have entered a notice on the Register.)

Quite naturally, the purchaser's solicitors would not go ahead with the purchase since the vendor could not grant vacant possession. The husband used his best endeavours to persuade his wife to remove her entry, but to no avail. The plaintiff sued for specific performance of the contract with vacant possession. The value of the house had increased from the agreed price of £6,000 at exchange of contracts, to £7,500 by the completion date. At the date of the hearing it was worth £11,500.

Megarry J explained that, where a vendor cannot give vacant possession, he must do all he can to obtain any necessary consents to sale, taking proceedings to obtain possession from any person who has no right to be in the property if needs be. The latter did not apply in this case as the wife did have a right under the Act to be there: 'The right is in essence a personal and non-assignable statutory right not to be evicted from the matrimonial home in question during marriage or until the court otherwise orders; and this right constitutes a charge on the estate or interest of the owning spouse ...'. The husband had done all he could reasonably do to try to obtain his wife's consent to the sale and, thus, the removal of the entry.

Megarry J refused to grant the purchaser his order for specific performance because to do so would result in the eviction of the husband, and probably the daughter of the family, but not the wife, thus splitting up the family. The purchaser was not left without a remedy, however: an order for damages was made against the husband, the amount being the difference between the value of the property at exchange of contracts and that at the date of the hearing, viz. £5,500.

Before making his decision, Megarry J explained to the wife the possible consequence of her husband being burdened with a judgment debt of this size. It could well result in her husband's bankruptcy. If her husband were to be declared bankrupt, the trustee in bankruptcy would be brought in and a trustee in bankruptcy would take the land free of the wife's right – even a right protected by entry on the register. This would, of course, mean that not only would the wife lose the home she had, but also it would be extremely difficult, if not impossible, for her husband to be able to obtain a new home for her and the family.

Having explained all this, Megarry J adjourned the hearing in order to give the wife the opportunity of removing her entry. However, a more obstinate person would be hard to find! Upon the resumption of the hearing the wife had still not removed her entry. Megarry J had no choice but to award the damages against the husband, pointing out that:

> As this case illustrates, Parliament has made it possible for the protected spouse to go far towards having his or her way as to not moving from the matrimonial home, at the expense of the other spouse and innocent purchasers. No doubt, too, the protected spouse may, by registering the statutory charge, and particularly by registering it at an inconvenient moment, require the owning spouse to buy off the charge. In some cases this may be very proper; in others it may be less so: but the power to do it is a unilateral power, free from any restraints.

It is fascinating to contemplate what effect all this had upon the marriage! It would be the final irony if it ended in divorce.

In *Barnett* v *Hassett* [1981] 1 WLR 1385 an order was made setting aside the registration of a Class F land charge, Wood J having found that the registration itself was a misuse of the right: 'It was abundantly clear that the husband did not intend to enter into or occupy the whole or any part of the matrimonial home. Was he therefore entitled to ask the Court to freeze any part of the proceeds of sale? I do not think so'.

Under the Civil Partnerships Act 2004, s 65, where

(a) a civil partner contributes in money or money's worth to the improvement of real or personal property in which or in the proceeds of sale of which either or both of the civil partners has or have a beneficial interest, and

(b) the contribution is of a substantial nature

(2) the contributing partner is to be treated as having acquired by virtue of the contribution a share or an enlarged share (as the case may be) in the beneficial interest of such an extent

(a) as may have been then agreed, or

(b) in default of such agreement, as may be seen in all the circumstances just to any court before which the question of the existence or extent of the beneficial interest of either of the civil partners arises.

Section 66 provides for applications where A claims that the other civil partner (B) has had in his possession or under his control,

(a) money to which, or to a share of which, A was beneficially entitled, or

(b) property (other than money) to which, or to an interest in which, A was beneficially entitled

and that either the money or other property has ceased to be in B's possession or under B's control or that A does not know whether it is still in B's possession or under B's control.

Section 67 allows for applications by a civil partner who is not in possession.

Section 77 and Schedule 5 make provision for financial relief upon dissolution or death, and s 71 and Sched 4 place civil partners in the same position as married couples in regard to wills, administration of estates and family provision.

It is important to note that the Act applies only to registered civil partnerships – the same-sex equivalent to a heterosexual civil marriage. *Sutton* v *Mishcon de Reya* (2004) *The Times*, 28 January, shows that whilst there is nothing contrary to public policy in a cohabitation agreement governing the property relationship between adults who intend to cohabit for the purpose of enjoying a sexual relationship, there is a need to distinguish between a property contract between two people whose sexual relationship involved them in cohabitation and a property relationship which sprang from the sexual relationship (the case concerned an agreement under which one party was to be the sex slave of the other).

Clearly the Act has met a real need: within four months of it coming into force more than 6,500 couples registered their civil partnerships (Source: *The Week*, 1 July 2006).

When and for how long?

Duration of interests behind trusts of land

With regard to trusts of land, we must look at two situations – where the equitable interests are held by joint tenants, and where they are held as tenants in common.

As between joint tenants – whether at law or in equity – the right of survivorship applies so that, upon the death of a joint tenant, the survivors together hold the fee simple absolute in possession. It is not possible, as we know, to sever the legal joint tenancy at all, or the equitable joint tenancy by will. Thus, where the legal estate to Blackacre is held by the maximum four trustees, on behalf of themselves as joint tenants in equity, and one of them dies, the fee simple absolute in possession is now held by the surviving three. Therefore, at the outset, the situation is as follows:

| LE | A + B + C + D | JT tenants and trustees for sale |
| EI | A + B + C + D | JT tenants |

Upon the death of B:

LE	A + C + D	JT tenants and trustees for sale
EI	A + C + D	JT tenants

It is important to note that the size of the cake never alters here; it is only the number of names within it that changes. Indeed, this is the only way in which the top layer of the cake – the legal estate – can ever alter (unless, of course, some other transaction has affected it, for example the formal appointment or retirement of trustees).

If the equitable interests had been held as tenants in common, then no right of survivorship would operate on them, each equitable share going as specified in its holder's will or under his intestacy:

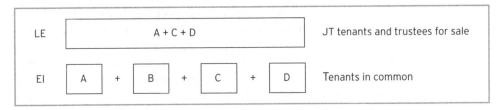

Upon the death of B:

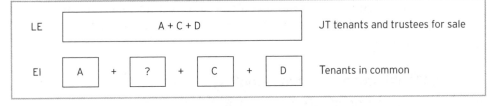

? having acquired his interest under B's will or intestacy.

It could be that though the equitable interests started out as a joint tenancy, there was an *inter vivos* severance, say by C selling his interest to P. How would B's death affect this situation?

At the outset, the position would be:

LE	A + B + C + D	JT tenants and trustees for sale
EI	A + B + C + D	JT tenants

Upon C's sale to P:

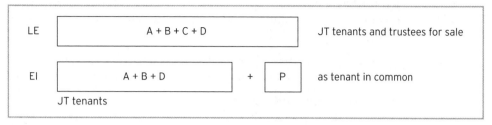

Upon B's death:

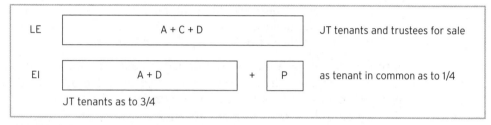

If D were to die, A could no longer remain a joint tenant and he would become a tenant in common as to three-quarters (by virtue of the right of survivorship), with P as tenant in common of one-quarter.

If A then dies, his equitable interest will go under his will or intestacy, but what of the legal estate? There is now only one trustee, but there are still two persons with equitable interests. It would appear, therefore, that another trustee would need to be appointed in order to overreach the beneficial interests. However, in unregistered land, the Law of Property (Joint Tenants) Act 1964, s 1 deals with this situation:

> For the purpose of section 36(2) of the Law of Property Act 1925 ... the survivor of two or more joint tenants shall in favour of a purchaser of the legal estate, be deemed to be solely and beneficially interested if he conveys as beneficial owner or the conveyance includes a statement that he is so interested.
>
> Provided that the foregoing provisions ... shall not apply if, at any time before the date of the conveyance by the survivor –
>
> (a) a memorandum of severance (that is to say a note or memorandum signed by the joint tenants or one of them and recording that the joint tenancy was severed in equity on a date therein specified) had been endorsed on or annexed to the conveyance by virtue of which the legal estate was vested in the joint tenants; or
> (b) [a bankruptcy order] made against any of the joint tenants, or a petition for such an order, had been registered under the Land Charges Act 1925, being an order or petition of which the purchaser has notice, by virtue of the registration, on the date of the conveyance by the survivor.

The 1964 Act only applies to unregistered land. In registered land, the need for a second trustee will depend upon whether a restriction has been entered on the register (there being, of course, no conveyance upon which a memorandum could be endorsed!).

The above relates, however, only to consequences brought about – voluntarily or involuntarily – by the tenants, yet it may be that a third party, such as a mortgagee, wishes to bring the trust to an end.

The Trusts of Land Act 1996, s 14 provides that 'any person who is a trustee of land or has an interest in property subject to a trust of land may make an application to the court ..., and upon such an application, the court may make any ... order –

(a) relating to the exercise by the trustees of any of their functions ..., or
(b) declaring the nature or extent of a person's interest in property subject to the trust,

as the court thinks fit' – s 14(2).

Section 4(1) provides that:

> [i]n the case of every trust for sale created by a disposition there is to be implied, despite any provison to the contrary made by the disposition, a power for the trustees to postpone sale of the land; and the trustees are not liable in any way for postponing sale of the land, in the exercise of their discretion, for an indefinite period.

Although there was a duty to sell under the old trust for sale, trustees also had a power to postpone sale. However, it was held in *Re Mayo* [1943] Ch 302 that such postponement could continue only so long as all the trustees were unanimous in that decision. In a trust of land, any trustee who wishes to sell where the other trustees wish to postpone, may, of course, apply to the court under s 14, as may any other person who has an interest in the land.

When considering such an application, the court must take into account, amongst others, those matters stipulated in s 15(1) – that is the intentions of the settlor; the purposes for which the property subject to the trust is held; the welfare of any minor who occupies or might reasonably be expected to occupy any land subject to the trust as his home, and the interests of any secured creditor of any beneficiary.

The legal estate

The fee simple, as we know, can be compulsorily acquired under a compulsory purchase order, lost by adverse possession or, obviously, disposed of by sale – either by trustees or others, eg mortgagees. There are two other ways in which the legal joint tenancy can be determined – partition and release.

(a) Partition. Partition can only occur between all joint tenants of full age, whether legal or equitable. In regard to the legal estate, of course, this will cause no difficulty, as only persons of full age can hold as legal joint tenants and trustees. The effect of partition is to separate the ownership completely, creating two (or more) separate entitlements. This is not the same as severance, though, where each tenant would become entitled to a specific share in the same piece of land. (Indeed, it is not, of course, possible to sever the legal estate.) Upon partition, each former joint tenant will hold title to the whole of his part of the estate. Thus, if Smith and Jones held 100 hectares of land upon a trust of land as joint tenants, and Jones severed the equitable joint tenancy by selling his half-share to Brown, Smith and Brown would each hold a half-share in the 100 hectares. However, if the legal estate were partitioned, Smith and Jones would each have the whole of the interest in 50 hectares, thereby creating two separate estates. Therefore, whereas with a tenancy in common all tenants enjoy the unity of possession, upon partition each is entitled to sole posession of his own piece of land.

Section 7(1) of the Trusts of Land Act 1996 provides that where the beneficiaries are of full age and absolutely entitled in undivided shares to land or any part of it being a trust of land, the trustees may partition the land. However, before exercising this power, the trustees must obtain the consent of each of the beneficiaries – s 7(3). Where a share in the land is absolutely vested in a minor, the trustee can still partition that share, in which case they will retain it in trust for the minor beneficiary until he reaches full age – s 7(5).

As not every piece of land can be easily divided between two owners, the joint tenants must come to some agreement as to how it should be divided so as to give each a title of equal value. If they cannot reach agreement between themselves, an arbitrator can be brought in.

It may be that disagreement arises from another source, namely other trustees or beneficiaries. Being persons interested in the land, they can, of course, seek a court order under the Trusts of Land Act, s 14.

(b) Release. Partition gives an individual title to both Smith and Jones. Release will give the whole title to one of them. Any joint tenant – legal or equitable – can release his interest to the other or others, thereby enhancing their existing interest.

The equitable interests

We have already seen how an equitable joint tenancy is severed and the effect it has upon the beneficial interests. However, we did not discuss all the ways in which severance can be effected. In the leading case of *Williams* v *Hensman* (1861) 1 John & H 546, Page Wood VC laid down three methods of severance at common law:

> A joint tenancy may be severed in three ways: in the first place, an act of any one of the persons interested operating upon his own share may create a severance as to that share .. . Secondly, a joint tenancy may be severed by mutual agreement. And, in the third place, there may be severance by any course of dealing sufficient to intimate that the interests of all were mutually treated as constituting a tenancy in common.

However, it is possible to identify several other methods too, the full range being – sale, partition, release, mutual agreement, a course of dealing, alienation, acquisition by one joint tenant of an interest greater than that of his fellow joint tenant or tenants, and finally killing another joint tenant (pretty final for him!). It must always be remembered, of course, that an equitable joint tenancy can only be severed *inter vivos*, never by will.

The Law of Property Act 1925, s 36(2) allows for severance in equity:

> provided that where a legal estate (not being settled land) is vested in joint tenants beneficially and any tenant desires to sever the joint tenancy in equity, he shall give to the other joint tenants a notice in writing of such desire or do such other acts or things as would in the case of personal estate have been effectual to sever the tenancy in equity ... [prior to the Act].

In *Harris* v *Goddard* [1983] 1 WLR 1203, the Court of Appeal held that a notice in writing of a desire to sever a joint tenancy under s 36(2) must take effect forthwith; therefore it has to evince an intention to bring about the desired severance immediately, not at some time in the future. However, a contrary intention can defeat an attempted severance. In *White* v *White* [2001] EWCA Civ 955, an equitable joint tenant had severed his share by service of a s 36(2) notice. However, when the property was originally purchased by the joint tenants, only the claimant had provided purchase money, the intention being that he would receive the entire beneficial interest when the other joint tenant died. Given the circumstances, the court held that the severance should be reversed so as to give effect to the original intention of the parties. This is another illustration of how important evidence of a common intention can be. On the facts of this case, it made the beneficial joint tenancy unseverable.

It was held in *Grindal* v *Hooper* [1999] EGCS 150 that failure to endorse the notice of severance at the time of service could not prevent it from operating between the co-owners as provided by s 36. (In regard to endorsement, see 'How Can You Protect Them?')

Such 'other acts or things' were laid down in *Williams* v *Hensman*, and they are those which we shall look at next. However, remember the different consequences which will result from such severance depending upon whether it is effected in favour of a stranger, or of a co-joint tenant (and note that we are looking only at dealings with beneficial interests).

It was held in *Kinch* v *Bullard* [1998] EGCS 126 that a s 36 notice had been validly served even though it had not been received by the addressee: once it had been posted by ordinary first-class mail and been delivered at the property, it could not be withdrawn by the sender.

(a) Mutual agreement. Whereas release occurs by the unilateral decision of one joint tenant, mutual agreement is, by definition, the decision of them all. Sir John Pennycuick stated in *Burgess* v *Rawnsley* [1975] Ch 429 that, 'The significance of an agreement is not that it binds the parties; but that it serves as an indication of a common intention to sever'. Therefore, severance can be effective even by an oral agreement which could not be specifically performed.

However, a distinction has to be made between this situation and that which arises under a course of dealing between a joint tenant and a 'stranger'; for example, where one joint tenant sells his interest to someone other than his fellow joint tenant. In this situation there must be at least a specifically enforceable agreement between the joint tenant and his purchaser.

(b) A course of dealing. As Page Wood VC laid down, such a course of dealing must be 'sufficient to intimate that the interests of all were mutually treated as constituting a tenancy in common'. The leading case here is *Burgess* v *Rawnsley*, a sad little tale. Mrs Rawnsley, a widow, met Mr Honick, a widower, at a scripture rally. Both were elderly and lonely. They became good friends, so good that they bought a house together, each paying half the purchase price and holding as legal and equitable joint tenants. Mr Honick harboured a desire to marry Mrs Rawnsley and intended the house to be their matrimonial home, but did not tell her so. Mrs Rawnsley, on the other hand, at no time intended marriage and eventually this was made clear to Mr Honick, who then began negotiations to buy her share. Initially, Mrs Rawnsley agreed to sell her interest to Mr Honick for £750, but later demanded a higher price. Mr Honick then died. The question was, then, had this course of dealings severed the joint tenancy? If it had not, Mrs Rawnsley would take everything

by right of survivorship. If it had, Mr Honick's estate would be entitled to his share. The Court of Appeal held that there had been a severance:

> I think there was evidence that Mr Honick and Mrs Rawnsley did come to an agreement that he would buy her share for £750. That agreement was not in writing and it was not specifically enforceable. Yet it was sufficient to effect a severance. Even if there was not any firm agreement but only a course of dealing, it clearly evinced an intention by both parties that the property should henceforth be held in common and not jointly – Lord Denning MR.

Lord Denning went further, in fact, stating that in his opinion there would still have been a severance where the parties contemplated different objects both of which failed. However, his fellow judges – Browne LJ and Sir John Pennycuick – did not agree.

The Court of Appeal held in *Harris* v *Goddard* [1983] 1 WLR 1203 that any notice of a desire to sever must show an intention to sever immediately, not in the future, and in *McDowell* v *Hirschfield Lipson and Rumney* (1992) 2 FLR 126, Judge Eric Stockdale held that in the absence of any express act of severance a party must prove a course of dealing in which both parties clearly intended to sever the joint tenancy.

Severance by a course of dealing is also referred to as severance by 'mutual conduct', in either case it refers to dealing or conduct of the existing joint tenants. This method looks very similar to that of mutual agreement, but, as Gray (1993, p 501) explains, 'severance, by "mutual conduct" requires neither an express act of severance, nor a contract, nor a declaration of trust. It requires merely a consensus between the joint tenants, arising in the course of dealing with the co-owned property which effectively excludes the future operation of a right of survivorship'.

(c) Alienation. The sale by one joint tenant to a stranger is a form of alienation, as is the granting of a mortgage by one joint tenant on his share, as in *First National Bank plc* v *Achampong* [2003] EWCA Civ 487. Another would be the granting by a joint tenant of a mortgage on his share as in *First National Securities Ltd* v *Hegerty* [1984] 3 WLR 769. A joint tenant's bankruptcy will also alienate his interest, which will vest in his trustee in bankruptcy. Remember that any disposition of an equitable interest in land must comply with the Law of Property Act 1925, s 53(1)(a), which provides that 'no interest in land can be created or disposed of except by writing signed by the person creating or conveying the same, or by his agent thereunto lawfully authorised in writing . . .'.

(d) One joint tenant acquires a greater interest than his fellow joint tenants. We saw the effect of this earlier. ('What is it?')

(e) Where one joint tenant kills another. This would seem to be the most extreme method of alienating one's interest! However, the killing must be unlawful. There is a general principle that no one may benefit at law from his crime. *Re Crippen* [1911] P 108 is a famous example. Dr Crippen, after murdering his wife, escaped to America with his mistress, Ethel le Neve. Dr Crippen was duly caught and hanged. He left all his property, some of which he had acquired under Mrs Crippen's intestacy, to Miss le Neve. It was held that, Dr Crippen being unable to benefit from his crime, Mrs Crippen's property passed to her next of kin. In fact such a situation gives rise to a classic constructive trust under which, prior to his death, Dr Crippen held his wife's property on trust for her next of kin.

Similarly, one joint tenant who murders or otherwise unlawfully kills his co-tenant cannot take the share of the co-tenant by right of survivorship – *Re K* [1985] Ch 85. However, in that case, where the wife was convicted of the manslaughter of her husband, relief was granted under the Forfeiture Act 1982. Under this Act the court has a discretion to waive the general rule in any case other than murder. Because the wife had, prior to shooting him with a shotgun, suffered dreadfully at the hands of her husband over many years, the court exercised its discretion.

(f) Merger of interests. A much more civilised method than the last! Merger occurs where one joint tenant acquires the share of another in a situation like *Wiscot's Case*, which we saw earlier.

In *Hunter* v *Babbage* (1994) 69 P&CR 548 the court was asked to determine whether any or all of the following documents operated to sever a joint tenancy of a former matrimonial home:

1 an application for a property adjustment order in respect of the house;
2 a sworn affidavit as to the defendant's intention to apply to the court for ancillary relief, including a property adjustment order;
3 an affidavit sworn by the plaintiff;
4 the draft consent order.

The defendant was the former wife of the (now deceased) plaintiff.

It was held that the joint tenancy had been severed at common law, the parties holding the property in equal shares. In reaching this decision, Mr John McDonnell QC considered various methods of severance. Although the defendant's affidavit was capable of being sufficient notice of intention to sever under s 36, as it expressed a desire to sever at some time in the future and was not expressed to take effect immediately, it was not a notice of severance for the purposes of s 36. The correspondence and affidavits showed that the parties did agree that the property would eventually be severed, although this agreement was never finalised. A mutual agreement at common law to sever a joint tenancy can include an agreement to deal with the property in a way which involves severance. The severance operates independently of the agreement itself being specifically enforceable. (Here the parties were the joint tenants, of course, not strangers to the joint tenancy.) As the agreement had never been implemented and had no legal effect as such, the result was that the parties held in equal shares and not on the terms of the proposed agreement. This is a good judgment to read.

In *Barracks* v *Barracks* [2005] EWHC 3077 (Ch), it was held that the parties, Y and Z, held as tenants in common. However, it was stated *obiter* that, even if there had been a joint tenancy, it would have been severed: (a) by alienation upon the grant of a mortgage by Y; (b) a written notice to sever under LPA 1925, s 36 (by way of a counterclaim by Z to litigation); and (c) by mutual agreement arising from a court judgment that Y should buy Z out. This being so, when Z died, the property belonged to Y and X (the sole beneficiary of Z's estate).

Of course, you can have a trust of land of property held under a lease. Where the tenancy is a periodic one and is held by more than one person as joint tenants, it may be terminated by notice to quit given by only one of them – *Hammersmith &*

Fulham LBC v *Monk* [1992] 1 AC 478. However, this does not apply to a statutory tenancy – *Hounslow LBC* v *Pilling* (1993) 25 HLR 305.

Monk was followed by the House of Lords in *Harrow London Borough Council* v *Johnstone* [1997] 1 All ER 929.

Consequences of severence

As Gray (1993) explains,

> In the absence of any contrary court order [eg under the Matrimonial Causes Act 1973] or agreement between the co-owners [eg a declaration of trust, see *Goodman* v *Gallant* [1986] Fam 106], the aliquot shares which result from severance are always equal in size, irrespective of the proportions in which joint tenants may have contributed initially towards the purchase price of the co-owned property – p 486.

Thus, as Walton J explained in *Nielson-Jones* v *Fedden* [1975] Ch 222, 'upon a severance the person severing will take 1/nth of the property beneficially, where "n" is the original number of the joint tenants'. (Strictly, of course, 'n' is the number of the original joint tenants who are still surviving.)

However, by contrast, in *Bernard* v *Josephs* [1982] Ch 391, the Court of Appeal held that where there is no express declaration of trust the presumption that the property was held in equal shares does not always apply. Lord Denning MR and Kerr LJ said that the court should look at the contributions and all the circumstances of the case; Griffiths LJ said the intention of the parties was what had to be considered, having regard to their contributions. On the facts, equal shares existed.

In *Goodman* v *Gallant,* there was a statement of beneficial interests in the conveyance: the property was expressly stated to be held 'upon trusts to sell ... as joint tenants'. This was held to be conclusive and the shares were, therefore, equal.

Where severance occurs, a memorandum to that effect, signed by at least one of the joint tenants, should be endorsed on or annexed to the conveyance which created the joint tenancy. (As we saw in 'When and For How Long?', this is an important consideration when the Law of Property (Joint Tenants) Act 1964 applies.) In registered land a restriction should be placed on the Register.

Partition. Partition operates on an equitable interest in the same way as it operates upon the legal joint tenancy. This is not, of course, really 'severance': severance separates the equitable joint entitlement but retains a tenancy in common of the land. Partition, on the other hand, separates the ownership of the land, not merely the equitable interest in it, thereby destroying the joint tenancy and preventing the creation of a tenancy in common.

Release. Again, release operates on an equitable interest in the same way as it operates upon the legal joint tenancy.

Waiver of priority of equitable interest. Though not severing an interest nor wholly releasing it, the holder of an equitable interest can waive its priority in favour of another, usually a mortgagee. Such a waiver may be expressed by signing a statement to the effect that,

> I, ... the undersigned, realise that I have or may have a claim on or interest in the property known as .... which .... [the mortgagors] are

mortgaging to .... [the mortgagee] as security for a loan. I consent to the mortgage and agree that the repayment of the mortgage loan shall be secured on the said property and have priority over any such interest of mine.

Signed ....

Witnessed ....

Such waiver may also be implied, as in *Paddington Building Society* v *Mendelsohn* (1985) 50 P&CR 244, where it was held that a beneficial interest owned by someone who knew that capital to purchase the property would have to be raised by way of a loan, will have to give priority to the lender. The waiver should be noted on the Land Register.

Bankruptcy

We have already seen that the bankruptcy of a joint tenant will sever the equitable joint tenancy. However, the bankruptcy can have far wider implications than this.

A trustee in bankruptcy, being a person interested in the land, can apply to the court for an order under the Trusts of Land Act 1996, s 14 and, when considering the application, the court must have regard to the interests of any secured creditor of any beneficiary – s 15(1). The court has a discretion whether or not to grant such an order, and in exercising it looks, amongst other things, for any secondary or collateral purpose attached to the trust; and that where such purpose can be found, and where it is still subsisting, the order may be refused. However, in cases of bankruptcy everything changes.

It is the duty of a trustee in bankruptcy to call in all the bankrupt's assets, including his debts, in order that the creditors may be paid out. A bankrupt's assets include his share in the matrimonial home. The fact that a house is a matrimonial home, even more so when it is a family home with children living in it, creates a secondary purpose which, in almost any other case, would suffice to enable the court to refuse an application for an order for sale. In such cases, however, where the person seeking the order is a building society, bank or other financial institution, and where the contest is between the wife and children on the one hand and the financial institution on the other, Lord Denning said in *Boland* that 'monied might' must not be allowed to prevail over 'social justice'. What, though, if the person seeking the order does not represent 'monied might', but rather several small businesses, all of which will fail if their bills are not settled? In all but the most exceptional case, the order will be granted.

In *Re Holliday* [1980] 3 All ER 385, of which Hoffmann J said, 'It would be difficult to imagine a more extreme case than this', the court had to balance the need of the wife to provide a home for herself and her children against that of the trustee in bankruptcy to realise the husband's share for the benefit of his creditors. It was held that an order for sale would not be granted without the wife's consent until July 1985, by which time the two eldest children would be over 17 years of age.

Re Lowrie (a Bankrupt) [1981] 3 All ER 353

This case provides an example of the more typical result in cases of this type. In distinguishing *Re Holliday* (which he described as a 'brilliant example' of a case of exceptional circumstances, the husband having presented the petition in bankruptcy himself 'as a tactical move, and quite clearly as a tactical move, to avoid a transfer of property order in favour of his wife . . . at a time when no creditors were pressing'), Walton J held that the mere fact that there are young children living in a house, and that it would be difficult for their father (as a bankrupt) to raise a loan for another home, did not amount to exceptional circumstances or exceptional hardship sufficient to postpone sale. The judge took time to:

> step back for a moment and look at the situation which must in these cases inevitably occur, or at any rate must occur so frequently as to be almost inevitable. The first one is of course that the whole family are going to be rendered homeless. That is not an exceptional circumstance. It is a normal cir-cumstance and is the result, the all too obvious result, of a husband having conducted the financial affairs of the family in a way which has led to bankruptcy. The second result almost invariably is that it is going to be incredibly hard and incredibly bad luck on the co-owner, the wife, who is in most cases a totally innocent person who has done nothing to bring about the bankruptcy. Of course, as against that, one has to realise that she has been enjoying over whatever period it may be the fruits of the debts which the bankrupt has contracted and which debts are not at the moment being paid. So that although it may be very bad luck on her, she at any rate has had some enjoyment of the fruits which led to the bankruptcy.

In *re Citro, Domenico (a Bankrupt), Re Citro, Carmine (a Bankrupt)* [1990] 3 All ER 952, Hoffmann J at first instance, taking into account all the problems which would affect the children, postponed an order for sale until the youngest child reached 16. The Court of Appeal overruled him, saying that the interests of the creditors must prevail over those of the wives and children whose circumstances, though dis-tressing, were not so exceptional as to warrant any postponement longer than six months. An order was made accordingly.

In fact these cases now come under the Insolvency Act 1986, s 335A providing that where any application is made by the trustee of a bankrupt's estate under the Trusts of Land Act 1996, s 14 for an order for sale of land,

> the court shall make such order as it thinks just and reasonable having regard to –
>
> (a) the interests of the bankrupt's creditors;
> (b) where the application is made in respect of land which includes a dwellinghouse which is or has been the home of the bankrupt or the bankrupt's spouse or former spouse –
>> (i) the conduct of the spouse or former spouse, so far as contributing to the bank-ruptcy,
>> (ii) the needs and financial resources of the spouse or former spouse, and
>> (iii) the needs of any children; and
> (c) all the circumstances of the case other than the needs of the bankrupt – (inserted under the Trusts of Land Act 1996, Sched 3, para 23).

The new s 335A applies to applications made before or after the Trusts of Land Act came into force, and has the effect of excluding ss 14 and 15 of the Trusts of Land and Appointment of Trustees Act (TOLATA) 1996, where an application is made by a Trustee in Bankruptcy.

It should be noted that s 335A applies only to married, or formerly married couples, and not to any other co-owners or cohabitors, and that from the day that a petition for bankruptcy is presented, nothing 'is to be taken as having given rise to any rights of occupation under the Matrimonial Homes Act 1983 in relation to a dwellinghouse comprised in the bankrupt's estate' – s 336(1). However,

> [w]here a spouse's rights of occupation under the Act of 1983 are a charge on the estate or interest of the other spouse, or of trustees for the other spouse, and the other spouse is adjudicated bankrupt ... the charge continues to subsist notwithstanding the bankruptcy and binds ... the trustee of the bankrupt's estate and persons deriving title under that trustee – s 336(2).

In effect, ss 335A and 336 do little more than reflect the view of equity, and thus the outcome of applications under them should usually be much the same.

In *Re Dennis (a Bankrupt)* [1993] Ch 73, Nicholls VC held that it is the moment of adjudication of bankruptcy that causes the property of a bankrupt to vest in his trustee, thereby causing an involuntary alienation of his property which results in the severance of any joint tenancy to which he might then be beneficially entitled: title is not vested retrospectively in the trustee in bankruptcy. By way of contrast, it was held in *Re Palmer (Deceased)* [1993] 3 WLR 877, that a bankruptcy order operated retrospectively and took effect just before death and, therefore, severed a joint tenancy immediately before the debtor's death, thus defeating the right of survivorship in favour of the other joint tenants. These decisions seem to be totally opposed, but in both cases the decision enabled the trustee in bankruptcy to take the bankrupt's share for the benefit of his creditors. In *Dennis* it was the non-bankrupt co-owner who had died and, unless the severance occurred prior to that, that is at the date of bankruptcy, the creditors' claims would be thwarted. However, in *Palmer* it was the bankrupt who had died and, unless the order was retrospective, his share would have devolved upon his co-owners by right of survivorship, again defeating the creditors. Therefore, it seems that the point at which the bankruptcy causes severance depends upon who dies first – the non-bankrupt co-owner or the bankrupt.

Barca v *Mears* [2004] EWCA Civ 2170

This case concerned not only s 335A but also Articles 1 and 8 of ECHR. Mr B owed some £135,595 to his creditors, £52,342.19 of this to Halifax plc. Mr B's house was valued at £140,000. His son, Lorenzo (who lived with him from Thursday to Monday each week) had special needs which, argued Mr B, would be severely affected if an order for sale of his house were made. Under s 335A(3), 'the court shall assume, unless the circumstances in the case are exceptional, that the interests of the bankrupt's creditors outweigh all other considerations'. Mr B claimed the consequences for Lorenzo of a sale would constitute exceptional circumstances'. Following *re Citro* [1991] Ch 142, Mr Strauss QC held that, Lorenzo's problem not being extreme and the fact that a sale of the house would not result in his having to change schools, sale should be ordered.

The next point to be addressed was whether such an order and sale would be a breach of Article 8 or 1. In response to this, Mr Strauss stated, *obiter*, that,

> it does seem to me to be questionable whether the narrow approach as to what may be 'exceptional circumstances' adopted in *re Citro*, is consistent with the Convention ... It seems to me that a shift in emphasis in the interpretation of the statute may be necessary to achieve compatibility with the Convention.

However, on the facts, he held that the creditors' interests must prevail and the house be sold.

It was estimated that a record 100,000 people would go bankrupt in 2006 – Source: *The Week*, 11 November 2006.

(Section 86 of the Land Registration Act 2002 provides for bankruptcy in registered land.)

How can you protect them?

Ensuring the interests are binding on third parties

In unregistered land

Being a legal estate, a fee simple absolute in possession, provided it is properly created, binds the world. It, therefore, needs no other form of protection.

However, as we have seen, equitable interests may be held under a strict settlement or behind a trust of land by persons who may not be the same as those who hold the legal estate. The protection afforded by the 1925 legislation for these family equitable interests is overreaching. So long as there are at least two trustees (or a trust corporation in the case of a strict settlement), and a minimum of two and a maximum of four trustees of the legal estate (in the case of a trust of land), who sign the receipt for the capital monies, then the beneficial interests will be swept off the title, the beneficiaries taking their proportionate interest in the proceeds of sale. You would think, then, that where there had been two or more trustees originally but now, by right of survivorship following the death or deaths of the others, only one trustee remains, another would have to be appointed to enable overreaching. However, in unregistered land only, and where there has been no memoranda of severance of beneficial interests endorsed on the conveyance to those trustees, then under the Law of Property (Joint Tenants) Act 1964, a purchaser can deal with the sole surviving trustee as if he were the absolute owner. (Of course, as between that trustee and any other beneficiaries, the trust remains, though now in the purchase price, not the land.) To enjoy the benefit of this provision, however, the purchaser must be 'in good faith for valuable consideration'. See *Grindal* v *Hooper* [1999] EGCS 150.

We have seen, though, that there are not always two trustees of a legal estate held under a trust of land and in such cases the overreaching mechanism cannot operate. In such cases the beneficial interests are protected by the doctrine of notice.

Caunce v Caunce [1969] 1 All ER 722

Here the husband was the sole legal owner. His wife, having contributed to the purchase price, had an equitable interest. The husband, having granted a legal mortgage on the property to Lloyds Bank (the money to be used to set up a new life for him and another woman), became bankrupt and disappeared; thus he was not only in default of his mortgage payments but, as the judge said, 'in default of appearance'.

Mrs Caunce was totally innocent of any collusion in or agreement with regard to the mortgage, and the bank had acted in good faith, having been unaware of Mrs Caunce's interest and, therefore, of the existence of the trust for sale. The question was, which of these two innocent parties, both duped by the same person - viz, Mr Caunce - should succeed?

Stamp J, in reaching his much criticised decision, ignored the obvious solution, namely that, as a single trustee for sale is unable to deal effectively with the legal estate, the mortgage was void. The only question then was whether the bank was bound by Mrs Caunce's equitable interest. Being a family interest, it was not registrable as a land charge; however, there being only one trustee for sale, it was not overreachable either. It was, then, subject to the doctrine of notice. (The situation will be exactly the same with trusts of land.)

The bank had no actual notice of Mrs Caunce's interest. Did it have constructive notice? Mrs Caunce's occupation of the house would be the obvious fact to fix the bank with notice, but Stamp J held that she had not been 'in apparent occupation or possession': she was living in the matrimonial home 'ostensibly because she was the husband's wife': she was a mere shadow of her husband. The bank took the land free of her interest therefore – although she did, of course, receive her proportionate interest in the proceeds of sale.

This decision continued to apply in unregistered land, notwithstanding the position of a wife in the same situation in registered land following *Boland*, until the following case.

Kingsnorth Finance Co Ltd v *Tizard* [1986] 2 All ER 54

Here again the legal estate was vested in the husband alone, but the wife had an equitable interest. Following the breakdown of the marriage, the wife would sleep at her sister's house when the husband was sleeping at the matrimonial home, but would sleep there herself when he was away. Each day she returned to cook their children's meals. Her personal belongings remained in the matrimonial home.

Without the wife's knowledge, the husband charged the property to the finance company in the sum of £66,000, describing himself on the application form as 'single'. While Mrs Tizard was at her sister's house, the finance company's surveyor called to inspect the premises and, during the conversation with him, Mr Tizard let it slip that he was in fact married, but separated from his wife. There were obvious signs of the children's occupation, but not of Mrs Tizard's.

Mr Tizard emigrated and the finance company sought possession of the property. Mrs Tizard claimed that it had constructive notice of her equitable interest and was, therefore, bound by that interest. Judge John Finlay QC agreed with her, finding that she was in actual occupation of the house. Furthermore, he held that occupation need not be perpetual physical presence, nor exclusive nor continuous and uninterrupted. Therefore, as Mrs Tizard was in the house at the same time every day, she was in occupation. More importantly, from her point of view, not only was she 'in occupation', but the finance company had constructive notice of such occupation due to the information given to the surveyor that Mr Tizard was, far from being single, a married man with children. The surveyor's constructive notice was imputed to his principals, for, as Lord Wilberforce said in *Boland*, 'the presence of the vendor, with occupation, does not exclude the possibility of occupation by others'. It was for the surveyor to look for signs of such occupation by another, namely Mrs Tizard. The inspection made by the surveyor did not amount to such an inspection as ought reasonably to have been made on the facts of the case.

Tizard brought the situation in unregistered land into line with that in registered land following *Boland*, so that now any person with a beneficial interest, even though he is not a trustee of the legal estate, may be able to defeat a purchaser, though, as we have seen, since *Abbey National Building Society* v *Cann*, *Boland* is now effectively limited to claims against second and subsequent mortgagees. In both systems, an equitable interest in the land must first be proved. In both systems it is likely that the interest holder must have been in actual occupation. To this extent, the situation looks identical, but it must be remembered that though both claimants will need to prove occupation (though, in unregistered land, anything which will fix the purchaser with notice will do) in order to protect their interest, they need to do so for different legal reasons. In unregistered land, occupation is the most likely fact that will fix a purchaser with notice, and if there is only one trustee of the legal estate, the interest is protected by the doctrine of notice. However, the doctrine of notice has (we are told) no role in the registered land system. In registered land, actual occupation is necessary to bring Sched 3, para 2 of the Land Registration Act 2002 into operation in order to convert an unprotected minor interest into an over-riding interest which will bind the purchaser – but only subject to the proviso.

As we have seen in *Carrick*, whether title to land is registered or unregistered is crucial, Sched 3, para 2 offering protection in registered land where the doctrine of notice may fail to protect in unregistered land, and vice versa. (However, owners of beneficial interests are well advised to enter a restriction, notwithstanding *Boland*.)

In registered land

The title to a fee simple absolute in possession must be registered, with the holders of the legal estate being entered as registered proprietors. There are three types of registered freehold title – absolute, possessory and qualified. The land registrar will determine which applies.

The absolute freehold

> A person may be registered with absolute title if the registrar is of the opinion that the person's title to the estate is such as a willing buyer could properly be advised by a competent professional adviser to accept – LRA 2002, s 9(2).

This is 'without doubt the most reliable and marketable title that exists, because it is virtually indefeasible and cannot be bettered' – Ruoff and Roper (1991). A registered proprietor with an absolute freehold holds the legal estate subject only to encumbrances entered on the register and any overriding interests.

A possessory freehold

A person may be registered with possessory title if the registrar is of the opinion –

(a) that the person is in actual occupation of the land, or in receipt of the rents and profits of the land, by virtue of the estate, and
(b) that there is no other class of title with which he may be registered – LRA 2002, s 9(5).

Where the title is possessory and has been entered in the register as such for at least 12 years, the registrar may upgrade it to an absolute title 'if he is satisfied that the proprietor is in possession of the land' – s 62(4).

A qualified freehold

A person may be registered with qualified title if the registrar is of the opinion that the person's title to the estate has been established only for a limited period or subject to certain reservations which cannot be disregarded under subsection (3) – s 9(4).

Section 9(3) provides that 'the registrar may disregard the fact that a person's title appears to him to be open to objection if he is of the opinion that the default will not cause the holding under the title to be disturbed'.

The registrar has the power to upgrade a qualified freehold title to absolute title under LRA 2002, s 62(1).

This is like a freehold absolute except that the title is subject to some defect or right specified in the register. Therefore the registered proprietor holds the legal estate subject to certain exceptions. Such titles are rare.

Beneficial interests

The equitable interests of beneficiaries under a strict settlement or behind a trust of land – beneficial interests – are minor interests and must be protected by the entry of a restriction. However, if a beneficial interest behind a trust of land has not been so entered, and the holder of the interest is in actual occupation of the land, then the unprotected minor interest may have become an overriding interest under paragraph 2 of Schedule 3 to the 2002 Act, except for

(a) an interest under a settlement under the Settled Land Act 1925 (c 18);

(b) an interest of a person of whom inquiry was made before the disposition and who failed to disclose the right when he could reasonably have been expected to do so;

(c) an interest –
  (i) which belongs to a person whose occupation would not have been obvious on a reasonably careful inspection of the land at the time of the disposition, and
  (ii) of which the person to whom the disposition is made does not have actual knowledge at that time;

(d) a leasehold estate in land granted to take effect in possession after the end of the period of three months beginning with the date of the grant and which has not taken effect in possession at the time of the disposition – para 2.

If the purchaser did enquire – and enquire of the right person – then whether or not the purchaser will be bound by the interest will depend upon the interest holder's response. If the purchaser was told of the interest, he knows of it, will be bound by it, and either goes ahead with the purchase or does not. If the interest holder denies having any interest, when he could reasonably have been expected to disclose it, the purchaser takes free of it.

It must always be remembered that Sched 3, para 2 can only bind the purchaser where there is only one trustee of the legal estate, for if there are two or more the interest will have been overreached – overreaching overrides overriding interests – as in *City of London BS* v *Flegg* [1988] AC 54. Even if there was only one trustee, the beneficial interest can only prevail where the interest holder is in actual occupation of the land, before or at the time of the relevant transaction – *Abbey National Building Society* v *Cann*. Rights in a family home by way of proprietary estoppel are also overreachable (but not commercial interests) – *Birmingham Midshires Mortgage Services Ltd* v *Sabherwal* (2000) 80 P&CR 256.

Under LRA 2002, beneficial interests continue to be protected by entry of a restriction; however, 'no notice may be entered in the register in respect of ... an interest

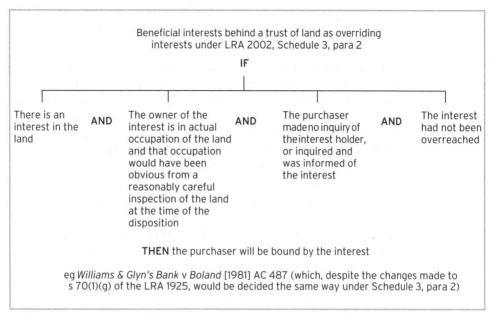

Figure 7.2

under a trust of land or a settlement under the Settled Land Act 1925' – LRA 2002, s 33.

Reform

The Law Commission had for some years been working on a Consultation Paper in regard to the question of home-sharing and the position of sharers upon the breakdown of the relationship, in an attempt to bring together the two areas of family law and property law, concluding in July 2002 that 'it is not possible to devise a statutory scheme for the determination of shares in the shared home which operate fairly and evenly across all the diverse circumstances which are now to be encountered'. This being so, the property law approach was advocated, based on the execution by the parties of a declaration of trust:

> where no express declaration of trust has been executed, we believe that the courts must continue to ask themselves what the parties' intentions were ... taking a broader view of the kinds of contributions from which they might infer 'common intention'. For instance, where a person who is living with the home owner has paid the household bills and thereby enabled the home owner to pay the instalments due under the mortgage, that should normally be sufficient to enable the courts to infer that the person was intended to obtain a share in the home. We also believe that it would be more just if courts adopted a broader approach to quantifying the value of the share – *Sharing Homes* (Law Com No 278).

The Law Commission returned to this particular fray in 2006 with its consultation paper, *Cohabitation: The Financial Consequences of Relationship Breakdown*. This time the emphasis will be on relationships (or, rather, what happens upon their breakdown) as opposed to strict property law principles, an approach which Elizabeth Cooke (2005) hopes, may bring us a new legal regime for cohabitants which will obviate the need to add any more slopes and peaks to the volcanic mountain landscape of the common intention constructive trust.

However, this project is not looking at all cohabitants: it is only looking at 'people who are living together in relationships bearing the hallmarks of intimacy and exclusivity, but who are not married to each other or who have not formed a civil partnership'. For these cohabitees, the Law Commission proposes a statutory discretion allowing for some form of limited but structured discretionary power to adjust the property rights of the specified classes of cohabitees.

For all others – married couples, civil partners, blood relatives, 'caring relationships', landlords and tenants, lodgers – the current property law will continue to apply. It is vital that these excluded categories of cohabitee, and their solicitors, heed Ward LJ's warning in *Carlton* v *Goodman* [2002] EWCA Civ 545 and make an express written declaration of what they intend their rights to be.

It can be seen from the included categories that emotional ties alone will not suffice under the new proposals: there must be a sexual relationship. Why is sexual activity to be the bedrock? It is very difficult to understand why people who have lived together for many years in companionable and/or caring relationships should be excluded. Why are they to be left on Elizabeth Cooke's 'volcanic mountains'?

The inevitable outcome of the proposals would be a triple tier of authority – the matrimonial legislation that applies to married couples and civil partners, the equitable remedies (resulting trusts, constructive trusts and proprietary estoppel) and the proposed statutory discretion. Given the nature of the distinctions that form the bases of these, what sort of enquiries will third parties have to make? Will the nature of everyone's personal relationship have to be broadcast to the world? As Martin Dixon (2006) rightly says, 'third parties need to know who owns what before they become involved, not who might own what if the cohabitants' relationship breaks down'. (His article looks at the case of *Abbey National Bank Plc* v *Stringer* [2006] EWCA Civ 338 – a curious case, but a very instructive one – one which would not fall within the Law Commission's proposed categories.)

Summary

In this chapter we have looked at the problems that can arise and how parties are affected by the following –

- Tenancies in common.
- Joint tenancies – the right of survivorship and its effect.
    - The four unities – possession, interest, time and title
    - The equitable presumptions
    - Severance .
- Party walls, hedges and ditches.
- The roles of trustees and the rights of beneficiaries –
    - Sale, postponement and purchase

- The need for consents
- The duty to consult
- Challenges by beneficiaries and guidance for trustees
- The right to occupy
- Delegation by trustees of their powers
- Appointment and retirement of trustees
- Protection of purchasers
- Powers of trustees.
- Acquisition –
  - Express trusts of land
  - Statutory trusts of land
  - Implied trusts of land –
    - Resulting trusts
    - Presumption of advancement
    - Constructive trusts –
    - Express common intention
    - Implied common intention.
- Quantification.
- Statutory rights.
- Civil partnerships.
- Duration of interests in trusts of land –
  - The legal estate –
    - Partition
    - Release
  - Equitable interests –
    - Modes of severance –
    - Mutual agreement
    - Course of dealing
    - Alienation
    - Acquisition of a greater interest
    - Killing of a joint tenant
    - Merger of interests
    - Notice under LPA 1925, s 36
  - Consequences of severance.
- Bankruptcy.
- Protecting the interests –
  - In unregistered land
  - In registered land.
- Reform.

References

Cooke, E, 'Cohabitants, Common Intention and Contributions (Again)' [2005] Conv 555.

Dixon, M, 'A Classic of our Time: Co-ownership and its Consequences' [2006] Conv 577.

Gray, K. and Gray S.F., *Elements of Land Law*, 4th edition, Oxford University Press, 2005.

Gray, K, *Elements of Land Law*, 2nd edition, London: Butterworths, 1993.

Gray, K.J. and Symes, P.D., *Real Property and Real People*, London: Butterworths, 1981.

Law Commission, *Sharing Homes* (Cm 5666) (Law Com No 278, July 2002).

Oakley, J.A., *Megarry's Manual of the Law of Real Property*, 8th edition, London: Sweet and Maxwell, 2002.

O'Hagan, P, 'Indirect Contributions to the Purchase of Property' [1991] 56 MLR 224.

Pascoe, S, 'Section 15 of the Trusts of Land and Appointment of Trustees Act 1996: A Change in the Law?' [2000] Conv 315.

Ruoff and Roper, *The Law and Practice of Registered Conveyancing*, London: Sweet and Maxwell, 1991.

Further reading

Trusts of Land and Appointment of Trustees Act 1996, s 15

Pascoe, S, 'Section 15 of the Trusts of Land and Appointment of Trustees Act 1996: A Change in the Law?' [2000] Conv 315.

Probert, R, 'Creditors and section 15 of the Trusts of Land and Appointment of Trustees Act 1996: first among equals?' [2002] Conv 61.

The right to occupy

Barnsley, D G, 'Co-owners' Rights to Occupy Trust Land' [1998] 57 CLJ 123.

Ross Martyn, J G, 'Co-owners And Their Entitlement To Occupy Their Land ...' [1997] Conv 254.

Resulting and constructive trusts

Dixon, M, 'Resulting and Constructive Trusts: The Mist Descends and Rises' [2005] Conv 79.

Express common intention

Dixon, M, 'A Classic of our Time: Co-ownership and its Consequences' [2006] Conv 577.

Lawson, A, 'The things we do for love: detrimental reliance in the family home' (1996) *Legal Studies* 218.

Implied common intention

Bottomley, A, 'Women and Trust(s): Portraying the Family in the Gallery', *Land Law Themes and Perspectives*, eds Susan Bright and John Dewar, Oxford University Press, 1998 (p 206).

Cooke, E, 'Cohabitants, Common Intention and Contributions list (Again)' [2005] Conv 555.

Dewar, J, 'Land, Law and the Family Home', *Land Law Themes and Perspectives*, eds Susan Bright and John Dewar, Oxford University Press, 1998 (p 327).

Gardner, S, 'A Woman's Work', [1991] 54 MLR 126.

Hayton, D, 'Equitable Rights of Cohabitees' [1990] Conv 370.

Hayton, D, 'Constructive Trusts of Homes – A Bold Approach' (1993) 109 LQR 484.

Lawson, A, 'The things we do for love: detrimental reliance in the family home' (1996) 16 *Legal Studies* 218.

Quantification

Barlow, A, 'A matter of trust: the allocation of rights in the family home' (1999) 19 *Legal Studies* 468.

Battersby, G, 'How not to judge the quantum (and priority) of a share in the family home' (1996) 8 CFLQ 261.

Cooke, E, 'Equitable Accounting between Co-owners' (1993) 23 FL 695.

Gardner, S, 'Quantum in Gissing v Gissing Constructive Trusts' (2004) 120 LQR 541.

Oldham, M, 'Quantification of Beneficial Interests in Land' [1996] CLJ 194.

O'Hagan, P, 'Quantifying Interests under Resulting Trusts' (1997) 60 MLR 420.

Sparkes, P, 'The Quantification of Beneficial Interests: Problems arising from Contributions to Deposits, Mortgages, Advances and Mortgage Instalments' (1991) 11 OJLS 39.

Severance

Fox, L, 'Unilateral Demise by a Joint Tenant: Does it Effect a Severance?' [2000] Conv 208.

Nield, S, 'To Sever or Not to Sever: the effect of a mortgage by one joint tenant' [2001] Conv 462.

Bankruptcy

Doyle, L, 'Bankruptcy, Insolvency and Matrimonial Property', Sol Jo, 18 September 1992, p 920.

Howells, J, 'Trusts of Land, Bankruptcy and Human Rights' [2005] Conv 161.

Reform

Cooke, E, 'Cohabitants, Common Intention and Contributions (Again)' [2005] Conv 555.

Dixon, M, 'A Classic of our Time: Co-ownership and its Consequences' [2006] Conv 577.

Mee, J, 'Property Rights and Personal Relationships: Reflections on Reform' (2004) 24(3) *Legal Studies* 414.

Riniker, U, 'The Fiction of Common Intention and Detriment' [1998] Conv 202.

Rotherham, C, 'The Property Rights of Unmarried Cohabitees: The case for reform' [2004] Conv 268.

8 Terms of years absolute

What's the problem?

Leases in context

> *Why dost thou pine within and suffer death,*
> *Painting thy outward walls so costly gay?*
> *Why so large cost, having so short a lease,*
> *Dost thou upon thy fading mansion spend?*
>
> William Shakespeare, Sonnets.

> *The kind of dwelling to be had for 7s or 8s [35p or 40p] a week varies in several ways.*
> *If it be light, dry and free from bugs, if it be central in position, and if it contain three*
> *rooms, it will be eagerly sought for and hard to find. Such places exist in some blocks of*
> *workmen's dwellings, and applications for them are waiting long before a vacancy occurs,*
> *provided, of course, they are in a convenient district. Perhaps the next best bargain after*
> *such rooms . . . is a portion of a small house. These small houses are let at rents varying*
> *from 10s to 15s [50p to 75p], according to size and condition and position. They are let*
> *to a tenant who is responsible to the landlord for the whole of the rent, and who sublets*
> *such rooms as she can do without in order to get enough money for the rent-collector . . .*
> *But there is always a serious risk attached to the taking of the whole house – the risk of*
> *not being able to sub-let, or, if there are tenants, of being unable to make them pay . . .*
>
> M P Reeves, *Round about a Pound a Week* (1989).

The above was describing the situation common in Lambeth at the beginning of the twentieth century, which gave rise to verminous conditions and a 'deplorably low' standard of sanitation.

Later in the century, in the late 1960s/early 1970s, a similar problem with the availability of rental accommodation, especially 'bedsits', gave rise to 'rackmanism', named after Peter Rackman, a landlord. Rackmanism is 'the unscrupulous intimidation and exploitation of tenants by a landlord' – *Longman's Dictionary of the English Language*, and under it occupiers, desperate for accommodation, are charged exhorbitant rents for atrocious living conditions, from which the landlord can evict them at any time.

In the late 1980s, a property owner granted the right to occupy a furnished four-bedroomed flat to four individuals who would each be entitled to a bedroom, and they would all share the rest of the flat, rather like a student house. Each was to pay a monthly 'rent'. Another property owner allowed a young unmarried but cohabiting couple to occupy a one bedroomed (double bed) flat. Under this agreement, the property owner was entitled at any time to use the rooms, together with the young couple, and to permit other persons to use all of the rooms too. In both cases the rents were reasonable and the premises in a reasonable condition. In both cases the property owner served notices to quit upon the occupants. What do these two cases have to do with rackmanism? What is the connection between them and the situation described by Reeves? What, if anything, do they have in common with the well-to-do occupiers of apartments in Mayfair who have a 99-year term, or a family living in a large suburban house under a 999-year tenancy? What has Shakespeare's Elizabethan mansion got to do with it?

Who cares?

Those who will be affected

The occupiers. We all need somewhere to live and would prefer comfortable accommodation in reasonable repair with good sanitation, but we may not be able to afford to buy the fee simple absolute in possession in a property. It may be that we could afford to do so but do not wish to take on such a commitment, possibly for financial reasons or maybe because we only need the accommodation for a short time. It may be that we can afford to buy the freehold but it is not for sale, though a portion if it, albeit a large portion, say 99 years, is on offer. In each case we need to know that we are secure in our accommodation in that we know exactly how long we can remain there and upon what terms we can leave or be required to quit the premises. If and when we decide to move, what are we entitled to take from the property? What if we need to move before the end of the agreed term? Will we still be liable in any way under the agreement with the owner?

Following the prolonged recession in the property market in the 1980s and 1990s and the rise of negative equity (where the property is worth less than any money owed on it), renting rather than buying private residential accommodation became much more popular. This, of course, needs an available supply of suitable rental accommodation.

The property owner. The property may be an investment to him: all he wants is to get as much money out of it for as little outlay as he can – Peter Rackman was the ultimate example! If someone comes along who is able and willing to pay double the current rent, the owner will want to remove the existing occupier as quickly as possible, or make him meet the increased offer. It may be that the owner merely went to live abroad for a year or two and now, upon his return, wishes to get back into his own house. Can he?

The owner of a freehold may grant a long term – 99 or 999 years – of some or all of his land to a builder, who wishes to build a housing estate on it. The builder then, naturally, sells the houses. Does the freehold owner have any rights in the land during the term he granted to the builder? Does the builder owe him any obligations, and, if so, for how long?: is he liable after he has sold all the houses? Are the purchasers of the houses under any obligation to the freehold owner (or the builder)?

As well as the question of regaining possession of his land, the owner will wish to ensure that his property retains its value during the term granted to the builder. The builder will probably have made promises in this regard but can the purchasers of the houses he built be made to keep his promises? What of any further sales of the houses, the original purchasers selling on? Can the original promises be made to bind the new occupiers?

The fee simple owner's heirs or assigns, that is, the people who take the fee simple by inheritance upon the original owner's death or who buy it from him. Can they take possession of the land or will they be bound by the arrangements the original owner made? If they are, can they enforce the benefits of the promises made to him? If so, against whom?

The original occupier. Can he stay for the whole of the term granted, or can he be made to leave sooner? Will any rent payable remain the same throughout the whole term or can it be altered? Who will be responsible for keeping the property in repair? If the original owner sells, can any obligations he entered into be imposed upon his successor in title? If the occupier sells all or part of the term granted to someone else, who will be responsible for any breach of any of the obligations imposed on the original occupier? Can he ever become the owner of the fee simple absolute in possession?

Purchasers from the original occupiers. What strings are attached to their occupation? Are they under any obligations? If so, to whom? Will it make any difference if they are buying only part of the occupier's time in the land rather than all of it? Can they enjoy the benefits which were granted to the person from whom they bought? Can they enforce them? If so, against whom? Will they be bound by any obligations entered into by previous occupiers?

The answers to all these questions will depend upon whether the occupier has a lease or merely a licence; whether any lease is legal or merely equitable; whether the purchaser takes an 'assignment' of the term or merely a 'sublease'; the date of the agreement; whether the property is business premises or residential; whether the term is short or long.

Lenders. If the term is a long one, the chances are that a loan was needed to pay for it. If the borrower fails to keep up with repayments on it, the lender will want to know whether any other terms of years have been granted and whether any rent is payable under them. This could prove important if the property becomes subject to negative equity: any rent would provide a continuing source of money to go towards paying off the loan and the presence of an occupier will probably prevent the property falling into disrepair: also, it usually makes the property more attractive to any prospective purchaser. (Of course, it could be that the borrower is the fee simple owner.)

What are they?

The nature and characteristics of leases

The term of years absolute is not, perhaps, a phrase with which you are familiar. However, you will have heard of a lease, and the two are synonymous. In fact several words or phrases are commonly used for the same thing – term of years absolute, term of years, leasehold, lease and tenancy. (In *Bruton* v *London & Quadrant Housing Trust* [2000] 1 AC 406, however, the House of Lords held that there can be circumstances where a lease may create the contractual relationship of landlord and tenant, but without the tenant gaining an estate in land. Although it must be said that such a set of circumstances would be **extremely** rare, *Bruton* was held to be such a case. As a general rule a tenant under a legal lease will have a legal estate – a proprietary right.)

A term of years absolute is a legal estate (since 1925), but it is less than a fee simple in that it is for a defined period. However, this period need not be for 'years' – it can be for a single year, or less than a year, or even from year to year, because:

> 'Term of years absolute' means a term of years … but does not include any term of years determinable with life or lives … and in this definition the expression 'term of years' includes a term for less than a year, or for a year or years and a fraction of a year or from year to year – Law of Property Act 1925, s 205(1)(xxvii).

(This definition is the same for registered land – LRA 2002, s 132.) However, the term or duration of the lease must be certain.

Lace v Chantler [1944] KB 368

A term created by a leasehold tenancy agreement must be expressed either with certainty and specifically or by reference to something which can, at the time when the lease takes effect, be looked to as a certain ascertainment of what the term is meant to be - Lord Greene MR.

Thus, a term 'for the duration of the war' did not create a lease. Nor, as we have seen, will a term for life or lives (though s 205(1)(xxvii) does provide that it does not matter that a lease may terminate before the end of the period, being 'either certain or liable to determination by notice, re-entry, operation of law, or by a provision for cesser on redemption').

We shall see shortly that leases can take many forms, one being a 'periodic tenancy' which may be from week to week, month to month, quarter to quarter or year to year. Obviously the ultimate length of this kind of lease cannot be determined at the outset; indeed it could go on forever. However, so long as each separate 'period' is definite, the test of certainty of duration is satisfied. The need for certainty of duration was reaffirmed by the House of Lords in *Prudential Assurance Co Ltd* v *London Residuary Body* [1992] 2 AC 386.

Section 205(1)(xxvii) also provides that a lease can be created 'whether or not at a rent …', but if it is subject to a rent, that rent must be certain.

Bostock v Bryant (1991) 22 HLR 449

The Court of Appeal held that 'rent' has to be a payment in money terms. Though 'rent' could be paid goods or services, it must have a certain monetary value; that is, it should be a quantified money payment, not a fluctuating sum such as the payment of electricity, gas or fuel bills. It was also noted that the Court will not infer that a payment made by the occupier of premises to the owner thereof amounts to rent if there is another more likely explanation of the payment. In that case the Court held that the inference was that the plaintiff was merely paying for the energy which he and his family had consumed, and was not paying rent.

It was stated in *Greater London Council* v *Connolly* [1970] 2 QB 100 that certainty as to the rent must exist, not at the date of the lease but at the time when payment is due.

In *Street* v *Mountford* [1985] AC 809 (HL), Lord Templeman stated that, '[t]o constitute a tenancy the occupier must be granted exclusive possession for a fixed or periodic term certain in consideration of a premium or periodical payments', ie rent, but, as we have seen, s 205(1)(xxvii) provides for leases 'whether or not at a rent'. The Court of Appeal in *Ashburn Anstalt* v *Arnold* [1989] Ch 1 confirmed that rent is not an essential characteristic of a lease and said that such a requirement was not introduced by *Street* v *Mountford*: indeed, '. . . the reservation of rent is not necessary for the creation of a tenancy' – Fox LJ. The House of Lords in *Prudential Assurance Co Ltd* v *London Residuary Body* overruled *Ashburn Anstalt* on other grounds, but the Court of Appeal in *Skipton Building Society* v *Clayton* (1993) 25 HLR 596 reaffirmed that it is possible to have a lease without the payment of rent. For the purpose of the Rent Act 1977 and the Housing Act 1988, however, rent must be payable.

[You may come across the following rents: chief rent – though generally extinguished by the end of 1935, the term is still used in some areas, eg Manchester, to describe rent secured on a freehold by way of a rentcharge; ground rent – this is secured on a long leasehold where a lump sum (a fine or premium) has been paid and a ground rent (representing the value of the land without the buildings upon it) is payable periodically, usually annually – such rent may be 'peppercorn', that is, purely nominal; rack rent, which is the market rent for a periodic tenancy.]

The person who grants a lease is called the lessor or landlord, and the person who acquires it, the lessee or tenant.

Types of lease

Fixed-term leases

Leases can be granted for any length of time, so long as the duration is certain. Thus, a fixed-term lease can be granted for three years or 3,000 years. The shorter the term, the more likely it is to be called 'a tenancy' rather than 'a lease'.

Where the lease is for a long period, commonly 99 years, the purchase of it is usually for a lump sum, or 'premium' or 'fine'. In fact, it is very similar to purchasing a fee simple. Just as a fee simple owner can mortgage his estate in order to pay for it, so too can the leaseholder. However, whereas the payment of the purchase price by the fee simple owner ends his financial liability to his vendor, the leaseholder is burdened with a continuing liability to the lessor in the form of a ground rent – albeit nominal as a rule – and any agreed service or management charges. The latter are especially common in purchases of leasehold flats.

As with a fee simple, the owner of a long leasehold has a valuable asset which he can alienate though, of course, the lease is a wasting asset in that it reduces with the passage of time until, eventually, there is nothing left to alienate.

Periodic tenancies

These are short leases, being weekly, monthly, quarterly or from year to year. The 'period' is measured by reference to the agreed (not the actual) mode of rental payment so that, if an agreement requires rent to be payable monthly, even if the tenant pays quarterly, he only has a monthly tenancy, and vice versa.

Perpetually renewable leases

As noted earlier, the granting of new periodic tenancies immediately upon the determination of the previous one can, in effect, create a perpetual lease. However, any attempt to grant a lease with a covenant for perpetual renewal will be converted, by the Law of Property Act 1922, s 145, into a contract to grant a lease for 2,000 years with the resultant term being subject to the covenants, conditions and provisions of the original lease.

Tenancy at will

These arise whenever a person occupies another's land as his tenant and with his consent, upon the understanding that either of them may determine the tenancy at any time. A tenancy at will can also arise where a term of years has ended and the tenant, with the consent of his landlord, remains on the land, as in *Dean and Chapter of the Cathedral and Metropolitan Church of Christ Canterbury* v *Whitbread* (1995) 72 P&CR 9.

The death of either party will cause the tenancy to terminate, as also will the assignment of either party's interest to another. However, it should be appreciated that, by its nature, a tenancy at will is not a tenancy at all, but merely a licence – a mere permission to do something that would otherwise amount to a trespass. The relationship between the parties is thus purely personal and, therefore, the 'tenant' has no 'interest' to assign.

Wheeler v Mercer [1957] AC 416

A tenant at will is regarded as being in possession by his own will and at the will, express or implied, of his landlord . . . a tenancy by their mutual agreement . . . A tenancy at will . . . has been properly described as a personal relation between the landlord and his tenant . . . - *per* Viscount Simonds

Unless the landlord has agreed that occupation shall be rent-free, compensation must be paid by the tenant for his period of occupation. The tenancy at will may become a legal periodic tenancy once the landlord accepts rent from the tenant, but it was held in *Javad* v *Aquil* [1991] 1 All ER 243 that whether a tenancy at will or a periodic tenancy has been created depends primarily on the intentions of the parties. Thus, in applying *Javad* in *London Baggage Co (Charing Cross) Ltd* v *Railtrack plc* [2000] EGCS 57, it was held there is no rule that a tender of rent by a holding-over tenant raises a presumption of a periodic tenancy; the intention of the parties has to be gathered from all the surrounding circumstances. The holding over by a tenant during negotiations was held to afford 'a classic instance calling for the implication of a tenancy at will'. (Whether the test to be applied is subjective or objective is unsettled.) Again, in *Ramnarace* v *Lutchman* [2001] 1 WLR 1651 (PC), it was held that where the possession was allowed in the course of negotiations, this will normally give rise to a tenancy at will. In *Walji* v *Mount Cookland Ltd* [2002] 1 P&CR 13, the defendants, appealing against the finding at first instance of a quarterly periodic tenancy, argued that Walji's possession and payment of rent were referable to negotiations for a new underlease. However, on the facts, the Court of Appeal dismissed the appeal and upheld the periodic tenancy. If a periodic tenancy does arise, the 'period' is measured by the mode of rental payment.

Tenancy at sufferance

This type of tenancy arises when a person remains in possession at the end of his term – either under a fixed-term lease or after the death of a life interest holder of whom he has an estate *pur autre vie*.

The tenant is not liable to pay rent, but he is liable to a money claim by the landlord for use and occupation of the land – a fine distinction! A tenancy at sufferance differs from a tenancy at will in that the landlord gives consent for the latter, but not the former.

Tenancy by estoppel

We have seen that it is only possible to grant what you have. If a person, having no estate in a piece of land, by reason, say, of not yet having completed his own purchase of it, as occurred in *Church of England Building Society* v *Piskor* [1954] Ch 553, purports to grant a tenancy of that land to another, both parties to the purported tenancy will be estopped from denying its existence. Thus, they will both be bound by the terms of the lease, as will their successors in title. If and when the landlord actually acquires the legal estate, this will (provided the tenancy by estoppel continues) 'feed the estoppel' so that the tenant also acquires a legal estate – *Rawlin's Case* (1587) Jenk 254. See *Bruton* v *London & Quadrant Housing Trust* [2000] 1 AC 406.

If the landlord did, in fact, have a legal estate in the land, then no estoppel would arise: the tenant would acquire either the full term agreed or such interest as the landlord had. For example, if the lease was for 50 years and the landlord had an estate greater than that, the tenant would get a lease for 50 years, but if the landlord only had an interest for 35 years, that is all that the tenant could acquire.

It was held in *First National Bank plc* v *Thompson* [1996] 1 All ER 140 that the doctrine of 'feeding the estoppel' operates without the need for an express representation of the grantor's 'title' and can apply to the creation of a legal charge, ie mortgage, of registered land.

We shall be looking next at the vital distinction which must be made between a lease and a licence, and the consequences which flow from it.

Bruton v *London & Quadrant Housing Trust* [1998] 3 WLR 438

Here, the question was whether Mr Bruton was a licensee of the housing trust, or was he its tenant by estoppel? The housing trust was a voluntary organisation concerned with the homeless. The local authority granted the trust a licence to use certain short-life properties, pending their redevelopment, as temporary accommodation for homeless people on its waiting list. The trust undertook to ensure that no occupier became a secure tenant without the prior consent of the council and that no occupier should gain any rights of security or other rights whilst in occupation. In 1989 Mr B signed an agreement with the trust for his occupation of a self-contained flat in one of these properties on a temporary basis on a weekly licence. Under the agreement, Mr B was to vacate the premises upon reasonable notice from the trust. In 1995 Mr B claimed that he was a tenant and the trust his landlord. Did he have a lease by estoppel? The Court of Appeal held (Sir Brian Neill dissenting) that a grant of exclusive possession by a grantor who had no capacity to do so did not create a tenancy and this principle extended also to where the grantor had no estate or interest in the land. Thus, a grant from a grantor like the trust, who had, and was known to have, no title and who had agreed to grant no more than a mere licence, did not bring a tenancy into being. Having excluded itself and those claiming through it from possession (as we shall see shortly, one of the essential requirements of a lease is exclusive possession of the premises), the trust had not purported to grant a tenancy and the parties had proceeded on the basis that it was a licence which was being granted. Therefore, there was no tenancy created by estoppel and Mr B was a mere licensee. If only matters had been allowed to rest here!

However, before we look at the outcome of Mr B's appeal to the House of Lords, we need to understand the meaning of 'exclusive possession'.

Essential characteristics of a lease

We have seen already that leases must be of definite duration, and that rent, if payable, must also be certain. However, the most important characteristic for a lease is that of exclusive possession. It is not surprising that this issue has created, and continues to create, a vast amount of case law for, unless exclusive possession has been granted, there can be no tenancy, only a licence. We shall see shortly that if you are to obtain any statutory protection against eviction, you must have a tenancy.

Whereas the definition of a lease in the Law of Property Act 1925 provides for a term of years absolute 'whether or not at a rent', the courts have long stated rent to be one of the three essential requirements of a lease. Thus exclusive possession for a fixed term at a rent will normally create a tenancy unless 'there had been something in the circumstances, such as a family arrangement, an act of friendship or generosity, or such like to negative any intention to create a tenancy' – Lord Denning in *Facchini* v *Bryson* (1952) 1 TLR 1386.

Facchini was applied by the Court of Appeal in *Addiscombe Garden Estates Ltd* v *Crabbe* [1958] QB 513, where it was held that the agreement taken as a whole, although described as a licence, on its true construction created the relationship of landlord and tenant and not that of licensor and licensee: the relationship was determined by the law and not by the label which the parties chose to put on it.

These exceptions became known as the '*Facchini* categories', and where any of them existed there could be no lease, merely a licence. On the other hand, where none of them existed, there could only be a tenancy. Obviously, this situation was not in the best interests of landlords, who wished to avoid the creation of a lease and any resultant statutorily protected tenancy. A commercial landlord could rarely claim to be acting as family, friend or charity! (Nonetheless, in *Marcroft Wagons Ltd* v *Smith* [1951] 2 All ER 271, Sir Raymond Evershed MR felt that the landlord had shown 'ordinary human instincts of kindliness and courtesy' and that therefore 'I should be extremely sorry if anything which fell from this court were to have the result that a landlord could never grant to a person in the position of the defendant [who had just lost her mother] any kind of indulgence, particularly in the circumstances'. It was held that a licence only had been granted.)

Following the introduction of the Rent Act 1977, with its extensive protection for tenants in the form of a statutory right to remain in possession (subject to and with the benefit of 'all the terms and conditions of the original contract of tenancy') after the expiration of the original term, and the imposition of a maximum 'fair rent', the desire by landlords to avoid creating tenancies took the form of challenges in the courts against the *Facchini* categories. In *Somma* v *Hazelhurst and Savelli* [1978] 1 WLR 1014 the landlord succeeded, the Court of Appeal holding that where both parties intended to create a licence only, and could 'frame any written agreement in such a way as to demonstrate that it is not really an agreement for a lease masquerading as a licence', the Court could see no 'reason in law or justice why they should be prevented from achieving that object'. The Court of Appeal rejected the *Facchini* categories altogether, Cumming-Bruce LJ stating that there was:

> no reason why an ordinary landlord not in any of these special categories should not be able to grant a licence to occupy an ordinary house. If that was what both he and the licensee intended and if they could frame a written agreement in such a way as to show that it was not really an agreement for a lease masquerading as a licence, there was no reason in law or in justice why they should be prevented from achieving that object. Their common intention should not be categorised as bogus or unreal or a sham merely because the Court disapproved of the bargain.

Thus the expressed intention of the parties replaced exclusive possession as the primary test as to whether a lease or a licence had been created. Only in cases of 'sham', that is 'the inclusion of written terms which are so inconsistent, incomprehensible or improbable as to raise a presumption that they cannot possibly represent the true intentions of the parties' – Kevin Gray (1993, p 726) – would the court prevent the parties from achieving their object of creating a licence. Given the real situation in the rented property sector at that time – under which a person seeking accommodation was in no position to argue the terms, let alone the nature, of any agreement – the upholding of a licence merely gave effect to the intention of one of the parties, namely the licensor. However, the Court of Appeal in *Street* v *Mountford* (1984) 81 LS Gaz 1844 applied the *Somma* test (notwithstanding that in doing so the Court allowed Mr Street to drive 'a coach and horses through the Rent Acts' – Lord Templeman).

This situation did not last for long, thankfully, for *Street* v *Mountford* went to the House of Lords the following year.

Street v *Mountford* [1985] AC 809

Their lordships reversed the Court of Appeal's decision and overruled that in *Somma*, holding the licence to be a sham. Lord Templeman confirmed that where:

> residential accommodation is granted for a term at a rent with exclusive possession, the landlord providing neither attendance nor services, the grant is a tenancy; any express reservation to the landlord

or limited rights to enter and view the state of the premises and to repair and maintain the premises only serves to emphasise the fact that the grantee is entitled to exclusive possession and is a tenant ... exclusive possession is of the first importance in considering whether an occupier is a tenant; exclusive possession is not decisive because an occupier may be a lodger or service occupier or fall within the other exceptional categories mentioned by Denning LJ in *Errington v Errington and Woods* [1952] 1 KB 290.

In the latter case Lord Denning noted that there were exceptional circumstances which negatived the prima facie intention to create a tenancy, notwithstanding the fact that the occupier enjoyed exclusive possession, the circumstances being where the parties did not intend to enter into legal relations at all; where the relationship between the parties is that of vendor and purchaser, or master and service occupier; where the owner had no power to grant a tenancy – for instance a requisitioning authority. On the facts of *Street v Mountford* the House of Lords found none of these exceptions applied. Indeed,

> if the observations of Denning LJ are applied to the facts of the present case it may fairly be said that the circumstances negative any intention to create a mere licence. Words alone do not suffice. Parties cannot turn a tenancy into a licence merely by calling it one – Lord Templeman.

This decision seems to bring us back to where we started. However, in recent cases the courts seem to be inconsistent in their attitude to the sham, the *Facchini* categories and, indeed, Lord Templeman's remarks in *Street* v *Mountford* in regard to 'exceptional circumstances' which may negate exclusive possession. In *Carr Gomm Society* v *Hawkins* [1990] CLY 2811 where the plaintiff was a charity with the aim of providing accommodation and support for lonely, single people, the County Court judge held the defendant a licensee notwithstanding that he enjoyed exclusive possession of a room in the plaintiff's home and did not have the services of a housekeeper, being 'impressed by the need for the charity to be able to move people on as needs be'. (There is, in fact, a provision in the Housing Act 1985 that, where a licence is granted by an almshouse charity, it does not create a secure tenancy.) *Hawkins* was distinguished and disapproved by the House of Lords in *Westminster City Council* v *Clarke* [1992] AC 288, where an occupant of a room in a council-run hostel for the homeless was held to be a licensee only. However, in the *Clarke* situation, occupants were not entitled to a particular room and could be required to share with other occupants. Visitors to the rooms were not allowed except with the permission of hostel staff. Taking these restrictions and other conditions imposed upon occupants, the House of Lords concluded that the council 'retained possession of all the rooms of the hostel' so that no individual occupier could claim to enjoy exclusive possession.

Clearly, then, we have to distinguish between 'exclusive possession' and 'exclusive occupation':

> 'The vital difference is that in acquiring exclusive possession, the occupier is deemed to have a "stake in the land", an authority to "exercise the rights of an owner of the land" which is consistent with an acquisition of a legal estate conferred only by the granting of a tenancy. Unlike an occupier with only the rights of exclusive occupation, an occupier with exclusive possession can "keep out strangers and keep out the landlord", should he be so minded' – Mark Pawlowski and Sarah Greer (2000) (with quotation from Lord Templeman in *Street*).

As Lord Templeman said, it is exclusive possession that turns a tenancy into an estate in land.

Clarke must be contrasted with *Family Housing Association* v *Jones* [1990] 1 WLR 779 where the provision of temporary accommodation at a rent less than market rent, together with advice and support for the defendant, did not fall within the *Facchini* exception of charity and therefore created a tenancy. Slade LJ recognised that 'the result must be substantially to reduce the choice of methods available to bodies such as the Family Housing Association for dealing with their always limited supplies of housing stock', even though he was 'not sure that this result will necessarily enure to the benefit of the class of homeless persons in this country viewed as a whole'.

Looking at this point, Millett LJ said in the Court of Appeal in *Bruton* v *London & Quadrant Housing Trust* [1998] 3 WLR 438:

> I have not overlooked the decision of this court [in *Jones*] which was approved by Lord Templeman in [*Clarke*]. The facts of the earlier case were closely similar to the present ... The arrangements were held to create a tenancy. But the fact that the grantor had no title was not referred to in argument or the judgments, and its significance appears to have been overlooked ... No consideration was given to the question whether the necessary conditions for the creation of such a tenancy existed ... In the circumstances we are not in my judgment precluded from considering these questions for ourselves.

As we saw earlier, the Court of Appeal held that no tenancy by estoppel arose as it had been clear to all parties that only a licence was being granted. Mr Bruton appealed to the House of Lords [1999] 3 WLR 150 where their lordships agreed there was no estoppel but held that Mr B had a tenancy – a lease!

In the Court of Appeal, Sir Brian Neill, whilst acknowledging that the solution reached by Kennedy and Millett LLJ to 'this difficult problem' was 'both socially desirable and eminently sensible', was nevertheless unable to agree with it. His dissenting judgment was founded on the Court of Appeal's earlier decision in *Jones*, which his lordship felt unable to circumvent. Indeed the facts of *Jones* were strikingly similar to those of *Bruton* – like Mr B, Mrs J occupied a self-contained flat under a 'licence' granted by a housing association, which had itself been granted a licence from the freeholder, another London Council. Basing its decision on the *Street* v *Mountford* test of exclusive possession, the Court of Appeal in *Jones* held that Mrs J was a tenant of the housing association, not merely its licensee, even though the association had retained a key to her flat to enable it to inspect the flat and to discuss with Mrs J any re-housing problems which she might have. Again, in *Jones*, as in *Bruton*, the housing association did not have any legal title out of which to grant Mrs J a lease.

However, as this point was not addressed in argument in *Jones*, Millett LJ felt able to distinguish *Jones* in *Bruton*. (This point – the lack of a title by either the housing association in *Jones* or the housing trust in *Bruton* – is one of great importance. The general rule is that you cannot grant what you do not have yourself – *nemo dat*. The Court of Appeal did not refer to *nemo dat* in *Jones* and, in the House of Lords in *Bruton*, Lord Hoffmann felt that the failure to consider the fact of the housing association's lack of title was easily explained: it was 'irrelevant to the issue in the case'.) Having concluded that the housing trust had granted Mr B a tenancy, their lordships decided that the question of a tenancy by estoppel did not strictly arise: it was 'the fact that the agreement is a lease which creates the proprietary interest. It is putting the cart before the horse to say that whether the agreement is a lease depends upon whether it creates a proprietary interest'. Thus, it is the fact that an agreement between the parties constitutes a tenancy which gives rise to an estoppel, not the other way round. In *Bruton*, therefore, the only question was whether the agreement conferred a tenancy on Mr B, or merely a licence. As a tenancy had been granted, Mr B had no need to rely on estoppel.

So, how did the House of Lords come to the conclusion that a tenancy and not a licence had been granted to Mr B? Controversially! Their lordships relied upon Lord Templeman's judgment in *Street* v *Mountford*, Lord Jauncey stating, 'it is the legal consequences of the agreement which is determinative rather than the label which the parties have chosen to attach to it'. However, as Bingham LJ had explained in *Antoniades* v *Villiers*, *Street* had not totally precluded the granting of a genuine licence where the terms in a written document were accepted as representing the true meaning of the agreement:

> [*Street*] has held that the true legal nature of a transaction is not to be altered by the description that the parties choose to give it. A cat does not become a dog because the parties have agreed to call it a dog. But in deciding whether an animal is a cat or a dog, the parties' agreement that it is a dog may not be entirely irrelevant.

In *Bruton*, there was, according to Lord Jauncey, 'no doubt that both parties . . . were under the impression and indeed intended that the legal consequences of the agreement should be those of a licence' which intention, in his lordship's view, was 'not unreasonable'.

In *Street*, Lord Templeman stated that, in order to constitute a tenancy, an occupier must be granted exclusive possession for a fixed or periodic term certain in consideration of a premium or periodical payments; regardless of the parties' intentions and of any label attached to the agreement. Of prime importance in distinguishing between a lease and a licence is the presence or absence of exclusive possession. His lordship stated that:

> In the case of residential accommodation there is no difficulty in deciding whether the grant confers exclusive possession. An occupier of residential accommodation at a rent for a term is either a lodger or a tenant. The occupier is a lodger if the landlord provides attendance or services which require the landlord or his servants to exercise unrestricted access to and use of the premises . . . There can be no tenancy unless the occupier enjoys exclusive possession; but an occupier who enjoys exclusive possession is not necessarily a tenant. He may be owner in fee simple, a trespasser, a mortgagee in possession, an object of charity or a service occupier.

Summarising Denning LJ's exceptional categories as laid down in *Errington* v *Errington & Woods* [1952] 1 KB 290, Lord Templeman identified three which would give rise to a licence only: (1) where the parties did not intend to enter into a legal relationship at all; (2) where the relationship between the parties was referable to some other relationship, such as vendor and purchaser, master and servant; and (3) where the grantor had no power to grant a tenancy.

Though arguments could be raised on other points (eg, the charitable status and objects of Quadrant, which could be said to make Mr Bruton 'an object of charity'), the obvious one in *Bruton* is Lord Templeman's third category, which was not limited to cases where the grantor had no capacity to grant a tenancy, but extended to cases where he had no estate or interest in the land out of which to make the grant. Thus, 'this exception has been controversially whittled down...' (Cheshire and Burn, 2000, p 394).

A further problem arising from Lord Hoffmann's judgment in *Bruton* is caused by his suggestion that the existence of a lease does not inevitably lead to the grant of a proprietary right. Lord Hobhouse expressed the view that the relationship between the parties was only 'contractual' (and, therefore, the lack of a title by Quadrant was not a bar to Mr Bruton's lease):

> But if Mr Bruton's tenancy is not 'good against all the world' and is purely contractual in nature, then surely the very essence of a tenancy, namely exclusive possession, is lacking unless, of course, exclusive possession in this context, may now mean exclusive possession as between grantor and grantee only! – Mark Pawlowski and Sarah Greer (2000).

As Martin Dixon (1999) rightly says:

> There is here, then, the apparent re-emergence of the lease as a right *in personam*. Of course, prior to *Bruton*, we would have called this 'personal lease' a licence! One cannot help surmising that, in its efforts to do justice to Mr Bruton (by giving him a tenancy), the House of Lords has taken a wrong turn. With due respect to Lord Hoffmann, the whole point of *Street* v *Mountford* was to distinguish proprietary rights which bind third parties from personal rights which do not. An example of the former are leases, the second are licences. If it is now possible to have a lease (proprietary), a lease (non-proprietary) and a licence, what is the difference between the last two? Does a lease (non-proprietary) benefit from legislation applicable to leases, even if that legislation is premised on the assumption that leases do bind third parties (eg, Landlord and Tenant (Covenants) Act)? [Also Law of Property Act 1925, s 54(2) and Land Registration Act 2002, Sched 3, para 2.] Hard cases make bad law. It is difficult to see the merit of this decision, unless you are Mr Bruton.

Mr Bruton, with a lease of a central London flat for a mere £18 per week, must be a very happy tenant indeed! However, Quadrant will not be the only unhappy landlord following this decision (which required them to expend large sums of money in order to comply with their obligation under an implied landlord's covenant to repair). All housing associations, trusts and charities must now be wondering how they can grant a licence only! The provision of services may be a possibility, but such provision could be deemed to be a sham. It will be fascinating to see how those representing *Bruton* 'landlords' seek to avoid a tenancy, and how (or if) the courts will attempt to distinguish instant cases from *Bruton*. Another possibility is that the government – several of whose policies, eg 'Care in the Community' and provision of accommodation for the homeless, are undermined by *Bruton* – will step in with a 'statutory overrule'.

Does C have any rights against A once B's licence has come to an end? In two cases – *Kay* v *Lambeth London Borough Council* [2004] EWCA Civ 926 and *London Borough of Islington* v *Green* [2005] EWCA Civ 56 – the Court of Appeal held that C does **not** have any interest in the land binding on A (though it could be different if B was deemed to be acting as A's agent).

Ward v *Warnke* (1990) 22 HLR 496

The Court of Appeal had to consider a family arrangement. The defendant and his wife had been allowed to move into a cottage purchased for holidays and as a retirement home by the wife's parents. The wife paid the rates, water rates, electricity and telephone bills, and a rent of £3.50 per week, increasing to £6 per week, whilst in occupation. The rent was paid into a building society account which initially named the defendant and his wife, and later the wife only, as beneficiaries. Upon the breakdown of her marriage, the daughter left the cottage but the defendant stayed on together with one of the four children of the marriage. The plaintiff mother sought possession of the premises. The Court of Appeal upheld the first instance decision that a tenancy, and not a licence, had been created on the ground that there was no basis for saying there was no intention to enter into legal relations. The fact that it was a transaction between members of a family did not prevent the creation of legal relations.

However, in *Monmouth Borough Council* v *Marlog* [1994] 2 EGLR 68, the appellant, Mrs Marlog, was held to be merely 'the lodger or licensee'. She claimed to be a sub-tenant of one of the council's tenants, having been allowed by him to share his house. When the tenant fell into arrears with his rent the council sought possession: the tenant moved out, but Mrs Marlog remained, claiming she had the right to do so because of the subtenancy. The Court of Appeal found for the council as there was no evidence to support an intention to create legal relations (Mrs Marlog and the tenant were not cohabiting). This is an example of one of the exceptions referred to by Lord Templeman in *Street* v *Mountford*.

With regard to sham agreements, the Court of Appeal in *Estavest Investments* v *Commercial Express Travel* (1988) 21 HLR 106 refused to find a sham where a landlord had let premises to company tenants rather than directly to the occupier in order to avoid creating a statutory tenancy under the Rent Act. Again, in *Hilton* v *Plustitle* [1989] 1 WLR 149 the Court of Appeal held that an agreement to let a flat to a company which then nominates an occupier in order to avoid creating a statutory tenancy is not necessarily to be treated as a sham. On the facts, as the agreement reflected the parties' intentions, it was upheld.

In *Aslan* v *Murphy* (*Nos 1 and 2*) [1990] 1 WLR 766, Lord Donaldson MR pointed out the need for courts to consider the possibilities of a pretence:

> What [the judge at first instance] should have done . . . was to consider whether the whole agreement was a sham and, if it was not, whether in the light of the factual situation the provisions were part of the true bargain between the parties or mere pretences.

In *Rowan* v *Dann* [1992] NPC 3, the Court of Appeal held that where an improper purpose was common to both sides and where the defendant had suffered no disadvantage, the plaintiff was entitled to resign from the transaction. The improper purpose had been the creation of leases, adjudged at first instance to be a sham to keep the land out of the hands of creditors. The Court of Appeal held in *Huwyler* v *Ruddy* [1996] EGCS 8 that if the purpose of access by a landlord was so trivial as to be a sham, the court would disregard it. In that case the defendant was entitled to services which included laundry and cleaning. By virtue of his obligation to provide these services, the plaintiff had unrestricted access to the defendant's room. On these facts the purpose of access did not amount to a sham. Again, there was held to be no sham in *Eaton Square Properties Ltd* v *O'Higgins* [2000] EGCS 118, where the Court of Appeal adopted the definition of 'sham' provided in *Snook* v *London & West Riding Investments Ltd* [1967] 2 QB 786:

> a sham is where the acts done, or documents executed, are intended by the parties to give to third parties or to the court the appearance of creating between the parties legal rights and obligations different from those the parties had in fact intended to create.

However, the following can only be licensees: lodgers – *Marchant* v *Charters* [1977] 1 WLR 1181 and *Otter* v *Norman* [1989] AC 129; service occupiers – *Norris* v *Checksfield* [1991] 4 All ER 327; purchasers allowed into occupation prior to completion.

The Mortgage Corporation v Ubah (1997) 73 P&CR 500

The Court of Appeal held that full protection under the Rent Act 1977 could not be claimed by someone who, under the terms of his agreement, shared the kitchen of the premises with the person who allowed him occupation, even though the latter was no longer using, or capable of using the kitchen. What matters is not 'whether the rights were in fact being exercised, but whether they were there to be exercised as and when the party entitled to them was capable of doing so' – Waite LJ. This could have serious consequences for occupiers of sheltered accommodation. However, the fact that there are no cooking facilities will not prevent premises being a 'dwellinghouse' for the purposes of the Housing Act 1988 – the House of Lords in *Uratemp Ventures Ltd* v *Collins* [2002] 1 All ER 46 (criticising Lord Templeman's dictum in *Westminster City Council* v *Clarke* [1992] AC 288).

(See also *Gray* v *Taylor* [1998] 1 WLR 1093 for a further example of a situation which created no lease, notwithstanding the right to exclusive occupation.)

It was held in *Venus Investments Ltd* v *Stocktop Ltd* [1996] EGCS 173 that the principle enunciated by Lord Templeman in *Street* v *Mountford* applies to commercial as well as to residential property.

However, if the Law Commission's proposals in its *Renting Houses Report* (Law Com No 297) become law, the lease/licence distinction will become obsolete. See Reform.

What is exclusive possession?

The House of Lords' decision in *Street* v *Mountford* did not halt attempts by landlords to avoid the creation of tenancies. Indeed it seems to have created another avenue for challenge – what is exclusive possession? In the first two cases since *Street* v *Mountford* to reach the House of Lords on this point, the House reversed both Court of Appeal decisions. The cases – *Antoniades* v *Villiers* and *AG Securities* v *Vaughan* – went on joint appeal (hence the identical references).

Antoniades v Villiers [1988] 3 WLR 1025

This case provides a clear illustration of sham. A one-bedroom flat was let to a young unmarried but cohabiting couple under separate but identical 'licence' agreements, executed simultaneously. It was emphatically stipulated that the couple were not to have exclusive possession. Indeed, clause 16 of the agreements stated that 'the licensor shall be entitled at any time to use the rooms together with the licensee and permit other persons to use all the rooms together with the licensee'. For good measure, the agreements stated that the real intention of the parties in all the circumstances was to create a licence which did not come under the Rent Acts. The Court of Appeal had found this to be a licence; the House of Lords found it to be a lease - the agreements were interdependent and were to be read as constituting a single transaction. The fact that the couple intended to occupy the flat as man and wife - an intention known to the lessor - created a joint tenancy, and the purported retention by the lessor of the right to share - or introduce others to share - the limited accommodation was clearly a pretence aimed at depriving the couple of Rent Act protection.

As Lord Templeman remarked in *Vaughan*:

> Parties to an agreement cannot contract out of the Rent Acts: if they were able to do so the Acts would be a dead letter because in a state of housing shortage a person seeking residential accommodation may agree to anything to obtain shelter.

Mikeover v *Brady* [1989] 3 All ER 618 also concerned an unmarried cohabiting couple. However, the Court of Appeal held in that case that they were not joint tenants because they were not jointly liable for the rent.

AG Securities v *Vaughan* [1988] 3 WLR 1025

This case, which must be contrasted with *Antoniades*, concerned a four-bedroom flat, let to four individual flat-sharers each of whom entered into a separate short-term 'licence' agreement, such agreements being made at different times, on different terms, with different rents. All the agreements provided that each occupant had 'the right to use [the flat] in common with others who have or may from time to time be granted the like right ... but without the right to exclusive possession of any part of the ... flat'. The licensor and the remaining licensees mutually agreed upon replacement occupants when any occupant left. The Court of Appeal had found these agreements to be leases; the House of Lords found them to be licences. As each occupant had exclusive possession of one room only - each bedroom, the rest of the accommodation being shared - they did not between themselves enjoy a collective joint tenancy.

This arrangement is, of course, very like that of a 'student house'. It became common for private landlords to grant students sharing a house 'assured shorthold tenancies' under the Housing Act 1988. Such tenancies had to be for a term of at least six months, and at the end of the agreed term the landlord was entitled to possession. The Housing Act 1996, s 98 now requires a landlord to serve two months' notice requiring possession of property let on an assured shorthold tenancy and such notice must be in writing.

From 28 February 1997 any assured tenancy which is entered into on or after that date, or which arises at the end of a fixed term assured tenancy which began on or after that date, is an assured shorthold tenancy – s 98. Section 99 provides that an order for possession may not be made so as to take effect earlier than six months after the beginning of the tenancy.

As Richard Smith (1996, p 150) says:

> Under the Housing Act 1988 the standard tenancy is the assured tenancy, whereas the assured shorthold is an exception which can be created only by complying with certain

conditions set out in s 20(1) [of the Housing Act 1988]. The Housing Act 1996 reverses this position. It inserts section 19A into the 1988 Act, the effect of which is that on or after [28 February 1997] any *new* assured tenancy will automatically be a shorthold tenancy unless it falls within certain exceptions.

One of these exceptions covers students occupying halls of residence owned by a 'specified educational institution or body of persons', which includes most publicly funded higher education institutions (Sched 1, para 8, of the 1988 Act).

The case of *Hadjicoulas* v *Crean* [1988] 1 WLR 1006 concerned an agreement very similar to that in *Villiers* made by two ladies in respect of a two-bedroom flat. However, the Court of Appeal distinguished the two cases, stating that a presumption of exclusive possession could not arise from the mere fact that two or more persons shared the occupation of a flat. Thus each case is dependent upon its own facts.

Stribling v *Wickham* [1989] 27 EG 81

Here the Court of Appeal laid down the facts which will be most relevant in deciding whether a lease or a licence has been created, and they are: the number of sharers; the nature and extent of the accommodation provided; the relationship between the sharers; the intended and actual mode of occupation; and the course of negotiations.

Another case, similar on its facts to *Villiers*, is *Nicolau* v *Pitt* (1989) 21 HLR 487 where an owner attempted to grant a licence to a married couple by inserting in the agreement a provision that 'the licensor is not willing to grant exclusive possession' and that occupation was 'in common ... with the licensor and such other licensee or invitees as the licensor may permit from time to time to use the said flat'. The Court of Appeal found this to be a lease as in reality the parties had contemplated that exclusive possession would be enjoyed.

In *Skipton Building Society* v *Clayton* (1993) 25 HLR 596, where the court found a sham, it was made clear that a bald statement that an agreement does not confer exclusive possession will be carefully scrutinised by the court in its attempts to identify the true intentions of the parties.

By way of contrast, the Court of Appeal found in *Westminster City Council* v *Basson* (1990) 23 HLR 225 that, the Council having made clear its intention not to grant a tenancy, a licence only was created notwithstanding a delay of more than a year by the Council in taking possession proceedings and the provision by it to the licensee in the meantime of a rent book and the grant of a rent rebate. Again, in *Ogwr Borough Council* v *Dykes* [1939] 1 WLR 295, the Court of Appeal found a licence and not a lease even though the occupier enjoyed exclusive possession: on the terms, any intention to create a tenancy was specifically and definitely negatived. See also *Camden London Borough Council* v *Shortlife Community Housing Ltd* (1992) 90 LGR 358.

The importance of the distinction between a lease and a licence, as we saw at the beginning of this section, arose with the introduction of the Rent Act 1977. Though the introduction of the Housing Act 1988 has reduced the flow of cases in this area, the debate continues as the Housing Act is not retrospective in effect (that is, it only applies to agreements entered into after it was passed) and it does itself provide for certain – though limited – circumstances in which the possession of a lease rather than a licence will afford some statutory protection.

However, a contractual licensee, even one not in occupation of land, may be entitled to claim possession against a trespasser if such a remedy is necessary to vindicate and give effect to the licensee's contractual rights of occupation, because, 'The contrary intention would be both disreputable and unjust, since it would mean that the law was powerless to correct a proved or admitted wrongdoing' – Court of Appeal in *Dutton* v *Manchester Airport plc* [1999] 2 All ER 675. (Of course, a licensee cannot exclude an occupier with an equal or superior claim to possession.)

Leases in registered land

Following objections to the proposal in the new Land Registration Rules in 2003 of a standard form of lease, a set of 14 standard clauses which must be incorporated in every lease for registration purposes was produced. These came into force on 9 January 2006, and they are as follows:

- LR1   the date of the lease
- LR2   the title number
- LR3   names of the parties to the lease
- LR4   the leasehold property
- LR5   statements (applicable to some residential and charity leases)
- LR6   the term of the lease
- LR7   any premium
- LR8   any restriction on the disposition
- LR9   any options to renew, offer to surrender clause or other such right of acquisition
- LR10   restrictive covenants over other land
- LR11   any easements granted or reserved
- LR12   any estate rentcharge
- LR13   standard Land Registry restrictions
- LR14   if the tenant is more than one person, a declaration of trust.

These clauses must appear (correctly numbered) at the very front of the lease and are compulsory in all residential or commercial leases granted on or after 19 June 2006 and which have to be registered, unless there is an implied surrender and regrant following variation of the lease or where the form of lease was 'expressly required' (in a specified form with no alteration permitted) under statute, a court order, any agreement or 'necessary licence or consent' before 19 June 2006.

How can they exist?
Classification: legal or equitable?

The term of years absolute is the other legal estate. We now know the requirements for a term of years absolute, and so long as these and the formal requirements are satisfied, a fixed-term or periodic lease will be legal. In registered land 'leases granted for a term not exceeding seven years' are overriding interests – Land Registration Act 2002, Sched 3, para 1; leases for more than seven years are registrable interests. Tenancies at will and sufferance have no definite timespan and cannot, therefore, be legal. Indeed, they are not really 'tenancies' at all, a tenancy at will being a personal licence and a tenancy at sufferance not even that because there is no permission. Tenancies by estoppel cannot be legal either. In fact the 'tenancy' in reality takes effect behind a licence. A term of years absolute which fails to satisfy the legal formalities may still be effective as an equitable lease because an equitable lease will be enforceable on exactly the same terms as the formally defective agreement. For this reason it is often said that an equitable lease is as good as a legal lease but, as we shall see, this is not strictly so.

The fee simple absolute in possession owner – or lessor – who granted the lease retains the freehold reversion of the lease, which he can assign. The lessee can also assign his interest – his term of years absolute. However, if the lessee conveys less than the time he has left in the term of years to X, then he (the lessee) also has a reversion of what will be left at the end of his grant to X, and X will be a subtenant. In this situation the fee simple absolute in possession owner, L, holds that and the leasehold reversion and is the head landlord; his tenant, T, holds under the head lease and is, in turn, landlord of X. X is the tenant of T under the underlease. Provided all the formal requirements are satisfied in each transaction, L, T and X each hold a legal estate in the same piece of land at the same time. In addition, landlords usually reserve to themselves a right to re-enter the property upon breach by the tenant of any of the covenants in the lease, especially failure to pay rent. 'Rights of entry exercisable over or in respect of a legal term of years absolute' fall within the Law of Property Act 1925, s 1(2)(e), and can, therefore, be legal. Thus, L and T may also have this legal interest. Such a situation highlights the flexibility provided by the old doctrine of estates which is retained by the 1925 legislation: 'A legal estate may subsist concurrently with or subject to any other legal estate in the same land in like manner as it could have done before the commencement of this Act' – Law of Property Act 1925, s 1(5). Under s 4 of the Landlord and Tenant (Covenants) Act 1995, the benefit of a landlord's right of re-entry is automatically annexed to the reversion, and the new landlord can exercise it in respect of a breach by the tenant prior to the assignment.

Who does what?

Roles of the parties

Who can grant a tenancy? Anyone who has himself some greater interest or time in the land than that which he is granting: you can only grant what you have (see, however, *Bruton* v *London Quadrant Housing Trust* [1998] 3 WLR 438). Therefore, the fee simple absolute owner can grant any period – he has forever, but a tenant can also grant a lease, so long as the term he grants is less than the time he has left: this would be a sublease. A tenant could, instead, assign his lease, that is convey the whole of the time he has left to someone else. (As we shall see later, the granting of a sublease or the assignment of the whole of the remaining term usually requires the landlord's consent.)

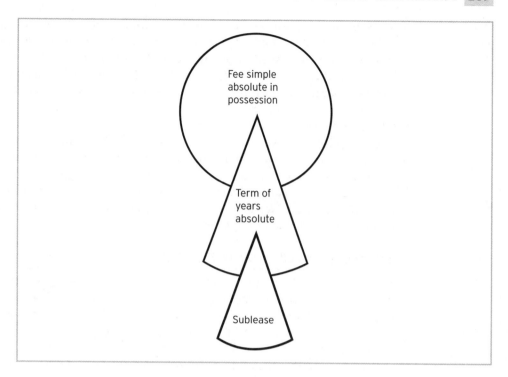

Therefore, there can be any number of legal estates all existing on the same piece of land at the same time – Law of Property Act 1925, s 1(5).

When a landlord grants a lease, a term of years to a tenant, both parties usually make promises each to the other in regard to certain matters. Promises made by deed are covenants and, not surprisingly, promises made in a lease are leasehold covenants! In addition to covenants expressly incorporated into the lease, others will be implied into all leases. Under the covenants the landlord and the tenant are bound to do or refrain from doing certain things: for example, the tenant will covenant to pay the rent and the landlord will covenant to keep the premises in repair. We need, therefore, to look at the various covenants – express and implied – entered into by landlords and tenants, and the rights and responsibilities which are imposed upon them. We shall be looking only at residential leases.

The landlord

Needless to say, as in any other legal contract or agreement, it is open to the parties to it to include any terms upon which they can agree: it is the same with covenants in leases. It is common, however, for landlords to enter into an express covenant to repair. In the absence of an express covenant to repair, such a duty will be implied at common law, and imposed by statute.

Covenant to repair

At the beginning of the term of the lease, the usual rule of *caveat emptor* (let the buyer beware) applies. Therefore, a tenant should inspect the premises carefully to see what he is taking on (for, as we shall see shortly, the tenant may himself be liable to repair). An exception to *caveat emptor* in the landlord/tenant relationship was established in *Smith* v *Marrable* (1843) 11 M&W 5 when the court implied a condition that any furnished dwellinghouse should be reasonably fit for human habitation at the commencement of the term. However, 'reasonably fit' has a very restricted meaning. In *Maclean* v *Currie* (1884) Cab & El 361 it was held not to apply to ordinary disrepair – in that case to cracked plaster: disrepair which merely makes habitation unpleasant or inconvenient will not suffice.

The exception relates only to the condition in which the premises were at the beginning of the term and only to residential, furnished accommodation. Even then, it was held not to extend to dangerous appliances, eg to electrocution by a faulty refrigerator in *Pampris* v *Thanos* [1968] 1 NSWR 56, nor to furnishings supplied by the landlord. Needless to say, given the contractual relationship, only the tenant can sue for breach of this covenant.

Liverpool City Council v *Irwin* [1977] AC 239

However, the result of this case is that local authority landlords of high-rise flats are under a contractual duty to 'take reasonable care to keep in reasonable repair and usability' all the common parts and facilities, eg stairs, lifts. In that case, the Council having shown that it had made considerable efforts to maintain such areas and facilities despite continuous acts of local vandalism, the House of Lords held it was not in breach of this contractual duty of care. Lord Salmon stated that the maintenance of such facilities as stairways, lifts and rubbish chutes could not be regarded as merely:

> conveniences: they are essentials of the tenancy without which life in the dwellings as a tenant, is not possible ... Can a pregnant woman accompanied by a young child be expected to walk up fifteen ... storeys in the pitch dark to reach her home? Unless the law imposes an obligation upon the Council at least to use reasonable care to keep the lights working properly and the staircase lit, the whole transaction becomes inefficacious, futile and absurd.

Again, however, this duty of care is enforceable by the tenant alone.

In the law of tort, landlords can find themselves liable for negligence in regard to personal injury or damage to property, though the House of Lords in *Cavalier* v *Pope* [1906] AC 428 held that the liability is limited to defects occurring after the beginning of the term: a landlord is not liable for the defective state of the premises at the commencement (a highly criticised ruling). Actions in tort are not limited to the tenant, but the usual rule as to foreseeability applies.

A landlord is also subject to the tort of nuisance in regard to his own acts or omissions: he is not normally liable for nuisance committed by his tenant, however.

There are certain statutory provisions in regard to repair to residential tenancies. Under the Landlord and Tenant Act 1985, s 8(1), two implied terms are imposed upon landlords under which a dwellinghouse must be 'fit for human habitation at the commencement of the tenancy' and must be 'kept by the landlord fit for human habitation during the tenancy'. These provisions cannot be excluded, but they have no application where the premises cannot be made fit for human habitation at reasonable expense. Added to this:

> the statutory rents limits on eligible tenancies now make the section virtually ineffective

except in respect of properties which are, in any event, fit only for total demolition rather than repair – Gray (2005, p 1458).

The Landlord and Tenant Act 1985, s 1 implies into leases of dwellinghouses for less than seven years certain covenants in regard to repair and maintenance. Again, however, the extent of the liability is restricted.

Quick v *Taff Ely BC* [1986] QB 809

Here Dillon LJ defined 'disrepair' as 'related to the physical condition of whatever has to be repaired, and not to questions of lack of amenity or inefficiency'. In that case 'very severe condensation' which made the living conditions 'appalling' was not covered, because, although there was lots of mould on the walls, there was no physical damage to them or to the windows: mere loss of amenity does not suffice for 'disrepair'.

The Court of Appeal in *Stent* v *Monmouth DC* (1987) 19 HLR 269 held that there can be no disrepair where there is no physical deterioration in the building. In that case a leaking door was not enough in itself to amount to disrepair. However, if the water does cause actual damage to the building, that may be sufficient to establish a breach of the landlord's obligation to repair.

Sanderson v *Berwick-on-Tweed Corporation* (1884) 13 QBD 547

Here the tenant's farm suffered flooding due to the drains of two neighbouring farms, which were also leased from the landlord, being blocked. The landlord was held liable for the damage caused by the flood which resulted from defective drains which the neighbouring tenant had been using properly, but not for the flood which resulted from excessive use of good drains. A landlord will only be liable for the lawful acts of other tenants. Thus, a landlord is not liable to one tenant for an excessively noisy neighbouring tenant, but he would be liable if the neighbour was making no more than a reasonable amount of noise which caused suffering to a neighbouring tenant because the partition walls were too thin and flimsy.

According to Megarry and Wade (2000 p 862):

> [u]sually there is no breach of the covenant unless the tenant suffers some physical interference with his enjoyment of the property. Thus where a landlord erected an external staircase which passed the tenant's bedroom windows and so destroyed his privacy, the tenant's action for damages failed.

The case referred to was *Browne* v *Flower* [1911] 1 Ch 219 and the decision is debatable. It can be contrasted with *Owen* v *Gadd* [1956] 2 QB 99, where the landlord, who had retained the top floor of the premises, erected scaffolding to repair the retained part, thereby obstructing access to the demised ground floor shop. The Court of Appeal held that this amounted to substantial interference; physical interruption was not necessary. The tenant succeeded (though he was awarded only minimal damages).

In addition, under the Protection from Eviction Act 1977, s 1 it is a criminal offence for any person to interfere with the peace or comfort of a residential occupier or his household, or to withdraw services reasonably required for residential occupation, if the intention is to drive the tenant out of the premises or to prevent him from exercising his rights.

Non-derogation from grant

The doctrine of non-derogation from grant means that 'a grantor having given a thing with one hand, is not to take away the means of enjoying it with the other' – Bowen LJ in *Birmingham Dudley & District Banking Co* v *Ross* (1887) 38 Ch D 295. A landlord impliedly covenants not to engage in activities which would frustrate the use of the land for the purposes for which it was let.

Aldin v *Latimer, Clark & Muirhead* [1894] 2 Ch 437

Construction on land retained by a landlord of buildings which prevented the free flow of air required by the tenant timber merchant to dry his timber was a derogation from grant.

In a more recent case, *Romulus Trading Co Ltd* v *Comet Properties Ltd* [1996] 2 EGLR 70, the question was whether leasing property to a tenant for banking and safe deposit purposes and then leasing nearby premises in the same block to another tenant for similar purposes amounted to a derogation from grant. The answer was no. Garland J provides an excellent review of cases on this point and his judgment is well worth reading in full. However, see *Lawson & Lawson* v *Hartley-Brown* (1996) 71 P&CR 242 where the Court of Appeal held there had been a derogation from grant.

The doctrine represents 'an implied rule of common honesty which is imposed in the interests of fair dealing between the parties' (Haley, 1997). It will arise only where the landlord retains part of the premises and seeks to restrict the use of the part let.

The doctrine is not limited to leases. (Indeed, we shall come across it again in regard to easements.)

Covenant for quiet enjoyment

Evans and Smith (2002, p 100) explain that such a covenant 'protects the tenant from acts which cause *physical* interference, whether those acts are done on the premises or not and from any conduct of the landlord or his agent interfering with the tenant's freedom of action in exercising his rights as tenant. It affords him no remedy in respect of acoustic or visual interference, for which his proper remedy, if any, would lie in tort'. Indeed, this has traditionally been the view taken, with much case law in support. However, the House of Lords, in a joint appeal, *Southwark London Borough Council* v *Mills*; *Baxter* v *Camden London Borough Council* [2001] 1 AC 1, held that although a breach of the covenant for quiet enjoyment requires a substantial interference with the tenant's lawful possession of the land, that interference need not be direct or physical, and a regular excessive noise could constitute such substantial interference. It was also explained that the covenant for quiet enjoyment is prospective in nature and does not apply to things done before the grant of the tenancy, even though they might have continuing consequences for the tenant: a tenant takes the property not only in the physical condition in which he found it, but also subject to the uses which the parties contemplated would be made of the parts retained by the landlord.

In regard to any claim in nuisance, their lordships held that a landlord cannot be held liable for authorising activities of his tenant if those activities did not in themselves constitute an actionable nuisance, and the ordinary use of residential premises is not in itself capable of amounting to a nuisance.

Article 8 of the European Convention on Human Rights protects a person's right to respect for his home and private life, and it is applicable to and enforceable between private parties as well as states – *X and Y v Netherlands* (1985) 8 EHRR 235. Section 6 of the Human Rights Act 1998 requires UK courts not to act in any way that is incompatible with any Convention right (unless required so to do in order to comply with primary legislation).

> The cumulative effect of these positive obligations under Article 8, together with the duty imposed on public authorities by Section 6 of the HRA 1998, may be that a public authority will be required to take action to prevent an interference to a person's home and private life by noise, nuisance or harassment, even where the actual perpetrator of the nuisance is a private person – Deborah Rook (2002).

On a number of occasions severe noise pollution has been held to constitute an interference under Article 8.

Southwark LBC v Mills [2001] 1 AC 1, [1999] 4 All ER 449

Here the noise levels were intolerable; the lack of effective soundproofing resulted in tenants being able to hear every sound from neighbouring flats – lights being switched on and off, doors being opened and closed, pans being placed on ovens, etc. Of course, *Mills* pre-dates the Human Rights Act, but would the decision have been different had it been heard today? Probably not, because the Council would claim that the financial burden upon it to rectify the matter would be prohibitive. The court would have to weigh the general interest of the community as a whole with the rights of the tenants in order to assess whether there was a fair balance. Given that a huge proportion of the Council's limited financial resources would be eaten up if the court found for the tenants, it is likely that they would not succeed. (However, if the court feels that financial resources are adequate to carry out the necessary work without beggaring the defendant, it may invoke Article 8 – see *Marcic v Thames Water Utilities Limited* [2001] 3 All ER 698.)

The tenant

It has to be said that it is the tenant, rather than the landlord, who carries most of the burdens. Indeed, most tenants' covenants amount to liabilities imposed upon the tenant for the benefit of the landlord.

Covenant to repair

As we saw when looking at the landlord's responsibility to repair, the covenantor (he who makes the promise, that is he who agrees to accept the burden of the covenant) must keep the premises in the condition in which they would be kept by a reasonably minded owner, taking into account the length of the lease, the locality, age and character of the premises at the time of the lease. Words like 'good', 'perfect' or 'substantial' do not increase the burden of repair. As with landlords, tenants are not required at the end of the term to give back to the landlord a building wholly different from that which he demised to the tenant. Thus, any renovations which are so substantial as to go beyond what any reasonable person would consider repair cannot be required of a tenant. The Queen's Bench Division held in *Fitzroy House Epworth Street (No 1) Ltd* v *Financial Times Ltd* [2006] EGLR 19 (applying *Commercial Union Life Assurance Co Ltd* v *Label Ink Ltd* [2001] L&TR 29) that 'material' does not mean simply 'non trivial' and that a breach of a repairing covenant would only be material 'if it jeopardised the landlord's ability to relet speedily the value of his reversion or his rental income'.

Ravenseft Properties Ltd v *Davstone (Holdings) Ltd* [1980] QB 12

Here the tenant covenanted in an underlease to 'repair, renew, rebuild ... the premises and every part thereof' and to repay to the landlord costs incurred in executing works to remedy want of such reparation. The building, a block of maisonettes, had been constructed in 1958–60 of a reinforced concrete frame with stone cladding. At that time it was not the usual practice to include expansion joints and none had been used for this building. Because no such joints had been used part of the stone cladding became loose and, by 1973, was in danger of falling. It became apparent that, in addition, the original contractors had not properly tied in the stones. By this time it had become common standard practice to use expansion joints in this type of construction and the costs of the necessary reparations was some £55,000, £5,000 of which was the cost for inserting the joints. The tenant was held liable under the express covenant to repair, the court holding that an express covenant to repair can extend to the remedying of an inherent defect in a building.

The question is one of degree – is the tenant being asked to do what can properly be described as 'repair', or is he being asked to give to the landlord a wholly different building?

Ravenseft was distinguished in *Post Office* v *Aquarius Properties Ltd* [1987] 1 All ER 1055, where the floor of a basement had been built defectively, but had not worsened. The tenant was held not to be liable under the covenant to repair as the building was in the same physical condition throughout and thus no lack of repair could be proved by the landlord.

Brew Brothers Ltd v *Snax (Ross) Ltd* [1970] 1 QB 612

This case provides another contrast with *Ravenseft*. A 14-year lease of a shop and dwelling which was bounded on one side by a filling station, contained a covenant by the tenant to 'repair, uphold, support, maintain ... and keep in repair' the demised premises and to 'pay on demand a reasonable share of the expenses ... of maintaining, repairing and cleansing all party walls, fences and drains' and to repair any want of repair due to the tenant's breach. A year after the commencement of the lease the foundations shifted due to seepage from broken drains: as a result a wall of the demised premises tilted and had to be temporarily shored up. To make the premises safe required the repair of the drains and the rebuilding of several walls, at a cost of £8,000. In spite of the repairing covenant, the Court of Appeal held the landlord was jointly liable with the tenants for the cost of the repairs, as they ought to have known of the dangerous state of the premises.

The question is whether the total work to be done amounts to renewal or replacement of defective parts, ie to a repair or, in effect, to renewal or replacement of
substantially the whole premises. This question cannot be answered by looking
simply at the component parts of the work required to be done, said the Court of
Appeal.

It is vital, therefore, that a prospective tenant draw up a schedule of repair at the
start of the lease, preferably with photographic evidence, particularly of any dilapidations. We shall see shortly that a tenant under leases created prior to 1 January
1996 remains liable upon covenants throughout the entire term of years, even if he
assigns the lease. Where a tenant contemplates subletting in the future, a schedule
of repairs and dilapidations at the start of his lease, and another at the date of assignment, is essential.

Following *Hill* v *Barclay* (1810) 16 Ves 402, although a landlord could not obtain
specific performance of a repairing covenant against his tenant, the tenant could
seek the remedy to force his landlord to execute repairs. However, Lawrence Collins
QC, sitting as a deputy judge of the High Court, held in *Rainbow Estates* v *Tokenhold*
[1998] 2 All ER 860 that the defendant tenants of a listed building were subject to
repairing obligations, and he made an order of specific performance against them.
In the judge's view, if, in some circumstances, a landlord's repairing covenant can be
made specifically enforceable against him, why not a tenant's? Each case should be
looked at individually and, provided the landlord is not trying to evade the tenant's
protection under the Leasehold Property (Repairs) Act 1938, there could be situations in which damages would be an inadequate remedy and specific performance
could be ordered. This case, where the landlord had no right of forfeiture for breach
of covenant and no right to enter and carry out repairs himself (an unusual omission) was such a situation. No doubt this case will go to appeal. If so, it will be
interesting to see whether the Appeal Court will take the opportunity to place both
parties on an equal footing.

Covenant against subletting or assignment

A tenant may be required to enter into a covenant not to sublet or assign, either at
all, or without the landlord's consent. In the latter case, unless the terms of the lease
absolutely prohibit assignment, the landlord's consent must not be unreasonably
withheld – Landlord and Tenant Act 1927, s 19(1). Prior to the Landlord and Tenant
(Covenants) Act 1995, parties to a lease were not allowed to agree between themselves what would or would not amount to unreasonableness. To get around this,
pre-conditions for assignment or underletting were inserted into the lease (see, for
example, *Adler* v *Upper Grosvenor Street Investments Ltd* [1957] 1 All ER 229). Since
1996, in cases of assignment (but **not** subletting), the parties can agree on the circumstances in which consent may be withheld. However, as Emma Slessinger (2005)
points out, 'pre-conditions continue to be relevant for several reasons. For forms of
alienation other than assignment (most obviously underletting), they are the only
way in which the parties can, in effect, agree in advance limitations on what will be
permitted'.

Ashworth Frazer Ltd v *Gloucester City Council* [2001] 1 WLR 2180

In this case the House of Lords held that the court neither could nor should determine by strict rules the grounds upon which a landlord might reasonably or unreasonably withhold consent and, although a landlord was not entitled to refuse consent on grounds which were 'wholly extraneous' to the relationship of landlord and tenant with regard to the subject matter of the lease, the question whether the landlord's conduct was reasonable or unreasonable depended in each case on its particular facts and fell to be determined by tribunal of fact, giving the concept of reasonableness a broad and commonsense meaning. The House of Lords, in *Ashworth Frazer*, laid down three 'overriding principles ... which apply in determining whether or not a landlord has unreasonably withheld consent' which are 'indubitably correct' – Peter Gibson LJ in *First Penthouse Ltd* v *Channel Hotels* [2004] EWCA Civ 1072. They are –

1. a landlord is not entitled to refuse his consent to an assignment on grounds which have nothing whatever to do with the relationship of landlord and tenant in regard to the subject matter of the lease;
2. it is not necessary for the landlord to prove that the conclusions which led him to refuse to consent were justified, if they were conclusions which might be reached by a reasonable man in the circumstances; and
3. in each case it is a question of fact, depending on all the circumstances, whether the landlord's consent to an assignment has been unreasonably withheld.

Under the Landlord and Tenant Act 1988, s 1(3) a landlord must, upon service by the tenant of a written application for consent, supply the requested consent 'within a reasonable time' or provide reasons why such consent is being withheld. Under s 1(6), the burden of proving the reasonableness of the refusal of consent rests with the landlord. *Orlando Investments Ltd* v *Grosvenor Estate Belgravia* (1990) 59 P&CR 21 provides an example of a reasonable refusal of consent to sublet. In that case there had been a history of extensive and longlasting breaches of repairing covenants by the tenant and it was held reasonable for the landlord to refuse consent to assign unless he could be reasonably satisfied that the assignee would remedy the breaches. The Landlord and Tenant (Covenants) Act 1995, s 22 inserts a new s 1A into the 1927 Act. This allows landlords, upon granting new leases, to specify the exact circumstances in which they may withhold consent to an assignment, or the conditions which they may attach to such consent. Where a landlord takes advantage of s 1A, a tenant cannot challenge the withholding of consent, or attaching of conditions, on the grounds of unreasonableness. As long as it is reasonable so to do, a landlord can insist that an assignor enter into an 'authorised guarantee agreement' requiring the assignor to guarantee the liabilities of his immediate assignee – s 16 of the 1995 Act. However, the guarantee does not extend to subsequent assignees.

On the other hand, it may be that a tenant has covenanted not to make improvements or alterations to the demised premises without the landlord's consent. In such a case also the landlord's consent must not be unreasonably withheld – Landlord and Tenant Act 1927, s 19(2).

Hagee v Co-operative Insurance Society (1991) 63 P&CR 362

Here the tenant covenanted not to cut any main walls or timbers of the building (which was a listed building) without the landlord's consent. The tenant employed independent contractors to renew an out-of-date air-conditioning system, instructing them to lay any necessary pipework above the upstairs floorboards. However, the landlord's advisers informed the contractors that this would not be acceptable. In view of this the contractors, without consulting or informing the tenant, cut a channel in the floor joists and laid the pipework within it. Upon hearing of this, the landlord refused to accept any further rent from the tenant and sought possession of the premises for breach of the covenant. It was held that, had the tenant carried out or authorised the cutting of the joists, he would have been liable for breach. However, as the work was carried out in breach of his instructions and without his knowledge, he was not liable. (As it turned out, the work as carried out did not affect the character of the building, and did not, therefore, contravene the planning Acts.)

Landlords are careful about tenants to whom they grant leases of their property. It is not unreasonable, therefore, that they should also wish to have a say in any assignee or sublessee. Indeed, in *Houlder Bros v Gibbs* [1925] 1 Ch 575 the Court of Appeal stated that if a refusal of consent is to be acceptable it must relate to the personality of the intented assignee or to the use which he is likely to make of the property. In *Gibbs* the landlord's reason for refusal was rejected because it was 'independent of the relationship between the lessor and the lessee, and on grounds which are entirely personal to the lessor and wholly extraneous to the lease'. In regard to the use which an intended assignee may make of the premises, the Court of Appeal in *Ashworth Frazer Ltd v Gloucester City Council* (2000) 80 P&CR 11 held that the belief of a landlord, no matter how reasonable, that the proposed assignee intends to use the demised premises for a purpose which would give rise to a breach of user covenant is not, in itself, a ground for withholding consent to assignment. Provided that, when giving consent to assignment, the landlord does not disable himself, necessarily and inevitably (by waiver, estoppel or otherwise), from continuing to insist on due observance of the user covenant by the assignee, he is in no worse position, following assignment, than he would have been if the assignor had himself proposed to use the demised premises for that purpose. However, the position would be different if the assignment inevitably gave rise to breach of the user covenant, and if consent to the assignment necessarily involved consent to the breach of the user covenant.

Balcombe LJ, in *International Drilling Fluids Ltd v Louisville Instruments (Uxbridge) Ltd* [1986] Ch 513, summarises the current law by providing seven propositions. See also *Straudley Investments Ltd v Mount Eden Land Ltd* [1996] EGCS 153 where the Court of Appeal provided two more. In *International Drilling Fluids* the Court of Appeal held that a refusal 'designed to achieve a collateral purpose unconnected with the terms of the lease' will fail. For a recent application of this, see *Norwich Union Life Insurance Society v Shapmoor Ltd* [1998] 3 All ER 32.

Covenants as to use of premises

Frequently leases contain covenants requiring the tenant either to use or not to use the premises for certain purposes, for example to use as a private dwelling only, or not to use for immoral purposes. It was held in *Marquis of Bute* v *Guest* (1846) 15 M&W 160 that a covenant not to use the premises other than for a specified purpose does not amount to a positive covenant to use the premises for that purpose; and in *Pulleng* v *Curran* (1982) 44 P&CR 58 it was held that no liability attaches to the tenant in such circumstances even if he makes no use whatsoever of the land.

Alarm bells rang when the Court of Appeal, in *Co-operative Insurance Society Ltd* v *Argyll Stores (Holdings) Ltd* [1996] 3 All ER 934, ordered a tenant to reopen its Safeway supermarket in the Hillsborough Shopping Centre, Sheffield. The store had been losing money and, in breach of covenant, the tenant closed it. As Lord Hoffmann said in the House of Lords, [1997] 3 All ER 297, however, it is settled practice that a court never grants mandatory injunctions requiring persons to carry on business, and the practice was not entirely dependent upon damages being an adequate remedy. One of the main reasons is the inability of the court to supervise the carrying on of the business, either at all or in a proper manner ('equity does nothing in vain'), and this applies even more so to orders of specific performance. Stating that the established practice of the court not to grant a mandatory injunction should only be departed from in exceptional circumstances, the House of Lords overruled the Court of Appeal's decision. Everyone breathed a sigh of relief (except the landlords)!

Covenant to pay rent

We have seen already that rent is one of the essential requirements of a lease. Obviously, then, every tenant enters into a covenant to pay rent. Unless the lease provides otherwise, rent is usually payable in arrears.

Prospective tenants should be careful to note any rent review clauses in the lease, under which the landlord can at certain points, for example every three years throughout the term or after seven years, alter the rent – usually in an upward direction! Such clauses do not usually specify the new rent and a tenant could, at the relevant time, find himself liable for a rent which he cannot afford. The imminence of a rent review will, of course, make any assignment or subletting more difficult.

Rent remains payable unless the lease has been frustrated, and this can be a difficult factor to prove.

In the absence of an express covenant to pay rent, one will be implied.

How can you acquire them?
Rules, principles and formalities

Generally, leases, to be legal, must comply with the requirement of the Law of Property Act 1925, s 52, which provides that:

> All conveyances of land or of any interest therein are void for the purpose of conveying or creating a legal estate unless made by deed.

However, to this general rule s 54(2) provides an exception in that: 'Nothing in the foregoing provisions of this Act shall affect the creation by parol of leases taking effect in possession for a term not exceeding three years ... at the best rent which can be reasonably obtained without taking a fine'. Therefore, a lease, even if it is created orally, can be legal if it is for three years or less, taken in possession (ie it must begin at the date of the grant), and for the best rent which can reasonably be obtained without taking a fine.

Long v *Tower Hamlets London Borough Council* [1996] 2 All 683

Here the need for the lease to be 'taken in possession' was illustrated. The tenancy document was executed on 8 September 1975 but the tenancy was not to commence until a future date – 29 September 1975. Not being by deed, the 'tenancy' document could not be a lease under s 54(2), even though the term was for less than three years. If it took effect at all, it was as a reversionary lease. (There was, however, on the facts a periodic tenancy due to the payment and acceptance of rent.)

It must be noted, however, that s 54(2) applies only to the original grant of a lease; it does not apply to assignments of leases – *Crago* v *Julian* [1992] 1 All ER 744.

As we have seen, the Law of Property (Miscellaneous Provisions) Act 1989, s 1 has made some amendments to the way in which deeds for the purpose of s 52 must be created after 30 July 1990 in order to be valid.

Contracts for leases

Failure to comply with the relevant formal requirement will, of course, render the purported legal lease void, but that is not to say that it will be of no effect at all.

As we have already seen, a formally invalid lease can give rise to a tenancy at will where the tenant has gone into possession with the landlord's consent. We also saw that if the landlord then accepts rent from the tenant, a periodic tenancy will be implied. However, under a tenancy at will, the landlord can give notice to quit at any time, and under a periodic tenancy, the tenant is only entitled to one rental period's notice (or four weeks minimum if it is a dwellinghouse), which will usually be far less than the tenant would have been entitled to under the lease, had it been valid. Yet, it may be that equity will secure for the tenant the originally agreed period of tenure.

It is crucial here to understand that before the completion stage of any transaction in land there is a contract stage. Until contracts have been 'exchanged' there is no legally enforceable agreement. Following exchange, traditionally about four weeks later, the actual conveyance or transfer will be completed. The formal requirements for contracts are different from those for deeds.

The starting point from which to claim equity's help is the contract for the defective lease. If the court would grant specific performance of this contract, the tenant will have a contract to create a lease – an estate contract. Whether or not specific performance will be granted depends upon several matters.

First, the contract for the lease must be valid. As we have seen, this will depend upon the date – if before 27 September 1989 it must comply with the requirements of the Law of Property Act 1925, s 40; if after 26 September 1989 it must comply with those of the Law of Property (Miscellaneous Provisions) Act 1989, s 2. It should be noted that whilst a *contract* for a lease of less than three years had, prior to 27 September 1989, to comply with s 40, any contract for such a lease made after 26 September 1989 does not need to comply with s 2 (and, probably, not with s 40 either).

If the contract is valid, the court will next decide whether or not to grant specific performance of it, but such a grant is purely discretionary and by no means guaranteed. Thus the tenant must have complied with all the maxims of equity, under which 'he who comes to equity must come with clean hands', 'he who seeks equity must do equity', 'equity will not assist a volunteer' and so on. Therefore, he must be bona fide and must have provided consideration. There must have been no undue delay on the tenant's part, for this will defeat his claim because of the doctrine of laches.

Coatsworth v *Johnson* (1886) 54 LT 520

The question was whether the court would have decreed specific performance in the circumstances of the case. As the plaintiff, the tenant, 'when he went to the court of equity and asked for specific performance, would have had to admit that ... he himself had failed to perform a material portion of the contract – in point of fact, that he had broken a portion of the agreement'. Lopes LJ stated: 'it is perfectly clear that the court of equity would have refused specific performance'.

If the court is willing to grant an order of specific performance, the landlord will have to do what he originally promised, that is, convey the legal estate to the tenant – but this time by way of a valid deed. Until such a deed has been executed, the tenant has an equitable interest – namely, an estate contract (a minor interest in registered land).

The rule in *Walsh* v *Lonsdale*

It will usually be the case that a tenant who is paying rent will have not only his contract for a lease, that is, an equitable lease, but also a legal periodic tenancy.

Walsh v *Lonsdale* (1882) 21 Ch D 9

The landlord granted a seven-year lease to the tenant under the terms of which the tenant was to pay rent yearly in advance. The lease was created in writing only, but the tenant entered into possession and paid the rent, though in arrear, thus becoming a legal periodic tenant. The landlord later demanded a year's rent in advance, as originally agreed, but the tenant refused to pay. The landlord seized the tenant's goods by way of distraint, whereupon the tenant sought damages for trespass and a decree of specific performance in respect of the informal lease. There was, then, a conflict between the tenant's legal periodic tenancy, under which rent was payable in arrear, and his equitable seven-year lease, under which rent was payable in advance. Whether the landlord was liable for trespass depended solely upon which lease - the legal periodic or the equitable - was held to prevail.

Following the Judicature Acts 1873-75, any conflict between the rules at common law and those in equity has to be resolved in favour of equity. Therefore, the lease was held to be equitable, for, as Jessel MR explained:

> There are not two estates as there were formerly, one estate at common law by reason of the payment of rent from year to year, and an estate in equity under the agreement. There is only one Court, and the equity rules prevail in it. The tenant holds under an agreement for a lease. He holds, therefore, under the same terms in equity as if a lease had been granted, it being a case in which both parties admit that relief is capable of being given by specific performance. That being so, he cannot

complain of the exercise by the landlord of the same rights as the landlord would have had if a lease had been granted.

Walsh v *Lonsdale* is a rare case because a tenant will usually be claiming an equitable lease, the landlord a legal periodic one.

What has now become known as 'the rule in *Walsh* v *Lonsdale*' has subsequently been given wider application, now being used to give effect in equity to informal grants of interests in land, for example easements and mortgages. Given the fact that the equitable lease arising from the application of the rule in *Walsh* v *Lonsdale* takes effect in exactly the same terms as those of the formally defective lease, it is often said that 'an equitable lease is as good as a legal lease', but this is not so for four reasons:

1 it depends for its existence upon the grant of specific performance which, being entirely discretionary, may not be granted even if the contract for the lease is valid;
2 it is not as secure against third parties;
3 there is no 'privity of estate' under such leases; and
4 equitable leases are not 'conveyances' for the purposes of the Law of Property Act 1925, s 62.

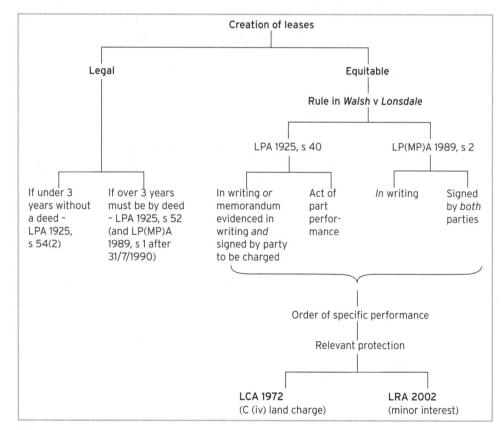

Figure 8.1

When and for how long?

Duration of leases and their covenants

A term of years must be for a definite term; that is, it must be clear from the outset when it will end, and in certain cases statute ensures that this is so by automatically converting uncertain terms into certain ones.

Leases determinable upon marriage or death

The Law of Property Act 1925 provides:

> Any lease or underlease, at a rent, or in consideration of a fine, for life or lives or for any term of years determinable with life or lives, or on the marriage of the lessee ... shall take effect as a lease, underlease or contract therefor, for a term of ninety years determinable after the death or marriage (as the case may be) of the original lessee, or of the survivor of the original lessees – s 149(6).

In *Skipton Building Society* v *Clayton et al* (1993) 25 HLR 596, an agreement, having been construed as a term of years for the joint lives of the second and third defendants and the life of the survivor of them, was held to come within s 149(6).

Reversionary leases

Section 149(3) of the Law of Property Act 1925 provides that any 'term, at a rent or granted in consideration of a fine ... to take effect more than 21 years from the date of the instrument purporting to create it, shall be void, and any contract ... to create such a term shall likewise be void'. However, 'Nothing in this Act affects the use of law that a legal term, whether or not being a mortgage term, may be created to take effect in reversion expectant on a longer term, which rule is hereby confirmed' – s 149(5). Leases frequently contain options to renew.

Re Strand & Savoy Properties Ltd [1960] Ch 582

The question arose whether such options are valid under s 149(3). The provision in that case was that the landlords would grant a further term of 35 years at the same rent 'at the written request of the lessee made 12 months before the expiration of the term hereby created'. Depending upon the time at which the option was exercised, this could well be a contract to take effect more than 21 years from the date of the lease. The option to renew was held to be valid:

> On [its true] terms the subsection is confined, so far as contracts are concerned, to contracts to create terms which, when created, will only take effect more than 21 years from the dates of the instruments creating them; that is to say, it invalidates contracts for the granting of leases which will, when granted, be reversionary leases, the postponement of the commencement of the term being for more than 21 years from the date of the lease - Buckley J.

As the option to renew, and thus the new term, would take effect immediately at the end of the lease, it was immaterial that it would be more than 21 years before the contractual right was exercised. This principle applies only to options to renew an already existing term at its termination.

What, though, if either of these two leases is not 'at a rent or in consideration of a fine'? Such a lease, if created before 1 January 1997, must take effect behind a strict settlement. If created after 31 December 1996, presumably such a lease will take effect under a trust of land, but the Act is silent on this point.

Perpetually renewable leases

The Law of Property Act 1922, s 145 provides that any contract which provides for the grant of a lease with a covenant for perpetual renewal shall operate as a contract to grant a lease for 2000 years. Perpetual renewals must be distinguished from limited renewals, as explained by Romer J in *Majorie Burnett Ltd* v *Barclay* (1985) 258 EG 642:

> In construing Clause 6 of the lease in the present case ... I must bear in mind that the leaning of the courts has been against perpetual renewals I have to find expressly in the lease a covenant or obligation for perpetual renewal. And I have to look ahead to see what the second lease will contain when the requirements of the covenant for renewal in the first have been duly observed.

On the facts, Romer J could find only a provision for the lease to be renewed twice. It was, therefore, not an attempt at perpetual renewal. However, in *Caerphilly Concrete Products Ltd* v *Owen* [1972] 1 WLR 372, a provision that the landlord would 'on the written request of the tenant ... grant to him a lease of the said demised land for the further term of five years from the expiration of the said term hereby granted at the same rent and continuing the life covenants and provisos as are here contained (including an option to renew such lease for the further term of five years at the expiration thereof)', was held by the Court of Appeal to amount to perpetual renewal. If a contract is so converted, the lessee or his successor in title may terminate the lease by giving at least ten days' notice in writing.

Periodic tenancies

These can be determined by the lessor giving notice to quit, the minimum length of the notice being one rental period. In express grants, rental periods are based upon the agreed, rather than the actual, mode of payment, so that if the agreement was for rent to be paid monthly, and the lessee paid quarterly, he would only be entitled to one month's notice. Where a periodic tenancy arises automatically, for example where a landlord accepts rent from a tenant at will, the period is measured by the actual mode of rental payment. The maximum under any periodic tenancy is six months' notice. However, these periods are subject to any protection afforded by various statutes, for example the Protection from Eviction Act 1977, s 5(1) of which provides that a minimum of four weeks' notice must be given to a tenant of a dwellinghouse, and though, generally, there is no common-law requirement that such notice be in writing, under s 5(1) notice to quit a dwellinghouse must be in writing, and must point out to the tenant the fact that he may be entitled to security of tenure under some other statutory provision. However, the Housing Act 1988 provides exempt categories, but for the most part these relate to persons who are not tenants proper, but more like lodgers. Under any assured tenancy or fixed-term assured tenancy entered into or beginning after 28 February 1997, an order for possession may not be made so as to take effect earlier than six months after the beginning of the tenancy – Housing Act 1996, s 99. The exempt categories under the Housing Act 1988 continue to apply.

The notice must comply strictly with the terms set out in the lease. It must state the correct date for the termination of the tenancy, or provide a formula by which the correct date can be ascertained with certainty, such as 'at the expiration of the year of your tenancy, which shall expire next after the end of one half year from the service of this notice'. That clause was accepted as a valid notice to quit in *Addis* v *Burrows* [1948] 1 KB 444. The notice must also be unconditional, unambiguous and relate to the whole of the premises. Therefore, a notice to quit part only of the premises is void. The House of Lords held in *Hammersmith & Fulham LBC* v *Monk* [1992] AC 478 that where one joint tenant of a periodic tenancy served notice to terminate the tenancy, it was effective even though the other joint tenant neither knew of nor consented to it. However, it is vital for the severing tenant to ensure he complies with all the necessary formalities under the lease and any relevant statutory provisions. In *Hounslow LBC* v *Pilling* (1993) 25 HLR 305 the Court of Appeal held that although the unilateral notice served by one joint tenant severed the joint tenancy, it was not sufficient to terminate the statutory tenancy as the notice did not comply with the Protection from Eviction Act 1977. (See Jones (1993).)

Statutory protection for periodic tenants

Residential tenancies. Most private sector residential tenancies created before 15 January 1989 gained protection from the Rent Acts. If a landlord terminated the contractual tenancy by serving notice to quit, the tenant became a statutory tenant and could only be evicted by a court order. The landlord had to establish one of the statutory grounds. Rents were also regulated by the Rent Acts, which did not apply to licences. 'The lease/licence distinction was therefore of crucial importance to landlords who wished to regain possession of their property' – Richard Royle, (2003, p 103).

Tenancies created after 14 January 1989 are mostly covered by the Housing Act 1988, under which landlords are able to grant assured shorthold tenancies which enable them to regain possession at the end of the term. The Housing Act 1996 makes all new tenancies shorthold tenancies unless the landlord expressly creates an assured tenancy. Landlords must give two months' written notice to recover possession. The lease/licence distinction has become less important since the introduction of assured shortholds, but there remain many tenants protected by the Rent Acts. (However, the Housing Act 1985 applies to public sector tenancies and licences, providing secure tenants with security of tenure on similar terms to those in the Rent Acts.)

Ghaidan v *Godin-Mendoza* [2004] 3 WLR 13

This case raised the question of the effect of the Human Rights Act on para 2(2) of Schedule 1 to the Rent Act 1977. The House of Lords held, in *Fitzpatrick* v *Sterling Housing Association* [1998] Ch 304, that para 2(2), which treated a spouse or a person living with the original tenant, as his or her wife or husband, did not include homosexual couples. In *Fitzpatrick*, the original tenant had died before the HRA came into force. However, in *Ghaidan*, the death of the tenant occurred after. Did *Fitzpatrick* still apply? The House of Lords in *Ghaidan* held by a majority that it was possible, without contradicting any cardinal principle in the 1977 Act, to read para 2(2) as extending to same-sex partners and thereby eliminate its discriminatory effect. Therefore, it did not fall foul of Articles 8 and 4 of the ECHR. Adopting such an interpretation, the defendant was entitled to succeed to the statutory tenancy of his late partner.

Another case concerning Article 8 was *Harrow LBC v Qazi* [2004] 1 P&CR 19, which raised the question whether the Council's termination of a tenancy infringed Article 8. The Court of Appeal held that it did, but the House of Lords declared that the object of Article 8 is 'to protect the individual against arbitrary interference by public authorities with his right to privacy, and is concerned with his home as an aspect of that. In addition, "home" for the purposes of Article 8 depends upon the factual circumstances' – it is not concerned, as such, with the protection of [the] right to own or to occupy property. Save in wholly exceptional circumstances, the requirements of Article 8(2) are met where the domestic law affords an unqualified right to possession on proof that the tenancy has been terminated. As Qazi's right to occupy the premises as his home arose from the tenancy, and as the tenancy had come to an end lawfully, the Council's unqualified right to possession was not in breach of Article 8.

Agricultural tenancies. The Agricultural Holdings Act 1986 provides limited statutory rights of security of tenure for agricultural tenants under which the tenant may acquire a right to renew his lease.

Business tenancies. Some protection is provided for commercial tenants under the Landlord and Tenant Act 1954, Part II in that landlords can only terminate a tenancy in accordance with the Act. If the landlord refuses to grant a renewal of a commerical tenancy without adequate grounds, the tenant can apply to the court.

Other tenancies

Tenancies at will

These can be determined at any time by either party.

Tenancies at sufference

Provided such a tenancy has not become a periodic tenancy, it can be ended by the landlord at any time. (However, if the tenant has been in possession for 12 years or more he may well have acquired the landlord's title by adverse possession.)

Tenancies by estoppel

If the estoppel which gave rise to the tenancy is 'fed' by the lessor acquiring the legal estate in the land, this will turn the tenant's equitable lease into a legal one but, as it will be subject to the same terms, it cannot extend the term.

Fixed-term tenancies

Subject to any statutory protection, where the term is for a fixed period the tenancy will, obviously, terminate at the end of the term. However, such leases frequently contain a 'break clause' under which either or both of the parties can determine the lease upon giving notice to the other prior to the expiration of the fixed term. The clause is usually exercisable at certain points throughout the term, commonly at the end of the third or seventh year, and upon notice being given of an intent to exercise the break clause.

Alternatively, the need for a notice to quit may be expressly provided for in a fixed-term lease.

Forfeiture

A landlord may forfeit a lease for the non-payment of rent or the breach of other covenants in the lease by the tenant, but he only has this right if the lease contains an express provision for forfeiture on the breach of covenant. Forfeiture may be effected either by serving a writ for possession or by peaceable re-entry, but if the premises are a dwellinghouse the landlord must, as we have seen, obtain a court order.

Re-entry

Mummery J stated in *Cowan* v *Department of Health* [1992] Ch 286 that a landlord's right of re-entry 'is what gives value and substance to the ... freehold reversion'. Coupled with the right to forfeit the lease, the right to re-enter the demised premises 'is the most draconian weapon in the armoury of the landlord whose tenant has committed a breach of covenant'. Most written leases contain an ample forfeiture clause which provides that, in the event of any breach by the tenant, 'it shall be lawful for the landlord to re-enter upon the demised premises and peaceably to hold and enjoy the demised premises thenceforth as if this lease had not been made and the term hereby granted shall absolutely determine' (Gray and Gray, 2000, p 1253).

However, the lease does not 'determine', ie it does not end automatically just because the tenant is in breach. If the lease contains a right of re-entry, then the breach renders the lease voidable only (at the landlord's option); it is only avoided upon re-entry – *Shevill* v *Builders Licensing Board* [1980] 2 BPR 9662. Upon the tenant's breach, the landlord must choose between enforcing forfeiture or waiving it: if he opts for forfeiture, he must re-enter – *Billson* v *Residential Apartments Ltd* [1992] 1 AC 494.

Re-entry requires some 'unequivocal act' such as changing the locks or padlocking the doors to the demised premises, which shows the landlord's intention to re-enter for the breach.

LPA 1925, s 146(1) refers to the enforcement of a right of re-entry 'by action or otherwise', that is by court action or 'peaceably'. Peaceable re-entry does, however, require the landlord to serve upon the tenant any statutory notice that he may be entitled to receive. However, peaceable re-entry is not available against a tenant of residential premises – s 2 of the Protection from Eviction Act 1977 provides that any re-entry exercised 'other than by proceedings in court while any person is lawfully residing in the premises' is unlawful. (Obviously, where the premises are non-residential, peaceable re-entry has the advantage of saving the landlord the time and money involved in seeking an order for possession.)

A right of re-entry is a proprietary right and it can be legal – LPA 1925, s 1(2)(e). The right must be expressly contained in the lease (it will only be implied into a legal lease in rare circumstances where the performance by the tenant of his obligations under the lease is deemed to be a condition upon which the continuance of the lease depends – *Doe d Henniker* v *Watt* (1828) 8 B&C 308). Curiously, however, a right to re-enter is implied into every equitable lease – *Hodgkinson* v *Crowe* (1875) 10 Ch App 622.

Where the premises are residential, there are serious consequences for a landlord who re-enters the demised premises without obtaining a duly executed court order for possession. We have already seen that the Protection from Eviction Act 1977 renders the landlord's action unlawful; indeed, it is a criminal offence (as is entry with a court order but without a proper bailiff, such as in *R* v *Brennan and Brennan* [1979] Crim LR 603, where the landlord employed 'a very large man and an alsatian dog'!).

The 1977 Act also makes the harassment by a landlord against a residential tenant a criminal offence – s 1(3). A tenant who suffers from acts by his landlord which fall under the Act can sue for damages in contract or tort, as well as under the remedies created by the Housing Act 1988 of damages under the statutory liability 'in the nature of a liability in tort' under s 27(4)(a) or of the right to continue in occupation under s 27(6)(b).

The Law Commission recommends that the law on peaceable re-entry should be reformed and 'placed on a statutory footing', which 'would preserve the remedy ... but with safeguards to ensure the protection of the legitimate interests of tenants' – Charles Harpum, Law Commissioner, *Termination of Tenancies by Physical Re-entry, A Consultative Document.*

We shall see later how landlords and tenants can seek to enforce compliance with the covenants, or the landlord seek forfeiture and the tenant relief. We shall also see that where the landlord wishes to forfeit for a breach of any covenant other than payment of rent, he must serve a written notice under the Law of Property Act 1925, s 146, stating the nature of the breach demanding it be remedied, if possible, and requiring the tenant to pay compensation (unless the landlord chooses to waive this). The landlord must wait for a reasonable time after service of the notice, giving the tenant the opportunity to remedy the breach. Of course, the breach must be capable of being remedied and certain covenants, usually negative ones, have, as we have seen, been held to be irremediable. In *Scala House and District Property Co Ltd* v *Forbes* [1974] QB 575 the Court of Appeal held that a covenant against assignment, underletting or parting with possession was incapable of remedy – 'It is a complete breach once for all'.

The Protection from Eviction Act 1977 provides that where premises are let as dwellings, and while the tenant remains in residence, the landlord cannot recover possession except with a court order. However, the protection does not apply to statutorily protected tenancies, which are covered by their own provisions, nor to 'excluded tenancies' as defined by s 3A of the Act, for example where the tenant shares accommodation with the landlord as part of the landlord's principal home. A property owner also needs a court order to remove squatters from his premises, notwithstanding they are there unlawfully – Criminal Law Act 1977, s 6(1).

Where the breach is remediable and the tenant fails to comply with the notice of forfeiture, the landlord can forfeit. However, as we shall see, the tenant or subtenant can apply to the court at any time before re-entry by the landlord for relief, and this the court may grant upon such terms as it thinks fit. Even if a tenant cannot himself apply for relief (say, for example, that he is a squatter), his subtenants, mortgagees or chargees may apply in his stead – *Tickner* v *Buzzacott* [1965] Ch 426. Relief should be sought by a tenant in possession within six months from the date of forfeiture. However, where a mortgagee of a leasehold interest seeks relief, it was held in *United Dominions Trust Ltd* v *Shellpoint Trustees* (1993) 64 P&CR 457 that he may do so after the six-month period, even though the tenant would be barred from so doing.

Alternatively, a landlord may choose to waive a breach of covenant and thus his right to forfeiture, either expressly or impliedly. Such waiver will not deprive the landlord of any claim that he may have in damages, however.

The Court of Appeal in *Billson* v *Residential Apartments Ltd* [1992] 1 AC 494 held that the court has no power to grant relief from forfeiture after peaceable re-entry has been effected for breach of covenant other than covenant to pay rent (see later under repairing covenants for full facts of this case). In *Bhojwani* v *Kingsley Investment Trust Ltd* (1992) 39 EG 138, the breach was of a covenant to pay rent and the landlord's re-entry was held to be lawful because of the rent arrears. What, though when

> [t]he landlord has forfeited the lease and recovered possession [and] he has found a new tenant and granted him a tenancy[?] What happens if the old tenant (or a sub-tenant or mortgagee) pops up and claims relief against forfeiture? Will the court grant relief and if so what will be the effect of the order on the new tenancy? – Webber (1997, p 82).

Where a landlord has forfeited for non-payment of rent, the general rule is that the court will grant relief from forfeiture to the tenant if he can pay the rent. As Lord Greene MR said in *Chandless-Chandless* v *Nicholson* [1942] 2 QB 321, the court's view is that the reservation by the landlord of a right of re-entry is 'merely security for payment of rent'. Similarly, where the breach is of any other covenant, relief is usually granted to one who makes good the breach.

In *Proudreed Ltd* v *Microgen Holdings plc* [1995] *The Times*, 17 July, the Court of Appeal held there had been no surrender of a lease by a landlord who had requested the return of keys of a dwellinghouse where there had been no other act which evidenced an intention to resume possession. However, in *Mattey Securities Ltd* v *Ervin & Others* [1998] EGCS 61, the Court of Appeal held that surrender by operation of law did not depend upon the intention of the parties and a clear distinction was to be made between the legal requirements for surrender, where intention was not a legal requirement, and an intention to enter into legal relations, where intention was highly relevant. In *Bolnore Properties Ltd* v *Cobb* [1996] EGCS 42, the delivery of the keys to the landlord by the tenant was held to be a symbolic delivery of possession with intent to surrender the lease (the tenant being faced with imminent eviction which he could avoid only by surrendering his existing tenancy and accepting a new shorthold one). Having complied with the statutory requirements for creating a shorthold tenancy, this would not be seen as a device to avoid the impact of the Rent Act, in other words it was not a sham.

Landlords and tenants may agree to vary the terms of the lease, indeed the original lease may itself have contained provision for this, for example a rent review clause. If the variation of the lease is such that it can, in reality, only take effect under a new lease, then both a surrender of the old lease (in so far as it has been rendered impracticable by the variation) and a grant of a new one (to give effect to the variation) may be implied. However, the Court of Appeal in *Friends' Provident Life Office* v *British Railways Board* [1996] 1 All ER 336, made it clear that such a regrant will only be implied in exceptional circumstances, where the variation affects the legal estate and either increases the extent of the premises demised or the term for which they are held. The changes in *Friends' Provident*, though extensive, did not vary the estate itself, thus there was no surrender and regrant. On the facts this meant that the tenant's obligations under the covenant to pay rent had not been brought to an end by the deed of variation.

Under LRA 2002, Sched 2, para 7, a notice in respect of a right of entry must be entered in the register, and the proprietor of the lease to which it relates must be registered as proprietor.

Surrender

It may be that, instead of the landlord wishing to remove the tenant, the tenant wishes to give up the remainder of his term to his landlord. One advantage of doing this is that the tenant's liabilities under the lease cease as from the date of surrender, though, of course, he remains liable for any breach or default prior to that.

Any surrender should be by deed, even if the lease was for less than three years (the exemption provided by the Law of Property Act 1925, s 54(2), applies to grants only). Needless to say, a defective deed may yet operate in equity under the rule in *Walsh* v *Lonsdale*. Equity may also take a hand by way of estoppel, in which case no deed would be necessary, as s 52(2)(c) provides an exception in cases of 'surrenders by operation of law, including surrenders which may, by law, be effected without writing'.

Any surrender must arise from the agreement – express or implied – of both parties; it cannot be by the act of just one of them. Thus, in *Cannan* v *Grimley* (1850) 9 CB 634, the return of keys by the tenant did not, in the absence of an agreement with his landlord, amount to a surrender.

Bellacourt Estates v *Adesina* [2005] EWCA Civ 208

The Court of Appeal approved the following statement of the law regarding surrender and abandonment by a tenant from Megarry and Wade (2000, at p 849):

> Abandonment of the premises by the tenant without more (even if rent is unpaid) is not a surrender, because the landlord may wish the tenant's liability to continue. Nor is the delivery of the key of the premises to the landlord enough by itself. Even if he accepts it, it must be shown that he did so with the intention of determining the tenancy ... and nor merely because he had no alternative.

In *Adesina*, T had entered into a lease in August 2000, vacating the premises shortly afterwards and paying no rent. L appealed against the first instance decision that it had accepted a surrender of her tenancy by T. Upholding the appeal, the Court of Appeal held that this was simply a case of a landlord not demanding rent arrears or service charges from a tenant and, as 'a mere omission to do something was not unequivocal conduct', there had been no acceptance of the purported surrender.

Break clauses

'Break clauses enable both landlords and tenants to free themselves from obligations which have proved onerous or which inhibit future planning' – H W Wilkinson, (1994, p 1637).

The House of Lords in *Mannai Investment Co Ltd* v *Eagle Star Life Assurance Co Ltd* [1997] 3 All ER 352, held that where a tenant served a notice purporting to exercise the break clause, the fact that the notice contained a minor misdescription – in that the determining date was one day out – would not render the notice ineffective, provided that, 'construed against its contextual setting it would unambiguously inform a reasonable recipient how and when it was to operate'. This was a landmark decision which effectively overruled a 157-year-old precedent.

It was made clear in *Peer Freeholds Ltd* v *Clean Wash International Ltd* [2005] EWHC 179 (Ch) that a break notice will be valid if it is sufficiently clear and unambiguous to leave a reasonable recipient in no reasonable doubt as to how and when it is intended to operate.

Merger

Merger occurs when the fee simple absolute and the reversion of the lease come together, for example where L leases land to T and later L sells the fee simple absolute to P, and T assigns his lease to P also; or where L leases land to T and T then acquires L's reversion.

Enlargement

A tenant can enlarge his lease into a fee simple provided that the original term was granted for no rent of money value, for not less than 300 years, of which there are still at least 200 years to run, and the term cannot be determined by re-entry for breach of covenant. The effect of enlarging such a lease, by virtue of the Law of Property Act 1925, s 153, is to provide the former tenant with a fee simple, but subject to all the terms of the lease.

Disclaimer

Under the Insolvency Act 1986, s 315, a tenant's trustee in bankruptcy can disclaim a lease which he finds onerous. This has the effect of bringing the lease to an end, but not of denying any third-party rights, so that if T mortgaged his term of years to M, the trustee in bankruptcy can disclaim the lease but the court may make a vesting order in favour of M. What's more, the Court of Appeal held in *Hindcastle Ltd* v *Barbara Attenborough Associates Ltd* (1994) *The Times*, 6 July, that the liability of the original lessee continues even after disclaimer of the lease by the liquidator of his assignee.

Frustration

National Carriers Ltd v Panalpina (Northern) Ltd [1981] AC 675

Here the House of Lords settled the vexed – not to say frustrating – question: are leases subject to the doctrine of frustration? Their Lordships held that in exceptional cases the doctrine could apply to a lease of land, though the event would have to be such that no substantial use that had been permitted by the lease and contemplated by the parties remained to be enjoyed by the tenant. In *Panalpina* the tenants had been prevented from using the leased premises for some 20 months out of a term of ten years. It was held that this did not amount to frustration.

A frustrating event will end the lease for both parties.

By statute

Under the Law of Property Act 1925, s 84(1), the Lands Tribunal has power 'from time to time, on the application of any person interested in any freehold land affected by any restriction under covenant or otherwise as to the user thereof or the building thereon, by order wholly or partially to discharge or modify any such restriction . . .'. Though this provision 'primarily applies to restrictions on freehold land . . . by subsection (12), as amended by the Landlord and Tenant Act 1954, [it] is made applicable to restrictions affecting leasehold land where a term of more than 40 years is created by the lease of which more than 25 years have expired' – Harman LJ in *Ridley* v *Taylor* [1965] 1 WLR 611. However, his Lordship went on to state that, 'it seems to me that it should be more difficult to persuade the court to exercise its discretion in leasehold than in freehold cases'. Notwithstanding this, since 1950 there have been more than a dozen cases reported in the *Property and Conveyancing Reports*, and in about two-thirds of them the tenant has succeeded.

Certain statutes enable tenants to extend their leases – Leasehold Reform Act 1967, Housing Act 1985, Landlord and Tenant Act 1987 and Leasehold Reform, Housing and Urban Development Act 1993. In addition, the Rent Act 1977 and the Housing Act 1980 provided protected 'shorthold tenancies' and the Housing Act 1988 an 'assured shorthold'. However, these have since been superseded by assured shorthold tenancies governed by the Housing Act 1996. These Acts truly cover landlord and tenant and housing law, not land law, and therefore the Acts themselves should be consulted for the various provisions affecting such 'statutory' tenancies.

The running of covenants

A covenant is, then, an agreement contained in a deed in which one party promises the other that he will do or not do certain things on or in relation to certain land. The person making the promise is the covenantor, and the person to whom he makes it, the covenantee. Thus the covenantor has the burden of the covenant, and his land is the servient tenement, whilst the covenantee has the benefit and his land is the dominant tenement.

Covenants arise in freeholds and leaseholds and are used mainly to retain the character and value of the property for the benefit of which they are made, or to define the obligations of the parties in relation to it.

Covenants can be positive or negative (negative covenants usually being called restrictive covenants). Not surprisingly, a positive covenant requires the covenantor to perform some specified act in relation to the land, whilst a negative one restricts him from doing something on his own land. An example of a positive covenant is the requirement to maintain property in good repair. In almost every case, a positive covenant will involve the covenantor in expenditure. An example of a negative, or restrictive, covenant is an obligation not to use a servient tenement for anything other than a dwellinghouse. In freehold land, a positive covenant cannot bind anyone other than the original parties to it. (This can cause difficulties, especially in regard to flats where the common parts, such as the stairs and landings, need to be maintained.)

Leasehold covenants continue, in normal circumstances, for the full duration of the term granted, though we have seen that breach of certain covenants may lead to a lease ending before its allotted time. We have also seen that fixed-term leases may contain a 'break clause', and it is also quite common to find, in the case of tenants' covenants to pay rent, a 'rent review clause'. Whilst this does not alter the length of time during which the covenant will run, it does provide for alteration of the amount of rent which will be payable during a given part of the term. In such clauses, rent is commonly reviewable every three, five or seven years.

A tenant, by definition, has a right to exclusive possession, but a landlord has a right of entry to the premises in order to effect repairs thereto. The right of entry is usually expressly reserved in the lease, but one will be usually implied into all leases where there is an obligation to repair.

As far as the original parties to a lease are concerned, there is no difficulty as they can sue each other in privity of contract. What, though, if either the landlord or the tenant assigns his interest to a third party – will the covenants run with the reversion (ie from the landlord to his assignee) or with the lease (ie from the tenant to his assignee)? We will have to consider two sets of rules, following the Landlord and Tenant (Covenants) Act 1995. This Act applies to all 'new' tenancies and, for the purposes of the Act, 'a tenancy is a new tenancy if it is granted on or after the date on which this Act comes into force otherwise than in pursuance of (a) an agreement entered into before that date, or (b) an order of a court made before that date' – s 1(3). The Act came into force on 1 January 1996. Where a lease is entered into pursuant to an agreement for lease, option agreement or court order made before the Act came into force the old rules apply.

In old leases, covenants must 'touch and concern' the land if they are to 'run'. In order to touch and concern the land, a covenant must affect the landlord *qua* landlord and the tenant *qua* tenant, that is, the landlord as a landlord, and the tenant as a tenant and not just personally. Thus, it was held in *Woodall* v *Clifton* [1905] 2 Ch 257 that an option to purchase the freehold reversion could not be such a covenant as it affected the parties as vendor and purchaser, but not as landlord and tenant. However, a covenant to renew the lease does run.

The statutory equivalent of 'touch and concern' the land requires that covenants contained in leases granted prior to 1 January 1996 have 'reference to the subject matter of the lease' – Law of Property Act 1925, ss 141(1) and 142(1). New leases created after 31 December 1995 are governed by the Landlord and Tenant (Covenants) Act 1995, which applies to a covenant 'whether or not the covenant has reference to the subject matter of the tenancy' – s 2(1)(a), and 'whether the covenant is express, implied or imposed by law' – s 2(1)(b). However, the covenant must be a covenant 'of a tenancy', though exactly what this expression means is not yet clear.

Covenants to pay rent, to repair the premises, not to use the premises for business purposes, not to assign the lease without the landlord's consent and so on are common in leases, though they may be express or implied. Where, as in most cases, a lease is preceded by a contract for that lease, there may be an express term that it will include 'the usual covenants'; these would include the landlord's usual covenant for quiet enjoyment (which means that the tenant's enjoyment of the property will not be disturbed), and the tenant's usual covenants to pay rent, rates and taxes, to keep the premises in repair and deliver them up to the landlord in such condition, and to allow the landlord to enter and view the state of repair.

Express covenants usually include the tenant's covenants to pay rent, not to assign, underlet or part with possession of the premises – either at all, or without the landlord's consent – and a covenant by the landlord or tenant to repair.

In regard to express covenants, the Court of Appeal affirmed in *Larksworth Investments Ltd* v *Temple House Ltd* [1996] EGCS 86 that the construction of covenants in leases should be ascertained from the parties' mutual intention from the contractual words used. The court should, therefore, determine what reasonable persons in their position would have intended. However, where a tenant has assigned, the obligations of the original tenant are not affected by any subsequent agreement by the landlord with the assignee under which the assignee takes on some obligation which was not contemplated in the original lease: *Friends' Provident Life Office* v *British Railways Board* [1996] 1 All ER 336 (but if the original lease had contemplated some future variation of its terms, such as by including a rent review clause, the original tenant may well find himself bound by any enlarged or enhanced obligations undertaken by his assignee).

Before we look at the rules for 'running' the benefit and burden of leasehold covenants beyond the original parties, however, we must first understand the difference between an assignment of a lease and the granting of a sub- or underlease. As Joyce J explained in *South of England Dairies Ltd* v *Baker* [1905] 2 Ch 631, 'An assignment of a term differs from an underlease in that the former means parting with the whole and the latter with only a portion of the lessee's interest. An assignment of a lease must necessarily embrace all the estate of the assignor'.

Example

If Tony is the fee simple owner of a house in Catherine Street and he grants a lease of it to Debbie for ten years, and after two years Debbie transfers it to Lorie, Lorie has the whole of the remaining term – eight years: this is an assignment. If, on the other hand, Debbie only grants Lorie three years, this is a sublease, which, as we shall see, can cause problems for Tony when it comes to the running and enforcement of the covenants in the lease against Lorie.

Brown & Root Technology Ltd v *Sun Alliance & London Assurance Company Ltd* (1997) The Times, 27 January

Here the meaning of 'assignment' was considered. Following *Gentle* v *Faulkner* [1900] 2 QB 267, the Court of Appeal held that 'assignment' means assignment of the legal estate, not of the beneficial interest. Transfer of the beneficial interest was held not to be relevant to the legal relationship between landlord and tenant. It is important, then, to remember that in registered land the legal estate will only pass on registration: until then it is deemed to remain with the registered proprietor, that is the vendor. The purchaser will, therefore, only have a beneficial interest, his vendor holding title on trust for him. The land in *Brown & Root* was registered land. The case concerned a licence to break the lease early (a personal right only). This right was non-assignable and ceased on assignment of the lease. Therefore, the point in time at which assignment occurred was vital. Being registered land, there was no assignment of the legal estate until title was registered in the name of the assignee. That had not occurred, so the right to break was still available to the tenant.

(Of course, where land is unregistered, title passes to the assignee on completion of the assignment.)

In its Consultation Document, *Land Registration for the Twenty-First Century* (Law Com 254 (1998)), the Law Commission proposes various options to avoid the problems caused by the decision in *Brown & Root*.

Where the tenant assigns his term

Tenancies granted before 1 January 1996

An assignment by the tenant must, then, be of the whole of the term remaining under his lease. Where T does assign his lease, he will be taken to have covenanted not only for himself but also on behalf of his 'successors in title' (assignees) and 'the persons deriving title under him' (subtenants) by virtue of the Law of Property Act 1925, s 79. Therefore, he remains liable to the landlord upon the covenants for the duration of the lease, notwithstanding that it was not he, T, who broke them and even though he now has no interest in the land. However, the House of Lords in *City of London Corporation* v *Fell* [1993] 3 WLR 1164, held that upon assignment of a lease the continuing liability of an original tenant upon covenants entered into with the landlord ceases upon the expiry of the agreed contractual term; where a lease continues by virtue of the Landlord and Tenant Act 1954, the liability of the original tenant ends with the original term. *Fell* was applied in *Friends' Provident Life Office* v *British Railways Board*, where it was held that obligations accepted by a lessee in his contract with the lessor could not be varied or increased by a subsequent agreement made by the lessor with an assignee.

We shall see that not only can L sue T for any breach committed during the duration of the lease, but usually he can choose instead to sue the actual perpetrator, that is, T's assignee. However, he cannot go against both of them in an attempt to recover twice! He can, though, 'sue either the original lessee or the assignee, or both at the same time' – Bedlam LJ in *Norwich Union Life Insurance Society* v *Low Profile Fashions Ltd* (1992) 64 P&CR 187, that is he can go against both to recover his loss – a useful ploy where neither one can, individually, pay the full amount due. Given the purpose of covenants – to keep up the value of the property – it is usually preferable for the landlord to go against the current tenant, A, as an order for specific performance (to force A to carry out the required tasks) or an injunction (to prevent him from acting in breach) will probably be more effective than mere damages, and cause the landlord less inconvenience. Of course, if the actual perpetrator has absconded, or if he is a man of straw, L would still be able to go against T for damages. It is for L to decide who to sue; if he chooses to go against T, so be it. T cannot complain, even if A is able to pay.

Re Mirror Group (Holdings) Ltd (1992) The Times, 12 November

Where there had been three assignments of the lease, T paid L arrears of rent due from assignees amounting to over £2 million, A1 and A3 being insolvent. T then tried to compel A1 to sue A2 and give the proceeds to T, or to assign his cause of action against him to T. The court held, there being no direct legal nexus between T and A2, that A1's obligation to T did not extend to acting upon his own right to sue A2. As T could not, therefore, compel A1 to sue A2, nor to assign the right so to do, the loss lay where it fell - with T.

If L decides to sue T, T can sue his assignee, A, because the Law of Property Act 1925, s 77, implies an indemnity clause into every assignment of a lease under which the assignee must indemnify his assignor for any breach of covenant. Therefore, it does not matter how many assignments there are because each assignor can sue his assignee under the chain of indemnity clauses which has been created.

Where the actual perpetrator is not the assignee of the tenant, but a subsequent assignee, T can go directly against him under the rule in *Moule* v *Garrett* (1871) LR 7 Ex 101 which states that 'where one person is compelled to pay damages by the legal default of another, he is entitled to recover from [that person] the sum so paid'.

Thus, where L grants a lease to T:

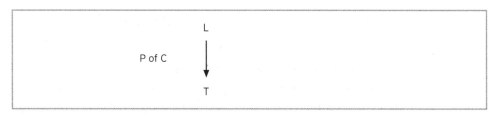

there is privity of contract (P of C) and continuing liability under s 79.

If T assigns the remainder of his term to A:

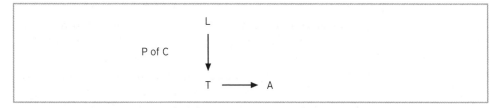

T remains liable to L in privity of contract, but so too does his assignee remain liable to T, because s 77 incorporates into every assignment of a lease an implied covenant by A that he will indemnify his assignor, T, for any breach of covenant which A commits. As this clause is implied into every assignment, it creates a chain of indemnity covenants, so that:

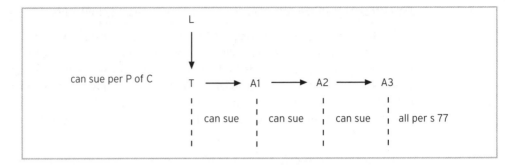

However, if A3 is the real perpetrator, T can, if he prefers, sue A3 direct under the rule in *Moule* v *Garrett*:

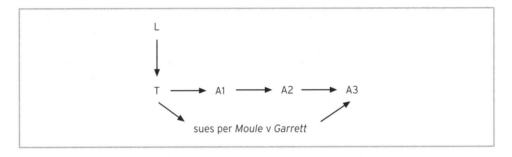

Tenancies granted after 31 December 1995

For the most part, the 1995 Act applies only to 'new' tenancies, that is those granted after 31 December 1995. However, ss 17–20 apply to all leases – new and old. The tenancy is 'granted' on the beginning of the day on which it is effectively executed: therefore, you cannot avoid the Act either by backdating a deed executed after the Act or by providing for the term to begin earlier than the date of execution of the lease.

'A tenancy granted pursuant to an agreement entered into before the Act, or following a court order made before it, is not a new tenancy' – s 1(3); nor is a tenancy which arises upon the exercise of an option to renew where the option was entered into before the Act – s 1(6). Curiously, 'option' for the purposes of s 1(6) includes 'the right of first refusal' – that is, a right of pre-emption – s 1(7).

However, a tenancy which arises from a deemed surrender and regrant is a new tenancy – s 1(5).

Section 5 of the Act abolishes the liability of a tenant for rent and other leasehold covenants after the whole of the premises have been assigned; that is, of course, when the tenancy of all the premises has been assigned for the whole of the remaining term. Section 5(2) provides that upon such an assignment the tenant 'is released from the tenant covenants of the tenancy' and 'ceases to be entitled to the benefit of the landlord covenants of the tenancy, as from the assignment'. However, s 11 provides that where an assignment is made in breach of covenant or by operation of law, then the liability of the assignor continues.

If the tenant assigns part only of the premises demised to him, then as from the assignment he 'is released from the tenant covenants of the tenancy, and . . . ceases to be entitled to the benefit of the landlord covenants of the tenancy, only to the extent that those covenants fall to be complied with in relation to that part of the demised premises' – s 5(3).

The only three exceptions to s 5 are: where the assignment was unauthorised release will not be automatic, though the assignor may obtain release if there is a later valid assignment – s 11. Assignments by operation of law – that is following death or insolvency – will also operate as for an unauthorised assignment. Finally, where lease terms are expressed to be made personal to a named person 'nothing in [s 3] shall operate ... to make the covenant enforceable by or (as the case may be) against any other person'.

Thus, '[a]fter 1 January 1996 the only former tenants or guarantors who can be held liable for the debts of a successor will be those holding under leases executed before that date, or former tenants under "new" leases who have given an authorised guarantee under s 16' (Charles Ward, 1995, p 18). Also, of course, a tenant who has assigned without consent will remain liable – s 11. Section 16 enables a landlord to insist that an assignor enter into an 'authorised guarantee agreement' requiring the assignor to guarantee the liabilities of his immediate assignee (but not subsequent assignees), so long as it is reasonable to do so: the reasonableness requirements of the Landlord and Tenant Act 1927, s 19, must be satisfied – *Wallis Fashion Group Ltd v GCU Life Assurance* (2000) 81 P&CR 393.

Neither former tenants nor guarantors shall be liable to pay any amount, however, unless notice (stating the amount due and the fact that the landlord intends to collect it from the former tenant or guarantor) has been served upon them within six months of the date the debt fell due: s 17. In addition, as Ward says, 'Section 19 strengthens the position of a former tenant or guarantor who is forced to pay the debts of a successor'. It does this by providing a new right to call for an 'overriding lease', under which the terms 'will be consistent with those in the original lease previously assigned and will be for the residue of the existing lease plus three days. The effect of an overriding lease is to make the defaulting assignee into an undertenant of the former tenant or guarantor, and give him all the rights and remedies of an intermediate landlord'. This means that the lease can then be forfeited and the former tenant or guarantor given control of the premises. An overriding lease can only be sought after the landlord has made a demand under s 17, and the former tenant or guarantor must make the request for an overriding lease within 12 months of the s 17 payment being made. A landlord, upon receiving a valid request for an overriding lease, must grant it within a reasonable time, though if there are competing applications (for example, where there is more than one former tenant) he is only obliged to grant one. As Ward explains, '[t]he rule is "first come, first served". Where two requests are received on the same day, a landlord must give former tenants priority over later ones'. Unless the original lease was itself a new lease, an overriding lease will not be a 'new' lease under the Act. Remember, ss 17–20 apply to all tenancies – new and old.

The effect of s 5, then, in regard to 'new' tenancies, is to render ss 77, 78 and 79 of the Law of Property Act 1925 and the rule in *Moule* v *Garrett* obsolete, so that all tenants, bar the current holder of the term of years, drop out of the picture.

Under the 1995 Act there is no rule that only covenants which touch and concern the land may pass to an assignee: the benefit and burden of all covenants in the lease will pass upon assignment unless they are expressly stated in the lease itself to be personal: s 3. The Court of Appeal held in *Edlington Properties Ltd* v *J H Fenner & Co Ltd* [2006] 1 WLR 1583 that a covenant, to pay rent is 'clearly within the ambit' of s 3. However, the Court of Appeal in *BHP Petroleum Great Britain Ltd* v *Chesterfield Properties Ltd* [2002] 2 WLR 672, held that a covenant that was expressed to be personal to the landlord was not a 'landlord covenant' for the purposes of s 28(1) of the Act, which defines 'landlord' (and 'tenant') as persons being landlord and tenant 'for the time being'. Given this decision, 'it is difficult to see what role this provision can have, [if] personal covenants are not landlord and tenant covenants in the first place' (Roger J Smith, 2003, p 441). *Chesterfield* was distinguished by the House of Lords in *Avonridge Property Co Ltd* v *London Diocesan Fund* [2006] 1 All ER 127, in which their lordships gave valuable advice on the meaning and application of certain sections of the Act: ss 5–8 are 'relieving provisions intended to benefit landlords or tenants to relieve them from a liability which would otherwise exist' which introduce a means, which cannot be ousted, 'whereby in certain circumstances without the agreement of the other party, a landlord or tenant could be released from the liability he had assumed'. Section 25 should be interpreted generously, but there is 'nothing in the Act to suggest that the statute was intended to exclude the parties' ability to limit liability under their covenants from the outset in whatever way they agreed' (whether the agreed limitation was contained in the lease itself, in a separate document by way of waiver or an agreement to release). As the risks involved were obvious on the face of the subleases and thus not concealed or obscured from the subtenant, the facts did not exemplify a loophole in the Act.

Though s 28(1) defines 'assignment' as including equitable assignments, and 'tenancy' as 'any lease or other tenancy', including a subtenancy and an agreement for a tenancy, it is doubtful whether this is enough to 'overrule' the long-established principle that the doctrine of privity of estate does not apply to equitable leases – *Purchase* v *Lichfield Brewery* [1915] 1 KB 184. As we shall see very shortly, the effect of this is that, if the 1995 Act does not apply to equitable leases, the purchaser from a landlord remains in a stronger position than the purchaser from a tenant.

Where L assigns his reversion

Tenancies granted before 1 January 1996

L's reversion is, of course, the fee simple absolute in possession subject to the remainder of the lease. As it is not only the tenant but also the landlord who enters into covenants, the landlord will also be liable for any breach by him. Liability to the tenant comes under privity of contract, such liability continuing even after assignment of the reversion by virtue of the Law of Property Act 1925, s 79.

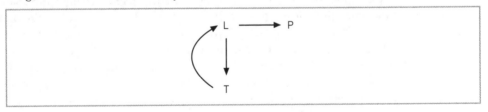

If T has assigned his term, his assignee can sue L:

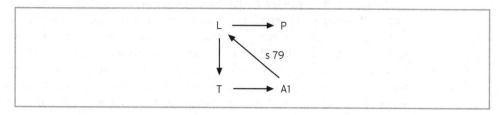

If A1 assigns his term to A2, A1 can still sue L for any breach committed by him during A1's tenancy, notwithstanding that A2 is now the tenant. However, once L has parted with his interest to P, he can no longer go against T – Law of Property Act 1925, s 141. However, in cases of 'new' leases under the Landlord and Tenant (Covenants) Act 1995, s 24(4) provides that '[w]here by virtue of this Act a person ceases to be entitled to the benefit of a covenant, this does not affect any rights of his arising from a breach of the covenant occurring before he ceases to be so entitled'. This would seem, therefore, to change the rule in regard to breaches prior to assignment of a new lease, so that a landlord can sue his former tenant for pre-existing breaches.

Having looked at the position between the original parties, we must now look at that of third parties. Can an assignee of L sue an assignee of T for breach of covenant? Whilst the original parties can enforce the covenants under privity of contract, assignees can enforce them if there is 'privity of estate' (P of E).

Privity of estate is, like privity of contract, a relationship and it occurs where the relationship between the assignees is that of landlord and tenant, notwithstanding that, as between themselves, there is no privity of contract. Therefore, as between the original parties there is both privity of contract and privity of estate, but as between assignees from them there can only be privity of estate, that is:

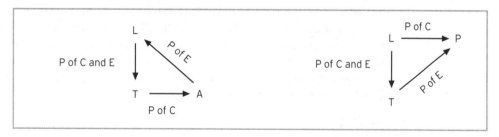

and where both original parties have assigned their interests:

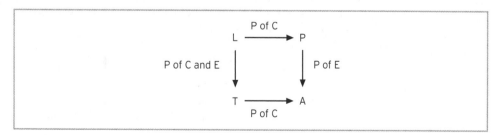

Thus, so long as there is an assignment of the fee simple reversion or of the whole of the term left in the lease, there will be privity of estate between the current landlord and tenant, no matter how many assignments there are of either.

Provided there is privity of estate, then by virtue of the Law of Property Act 1925, ss 141 and 142, the benefit and burden respectively of the covenants run with the reversion of the lease, provided the covenants had 'reference to the subject matter of the lease' – that is, provided they touch and concern the land. In other words, they must affect the landlord as a landlord and the tenant as a tenant, and not merely personally, so that covenants of a purely personal nature will not pass, nor will any which do not fall within the landlord and tenant relationship. Thus, a covenant by a landlord to grant his tenant an option to purchase the freehold reversion would not pass because it creates a relationship of vendor and purchaser, not one of landlord and tenant. Obviously, a covenant to keep the premises which are the subject matter of the lease in repair does touch and concern the land, but a covenant to keep other premises in repair does not – *Dewar* v *Goodman* [1909] AC 72.

Where it is the tenant who assigns, covenants will run with the lease, binding the assignee, under the rule in *Spencer's Case* (1583) 5 Co Rep 16a, provided the covenants touch and concern the land. Under the rule the original covenantor must have covenanted on behalf of himself, his assigns and successors in title but, as we have seen, this is not a problem today as s 79 implies it – though it can be excluded by express words.

Not only does the assignee have the burden of the covenants imposed upon him under the rule, but he can also enforce the benefit of the landlord's covenants – provided they also touch and concern the land. With regard to the benefit, s 78 implies the necessary words as to the assignees and successors in title but, unlike s 79, they cannot be excluded.

It must be noted, however, that where the lease is merely equitable, though the benefit of any of the tenant's covenants may pass upon assignment of it, the burden cannot because *Spencer's Case* does not apply to equitable leases: *Purchase* v *Lichfield Brewery*. This means that the landlord will only be able to sue his original tenant – another reason why an equitable lease is not as good as a legal lease! On the other hand, if the assignment is of the reversion, it will not matter whether the lease is legal or equitable because ss 141 and 142 apply to both. Therefore, a purchaser from the landlord takes both burden and benefit.

Subtenants

A problem arises where, instead of assigning the whole of his remaining term, the tenant transfers only part of it. This is a sublease and this creates no privity of estate between the subtenant and the original (head) landlord, between whom, of course, there is no privity of contract either.

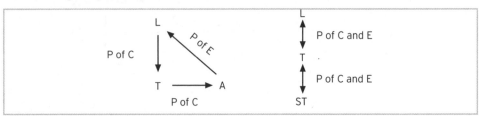

L has privity of contract and privity of estate with T, and T has privity of contract and privity of estate with ST, but there is no relationship at all between L and ST. Therefore, the covenants cannot be directly enforced by L or ST under *Spencer's Case*. Of course, T remains liable to L throughout his term and he will, therefore, usually incorporate into the sublease to ST all the covenants which appear in T's lease from L. T can then sue ST upon himself being sued by L.

As Joyce J explained in *South of England Dairies Ltd v Baker*:

> The original lessor has no right of action against the underlessee personally for the breach of any positive covenant of the lessee's contained in the original lease. The original lessor's remedy in such a case is against the original lessee, who is liable for breach of the covenant. The underlessee is liable, however, in equity to be restrained from breach of a negative or restrictive covenant contained in the original lease of which he had notice, express or imputed, when the underlease was granted.

A positive covenant is one which will involve the covenantor (the party with the burden of the covenant) in expense, such as a covenant to repair. In freehold land, the burden of a positive covenant can never run with the land, but in leasehold land it can – as between the original parties or where there is privity of estate: where a sublease has been created, the burden of a positive covenant cannot be enforced directly against the subtenant by the landlord. As Joyce J says, however, there is a way in which L can sue, and be sued by ST directly in equity for the breach of negative covenants, and that is under the rule in *Tulk v Moxhay* (1848) 2 Ph 774. *Hemingway Securities Ltd v Dunraven Ltd* [1995] 1 EGLR 61 illustrates this. We shall see, however, that even if a negative covenant runs, it may be unenforceable. In regard to the rule in *Tulk v Moxhay* though, s 3(5) of the Landlord and Tenant (Covenants) Act 1995 may prove to be crucial. It provides that:

> Any landlord or tenant covenant of a tenancy which is restrictive of user of land shall, as well as being capable of enforcement against an assigneee, be capable of being enforced against any other person who is the owner or occupier of any demised premises to which the covenant relates, even though there is no express provision in the tenancy to that effect.

Clearly, then, under s 3(5) the head landlord can enforce negative covenants directly against a subtenant: he will not have to turn to *Tulk v Moxhay*. It would seem, however, that the rule in regard to transmission of positive covenants remains the same; that is, they are not enforceable by a head landlord directly against a subtenant. (In regard to the *benefit* of covenants in a lease created after 11 May 2000, a subtenant may be able to enforce them directly against the landlord under the Contracts (Rights of Third Parties) Act 1999.)

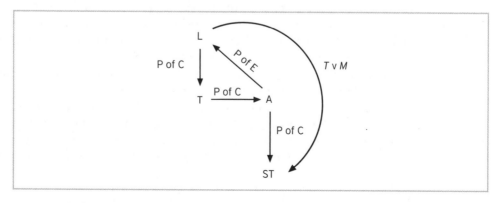

Neuberger J stated *per curiam* in *PW & Co v Milton Gate Investments Ltd* [2004] Ch 142 that, in light of s 3 of the Human Rights Act 1998, ss 141 and 142 could be construed in such a way as to enable covenants in a subtenancy to be enforceable as between a head landlord and subtenant in the event of the head tenancy being determined by break notice.

Tenancies granted after 31 December 1995

We have seen that under the Landlord and Tenant (Covenants) Act 1995 the privity of contract which bound an original tenant throughout the term of a lease has been abolished for new leases. The landlord, too, can be released from his obligations upon sale of the reversion under s 7 of the 1995 Act. However, release in the case of a landlord is **not automatic**. If a landlord is to be released he must serve notice on the tenant before or within four weeks of completion of the assignment of the reversionary interest. Section 8 of the Act lays down the procedure for seeking release from the covenants. Provided the tenant does not object within 28 days, the landlord will obtain the release: he will also be released if the tenant, having initially objected, subsequently withdraws his objection or if it is overruled by a county court. Thus, ss 7 and 8 render ss 141 and 142 of the Law of Property Act 1925 and the rule in *Spencer's Case* obsolete in respect of new tenancies. As mentioned previously, the 1995 Act applies to equitable as well as legal leases.

The 1995 Act has clearly made the running of leasehold covenants a great deal easier. It is, however, unfortunate that it applies to all express covenants in a lease, regardless of whether they touch and concern the land or not. Unless the original parties to the lease expressly provide that a covenant is personal to them only, any covenant, no matter how whimsical, will run to the successors in title of the original landlord and tenant. The need for covenants to touch and concern the land is well founded: as Gray (1993) says, '[n]o purchaser would wish to buy land under circumstances where its future use had already been fettered by trivial or obscure covenants governing the activities permissible on the land' – p 1125. Under the 1995 Act this is the situation that an assignee of a landlord or tenant may face.

Enforcement

Having proved that the benefit of a covenant runs, the covenantee will wish to enforce it against the covenantor. We need to consider the position of both landlord and tenant as each will have entered into covenants for the benefit of the other, although to some extent '. . . the remedial rights of landlord and tenant have been distributed most unevenly' (Gray, 1993, p 777). Whilst the landlord, if he has retained such a right in the lease, usually has a right to forfeit the lease if the tenant defaults on his covenants, the tenant has no reciprocal right, such as 'to take part in a "rent strike" in order to bring pressure to bear upon a defaulting landlord' (Gray, p 777, again). The tenant must, therefore, seek damages, an order of specific performance or an injunction to obtain redress against any breach of the landlord's covenants. If he does try to force compliance by withholding rent, the landlord could sue him for non-payment and seek forfeiture of the lease! If the 'lease' was, in fact, only a contract for a lease, the breach by the tenant could prevent his obtaining the necessary order of specific performance to transform the contract into an equitable lease: *Coatsworth* v *Johnson* (1886) 54 LT 520.

Covenants may be positive or negative and it had long been thought that negative covenants were not capable of being remedied (see, for example, *Rugby School (Governors)* v *Tannahill* [1935] 1 KB 87 and *Scala House & District Property Co Ltd* v *Forbes* [1974] QB 575, below). However, in *Expert Clothing Service & Sales Ltd* v *Hillgate House Ltd* [1986] Ch 340, a case concerning two positive covenants, the Court of Appeal made *obiter dicta* to the effect that very often negative covenants are capable of remedy by forcing compliance, say by ordering a certain activity to be discontinued.

Savva v Houssein (1996) The Times, 6 May

Here the Court of Appeal confirmed this approach. The covenants in question - not to put up signs or alter the premises without the landlord's consent - were negative covenants. The Court held that breach of these covenants could be remedied by the removal of the signs and by the restoration of the property to its original condition. In so finding, the Court stated that nothing in the Law of Property Act 1925, or in logic, required the court to make a distinction between negative and positive covenants when deciding whether compliance with them, notwithstanding it be retrospective, would (with or without additional financial compensation) remedy the harm caused by the breach.

If the landlord seeks to enforce the burden of covenants against the tenant, the method or procedure to be followed will vary according to the nature of the covenant in question. Ultimately, of course, he could seek to forfeit the lease.

Repairing covenants

The landlord can sue in contract in damages, but these cannot be greater than the diminution in value of the reversion; that is he cannot claim more than his loss – Landlord and Tenant Act 1927, s 18. The Court of Appeal held in *Culworth Estates Ltd* v *Society of Licensed Victuallers* (1991) 62 P&CR 211 that the measure of the damages depends upon the landlord's intention. If he intends to repair the premises, the measure of damages is the cost of those repairs; if he intends to sell the property in its unrepaired state, the measure of damages is the diminution in the capital value of the property. Of course, if he intended to demolish the property in any case, he has suffered no loss and will receive nothing.

If the landlord incorporated a forfeiture clause in the lease, he could seek to forfeit the lease for breach of a repairing covenant. First, however, he would have to serve a notice upon the tenant under the Law of Property Act 1925, s 146 specifying the breach complained of, that he requires it to be remedied if possible (breaches of repairing covenants are capable of remedy), and requiring the tenant to pay compensation if the landlord so wishes. The tenant must be given a reasonable time in which to remedy the breach: three months is usual.

Where the landlord can claim damages and forfeiture, as in breaches of repairing covenants, the tenant can claim relief under the Leasehold Property (Repairs) Act 1938, if the original term was for more than seven years, of which at least three years are left to run. Under this Act the landlord must serve a notice on the tenant, who can serve a counter-notice on the landlord within 28 days. If the tenant does so, the landlord cannot proceed further without leave of the court, such leave being granted in only limited circumstances.

The landlord could, of course, enter the premises and effect the repairs himself, charging the tenant therefor.

However, '[n]o matter how well drafted the repairing obligations imposed upon a tenant by a lease, the landlord is likely to encounter serious difficulties in ensuring their performance' – R Mitchell and S Williams (*see* Further reading, below). The 1938 Act may require the landlord to obtain leave of the court, but such leave is not easy to obtain, and if damages are awarded they are usually limited by the Landlord and Tenant Act 1927 to the amount by which the breach has affected the value of the landlord's reversion.

Jervis v *Harris* [1996] 1 All ER 303

In this case, the Court of Appeal's decision has done much to improve the landlord's position. The case concerned a long lease under which the tenant was obliged to maintain and repair the property. As is usual, the lease reserved to the landlord the right to enter the property so as to check its state of repair and to carry out any necessary repairs himself should the tenant fail to do so within a specified period. Any costs or expenses so incurred could be recovered from the tenant. The question arose as to whether such recovery amounted to a claim for damages for the tenant's breach: if so, the 1938 Act would apply. In a unanimous decision, the Court of Appeal held that such recovery of costs for work carried out by the landlord was not a claim for damages: rather, it was a claim for a debt and such a claim does not fall under the 1938 Act. Therefore the landlord did not require leave of the court before entering, repairing and recovering his losses. As a result, say Mitchell and Williams, '[l]and-lords are now in a much better position to secure full compliance with repairing obligations in leases which contain provisions of this nature'.

Where it is the landlord who is in breach of the repairing covenant, the tenant can apply for specific performance under the Landlord and Tenant Act 1985, s 17. Like the landlord, the tenant could employ the self-help remedy of carrying out the repairs himself, deducting the cost of them from his rent. This is known as a set-off and certain conditions must be met if it is to be employed. These were laid down in *Lee-Parker* v *Izzet (No 1)* [1971] 1 WLR 1688: the landlord must be in breach of the covenant; the tenant must have given him proper notice of the need for the repair; the cost of carrying out the repairs must be no more than is reasonable; and the amount to be deducted from the rent must be certain.

Section 146(2) enables tenants to apply for relief from forfeiture wherever and however the landlord claims the lease has been determined by breach of covenant.

Billson v *Residential Apartments Ltd* [1992] 1 AC 494

This case concerned breach of a covenant against alteration or addition without the land-lord's consent. Immediately upon assignment of the lease to them the tenants began major works of reconstruction to convert the premises into self-contained flatlets, neither seeking nor obtaining the landlord's consent. The landlord duly served a s 146 notice requesting the tenants 'within a reasonable time to remedy the said breaches in so far as they are capable of remedy'. Two weeks later, at 6 am, agents of the landlord peaceably re-entered the property, which was vacant, by changing the locks. Four hours later that same day the tenant's workmen regained possession of the premises. Section 146(2) provides that '[w]here a lessor is proceeding, by action or otherwise, to enforce a right of re-entry or forfeiture, the lessee may . . . apply to the court for relief'. Could the tenant apply for relief against forfeiture **after** the landlord had re-entered without a court order? The tenants claimed that, having re-entered, the landlord was no longer 'proceeding' to enforce his rights, having actually enforced them. The Court of Appeal accepted this argument, but the House of Lords held otherwise: s 146(2), according to Lord Templeman, gives tenants a right to apply for relief against forfeiture 'where a landlord proceeds by action or otherwise' to enforce a right of re-entry. His lordship much preferred 'the civilised method of determining the lease by issuing and serving a writ' to 'the dubious and dangerous method of determining the lease by re-entering the premises', but noted that the 'dawn raid' carried out by the landlords, who were 'perhaps incensed' by the flagrant breach of the covenant, had 'fortunately . . . not resulted in bloodshed'. Parliament could not have intended that a tenant would be entitled to relief where the landlord employed the 'civilised method' of determining the lease, but debarred from it if the landlord employed 'the dubious and dangerous method'.

Upon receipt of notice under s 146, the tenant can apply to the court for relief under s 147, which gives the court discretion to relieve him, wholly or partially, from the liability for the repairs if the notice was unreasonable. (This relief is not available to a tenant who expressly covenanted to put the premises in repair, and who has never done so.) In deciding whether or not to grant relief, the court will consider the conduct of the parties and any other circumstances, as it thinks fit. The court, even if it grants relief, may order the tenant to pay compensation to the landlord, plus costs, or grant the landlord an injunction to restrain any breach in the future (though an injunction is not appropriate where the tenant is no longer in occupation).

Covenant against subletting

The covenant may be conditional, that is no subletting without the landlord's consent, or absolute. (We have seen already that the landlord cannot withhold his consent unreasonably.) If the lease is silent, the tenant is entitled to assign or underlet, the landlord having no veto.

A covenant not to sublet is a negative obligation and one the breach of which cannot generally be remedied – but see *Savva* v *Houssein* above. Therefore, relief against forfeiture will rarely be granted to the tenant and the landlord need only give the tenant a short period of notice: in *Scala House* v *Forbes* [1974] QB 575 the period was only 14 days. However, the landlord must serve the s 146 notice on the right person! The Court of Appeal in *Buller* v *Judy Properties* (1992) 64 P&CR 176 held that a notice served upon the original tenant was ineffective as it should have been served on the assignee, notwithstanding that the assignment was in breach of the covenant against subletting without the landlord's consent.

Willowgreen Ltd v *Smithers* (1993) The Times, 14 December

The Court of Appeal's decision shows that it is equally important to send the notice to the right place. In a long lease of premises let to the defendant and his mother the agreement provided that 'any demand for payment, notice or other document required or authorised to be given to the tenant shall be well and sufficiently given if sent by the lessor through the post addressed to the tenant by name ... or may be left for the tenant at the premises'. The defendant did not live at the premises; indeed, he had not even visited them for some time prior to the date upon which proceedings for possession were issued. The papers in connection with these proceedings were sent by the court to the defendant at the premises but he did not receive them. Some months later judgment was entered against him: he applied to have the judgment set aside. The Court of Appeal allowed his appeal against the first instance refusal, stating that it is necessary for a landlord to state in the Request for Issue of Summons the defendant's 'address', that is the place where the defendant lives, not 'a place at which the defendant was never present'.

John Hewitt, in his article 'More Trouble Dead than Alive' (1992), asks the question: 'What should a landlord do when a tenant dies and he needs to enforce his rights under a lease requiring him to serve formal notice?' The most obvious persons upon whom to serve the notice are the personal representatives of the deceased tenant. However, it is important to remember that though an executor's authority arises under the will, an administrator's does not arise until his appointment. Where there is any doubt as to the identity or authority of the personal representatives, Hewitt suggests that '[t]he answer in practical terms is that the landlord ought to send out copies of the s 146 notice to just about all and sundry in the expectation that one of the copies will end up with someone on whom service is permitted by the relevant legislation'. A wise precaution.

In *Sanctuary Housing Association* v *Baker* (1997) 74 P&CR D28, the Court of Appeal had to consider what, if any, remedy a landlord has against the assignee of a lease where the landlord's consent to such assignment was obtained by the deception of both the assignor and the assignee. Auld LJ concluded that although as between the landlord and the assignor,

> it may well be that the deception would vitiate the consent, it does not necessarily follow that it vitiates the assignment. It seems to me arguable that ... the assignor's interest is validly passed to the assignee and that the landlord's only remedy is to proceed against the assignee for forfeiture for breach of covenant.

Covenants against certain uses

Again, a covenant not to use the premises for certain purposes is a negative one and is generally incapable of remedy other than forfeiture but see *Savva* v *Houssein* above.

Rugby School (Governors) v *Tannahill* [1935] 1 KB 87

A covenant against use of school premises for immoral purposes was breached when the property was used for a brothel! Having already occurred, the breach was not capable of remedy – the stigma, which would not readily disappear, had already attached to the property.

However, a different conclusion was reached in *Glass*:

Glass v *Kencakes Ltd* [1966] 1 QB 611

Where subtenants used the demised premises for immoral purposes in breach of the tenant's covenant, the tenant not knowing of the use nor having any reason to know of it, the judge refused to grant forfeiture, granting relief to the tenant instead as he was not morally to blame.

Again in *Ropemaker Properties* v *Noonhaven* [1989] 34 EG 40, the court granted relief to a tenant against forfeiture sought by the landlord for breach by subtenants of a covenant not knowingly to use or permit the premises to be used for any immoral or illegal purposes. The court took account of the substantial value of the lease and the substantial loss which forfeiture would cause to the tenant – a loss greatly out of proportion to the harm done. In addition, the immoral use had already been brought to an end and was unlikely to recur.

Covenant to pay rent

Rent is normally payable in arrears, though the lease can provide otherwise, as it did in *Walsh* v *Lonsdale*. Rent continues to be payable throughout the term of the lease unless the lease has been frustrated. There are three ways in which a landlord can enforce the payment of rent – by an action for money; by distress, that is by seizing and selling enough of the tenant's goods on the premises to meet the arrears (exercisable by the landlord himself or by bailiffs certified by the court); or by threat of forfeiture. In the case of distress, Lightman J, in *Fuller* v *Happy Shopper Markets Ltd* [2001] 1 WLR 1681, warned landlords of the risk of being in breach of a tenant's human rights where they employ distress without giving notice of their intention and without checking that there are no possible cross-claims. The procedure for forfeiture for non-payment of rent is different from that for any other breach. Section 146 does not apply here.

In regard to rent, the landlord must make a formal demand at the demised premises for the rent on the date it is due at such hour before sunset as gives the landlord time to count the money before the sun goes down! However, if the landlord provides in the lease for forfeiture for breach of payment of rent, whether the rent is formally demanded or not, he can avoid this inconvenient procedure. Alternatively, if at least six months' rent is in arrears and there are not enough goods of the tenant available for distress, the landlord can dispense with the formal demand under the Common Law Procedure Act 1852, s 210. Under s 211, if the rent is six months in arrears and there are insufficient goods against which a landlord can distrain, he can, provided a right of re-entry was reserved in the lease, recover the premises by making a formal demand for rent within the time stipulated in the reservation. In fact, if a power of re-entry for non-payment of rent was incorporated in the lease, and it was stated to be enforceable 'whether rent is formally demanded or not', the landlord can re-enter. Under s 212 of that Act, the tenant can apply to the High Court to stay any proceedings by paying any rent due plus the landlord's costs, provided he is at least six months in arrears. At any time up to six months following re-entry by the landlord, the tenant can apply for relief against forfeiture under the Administration of Justice Act 1985, s 55.

If before trial or within six months of judgment against him, the tenant pays the rent due and the landlord's costs, the court will, if it is just and equitable so to do, grant the tenant relief, the tenant then continuing under his old lease. Such relief may be granted on terms, for example that the tenant execute outstanding repairs, as in *Newbolt* v *Bingham* (1895) 72 LT 852.

Section 17 of the Landlord and Tenant (Covenants) Act 1995, which applies to 'both new and other tenancies', and thus to leases created before 1 January 1996, provides that a landlord cannot recover arrears of rent or other fixed payments (for example, service charge) from a former tenant unless, within six months of the money having become due, he notifies the former tenant of the fact that he intends to recover the money, and the amount due. This will stop landlords allowing arrears to accumulate for long periods before seeking to recover from a former tenant (who may not even know that the current tenant is in breach).

Though they are usually incorporated into commercial leases only, you should be aware of rent review clauses. These are employed by landlords:

> [b]asically because in times of inflation, a landlord will only feel able to grant a lease of any length if he is confident that, throughout the term, he will get a proper return – Christine Hughes (1992, p 20).

In *British Gas Corporation* v *Universities Superannuation Scheme Ltd* [1986] 1 EGLR 1120 it was said that the normal commercial purpose of a rent review was to reflect the changes in the value of money and real increases in property value long term, giving rise to the 'presumption of reality'.

Thus, a rent review clause calls for review of the rent at defined periods, usually every three, five or seven years throughout the term. Therefore, a tenant, more particularly an assignee, should always check for the inclusion of rent review clauses. However, during the 1990s the property market had been anything but inflationary, with rents in most city centres plummeting, sometimes to as low as half the peak rate. In that climate, the then Department of the Environment became concerned at, and sought representations on the prevalence of upwards only rent reviews, though the government stressed that the Consultation Paper was not a forerunner to legislation. In the meantime, tenants and assignees should try to ensure that any rent review clauses they may be subject to operate in a downwards as well as an upwards direction.

In *Co-operative Wholesale Society Ltd* v *National Westminster Bank plc* [1995] 1 EGLR 97 it was said that, in construing rent review clauses, the court will have regard to the language used in the context of the material surrounding circumstances, and will bear in mind the normal commercial purpose of such a clause.

Subtenants: right to relief against forfeiture

What is the position of subtenants if the landlord forfeits the tenant's lease? The termination of the one automatically brings the other to an end too. However, the subtenant can seek relief under s 146(4). The reasons for the forfeiture are irrelevant to the subtenant's right to relief, thus he can seek relief where the tenant could not. If it grants relief, the court can order the landlord to grant the subtenant a lease for a period not exceeding the remainder of the original sublease. Conditions may be imposed upon the subtenant, such as specifying a higher rent. Sometimes a claim for relief under s 146(4) may not provide everything the subtenant could hope for: this is because orders under s 146(4) cannot be made retrospective. This could result in a period between forfeiture and relief, so that in the interim the subtenant is trespasser and thus liable to pay additional sums to the head landlord. Tenants seek relief under s 146(2) where orders can be made retrospectively, avoiding the problem. In *Escalus Properties Ltd* v *Dennis* [1995] 3 WLR 524 the Court of Appeal held that subtenants, as well as tenants, can seek relief under s 146(2), due to the definition of 'lessee' under s 146(5)(b) which includes 'persons deriving title under a lessee'.

The Landlord and Tenant Act 1988 applies to qualified and fully qualified covenants against assignment and underletting.

It is not only subtenants (and, of course, tenants) who can apply for relief from forfeiture. The Court of Appeal in *Croydon (Unique) Ltd* v *Wright* [1999] 4 All ER 257 held that the holder of a charging order (eg creditors of the tenant who have charged the lease with the debt) are entitled to apply for relief.

Waiver

The landlord may decide not to exercise any of the above rights and waive the breach. There are two requirements for waiver – the landlord must be aware of an act by the tenant giving rise to forfeiture, and the landlord must carry out some positive act amounting to a recognition of the continuance of the tenancy. In *Van Hazarlem* v *Kasner* (1992) 36 EG 135 a landlord who, with notice of a tenant's breach, demanded and accepted rent from the tenant, was held to have waived the breach. Obviously, granting a new lease to a defaulting tenant will amount to waiver. The landlord loses his right to re-enter in respect of breaches which he has waived, but not of subsequent breaches.

It is only common sense that where the breach is of a covenant to pay rent and the landlord demands the rent, this will not amount to a waiver (in fact, a formal demand for rent is essential for any forfeiture proceedings). However, in *Re a Debtor* [1995] 1 WLR 1127 it was held that a demand for a later quarter's rent indicated that the landlord did not regard the lease as ended but as continuing into that quarter. Therefore, he waived his right to forfeit for breach in regard to an earlier quarter's rent.

It may be possible for another *tenant* to enforce it under the Contracts (Rights of Third Parties) Act 1999, if the lease was created on or after 11 May 2000 (see Chapter 14 for a fuller explanation of how the Act works), or under the following decision of the Court of Appeal.

Williams v *Kiley* [2002] EWCA Civ 1645

In this case the court, apparently for the first time, gave effect to a letting scheme relating to commercial property. A letting scheme is the leasehold equivalent of a freehold building scheme (which is explained in Chapter 14). The effect of a letting scheme is to enable one tenant to take direct action against another tenant within the scheme to enforce compliance with the obligation under the covenant. In *Williams*, the covenant in question restricted use of shops in an arcade. Williams ran a newspaper/sweetshop, which also sold cigarettes. Each lease contained a clause which permitted a specified use and expressly excluded uses for which the neighbouring shops were to be let. Both Williams' and Kiley's leases contained this clause, with Williams being permitted to use his shop 'for the trade or business of a newsagent sugar confectioner tobacconist and (if so required) as a subpost office (which term shall not include . . . grocer or general stores . . .)'. Kiley's lease, on the other hand, permitted use of his shop as 'a grocery and general store (which term shall not include . . . newsagent sugar confectioner tobacconist . . .)' The landlord of both shops was Swansea City Council, but it declined to enforce the covenant against Kiley. If Williams could prove (a) the existence of a letting scheme, and (b) breach of the covenant by Kiley, he could enforce the covenant against Kiley. The Court of Appeal held that a letting scheme did exist, that Kiley was in breach and that Williams could sue him.

Abandonment

In *Attorney General for Hong Kong* v *Fairfax Ltd* [1997] 1 WLR 149, the Crown claimed that a proposed development would constitute a breach of a covenant restricting any buildings to villa residences only. A premium for waiver of its right under the covenant was demanded by the Crown. However, over a period of 40 years, multi-storey apartment blocks had been built on almost all the rest of the land, which had been subdivided. The Privy Council held that the covenant had been abandoned by the Crown, which had, therefore, lost the benefit of it.

The tenant's right to buy

So, a tenant may lose his lease other than by simple effluxion of time, that is by forfeiture. He can, of course, 'lose' it voluntarily by surrendering his tenancy. A frustrating event would end the lease for both the tenant and his landlord.

On the other hand, the landlord may be forced to part with the reversion, that is the fee simple absolute in possession, on exercise by the tenant of the various statutory provisions creating a right to buy: alternatively, the landlord may be forced thereunder to grant a longer term of years.

Various legislation has enabled tenants to acquire the freehold of their dwellings, or to extend the term of years. These rights are contained in the Leasehold Reform Act 1967, the Housing Act 1980, the Housing Act 1985, the Landlord and Tenant Act 1987, the Leasehold Reform, Housing and Urban Development Act 1993 and the Housing Act 1996.

Very briefly, the rights conferred by these Acts are as follows:

Under the Leasehold Reform Act 1967, a qualifying tenant has two rights: (i) a right to call for his current tenancy to be replaced by a new one which will continue for 50 years beyond the expiry of the current lease; and (ii) the right to 'enfranchise' his lease, that is to purchase the freehold, by compulsorily forcing the landlord to sell it to him. In order to qualify for either right, the tenancy must be of a 'house': individual flats and tower blocks are, therefore, excluded. The Court of Appeal in *Duke of Westminster* v *Birrane* [1995] 3 All ER 416, held that a 'house' for the purposes of the Act did not have to be structurally detached or solely designed or adapted for living in and the use or lack of it which the tenant made of the premises or part of them was irrelevant in determining whether the building could reasonably be called a 'house'. However, the tenant's right to enfranchise is excluded where part of the

house is sufficiently substantial or significant as to make it likely that enfranchisement would prejudice the enjoyment of the house or another part of the structure,
whether by reason of the inability of one freehold owner to enforce positive obligations against successors in title of the other or otherwise. In *Malekshad* v *Howard
de Walden Estates Ltd* [2001] 3 WLR 824, the Court of Appeal accepted that although
s 2(2) of the Act does treat some tenants differently to others, this is not a breach of
Article 8 of the European Convention on Human Rights as it is 'objectively justifiable and proportionate', and there are clear and acceptable policy reasons for s 2(2).
See also *James* v *UK* (1986) 8 EHRR 123, ECtHR, a case which

> addressed an important principle that had widespread long-term social and economic
> effects for the parties involved, and for society as a whole ... [where] the principles enun-
> ciated ... are and will continue to be of importance in the light of further proposals for
> reform of English land law in respect of enfranchisement and commonhold' – Peter
> Halstead (2002).

The original lease must have been for a period of more than 21 years and be at a
'low rent' (calculated on a combination of specified rateable values and the 'letting
value' of the property). The tenant must show either that he has lived in the rented
house as his only or main residence for at least three years prior to giving notice of
his desire to exercise his rights under the Act, or that his residence during ten years
prior to the notice totals three years. If he opts to extend his lease, the tenant continues to pay rent as payable under the current lease: no fine or premium is due. If
he chooses to enfranchise, the price for the freehold reversion will be that which a
willing seller would be expected to receive on the open market. Under the Housing
Act 1996, the low-rent test changes: long leaseholders with a long lease which is
either at a low rent, or those with a 'particularly long lease', normally one granted
for a term of 50 years or more, will qualify. It is expected that this new provision will
relieve most leaseholders from the low-rent test.

The Housing Act 1985 incorporates the tenant's 'right to buy' his own home. Here
a 'secure tenant' has the right to buy either the freehold or a long leasehold term in
the property in which he lives. As Alan Harrison (1997) says:

> A secure tenancy is a very splendid thing. Deliberately easy to create, rather more difficult
> to bring to an end, it can survive the death of the tenant. It can also entitle the holder to
> the purchase of a capital asset at a substantial discount ('the right to buy') – p 540.

The right has been extended to certain housing association tenants by the 1996 Act.
As Nourse LJ observed in *Dance* v *Welwyn Hatfield DC* [1990] 1 WLR 1097, it is a right
which bears 'a strong resemblance to an option to purchase'.

The conditions governing who is a secure tenant and who is eligible to exercise
the rights conferred by the Act are (as Gray points out) 'complex', and you are
advised to refer to the Act if you need to know these details. If he opts to exercise
either right, the price will be whatever could be obtained for the interest on the open
market, less a discount calculated with reference to the length of the tenant's previous (secure) tenancy of the property. Should the tenant decide to sell the property
within three years of exercising the right to buy, either freehold or long lease, some
or all of this discount will be repayable. Again, the property must be a 'house' of
which the landlord owns the freehold. However, if the tenant's home is a flat, or if
his landlord is not the freehold owner, the tenant can call for the grant of a long

lease, normally not less than 125 years, at a (ground) rent not exceeding £10 per annum, provided he is a 'secure' tenant, the price to be calculated as above.

'The grant of a lease in pursuance of Part 5 of the Housing Act 1985 (the right to buy) out of an unregistered legal estate in land' must be registered under LRA 2002, s 4(1)(e) – as, of course, must any such lease granted out of a registered title.

The Landlord and Tenant Act 1987 comes to the aid of tenants of blocks of flats and provides them with a limited right of pre-emption, rather than an option to purchase, in that they have a right of first refusal should the landlord decide to dispose of his interest. If a landlord does so decide, he must serve notice of such intention and his asking price upon all 'qualifying' tenants, giving them two months in which to exercise the right by accepting the landlord's offer, or making a counter-offer, or rejecting it. If they reject, the landlord can sell elsewhere at a price not less than that offered to the tenants, within a period of 12 months.

Most private sector tenancies created after 14 January 1989 are subject to the Housing Act 1988 under which an 'assured tenant' has rights similar to those under the Rent Acts, except that rents are not regulated under the 1988 Act. Provided the tenancy is for not less than six months and the landlord serves notice on the tenant in the form prescribed by the Act at the start of the tenancy, an assured shorthold tenancy may be granted under s 20(1). The 1988 Act imposes a much stricter test of occupation than under the Rent Act 1977. Under the 1988 Act the tenant must occupy the dwellinghouse as 'his only or principal home'.

The Leasehold Reform, Housing and Urban Development Act 1993 also gives tenants of flats the opportunity to buy their home, thus remedying 'one of the alleged shortcomings of the Leasehold Reform Act 1967 . . . that it has no application to the leasehold estate in a flat as distinct from a house' (Gray, 1993, p 770). The 1993 Act introduced a 'right of collective enfranchisement' for special categories of qualifying tenants of blocks of flats, or buildings in two or more flats occupied by qualifying tenants. The Act will not assist tenants of flats over shops as premises which have an internal area of more than 10 per cent designated to non-residential purposes do not come within the Act. Also excluded are premises with less than five flats or units, and premises with a resident landlord. At least two-thirds of the qualifying tenants in a block or building must opt to exercise the right. If such a majority does go ahead, any qualifying tenant who decides not to join in the enfranchisement will become the tenant of those who do. As a 'qualifying tenant' is one who holds a 'long lease', that is one granted originally for a term of more than 21 years, and at a 'low rent', the right is not universally exerciseable. In addition, a 'qualifying tenant' must have occupied his flat as 'his only or principal home' for the 12 months preceding his application, or for a total of three years out of the preceding ten. All these requirements exclude many tenants from the right.

The cost of the purchase, which has to be conducted by the qualifying tenants through a 'nominee purchaser', is laid down in the Act and governed by criteria which assume sale by a willing seller on the open market. An important factor is the 'marriage value', that is the increased value which results from the merger of the leasehold and freehold interests, which is intended to compensate the landlord for having to compulsorily sell his reversion.

Finally, the Housing Act 1996 has been mentioned where relevant, but it is worth noting that it:

had at times a turbulent legislative passage. The debates on the provisions which reduce the rights of the homeless aroused much controversy and have attracted much publicity. But what has so far received little attention are the changes the 1996 Act makes to assured tenancies. This is a surprise, since the new rules which govern assured shorthold tenancies may herald the deregulation of the privately rented sector. For the first time since 1915 a landlord will be able to convert a statutorily regulated tenancy to one with limited security – James Driscoll (1996, p 1699).

It can be seen, then, that these Acts will fail to enable many tenants to buy their homes. The other side of the coin, however, is that those who can, compulsorily take away the landlord's estate in the land. Therefore, either way, they are controversial and seem to leave everyone unsatisfied! However, collective purchase of the freehold is made easier by the Commonhold and Leasehold Reform Act 2002, s 71(1) of which simplifies the criteria for eligibility for the exercise of the right (and thus reduces the cost of doing so). The rights of tenants of flats under the Leasehold Reform Act 1967 to extend their lease and buy a new longer lease or the freehold are enhanced, as is the right of a tenant of a house who has already extended his lease under the 1967 Act. He has the right to buy the freehold or gain security of tenure once his extended lease expires. Section 71 also contains a new right enabling leaseholders of flats to take over the management of their building, and enables the setting up of 'RTMs' – right to manage companies. These will be made up of 'qualifying tenants' (defined in s 75). The RTM can enforce the covenants in the lease, acting, in effect, as a single owner on behalf of all the joint owners. The right can be used even where there is no proof of shortcomings on the part of the landlord, and there is no need for the tenants to pay compensation.

How to protect them

Ensuring rights under leases against third parties

In unregistered land

Provided they are legal, terms of years absolute bind the world. However, if the term of years is merely equitable, under the rule in *Walsh* v *Lonsdale*, the contract which gives rise to it must be registered as a Class C(iv) land charge: an estate contract.

In registered land

Under the LRA 2002, all legal terms of years for more than seven years must be registered – s 4(1)(c).

There are four types of leasehold title: absolute, good, possessory and qualified. Again, it is for the land registrar to decide which will be granted.

An absolute leasehold

A person may be registered with absolute title if –

(a) the registrar is of the opinion that the person's title to the estate is such as a willing buyer could properly be advised by a competent professional adviser to accept, and

(b) the registrar approves the lessor's title to grant the lease – LRA 2002, s 10(2).

This will only be granted if the freehold or the term of years absolute out of which the lease to be registered has been created is itself already registered at HM Land Registry, or has been deduced to the satisfaction of land registrar. It is the most secure of the leasehold titles.

A good leasehold

A person may be registered with good leasehold title if the registrar is of the opinion that the person's title to the estate is such as a willing buyer could properly be advised by a competent professional adviser to accept – s 10(3).

This arises where the fee simple absolute or the term of years out of which the lease to be registered was granted has not been or cannot be investigated, and therefore no guarantee can be given as to the lessor's right to grant it. A good leasehold is, then, subject to any right which detracts – derogates – from the lessor's title to grant it, such as the rights of beneficiaries under a strict settlement where the tenant for life has granted the lease in breach of his powers under the Settled Land Act.

A possessory title

A person may be registered with possessory title if the registrar is of the opinion –

(a) that the person is in actual occupation of the land, or in receipt of rents and profits of the land, by virtue of the estate, and
(b) that there is no other class of title with which he may be registered – s 10(6).

This is the same as a possessory freehold, in that the holder of it is subject to any rights which existed at first registration.

A qualified title

A person may be registered with qualified title if the registrar is of the opinion that the person's title to the estate, or the lessor's title to the reversion, has been established only for a limited period or subject to certain reservations which cannot be disregarded under subsection (4) – s 10(5).

Section 10(4) enables the registrar to disregard 'the fact that a person's title appears to him to be open to objection if he is of the opinion that the defect will not cause the holding under the title to be disturbed'.

This is only granted when the registrar feels unable to grant any of the other titles. It is not possible for the lessee to apply for such a title, but the registrar may, with the lessee's consent, grant it. The effect of a qualified title is virtually the same as that of an absolute title. Hayton estimates that such titles arise 'perhaps once in 100,000 cases'.

As with freehold titles, the registrar has the power to upgrade leasehold titles under LRA 2002, s 62. Thus the registrar can upgrade a good leasehold to an absolute title 'if he is satisfied as to the superior title' – s 62(2). A possessory title can be upgraded to a good leasehold if the registrar is satisfied as to the title to the estate – s 62(3), and that the possessory title has been registered for at least 12 years and the proprietor is in possession of the land – s 62(5). Finally, a qualified title can be entered by the registrar as an absolute leasehold, if he is satisfied both as to the title to the estate and as to the superior title – s 62(3).

Registrable, overriding and minor interests

For every lease, or assignment of a lease, of more than seven years, there must be a separate registered title, plus, of course, the registered title of the fee simple absolute in possession out of which it was granted.

A legal lease under seven years for purposes of LRA 2002, Sched 3, para 1, is an overriding interest.

An equitable lease, or an agreement for a lease, takes effect as a minor interest and must be protected by the entry of a notice under LRA 2002. However, if such entry has not been made and the lessee is in actual occupation, it could be an overriding interest under Sched 3, para 2.

Leasehold covenants, in both unregistered and registered land (LRA 2002, s 28), take their protection from the lease itself. However, there appears to be one exception to this, for, although previously held to run with the lease, it was held by the Court of Appeal in *Phillips* v *Mobil Oil Co Ltd* [1989] 3 All ER 97 that an option to renew a lease is registrable under the Land Charges Act 1972 as a Class C(iv) land charge, being void for non-registration only against a purchaser for value. In registered land, it is a minor interest.

Where a lease is merely equitable, only the benefit of the covenants will run, that is, pass on to a successor in title of the covenantee. The burden of them cannot be imposed upon a successor of the covenantor.

As we have seen, certain covenants, for example a covenant for quiet enjoyment in favour of the lessee, may or will be implied into every lease.

A lease granted under Part 5 of the Housing Act 1980 (right to buy) must be registered (even though the lease is granted out of an unregistered legal estate) – LRA 2002, s 4(1)(e).

We have seen that it is usual for landlords to reserve a right of entry in the lease. Rights of entry can be legal interests (LPA 1925, s 1(2)(e)) and, being contained in the lease, the right of entry will be legal if the lease is. In unregistered land it will, therefore, bind the world. In registered land it is a registrable interest and 'does not operate at law until the relevant registration requirements are met' – LRA 2002, s 27(1) and (2)(e).

Reform

The Law Commission has published many reports on the law of landlord and tenant, the most recent of which – *Renting Homes: The Final Report* (Law Com No 297) – was published in 2006. It addresses the fact that though over 6 million households in England and Wales (a third of the population) rent their homes 'the law governing the relationship with their landlords is an irrationally complicated mess'. Thus, the Commission's aim is to 'replace it with a modernised, understandable and just legal structure'. To this end, Vol 1 of the Report provides an 'illustrative model secure contract and standard periodic contract'. Volume 2 contains the draft Rented Homes Bill.

The recommendations would allow for the abolition of secure, assured, assured shorthold, introductory and demoted tenancies as well as 'various varieties of common law tenancies'. They would also render the lease/licence distinction obsolete.

The main benefits for both landlords and occupiers are listed as follows:

■ Identical contracts for council and housing association tenants. This will increase the security of housing association tenants.

■ Improvements to council and housing association tenants' rights, eg better succession rights and the right to apply to add a partner or flatmate to the contract.

■ Government approved model contracts to make private renting easier, cheaper and more flexible.

■ A clear and practical legal framework for supported housing, which provides accommodation for people who have drink, drug or mental health problems, women's refuges, etc.

The Law Commission also has three projects in hand:

1 'Housing: Ensuring Responsible Renting', looking at the promotion of 'responsible behaviour by landlords' and control of 'anti-social behaviour by tenants in the private sector'.

2 'Housing: Proportionate Dispute Resolution', reviewing 'the law and practice on how housing disputes are resolved, with the aim of reforming it to make it simple, effective, fair and proportionate'. Proposals for a 'more coherent system of housing dispute resolution' include the use of 'a "triage plus" process, diagnosing individual and wider housing problems, referring them to appropriate resolution methods, and collecting information about housing problems and how they are resolved; use of dispute resolution mechanisms such as mediation, ombudsmen and managerial techniques; and, where needed, use of a court of tribunal.

3 'Termination of Tenancies for Tenant Default', looking 'to reform the means by which a landlord can terminate a fixed-term commercial or residential tenancy where the tenant has not complied with their obligations'. The provisional proposals are to abolish the current law of forfeiture of tenancies and the related doctrine of tenure; to create a new statutory scheme for termination of fixed-term commercial and residential tenancies of 21 years or more; to require landlords to give pre-action notice to tenants and any qualifying derivative interest holders (including subtenants and mortgagees) of their intention to terminate a tenancy for tenant default; to give the courts a structured discretion to make a range of orders in addition to termination (including an order requiring the tenant to remedy the default) to ensure that the remedy is proportionate to the default; to provide a modified regime whereby landlords may recover possession unilaterally, subject to safeguards (particularly for residential tenants).

As with all Law Commission papers, a full explanation of the current state of the law and the reasons why reform is necessary is given in the Scoping Paper.

Summary

In this chapter we have looked at the following:

- Types of leases – fixed term, periodic tenancies, perpetually renewable leases, tenancies at will, at sufferance and by estoppel
- Essential characteristics of a lease –
  - A term certain
  - Exclusive possession
  - Rent.
- Classification of leases – legal or equitable.
- The roles of the parties –
  - The landlord –
    - Covenant to repair
    - Non-derogation from grant
    - Covenant for quiet enjoyment
  - The tenant –
    - Covenant to repair
    - Covenant against assignment or underletting
    - Covenants as to use of the premises
    - Covenant to pay rent.
- Rules, principles and formalities for acquisition –
  - Contracts for leases
  - The rule in *Walsh* v *Lonsdale*.
- Duration of leases –
  - Leases determinable upon marriage or death
  - Reversionary leases
  - Perpetually renewable leases
  - Periodic tenancies
  - Agricultural and business tenancies
  - Tenancies at will
  - Tenancies at sufferance
  - Tenancies by estoppel
  - Fixed-term tenancies
  - Re-entry
  - Forfeiture
  - Surrender
  - Disclaimer

- – Frustration
- – By statute.
- ■ The running of covenants in leases –
    - – Where the tenant assigns his term
        - – Pre and post 1 January 1996
        - – Position of subtenants
    - – Where the landlord assigns his reversion –
        - – Pre and post 1 January 2006
        - – Position of subtenants.
- ■ Enforcement –
    - – Repairing covenants
    - – Covenants against subletting
    - – Covenants as to use of premises
    - – Covenant to pay rent
    - – Subtenants' right to relief against forfeiture
    - – Waiver
    - – Abandonment.
- ■ Tenants' right to buy.
- ■ Protecting rights under leases –
    - – In unregistered land
    - – In registered land.
- ■ Reform.

References

Burn, E H, *Cheshire and Burn's Modern Law of Real Property*, 16th edition, London: Butterworths, 2000.

Dixon, M, 'Leases and licences: new headaches' (1999) 28 *Student Law Review* 60.

Driscoll, J, 'New assured tenancies – new dangers?' NLJ, 22 November 1996, p 1699.

Evans, D.L. and Smith, P.F., *The Law of Landlord and Tenant*, 6th edition (revised), Oxford University Press, 2002.

Gray, K. and Gray S.F., *Elements of Land Law*, 4th edition, Oxford University Press, 2005.

Gray, K, *Elements of Land Law*, 2nd edition, London: Butterworths, 1993.

Gray, K and Gray, S F, *Elements of Land Law*, 3rd edition, London: Butterworths, 2000.

Haley, M, 'Trespass, Breach of Covenant and Interim Rent' [1997] Conv 304.

Halstead, P, 'Human Property Rights' [2002] Conv 153.

Harpum, C, Megarry and Wade, *The Law of Real Property*, 6th edition, London: Sweet and Maxwell, 2000.

Harrison, A, 'Security Scare', Sol Jo, 6 June 1997, p 540.

Hewitt, J, 'More Trouble Dead than Alive', Sol Jo, 31 July 1992, p 751.

Hughes, C, 'Drafting Rent Review Clauses – the Basic Principles', *Law Notes*, March 1992, p 20.

Jones, S, 'Termination of Joint Tenancies in the Light of *Pilling*' NLJ, 20 August 1993, p 1236.

Law Commission, *Land Registration for the Twenty-First Century* (Law Com No 254, 1998).

Law Commission, *Renting Homes: The Final Report* (Law Com No 297, 2006).

Pawlowski, M and Greer, S, 'Leases, Licences and Contractual Tenancies' (2000) 9(1) *Nottingham Law Journal* 85.

Reeves, M P, *Round about a Pound a Week*, London: Virago, 1989.

Rook, D, 'Property Law and the Human Rights Act 1998: A Review of the First Year' [2002] Conv 316.

Royle, R, *Briefcase on Land Law*, 4th edition, London: Cavendish, 2003.

Slessinger, E, Precedent Editor's Notes [2005] Conv 374.

Smith, R, 'New Rules for Assured Shorthold Tenancies' (1996) *Estates Gazette*, 19 October, p 150.

Smith, R J, *Property Law*, 4th edition, London: Longman, 2003.

Ward, C, 'The Landlord and Tenant (Covenants) Act 1995', Legal Exec Jo, October 1995, p 18.

Webber, G, 'Relief from Forfeiture', Sol Jo, 31 January 1997, p 82.

Wilkinson, H W, 'Break Clauses in Leases', NLJ, 25 November 1994, p 1637.

Further reading

Nature and characteristics of leases

Cooke, E, 'Touching The Time of The Beginning of a Lease For Yeares' [*sic*] [1993] Conv 206.

Smith, P F, 'What is Wrong with Certainty in Leases?' [1993] Conv 461.

Sparkes, P, 'Certainty of Leasehold Terms' [1993] 109 LQR 93.

Exclusive possession

Bright, S, 'Beyond Sham and into Pretence' [1991] 11 *Oxford Journal of Legal Studies* 138.

Morgan, J, 'Exclusive Possession and the Tenancy by Estoppel: A Familiar Problem in an Unusual Setting' [1999] Conv 493.

Routley, P, 'Tenancies and Estoppel: After *Bruton* v *London & Quadrant Housing Trust*' (2000) 63 MLR 424.

Covenants for assignment and underletting

Hopkins, N, 'Surrender as an Assignment and the Protection of Third Parties' [1996] Conv 284.

Slessinger, E, Precedent Editor's Notes [2005] Conv 374.

Running of covenants

Bridge, S, 'First Tenant's Liability' [1994] CLJ 29.

Bridge, S, 'Former Tenants, Future Liabilities and the Privity of Contract Principle: The Landlord and Tenant (Covenants) Act 1995' [1996] CLJ 312.

Davey, M, 'Privity of Contract and Leases – Reform at Last' [1996] 59 MLR 78.

Enforcement

Bright, S, 'Possession Orders and Rent Arrears' [1997] 113 LQR 217.

Haley, M, 'Rent Reviews and Time Limits: A Cautionary Tale?' [1993] Conv 382.

Hewitson, R, 'Landlord's Self Help Clauses' [1997] Conv 299.

Mitchell, R and Williams, S, 'Tenants' repairing obligations in leases - a recent change', Sol Jo, 2 August 1996, p 788.

Right to Buy

Bright, S, 'Enfranchisement - A Fair Deal for All or None?' [1994] Conv 211.

Clarke, D N, 'Leasehold Enfranchisement - Leasehold Reform, Housing and Urban Development Act 1993' [1993] Conv 223.

Davey, M, 'The Onward March of Leasehold Enfranchisement' (1994) 57 MLR 773.

Driscoll, J, 'Assured tenancies: the new law', Sol Jo, 14 February 1997, p 130 and 21 February 1997, p 156.

Driscoll, J, 'New rights for leaseholders (1)', Sol Jo, 5 September 1997, p 812 and (2), Sol Jo, 12 September 1997, p 840.

Madge, N, 'The Housing Act 1989: The Private Sector', *Legal Action*, January 1989, p 14.

Ward, C, 'When a shorthold tenancy goes wrong', *Estates Gazette*, 19 October 1996, p 150.

Smith, R, 'New rules for assured shorthold tenancies', *Estates Gazette*, 19 October 1996, p 150.

Reform

Bridge, S, 'Putting it Right? The Law Commission and the Condition of Tenanted Property' [1996] Conv 342.

www.lawcom.gov.uk

9 Commonhold

What's the problem?

Commonhold in context

We know that a term of years absolute, a lease, is a wasting asset, with the owner of it having less and less as time goes by. As Stuart Bridge puts it in *Residential Leases* (1994, p 155),

> The long leaseholder is both an embittered and an endangered species: embittered because the long lease, as its term comes to its close, is a depreciating asset; endangered because the latter half of this century has seen legislative intervention entitling many long leaseholders to purchase their landlord's interest ('to enfranchise') and become freeholders. (See Chapter 8, The tenant's right to buy.)

Where the lease has not been converted into a freehold, its term gets shorter by the day, leaving less for the tenant to sell on (assign) and therefore less security upon which a lender can accept a mortgage. We have seen that although covenants – both positive and negative – can 'run' in leaseholds, there are difficulties with regard to running covenants in freehold land. In particular, positive covenants cannot run with freehold land. Many of the covenants which appear regularly in leases are, in fact, positive (for example the covenant to repair). This is the reason why the vast majority of flats are held on leaseholds.

It is possible to hold a flat on a freehold, for there is nothing 'to prevent a fee simple existing in an upper storey of a building, separate and distinct from the rest' – Report of the Welsh Consumer Council, November 1984. Where they are held in this way they are known as 'flying freeholds'. These are not a modern invention: Coke held long ago that a 'man may have an inheritance in an upper chamber though the lower buildings and soil be in another'. Thus, a legal estate 'can exist in what has become mere airspace'; indeed,

> Documents creating freehold flats are drafted on the basis that the freehold estate which they confer is capable of lasting beyond the life of the building itself – that is to say, that the estate does not terminate when the building is demolished at the end of its natural life, or is destroyed prematurely in some other way' – *Transfer of Land: The Law of Positive and Restrictive Covenants* (Law Com No 127, 1984), para 4.6.

In *Grigsby* v *Melville* [1974] 1 WLR 80 a claim was made to a 'subterranean flying freehold' of a cellar! Clearly, the owners of flying freeholds need to be able to impose covenants – especially positive covenants – upon adjacent properties (whether above, below or adjoining sideways) because of their vulnerability to structural damage should, for example, a flat above collapse from lack of maintenance. Estate rentcharges are usually employed to solve the problem. In *Abbahall Ltd* v *Smee* [2003] 1 All ER 465, the Court of Appeal held that, in the case of a flying freehold, where the roof, which seemed equally to protect both premises, had been allowed to fall into disrepair, so that water leaked into the ground floor creating a danger of masonry falling onto visitors to the ground floor, commonsense and common justice and reasonableness as between the neighbours suggested that those who were to benefit from the repair works should also shoulder the burden of paying for them. If parties were to derive an equal benefit they should usually contribute equally: if they were to benefit unequally, then they should each contribute proportionately to their benefit – this evaluation would depend on the particular circumstances as in each case, and should be calculated on a broad basis and by a broad, rather than a detailed, assessment: 'fine calculations' are not appropriate. The state of each party's means is irrelevant. On the facts, the cost of repairing the roof was to be shared equally.

To address both these problems – the wasting nature of leases and the impossibility of running positive covenants with freehold land – a proposal for 'a scheme of freehold ownership known as "commonhold"' which arises from the 'ever-increasing concern with the difficulties that confront leaseholders in selling leases whose outstanding periods have decreased significantly since their grant' was introduced by the Law Commission in 1987 (in the Aldridge Report – *Commonhold, Freehold Flats*, Cm 179). Commonhold finally became a reality when the Commonhold and Leasehold Reform Act 2002 received Royal Assent on 1 May 2002, and came into effect on 27 September 2004.

Commonhold is not limited to developments of residential flats, however; it is also available for commercial or mixed-use developments including offices or business parks.

Who cares?

Those who will be affected

Commonhold has been introduced to help two people, mainly – the tenant and the mortgagee.

In regard to the tenant,

> In addition to providing owners in multi-occupier developments with the means of owning the freehold in their premises, commonhold will furnish them with a system for the efficient management of the development as a whole. As a result, commonhold will have the dual advantages of affording owners a measure of control and security which is often felt to be lacking in long leasehold developments, whilst avoiding the difficulties which attach to so-called 'flying freehold' schemes – Consultation Paper on Commonhold produced by the Lord Chancellor's Department in July 1996.

As for the mortgagee, a freehold title obviously provides a better security for the loan than a leasehold. Also, as we shall see shortly, each Commonhold development will be governed by a Commonhold Community Statement which, amongst other things, will make provision for the rights of, and impose duties upon, each 'unit-holder'. In addition, s 16(1) provides that, if a unit-holder transfers his interest in his unit to another person, 'any right or duty conferred or imposed by the commonhold community statement shall affect a new unit-holder in the same way as it affected the former unit-holder': further, s 16(2) provides that a former unit-holder cannot be held responsible for any breach which arises after he has transferred his interest (nor, of course, can he take any benefit under it). This should cure the problem of enforcing covenants, especially positive ones.

It is estimated that, once in force, Commonhold will enable more than 1.5 million people to own their flats outright – that is, to own a fee simple in the flat rather than holding it on leasehold.

What is it?

The nature and characteristics of commonhold

Commonhold was described in the White Paper produced in 1990 (Cm 1345) as,

> a freehold development of two or more 'units' which share services and facilities and so require a system, for communal management, and for the ownership of any common parts. A commonhold must consist of at least two units because the concept of shared services and facilities is of the essence of the commonhold system. The 'promoter' of a commonhold (ie the person who establishes it) might be the developer of a new development, or the persons interested in an existing one, such as the freeholder and leaseholders of a block of long-leasehold flats. The most obvious example of a commonhold is that of a block of flats where, at present, the flats would be owned on a long-leasehold basis. But there would be nothing in the commonhold legislation to prevent commonholds from being established for non-residential purposes . . .

Section 1(1) of the Act provides that land is commonhold if:

(a) the freehold estate in the land is registered as a freehold estate in commonhold land,
(b) the land is specified in the memorandum of association of a commonhold association as the land in relation to which the association is to exercise functions, and
(c) a commonhold community statement makes provision for rights and duties of the commonhold association and unit-holders (whether or not the statement has come into force).

Thus, commonhold can only be created out of registered land. There must be a commonhold association, that is a private company limited by guarantee and registered at Companies House. Finally, there must be a commonhold community statement, providing the rules and regulations under and by which the commonhold will operate and be managed. Though most community statements will have much in common, each statement will be specific to the individual commonhold. The duties of a unit-holder, that is the covenants, may be specified in the community statement and s 31(5) states that 'duty' includes, 'in particular', a duty to pay money, to undertake works, to grant access, to give notice, to refrain from entering into certain transactions, to refrain from using the whole or part of the unit for a specified purpose, to refrain from undertaking works (including alterations) of a specified kind, to refrain from causing nuisance or annoyance, to refrain from specified behaviour, to indemnify the commonhold association or a unit-holder in respect of costs arising from the breach of a statutory requirement. In other words, both positive and negative obligations, or 'duties', or covenants can be enforced under the community statement.

In addition, s 39(1) provides that the commonhold community statement must make provisions:

(a) requiring the directors of the commonhold association to establish and maintain one or more funds to finance the repair and maintenance of common parts;
(b) requiring the directors of the commonhold association to establish and maintain one or more funds to finance the repair and maintenance of commonhold units.

Section 35 imposes a further duty upon the directors of a commonhold association under which they

shall exercise their powers so as to permit or facilitate so far as possible

(a) the exercise by each unit-holder of his rights, and
(b) the enjoyment by each unit-holder of the freehold estate in his unit.

The commonhold is made up of commonhold 'units' and 'common parts'. Units are defined in s 11(1) as 'a commonhold unit specified in a commonhold community statement'. Section 11(2) provides that a commonhold community statement must:

(a) specify at least two parcels of land as commonhold units, and
(b) define the extent of each commonhold unit.

Section 11(4) provides that a 'commonhold unit need not contain all or any part of a building'. However, 'it shall not be possible to create an interest in part only of a commonhold unit' – s 21(1), nor shall it be 'possible to create a charge over part only of an interest in a commonhold unit' – s 22(1).

Common parts are defined in s 25(1) as 'every part of the commonhold which is not for the time being a commonhold unit in accordance with the commonhold community statement'. In practice, they will be very much the same as common parts of leasehold blocks – stairways, walkways, corridors, etc.

The commonhold itself 'may include two or more parcels of land, whether or not contiguous' – s 57(1). However, Schedule 2 provides a list of types of land which may not be registered as commonhold, most importantly,

an application [to register a commonhold] may not be made . . . wholly or partly in relation to land above ground level ('raised land') unless all the land between the ground and the raised land is the subject of the same application – para 1(1).

Thus, there can be no commonhold of a block of flats over a row of shops, where the shops are leasehold – there can be no 'flying commonholds'!

The Act clearly anticipates most commonholds to arise in new developments, but there will be provision for converting an existing leasehold into a commonhold – but only if certain conditions are satisfied. The most important of these is the need to obtain the consent to the conversion to commonhold of 100% of the existing leaseholders (and of any other owners of what would become units in the new commonhold). Further details are provided in the Commonhold Regulations 2004.

How can they exist?

Classification: legal or equitable?

As we have seen, land is only commonhold if it is registered as a freehold estate in commonhold land – s 1(1). In addition, 'The Registrar shall register a freehold estate in land as a freehold estate in commonhold land . . . ' – s 2(1). Therefore, commonhold is freehold – or is it?

Although defined as a freehold, it

> is really an entirely new and essentially separate form of land holding that deserved to be treated independently of aspects of standard freehold and leasehold' – David N Clarke (2002).

Not only that, but, as we know, a freehold estate can have no conditions attached to it, yet, as we have already seen in ss 21(1) and 22(1), there are conditions attached to commonhold units. Section 17 provides a further limitation upon residential units: 'It shall not be possible to create a term of years absolute in a residential commonhold unit unless the term satisfies prescribed conditions'. These may relate to length of term, the circumstances in which the term was granted or any other matter – s 17(2). A further condition is imposed by s 20. Although s 20(1) forbids anything in the commonhold community statement from preventing or restricting 'the creation, grant or transfer by a unit-holder of an interest in the whole or part of his unit, or a charge over his unit', s 20(3) provides that no interest, other than a charge, can be created without the written consent of the commonhold association, or it being made a party to the grant. So, no, it is not really a freehold. In truth it is a third legal estate – a hybrid of the fee simple absolute in possession and the term of years absolute.

How can you acquire them?

Rules, principles and formalities

Under s 2(1),

> The Registrar shall register a freehold estate in land as a freehold estate in commonhold land if –
>
> (a) the registered freeholder of the land makes an application under this section, and
> (b) no part of the land is already commonhold land.

An application under s 2 must be accompanied by the documents specified in Schedule 1 to the Act. These include the commonhold association's certificate of incorporation under the Companies Act 1985, the memorandum and articles of association of the commonhold association, the commonhold community statement and any consents required by the Act.

Section 2(3) states that

> [a] person is the registered freeholder of the land for the purposes of [Part 1 of the Act] if –
>
> (a) he is registered as the proprietor of a freehold estate in the land with absolute title, or
> (b) he has applied, and the Registrar is satisfied that he is entitled, to be registered as mentioned in paragraph (a).

Section 3(1) specifies that:

'An application under section 2 may not be made in respect of a freehold estate in land without the consent of anyone who –

(a) is the registered proprietor of a leasehold estate in the whole or part of the land,
(b) is the registered proprietor of a leasehold estate in the whole or part of the land granted for a term of more than 21 years,
(c) is the registered proprietor of a charge over the whole or part of the land, or
(d) falls within any other class of person which may be prescribed.

Under s 5, the Registrar 'shall ensure that in respect of any commonhold land' certain documents are kept in his custody and referred to in the register, including prescribed details of the commonhold association and of the registered freeholder of each commonhold unit, and copies of the commonhold community statement and memorandum and articles of association of the commonhold association.

Schedule 3, para 7 provides that:

[a] person is entitled to be entered in the register of members of a commonhold association if he becomes the unit-holder of a commonhold unit in relation to which the association exercises functions –

(a) on the unit becoming commonhold land by registration with unit-holders . . . or
(b) on the transfer of the unit.

The same applies to joint unit-holders – para 8(1).

The effect of registration is that,

[a] person who is entitled to be entered in the register of members of a commonhold association becomes a member when the company registers him in pursuance of its duty [to maintain a register of members under the Companies Act 1985].

In compliance with the principles of the Land Registration Act 2002, a title to commonhold is created by registration of it.

When and for how long?

Duration of commonholds

Individual unit-holders are bound to comply with the commonhold regulations during their ownership of the unit. If a unit-holder transfers his interest in the unit to another person, as 'any right or duty conferred or imposed by the commonhold community statement shall affect a new unit-holder in the same way as it affected the former unit-holder' (s 16(1)), and a 'former unit-holder shall not incur a liability or acquire a right under or by virtue of the commonhold community statement' (s 16(2)), both his rights and obligations cease upon transfer.

In regard to the commonhold itself, provision is made for both voluntary and compulsory winding up. Sections 43 to 49 cover voluntary winding up, sections 50 to 56, compulsory.

How can you protect them?

Ensuring rights under commonholds against third parties

As we have seen, commonhold can only exist in registered land, and, in order to be registered, the commonhold community statement (amongst several documents) must be deposited. As the community statement contains all rights, obligations and duties of the commonhold association and of the unit-holders, all of which are binding on them both, then notice of them is given to any prospective purchaser.

Both the commonhold and the units within it are registered as legal estates – freehold estates in commonhold land. In accordance with the principle of the Land Registration Act 2002, there can be no legal interest until registration.

We have seen that, in addition, a unit-holder is protected in the exercise and enjoyment of his rights and his unit under s 35. Also, s 37 states that 'regulations may make provision' for enforcement of duties and compensation or infringement of rights contained in the commonhold community statement, the memorandum or articles of the community association, or any provision made under the Act. The regulations may, for example, make provision requiring compensation to be paid where a right is exercised in specified cases or circumstances, or where a duty is not complied with; or enabling recovery of costs where work is carried out for the purpose of enforcing a right or duty, or in consequence of a failure to perform a duty. Section 37 can, of course, be relied upon by either the unit-holder or the commonhold association, depending upon the facts.

Finally, s 42 provides that a commonhold association must be a member of an approved ombudsman scheme.

Summary

In this short chapter we have looked at the following aspects of commonhold:

- The reason for its introduction.
- Those who will be affected by creation of a commonhold.
- Its nature and characteristics.
- The fact that commonholds can only be legal.
- Rules, principles and formalities of creation.
- Duration.
- Ensuring that interests under a commonhold bind third parties.

References

Bridge, S, *Residential Leases*, London: Blackstone Press, 1994.

Clarke, D N, 'The Enactment of Commonhold: Problems, Principles and Perspectives' [2002] Conv 349.

Law Commission, *Transfer of Land: The Law of Positive and Restrictive Covenants* (Law Com No 127, 1984).

Law Commission, *Commonhold, Freehold Flats* (Cm 179), 1987.

Further reading

Clarke, D. N, 'The Enactment of Commonhold: Problems, Principles and Perspectives' [2002] Conv 349.

PART 3

Interests in land
The buyer beware

10 Introduction to interests in land

We have spent a long time looking at the legal estates – what they are, the people they affect, how they are acquired, who does what in regard to them, when they arise and how long they can last, how they are protected, etc. Whilst considering the fee simple absolute in possession, we considered the situation in regard to the beneficial interests in land which exist behind a trust and we now know that those interests relate to the real ownership of the land (or as near to actual ownership of the land as it is possible to get).

What we have to look at now are the third-party interests, those which exist over rather than in the land. Though any interest in land is important, these do not give any form of ownership in the land over which they operate, though they may give the right to end ownership, for example the mortgagee's right to seek possession of the land upon which the loan was secured and his right to sell it.

We know that there are very few interests in land capable of being legal and that all others can exist only as equitable interests: Law of Property Act 1925, s 1(2) and (3). Thus, restrictive covenants, which are very important interests in land, can only be equitable, whilst an easement can be legal, though it may be equitable.

Whether an interest is legal or equitable will depend for the most part upon the way in which it was acquired. As a general rule, an interest can only be legal if it is equal in time to one or other of the two legal estates and it is created by deed. However, to all general rules there are exceptions, as we shall see in Chapter 12, Easements. Of course, if an interest is not capable of being legal, that is to say it is not contained in s 1(2), it will be equitable no matter how long it lasts and whether or not created by deed; restrictive covenants would fall into this category. There will also be additions to the general rule, special rules which apply only to specific interests; again, easements will provide us with examples.

Where an interest is not capable of being legal, or where it fails to comply with the legal requirements, we shall have to look at methods of acquisition in equity. In addition to these there is, as we have seen, proprietary estoppel which may give rise in equity to whatever interest was promised (provided, of course, all the requirements of the doctrine are satisfied).

The land over which a third party has an interest is burdened land; it is land subject to a disability in that the owner of it must allow the owner of the interest to exercise the benefit of that interest. Such rights are usually unattractive to any prospective purchaser of the burdened land, especially those which cannot be removed before completion of the sale. Any purchaser, or his solicitor, must ensure that any mortgage on the land in question is discharged (paid off) before the purchaser becomes the new owner. Failure to do so will leave the purchaser with land still subject to his vendor's mortgage liabilities (as well as those under any mortgage he himself granted in order to raise the purchase price). Interests in land are just that, interests **in land**. Therefore, they attach to the benefited land, not merely the person who currently owns (holds title to) that land. They are like the barnacles on a ship, which go wherever the ship goes, regardless of who the captain is. The only way to get rid of them is to go into dry dock and have them scraped off. So with interests in land, they will attach to the land, and whoever buys the land to which they attach will take the land subject to them. However, there are ways of 'scraping them off', as we shall see. We shall also see that an interest-holder who fails to protect his interest in the required manner will find, more often than not, that he has destroyed the interest himself in that it will not be binding on any subsequent purchaser of the burdened land. The benefit of an interest is of no use unless the burden of it is attached to the appropriate piece of land. Indeed, once an interest ceases to be capable of binding third parties, it ceases to be a proprietary right. A proprietary right, a right in land, a right *in rem*, is one which is capable of binding third parties. It is, as we saw at the very beginning, this characteristic which differentiates it from a mere personal interest, a right *in personam*.

A proprietary right is far superior to a personal one. With a proprietary right, you can claim against the land itself, but with a personal right you can only sue the person who is depriving you of it. What if that person is a man of straw? What use is a right against someone who has no money with which to compensate you? To sue him would be to throw good money after bad. Effectively, therefore, if he has no money, you have no remedy. If, on the other hand, you have a proprietary right, a right in land, you are sure to have something real to sue against; that is why mortgagees always insist upon taking land as security for the monies they are lending. Even if the property is subject to negative equity, the mortgagee should recoup some, if not all, of his money (unless he himself failed to protect his interest and finds he is bound by a later one).

All in all, then, we shall have to consider most of the same questions in regard to the interests in land that we looked at in regard to the estates: what are they?, who cares?, how can you acquire them?, when and for how long?, and how can you protect them? (which may well depend upon how they can, and do, exist).

As most of us can only hope to acquire a legal estate with the aid of a loan, and as that loan will more than likely be secured on the land, we shall start with mortgages.

Summary

In this brief introduction to Interests in Land we considered the concept of third parties and proprietary rights.

11 Mortgages

What's the problem?

Mortgages in context

Who remembers Winston Graham's character, Captain Ross Poldark, who, in the late eighteenth and early nineteenth centuries, seemed always to be swimming against the financial tide? His land, Nampara, was continually being used as security to raise desperately needed cash to shore up his mining venture. With the cash, however, came indebtedness to the wicked banker, George Warleggan, and the ever present fear of losing all – the mine, the land, his home – if the next payment of interest could not be met.

In 1938, Noël Coward wrote of:

> The Stately Homes of England,
> How beautiful they stand,
> To prove the upper classes
> Have still the upper hand;
> Though the fact that they have to be rebuilt
> And frequently mortgaged to the hilt
> Is inclined to take the gilt
> Off the gingerbread,
> And certainly damps the fun
> Of the eldest son.

So, landowners in the eighteenth and nineteenth centuries and stately home owners in the twentieth: what have their problems to do with most of us in the new millennium? An all too common tale of the late 1980s/early 1990s was that of the couple who borrowed money from a building society or bank in order to buy their dream house. The price they paid was probably hugely inflated. Interest rates rose steadily to record levels and, at the same time, unemployment rose too. Many people found they could not keep up with the agreed monthly repayments to the lenders. As the capital sum and accumulating interest arrears continued to attract ever more interest, with the only means of repayment being the sale of the house, house prices began to slump. Some people, in total despair, were simply moving out of their homes and posting the keys through the lenders' letterboxes (thereby making themselves 'intentionally' homeless, which meant that a local authority could not rehouse them). Though matters eased somewhat from the mid-1990s, as recession continued, more and more owners of small companies mortgaged or remortgaged their homes in order to raise capital to bolster ailing businesses – back to Poldark! The initial desperate desire to obtain the benefit of the loan became an even more desperate need to be freed of its burden. Shakespeare was right, then; it is best to 'neither a borrower, nor a lender be' (*Hamlet*). However, in the real modern world most of us could not hope to own our own homes without the aid of a loan; neither would anyone be willing to lend such large sums without real security.

Who cares?

Those who will be affected

Everybody!

The borrower who, when he needed the money to buy or improve his house, set up or subsidise his business, wanted someone willing and able to lend him the money. In the UK, approximately 70 per cent of houses are owner-occupied and almost all of these houses will have been bought with the aid of a loan from a building society or a bank. If it were not for these lending institutions we should not be what Lord Diplock described as 'a property-owning, particularly a real-property-mortgaged-to-a-building-society-owning, democracy' – *Pettit* v *Pettit* [1970] AC 777.

The borrower's spouse, usually the wife. Remember Mrs Boland? – *Williams & Glyns Bank Ltd* v *Boland* [1981] AC 487: she knew nothing of the arrangement made with the bank by her husband. The first she learnt of it was when the Bank sought to enforce its security and gain possession of her home. Commonly, the mortgagor's spouse is the co-mortgagor, especially where the mortgage was granted in order to raise money to buy the house. Here both mortgagors will have executed the mortgage deed which, as we saw in *City of London Building Society* v *Flegg* [1988] AC 54, can make all the difference. In any event, in such cases the spouse cannot claim to be ignorant of the mortgage transaction: this too can be a crucial factor – see *Paddington Building Society* v *Mendelsohn* (1985) 50 P&CR 244. However, as we shall see, Mrs O'Brien – *Barclays Bank plc* v *O'Brien* [1993] 3 WLR 786 – showed that a wife, with knowledge of the transaction, may still avoid the consequences of failing to repay the loan.

The lender, usually a building society or bank. It has lent the money, taking the house as security for the loan. If all had gone according to plan, the loan would have been paid off in due course, usually by the payment of monthly instalments over an agreed period of years. However, when the borrower defaults, the lender will seek to get its money back. As we shall see, there are several ways open to a lender by which it can do this, but the most common in regard to loans secured on dwellinghouses is to seek possession of the house and then sell it. Due to falling house prices, though, the property may now be worth less than the debt – this is negative equity. What then? Will the loss of the borrower's home wipe out the indebtedness to the lender? No. The dream has become a nightmare.

Subsequent lenders. Frequently, as trouble mounts, borrowers will raise more money on the security of their home, not always from the same lender as before. Again, if all goes well, all the lenders will be paid. However, if the borrower gets into difficulties and cannot make repayments on the later loan, what can the second lender do? This is a crucial question in cases of negative equity: here the conflict becomes one between lender and lender, not lender and borrower. Will the second lender get all, or any, of its money back? We have mentioned Mrs Boland: since *Abbey National Building Society* v *Cann* [1990] 1 WLR 832, such a claim is only likely to succeed against a subsequent lender.

Purchasers of mortgaged property. Unless it is a brand new house, the chances are that there is a mortgage on the house which you are buying, as your vendor had to borrow the money he used to buy it himself. A mortgage is an interest in land (usually a legal interest) and as such it is capable of binding purchasers. Therefore, a purchaser of a house which is subject to a subsisting mortgage must ensure that the full indebtedness to the lender is paid off before he completes the purchase.

If not, he will find himself with a house which is subject to two mortgages – his vendor's and his own. (It may be that you are buying from the lender, who has taken possession of the house and is selling to recoup the monies lent to the previous owner. Although, as we shall see, the lender is under a duty to obtain the best price in all the circumstances, it may be that a purchaser from it will get the house at a relatively cheap price.)

Politicians and the general public. A prolonged slump in the housing market directly affects the entire economy. If mortgagees flood an already depressed market with repossessed houses, house prices will fall even further. This affects the security and investment of all home owners. In addition, the lenders' security in repossessed housing stock will be devalued, leaving less capital available for lending. Home owners who have been dispossessed must be rehoused: where is the money to come from? It could well have to come from the taxpayer.

We can see, then, that of all interests in land none affects us all – economically (it is probably the greatest financial obligation the majority of us will ever undertake), socially or politically – as much as mortgages. For these reasons '... the sheer number of mortgages now subsisting at any time magnifies the importance of every defect in the law. Any unsatisfactory feature of mortgage law now affects a large number of people even if it arises in only a tiny proportion of cases' – the Law Commission in 1986 in its Working Paper No 99, *Land Mortgages*. Given the number of home owners in the UK, the proportion of those who fall into difficulties may well be 'tiny' but, as we are about to see, it still amounts to a large body of case law: just like the usual domestic mortgage term, this chapter may seem interminable!

What are they?

The nature and characteristics of mortgages

A mortgage must be the one right in or over land that everyone has heard of. However, almost all forms of property and the interests therein, including a mortgage itself, can be the subject of a mortgage.

What, then, is a mortgage?

Santley v *Wilde* [1899] 2 Ch 474

This classic definition was given by Lindley MR: 'A mortgage is a transaction under which land or chattels are given as security for the payment of a debt or the discharge of some other obligation'.

Nowadays, the security offered is usually a house, and the obligation undertaken is the repayment of the mortgage advance plus interest. As a result of this obligation:

> The institution of the mortgage exerts a profound effect upon ordinary people in a variety of ways. From the point of view of the private individual, his mortgage commitment can indeed become a central concern in his life ... a mortgage transaction will almost certainly represent the largest single form of financial indebtedness incurred by the ordinary individual during his lifetime, and the discharge of this obligation will probably rank as his most important financial responsibility – Gray and Symes (1981, p 507).

It is the mortgagor – the borrower – who grants the mortgage, the lender being the mortgagee. Whilst it used to be that the mortgagee obtained the whole of the mortgagor's fee simple (which the mortgagee would reconvey to the mortgagor upon payment of the capital sum and interest) as security for the loan, today the mortgagor retains his legal estate, the mortgagee acquiring a legal (or equitable) interest in it. If, however, the mortgage is granted upon or by way of a leasehold, the mortgagee will have a legal estate in the mortgagor's land, that is a term of years absolute, though the mortgagee's lease will be shorter than that of the mortgagor (or, of course, his fee simple absolute in possession, if the mortgage was granted on a freehold). Thus, the mortgagor retains his legal estate in reversion.

In effect, then, a mortgage is:

> an invisible label on a piece of land (either freehold or leasehold) which states that, unless a sum of money is repaid on or by a certain day (or, often, by monthly instalments), the land itself will be sold to repay the loan. The mortgage is a charge (burden) imposed on land as security for debt. There may be several mortgages on one piece of land – Hilary Lim and Kate Green (1995, p 130).

The Law of Property Act 1925, s 1(2)(c) refers to a 'charge by way of legal mortgage' and 'mortgage' is defined in s 205(1)(xvi) as including 'any charge or lien on any property for securing money or money's worth'; '"legal mortgage" means a mortgage by demise or subdemise or a charge by way of legal mortgage'. In the Land Registration Act 2002, 'charge' means any mortgage, charge or lien for securing money or money's worth, and 'legal' mortgage has the same meaning as in the LPA – LRA 2002, s 132.

Looking after the mortgagor: rights of mortgagors

The governing maxim is 'once a mortgage, always a mortgage', and equity jealously guards against any attempt by a mortgagee to acquire anything other than security for his loan by the imposition of certain restrictions, though we shall see that the application of the rules governing these varies according to the nature of the relationship between the parties. Where the parties are of equal bargaining power or where 'the resulting agreement was a commercial agreement between two different corporations experienced in such matters ... made between two competent parties, acting under expert advice and presumably knowing their own business best' – Sir Wilfred Greene MR in the leading case of *Knightsbridge Estates Trust Ltd v Byrne* [1939] Ch 441 – the court may be unwilling to disturb a perfectly reasonable commercial transaction, but will not hesitate to protect the unwary from oppression.

All the principles governing the validity of terms in a mortgage agreement are directed towards protecting the mortgagor and his 'equity of redemption' – the sum total of the mortgagor's rights in his mortgaged realty. The right to redeem – the mortgagor's right to pay off the loan and free his estate from the mortgagee's interest therein – is just one, though probably the most important, aspect of the equity of redemption.

The equity of redemption itself is:

> an estate in the land, for it may be devised, granted, or entailed with remainders, and such cannot be considered a mere right only ... the person therefore entitled to the equity of redemption is considered as the owner of the land ... The interest of the land must be somewhere, and cannot be in abeyance, but it is not in the mortgagee, and therefore must remain in the mortgagor – Lord Hardwicke LC in *Casborne* v *Scarfe* (1738) 1 Atk 603.

In *Re Sir Thomas Spencer Wells* [1933] Ch 29 the right of the Crown to claim an equity of redemption as *bona vacantia* was upheld, thus clearly establishing it as a proprietary right,

> [the] effective value of this right [being] the difference at any given point in time between the market value of the land and the sum of the mortgage debt currently outstanding ... The value of that equity will steadily increase as the mortgage debt is gradually discharged ... Such is the significance of the mortgagor's 'equity of redemption' that the contractual date for repayment of the mortgage loan is rendered entirely academic in this context, and for this reason most mortgage deeds contain a clause which requires repayment of the entire capital sum within a short period (eg six months) of the granting of the loan – Gray and Symes (1981, p 518).

We must now look at the principles under which equity protects the equity of redemption. They have evolved over a long period. Indeed,

> For three centuries, the Courts of Equity have shown a readiness to interfere with the freedom to contract between mortgagor and mortgagee. The inequality of bargaining power which exists between the parties has fostered a paternalistic approach under which the mortgagor is to be protected against exploitation and unconscionable treatment – Michael Haley (1997).

There must be no oppressive or unconscionable terms

This principle is all-embracing and applies to all terms in the mortgage agreement. The standard of what is or is not oppressive or unconscionable may vary according to the circumstances, especially the relationship of the parties. However, as Sir Wilfred Greene MR stated in *Knightsbridge Estates Trust Ltd* v *Byrne*:

> [whilst] equity may give relief against contractual terms in a mortgage transaction if they

are oppressive or unconscionable ... equity does not reform mortgages because they are unreasonable. It is concerned to see two things – one that the essential requirements of a mortgage transaction are observed and the other that oppressive or unconscionable terms are not enforced – subject to this, it does not, in our opinion, interfere.

The most likely source of oppression or unconscionability lies in the imposition of interest rates, but, as Gray and Symes (1981) point out:

> The modern domestic mortgage is a quite remarkable form of transaction. Most mortgages of residential property are concluded between an owner-occupier and a building society. Such mortgages are, of course, covered by the general law relating to mortgages, but they differ slightly from the ordinary mortgage of realty in that they are affected by certain rules which apply specifically to transactions entered into by building societies ... All building societies reserve the right, on serving notice on their borrowers, to alter the rate of interest payable on mortgage loans. In other words, the rate of interest payable by the mortgagor is not fixed throughout the period of the loan, but fluctuates in accordance with the rate stipulated from time to time by the society itself.
>
> The open-ended contract thus concluded between the mortgagor and mortgagee is nothing short of astonishing. The mortgagor agrees to pay *any* rate of interest demanded by the lender of the money – p 525.

Indeed, by the time a mortgagor has redeemed his domestic repayment-by-instalments mortgage, he will usually have paid almost three times the original capital sum.

Such a condition, if imposed by an individual mortgagee or any 'fringe' financial institution would, without doubt, be struck down, and even where imposed by a building society – Wurtzburg and Mills (1976, p 616) consider it would be 'open to doubt if an unlimited power simply to vary the interest rate at discretion would be legally binding'. However, most building societies, when they raise their interest rates, are prepared to allow their borrowers to extend the repayment period for the loan, thereby enabling them to continue with their repayments at the rate of interest in force before the increase. Gray and Symes (1981, p 525) offer justification for the privileged position enjoyed by the building societies by virtue of the fact that their interest rates are 'subject to an element of quasi-public control, in the sense that the variation of interest rates is now closely related to the general economic strategy of the government of the day'. The same could be argued on behalf of the major banks. (However, under the Unfair Terms in Consumer Regulations 1994, which bring into effect EC legislation, 'certain time honoured clauses containing legal terms of art which have gone unquestioned in standard conditions may now be voidable' – Rex Newman and Clive Halperkin (1995), whose article sets out the terms which could potentially fall under the new Regulations.)

The two leading cases in this area provide examples of the different attitude adopted by the courts according to whether the transaction is between parties of equal or unequal bargaining strengths.

Multiservice Bookbinding Ltd v *Marden* [1979] Ch 84

Browne-Wilkinson J upheld an agreement notwithstanding the fact that:

> The defendant made a hard bargain. But the test is not reasonableness. The parties made a bargain which the plaintiffs, who are business men, went into with their eyes open, with the benefit of independent advice, without any compelling necessity to accept a loan on these terms and without any

sharp practice by the defendant. I cannot see why there was anything unfair or oppressive or morally reprehensible in such a bargain entered into in such circumstances. The need for the defendant to invest his money in a way which preserved its real purchasing power provides an adequate explanation of all the terms of the mortgage.

Repayment of the loan was, in fact, index-linked to the Swiss franc. This had the effect of causing an initial loan of £36,000 to require a repayment of £133,000 upon redemption. However, the value of the commercial premises upon which the loan was secured had trebled in this time.

Cityland & Property (Holdings) Ltd v *Dabrah* [1968] Ch 166

Marden must be contrasted with this case, where the mortgagor was a tenant of limited means buying the freehold from his landlord with the aid of a loan from the landlord. Not only was there unequal bargaining strength between the parties, but the fact that the tenant had been threatened with eviction at the expiry of his lease did not enhance his position. The landlord lent the tenant £2,900 which, on the terms of the agreement, required a repayment of £4,553 for redemption, the difference of £1,653 being described as a 'premium' in lieu of interest. This represented an annual interest rate of 19 per cent which Goff J held to be 'unfair and unconscionable'. A rate of 7 per cent per annum was imposed as representing a 'reasonable' rate of interest.

Two other cases which illustrate the more zealous application of this principle where there is inequality of bargaining strength are *Wells* v *Joyce* [1905] 2 IR 134, where the court was willing to assist a Connemara farmer of 'rustic mind', and *Carrington Ltd* v *Smith* [1906] 1 KB 79 where it was unwilling to assist an 'intelligent . . . man of business' who had entered into a mortgage with an interest rate of 50 per cent.

Interest rates which are imposed as a penalty will be declared void if they take no genuine account of the likely damage which would be suffered by the mortgagee should the mortgagor default. Thus, any attempt to charge a higher rate of interest for failure to make regular payments at the agreed rate will usually be struck down (though such an agreement could be achieved quite legally by agreeing to reduce the rate for prompt payment).

Whilst we have used cases on interest rates to illustrate this point, the rule against oppression or unconscionability applies to all terms, for the court will set aside 'any oppressive bargain, or any advantage exacted from a man under grievous necessity and want of money' – Stuart VC in *Barrett* v *Hartley* (1866) LR 2 Eq 789, as it did in *Horwood* v *Millars Timber Trading Co Ltd* [1917] 1 KB 305 where the mortgagor had been reduced to a condition 'savouring of slavery'.

It is not uncommon for mortgage loan agreements to contain a variable interest clause but, in *Paragon Finance Plc* v *Nash* [2002] 1 WLR 685, the Court of Appeal held that the power of the mortagagee to set new interest rates from time to time was not completely unfettered: in order to give effect to the reasonable expectation of the parties, it is an implied term that the discretion to vary the interest rate should not be exercised dishonestly, for an improper purpose, capriciously, arbitrarily or in a way in which no reasonable mortgagee, acting reasonably, would do. That being the case, it would not be a breach by a mortgagee of that implied term if, as a commercial organisation, it raised interest rates to be paid by mortgagors in order to overcome financial difficulties encountered by the mortgagee in regard to the agreement. In both *Staunton* and *Paragon Finance Plc* v *Nash* (heard as a joint appeal with *Staunton*) there was no evidence that the decision to widen the gap between the rates charged and the standard rates had been motivated by anything other than purely commercial considerations, and therefore the mortgagee was not in breach of the implied term.

A standard clause in domestic mortgages requires that the mortgagor agree not to let the mortgaged property without the prior written consent of the mortgagee.

Citibank International plc v Kessler (1999) 78 P&CR D7

This standard covenant was incorporated into a mortgage granted on a dwellinghouse owned by the Kesslers. Mr K went to work in Germany and fell into arrears with the mortgage repayments. Due to an unresolved boundary dispute and structural defects, the property became unsaleable and could not be remortgaged. The result of this was that Mr K could no longer afford to work in Germany, and he had to refuse work there. He and Mrs K claimed that the clause was in breach of Article 48 of the EC Treaty's guarantee of freedom of movement of workers within the Community. The Court of Appeal held that Article 48 did not apply: . . . it was aimed at regulating 'in a collective manner gainful employment and the provision of services' - Chadwick LJ. To hold otherwise would lead to 'a danger that banks would be less willing to lend to those whose occupation was such that they might move between member states to seek employment, if there were a wish that provisions included in the loan documentation to protect the lender would be held unenforceable in those circumstances. Far from promoting freedom of movement of workers by facilitating the ability to obtain funds for the acquisition of residential property in any member state in which they were working [the K's agreement] would be likely to impede such freedom of movement' - Chadwick LJ.

(For another aspect of unconscionability – though not necessarily on the part of the mortgagee – see undue influence later in this chapter.)

There must be no clogs or fetters on the right to redeem

> A clog or fetter is something which is inconsistent with the idea of security: a clog or fetter is in the nature of a repugnant condition . . . If I give a mortgage on a condition that I shall not redeem, that is a repugnant condition. The Courts of Equity have fought for years to maintain the doctrine that a security is redeemable. But when and under what circumstances? On the performance of the obligation for which it was given. If the obligation is the payment of a debt, the security is redeemable on the payment of that debt. That, in my opinion, is the true principle applicable to the cases, and that is what is meant when it is said there must not be any clog or fetter on the equity of redemption' – Lindley MR in *Santley* v *Wilde* [1899] 2 Ch 474.

In other words, the mortgagor must be free to redeem (pay off) the mortgage loan merely by paying back the capital which he borrowed and the interest thereon. As Walker L J said in *Browne* v *Ryan* [1901] 2 IR 653:

> where a transaction appears, or has been declared to be a mortgage . . . the mortgagor is entitled to get back his property as free as he gave it, on payment of principal, interest, and

costs, and provisions inconsistent with that right cannot be enforced. The equitable rules, 'once a mortgage always a mortgage', and that the mortgagee cannot impose any 'clog or fetter on the equity of redemption', are merely concise statements of the same rule.

Thus, the 'one matter that the mortgagor can insist upon is that, on redemption by payment, he gets back his security' – Lord Browne-Wilkinson in *Cheah v Equitcorp Finance Group Ltd* [1992] 1 AC 472.

Two contrasting cases provide good examples on the point.

Samuel v Jarrah Timber & Wood Paving Corporation Ltd [1904] AC 323

Jarrah granted a mortgage on £30,000 worth of debenture stock to Samuel at 6 per cent interest to secure a loan of £5,000, the principal and interest being payable on 30 days' notice from either side. A term in the mortgage gave Samuel (ie the mortgagee) 'the option to purchase the whole or any part of such stock at 40 per cent at any time within 12 months'. When Samuel tried to exercise this option, Jarrah claimed that as it excluded his right to redeem it was illegal and void. The House of Lords, reluctantly, agreed with him. Notwithstanding the fact that the whole arrangement amounted to a 'perfectly fair bargain', and the decision could lead to 'it being used as a means of evading a fair bargain come to between persons dealing at arms' length and negotiating on equal terms . . .' – Lord Macnaghten – their lordships upheld the rule, as stated by Lord Henley in *Vernon v Bethell* (1762) 2 Eden 110, 'that a mortgagee can never provide at the time of making the loan for any event or condition on which the equity of redemption shall be discharged and the conveyance absolute'.

The words 'at the time of making the loan' are crucial, for 'there is great reason and justice in this rule, for necessitous men are not, truly speaking, free men, but to answer a present exigency will submit to any term that the crafty may impose upon them' – Lord Henley again. Therefore, if, once the mortgage has been completed, the mortgagor is no longer a 'necessitous man', he is free to decide whether or not to grant the option.

Reeve v Lisle [1902] AC 461

In contrast to *Jarrah*, here the grant of an option to purchase part of property upon which a mortgage loan was secured was held to be valid as it had been granted 10 days after the mortgage and was, therefore, a transaction which was separate from and independent of the mortgage.

Of course, a mortgagee could not get around the rule merely by taking the mortgage and the option in different instruments and at different dates if the mortgagor was, in truth, a 'necessitous man'. Thus, if the reality was that the mortgage loan was only advanced subject to the grant of the option – albeit post-dated – it would fall within *Jarrah*, which is a classic example of an application of the maxim 'once a mortgage, always a mortgage', as the option turned the transaction into what amounted to a sale.

Lewis v Frank Love [1961] 1 WLR 261

Therefore, where a mortgage and an option to purchase were granted by way of two separate documents, but on the same day and for the same consideration, the court held the two documents must be read together. This brought the option into a *Jarrah* situation: the option was invalid.

Lewis was distinguished by Aiden J in *Pye* v *Ambrose* [1994] NPC 53, where he found that an option did not constitute a clog on the equitable right to redeem the mortgage as the obligation to repay the loan only arose when the option was no longer exercisable.

Clogs and fetters upon the equity of redemption thus deprive the mortgagor of his right to redeem. However, clauses which, though they do not totally exclude the right, nevertheless render it virtually unattainable, are also subject to the scrutiny of the courts.

For an excellent review of cases on this point see the judgment of Chadwick LJ in *Jones* v *Morgan* [2001] EWCA Civ 995.

There must be no postponement of the right to redeem

Fairclough v *Swan Brewery Co Ltd* [1912] AC 565

'Is there a difference between forbidding redemption and permitting it, if the permission be a mere pretence?' – Lord Macnaghten. In this case the terms of a mortgage of the 17½ years which remained of a 20-year lease meant that upon redemption there would be only six weeks of the lease left, rendering the provision for redemption 'nugatory . . . For all practical purposes this mortgage is irredeemable. It was obviously meant to be irredeemable. It was made irredeemable in and by the mortgage itself'. Therefore, as 'equity will not permit any device or contrivance being part of the mortgage transaction or contemporaneous with it to prevent or impede redemption' – Lord Macnaghten again – it was void.

Knightsbridge Estates Trust Ltd v *Byrne* [1939] Ch 441

However, as Sir Wilfred Greene MR stated, although:

> [i]t is indisputable that any provision which hampers redemption after the contractual date for redemption has passed will not be permitted . . . [and that] further it is undoubtedly true to say that a right of redemption is a necessary element in a mortgage transaction, and consequently that, where the contractual right of redemption is illusory, equity will grant relief by allowing redemption . . . [and] moreover, equity may give relief against contractual terms in a mortgage transaction if they are oppressive or unconscionable

the court may, in the case of 'a commercial agreement between two important corporations experienced in such matters' which has 'none of the features of an oppressive bargain where the borrower is at the mercy of an unscrupulous lender', be unwilling 'to view the agreement made as anything but a proper business transaction'. This being so, the Court of Appeal upheld as valid a term providing for a redemption date 40 years after that of the mortgage agreement.

There must be no collateral advantages

Just as there must be no clogs or fetters, there must be no other collateral advantages to the mortgagee. 'A covenant is collateral where an obligation is placed on the mortgagor which is independent of that for the performance of which land is charged' (Burn, 2004, p 811).

Noakes & Co Ltd v Rice [1902] AC 24

'[W]hen the money secured by a mortgage of land is paid off, the land itself and the owner of the land in the use and enjoyment of it must be as free and unfettered to all intents and purposes as if the land had never been made the subject of the security ...' - Lord Macnaghten.

Therefore, any collateral advantage to the mortgagee which continues beyond redemption is void. However, a collateral advantage which lasts only whilst the mortgage continues, so long as it is not unconscionable, will be valid.

Biggs v Hoddinott [1898] 2 Ch 307

This case concerned a mortgage of a public house granted by publicans to a brewer, which contained a covenant by the mortgagors that during the continuance of the mortgage they would take all their beer from the mortgagee - a *solus* agreement, in other words. In reply to what Lindley MR described as 'a very ingenious and learned argument' made on behalf of the mortgagor, the Court of Appeal upheld the term as valid, for:

> it is not stipulated that damages for breach of the covenant shall be covered by the security, and redemption takes place quite independently of the covenant; so this is not a case where the right to redeem is affected ... here the right of the mortgagors to redeem on payment of principal, interest and costs is maintained ... I think the cases only establish that the mortgagee shall not impose on the mortgagor an unconscionable or oppressive bargain. The present appears to me to be a reasonable trade bargain between two business men who enter into it with their eyes open, and it would be a fanciful doctrine of equity that would set it aside - Chitty LJ.

However, the provision must not amount to a restriction of trade, as 'A mortgage is subject to the common law doctrine that invalidates any contract in restraint of trade which places an unreasonable restriction upon the freedom of a man to pursue his trade or profession' (Burn, 2000, p 683).

Esso Petroleum Co Ltd v Harper's Garage (Stourport) Ltd [1968] AC 269

The House of Lords stated that *solus* agreements are within the category of agreements in restraint of trade and must be justified on the grounds of reasonableness. Thus the test in these cases is unreasonableness, not unconscionability, so that a term which was upheld as being not oppressive may yet fail for being an excessive restraint of trade.

The Court of Appeal in *Alec Lobb (Garages) Ltd v Total Oil (Great Britain) Ltd* [1985] 1 WLR 173 felt it was very much 'a rule of thumb', each case depending on its own facts, with the courts looking not only at the interests of the parties but at the public interest as well. In *Texaco Ltd v Mulberry Filling Station Ltd* [1972] 1 All ER 513, a *solus* agreement was upheld as valid because the restraints were reasonable in reference to the interests of the parties, being no more than were required for the protection of the covenantee. They were part of a commercial contract in which there was equality of bargaining strength between the parties, and reasonable in reference to the interests of the public. See also *Young* v *Evans-Jones* [2002] 1 P&CR 14.

G & C Kreglinger v New Patagonia Meat & Cold Storage Co Ltd [1914] AC 25

Yet, as Viscount Haldane LC explained:

> it is inconsistent with the objects for which they were established that these rules should crystallize into technical language so rigid that the letter can defeat the underlying spirit and purpose. Their application must correspond with the practical necessities of the time. The rule as to collateral advantages, for example, has been much modified . . . by the recognition of modern varieties of commercial bargaining . . . . Unless such a bargain is unconscionable it is now good. But none the less the other and wider principle remains unshaken, that it is the essence of a mortgage that in the eye of a Court of Equity it should be a mere security for money, and that no bargain can be validly made which will prevent the mortgagor from redeeming . . . . Thus any bargain framed in such a way that 'the right to redeem was cut down' would itself be cut down. However, the parties to a mortgage are entirely free to 'stipulate for a collateral undertaking, outside and clear of the mortgage'.

In this case the House of Lords found the provision in question, which required the mortgagor to sell his produce (sheepskins) only to the mortgagee, so long as the mortgagee paid the best price for them, to be, in fact, independent of the mortgage transaction and valid, notwithstanding that it continued for two years after redemption. As Viscount Haldane explained, 'The question is one not of form but of substance, and it can be answered in each case by looking at all the circumstances, and not by mere reliance on some abstract principle'. Lord Mersey compared the doctrine against clogging the equity of redemption with 'an unruly dog which, if not securely chained to its own kennel, is prone to wander into places where it ought not to be'! For an excellent review of cases on this point, see Chadwick LJ's judgment in *Jones* v *Morgan* [2001] EWCA Civ 995.

Finally, the Building Societies Ombudsman Scheme, established in 1987, provides a possible means of redressing a grievance against a building society mortgagee outside the courts. All building societies are members of the scheme, which is administered by an independent body. In every annual report since it was established, most complaints to the Ombudsman concern mortgages, complaints about investments being the second largest. A good explanation and discussion of the Scheme is provided by Rhoda James and Mary Seneviratne (1992) in their article 'The Building Societies' Ombudsman Scheme'. A ruling by the Financial Ombudsman in February 2002 that 'dual rate policies' discriminated against borrowers on older agreements caused a flurry of activity. A 'dual rate policy' is one under which new mortgagors enter into agreements at a new lower variable rate than mortgagors on older agreements. The Building Societies' Association consulted their lawyers as to the possibility of challenging, on human rights grounds, the fact that there is no independent appeal process against the Ombudsman's rulings. However, within a few weeks of it, the two largest building societies agreed to pay over 400,000 borrowers compensation.

The Financial Services Authority is currently looking into claims against financial services companies of mis-selling, especially in regard to endowment mortgages.

A mortgagor remains bound by his obligations until he redeems the mortgage. As we have seen, his right to redeem must not be fettered in any way by the mortgagee.

Looking after the mortgagee: remedies for mortgagees

If a mortgagor has his rights, so too does a mortgagee. Although there are several ways in which a mortgagee can enforce them, his rights all amount to the same thing – an ability to recover his money should the mortgagor default on the mortgage. The same rights are available to both legal and equitable mortgagees, but they differ somewhat in their application. They are a right to sue on the mortgagor's covenant to repay, the power of sale, the right to possession, the right to appoint a receiver and the right to foreclosure. We shall take each of the rights in turn as they apply to legal mortgagees, noting the differences in application where the mortgagee is equitable. A mortgagee's rights are exercisable concurrently, so that he may claim possession and sale and, if sale does not wipe out the debt, sue the mortgagor personally on his covenant to pay the debt. In regard to a money claim, the Court of Appeal held in *Cheltenham & Gloucester Building Society* v *Johnson & Sunshine* (1997) 73 P&CR 293, that a mortgagee can not be in a worse position than if he had lent unsecured. He was, therefore, entitled as of right to a judgment for whatever sum of money was due and payable under the terms of the mortgage. See also *Cheltenham & Gloucester Building Society* v *Grattidge* (1993) 25 HLR 454.

Naturally, with rights go duties, and we shall look also at the duties imposed upon mortgagees in the exercise of their rights.

Palk v Mortgage Services Funding plc [1993] 2 WLR 415

Nicholls VC, following Lord Templeman in *China & South Sea Bank Ltd* v *Tan Soon Gin* [1900] 1 AC 536, stated that the overriding duty is to be fair:

> a mortgagee can sit back and do nothing. He is not obliged to take steps to realise his security. But if he does take steps to exercise his rights over his security, common law and equity alike have set bounds to the extent to which he can look after himself and ignore the mortgagor's interests. In the exercise of his rights over his security the mortgagee must act fairly towards the mortgagor ... he is not entitled to conduct himself in a way which unfairly prejudices the mortgagor: there is a legal framework which imposes some constraints of fairness on a mortgagee ... exercising his remedies over his security.

The right to sue on the covenant

When the mortgagor granted the mortgage he undertook to repay the money lent by the mortgagee, together with any interest thereon. If the mortgagor fails to repay as agreed, he or she is in breach of the covenant and can be sued at common law. Under the Limitation Act 1980 any action to recover the principal monies and any interest owing must be brought by the mortgagee within 12 years from the date when the right to receive the money arose. However, this period will begin to run afresh each time the mortgagor either pays off some of the capital or interest, or acknowledges in writing his liability to pay it.

The mortgagor remains liable on this covenant notwithstanding that he may have transferred his interest in the secured land to someone else. However, in practice, the mortgagor would require his transferee to indemnify him.

Given the fact that the mortgagee can only sue the mortgagor on the covenant if the mortgagor is actually in arrears, it may seem that he is something of a 'man of

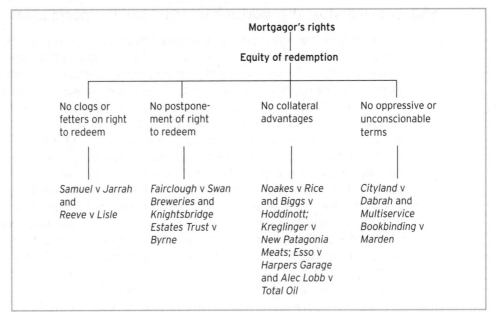

Figure 11.1

straw', in which case the mortgagee may be throwing good money after bad. However, even if the mortgagee exercises one of his other rights, the right to sue remains. It may be useful, therefore, if the security fails to satisfy the whole debt. This, unfortunately, is a situation in which many people are finding themselves at present, for although interest rates are at their lowest for many years, a great many houses still represent a negative equity (that is, the current value (market price) is less than the sums owed on it). When a house is not worth what was paid for it, which usually means it is not worth what was borrowed on it, sale will not wipe out the mortgagor's indebtedness. The mortgagee can then sue for the balance, *in personam*. In many cases this will result in the mortgagor being declared bankrupt. As Nicholls VC explained in *Palk*, a case of negative equity, there was:

> not merely a disagreement between the mortgagor and a mortgagee about the likely future trend of house prices ... probably another feature is a difference in their attitudes towards taking risks. . . . A substantial lender may be prepared to take risks that would be imprudent for a householder with limited financial resources.
>
> In addition, there is also the further feature that the interests of the mortgagor and the mortgagee do not march hand in hand in all respects. The security afforded by the house is not the only remedy possessed by [the mortgagee]. The company also has a personal claim against Mrs Palk. If the property market does not improve as [the mortgagee] hopes, and so the shortfall becomes larger than it is now, the company can have recourse against Mrs Palk for the increased shortfall. Hence, it is said, [the mortgagee] is intent on speculating at Mrs Palk's expense. If its gamble on property prices fails, the company can still go against Mrs Palk.

Equitable mortgagees

An equitable mortgagee can sue on the covenant in the same way as a legal mortgagee.

The House of Lords confirmed, in *West Bromwich Building Society* v *Wilkinson* [2005] 1 WLR 2303, that a mortgagee's right to sue the mortgagor on his covenant to repay arises on the first default of payment of instalments, and confirmed that the limitation period for commencement of an action to recover that shortfall on sale of the repossessed property was 12 years. On the facts, the mortgagee's claim was statute barred.

The power of sale

The Law of Property Act 1925, ss 101 to 107, provides the mortgagee with the power of sale. It is the most frequently utilised right, and is usually exercised in conjunction with the right to possession.

No court order is required for the exercise of the power, but certain requirements must be satisfied before it can be used. First, the power of sale must have *arisen*. It arises when the requirements of s 101 are satisfied. There are three requirements, all of which must be met:

(a) the mortgage must be made by deed; and

(b) there must be no contrary provision expressed in that deed; and

(c) the mortgage money must have become due. In other words the legal date for redemption must have passed. The legal date for redemption is stated in every mortgage and is usually six months after the date of execution.

(In regard to (a), the Law Commission, in its Consultation Document, *Land Registration for the Twenty-First Century* (Law Com No 254, 1998)), recommended that the power of sale (and power to appoint a receiver) should be exercisable by the proprietor of a registered charge, whether or not the charge was created by deed.)

Twentieth Century Banking Corporation Ltd v *Wilkinson* [1977] Ch 99

The mortgage of the defendant's house provided for payment of interest on the sum borrowed but gave the mortgagee no right to demand capital until the end of the 15-year mortgage term, ie until 1988. The mortgagor, who had an option to begin paying the capital after the fourth year, defaulted before then in his interest payments. The mortgagee sought payment of the debt with interest, possession of the property and sale or foreclosure. Templeman J (as he then was) held that s 101 confers on a mortgagee a power of sale only when the mortgage money becomes due. On this mortgage, that was not until 1988 and an action for sale could not, therefore, be sustained.

As soon as these three conditions are met, the power of sale arises. However, the power must also be *exercisable*, and this occurs when any one of the three requirements in s 103 is satisfied. They are:

(a) having had a notice requiring payment served upon him, the mortgagor is in default of three months' repayments after such service; or

(b) the interest payable is at least two months in arrears; or

(c) the mortgagor is in breach of either a covenant in the mortgage deed (other than the covenant to repay), or of some provision which ought to have been complied with by the mortgagor (or someone else who concurred in making the mortgage) under the Law of Property Act 1925.

Remember that all three requirements of s 101 must be complied with, but only one of s 103.

The mortgagee has no right to sell until the power of sale has at least arisen under s 101, and it is the duty of the purchaser to ensure that the power has arisen. However, as soon as the requirements of s 101 are satisfied and the power of sale has arisen, the mortgagee can convey a good title to a bona fide purchaser even though the power has not yet become exercisable (but a purchaser who knows that the power was not exercisable will not take a good title).

If a mortgagee does sell before the power has become exercisable under s 103, the mortgagor can sue the mortgagee for damages under s 104. Under this right a mortgagor could claim for such things as the costs of removal, or for accommodation between the date of sale and the time when the power did become exercisable.

Section 105 sets out the duties of a mortgagee in his application of the proceeds of sale: the money shall be held by him in trust to be applied by him, first, in payment of all costs, charges and expenses properly incurred by him as incident to the sale or any attempted sale, or otherwise; and secondly, in discharge of the mortgage money, interest and costs, and other money, if any, due under the mortgage; and the residue of the money so received shall be paid to the person entitled to the mortgaged property, or authorised to give receipts for the proceeds of the sale thereof. In registered land, for the purposes of s 105, 'a person shall be taken to have notice of anything in the register immediately before the disposition on sale' – Land Registration Act 2002, s 54.

The Court of Appeal held in *Raja* v *Lloyds TSB Bank plc* (2001) 82 P&CR 16 that the duties of a mortgagee in possession to obtain the best price reasonably available and to incur no more than reasonable expenses in the marketing and sale of the property arise in equity, and not in contract or tort. Thus these duties do not depend upon the existence of an enforceable contract between the parties and are owed by each mortgagee to each subsequent mortgagee, as well as to the mortgagor. Receivers owe an identical duty. The relevant limitation period is 6 years here, not 12. Where a mortgagee is held to be in breach of its statutory duty under s 105 by selling the secured property at an undervalue, the prima facie measure of damages is the reduction in the value of the equity of redemption – *Adamson* v *Halifax plc* [2003] 1 WLR 60.

In *Barclays Bank plc* v *Burgess* [2002] unreported, the Court of Appeal held that where husband and wife had executed an all monies charge on their home, the bank was not entitled under s 105 to debit the whole of the joint indebtedness against the wife's half share in the proceeds of sale, since she was not liable for two business loans, which were held not to have been secured by the legal charge.

A mortgagee, provided he has priority over any subsequent mortgagees, can convey the whole of the mortgagor's estate, even if the mortgagor only granted a term of years. If there are any other mortgages which rank above the mortgagee's, any sale will, of course, be subject to them (unless the prior mortgagees concur in the sale).

While no specific mode of sale is necessary, a mortgagee must act in good faith. Provided he takes reasonable care, no liability will attach to the mortgagee so long as he is not negligent in obtaining 'the true market value' in the case of a non-building society mortgage – *Cuckmere Brick Co Ltd* v *Mutual Finance Ltd* [1971] Ch 949. This does not mean that the mortgagee must hold off selling until the market peaks: as Salmon LJ explained in *Cuckmere Brick*, the mortgagee must 'take reasonable precautions to obtain the true market value of the mortgaged property at the date on which he decides to sell'. (It goes without saying, however, that if mortgagees flood an already depressed market, prices will be low.) It is for the mortgagor to prove that the mortgagee has breached its duty.

It is always a question of fact whether a mortgagee has fulfilled his duty of care.

Parker-Tweedale v *Dunbar Bank plc* [1991] Ch 12

The mortgagee bank, in exercise of its power of sale, sold the secured land, with the mortgagor's consent, for £575,000 and the land was resold the next week for £700,000. The bank was held not to be in breach of its duty to take reasonable care to obtain a proper price. At the time of sale, it had relied upon an estate agent's valuation for the land of between £380,000 and £450,000. It was further held that, as the mortgagee's duty arises from a 'particular relationship' with the mortgagor, a trust beneficiary holding under the mortgagor is not owed any independent duty of care additional to that owed to the mortgagor by the mortgagee.

Palk v *Mortgage Services Funding Plc* [1993] 2 WLR 415

'[I]f he sells the property, [the mortgagee] cannot sell hastily at a knock down price sufficient to pay off his debt. The mortgagor also has an interest in the property and is under a personal liability for the shortfall. The mortgagee must keep that in mind. He must exercise reasonable care to sell only at the proper market value'. – Nicholls VC

Similarly, if a mortgagee lets the secured property, he must do so at a proper market rent.

AIB Finance Ltd v *Debtors* [1997] 4 All ER 677

When exercising his power of sale, a mortgagee whose security included a business carried on on the property charged, had a duty to ensure that the value of the combined asset was maximised. Accordingly, although he had a free choice as to the timing of the sale, once he had decided to exercise his power to repossess and sell the property the mortgagee had to take into account the effect of that on the value of the goodwill of the business. In such circumstances, therefore, he had a duty to safeguard and maintain the business and should normally make arrangements to ensure continuity before physical possession, as otherwise there would inevitably be a break in the business and consequent damage to its value as a going concern. However, no such duty could exist where the business had ceased before the lender obtained possession of the premises.

In the case of a building society mortgage, there will be no liability provided the mortgagee acquires 'the best price which can reasonably be obtained' – the Building Societies Act 1986, s 13 and Sched 4.

Skipton Building Society v Stott [2000] 2 All ER 779

Here, the Court of Appeal had to consider the mortgagee's duty under this provision. It held that the correct approach in deciding whether the mortgagee had sold for too low a figure is to compare the amount recovered by the mortgagee with an assessment of the market value of the property, the market price being established by the party with the burden of proof. On the facts of *Stott*, it was clear that the market value was considerably higher than the amount Skipton sold for. It was held that the building society had to give credit for the higher amount (which took Stott out of the negative equity trap).

An interesting situation arose in *Polonski* v *Lloyd's Bank Mortgages Ltd* (1997) *The Times*, 6 May. Mrs Polonski owned a house in a run-down and rough area. The house was subject to a mortgage, payments on which were being met by income support. Mrs P was not in arrears, but she did wish to move to a more pleasant area and one which would offer better schools for her young children. A housing association had offered to buy her house but the price it was willing to pay was £12,000 short of the mortgage debt. There was no prospect of Mrs P being able to find the shortfall. The bank, naturally, was not happy with this arrangement and Mrs P sought an order for sale under the Law of Property Act 1925, s 91(2), which provides that:

> In any action, whether for foreclosure, or for redemption, or for sale, or for the raising and payment in any manner of mortgage money, the court, on the request of the mortgagee, or of any person interested either in the mortgage money or in the right of redemption . . . may direct a sale of the mortgaged property, on such terms as it thinks fit . . .

Referring to *Palk*, which Jacob J felt gave the court an unfettered discretion to do what is considered to be fair, the order was made. However, in *Palk*, Sir Michael Kerr had said:

> . . . it must only be in exceptional circumstances that the power will be exercised against the mortgagee's wishes when a substantial part of the mortgage debt will nevertheless remain outstanding. Whenever a mortgagee can demonstrate a real possibility, let alone a probability, that a refusal or postponement of a sale would be financially beneficial, because of the property's likely increase in value . . . then the mortgagor's request will no doubt be refused out of hand . . . .

As M P Thompson (1998) says:

> This seems to meet exactly the facts of [*Polonski*] . . . What this seems to say is that in any case of negative equity, a mortgagor can expect the court to order a sale of the property, against the mortgag[ee]'s will, thereby depriving it of its status of being a secured creditor, and leaving it to the dubious prospect of successfully pursuing a personal action against the erstwhile mortgagor. This seems very difficult to justify . . . It is thought that the decision in *Polonski* must be treated with considerable reserve.

T E Bergin and A Davies (1997) conclude that, 'The combined effect of *Krausz* [see later] and *Polonski* must be to encourage mortgagees of properties in the negative equity trap to take steps to obtain possession and sell the property as soon as possible after default by the mortgagor'.

Though it is a long established rule that a mortgagee shall not sell to himself – 'a sale by a person to himself is no sale at all', Lindley LJ in *Farrar v Farrars Ltd* (1888) 40 Ch D 395 – in *Tse Kwong Lam* v *Wong Chit Sen* [1983] 1 WLR 1349, the Privy Council held that there was no inflexible rule that a mortgagee exercising his power of sale under a mortgage could not sell to a company in which he had an interest. However, the mortgagee and the company had to show that the sale was made in good faith and that the mortgagee had taken reasonable precautions to obtain the best price reasonably obtainable at the time, namely by taking expert advice as to the method of sale, the steps which ought reasonably to be taken to make the sale a success and the amount of the reserve. The mortgagee was not bound to postpone the sale in the hope of obtaining a better price or to adopt a piecemeal method of sale which could only be carried out over a substantive period or at some risk of loss. The burden is on the mortgagee to prove that all reasonable steps have been taken to obtain the best price reasonably obtainable. On the facts, the mortgagee failed to establish this. As Lord Templeman stated:

> Where a mortgagee fails to satisfy the court that he took all reasonable steps to obtain the best price, the court will, as a general rule, set aside the sale and restore to the borrower the equity of redemption of which he has been unjustly deprived. But the borrower will be left with his remedy in damages against the mortgagee for the failure of the mortgagee to secure the best price if it will be equitable as between the borrower and the purchaser for the sale to be set aside.

As we have seen, having sold the property, the mortgagee is a trustee of the purchase monies which must be laid out in the order set out in s 105.

It was held by the Court of Appeal in *Halifax Building Society* v *Thomas* [1996] 1 WLR 63 that a mortgagee exercising its power of sale is not entitled to keep surplus proceeds of sale after discharging the mortgage even where the borrower fraudulently induced the building society to grant him the loan by way of mortgage.

If for any reason a mortgagor cannot sell under ss 101 and 103, a foreclosure order can be sought in order to give the court the opportunity to order a sale instead of granting such an order – Law of Property Act 1925, s 91. An example of the sort of situation in which such a need could arise is provided by *Twentieth Century Banking Corporation Ltd* v *Wilkinson*, where, as we saw earlier, the statutory power of sale under s 101 had not arisen. The predecessor to s 91 empowered a court to make an order for sale only in the course of foreclosure proceedings, but under s 91 the court can direct a sale at any time. In *Palk* v *Mortgage Services Funding plc* it was the mortgagor who made a s 91 application: the mortgagee had not intended to sell the property immediately but instead had sought to gain possession and delay sale until the market improved. The Court of Appeal held that as the mortgagee could itself buy the property if it wished to speculate on an increase in its value, in the interests of fairness the mortgagor should be allowed to sell. In *Cheltenham & Gloucester Building Society* v *Krausz* [1997] 1 All ER 21 Mr and Mrs Krausz had fallen into arrears and the building society sought an order for possession. A valuation of their home obtained by Mr and Mrs K put its value at 'no more than £65,000'. They then contacted a local charity which bought properties with a view to renting them back to their former owners. The charity offered to buy the house at the valuation, but the building society refused to agree to the sale, claiming that the house was worth around £90,000. Mr and Mrs K made an application for sale under s 91. Phillips LJ, referring to *Union Bank of London* v *Ingram* (1882) 20 Ch D 463, stated that the purpose of s 91 is to allow the borrower, whose property is worth more than the mortgage debt, to obtain a sale and get the benefit of the surplus. Until *Palk*, a mortgagor could only make such an application where the proceeds of sale were expected to be sufficient to discharge the entire mortgage debt, but *Palk* had established that a mortgagor can make a s 91 application even though the property is subject to negative equity. However, his lordship did acknowledge that, 'There will be a danger, if the mortgagee does not obtain possession, that the mortgagor will delay the realisation of the property by seeking too high a price, or deliberately procrastinating on completion'. Also, the mortgagee could not be expected to monitor effectively the negotiations of the mortgagor.

The Court of Appeal made it clear in *Corbett* v *Halifax plc* [2003] 2 All ER (Comm) 384 that equity will not intervene to set aside a conveyance by a mortgagee under the statutory power of sale of a secured legal estate unless there was some element of impropriety or bad faith on the part of the mortgagee in the exercise of that power. In addition, the mere fact that the sale was at an undervalue would not be enough to set it aside. Only if the purchaser had knowledge of, or participated in, an impropriety in the exercise of the power would the sale be vulnerable. Circumstances of which a mortgagee had no knowledge would not give rise to improper or irregular exercise of the statutory power.

Equitable mortgagees

As the result of the first requirement of s 101, an equitable mortgagee will only have a statutory power of sale if the mortgage was made by deed. An equitable mortgage by deposit of title deeds would satisfy this requirement provided the deposit was accompanied by a memorandum in the form of a deed. (You may well wonder why this would still be an equitable mortgage! The distinction lies in the contents of the deed. In order to be legal, the deed would have to either grant the mortgagee a term of years absolute, 'subject to a provision for cesser on redemption' – s 86, or be a charge 'expressed to be by way of legal mortgage' – s 87. A memorandum recording the fact that the deposit was intended to create an equitable mortgage would satisfy neither requirement. Equitable mortgages by deposit of title deeds are rare and today, given the simplicity of the form of legal charge, it is as easy to create a legal mortgage.)

It was held in *Re Hodson and Howes' Contract* (1887) 35 Ch D 668 that even where there is a deed, the mortgagee has power to sell the equitable interest only. The power can be extended to enable the mortgagee to sell the legal estate by the insertion in the mortgage deed of a power of attorney, or a declaration of trust under which the mortgagor declares himself to be trustee of the legal estate for the mortgagee and empowers the mortgagee to appoint himself (the mortgagee) or some other person as trustee in place of the mortgagor. This would enable the effective transfer of the legal estate to a purchaser.

Just as with a legal mortgagee, the court can order a sale instead of granting a foreclosure order – s 91.

Right to possession

Unlike the two previous rights (which enable a mortgagee to recover his money), the right to possession enables him to gain the property in order that it may be sold.

The Law of Property Act 1925, s 95(4) provides that the mortgagee has a right to possession as soon as the mortgage is executed, and, in *Four-Maids Ltd* v *Dudley Marshall (Properties) Ltd* [1957] Ch 317, Harman J explained further that the mortgagee 'may go into possession before the ink is dry on the mortgage unless there is something in the contract, express or by implication, whereby he has contracted himself out of that right'. It is quite common for building society mortgagees to expressly grant the mortgagor a right of possession until default, thus bringing the mortgagee's right within Harman J's proviso, and, in the case of instalment mortgages, Walton J accepted in *Esso Petroleum Co Ltd* v *Alstonbridge Properties Ltd* [1975] 1 WLR 1474 that, provided the mortgagor was not in default in the payment of one of his instalments, the court would be particularly ready to find an implied term entitling him to remain in possession (though, in order to so find, 'there must be something upon which to hang such a conclusion in the mortgage other than the mere fact that it is an instalment mortgage.') (It was held in *Birch* v *Wright* (1786) 1 Term Rep 378 that a mortgagor who resists his mortgagee's demand for possession automatically becomes a trespasser, but see below where the property is a dwelling-house.) Thus, a mortgagee can take possession without first obtaining a court order, but in practice it is most unusual for a mortgagee to do so. However, Lord Denning stipulated in *Quennell* v *Maltby* [1979] 1 WLR 318 that:

> a mortgagee will be restrained from getting possession except when it is sought bona fide and reasonably for the purpose of enforcing the security and then only subject to such conditions as the court thinks fit to impose.

Applying this *dictum*, the Court of Appeal held, in *Albany Home Loans Ltd* v *Massey* [1997] 2 All ER 609, that although the court had power to make an order for possession against one of two joint mortgagors, it would not, in general, be appropriate to do so where it would be of no benefit to the mortgagee, especially where the mortgagors were husband and wife. There was no benefit to the mortgagee, therefore, in ejecting Mr M whilst Mrs M could remain in the secured property. Following the case of *Western Bank Ltd* v *Schindler* [1976] 2 All ER 393, where the Court of Appeal held that s 36 applications under the Administration of Justice Act 1970 (see below) could be granted whether or not there is any sum due or other default under the mortgage agreement, Michael Haley (1997) quite rightly states that, 'The extension of relief to non-default cases, in effect, converts the mortgagee's absolute right to possession into a right which is exercisable only with the permission of the court and on good cause being shown'. However, the Court of Appeal, in *Ropaigealach* v *Barclays Bank plc* [1999] 4 All ER 235, stressed that s 36 does not abolish the common law right of the mortgagee to take possession; it provides merely a judicial discretion.

Yet, if possession is sought bona fide there is no requirement that the mortgagor be in default. It is as well then that, unlike the power of sale (which, as we have seen, arises and becomes exercisable automatically upon the fulfilment of the requirements of ss 101 and 103), the mortgagee must obtain a court order enabling him to exercise his right to possession. There is no automatic right to such orders which, as we have seen in *Boland*, may well be refused if the court feels that someone else has a higher claim to its protection. Of course, Mrs Boland was completely innocent, knowing nothing of the mortgages granted to Williams & Glyn's Bank by her husband. Had she known, concurred or colluded in any such mortgage she would, quite rightly, have lost her claim to protection in equity.

Paddington Building Society v *Mendelsohn* (1985) 50 P&CR 244

A mother who knew of, and was in favour of her son, the legal owner's intention to raise the balance of purchase monies for their home by way of mortgage, though she was held to have an equitable interest in the property, could not prevent the building society gaining possession. (Under the Family Law Act 1996, s 30(3), a spouse of a defaulting mortgagor can make repayments to the mortgagee even though he is not a legal owner, and such repayments would be 'as good as if made or done by the other spouse'. Of course, this right will only be of use to a spouse who is aware of the true situation and has the means to make such payments.) See also *Bristol Building Society* v *Henning* [1985] 1 WLR 778.

Realistically, there is little point in a mortgagee seeking possession unless there has been some default, as a mortgagee cannot sell until the requirements of ss 101 and 103 are satisfied. Indeed it is rare for an order to be sought where the mortgagor is not in arrears. Building society mortgages, which represent the vast majority of all mortgages granted, specifically state that the right of possession will only be exercised in cases of default.

However, 'Mortgagees are interested in their money, they are not interested in turning people out of their homes unless they think it is the only way of getting their money' – Glidewell LJ in *Mortgage Corporation Ltd* v *Drinkwater* (1994) unreported.

Where the mortgaged property is a dwellinghouse

When the loan is secured on a dwellinghouse,

> the tension between the commercial interests of the mortgagee and the need for the mortgagor to maintain a home persists. Although the court must attempt to achieve a balance between these competing claims, ... this is not a simple task. The judicial stance must necessarily reflect individual circumstances and broader notions of public interest, social and economic policy and parliamentary purpose – Michael Haley again.

As Waite LJ said in the leading case of *Cheltenham & Gloucester Building Society* v *Norgan* [1996] 1 All ER 449, '... the court is bound to be even-handed in its approach to the claims of each side'.

Where an order for possession is sought of a dwellinghouse, a mortgagor may be able to seek relief under the Administration of Justice Act 1970, s 36, which provides that the court:

(a) may adjourn the proceedings, or

(b) on giving judgment, or making an order, for delivery of possession of the mortgaged property, or at any time before the execution of such judgment or order, may –

   (i) stay or suspend execution of the judgment or order, or

   (ii) postpone the date for delivery of possession,

     for such period or periods as the court thinks reasonable.

There was a problem with s 36, however, because the court's discretion could only be exercised where 'it appears to the court that in the event of its exercising the power the mortgagor is likely to be able within a reasonable period to pay any sums due under the mortgage or to remedy a default consisting of a breach of any other obligation arising under or by virtue of the mortgage'.

'Any sums due under the mortgage' usually meant, in fact, the whole of the mortgagor's indebtedness to the mortgagee – not only arrears, but the whole of the unpaid capital sum plus interest – because the whole of the debt under the usual terms of a mortgage becomes 'due' upon a mortgagor falling into arrears. Had he been able to pay that, he would not, presumably, have been in arrears! The unavoidable result was illustrated in *Halifax Building Society* v *Clark* [1973] Ch 307. The mortgagor, who had deserted his wife, was £100 in arrears on the mortgage of the matrimonial home. Even if the wife had taken advantage of the right to have payments made by her accepted by the building society under the Matrimonial Homes Act 1967, s 1(5) (now Family Law Act 1996, s 30(3)), she was not in a position to be able to repay the whole of the capital and interest owing, which amounted to £1,400, within 'a reasonable period'. The building society was, therefore, granted its order for possession.

This problem was solved by the Administration of Justice Act 1973, s 8(1), which provides that:

> Where by a mortgage of land which consists of or includes a dwellinghouse, or by any agreement between the mortgagee under such a mortgage and the mortgagor, the mortgagor is entitled or is to be permitted to pay the principal sum secured by instalments or otherwise to defer payment of it in whole or in part, but provision is also made for earlier payment in the event of any default by the mortgagor or of a demand by the mortgagee or otherwise, then for the purposes of section 36 of the Administration of Justice Act 1970 (under which a court has power to delay giving a mortgagee possession of the mortgaged property so as to allow the mortgagor a reasonable time to pay any sums due under the mortgage) a court may treat as due under the mortgage on account of the principal sum secured and of interest on it only such amounts as the mortgagor would have expected to be required to pay if there had been no such provision for earlier payment.

In effect, then, s 8(1) overrules *Clark* and gives effect to what was surely the original intention of s 36 of the 1970 Act.

Cheltenham & Gloucester Building Society v *Norgan* [1996] 1 All ER 449

This case may well have taken things much further than was intended by the legislature. The Court of Appeal addressed a fundamental question: what is a 'reasonable period' under s 36? *The Supreme Court Practice*, which provides guidance to judges, stated that 'in any ordinary case a period of at least two years will be allowed to the borrower if it appears that he is likely to be able to clear off the arrears in that time and he may be allowed a much longer time'. It is common practice to allow between two and four years, and borrowers can make repeated applications. Counsel for the Building Society argued that periods from two to six years' deferment would be a just and fair exercise of the discretion under s 36, but Waite LJ stated that, 'the starting point for determining the reasonable period for repayment of the outstanding arrears is the outstanding term of the mortgage'. This being so, the court should 'pose at the outset the question: would it be possible for the mortgagor to maintain payment-off of the arrears by instalments over that period?'

The case concerned a 'term mortgage', that is one under which the capital is to be repaid only at the end of the term. (A mortgage secured by way of endowment is very similar to a term mortgage.) Where regular payments of capital and interest are required, the mortgage is a repayment mortgage. Obviously, then, the mortgagee of a term or endowment mortgage does not expect to be paid the capital sum until the end of the agreed mortgage term, say 25 years. Given this and the policy statement of the Council of Mortgage Lenders that 'lenders seek to take possession only as a last resort. They are in business to help people to buy homes, not to take their homes away from them', Evans LJ agreed with Waite LJ that it is appropriate to take account of the whole remaining part of the original term when assessing a 'reasonable period' for payment of arrears. Evans LJ went on to suggest several relevant considerations for a court when applying its discretion under s 36:

(a) How much can the borrower reasonably afford to pay, both now and in the future?
(b) If the borrower has a temporary difficulty in meeting his obligations, how long is the difficulty likely to last?
(c) What was the reason for the arrears which have accumulated?
(d) How much remains of the original term?
(e) What are relevant contractual terms, and what type of mortgage is it, ie when is the principal due to be repaid?
(f) Is it a case where the court should exercise its power to disregard accelerated payment provisions (s 8 of the 1973 Act)?
(g) Is it reasonable to expect the lender, in the circumstances of the particular case, to recoup the arrears of interest (1) over the whole of the original term, or (2) within a shorter period, or even (3) within a longer period, ie by extending the repayment period? Is it reasonable to expect the lender to capitalise the interest, or not?
(h) Are there any reasons affecting the security which should influence the length of the period for payment?

In the light of the answers to the above, the court can proceed to exercise its overall discretion, taking account also of any further factors which may arise in the particular case.

Leave to appeal to the House of Lords was refused, which is 'regrettable ... This socially important point of principle on the proper interpretation of s 36 ought to be considered at the highest judicial level. As matters stand, it is not clear whether the decision of the appeal court represents debtors' delight or defaulters' delusion' (H W Wilkinson, 1996, p 252). As Wilkinson so rightly says, this decision effectively reverses

> the burden of proof in mortgage repossession cases. Borrowers who are undeniably in default under the contractual terms of their mortgage, and are in consequence in most cases liable to repay both capital and interest at once, formerly had to find reasons why the court should not make or should suspend a possession order. Now there is to be a presumption that they have the full term in which to pay and the lenders will have to show why there should be a lesser term.

National and Provincial Building Society v *Lloyd* [1996] 1 All ER 630

Hot on the heels of *Norgan* came this case, where, again, the Court of Appeal had to consider the discretion under s 36. On the basis that it appeared that Mr Lloyd would be likely to be able within a reasonable period to pay the sums due under the mortgage, execution of an order for possession had been suspended. The likelihood of Mr Lloyd being able to repay the loan was based upon the fact that the mortgaged land could be sold for sums in excess of the amount due to the building society. The society appealed against the suspension, arguing that an order for possession of mortgaged property should be deferred only where a sale would take place within a short period of time. The Court of Appeal held that there was no rule of law to the effect that an order for possession of mortgaged property would only be adjourned or suspended if a sale would take place within a short period of time. Accordingly, if there were clear evidence that the completion of the sale of a property, perhaps by piece-meal disposal, could take place in six or nine months or even a year, there was no reason why a court could not come to the conclusion in the exercise of its discretion under s 36 that the mortgagor was 'likely to be able within a reasonable period to pay any sums due under the mortgage' and, in each case, the question of what was 'a reasonable period' would be a question for the court. Where a mortgaged property was to be sold and there were no other known assets, the question was whether it was likely that the mortgagor would be able within a reasonable period to pay all the sums due under the mortgage, including the capital sum.

The Court of Appeal in *Bristol and West Building Society* v *Ellis* (1996) P&CR 158 held that where, in a claim by a lender for a warrant of possession, there was insufficient evidence before the court to show that the borrower could sell the property within three to five years, or that the sale proceeds of the property would be sufficient to discharge the mortgage debt and any arrears, the court should grant an order of immediate possession. Auld LJ restated the starting point for the reasonableness of the period of three to five years for payment of the sums due under the mortgage as the outstanding period of the mortgage, in the absence of unusual circumstances and where discharge of all arrears by periodic payments were proposed, as in *Norgan*. However, his lordship went on to state that that starting point is not available to a mortgagor who could not discharge the arrears by periodic payments and whose only prospect of repaying the entire loan and accrued and accruing interest was from sale. In such a case the question of reasonableness is one for the court in the circumstances of the case, applying *Lloyd*.

His lordship stated that, in considering this question, the most important factors are likely to be the extent to which the mortgage debt and arrears are secured by the value of the property and the effect of time on that security. Where the property was already on the market and there was some indication of delay on the part of the borrower, it might be that a short period of suspension of the order for possession of only a few months would be reasonable. Where there was likely to be considerable delay in selling the property and/or its value was close to the total of the mortgage debt and arrears so that the mortgagee was at risk as to the adequacy of the security, immediate possession or only a short period of suspension might be reasonable. Where there had already been considerable delay in realising a sale and/or the likely sale proceeds were unlikely to cover the mortgage debt and arrears or there was simply not sufficient evidence as to sale value, the normal order would be for immediate possession, as in *Lloyd*.

In *Cheltenham & Gloucester Building Society* v *Krausz* the Court of Appeal summed up the position: though the right of a mortgagee to enter in possession is, at common law absolute and indefeasible, the rigours of this approach are mitigated by s 36, which offers the court the wide discretion to suspend possession where the borrower is in a position to pay arrears of instalments within a reasonable period.

However, if the mortgagor intends instead to sell the mortgaged property, the court must be satisfied that the proceeds will be sufficient to discharge the debt in its entirety. Phillips LJ went on to explain the relationship between ss 36 and 91 which, 'before the decision in *Palk*, [were thought to be] complementary'. However, *Palk*

> established, for the first time, that the court has power under s 91(2) to make an order for sale on the application of a mortgagor, notwithstanding that the proceeds of sale will be insufficient to discharge the mortgage debt . . . It is, however, quite clear that s 36 does not empower the court to suspend possession in order to permit the mortgagor to sell the mortgaged premises where the proceeds of sale will not suffice to discharge the mortgage debt, unless of course other funds will be available to the mortgagor to make up the shortfall . . .
>
> A mortgagor seeking relief in the circumstances of *Palk* is thus unable to invoke any statutory power to suspend the mortgagee's right to enter into possession . . .
>
> In my judgment the very specific delimitation of the power given by s 36 makes it clear that the legislature did not intend that the court should have any wider jurisdiction to curtail the mortgagee's right to possess . . .
>
> I recognise the principle of the inherent jurisdiction of the court . . . but I question whether that principle can justify the court in exercising its power to order a sale of mortgaged property under s 91 in the circumstances where the mortgagee is seeking to enter into possession in order to sell property in which there is negative equity and where the sole object with which the mortgagor seeks that order is to prevent the mortgagee exercising his right to possession so that the mortgagor can negotiate his own sale while in possession.

National Home Loans Corporation plc v *Yaxley* (1997) 73 P&CR D41

The Yaxleys sought a stay of possession proceedings under s 36 on the ground that 'in the not too distant future' a case brought by them against their original mortgagee and NHL would be heard. The Yaxleys were the victims of a fraud which had resulted in their defaulting on the mortgage. If they were to succeed in their claim, however, they would be able to pay off all the arrears. At first instance the judge held that though there may have been some prospect of their winning the case, it did not mean that they would be likely within a reasonable time to pay the sums due under the mortgage. Though the Yaxleys' application was also refused by the Court of Appeal, Walker LJ suggested that the mortgagee might, as an act of humanity, forbear from enforcing the possession order until the Yaxleys' action had been heard.

Generally, once a mortgagee is granted an order for possession, sale follows as soon as possible. However, in *Cheltenham & Gloucester plc* v *Booker* (1997) 73 P&CR 412, the Court of Appeal held that if the court was satisfied that:

(a) possession would not be required by the mortgagee pending completion of the sale but only by the purchasers on completion;
(b) the presence of the mortgagor pending completion would enhance, or at least not depress, the sale price;
(c) the mortgagor would cooperate in the sale of the property; and
(d) that vacant possession would be given on completion;

then an order for possession in favour of the mortgagees could, at their request, be suspended for a short time, leaving the mortgagors in occupation, and thus enabling the property to be sold by the mortgagee. However, such an order would be a rarity, made only where the necessary conditions were satisfied. *Booker* was not such a case.

This ratio and decision will no doubt please Michael Haley (1997) who argues that, 'there is no doubt that the court's discretion to postpone the mortgagee's right to possession is a necessary safeguard. Nevertheless, in order to achieve a balance between the disparate interests of the parties, it is vital that such discretion should remain flexible and be exercised with good reason'.

It was held in *Bank of Scotland* v *Grimes* [1985] 2 All ER 254 that s 36 applies not only to instalment mortgages, but to endowment mortgages too (applied by the Court of Appeal in *Royal Bank of Scotland* v *Miller* (2001) 82 P&CR 31 – a case which provides a very good explanation of the meaning of and interrelationship between ss 36 and 8). However, it does not apply to a mortgage to secure an overdraft: *Habib Bank Ltd* v *Tailor* [1982] 1 WLR 1218. In *Cheltenham & Gloucester Building Society* v *Johnson & Sunshine* (1993) 25 HLR 454 the Court of Appeal declared that s 36 deals solely with the power to suspend an order for possession. It has no direct bearing upon the power to suspend a money judgment; that is a separate discretion. However, following *Cheltenham & Gloucester Building Society* v *Grattidge* (1997) 73 P&CR 293, in principle though a mortgagee is entitled to a money judgment, it may be suspended on the same terms and in line with the suspension of possession order under s 36(2).

In repossessing mortgaged property the mortgagees may well, then, find that the property value has fallen, sometimes remarkably so. This is bad news for the mortgagor for, if the property does not yield enough funds to satisfy the mortgage debt, he will be personally liable for the balance, leaving him with no home and a large debt. The courts have recognised this and two cases show how they have tried to assist the mortgagor. As we have seen in *Palk* v *Mortgage Services Funding*, the mortgage debt exceeded the value of the house by about £70,000. The mortgagor wanted to sell in order to stem the arrears which were accumulating rapidly, but the mortgagee wanted to let the house until the market improved. Under its discretion under the Law of Property Act 1925, s 91(2), the Court of Appeal ordered sale as it would have been unfair to refuse sale, thereby increasing the mortgagor's eventual loss. In *Target Home Loans* v *Clothier* (1992) 25 HLR 48 it was the mortgagee who wanted to gain possession in order to sell the house. The mortgagor wanted a chance to sell the house himself. The Court of Appeal, in recognising that his difficulties were in no way caused by dishonesty, gave the mortgagor the opportunity to achieve a sale by adjourning the possession proceedings for four months.

It was held in *Royal Bank of Scotland* v *Miller* (2001) 82 P&CR 31, that the time at which the land is required to consist of or include a dwellinghouse, so as to attract the benefits of s 36(1), is the time when the mortgagee brings an action for possession of the mortgaged property.

Finally, the court cannot stay an order for possession under s 36 in respect of part only of a mortgaged property – *Barclays Bank plc* v *Alcorn* (2002) unreported.

Equitable mortgagees

An equitable mortgagee has no right to possession unless such a right has been expressly reserved or a court order for possession is granted.

When a mortgagee takes possession

Unfortunately, though probably inevitably given rises not only in property prices but also in interest rates and fuel costs, repossessions are on the increase – up 9 per cent in the first half of January 2007 and the highest for over a decade (source: Ceefax, 31 January 2007). If PricewaterhouseCoopers' warning of 'a 50–50 chance that house prices will be lower in real terms by 2010' (based on a forecast that 100,000 people would go bankrupt in 2006, an all time record) proves to be correct, the outlook is depressing – source: *The Week*, 11 November 2006.

Once a mortgagee takes possession he will usually sell the property. We have already seen how the proceeds of sale must be distributed. If the market is depressed the mortgagee may be willing to grant a lease. Whichever course is followed, the mortgagee is under a duty to account strictly for all proceeds from the sale or lease. The duty is owed to all persons entitled after him, and liability arises for any negligence.

Obviously, the mortgagee must sell for the best price that can reasonably be obtained, or lease for the best rent. Should even the best price or rent fail to raise sufficient money to satisfy the debt of the mortgagee, or of any subsequent mortgagee, an action can, of course, be brought by any of them on the mortgagor's personal covenant to pay. If the mortgagee decides to occupy the property personally, he must not only pay rent equivalent to the best that could reasonably be obtained from any other tenant, but also maintain the property in a reasonable state of repair. A mortgagee must never acquire any personal advantage from his powers of possession or sale.

Subrogation

As we have seen, in many cases more than one lender has been granted a mortgage over the same piece of land. However, subrogation is a remedy which invariably is relied upon by a re-mortgagee, that is one whose loan is used to pay off a previous mortgage.

> If a mortgagee cannot establish a right to possession relying on his own security, he may still be able to establish a right to possession relying on a previous mortgagee's security if he can show, by evidence, that his advance was used to redeem an existing loan. Such an entitlement relies on the remedy of subrogation – Miller and Klein (1996)

Subrogation is an equitable remedy: it is not a cause of action. However, 'It is available in a wide variety of difficult factual situations in which it is required in order to reverse the defendant's unjust enrichment', Millet LJ in *Boscawen* v *Bajwa* (1995) 70 P&CR 391. Be warned, however, for behind 'this apparently simple statement of general principle, the body of case law on mortgagee subrogation is complex': Miller and Klein. Indeed, 'It is impossible to formulate any narrower principle than that the doctrine will only be applied when the courts are satisfied that reason and justice demand it should be': Lord Salmon in *Orakpo* v *Manson Investments Ltd* [1978] AC 95.

Bankers Trust Co v *Namdar* [1997] ECGS 20

The Court of Appeal held that the plaintiffs could not invoke the doctrine because the wife had no knowledge of the refinancing of the family home and because the plaintiffs had at no time provided their own money towards the discharge of the mortgage.

The appointment of a receiver

There are two situations in which a mortgagee most frequently chooses to appoint a receiver rather than exercise the power of sale: where the secured property is a business which still has some 'life' in it, and where the mortgaged property has been leased by the mortgagor and the mortgagee wants to ensure that the rent payable is not in fact paid to the mortgagor.

Just as with sale, the power to appoint a receiver must both 'arise' and 'become exercisable' by satisfying the requirements of ss 101 and 103. No court order is required, therefore.

If the land is registered the mortgagee must be registered as proprietor before a receiver can be appointed – *Lever Finance Ltd* v *Needleman's Trustee and Kreutzer* [1956] Ch 375.

Silven Properties Ltd v *Royal Bank of Scotland plc* [2004] 1 WLR 997

Here, the Court of Appeal explained the relative positions of a receiver, the mortgagor and the mortgagee. The receiver is in a different position to that of the mortgagee; whereas a mortgagee has no duty at any time to exercise its power to enforce its security, in the absence of any provision to the contrary in the mortgage or in terms of his appointment, a receiver has to be active in the protection and preservation of the mortgaged property. Where the receiver has been appointed by the mortgagee as an agent of the mortgagor, the receiver's primary duty is to ensure that the secured debt is paid (though his core duty is still to account to the mortgagor).

Like the mortgagee, the receiver is entitled to sell the secured property in the condition in which it was without awaiting or effecting any increase in value or improvement in the property.

Once appointed, the receiver is deemed to be the agent of the mortgagor – s 109(2). Thus, for example, the mortgagor could not sue the mortgagee if the agent were negligent. A receiver owes a duty to get the best price and should also exercise some care as to the time of the sale. In *Gosling* v *Gaskell* [1897] AC 575 it was held that if there was a breach of this duty, and a sale at an undervalue, credit should be given to the mortgagor (or any guarantor) for the amount that should have been received. A receiver has power to recover income arising from the property – rent for example – by action or distress, and to give proper receipts. Just as a mortgagee who sells must lay out the proceeds of sale in a particular order, a receiver must apply any income as follows:

(1) by paying all outgoings, for example local taxes;
(2) by settling any prior claims;
(3) by paying his own commission and any expenses incurred by complying with requests of the mortgagee, for instance to effect repairs;
(4) by paying the interest due under the mortgage;
(5) by paying the capital sum due under the mortgage, if directed in writing to do so by the mortgagee;
(6) by paying anything left to the mortgagor.

– Law of Property Act 1925, s 109

The Court of Appeal explained the nature of the duty of a receiver in *Medforth* v *Blake* [1999] 3 All ER 97: the receiver's primary duty is to attempt to create a situation where the interest on the secured debt can be paid and the debt itself repaid. If he attempts to do this by managing the secured property (a pig-farming business, in this case), then he owes a duty to manage the property with due diligence, subject to his primary duty. Due diligence does not oblige the receiver to continue a business at the mortgaged property, but it does require him to take reasonable steps to manage it profitably if he does choose to continue that business. The Court also made a *per curiam* statement: a receiver cannot be in breach of his duty of good faith to the mortgagor in the absence of some dishonesty, improper motive or element of bad faith.

Equitable mortgagees

Where the mortgage is created by deed an equitable mortgagee has the same power as a legal mortgagee.

If there is no deed, the mortgagee can petition the court to appoint a receiver – Supreme Court Act 1981, s 37. A receiver appointed in this way is personally liable for his actions in that capacity – he is not an agent.

Foreclosure

For some reason better known to themselves students always begin with this, the oldest and most Draconian right of the mortgagee. From the mortgagor's point of view it is the worst of all possible nightmares, for the effect of foreclosure is to deprive him of not only his house but also the whole of his equity of redemption. In other words, if a mortgagee forecloses the mortgagor will not even be entitled to any surplus monies remaining after payment of all debts. Any surplus will go to the mortgagee.

However, as we have seen, the court has the power under the Law of Property Act 1925, s 91, to make an order for sale instead of foreclosure. It was stated in *Palk* v *Mortgage Services Funding plc* that the principle is to strike a fair balance between the interests of the parties. However, as explained by Sir Michael Kerr:

> ... [section 91(2)] not only places no restriction on the exercise of the court's powers, but ... it confers these expressly even when 'any other person' dissents, or when the mortgagee does not appear at all ... The position is therefore that section 91(2) deliberately places no restriction on the power of the court other than the inherent and necessarily implied obligation to exercise the power judicially. Thus, the judicial availability of the power does not depend on whether the mortgagee has taken some steps to exercise his rights over the mortgaged property ... Nor does it matter whether the mortgagee's dissent and objection are based on express contractual rights, or on the statutory rights provided by sections 99 and 101 of the Law of Property Act 1925, or on their express incorporation with variations into the mortgage deed.

It was held in *Arab Bank plc* v *Mercantile Holdings Ltd* [1994] 2 All ER 74 that, in exceptional circumstances, a court may grant an order for sale under s 91(2), even though the mortgagee had a perfectly valid power of sale and even though a purchaser from the mortgagee would be protected from the mortgagor by an exercise of this normal power.

A foreclosure order can be requested by the mortgagor, the mortgagee or any other person interested in either the mortgage monies or the equity of redemption, for example, a subsequent mortgagee.

As Sir Donald Nicholls VC said in *Palk*, 'foreclosure actions are almost unheard of today and have been so for many years. Mortgagees prefer to exercise other remedies'. However, where there is negative equity but a real possibility that the value of the security will increase in the future, a mortgagee may find foreclosure an attractive option. In *Merchant Banking Co of London* v *London & Hanseatic Bank* (1886) 55 LJ Ch 479 a first mortgagee sought a foreclosure order and the second mortgagee asked the court to order sale, but postpone it for a year or two. The request for sale on such conditions was refused and the foreclosure order made.

Apart from s 91, another reason why foreclosure is an unpopular option with mortgagees could be that even when the court does make an order for foreclosure, in special circumstances it may reopen it, for instance where the value of the property far exceeds the debt, but only if the mortgagor can find the money to pay off the mortgage.

As we have already seen, if, for some reason, the lender is unable to exercise its power of sale, 'if the lenders are entitled to foreclosure, [the court] may order a sale instead' – Templeman J in *Twentieth Century Banking Corporation Ltd* v *Wilkinson*.

The mortgagee must obtain a court order. If the court decides to grant this request it will first order a foreclosure order *nisi*, under which the mortgagor will be allowed time in which to repay the loan – usually six months. If the loan is not repaid within the specified time the court will make a foreclosure order absolute, and this has the effect of vesting the whole of the mortgagor's estate and interest in the property in the mortgagee, thereby extinguishing the equity of redemption. This, of course, makes the mortgagee the sole legal and equitable owner.

The right to a foreclosure order does not arise until the legal date for redemption has passed, or there has been a breach of some covenant which has the effect of destroying the mortgagor's right of redemption. It may be that no date for redemption has been fixed. In such cases (which are rare) the right to foreclose arises after a reasonable time has elapsed following a demand by the mortgagee for repayment. The same applies where the loan is repayable on demand.

If several mortgages have been granted on the same piece of land, any of the mortgagees can apply for a foreclosure order, as can an assignee from them. Every person interested in the land, including the mortgagor, should be joined in as parties to the action and any of the defendants may redeem the mortgage within the time allowed under the order *nisi*. If a subsequent mortgagee obtains the order for foreclosure, the rights of any prior mortgagees will not be affected but, upon the order being made absolute, all subsequent mortgages are also foreclosed.

Example

If three mortgages have been granted on the security of a house, 'Crumblestones', to the Priority Building Society, the Improvident Bank plc and Foolish Finances Ltd (being executed and registered in that order), any of the three mortgagees can apply for a foreclosure order. If the building society is granted an order absolute, all the mortgages are foreclosed. If the order is awarded to the bank, the mortgages held by the bank and Foolish Finances are foreclosed, but not the building society's mortgage. If Foolish Finances obtains the order, only its mortgage is foreclosed. Where some of the mortgages have not been foreclosed, the mortgagees holding them retain their rights.

If foreclosure fails to raise the necessary sums, any of the mortgagees can sue the mortgagor on his covenant to repay. This has the effect of reviving his right of redemption and cannot be used, therefore, if the mortgagee has done anything which would prevent such a revival. The most obvious example would be where the mortgagee has sold the property.

However, despite the various remedies available to mortgagees there are almost as many pitfalls. We have already seen the threat posed by a Mrs Boland and we shall come to that posed by a claim of undue influence shortly, but there are more.

Mrs Boland's threat arises from the fact that, with only one trustee signing the receipt for the mortgage monies, her interest had not been overreached. Furthermore, it was binding on the mortgagee bank. However, in some cases even where the relevant number of signatures have been obtained, the mortgagee has still failed to realise its security. These are the fraud cases where, usually, not only the mortgagee but also an innocent owner of the secured property have been defrauded.

First National Securities v *Hegerty* [1985] QB 850

A husband and wife were joint owners at law and in equity of the matrimonial home. When obtaining a mortgage advance on the property, the husband forged his wife's signature and then left the country with the loan money. Needless to say, he defaulted on the repayments! When the mortgagee brought proceedings it found that it was bound by Mrs Hegerty's interest, because for overreaching to operate, the signatures must be those of the trustees of land, being at least two in number – not merely two signatures. Mrs Hegerty, the second and all-important trustee, had not signed.

Skipton Building Society v *Clayton* (1993) 25 HLR 596

This case caught the mortgagee out on several fronts. Mr and Mrs Browne, the original owners of a leasehold flat, transferred it to Clayton at below market value. In return, the Brownes received a 'licence' to occupy the premises for life. Clayton mortgaged the land to Skipton. Mr Browne signed a document renouncing any interest in the flat; he also forged his wife's signature on the same document. The Brownes were, as part of this process, re-granted a licence for life. The purpose of this was to encourage the building society to grant the loan. Their surveyor duly visited the flat and concluded it was unoccupied, notwithstanding it was furnished. Clayton defaulted on the mortgage repayments and the building society sought possession. The Brownes claimed that they had a lease of the flat which was binding on the building society by virtue of the Land Registration Act 1925, s 70(1)(g). The building society claimed the Brownes merely had a licence and, therefore, no interest in the land, and also that they had impliedly consented to the mortgage. The Brownes were held to have a lease – the 'licence' being a sham. As they had a lease (which was converted into a lease for 90 years under the Law of Property Act 1925, s 149(6)), an interest in land, and they were in actual occupation, and as the building society had made no enquiry of them, the Brownes were held to have an overriding interest under s 70(1)(g). It was also held that neither Mr nor Mrs Browne had given any consent – express or implied – to the mortgage: Mrs Browne did not know anything about it and Mr Browne's knowledge did not amount to a consent that Skipton's interest take priority over his own.

So … another case showing once again the need for careful, not to say exhaustive, inspections by potential mortgagees of property offered as security. Of course, no matter how diligently they inspect, mortgagees – and any other purchaser – will be bound by any overriding interests, whether or not such investigations bring them to light. The only possible escape from s 70(1)(g) is the making of an enquiry of the right person and where any interest is denied. Thus:

> … a wise purchaser or lender will take no risks. Indeed, however wise he may be, he may have no ready opportunity of finding out. But, nevertheless, the law will protect the occupier. Reliance upon the untrue [unsupported assertion] of the vendor will not suffice – Russell LJ in *Hodgson* v *Marks* [1971] Ch 892.

In that case the plaintiff was:

> there for Mr Marks to see and he saw her on two occasions [but] it is plain that [the second defendant, a building society who had advanced the money to Marks] made no inquiries on the spot save as to repairs; it relied on [Marks], who lied to it; and I waste no tears on it – Russell LJ.

The same warning applies to Sched 3, para 2 of the 2002 Act.

Finally, domestic mortgages commonly contain a standard clause under which the borrower agrees not to let the mortgaged property without the prior consent of the mortgagee.

In regard to a mortgagee's duty of good faith to a mortgagor, the Court of Appeal held, in *Starling* v *Lloyds TSB* (1999) *The Times*, 12 November, that this duty does not

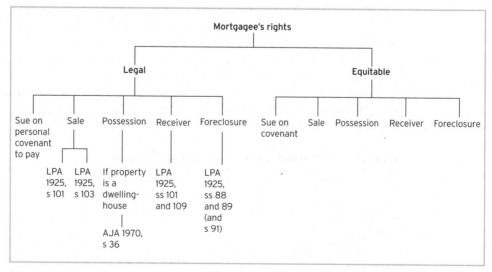

Figure 11.2

include a duty to consider reasonably a mortgagor's request for permission to lease out the mortgaged property. In the absence of bad faith, improper motive or dishonesty, no action can arise from an unreasonable refusal to give such consent. Furthermore, the Court of Appeal held in *Citibank International plc* v *Kessler* (1999) 78 P&CR D7, that a refusal by a mortgagee to consent to the letting of mortgaged property by the mortgagor did not breach Article 48 of the EC Treaty of Rome (which guarantees freedom of movement of workers within the Community).

Undue influence
(or, looking after the mortgagor and the mortgagee!)

We have seen that any oppressive or unconscionable term imposed by a mortgagee will be struck down. In addition, in connection with the mortgagee's right of possession, more especially so since *Williams & Glyn's Bank* v *Boland* [1981] AC 487, the doctrine of undue influence may come into play. Undue influence looks not at the terms of the mortgage, but the way in which agreement to it was obtained. As we shall see, the undue influence need not have come from the mortgagee, yet he may be bound by the consequence of it.

Royal Bank of Scotland v *Etridge* [2001] 4 All ER 449

Undue influence is one of the grounds of relief developed by the courts of equity as a court of conscience. The objective is to ensure that the influence of one person over another is not abused. In everyday life people constantly seek to influence the decisions of others. They seek to persuade those with whom they are dealing to enter into transactions, whether great or small. The law has set limits to the means properly employable for this purpose - Lord Nichols in the House of Lords.

The Court of Appeal held in *Pesticcio* v *Huet* [2004] EWCA Civ 372 that the law of undue influence is not concerned with dishonest or wrongful acts, but, as a matter of public policy, with the presumed influence arising from a relationship of trust and confidence which should not disadvantage the victim if the transaction was not satisfactorily explained by ordinary motives. It is the nature of the continuing relationship between the parties, rather than any specific act on the part of the recipient, that is relevant when considering undue influence.

In *Lloyds Bank Ltd* v *Bundy* [1975] QB 326, Lord Denning stated that as a general principle there could be no relief for a mortgagee where an 'inequality of bargaining power' was shown.

National Westminster Bank plc v *Morgan* [1985] AC 686

The House of Lords, in disapproving *Bundy*, stated that, as a court of conscience, the court must decide each case on its particular facts before deciding whether there has been unconscionability. Mere absence of equality of bargaining strength alone would not suffice.

In *Morgan* a wife was claiming undue influence by the bank manager, Mr Barrow, in obtaining her signature to the mortgage deed. However, said Lord Scarman, if a transaction is to be set aside on the ground of undue influence, it must 'constitute a disadvantage sufficiently serious to require evidence to rebut the presumption that in the circumstances of the relationship between the parties it had been procured by the exercise of undue influence'. Quite apart from constituting a serious disadvantage to Mrs Morgan, the mortgage had in fact rescued her home from repossession by another mortgagee. In addition, their Lordships could not agree with Mrs Morgan's contention that her relationship with Mr Barrow 'had assumed a very different character' than that of bank manager and customer. There was no undue influence. *Morgan* was considered in *Etridge*, where the House of Lords held that a transaction that is not readily explained by the relationship of the parties is still one of the two elements needed to give rise to a rebuttable evidential presumption of undue influence, shifting the evidential burden of proof from the party alleging undue influence to the party who is denying it. Thus the person claiming undue influence must 'prove in the first instance sufficient facts to give rise to the presumption' – Lord Scott. In *Morgan*, Lord Scarman concluded that 'manifest disadvantage' to the claimant would have to be shown in order to raise the presumption, but Lord Nicholls stated in *Etridge* that, 'this label has been causing difficulty ... experience has now shown that this expression can give rise to misunderstanding', consequently, it should be discarded. However, 'a disadvantage sufficiently serious to require evidence to rebut the presumption that in the circumstances of the parties' relationship, it was procured by the exercise of undue influence' is necessary; 'the greater the disadvantage to the vulnerable person, the more cogent must be the explanation before the presumption will be regarded as rebutted' – Lord Nicholls, here adopting Lord Scarman's approach in *Morgan*.

The matter arose again in *Kings North Trust Co Ltd* v *Bell* [1986] 1 WLR 119. This time the wife claimed that the undue influence had come from her husband. Mrs Bell, though not a legal owner, had an equitable interest in the matrimonial home. A second mortgage of the house expressly stated that all of Mrs Bell's interest was charged under the mortgage, and that she concurred in the mortgagee having priority over her right of occupation. Mrs Bell signed the deed upon her husband's assurances that the mortgage was to cover a short-term loan only and that it carried little, if any, risk. Neither statement was true. The Court of Appeal held that Mrs Bell's rights took priority over those of the mortgagee. She had signed the mortgage having been misled by her husband as to the true purpose of the loan. As Kings North had left it to Mr Bell to secure his wife's signature, the mortgagee was in the same position as Mr Bell. As Dillon LJ warned:

> The moral was that where a creditor (or intending creditor) desired the protection of a guarantee or charge on property from a third party other than the debtor and the circumstances were such that the debtor could be expected to have influence over the third party, the creditor ought for his own protection to insist that the third party had independent advice. That was the obvious means of avoiding the risk that the creditor would be held to have left it to the debtor to procure the execution of the relevant guarantee or security document by the third party.

His Lordship also explained that 'there was no presumption of law that a transaction between husband and wife for the husband's benefit was procured by undue influence on the part of the husband and there was no rule that such a transaction could not be upheld unless the wife had independent advice'. In regard to the first part of this statement, the House of Lords in *Etridge* agreed, stating that, in the ordinary course, a wife's guarantee of her husband's business debts is not to be regarded as a transaction which, failing proof to the contrary, is explicable only on the basis that it has been procured by the exercise of undue influence by the husband. Indeed, such transactions 'as a class' are not to be regarded as prima facie evidence of the exercise of undue influence by the husband – 'though there will be cases which call for an explanation'. As for the need for independent advice, we are coming to that next.

Mrs Bell's success was to prove a rare one: in each of a string of later cases, the claim to undue influence failed – until Mrs O'Brien!

Barclays Bank plc v *O'Brien & Another* [1993] 3 WLR 786

Here, the House of Lords upheld a wife's claim of undue influence, stating *per curiam* that the same principles apply to all cases where one cohabitee stands surety for the other cohabitee's debts and the creditor is aware that there is an emotional relationship between the cohabitees: the principles are not limited, therefore, to married couples. In addition, the principles are applicable to other relationships where the creditor is aware that the surety reposes trust and confidence in the principal debtor. In *O'Brien*, Mr O'Brien and his wife agreed to execute a second mortgage of their matrimonial home as security for an overdraft facility provided by the bank to a company in which Mr O'Brien, but not Mrs O'Brien, had an interest. The branch manager of the bank sent the documentation to another branch for execution with instructions to ensure that both Mr and Mrs O'Brien were fully aware of the nature of the documents and that, if in doubt, they should consult their solicitors before signing. These instructions were not carried out, however and, in reliance on her husband's false representation that the lending facility was limited to £60,000 and would last for only three weeks, Mrs O'Brien signed the deed without reading it.

When the company's overdraft exceeded £154,000 the bank applied for and obtained an order for possession. Mrs O'Brien appealed and the Court of Appeal found for her, holding that the legal charge was only enforceable against her to the extent of £60,000. The bank appealed. The House of Lords, whilst upholding the decision of the Court of Appeal, did so on different grounds: the *ratio* was different. In the only reasoned judgment, Lord Browne-Wilkinson stated that a wife who was induced to stand as surety for his debts by her husband's undue influence, misrepresentation or other legal wrong, has, *as against her husband*, an equity. However, in Mrs O'Brien's situation this is of little use unless the equity is binding upon the third party - the bank. Whether or not the equity will bind a third party will, said Lord Browne-Wilkinson, depend upon several factors:

1 Was the mortgagor acting as agent of the mortgagee?
2 Did the mortgagee have actual or constructive notice of the facts which gave rise to the equity?

If, on the facts, the mortgagee is put on enquiry as to the circumstances in which the surety (eg, Mrs O'Brien) agreed to stand surety, it will be bound by constructive notice. In the case of spouses, a combination of two matters may put a mortgagee upon enquiry:

1 Where, on the face of it, the transaction is not to the financial advantage of the wife; and

2 Where the transaction carries with it substantial risk that the wife may, due to a legal or equitable wrong of her husband, call for the transaction to be set aside.

In other words, any mortgagee who is put on enquiry, on the facts, and fails to take reasonable steps to satisfy itself that the wife's agreement to stand surety was obtained properly, will have constructive notice of the wife's rights and be bound by them. How then, if at all, can a mortgagee avoid being bound? Lord Browne-Wilkinson suggested that the mortgagee:

1 take steps to bring home to the wife the risk that she is running by standing surety for her husband's debt, and

2 advise her to take independent advice. Indeed, the mortgagee must insist that the wife be separately advised where it is aware of facts which make it not only possible, but probable, that the wife will be subjected to her husband's undue influence.

Each case must be decided on its own facts and although such cases will usually involve an attempt by a wife to prevent a mortgagee from gaining possession of her home due to the non-payment of mortgage repayments by her husband, the principles laid down in *O'Brien* apply whenever the mortgagee knows that the surety is cohabiting with the mortgagor – whether the relationship be legal or merely 'common law', whether it be hetero- or homosexual.

CICB Mortgages plc v *Pitt* [1993] 3 WLR 802

On the same day as the *O'Brien* judgment was delivered the same panel of judges delivered judgment in this case. Mr and Mrs Pitt's matrimonial home, which they owned jointly, was valued at £270,000 with a mortgage of £16,700 outstanding to a building society. In 1986 Mr Pitt told his wife that he wanted to take out a loan, using the house as security, to buy shares on the Stock Market so as to improve her standard of living. Mrs Pitt was not happy about the loan but, under pressure from Mr Pitt, she agreed. CICB made a loan to the Pitts of £150,000 for 19 years secured on the house by way of a remortgage, on the basis that the money was to be used to buy a second property. The Pitts executed a legal charge in favour of CICB, Mrs Pitt not having read any of the documents which she had signed. CICB paid the advance to solicitors who were acting for both CICB and the Pitts. The solicitors redeemed the building society mortgage and paid the balance of the loan monies to the Pitts, who paid it into their joint bank account. As intended, Mr Pitt used the money to buy shares, doing so in his own name. He then charged those shares to borrow more money, and bought more shares. Initially, he was very successful, becoming something of a paper millionaire, but in the Stock Market crash of 1987 he lost it all and fell into arrears with the repayments to CICB, who brought proceedings for possession of the family home. Mrs Pitt's claim of undue influence and misrepresentation were dismissed at first instance, and the Court of Appeal dismissed her appeal - as did the House of Lords. Holding that a person who could prove the exercise of actual undue influence by another in carrying out a transaction was entitled as of right against that other person to have the transaction set aside without proof of manifest disadvantage (thereby overruling the earlier case of *Bank of Credit & Commerce International SA* v *Aboody* [1990] 1 QB 923 in which the Court of Appeal had sought to interpret *Morgan*), the House of Lords held that Mrs Pitt had established undue influence as against her husband. Was CICB affected by, and thus liable for, this undue influence? Their

Lordships held that CICB would not be affected by Mr Pitt's undue influence on his wife, unless either Mr Pitt was acting as CICB's agent in procuring Mrs Pitt's agreement, or CICB had actual or constructive notice of the undue influence. Finding that Mr Pitt was not acting as their agent, and that CICB had no actual notice of the undue influence, was there constructive notice? As there was no indication that the transaction was anything other than a normal advance to a husband and wife for their joint benefit, CICB was not put on enquiry and could not be fixed with constructive notice of the undue influence. CICB were, therefore, entitled to enforce the legal charge.

The House of Lords distinguished *Pitt* from *O'Brien* on the ground of notice, Lord Browne-Wilkinson again providing the only reasoned judgment, but adopting the following reasoning of Peter Gibson LJ in the Court of Appeal:

> We are concerned with the application of equitable principles. I start with the fact that equity does not presume undue influence in transactions between husband and wife. Further, bona fide purchasers for value without notice are recognised in equity as having a good defence to equitable claims. On principle therefore a creditor who is not on notice of any actual or likely undue influence in a transaction involving a husband and wife ought not to be affected by the exercise of undue influence by the husband. Of course if the creditor leaves it to the husband to procure the wife's participation in the transaction or otherwise makes the husband the creditor's agent, whether in a strict or some looser sense, then the creditor is affected by the acts of the agent and notice of undue influence by the husband can be imputed to the creditor. By reason of the *O'Brien* case, I must accept that in a case where a wife provides security for a husband's debt, the creditor, unless it takes steps to ensure that the wife understands the transaction and that her consent was true and informed, may be affected by any undue influence executed by the husband to procure the wife's actions, even if the creditor has no knowledge of the undue influence; but that is explicable on the basis that such a transaction, favouring a husband at the expense of his wife, on its face puts the creditor on notice of the possibility of undue influence by the husband. By parity reasoning, if there is a secured loan to the husband and wife but the creditor is aware that the purposes of the loan are to pay the husband's debts or otherwise for his (as distinct from their joint) purposes, the creditor, without taking precautionary steps, may be affected by the husband's misconduct.

In undue influence cases the co-mortgagor or surety claims only to have joined in the transaction because of the undue influence exercised upon her. Having joined in the transaction, of course, the co-mortgagor or surety has waived priority of her interest in the secured property in favour of the mortgagee, either because she was a legal co-owner and therefore overreached her interest when executing the deed and receipt, or as an acknowledged equitable interest holder who agreed to the transaction. These cases, then, are different from those like *Boland* and *Flegg* where non-legal owners sought to prove the existence of an equitable interest which would bind the mortgagee, the interest holder being unaware of the mortgage. The principles evolved to meet those circumstances which would not avail a person who had joined in the mortgage transaction. Thus, Mrs O'Brien refreshes the parts that Mrs Boland cannot reach!

As the House of Lords stated, however, the principles laid down in *O'Brien* and *Pitt* are not limited to married couples (indeed, the same is true of the *Boland* principles) – see *Cheese* v *Thomas* [1994] 1 WLR 129, where the Court of Appeal had to decide:

> . . . a most unfortunate case. It arises out of the all too familiar situation where different generations of a family join to provide the older member with a home. Both sides have the best of intentions, but the arrangement breaks down. Difficulties then arise in unravelling what

has been done. Here, two members of a family have become involved in proceedings which ought never to have seen the door of a court – Sir Donald Nicholls VC.

'Since [*O'Brien*], many cases have come before the courts, testing the implications of the *O'Brien* decision in a variety of different factual situations' – Lord Nicholls in *Etridge*.

Royal Bank of Scotland v *Etridge* [2001] 4 All ER 449

Etridge itself considered appeals in eight cases, each of which

> arises out of a transaction in which a wife charged her interest in her home in favour of a bank as security for her husband's indebtedness or the indebtedness of a company through which he carried on business. The wife later asserted she signed the charge under the undue influence of her husband – Lord Nicholls.

In considering these eight appeals, the House of Lords has provided us with what amounts to the definitive statement of law in this area. Although all eight appeals were made by wives against their husbands, exactly the same principles apply to every case where there is an emotional relationship between the parties, even if they are not cohabiting – *Massey* v *Midland Bank plc* [1995] 1 All ER 929 (where there was a long-standing emotional and sexual relationship, but the couple did not live in the same house); and in the case of a brother and sister in *Barclays Bank plc* v *Rivett* [1997] NPC 18. However, a lender

> has no business inquiring into the personal relationship between those with whom it has business dealings or as to their personal motives for wanting to help one another. A bank is not to be treated as a branch of the social services agencies – Sir Richard Scott VC in *Banco Exterior Internacional SA* v *Thomas* [1997] 1 WLR 221.

In *Etridge*, the House of Lords, and especially Lord Nicholls (whose opinion 'it is plain . . . commands the unqualified support of all members of the House' – Lord Bingham), deals with three aspects:

1 the steps which the lender should have taken in respect of past transactions; and
2 the steps which the lender should take in future transactions in order to protect itself; and
3 the steps which solicitors should take to discharge their duty.

In setting out the principles and guidelines, their Lordships were only too well aware, as Lord Bingham stated, that

> the transactions which give rise to these appeals are commonplace but of great social and economic importance. It is important that a wife (or anyone in a like position) should not charge her interests in the matrimonial home to secure the borrowing of her husband (or anyone in a like position) without fully understanding the nature and effect of the proposed transaction and that the decision is hers, to agree or not to agree. It is important that lenders should feel able to advance money, in run-of-the-mill cases with no abnormal features, on the security of the wife's interest in the matrimonial home in reasonable confidence that, if appropriate procedures have been followed in obtaining the security, it will be enforceable if the need for enforcement arises. The law must afford both parties a measure of protection. It cannot prescribe a code which will be proof against error, misunderstanding or mishap. But it can indicate minimum requirements which, if met, will reduce the risk of error, misunderstanding or mishap to an acceptable level. The paramount need in this important field is that these minimum requirements should be clear, simple and practically operable.

The House of Lords held that a lender is put on inquiry to take reasonable steps to satisfy itself that the 'wife' had understood and freely entered into the transaction whenever a wife offers to stand surety for her husband's debts or those of his business, or of a company in which they both have a shareholding, when the wife is a director or secretary of the company.

> The position is likewise if the husband stands surety for his wife's debts. Similarly, in the case of unmarried couples, whether heterosexual or homosexual, where the bank is aware of the relationship. Cohabitation is not essential – Lord Nicholls.

A lender is not put on inquiry where money is being or has been advanced on the 'husband and wife' jointly **unless** the lender is aware the loan is being made for the husband's purposes. Once put on inquiry,

> the furthest a bank can be expected to go is to take reasonable steps to satisfy itself that the wife has had brought home to her, in a meaningful way, the practical implications of the proposed transaction. This does not wholly eliminate the risk of undue influence or mis-representation. But it does mean that a wife enters into a transaction with her eyes open so far as the basic elements of the transaction are concerned – Lord Nicholls.

With regard to future transactions, then, a lender 'once it has been put on inquiry' should take the following steps for its own protection:

1 It should communicate directly with the wife, informing her that for its own protection it will require written confirmation from a solicitor acting for her, to the effect that the solicitor has fully explained to her the nature of the documents and the practical implications they will have for her.

2 She should be told that the purpose of that requirement is that thereafter she should not be able to dispute that she is legally bound by the documents once she has signed them.

3 She should be asked to nominate a solicitor whom she is willing to instruct to advise her, separately from her husband, and act for her in giving the bank the necessary confirmation.

4 She should be informed that, if she wishes, the solicitor may be the same solicitor who is acting in the transaction for her husband. If a solicitor is already acting for the husband and the wife, she should be asked whether she would prefer a dif-ferent solicitor to act for her regarding the bank's requirement for confirmation from a solicitor. The bank should not proceed with the transaction until it has received an appropriate response directly from the wife.

If the bank is unwilling to undertake the task of explaining the husband's financial affairs to the wife, it must provide the solicitor with the financial infor-mation he needs for that purpose. The information required will depend on the facts of the case. Ordinarily, it will include information on the purpose for which the pro-posed new facility has been requested, the current amount of the husband's indebtedness, the amount of his current overdraft facility, and the amount and terms of any new facility. If the bank's request for security arises from a written appli-cation by the husband for a facility, a copy of the application should be sent to the solicitor. The bank will, of course, need to obtain the consent of its customer to that circulation of confidential information. If that consent is not forthcoming, the transaction will not be able to proceed. Where, exceptionally, the bank believes or suspects that the wife has been misled by her husband or is not entering into the transaction of her own free will, it must inform the wife's solicitor of the facts giving rise to such a belief or suspicion.

In every case the bank should obtain from the wife's solicitor a written confirmation to the effect mentioned above. In respect of past transactions, the bank will ordinarily be regarded as having discharged its obligations if a solicitor who is acting for the wife in the transaction has given its confirmation to the effect that he has brought home to her the risks she was running by standing as surety.

Finally, in future, banks should regulate their affairs on the basis that they are put on inquiry in every case where the relationship between the surety and the debtor is non-commercial, and must, therefore, always take reasonable steps to bring home to an individual guarantor the risks she is running by standing as surety. If the bank or other creditor does not take such steps, it will be deemed to have notice of any claim the guarantor may have that the transaction was procured by undue influence or misrepresentation on the part of the debtor.

However, it is not only the lender who needs to take precautions: so too does any solicitor who advises the wife – in which capacity the solicitor is acting not as the lender's agent, but solely for the wife.

As a first step the solicitor will need to explain to the wife the purpose for which he has become involved at all. He should explain that, if it ever becomes necessary, the bank will rely upon his involvement to counter any suggestion that the wife has been overborne by her husband or that she has not properly understood the implications of the transaction. The solicitor will need to obtain confirmation from the wife that she wishes him to act for her in the matter and to advise her on the legal and practical implications of the proposed transaction. Once such an instruction is obtained, the content of the advice required from the solicitor will be dictated by the facts of the case.

Generally, a solicitor's advice will need to cover the following as a 'core minimum' – an explanation of the nature of the documents and the practical consequences they will have for the wife if she signs them; the seriousness of the risks involved; the purpose of the proposed new lending facility, its amount and principal terms and the fact that the lender may increase the amount of the facility, or change its terms, or grant a new facility, without further reference to her. She should be told the amount of her liability under the guarantee.

The wife's financial means, including her understanding of the value of the property being charged, and whether she and her husband have any other assets out of which payment could be made if the husband's business fails should be discussed.

The solicitor must state clearly that the wife has a choice: the decision is hers and hers alone. However, it must be an informed decision, and therefore, in explaining the choice before her, some discussion of the present financial position, including the amount of her husband's present indebtedness, and the amount of his current overdraft facility, will be necessary. The solicitor should then check to see whether the wife wishes to proceed, and ask her if she is content that he write to the lender confirming that he has explained to her the nature of the documents and the practical implications they may have for her, or whether she would prefer him to negotiate with the lender on the terms of the transaction. No confirmation should be given to the lender without the wife's authority. This discussion with the wife should take place at a face-to-face meeting, in the absence of the husband, and be conducted in non-technical language.

Obviously, the solicitor must obtain any information from the lender that he needs, and if, for any reason, the lender fails to provide it, the solicitor should decline to provide the confirmation sought by the lender. However, as a general rule, it is not for the solicitor to veto the transaction by declining to confirm to the lender that he has explained the documents, their consequences and the potential risks to the wife. If he considers the transaction would not be in the wife's best interests, the solicitor should give her reasoned advice to that effect, but the decision whether to proceed or not is the wife's not the solicitor's: a wife must not be prevented from entering into a financially unwise transaction if, for her own reasons, she wishes to do so. (However, if it is glaringly obvious that the wife would be grievously wronged by going ahead, the solicitor should decline to act further.)

As already mentioned, the same solicitor may act for both the wife and the husband, but he must be satisfied that this is in the wife's best interests and that his acting for both will not give rise to any conflict of duty or interest. If at any stage he becomes concerned that there is a real risk that other interests or duties may inhibit his advice to the wife, the solicitor must cease to act for her.

Clearly, *Etridge* is a case which should be read in full!

The Court of Appeal stated in *Pesticcio* v *Huet* [2004] EWCA Civ 372, however, that the participation of a solicitor would not rebut the presumption of undue influence in every case.

Once undue influence affects a wife's decision, it is irrelevant that the transaction would have been entered into anyway – *UCB Corporate Services Ltd* v *Williams* [2002] EWCA Civ 555 (where it was also held that a lender will not escape liability just because it knows that the wife has been advised by a solicitor).

As mentioned earlier, these principles apply to any lender (not just a bank), and to any surety or guarantor (not just a wife), and to any debtor (not just a husband). In effect, both lenders and solicitors have been put on notice that they must no longer treat 'a couple' as a single unit, but as two separate (and potentially conflicting) individual interests. All the appeals in *Etridge* related to wives and husbands, but throughout the judgments it was stated that the principles would apply to any emotional, non-commercial relationships. However, there are other relationships where it is applicable. In *Credit Lyonnais Bank Netherland NV* v *Burch* [1997] 1 All ER 144, the Court of Appeal held that a relationship of trust and confidence between an employer and her employee was capable of giving rise to a presumption of undue influence in the context of a mortgage entered into by an employee as security for the employer's debts. (On the facts, a case could well have been made for setting the transaction aside as an unconscionable bargain. Miss Burch had not only pledged her home as security for an extension on her employer's overdraft, but she was also required to guarantee without limit repayment of all her employer's borrowings from the bank – past, present and future – together with interest, commission, charges, legal and other costs!) Holding that on the facts it was not just necessary for the bank to recommend that independent advice be taken, it was necessary at the very least that the employee have taken advice, the transaction was set aside. Millett LJ stated that it is not 'a universal panacea for a bank to advise that independent advice should be taken', because even if the defendant had taken individual advice, that would not necessarily have meant that the transaction could not be set aside. Legal advice is 'neither always necessary nor always sufficient', and the quality of such advice, where given, would always be examined by the courts. It was not enough that a person in Miss Burch's place understood the nature of the transaction being proposed. The question was not whether she knew what she was doing, but how her consent to the transaction had been procured. It was necessary to show that by receiving independent advice, the defendant had been put in the same position as if she was free from the undue influence. That involved her being advised as to the propriety of the transaction by an adviser fully informed of all the material facts. *Burch* was approved by the House of Lords in *Etridge*.

The Court of Appeal in *Steeples* v *Lea* [1998] 1 FLR 138 (another case where an employee acted as surety for his employer's loan) set out what is necessary for a successful defence based upon undue influence. The defendant must establish:

1 that a relationship of trust and confidence existed as between the defendant and the person inducing the loan such as would enable him to influence the defendant into effecting the mortgage;
2 the mortgage was manifestly and unfairly disadvantageous to the defendant;
3 the defendant's execution of the mortgage was not her spontaneous act in circumstances which enabled her to exercise an independent will; and
4 that the plaintiff had actual or constructive notice of the first three matters.

It was also stated *per curiam* that although the solicitor advising the lender had been under no duty to advise the surety, he had been under a duty to ensure that his own client, the lender, obtained good security for his advance, that is a security which was not liable to be impugned. He ought, therefore, to have advised his client not to proceed with the transaction unless the defendant had taken independent legal advice. The onus, then, is not only on the lender to ensure that the surety takes independent legal advice, but also upon the lender's solicitor. (Knowing this, of course, the lender's solicitor could give such advice to the surety.)

See also *Bristol & West Building Society* v *Mothew* (1997) 75 P&CR 241; *Mortgage Express Ltd* v *Bowerman* [1996] 2 All ER 836; *National Home Loans Corporation plc* v *Giffen Couch & Archer* (1997) *The Times*, 9 October.

In *National Westminster Bank plc* v *Amin* (1999) 77 P&CR D35, the Court of Appeal was asked to consider whether a higher duty is placed upon a lender when dealing with borrowers who do not speak or understand English. Mummery LJ concluded that they did not:

> [W]here a lender is seeking to enforce his rights over the security, the question whether or not the lender has constructive notice of such matters as the exercise of undue influence depends on how the transaction appeared to the lender at the time when it was entered into ... In this case the certificate which was given by the solicitors ... could not have been clearer. It expressly confirmed that the terms and conditions of the legal mortgage had been explained ... Of course, the bank *could* have inquired further into the particular circumstances of Mr and Mrs Amin, their ability to speak, write and understand English ... but .. . the bank was not obliged ... to conduct further inquiries in order to avoid being fixed with constructive notice as of such matters as undue influence by one member of the family over another or other members of the family.

The Court of Appeal held in *Yorkshire Bank plc* v *Tinsley* [2004] 1 WLR 2386 that, where two mortgages are inseparably connected and the first is voidable for undue influence, the second mortgage is also voidable. On the facts, the order of possession granted to the mortgagee was discharged.

However, the House of Lords in *Etridge* recognised (as did the Court of Appeal in *Britannia Building Society* v *Pugh* [1996] ECGS 128) that if third parties were to be fixed with constructive notice of undue influence in relation to every transaction between husband and wife, mortgage transactions would become almost impossible. A distinction has to be made between cases like *O'Brien* where the wife stands surety for the debts of her husband, which will put the lender on inquiry of any rights she may have against her husband to set aside the transaction by virtue of the trust and confidence which a wife often has in her husband in relation to their financial affairs, and cases like *Pitt* where the loan was made to husband and wife jointly and which appeared to the lender to be a normal advance to a husband and wife for their joint benefit.

How can they exist?
Classification: legal or equitable?

The Law of Property Act 1925, s 1(2)(c), provides that 'a charge by way of legal mortgage' is capable of being a legal interest, but mortgages can also exist in equity. The intention of the parties and the way in which the mortgage is created will usually determine whether it is legal or equitable. However, if the mortgagor has granted a mortgage of an equitable interest only, and not of the legal estate, the mortgage itself can only be equitable, regardless of the method of creation. In registered land, every legal mortgage is a registrable interest and every equitable one, a minor interest. However, in the registered land system, interests only become legal upon registration or entry on the register and, therefore, even a legal mortgage, until it is registered, will remain equitable.

How can you acquire them?
Rules, principles and formalities

There are several ways in which a mortgage can be acquired and each defines the nature of the mortgage and governs the relevant mortgagees' remedies.

Legal mortgages

There are two ways in which legal mortgages can be created. As the Law of Property Act, s 85(1), states: 'A mortgage of an estate in fee simple shall only be capable of being effected at law either by a demise for a term of years absolute subject to a provision for cesser on redemption, or by a charge by deed expressed to be by way of legal mortgage'. In registered land, no legal charge will be created until it has been registered – LRA 2002, Sched 2, para 8.

Grant by lease

It is therefore no longer possible to create a mortgage by transferring the fee simple to the mortgagee upon his promise to reconvey it to the mortgagor upon repayment of the loan for which it was granted. Any such attempt will result in the creation of a lease for 3,000 years from the date of the mortgage – s 85(2). However, as it is possible to create a legal mortgage 'by a demise for a term of years absolute', the mortgagee may, by virtue of the mortgage, still acquire a legal estate in the mortgaged land.

If the mortgagor has the fee simple absolute in the property to be mortgaged, he can grant to the mortgagee a term of years absolute of any duration, but if he merely holds a term of years absolute he can only grant the mortgagee a term less than that which he (the mortgagor) actually has.

No matter how long the terms granted, it is usual to provide that the mortgage monies be repaid within one year of the mortgage date, thus creating no clog or fetter on the mortgagor's right of redemption. Once the mortgage monies and any interest thereon have been paid, the mortgage and the lease terminate and the mortgagor once again has the whole of his legal estate. Of course, even though he granted a legal estate to the mortgagee, because it was less than his own legal estate the mortgagor retained the reversion. If he retains sufficient reversion, it is quite possible for the mortgagor to grant a second, and even a third, legal mortgage in this way. Where this is done it is usual to grant to each subsequent mortgagee a term slightly longer than that of his immediate predecessor, if only by one day.

Where the mortgagor only has a term of years absolute in the mortgaged property he does, of course, grant a sublease to the mortgagee for, as the Law of Property Act 1925 states:

> Any purported assignment of a term of years absolute by way of mortgage ... shall operate as a subdemise of the leasehold land to the mortgagee for a term of years absolute but subject to cesser on redemption, in manner following, namely:
>
> (a) the term to be taken by a first or only mortgagee shall be ten days less than the term expressed to be assigned;
>
> (b) the term to be taken by a second or subsequent mortgagee shall be one day longer than the term vested in the first or other mortgagee whose security ranks immediately before that of the second or subsequent mortgagee, if the length of the last mentioned term permits, and in any case for a term less by one day at least than the term expressed to be assigned – s 86(2).

'Cesser on redemption' simply means that the lease will end and the term of years revert to the mortgagor when he pays to the mortgagee all monies borrowed and all interest payable thereon.

Grant by way of charge by deed

This is by far the more common means of granting a legal mortgage and the Law of Property Act 1925 states:

> Where a legal mortgage of land is created by a charge by deed expressed to be by way of legal mortgage, the mortgagee shall have the same protection, powers and remedies (including the right to take proceedings to obtain possession from the occupiers and the persons in receipt of rents and profits, or any of them) if –
>
> (a) where the mortgage is a mortgage of an estate in fee simple, a mortgage term for three thousand years without impeachment of waste had been thereby created in favour of the mortgagee; and

(b) where the mortgage is a mortgage of a term of years absolute, a subterm less by one day than the term vested in the mortgagor had been thereby created in favour of the mortgagee;

it had been created by granting a term of years absolute – s 87.

The Land Registration Act 2002, s 23(1) provides that the owner of a registered estate has the 'power to make a disposition of any kind permitted by the general law in relation to an interest of that description, other than a mortgage by demise or sub-demise . . .', in other words, s 23(1) excludes the powers given by the Law of Property Act 1925, ss 85 and 86. However, the exclusion is prospective only – it will not affect any existing charges granted under ss 85 or 86.

Of course, where a mortgage is granted by way of a charge by deed, no legal estate is vested in the mortgagee, merely a legal interest. This form of creation applies to mortgages of both legal estates, and it is far simpler. An example of a charge by deed can be seen in the Fifth Schedule to the Law of Property Act 1925 (Form No 1).

A legal mortgage which is not protected by a deposit of the title deeds is called a 'puisne' mortgage.

We have been looking, so far, at mortgages granted expressly by all holders of the legal estate. What, though, where one only of two joint tenants purports to grant a mortgage? Is that an equitable mortgage of the severed beneficial interest?

First National Securities Ltd v *Hegerty* [1984] 3 WLR 769

A matrimonial home was held jointly by the husband and wife. H forged W's signature on the mortgage deed which purported to charge the jointly owned legal estate in favour of the lender. H then took the money and went abroad. It goes without saying that he then defaulted on the repayments. The mortgagees applied for a charging order on H's beneficial share. Bingham J held that the fraudulent legal charge, though not sufficient to affect W's equitable share, was effective against H's, thus giving the lender a valid equitable charge over H's equitable interest. The Court of Appeal agreed. (By virtue of the equitable charge, the mortgagee had an interest in the land under which it could make application for an order for sale under the Law of Property Act 1925, s 30 (now s 14 of the Trusts of Land and Appointment of Trustees Act 1996). If sale were ordered, the mortgagee would recover the loan monies only from H's half share in the proceeds. Stephenson LJ stated that any hardship caused to W and her children was not a circumstance which would justify the court in refusing to grant the charging order.)

Equitable mortgages

There are several ways in which an equitable mortgage can be created.

An agreement for a mortgage

Needless to say, when a legal mortgage is created under s 86 or s 87, the deed must comply with all necessary formal requirements. If for any reason the deed does not so comply, the mortgage may still succeed as an equitable mortgage under the rule in *Walsh* v *Lonsdale*, giving effect once again to the maxim 'equity deems to be done that which ought to be done'.

Just as with equitable leases, the contract for the mortgage must be one of which the court would grant an order for specific performance, and this in turn depends, as we have seen, upon its date. However, even if the contract is valid, there will be no order for specific performance of a contract where the mortgage monies have not been advanced, for equity will not force a man to make a loan.

Mortgage of an equitable interest

Again, it goes without saying that if the interest to be mortgaged is itself only equitable, then any mortgage of it cannot be legal. Therefore, if the interest is for less than the equivalent of a fee simple absolute in possession or term of years absolute, a mortgage of it will only be equitable. Thus, if the tenant for life under a strict settlement wishes to mortgage his own beneficial life interest (as opposed to the legal estate), or if a beneficiary who is not a trustee of the legal estate under a trust of land wishes to mortgage his equitable interest, only an equitable mortgage can be created. Any 'disposition of an equitable interest or trust ... must be in writing signed by the person disposing of the same, or by his agent ... or by will' – Law of Property Act 1925, s 53(1)(c). Thus, no deed is required, but the mortgage must be in writing.

Equitable charge

It may be that, unlike the situation where an agreement for a mortgage is created, all the mortgagor intended to create was an equitable charge, and he can achieve this by showing an intention to charge specific property with the repayment of a debt or some other obligation. This form of mortgage is very rare, but in *Matthews* v *Goodday* (1861) 31 LJ Ch 282, Kindersley VC held that writing by which R charged his property to E in the sum of £500 amounted to 'a security by which he equitably charged his land with the payment of a sum of money'.

Informal deposit of title deeds

It was held in *Russel* v *Russel* (1783) 1 Bro CC 269 that where a deposit of the title deeds is made with the intention that they be held as security for a loan, an equitable mortgage will arise. There is no need for a written memorandum (though some written record would usually accompany the deposit), because the deposit itself provides sufficient act of part performance – but therein lies the problem, for there is no role for part performance where the Law of Property (Miscellaneous Provisions) Act 1989, s 2 applies. Indeed, it was held by the Court of Appeal in *United Bank of Kuwait plc* v *Sahib & Ors* [1996] 3 All ER 215 that:

> [t]he rule that a deposit of title deeds for the purpose of securing a debt operated without more as an equitable mortgage had not survived the enactment of section 2 ...

(See, however, Neill LJ in *Singh* v *Beggs* (1996) 71 P&CR 120.)

Chadwick J went on to say that, in any event, the Law of Property Act 1925, s 53(1)(c) would have rendered void the disposition of any equitable interest thus created, as it was not in writing signed by the person disposing of the interest or by his lawfully authorised agent. Although a resulting or constructive trust would be saved in this regard by s 53(2), neither could arise on the facts.

If the deposit is accompanied by a written contract, then no doubt the rule in *Walsh* v *Lonsdale* would be applied, and if the deposit were accompanied by a deed which recorded the transaction, the same would apply. Of course, if the deed stated that the mortgage was to be 'by way of legal mortgage' it would comply with the requirements of the Law of Property Act 1925, s 85(1), and be legal.

However, the mortgagor must be entitled to so deposit the land or charge certificate.

Thames Guaranty Ltd v *Campbell* [1984] 2 All ER 585

A husband and wife were joint tenants of their matrimonial home. H agreed an overdraft facility with the plaintiffs, and this was secured on the matrimonial home. A month later, H, without the consent or knowledge of W, deposited the land certificate with the mortgagees who registered a notice of the deposit. The overdraft facility was renewed and increased and continued to be secured by the charge over the house. Had this deposit of the land certificate effected an equitable charge? The Court of Appeal held that it had not for, 'Even if Mr Campbell had had a beneficial interest in the property, he would not have been entitled to part with the land certificate without the consent of Mrs Campbell as joint owner of the legal estate'.

Estoppel

It is possible to 'create' a mortgage by estoppel.

First National Bank plc v *Thompson* [1996] 1 All ER 140

Mr Thompson and a Mrs McMahon had, by a legal charge dated 10 July 1991, purported to charge a property by way of legal mortgage to the bank. There was just one problem: at that date neither of them was, or was entitled to be, registered as proprietor of the property. Mr T had agreed in principle with the registered proprietor to buy his interest in the property, but the legal estate had not passed. In September 1991, the registered proprietor did execute a transfer of the property to Mr T and he was registered as proprietor in December 1991. In July 1992, the bank applied to have the legal charge registered but Mr T objected. At first instance the judge held that the bank could not have the charge of July 1991 registered and that it would have to submit a fresh legal charge for registration. The bank objected: in having to cancel the original charge and submit a fresh one, it would lose its priority as at 10 July 1991. The bank claimed that it had, in fact, a mortgage by estoppel in that although Mr T could not create a legal charge on 10 July 1991, he was estopped from denying the grant of one to the bank on that date. When Mr T subsequently acquired the legal estate in September 1991, this 'fed the estoppel', and the bank was then entitled to register the original charge. The Court of Appeal held that the bank was entitled to register the original charge. It was also declared that the doctrine of 'feeding the estoppel' applied in unregistered, as well as in registered, land.

In registered land

In the registered land system, interests only become legal upon registration at the land registry. Therefore, in the period following execution and completion of the transfer, but before its registration, a mortgage can only be equitable. See *Mortgage Corporation Ltd* v *Nationwide Credit Corporation Ltd* [1993] 4 All ER 623.

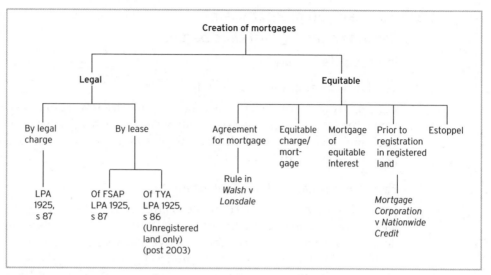

Figure 11.3

When and for how long?

Duration of mortgages

A mortgagor remains bound by his obligations until he redeems the mortgage. However, his right to redeem must not be fettered in any way by the mortgagee. As we have seen, it was held in *Barclays Bank plc* v *Zaroovabli* [1997] 2 WLR 729 that where a protected contractual tenancy existed at the date the mortgage was granted, it was binding on the mortgagee, and any statutory tenancy which came into existence on the termination of the contractual one was also binding on the lender.

Further, in *Woolwich Building Society* v *Dickman* [1996] 3 All ER 204 the Court of Appeal held that although an express agreement by an occupier to postpone his right of occupancy in favour of the mortgagee would normally bind the occupant, where a protected tenancy was in existence at the date of the grant of mortgage, the written consent would be ineffective. However, if the tenancy was not granted until after the mortgage, the rights of the mortgagee would override those of a protected and statutory tenancy – *Britannia Building Society* v *Earl* [1990] 1 WLR 422(CA).

Similarly, if, at the time of moving into the property, a tenant knew that the property was to be purchased with the aid of a mortgage, his interest would be subject to those of the mortgagee (see, eg, *Paddington Building Society* v *Mendelsohn* (1985) 50 P&CR 244).

A mortgagee is entitled to repayment of the capital monies and interest thereon during the continuance of the mortgage, it being redeemed upon the mortgagor paying off all sums due. However, as we know, a mortgagee can cause a mortgage to determine earlier upon exercising one or more of his rights – though this does not usually happen unless the mortgagor is in arrears with his repayments or in breach of some other covenant under the mortgage agreement. A mortgagee is statute barred from recovering principal monies or any interest under a mortgage after 12 years from the date when the right to receive such money arises.

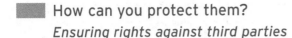 ## How can you protect them?

Ensuring rights against third parties

In unregistered land

Legal mortgages of the legal estate

Legal mortgages protected by the deposit of title deeds will bind the world. However, where the legal mortgage is not accompanied by such a deposit, it is a puisne mortgage and must be protected by registration as a Class C(i) land charge under the Land Charges Act 1972 (LCA 1972).

Equitable mortgages of the legal estate

Equitable mortgages protected by the deposit of title deeds cannot be registered as a land charge – Land Charges Act 1972, s 2(4)(iii)(a) – and are, therefore, subject to the doctrine of notice. Of course, the very fact that someone other than the vendor or mortgagor holds the deeds will give notice.

An equitable mortgage arising under the rule in *Walsh* v *Lonsdale* is an estate contract and must be registered as a Class C(iv) land charge, being void for non-registration only against a purchaser for value.

Equitable mortgages of equitable interests

An equitable mortgage of an equitable interest is not registrable as a land charge – Land Charges Act 1972, s 2(4)(iii)(b) – being subject to the rule in *Dearle* v *Hall* (1823) 3 Russ 1, under which the relevant date is that upon which the trustees of the **legal estate** were notified of the mortgage.

A mortgage which arises 'by way of indemnity against rents equitably apportioned or charged exclusively on land in exoneration of other land and against the breach or non-observance of covenants or conditions' – Land Charges Act 1972, s 2(4)(iii)(c) – is not only unregistrable as a land charge, but also very rare! When and if they ever do arise, they are subject to the doctrine of notice.

All other equitable mortgages are general equitable charges and registrable as Class C(iii) land charges.

In registered land

As mortgages do not have titles of their own, all legal charges must be entered on the existing registered title of the secured land – LRA 2002, s 59(2), with the chargee or his successor in title being entered as the proprietor of the charge. Until registration the mortgage takes effect in equity only (see *Mortgage Corporation Ltd* v *Nationwide Credit Corporation Ltd* [1993] 4 All ER 623).

An equitable mortgage of an equitable interest is, as in unregistered land, subject to the rule in *Dearle* v *Hall* – Land Registration Act 1986, s 5(1), and would appear to remain so under LRA 2002.

Where the mortgagee is in actual occupation of the secured property, the mortgage *may* be an overriding interest under Sched 3, para 2.

All other equitable mortgages are minor interests.

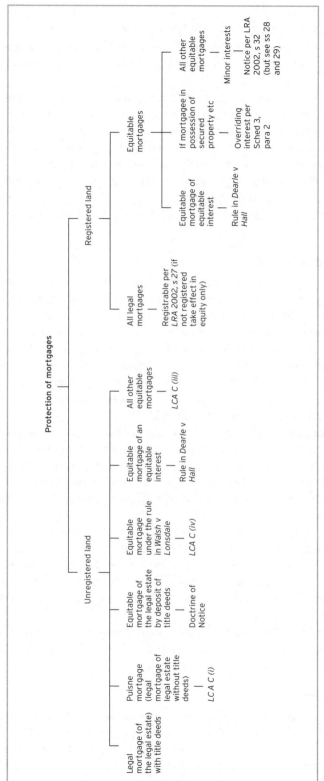

Figure 11.4

Priority

As Elizabeth Cooke (2003) says, 'the priority of mortgages between themselves is immensely important (especially if the market falls and there is not enough money to pay all the mortgagees ... mortgagees are among the most important purchaser' – p 91.

Where more than one mortgage has been granted on the same piece of land, the question of priorities arises. Which mortgagee will be paid out first if the mortgagor defaults? No matter which mortgagee exercises which right, for instance, to sell, in order to retrieve the money lent, the several mortgagees must be paid out in order. The rules of priorities govern this order. Therefore, a mortgagee who is quite low in the priority order may not be paid out in full, or at all – even if it was he who took the necessary steps to gain the property.

The subject of priorities can be very complicated and we shall deal with it only simply.

In unregistered land

Legal mortgages protected by deposit of title deeds have priority over all others from the date of deposit. If there is more than one (say each mortgagee has some of the deeds), the order will be determined by reference to the dates of creation. If the legal mortgage is a puisne mortgage it must be registered as a Class C(i) land charge.

Class C(i) and C(iii) land charges rank as against each other by date of registration, not date of creation. A Class C(i) land charge has no priority over a Class C(iii) land charge, other than by virtue of having been registered earlier. However, any unregistered registrable mortgage is void as against a purchaser – including a mortgagee – of the land charged with it – LCA 1972, s 4(5).

Equitable mortgages, other than C(iii) land charges, rank in accordance with the rules which govern them. Thus, an equitable mortgage created by the deposit of title deeds is protected by the doctrine of notice, so that any subsequent mortgagee with notice of it takes subject to that mortgage. As the subsequent mortgagee will need to see the deeds, he will be fixed with notice by the fact that he had to obtain the deeds from someone other than the mortgagor.

However, an equitable mortgagee of an equitable interest will not get the title deeds, but this situation is covered by the rule in *Dearle* v *Hall* under which the relevant date is that upon which all of the trustees of the legal estate were notified of the mortgage (unless the later mortgagee had notice of the earlier mortgage).

As between themselves, all other equitable mortgages are governed by the 'first in time (ie creation) prevails'.

Having identified the relevant dates, you simply place them in chronological order, and this is the order in which the mortgagees will be paid out from the proceeds of sale of the secured property.

In registered land

Other than equitable mortgages of equitable interests, which are governed by the rule in *Dearle* v *Hall* as above, all mortgages should have been registered, or entered on the register by way of a notice. A mortgage will, as we know, only be legal if it has been registered – LRA 2002, s 27(1) – and thus a registered disposition. As between legal mortgages (registered charges) themselves, the effect of ss 29 and 30 (s 29 relates to mortgages granted on the legal estate; s 30 relates to dealings on the mortgage itself, eg sale-on of the debt) is that they rank in order of registration – taking subject to any other interest recorded on the register and any overriding interest (in the case of Sched 3, para 2, any which has not been overreached). See also s 48.

However, if a later disposition is not for value, it takes subject to all earlier interests – whether or not they were registered or entered by notice.

If the later disposition is for value, then, where a later mortgage is equitable, and is therefore a minor interest, it too will be bound by any earlier registered charge, interest protected by notice and overriding interest. If the earlier interest is none of these, it will lose its priority and fall under the general rule of 'the first in time (ie of creation) prevails' under s 28.

Section 28 provides that –

(1) Except as provided by sections 29 and 30 the priority of an interest affecting a registered estate or charge is not affected by the disposition of the estate or charge.
(2) It makes no difference for the purposes of this section whether the interest or disposition is registered.

As between competing equitable mortgages, therefore, s 28 operates and the order is governed by the dates of creation: neither s 29 nor s 30, will affect this. Thus notices will warn against subsequent entries but will not protect against earlier interests.

In registered land, where does a mortgage (which must in such circumstances be equitable) stand if the mortgagee has failed to register or enter his interest? It depends upon whether the later mortgage is legal or equitable. If it is legal (and must, therefore, by definition, have been registered), the later mortgage will take priority. If it is equitable, even if it has been entered as a minor interest, the later mortgage will still be subject to the general rule: 'the first in time prevails' – s 28.

Mortgage Corporation Ltd v *Nationwide Credit Ltd* [1993] 4 All ER 623

On 10 July 1989, the plaintiffs, M, advanced £367,500 to L who executed a legal charge in their favour. On 31 July, L executed a further legal charge, this one in favour of the defendants, NCC, to secure an advance of £60,000. On 14 August, NCC entered a notice on the land register. M did nothing to protect its charge. It being registered land, both mortgages should have been substantively registered in order for them to be legal. As it was, both were equitable only. Subsequently L defaulted on both mortgages and M obtained a possession order and sold the property for £300,000. In order for this sale to go ahead, NCC had withdrawn its notice. M and NCC had agreed to allow the court to decide the issue of priority. Clearly, this was a case of negative equity. If M took priority they would take the whole £300,000, NCC nothing. If NCC took priority it would get its £60,000, M £240,000. The Court of Appeal held that M's charge took priority. Though NCC had entered a notice, its charge took effect only in equity and so M's charge, being the first in time, prevailed. NCC got nothing.

This case clearly illustrates two cardinal principles of the registered land system: first, that only registered registrable interests will be legal; second, that any entry of an equitable mortgage only affects subsequent purchasers, it does not affect priority in relation to earlier charges. In this regard, Dillon LJ stated that 'notice is indeed notice, but it does not give priority which would not, apart from the 1925 Act, have been there. Therefore, the plaintiff's charge has priority to the defendant's charge'.

LRA 2002, s 28 confirms this and *Mortgage Corporation* would be decided the same way under LRA 2002. Once e-conveyancing comes on line, the problem caused by this rule for parties in the position of National Credit should, to a large extent, be improved: due to compulsory electronic entries, most interests will not exist until they are entered on the register (but not all interests will be governed by the electronic entry rules).

The danger for mortgagees of not registering their mortgage promptly was highlighted in *Barclays Bank plc* v *Zaroovabli* [1997] 2 WLR 729.

However, as Elizabeth Cooke says (2003, at p 92), 'interests that are not recorded, and are therefore overridden by registered dispositions, nevertheless remain valid between the parties themselves, and remain proprietary rights which may take priority to other interests under the general rule [ie s 28]'.

It is important also to remember that mere equities and rights by way of proprietary estoppel now rank in order of creation, being minor interests – s 116.

Example

Say A makes a loan by way of legal mortgage on a piece of land on 1 April, and B makes a further loan on that same land, again by way of legal mortgage, on 1 June, and later, the property has to be repossessed and sold, but the sale fails to realise enough to pay off both debts, which will be paid first, A or B?

If both mortgages were registered in the order in which they were created, A would be paid first, B second; but, if A had not registered his mortgage until after B's was granted and registered, B would be paid first – first by registration. If neither had registered their mortgage, then both mortgages would take effect in equity only, as minor interests, and A would be paid first under s 28 – even if B had entered a notice. Thus, A would be paid first whether or not any notice was entered either by himself or B.

An interesting question would be, what if a legal mortgage had been granted to and registered by C on the same property on 1 August? B's notice would protect him against C – s 29, and so the order would be B–C–A, A's interest not prevailing over C's registered charge.

As Gray and Gray say (2005, p 191, para 12-67), s 28 is 'somewhat inelegantly expressed', and

> an important key to understanding the 'basic rule' of priority under the Land Registration Act 2002 is the realisation that its ulterior purpose is the governance of registered land interests *after* the introduction of the forthcoming regime of electronic conveyancing. It is at this point that the 'basic rule' will actually come into its own.

Tacking

A mortgagee may be able to modify his position under the rules as to priority by 'tacking', but only where he holds more than one mortgage from the same mort-

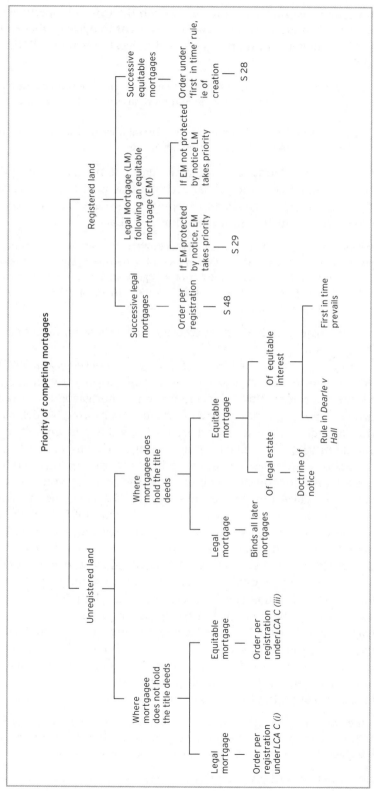

Figure 11.5

gagor on the same property. However, though the Law of Property Act 1925, s 94(1) provides that 'a prior mortgagee shall have a right to make further advances to rank in priority to subsequent mortgages (whether legal or equitable)', that right is only exercisable:

(a) if an arrangement has been made to that effect with the subsequent mortgagees; or
(b) if he had no notice of such subsequent mortgages at the time when the further advance was made by him; or
(c) whether or not he had such notice as aforesaid, where the mortgage imposes an obligation on him to make such further advances.

Under rule (c), the mortgagee would therefore be bound by any prior mortgages which were registered either as land charges or at the Land Registry. However, s 94(2) (as amended) provides an exception (eg where the mortgage is granted in order to secure a loan account or overdraft), so that:

> In relation to the making of further advances after the commencement of this Act a mortgagee shall not be deemed to have notice of a mortgage merely by reason that it was registered as a land charge . . . if it was not so registered at the [time when the original mortgage was created] or when the last search (if any) by or on behalf of the mortgagee was made, whichever last happened.

Thus, a bank which holds deeds as security for an overdraft need not search the register before granting the facility.

The Privy Council held, in *Cheah* v *Equitcorp Finance Group Ltd* [1991] 4 All ER 989, that where there are two mortgages on the same property, the mortgagees can agree to alter their priority without the consent of the mortgagor. It was stated *per curiam* that where a mortgagor has a genuine interest in ensuring his debts are satisfied in a particular order – for example where there are different interest rates – he could and should insist on a specific provision within the contract which would preclude the alteration of priorities. The reason behind the decision was that in the majority of cases a mortgagor will not be affected by the order in which his debts are satisfied, and a mortgagee can choose which of his various remedies he wishes to pursue.

The case of *Equity & Law Home Loans Ltd* v *Prestidge* [1992] 1 All ER 909, concerned the question of priorities as between the mortgagee and the holder of an equitable interest in the secured property. It has been clear since *Paddington Building Society* v *Mendelsohn* (1985) 50 P&CR 244 that if a person knows and approves of the fact that property in which he holds a beneficial interest is to be mortgaged, an intention will be inferred that the mortgagee's interest should take priority over the beneficial interest. However, the consequence of *Prestidge* would seem to be that consent to a mortgage to X will extend to a replacement mortgage to Y 'provided that [the new mortgage to Y] did not change the [beneficial interest holder's] position for the worse'. The Court of Appeal took the same view as the Privy Council in *Cheah*, that is that one mortgage is very much like another.

In registered land, the Land Registration Act 2002, s 49 provides:

(1) the proprietor of a registered charge may make a further advance on the security of the charge ranking in priority to a subsequent charge if he has not received from the subsequent chargee notice of the creation of the subsequent charge.

The notice here will be given by the chargee, not by the Land Registry. Section 49(2) provides that notices given under (1) 'shall be treated as received at the time when, in accordance with rules, it ought to have been received'.

Section 49(3) provides that

> the proprietor of a registered charge may also make a further advance on the security of the charge ranking in priority to a subsequent charge if –
>
> (a) the advance is made in pursuance of an obligation, and
> (b) at the time of the creation of the subsequent charge the obligation was entered in the register in accordance with rules.

In addition, such a proprietor may also make a further advance on such security if:

> (a) the parties to the prior charge have agreed a maximum amount for which the charge is security, and
> (b) at the time of the creation of the subsequent charge the agreement was entered in the register in accordance with the rules – s 49(4).

Finally, subsection (6) provides that 'tacking in relation to a charge over registered land is only possible with the agreement of the subsequent chargee'.

Of course, certain interests will not appear on the register – overriding interests, and yet such interests may bind the mortgagee – remember Mrs Boland? Following *Williams & Glyn's Bank Ltd* v *Boland* [1981] AC 487, deeds or notices of postponement came into practice. The purpose of these is to postpone any rights which occupiers, other than mortgagors, of the secured property may have and thus defeat claims under LRA 2002, Sched 3, para 2. The non-mortgagors sign the consent, a typical example of which would be:

> I, ..., understand that the [mortgagee] proposes to lend money on the security of [the secured property] AND I agree with the [mortgagee] that any right of occupation which I have or may have is postponed to the rights of the [mortgagee].

Woolwich Building Society v *Dickman* [1996] 3 All ER 204

Mr Dickman had bought a leasehold flat and then granted a tenancy of it to Mr and Mrs Todd, his parents-in-law. Their tenancy was protected under the Rent Acts. Subsequently, Mr D granted a mortgage on the property to the bank. Later he fell into arrears and the bank sought possession. The Todds had signed a consent – which warned them that 'This document is important. If you are uncertain of its effect, please take legal advice before signing it' – in favour of the bank. Was it enough to give the bank priority and defeat the Todds' statutory tenancy? The Court of Appeal held that where an occupier's written consent to postpone his rights of occupancy had been 'carefully drawn and clearly relied upon by the society as an essential pre-condition of the mortgage', it could not be read as anything other than an express agreement that the tenancy rights of occupation were to be subjected to the possessory rights of the society.

However, where, as in *Dickman*, a protected tenancy was in existence at the date of the grant of the mortgage, a written consent was not effective to subordinate the rights of the tenants to the rights of the mortgagee. The tenancy was, in fact, an overriding interest notwithstanding their consent. Waite LJ explained:

However effective the consents may otherwise have been to override the rights of the Todds as persons in actual occupation of the flat, they could have no effect upon the mandatory rights they enjoyed under s 70(1)(g) unless a provision to that effect was 'expressed on the register'. No such provision is there expressed.

Morritt LJ agreed, as:

Nothing to 'the contrary [was] expressed on the register in relation to the letters of consent ... it must follow that whatever the result of the letters as between the building society and the Todds as persons, they had no effect on the property or charges register in the land registry so as to preclude the Todds' tenancy being an overriding interest. Accordingly, the property was subject to that overriding interest at the time of the charge and was an interest subject to which the charge was granted and took effect ... It follows that the relationship of landlord and tenant between the building society and the Todds, which would clearly have arisen in the absence of those letters, came into existence [at the time of the charge] in spite of them.

Barclays Bank plc v *Zaroovabli* [1997] 2 WLR 729

Here the bank sought possession against the Zs and their tenant, Mrs Pourdanay. The mortgage predated Mrs P's tenancy, which was a statutory tenancy under the Rent Acts. However, the bank's charge was not registered until some five years after the Zs had been registered as proprietors and charged the property to the bank. For an overriding interest under s 70(1)(g) (now replaced and amended by LRA 2002, Sched 3, para 2) Mrs P's tenancy had to have existed prior to the mortgage - *Abbey National Building Society* v *Cann* [1990] 1 WLR 832 - which it did not. However, was she protected by s 70(1)(k) (now replaced and amended by LRA 2002, Sched 3, para 1), having a lease of less than three years? Following *Dickman*, recovery of possession by a mortgagee in all cases where the relevant tenancy predates the mortgagee's mortgage is prohibited. However, in *Zaroovabli*, the question was whether Mrs P's tenancy, which predated the registration of the bank's charge, but not the grant of it, was binding on the bank? [In *Dickman*, the Todds' tenancy had predated both the grant and registration.] Sir Richard Scott VC held that Mrs P's tenancy was an overriding interest under s 70(1)(k) and that it took priority over the mortgagee's unregistered charge. Further, it was not overreached when the charge was eventually registered. Therefore, the bank was bound by Mrs P's statutory tenancy.

The Vice-Chancellor also confirmed that the date generally applicable under s 70(1) was that of registration, which applied to all overriding interests, not merely to subsection (g) – presumably, this will continue to be the case under LRA 2002.

So, another potential problem for mortgagees, but 'Mortgagees deserve no sympathy at all when their own slackness is the cause of their loss. The moral for mortgagees is obvious, the solution is very simple. Do not delay registering your charge' (Barnsley, 1997). Indeed, mortgagees need to ensure that their charges are registered, and not merely entered by notice: *Mortgage Corporation Ltd* v *Nationwide Credit Corporation Ltd*.

It is probably fair to say, however, that in regard to postponement notices, until *Dickman* most, if not all, mortgagees were unaware of the need to enter a notice. One case which offered a crumb of comfort to mortgagees, albeit a small one, was *Hypo-Mortgage Services Ltd* v *Robinson* [1997] 2 FLR 71, where the Court of Appeal held that minor children of legal estate holders are generally not capable of being 'in occupation' for the purpose of s 70(1)(g): they must have an interest of their own in the property – this will be the same under LRA 2002.

Reform

In its report and draft bill *Transfer of Land: Land Mortgages* (Law Com No 204 (1991)), the Law Commission addresses several areas of law of mortgages – creation, protection, mortgagor's rights and mortgagee's rights. The report calls mortgages by an individual owner/occupier of residential property a 'protected mortgage' and in regard to these the Law Commission proposes that the court should have entirely new powers in regard to interest rates. Penalty clauses, that is where the interest rate increases where the mortgagor is in default, would be void (are they not already at common law?). In addition, the court would have powers to alter the interest rate payable on a protected mortgage in certain circumstances where the mortgagee is deemed to be guilty of unreasonableness, especially where the mortgage is subject to a variable interest rate (that is the vast majority of the approximately 8 million mortgages): it would be for the mortgagor to prove unreasonableness. Given the number of building societies which have become profit-making concerns, this reform would be welcome: there are few mortgages which continue to fall under the Building Societies Act provisions.

Under a proposal relating to all mortgages, the court would be given new jurisdiction to vary or set aside the terms of a mortgage.

In regard to the creation of mortgages, the Commission proposes all the current methods of creating mortgages – whether legal charge or equitable mortgage – be abolished (with the exception of the charging order and the floating charge), to be replaced by a 'formal land mortgage' and an 'informal land mortgage', both to be governed entirely by statute (which would, however, have to be interpreted by the courts!). The formal land mortgage must be created by deed but could be granted over any legal or equitable interest in land, as could the informal land mortgage, which could be created either by deed or by valid contract. The equitable mortgage by deposit of title deeds would be abolished (a recommendation pre-empted somewhat by the decision in *United Bank of Kuwait plc* v *Sahib & Others*).

The formal land mortgage would be protected in registered land in the same way as a legal charge is now, but in unregistered land all formal land mortgages would have to be registered as C(i) land charges, whether or not accompanied by deposit of title deeds. The informal land mortgage would, in registered land, be entered as a minor interest by way of notice or caution. In unregistered land, they would be registrable as C(iii) land charges. However, to these rules there would be an exception – land mortgages, formal or informal, granted on beneficial interests under a trust of land would be unregistrable, as now, thus remaining subject to the rule in *Dearle* v *Hall*.

Proposals in regard to mortgagees' rights reflect the Commission's desire to introduce a far greater degree of consumer protection in the field of mortgages. Of course, in attempting to curb excessive powers of mortgagees, regard must always be given to the reality that there would be no lending to enable people to buy their homes if the mortgagees could not be guaranteed a fair and secure return on their money.

It is proposed that the mortgagee's right to possession 'before the ink is dry on the mortgage deed', with or without default, be abolished, to be replaced by the need for a court order in the case of a protected mortgage, and a limitation in regard to all other property that the right to possession would only arise and continue for as long as necessary to protect the mortgagee's security, that is the value of the secured premises.

Before the power of sale could be exercised in regard to a protected mortgage, the Lord Chancellor suggests that the mortgagee would first have to serve an enforcement notice in prescribed form on the mortgagor, specifying the default and the action required to remedy it, explaining the consequences of default and how and where to obtain advice and assistance. A more radical proposal and a potentially controversial one, is that, in the case of a protected mortgage, the mortgagee must obtain the leave of the court to exercise any power of sale, the court having the power to refuse to order sale where there is no subsisting default or threat to the mortgagee's security. In addition, the court would have the power to reschedule mortgage repayments in terms of amount and/or time.

In regard to the appointment of receivers, the Commission proposes that only those who meet qualification standards to be laid down should be appointed as receivers, and even then only in similar circumstances to those where enforcement would be allowed generally. However, a right for a mortgagee to appoint a receiver would be automatically implied into mortgages unless expressly excluded.

Foreclosure, that most draconian of measures, would be abolished, to be replaced by a power under which a mortgagee could, with leave of the court, sell to itself. Such leave would only be granted where the court was satisfied that sale to the mortgagee would be the best way of realising the security.

Finally, we saw earlier that mortgagees can agree between themselves to transfer mortgages, or vary the priority of them. The Law Commission proposes that a mortgagee should only be able to transfer a protected mortgage with the mortgagor's written consent. (It should be noted, however, that the report will not be implemented in its present form – (1998) 587 HL Deb WA 213.)

Summary

In this chapter we have considered the following;

■ The nature and characteristics of mortgages.

■ The mortgagor's rights –

- No oppressive or unconscionable terms

- No clogs or fetters on the right to redeem

- No postponement of the right to redeem

- No collateral advantages to the mortgagee.

■ The mortgagee's rights –

- Right to sue on the mortgagor's covenant to repay

- The power of sale

- The right to possession
  - AJA 1970, s 36 (as amended)
  - Undue influence
- Appointment of a receiver
- Foreclosure.

■ Classifying mortgages as legal or equitable.

■ Rules, principles and formalities of acquisition.

■ Duration of mortgages.

■ How to protect rights under mortgages against third parties –
  - In unregistered land
  - In registered land
  - Tacking.

■ Reform.

References

Barnsley, D G, 'Mortgagees and the Dangers of Delayed Registration' [1997] CLJ 497.

Bergin, T E and Davies, A, 'Mortgagors and negative equity: application of the *Palk* doctrine', Sol Jo, 27 June 1997, p 618.

Burn, E.H., *Cheshire and Burn's Modern Law of Real Property*, 16th edition, London: Butterworths, 2000.

Burn, E H, *Maudsley & Burn's Land Law Cases and Materials*, 6th edition, London: Butterworths, 8th Edn, OUP, 2004.

Cooke, E, *The New Law of Land Registration*, Oxford: Hart Publishing, 2003.

Gray, K, *Elements of Land Law*, 2nd edition, London: Butterworths, 1993.

Gray, K and Gray, S F, *Elements of Land Law*, 4th edition, Oxford: Oxford University Press, 2005.

Gray, K.J. and Symes, P.D., *Real Property and Real People*, London: Butterworths, 1981.

Haley, M, 'Mortgage Default: Possession, relief and judicial discretion' (1997) 17(3) *Legal Studies* 481, vol 17(3), p 483.

James, R and Seneviratne, M, 'The Building Societies' Ombudsman Scheme' (1992) 11(2) *Civil Justice Quarterly* 157.

Law Commission, *Land Mortgages* (Working Paper No 99, 1986).

Law Commission, *Transfer of Land: Land Mortgages* (Law Com No 204, 1991).

Law Commission, *Land Registration for the Twenty-First Century* (Law Com No 254, 1998).

Law Society Gazette, No 22, 12 June 1991.

Lim, H and Green, K, *Land Law Cases and Materials*, 2nd edition, London: Pitman Publishing, 1995.

Miller, S and Klein, J, 'Mortgagees and the remedy of subrogation', Sol Jo, 5 April 1996, p 326.

Newman, R and Halperkin, C, 'Fair Enough?' Sol Jo, 30 June 1995, p 632.

Thompson, M P, 'When Mortgaged Property Should be Sold' [1998] Conv 125.

Wilkinson, H W, 'Mortgage repayments – in your own time?' NLJ, 23 February 1996, p 252.

Wurtzburg, E.A. and Mills J., *Building Society Law*, 14th edition, London: Blackstone, 1976.

Further reading

Generally

Palk v *Mortgage Services Funding* [1993] 2 WLR 415.

Mortgagors' rights

Jones v *Morgan* [2001] EWCA Civ 995, judgment of Chadwick LJ.

Knightsbridge Estates Trust Ltd v *Byrne* [1939] Ch 441, judgment of Sir Wilfred Green MR.

Multiservice Bookbinding Ltd v *Marden* [1979] Ch 84, judgment of Browne-Wilkinson LJ.

Mortgagees' rights
Power of sale

Dixon, M, 'Mortgage Duties and Commercial Property Transactions [2006] Conv 278.

Right to possession

Dixon, M, 'Combating the mortgagee's right to possession: new hope for the mortgagor in chains?', (1998) 18 *Legal Studies 279*.

Haley, M, 'Mortgage default: Possession, relief and judicial discretion' (1997), 77(3) *Legal Studies* 483.

Undue influence

Royal Bank of Scotland v *Etridge* [2001] 4 All ER 449.

Capper, D, 'Undue Influence and Unconscionability: A Rationalisation', [1998] 114 LQR 479.

Dixon, M, 'The Special Tenderness of Equity: Undue Influence and the Family Home' [1994] CLJ 21.

Dixon, M and Harpum, C, 'Fraud, Undue Influence and Mortgages of Registered Land' [1994] Conv 421.

Douzinas, C and Warrington, R, 'Building Societies and the Unsuspected Hazard' [1991] 54 MLR 142.

Draper, M J, 'Undue Influence: A Review' [1999] Conv 176.

Fehlberg, B, 'The Husband, the Bank, the Wife and her Signature' [1994] 57 MLR 467.

Fehlberg, B, 'The Husband, the Bank, the Wife and her Signature - the sequel' [1996] 59 MLR 675.

Rickett, C E F, 'The Financier's Duty of Care to a Surety' [1998] 114 LQR 17.

Sparkes, P, 'The proprietory effect of undue influence' [1995] Conv 250.

Thompson, M P, 'Mortgagees and Wives: Proceed with Caution' [1994] Conv 443.

Thompson, M P, 'Is Mortgage Fraud a Crime?' (Casenote on *R* v *Preddy* [1996] 3 All ER 481), [1996] Conv 441.

Tjio, H, 'O'Brien and Unconscionability' [1997] 113 LQR 10.

Wong, S, 'No Man Can Serve Two Masters: Independent Legal Advice and Solicitors' Duty of Confidentiality' [1998] Conv 457.

Protection

De Laay, J, 'The Priority Rule of *Dearle* v *Hall* Restated' [1999] Conv 311.

Omar, P, 'Equitable Interests and the Secured Creditor: Determining priorities' [2006] Conv 509.

12 Easements

What's the problem?

Easements in context

If you have seen the film *Oliver*, you will remember the scene where the young boy, having been rescued from the streets, is leaning out of the upper floor window overlooking a Victorian 'lock up' park across the road. In London especially such parks or gardens are quite common. Although the road in the film was crescent shaped and the park circular, the more usual layout is square or rectangular with large Victorian terraces on each side.

The leading case of *Re Ellenborough Park* [1956] Ch 131 concerned such a park in Weston-super-Mare. Here the park faced the seafront on one side with houses facing the park on the other three, a road separating the houses from the park. In the conveyance of the fee simple in each house the purchaser was granted certain easements for the use of roads, footpaths and drains 'and also the full enjoyment . . . at all times hereafter in common with all persons to whom such easements may be granted in the pleasure ground set out and made in front of the said plot of land . . . in the centre of the square called Ellenborough Park'. The vendors covenanted (promised) on behalf of themselves and their heirs, executors and assigns to keep the park as an ornamental pleasure ground and not to build upon it. In turn, the purchasers covenanted to pay a fair proportion of the expenses of keeping the park in good order and well stocked with plants. As well as the houses facing the park, there were some nine or ten others which did not: these were separated from the road which surrounded the park by those houses which did. The purchasers of these other houses were granted similar rights.

Where these parks exist, the houses which surround them seldom have anything in the way of a garden: the park is, then, a common 'garden' for all the houses.

Who cares?

Those who will be affected

The purchasers of the houses. The availability of a garden greatly enhances the enjoyment of each house: it also enhances the value and marketability of them. Can they enforce the right against any purchaser from their vendor?

The original vendor and the builder (usually the same person). The provision of the park makes the houses a more attractive proposition to potential purchasers. In addition, the covenants entered into by both parties will ensure that the park and the surrounding area remains attractive. If the original vendor has retained neighbouring land, obviously he will want to maintain the character of the area. The original builder will wish to retain his reputation for providing attractive houses.

Successors in title to the original purchasers. Can they take the benefit that their vendor enjoyed? Can the burden be imposed upon any purchaser of the park?

The successors in title to ownership of the park. Must they continue to let the house-owners use the park? Clearly, from their point of view the arrangement is a huge disadvantage: they cannot use the land to build upon, they must maintain it and share it with 'all persons to whom such easements may be granted'. In *Re Ellenborough Park*, as so often happens, all went well until one of the original parties – the owner of the park itself – died. His trustees wanted to know whether the owners of the houses had any enforceable rights over the park against his heirs or successors in title, and if so what.

What are they?

The nature and characteristics of easements

Easements are rights exercised by one person over the land belonging to another and they are incorporeal hereditaments. Easements can be positive or negative. A positive easement is a right to do something on someone else's land, for example, the right to walk over that land, or to place an advertising board upon it. A negative easement, on the other hand, prohibits a 'land owner' from using his own land in a certain way. If N, a neighbour of S, has an easement of light over S's land, then S cannot erect any building on his 'own' land which would interfere with that right. We shall see, however, that it is not possible to have a general right to light, only a limited right to light. There is no exact definition of easements. In fact we have to look at case law to see what rights have been held to be easements, but it must be emphasised that these cases in no way provide a finite list, for the categories are not closed. Indeed, they 'must alter and expand with the changes that take place in the circumstances of mankind' – Lord St Leonards in *Dyce* v *Lady Hay* (1852) 1 Macq 305. However, it has to be said that the courts are reluctant to add new kinds of rights to the list. For example in *Phipps* v *Pears* [1965] 1 QB 76, the court having said that the creation of new negative easements would not be readily accepted, it was held there could be no easement for protection from the weather. (However, in *Leakey* v *National Trust* [1980] QB 485 the owner of one property was ordered to pay for the weatherproofing of adjoining property as he owed to his neighbour a duty of care in tort not to damage his property. *Phipps* was distinguished on the ground that the houses in that case were not adjoining, whereas in *Leakey* they were.) Whilst easements are rights over land, and thus proprietary, they are also 'personal' in the ordinary sense of the word in that they are personal to the person whose land enjoys the right, in that they are not public rights, local customary rights or natural rights.

Re Ellenborough Park [1956] Ch 131

Although it is difficult to define easements, it is not quite so difficult to decide whether or not a claimed right is capable of being one because Danckwerts J, in this, the leading case, laid down the following four essential requirements:

1 there must be a dominant and a servient tenement;
2 the right claimed must accommodate the dominant tenement;
3 the dominant and servient tenements must be owned or occupied by different persons;
4 easements must be capable of forming the subject matter of a grant.

Each of these needs some explanation.

A dominant and a servient tenement

Obviously, if an easement is a right over someone else's land, there must be two pieces of land – a dominant and a servient tenement. It is crucial to understand that a tenement is a piece of land, not the person who owns it. (Nothing annoys examiners more than to be told that 'French is the dominant tenement and Saunders the servient'. Apart from anything else it shows that you have failed to grasp the nature of an easement; it is an interest in land.)

The dominant tenement enjoys the benefit of the easement and the servient tenement carries the burden of it.

> ### Example
> If Jack grants his neighbour Jill an easement to cross his land in order to reach the main road, Jack's land is the servient tenement and Jill's is the dominant.

Because there must be both a dominant and a servient tenement, an easement cannot exist 'in gross', that is without a dominant tenement. There must, therefore, be land to which the benefit of the easement can attach. However, it is possible for a servient tenement to serve more than one dominant tenement, provided that in each case the land is benefited.

> ### Example
> If Jack had also granted a right of way over his land to his other neighbour Fred, Fred's land, like Jill's, would be a dominant tenement and Jack's would be the servient in both cases.

On the other hand, however, a right granted for the benefit of a defined piece of land cannot be exercised in favour of another piece of land.

Tenements can be connected horizontally, as between flats on different storeys, or vertically, as between adjoining houses.

The need for a dominant as well as a servient tenement was reiterated by the Court of Appeal in *London & Blenheim Estates Ltd* v *Ladbroke Retail Parks Ltd* [1994] 1 WLR 31.

Accommodating the dominant tenement

The right claimed must accommodate the dominant tenement. This means that the right must benefit the dominant tenement – and not merely the tenement owner – in that it makes it 'a better and more convenient property'.

Re Ellenborough Park [1956] Ch 131

a right enjoyed by one over the land of another does not possess the status of an easement unless it accommodates and serves the dominant tenement, and is reasonably necessary for the better enjoyment of that tenement, for if it has no necessary connexion therewith, although it confers an advantage upon the owner and renders his ownership of the land more valuable, it is not an easement at all, but a mere contractual right personal to and only enforceable between the two contracting parties ... it is not sufficient to show that the right increased the value of the property conveyed, unless it is also shown that it was connected with the normal enjoyment of that property ... whether or not this connexion exists is primarily one of fact, and depends largely on the nature of the alleged dominant tenement and the nature of the right granted - Evershed MR.

Two contrasting cases illustrate this point nicely – *Re Webb's Lease* and *Moody* v *Steggles*.

Re Webb's Lease [1951] Ch 808

An advertisement for matches was held to be of no benefit to a butcher's shop and therefore not an easement.

Moody v *Steggles* (1879) 12 Ch D 261

Here the right to affix a signboard for a public house to adjoining premises was upheld as an easement because the sign related to the public house. *Steggles* also illustrates the fact that where the dominant tenement is a business, the right can create an easement where it accommodates the business. As Fry J explained:

> It is said that the easement in question relates, not to the tenement, but to the business of the occupant of the tenement, and that therefore I cannot tie the easement to the house. It appears to me that that argument is of too refined a nature to prevail, and for this reason, that the house can only be used by an occupant, and that the occupant uses the house for the business which he pursues, and therefore in some manner (direct or indirect) an easement is more or less connected with the mode in which the occupant of the house uses it.

Where an easement accommodates business premises, then once it has been acquired (as opposed to being in the course of acquisition, where excessive user of a purported servient tenement can defeat a claim to the right), 'a mere increase in user and not user of a different kind or for a different purpose' will not extinguish it – Ploughman J in *Woodhouse & Co Ltd* v *Kirkland (Derby) Ltd* [1970] 1 WLR 1185. Such easements are usually fairly specific in the nature and extent of the right concerned but easements, especially rights of way, can be very general.

British Railways Board v *Glass* [1965] Ch 587

'A right of way for this purpose or that has never been to my knowledge limited to a right to use the way only so many times a day or for such and such a number of vehicles so long as the dominant tenement does not change its identity' - Harman LJ. Here the grant was of 'a right of crossing the railway . . . with all manner of cattle' to a farmer. Years later the farmer allowed a few caravans on his farm, six of which were there for at least 20 years (a magic term as we shall see later). The Board complained when the number of caravans increased to 29, all crossing the railway. It was held that the Board could not prevent the use of the right.

Both *Woodhouse* and *Glass* concerned easements acquired by prescription.

We shall see later that the extent of an easement depends upon the way in which it was acquired: easements of necessity are strictly limited to the circumstances of the necessity which prevailed at the time of the grant. On the other hand, where an easement is acquired by prescription, the extent of it depends upon the nature and extent of the user at the time of the grant; if this remains constant, as in *British Rail* v *Glass*, there is no objection to an increase in that same user.

Attwood v *Bovis Homes Ltd* [2000] 4 All ER 948

Neuberger J stated *per curiam* that, where a right of way has been acquired by prescription, the rule may be that the dominant owner can only continue to use the right if he can satisfy the court that the change cannot result in the use of the way being greater in quantum, or different in character to, the use during the 20 or 40 years' continuous use necessary for acquisition of the right by prescription. The onus on the dominant owner will normally be difficult to satisfy. *Attwood* itself concerned an easement of drainage acquired by prescription and Neuberger J held that such a right would not be destroyed by a substantial change in the nature of the dominant tenement unless the servient owner could prove that the change had substantially increased, or changed the nature of, the burden on his land. On the facts, the dominant owners changed the use of the dominant land (which had the benefit of an easement of drainage) from agricultural to substantially residential and commercial. The servient owner claimed that the radical change in the nature of the use of the dominant tenement destroyed the right, relying upon authorities in regard to rights of way acquired by prescription. However, Neuberger J held that easements of drainage are not comparable to rights of way, but to rights of support, and a change in the nature of the dominant tenement would destroy a right of support only if the servient owner established that it had increased the burden on his land. As the change in use of the dominant tenement would not increase the amount of water coming onto it, it would not automatically be expected to alter the amount of water passing from the dominant tenement to the servient tenement. Thus the right of drainage remained. This case provides a useful review of this area.

Jelbert v *Davis* [1968] 1 All ER 1182

In contrast to the facts of *Glass*, J had a right of way over a strip of land belonging to D. The original conveyance provided 'the right of way at all times and for all purposes over the driveway . . . leading to the main road, in common with all other persons having the like right'. Subsequently, J obtained planning permission to use part of his land for a camping and caravan site for up to 200 caravans and/or tents. D objected to the proposed change in user of the land. Lord Denning MR held that the contemplated user of 200 camping units was excessive. The question was one of fact and degree, but 'no one of those entitled to a right of way must use it to an extent which is beyond that which is contemplated at the time of grant'.

Clearly, this was a case of express grant, as also was *White* v *Grand Hotel Eastbourne Ltd* [1913] 1 Ch 113. In that case a right of way benefiting a dominant tenement was held not to be limited to purely domestic use, so that when the dominant tenement became a hotel, and, consequently, the right was more heavily used (the path led to the guests' garage), the easement was not extinguished. (Had there been express words of limitation in the grant, it could have been different.)

Where the grant (or reservation) of the easement has been implied, the scope of the right is limited to the use contemplated at the date of the conveyance or transfer – *Nickerson* v *Barraclough* [1981] 2 WLR 773, but any use beyond grant will not be excessive if it was clearly contemplated by the parties at the date of grant – *Stafford* v *Lee* (1992) 65 P&CR 172. See also *Fairview New Homes plc* v *Government Row Residents Association Ltd* [1998] EGCS 92.

In *British Rail* v *Glass*, of course, there was no change of user, merely a greater use for the same purpose. Similarly, merely extending the size of the dominant tenement, but not altering the user of it, will not extinguish an easement, so long as 'the character and extent of the burden imposed on the servient tenement' is not enlarged – Purchase LJ in *Graham* v *Philcox* [1984] QB 747.

However, the right must not be too general. A right of way 'for all purposes' was held in *Ackroyd* v *Smith* (1850) 10 CB 164 to be too wide in that it could enable use for purposes not connected with the dominant tenement. Going back to the 'advertisement' cases, in *Clapman* v *Edwards* [1938] 2 All ER 507 a right 'for advertising purposes' failed on the same ground – that it was not restricted to user for the business carried out at the dominant tenement. In both cases slightly different wording, such as 'for all purposes connected with [the dominant tenement]' would have saved the right. By contrast, however, the Court of Appeal held in *White* v *Richards* [1993] RTR 318 that a right 'at all times hereafter to pass and repass on foot and with or without motor vehicles' over a dirt track 2.7 metres wide and 250 metres long did not entitle the dominant tenement owner to take an average of 15 juggernaut lorries over the track daily! Notwithstanding a right of way is granted in wide terms, it may be limited by the physical characteristics of the path over which it subsists. (However, 'a right of way expressly granted is not necessarily limited by the physical characteristics of the site of the easement at the time of the grant . . . the language of the grant may be such that the topographical circumstances cannot properly be regarded as restricting the scope of the grant according to the language of it' – Mummery LJ in the Court of Appeal in *West* v *Sharp* (2000) 79 P&CR 327.) West was followed in *B&Q plc* v *Liverpool & Lancashire Properties Ltd* [2000] EGCS 101 where Blackburne J held that there is no actionable interference with a right of way if the right could be substantially and practically exercised as conveniently after the occurrence complained of as before it.

In *Stafford* v *Lee* (1992) 65 P&CR 172, the Court of Appeal held that an easement granted giving the right to use a roadway for access to a piece of woodland may be taken as implying a right of way on foot or by vehicle for the purpose of building a house if, on the balance of probabilities, this is what the parties intended when the original easement was granted. It was held in *Greenwich Healthcare National Health Service Trust* v *London & Quadrant Housing Trust and others* [1998] 3 All ER 437 that a servient owner has no right to alter the route of an easement unless such a right was an express or implied term of the grant of the easement, or was subsequently conferred upon him. (On the facts, however, as no reasonable objection could be made to the proposed realignment, and all who could claim the benefit of the right of way had notice of the proposal but had not objected, and the realignment was necessary to achieve an object of substantial public and local importance and value, the defendants were not entitled to an injunction to restrain the plaintiff from proceeding with it. Thus, although the plaintiff had no right to alter the route of an easement, no injunction would be granted to prevent him from so doing!)

Supermarkets have become a way of life for most people nowadays and a case which concerned the rights of shoppers in regard to shopping trolleys was *Soames-Forsythe Properties Ltd* v *Tesco Stores Ltd* [1991] EGCS 22. Here a grant of 'full and free right of way on foot only' over land from a supermarket to the car park was held to include the right to push supermarket trolleys along it and also a right by way of an estoppel in the nature of an easement to park the trolleys on the walkway.

Any right which merely benefits the owner of the purported dominant tenement, and not the land itself (or the business thereon) cannot be an easement.

Hill v *Tupper* (1863) 2 H&C 121

Here the owner of a canal leased land on its bank to Hill, granting him also the exclusive right of putting pleasure boats on the canal itself. All went well until Tupper (without authority) put his own pleasure boats on the canal in competition with Hill. Could Hill stop him? That depended upon whether Hill had an easement - if he did, he could sue anyone, including Tupper, who interfered with it; if not, Hill could do nothing about it. The question, therefore, was whether or not Hill had an easement, and it was held that he did not. The right did not improve the 'dominant' land, nor was his business attached to it. Therefore, it was a purely personal advantage to Hill. (Of course, the canal owner could have sued Tupper for trespass.) Had the grant to Hill been of a right to cross and recross the canal, to and from his own land, it would have been a different matter.

There can be no easement for purely recreational purposes or personal amusement. This was stated by Martin B in *Mounsey* v *Ismay* (1865) 3 H&C 486: the right 'must be a right of utility and benefit, and not one of mere recreation and amusement'.

Re Ellenborough Park [1956] Ch 131

As this leading case illustrates, the easement may include recreational purposes - in that case the use of a 'garden'. As long as the right accommodates the dominant tenement - the land - and not merely the persons who occupy it, it is capable of being an easement and Evershed MR stated that 'the use of a garden undoubtedly enhances, and is connected with, the normal enjoyment of the house to which it belongs'. The 'garden' in question was a communal one, the use of which the Court of Appeal felt was 'for the purposes, not only of

exercise and rest but also for such domestic purposes as ... taking out small children in per-
ambulations or otherwise' and this 'is not fairly to be described as one of mere recreation or
amusement, and is clearly beneficial to the premises to which it is attached'.

In the more recent case of *Mulvaney* v *Gough* [2002] EWCA Civ 1078, the Court of
Appeal upheld the use of land as 'a communal garden for recreational and amenity
purposes' as an easement, but Latham LJ explained that this would not exclude the
servient owners

> from any use which they might wish to make of the land. It restricted that use only to the
> extent necessary to ensure that the servient land as a whole could still be enjoyed by the
> dominant owners as a communal garden for recreational and amenity purposes.

Thus, the 'enjoyment' of an easement does not necessarily mean the owner of it can
have fun! However, the deciding factor will be whether the dominant land is benefited by the right: permission to ride a horse over a neighbour's land may be purely
recreational, and therefore not an easement but a mere licence; on the other hand,
it may be a right of way on horseback, and capable of being an easement.

What of those houses in *Re Ellenborough Park* which did not face the park? Was
there sufficient 'connexion' with them as dominant tenements?

> The result is not affected by the circumstance that the right to the park is in this case
> enjoyed by some few houses which are not immediately fronting on the park ... the test is
> satisfied as regards these few neighbouring, though not adjacent, houses ... the extension
> of the right of enjoyment to these few houses does not negative the presence of the
> necessary 'nexus' between the subject-matter enjoyed and the premises to which the enjoy-
> ment is expressed to belong ...

However the tenements must not be too far apart: 'There cannot be a right of way
over land in Kent appurtenant to an estate in Northumberland' – Willes J in *Bailey*
v *Stephens* (1862) 12 CBNS 91.

In *Jobson* v *Record & Record* (1997) 75 P&CR 375 the question was whether the
Records could use an easement in favour of their farmhouse over a private roadway
for the purpose of transporting timber felled on another piece of land. The Court of
Appeal held that they could not: a right of way granted to benefit one defined area
could not be used to benefit another (see also *Harris* v *Flower* (1905) LJ Ch 127).

It can be seen that, whilst they need not be actually adjoining, the dominant and
servient tenements need to be reasonably 'contiguous' – close – though certain
bodies do enjoy exceptional powers under statute to acquire easements over land
many miles away from the dominant tenement, for example the Central Electricity
Generating Board to erect pylons on servient tenements far removed from the dominant tenement housing the generating station.

Ownership of the dominant and servient tenements

The dominant and servient tenements must be owned or occupied by different
persons. As an easement is a right over someone else's land, it should be obvious that
you cannot have an easement over your own land. Indeed, a person who holds an
estate in the land does not, so long as he is both owner and occupier of all of it,
need an easement to cross over it. However, any 'rights' that the owner habitually

exercises which would, if exercised by someone else, be an easement, are called 'quasi-easements' and these can, in certain circumstances, become easements proper. If there is one fee simple owner but separate occupation, for example by two tenants, then one tenant can have an easement over the other tenant's land.

Capable of grant

Easements must be capable of forming the subject matter of a grant. This means that the right claimed must be capable of sufficiently certain definition in a deed. The classic easement is a right of way, but easements can take many diverse forms. The following are just some of the rights which have been held capable of being easements: the right to use someone's kitchen in *Haywood* v *Mallalieu* (1863) 25 Ch D 357, the right to use a neighbour's toilet in *Miller* v *Emcer Products Ltd* [1956] Ch 304 (but this is not an easement of necessity!), the right to use a garden in *Re Ellenborough Park*, the right to hang clothes on a line which crosses over neighbouring land in *Drewell* v *Towler* (1832) 3 B&Ad 735, the right to have a fence maintained by an adjoining owner in *Crow* v *Wood* [1971] 1 QB 77, the right to nail trees to a neighbour's wall in *Hawkins* v *Wallis* (1763) 2 Wils 173.

The possibility of an easement for car parking is a relatively recent development.

Newman v *Jones* (1982) unreported

This was the first case where such a right was recognised, but only as a right to park a car anywhere on a marked out parking area, not in a particular defined space.

In *London & Blenheim Estates Ltd* v *Ladbroke Retail Parks Ltd* (1994) the right to park a car on any available space in a car park was upheld, provided that it would not leave the servient owner without any reasonable use of his land. However, it was held by the Court of Appeal in *Das* v *Linden Mews Ltd* [2002] EWCA Civ 590 that an easement could not be extended in order to accommodate 'ancillary use' for the dominant tenement – in this case a right of access to a property could not be extended so as to enable the carriageway to be used to gain vehicular access to adjacent land for the purpose of parking.

Saeed v *Plustrade Ltd* [2001] EWCA Civ 2011

there has in the past been some doubt as to whether a right to park in a car park can exist in law as an easement. More recent authorities of courts of first instance, cited by Judge Paul Baker QC in *London & Blenheim Estates Ltd* v *Ladbroke Retail Parks Ltd* [1994] ... and his own decision in that case appear to establish that it can, provided only that it does not amount to a claim to the entire beneficial user of the servient area, in which case the grant would not be that of an easement, though it might be of some larger or different grant; see also *Batchelor* v *Murphy* 11th May 2000 (unreported). However, the Court of Appeal in the first-mentioned case identified, but did not answer, the question whether the right to park could exist as a valid easement and no other Court of Appeal decision relating to the question has been cited to us. In the circumstances and in the absence of full argument, I would prefer to leave the question open, without intending in any way to suggest that Judge Paul Baker QC's decision was wrong - Sir Christopher Slade.

Thus the question remains open.

This issue was addressed again by the Court of Appeal shortly afterwards in *Batchelor* v *Marlow* (2001) 82 P&CR 36, where it held that user which rendered use by a servient owner 'illusory' could not be an easement. However, even though the right claimed in this case would result in the servient owner himself being able to park only at night or at weekends, as it was limited in time, it did not leave the servient owner without any reasonable use of his land, thus affirming *London & Blenheim*. The easement was acquired by prescription.

The right to place stones on adjoining land in order to prevent sand being washed away by the sea in *Philpot* v *Bath* (1905) 21 TLR 634, and the right of a landowner to use a particular seat in a parish church in *Re St Mary's Banbury* [1986] 2 All ER 611 were also upheld as easements. In *Leakey* v *National Trust* [1980] QB 485 the right to support of buildings by adjoining buildings or land was upheld, and in *Bradburn* v *Linsay* [1983] 2 All ER 408, even though there was no easement, the owner of an adjoining house was held to be under a duty in nuisance to maintain his own house so as to prevent damage to the adjoining one. He was, therefore, held liable for the cost of providing support for and weather-proofing of the dividing wall. See also *Green* v *Lord Somerleyton* [2004] 1 P&CR 520, applying *Leakey*. These decisions must be contrasted with that in *Phipps* v *Pears* [1965] 1 QB 76 where the two properties, though very close (only inches apart), were not adjoining. There it was held that there was no right to support of a non-party wall, and no right to protection from the weather.

As we have seen already, these cases in no way provide a finite list of what can exist as an easement: the categories are not closed; they 'must alter and expand with the changes that take place in the circumstances of mankind' – Lord St Leonards in *Dyce* v *Lady Hay*.

The right claimed must be certain enough to enable reasonable definition. Thus there is no general right to light, though you can have an easement of light through a defined aperture – *Wheeldon* v *Burrows* (1879) 12 Ch D 31. Similarly, there is no general right to air, but you can have an easement of air through a defined duct or channel – *Wong* v *Beaumont Property Trust Ltd* [1965] 1 QB 173.

Allen v *Greenwood* [1980] Ch 119

Here the plaintiffs were the owners of a house with a greenhouse in the garden. The defendants erected a fence which left enough light to enable the plaintiff to work in the greenhouse, but not enough for growing plants. The Court of Appeal granted the plaintiff an injunction. Goff LJ's view was that:

> [i]t cannot, I think, be right to say that there is no nuisance because one can see to go in and out of a greenhouse and to pot plants which will not flourish, and to pick fruit which cannot properly be developed and ripened, still less because one can see to read a book.

Lord Goff accepted the plaintiff's claim that 'warmth is an inseparable product of daylight' but left open the question whether a right to light would include properties from the sun in regard to solar heating.

Although the existence of a right to light was recognised long ago in *Aldred's case* (1610) 9 Co Rep 57b the question: 'if there is no general, that is unlimited right, to light, how much light is one entitled to?' frequently arises.

Deakins v *Hookings* [1994] 14 EG 133

Whilst only a county court decision, this interesting case, concerning two adjoining terraced houses with an L-shaped area at the rear which backed on to a narrow courtyard provides a thorough examination of the modern law in this area. The defendant bought one of the houses and extended it at the rear to provide an upstairs flat and a hairdressing salon downstairs. The court had to determine whether the light remaining to the adjoining house was sufficient for 'ordinary purposes of inhabitancy … according to the ordinary notions of mankind' as laid down by Lord Lindley in *Colls* v *Home & Colonial Stores Ltd* [1904] AC 179. Although it is not for the court to assess how much light there was before the obstruction and by how much it has been reduced, such factors are, of course, relevant. In *Deakins*, light to the living room of the adjoining house had been reduced. Light to that room had never been brilliant(!), only 51 per cent of it being well-lit previously, but this area had been reduced to 41 per cent. The kitchen had previously been well lit up to 88 per cent, but this was now 55–57 per cent. Cooke J took the approach that in an ill-lit room every bit of light is precious so that, although the drop in light to the living room was slight, because the light had been poor from the outset, the reduction to below 50 per cent took it below that which was acceptable. The judge accepted the plaintiff's evidence showing the effect upon her beneficial occupation to be 'real and deleterious'. He found the reduction of light to the kitchen to be substantial, though it did leave over 50 per cent well lit. However, realistically it left the rest of the kitchen – the 'circulation area' – unusable for any other purpose in any circumstances. Taking all this into consideration, Cooke J held that the reduction in light to the living room constituted an actionable nuisance, but not that to the kitchen.

There is no right to privacy – *Browne* v *Flower* [1911] 1 Ch 219, nor to a view because 'the law does not give an action for such things as delight' – *Aldred's Case*. On this ground there can be no easement to ride a horse upon another's land, unless it is being ridden over the land as a right of way (*Re Ellenborough Park*). Of course, 'such things as delight' are of a purely personal benefit and do not accommodate the dominant tenement.

The right claimed must not amount to joint user of the servient tenement by the dominant owner, so that his use of it amounts to, or prevents that of the servient owner.

Copeland v *Greenhalf* [1952] Ch 488

The defendant, a wheelwright, and his father before him had for many years used a strip of the plaintiff's land for storing and repairing vehicles, notwithstanding that they always left room for the plaintiff to reach his orchard, Upjohn J held that there could be no easement because:

> The right claimed goes wholly outside any normal idea of an easement, that is the right of the owner or occupier of a dominant tenement and a servient tenement. This claim … really amounts to a claim to a joint user of the land by the defendant. Practically, the defendant is claiming the whole beneficial user of the strip of land on the south-east side of the track there; he can leave as many or as few lorries there as he likes for as long as he likes; he may enter on it by himself, his servants and agents to do repair work thereon. In my judgment, that is not a claim which can be established as an easement. It is virtually a claim to possession of the servient tenement, if necessary to the exclusion of the owner; or, at any rate, to a joint user.

Similarly,

Re Ellenborough Park [1956] Ch 131

> a privilege of wandering at will over all and every part of another's field or park and which, though easily intelligible as the subject-matter of a personal licence, is something substantially different from the subject-matter of the grant in question, namely the provision for a limited number of houses in a uniform crescent of one single large but private garden ... for the right conferred no more amounts to a joint occupation of the park with its owners, no more excludes the proprietorship or possession of the latter, than a right of way granted through a passage, or than the use by the public of the gardens of Lincoln's Inn Fields ... amount to joint occupation of that garden with the London County Council, or involve an inconsistency with the possession or proprietorship of the Council as lessees.
>
> The right to full enjoyment of Ellenborough Park was, in substance, no more than a right to use the park as a garden in the way in which gardens are commonly used ... A private garden ... is an attribute of the ordinary enjoyment of the residence to which it is attached, and the right of wandering in it is but one method of enjoying it – Evershed MR.

Grigsby v Melville [1973] 1 All ER 385

Here it was held that a claim to a right of unlimited storage within a confined or defined space amounted to a claim to the whole beneficial user of the servient tenement and could not, therefore, be an easement. The confined space was a cellar beneath one of two adjoining cottages, Grigsby's. Melville claimed the right of storage for the benefit of his cottage but, as Brightman J said, 'A purchaser [Grigsby had bought the cottage from Melville] does not expect to find the vendor continuing to live mole-like beneath his drawing room floor'!

Newman v *Jones* (1982) (unreported) is in line with this ruling in that no easement will arise for the use of a specific or defined car space. However, a case which is often raised on this point – *Wright* v *Macadam* [1949] 2 KB 744, where the right of a tenant to store her coal in a shed on the landlord's land was upheld – is out of line. Indeed the case is very particular on its facts and, as Brightman J pointed out in *Grigsby*, 'The precise facts in *Wright* v *Macadam* in this respect are not wholly clear from the report and it is a little difficult to know whether the tenant had exclusive use of the coal shed or of any defined portion of it. To some extent a problem of this sort may be one of degree'. Whichever way one looks at it, *Wright* v *Macadam* is out of line with other authority, thus indicating that:

> it may be that the courts have in fact used the supposed requirement of non-exclusive user as a smokescreen for judicial discretion, invoking the requirement in order to strike down claims felt to be unmeritorious while suppressing the requirement in cases where it has been felt that a remedy should be given – Gray and Symes (1981, p 589).

The problem of exclusive and permanent possession of a small portion of land arises in regard to pipes. It is possible to have an easement of drainage, but does this extend to the drainpipe itself? The running of drainage – water, sewage, etc – will be intermittent, but the pipe uses the land permanently. Given the appropriate circumstances in a particular case, Buckley J in *Simmons* v *Midford* [1969] 2 All ER 1269 felt that the pipe may be a fixture appurtenant to the dominant land, even though the pipe passes through or under the servient tenement also. Of course, the servient owner can always grant a licence in regard to the pipe: whilst the easement for drainage continues, this licence would be irrevocable as, without it, the easement would be useless. The same principles would apply to gas pipes. (The public utility companies have statutory rights in regard to laying pipes, etc.)

For the purposes of this fourth essential requirement there must be a capable grantor and a capable grantee – the servient owner being the grantor, the dominant owner the grantee. In order to be a capable grantor, the servient owner must, at the date of creation, have been of full legal capacity and competent to grant such a right. This is usually not a problem, although a statutory corporate body may not have the necessary power endowed upon it by its constituting instrument, as in *Mulliner* v *Midland Railway Co* (1879) 11 Ch D 611 where the company was held to have acted *ultra vires* in purportedly granting an easement over part of its land.

A person claiming to be a capable grantee must also be a legal person capable of receiving a grant. Here again, corporate bodies must be endowed with such power. The grantee must also be definite, so that a fluctuating body of persons, such as 'the inhabitants for the time being of Knotty Ash' is not a capable grantee, though they may acquire a similar right by custom, and even though it is for purely personal pleasure, for example a right to play games as in *New Windsor Corporation* v *Mellor* [1974] 1 WLR 1504. A successful claim for a customary right requires that the custom be certain, in that the persons entitled to the right must be certain; and it must not be unreasonable; it must have continued uninterrupted from time immemorial within a particular district. The latter requirements are the most important, that is time and place. Though 'time immemorial' strictly means since 1189, according to Tindal CJ in *Lockwood* v *Wood* (1844) 6 QBD 50:

> As to proof of custom, you cannot, indeed, reasonably expect to have it proved before you that such a custom did in fact exist before the time of legal memory, that is, before the first year of the reign of Richard I; for if you did, it would in effect destroy the validity of almost all customs; but you are to require proof, as far back as living memory goes, of a continuous, peaceable, and uninterrupted user of the custom.

Under the Commons Registration Act 1965, rights of common can be asserted if registered (by 1970) under the Act, registration being conclusive. Even rights not registered by 1970 can be created and then registered, and, as shown in *R* v *Oxfordshire CC, ex parte Sunningwell PC* [2000] 1 AC 335, rights may continue to be enjoyed if shown to have been enjoyed for 20 years or more, though not registered.

The Countryside and Rights of Way Act 2000 now provides the general public with rights of access over common land and 'open country'. (This Act may burden hundreds of property owners, including parish councils and the National Trust, with 'hefty bills they had not planned for'.) In 1930, driving on common land was made illegal but many landowners 'turned a blind eye' to such trespassing. The 2000 Act introduces new charges for the offence. See *The Week*, 25 March 2002, *Country Matters*. There may well be a public right of way which includes the possibility of a public right to navigate a river.

Hamble Parish Council v *Haggard* [1992] 4 All ER 147

This case shows the importance of knowing who the grantee is. The easement was an unrestricted right of way giving access to a burial ground. The grant was made to the vicar and whoever was his successor in title to the dominant land. The defendants had mistakenly assumed that the grant was to the vicar and his successor as vicar. The successor in title to the vicar was the parish council, which Millett J held was entitled to the right of way.

An easement must not involve the servient tenement owner in any positive burden. All that is required of him is that he allow the dominant owner to exercise his right. Thus an easement must not normally involve the servient owner in expenditure. In *Regis Property Co Ltd v Redman* [1956] 2 QB 612, therefore, it was held there could be no easement to maintain a supply of hot water: this would require the 'servient' owner to supply the water, and also to heat it. Also:

> [a]part from any special local custom or express contract, the owner of a servient tenement is not bound to execute any repairs necessary to ensure the enjoyment of the easement by the owner of the dominant tenement. The grantor of a way over a bridge is not by common law liable, nor does he impliedly contract, to keep the bridge in repair for the convenience of the grantee – Gale (1986, p 49).

(Of course, the grantor may find himself liable under some other area of law, eg under the Occupiers' Liability Act 1984, s 1.) In regard to drains no duty lies with the servient tenement owner to keep the drains in repair, even if it serves the servient tenement also – *Buckley (R H) & Sons Ltd v Buckley (N) & Sons Ltd* [1898] 2 QB 608. To this rule there is one exception.

Crow v *Wood* [1971] 1 QB 77

Here it was held that the right to have a fence maintained and repaired by the servient owner was 'a right which is capable of being granted at law ... because it is in the nature of an easement'. However, '[i]t is not an easement strictly so called because it involves the servient owner in the expenditure of money. It was described by Gale [*Easements*, 11th edition, p 422] as a "spurious kind of easement" ... there seems to be little doubt that fencing is an easement' - Lord Denning.

Where the parties to an easement have expressly or impliedly agreed that the servient owner shall bear the cost, the agreement may be enforced. In *Liverpool City Council v Irwin* [1977] AC 239, the Council, the owner of a high-rise block of flats, was held liable to maintain the common parts by way of implied contract with the tenants.

Again, in *Miller v Hancock* [1893] 2 QB 177, the Court of Appeal held that, although maintenance of a right of way is normally the responsibility of the grantee (dominant tenement owner), on the facts 'it must have been intended by necessary implication' that the landlord (the servient owner) should have duty to repair and maintain the staircase.

If the servient tenement owner is not generally liable to maintain and/or repair the subject matter of the easement, can the dominant owner carry out the necessary work? According to Gale:

> [t]he question of ancillary easements commonly arises in connection with repairs. Thus the grantee of an easement for a watercourse through his neighbour's land may, when reasonably necessary, enter a neighbour's land for the purposes of repairing, and may repair such

watercourse (Parker J, *Jones* v *Pritchard* [1908] 1 Ch 630). If a man gives me a licence to lay pipes on his land to convey water to my cistern, I may afterwards enter and dig the land to mend the pipes, though the soil belongs to another and not to me (*Pomfret* v *Ricroft* (1669) 1 Wms Saund, 6th ed., 321). The owner of a building entitled to support from an adjoining building is entitled to enter and take the necessary steps to ensure that the support continues by effecting repairs, and so forth, to the part of the building which gives the support (*Bond* v *Nottingham Corporation* [1940] Ch 429).

Repair for this purpose includes making and improving the subject of the easement (*Newcomen* v *Coulson* (1877) 5 Ch D 133); alteration to meet altered conditions (*Finlinson* v *Porter* (1875) LR 10 QB 188); also replacement (*Hoare* v *Metropolitan Board of Works* (1874) LR 9 QB 296) – *Gale on Easements* (1986, p 46).

However, 'a dominant owner is not bound to keep the subject of his easement in repair'. Here again, though, the dominant tenement owner may find himself liable in other areas of law: for instance, failure to maintain a pipe may lead to sewage contaminating the servient land and the dominant owner being liable to the servient owner in the tort of nuisance. Also he may be forced to repair in order to avoid trespassing, by using an alternative path, for example.

It was held in *Gerrard* v *Cooke* (1806) 2 Bos & PNR 109 that grantees of express grants can also develop or improve, for example, a path so as to improve the accommodation of the dominant tenement. However, where the easement was acquired by prescription, the grantee has no such additional right – *Mills* v *Silver* [1991] Ch 271.

Usually, if repairs are necessary and the dominant owner wishes them to be carried out, it is up to him to repair, unless there is a contrary indication: *Miller* v *Hancock* [1893] 2 QB 177.

However, in *Duffy* v *Lamb* (1997) 75 P&CR 364, the Court of Appeal held that though a servient tenement owner was not under any duty to ensure that a supply of electricity was maintained, he was under a duty to take no positive step which would prevent the passage of electricity on to his land as well as its subsequent passage through the servient land to the dominant land. In switching off the plain-

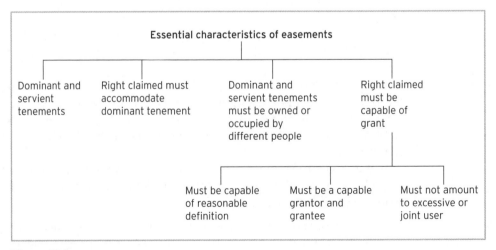

Figure 12.1

tiff's supply, the defendant servient owner was in breach of that duty. In so finding, the Court of Appeal applied *Rance* v *Elvin* (1985) 50 P&CR 9, the facts of which were identical to *Duffy* except that the easement in that case concerned the supply of water. In each case the crucial distinction between a right to a supply of water or electricity and the right to an uninterrupted passage of water or electricity had to be made. In each case the right had been one of passage. By disconnecting the supplies, the servient owners were liable.

It can be seen, then, that each claim to an easement must be considered on its own facts and, though it is difficult to define exactly what an easement is, it is not quite so difficult to decide whether or not a claimed right is capable of being one, thanks to the essential requirements laid down in *Re Ellenborough Park*.

How can they exist?

Classification: legal or equitable?

'An easement, right, or privilege in or over land for an interest equivalent to an estate in fee simple absolute in possession or a term of years absolute' are capable of being legal – Law of Property Act 1925, s 1(2)(a). They can, of course, also be equitable. An easement for life could only be equitable.

We shall see next that easements can be acquired in several ways, one of which is by prescription. An easement acquired by prescription or implied by virtue of the Law of Property Act 1925, s 62, if capable of subsisting as a legal interest, will be legal, even though it was not granted by deed. An easement under the rule in *Wheeldon* v *Burrows* is also legal.

How can you acquire them?

Rules, principles and formalities

There are several ways in which an easement can be acquired, each with its own rules. They fall under three heads: express, implied and presumed.

Express easements

There are three ways in which express easements can be created – by statute, by grant or by reservation.

By statute

If an electricity board needs to erect pylons to carry electricity cables across a field, it will require an easement over the farmer's land. Likewise, a gas board or water company may need an easement over someone else's land in order to effect maintenance and repairs to pipes and so on. In such circumstances public utilities can acquire the necessary right by way of a statutory grant. A local Act of Parliament may also create a statutory easement, for instance by giving a right of support to a canal constructed under statutory powers. Easements created by statute are legal.

By grant

The express grant of an easement is usually made by the use of express words in the conveyance of the legal estate in the dominant tenement. Provided, therefore, that it is equal in time to either of the legal estates and the conveyance itself complies with the formal requirements, such easements are legal.

Needless to say, if the easement is for a shorter time than either of the legal estates, or if the conveyance is formally defective, the easement cannot be legal. However, in the latter case, it may well succeed as an equitable easement under the rule in *Walsh* v *Lonsdale*. In addition, even an oral grant has succeeded as an equitable easement, when supported by an act of part performance – *McManus* v *Cooke* (1887) 35 Ch D 681 and *May* v *Belleville* [1905] 2 Ch 605. However, it is probable that this method has now been lost due to the Law of Property (Miscellaneous Provisions) Act 1989, s 2 (though similar facts may give rise to proprietary estoppel).

However, as we saw earlier in *White* v *Richards* (where the Court of Appeal held that the nature and extent of a right of way reserved in a conveyance must be ascertained from the words of the reservation read in the light of the surrounding circumstances, which included the width and physical characteristics of the track in question), even apparently well drafted express grants can cause difficulties.

IDC Group Ltd v *Clark* (1992) 08 EG 108

This case, which concerned a fire escape route between adjoining properties, provides another example. The right of way, through a doorway in a party wall, had been created by deed. The doorway had subsequently been blocked up. The successors in title to the original grantee sought a mandatory injunction, claiming an express easement which was binding on the defendant, the successor in title of the grantor. However, the court found that the words of grant in the deed were not sufficient to create an easement: notwithstanding it had been drafted by professionals, the right was described as a licence. The court held that words of grant must be used to create a legal easement.

We shall see shortly that it is imperative to use specific words for a successful express reservation, but *Clark* shows that this is equally true of express grants.

> The grant of an easement is also the grant of such ancillary rights as are reasonably necessary to its exercise or enjoyment. Where the use of a thing is granted, everything is granted by which the grantee may have and enjoy such use. The ancillary right arises because it is necessary for the enjoyment of the right expressly granted – Gale (1972, p 44).

Thus, in *Central Electricity Generating Board* v *Jennaway* [1959] 1 WLR 937, where the Board had statutory powers to place electric lines over J's land, a right also to place towers on J's land to support the lines was upheld. As we saw earlier, this point often arises in connection with repairs.

It must be understood that a merely friendly agreement between neighbours will not give rise to an easement, though in *Thatcher* v *Douglas* [1996] NLJ 1 an oral grant was upheld (it predated the Law of Property (Miscellaneous Provisions) Act 1989, s 2).

By reservation

Whether an easement (or profit *à prendre*) has been granted or reserved depends upon who gains the benefit.

> ## Example
>
> If V, the owner of Blackacre and Whiteacre, sells Whiteacre to P, whether there is a grant or a reservation will depend upon whether V wishes to retain, that is reserve for himself, a right of way over Whiteacre, or grant to P a right of way over Blackacre. The reservation of an easement by V over land which he has now sold to P is 'a derogation from grant' - granting P the fee simple, but holding back some interest in the land.

The courts do not look kindly upon derogations. Because of this attitude, an express reservation must be in the clearest possible terms (see *White* v *Richards*). As Morritt LJ explained in *Mills* v *Blackwell* (1999) 78 P&CR D43, a reservation has to be construed in the context of the deed as a whole and in the light of surrounding circumstances 'as they existed at the time of the execution of the deed, not confined to, but principally, the physical layout'.

The Court of Appeal held in *Partridge* v *Lawrence* [2004] 1 P&CR 14 that, in construing the terms of an express reservation, the deed had to be construed against the background knowledge which would have been available to the parties and, to that extent, extrinsic evidence as to what is the background is always admissible.

Implied easements

By reservation

Given the courts' attitude to the reservation of easements, it is not surprising that the general rule is that there can be no implied reservation of easements. However, there are always exceptions, and in this instance there are two – necessity and common intention. It must be clearly understood, though, that these are the only exceptions – any other methods of implied acquisition apply to grants only.

Peckham v *Ellison* [1998] EGCS 174

Here the Court of Appeal confirmed the traditional position, but on the special facts of the case held that an easement could be implied on the basis of common intention, following *Re Webb's Lease* [1951] Ch 808. The special facts of *Peckham* were that the 'servient owner' believed the claimed right already existed; that 'the right' had been exercised for more than 30 years; the existence of the claimed path had been disclosed in pre-contract enquiries; that the 'dominant owner' had continued to use the path for 10 months after the purchase of the 'servient tenement' by its new owners; that the original owners of the houses (the local council) had mistakenly omitted to deal properly with the right of way when conveying the properties; and the existence of a 'minor' path to the other property.

(a) Necessity. Cases of necessity are **very rare**. They only arise where a vendor has retained land which is totally surrounded by the land which he has sold, so that he has 'landlocked' himself completely. In other words, he has no access to his retained land. '"Necessity" is, therefore, not the same as "necessary". If there is **any** means of access to the retained land, no matter how distant or inconvenient, there can be no necessity' – Stirling LJ in *Union Lighterage Co* v *London Graving Dock Co* [1902] 2 Ch

557. This was also shown by the Privy Council in *Manjang* v *Drammeh* (1991) 61 P&CR 194, where it held that as there was an available access to land by water, namely the River Gambia, though it was many miles away, there could be no right to an easier or more convenient route by necessity. Therefore, an easement for the use of a neighbour's toilet is not an easement of necessity!

Stirling LJ, in *Union Lighterage Co* v *London Graving Dock Co*, explained that 'an easement of necessity . . . means an easement without which the property retained cannot be used at all and not one merely necessary to the reasonable enjoyment of that property'. Therefore, 'necessity' must always be distinguished from 'necessary': more about this when we come to the rule in *Wheeldon* v *Burrows*.

It was held in *Hillman* v *Rodgers*, 19 December 1997 (unreported) by the Court of Appeal that it is possible to exclude easements of necessity by a contrary intention, but only very clear words will do, and in *Holaw (470) Ltd* v *Stockton Estates Ltd* [2000] EGCS 89, Neuberger J, applying *Re Webb's Lease* [1951] Ch 808, held that, in the absence of a valid claim to an easement of necessity, the reservation of an easement would not normally be implied. A rare exception could be made where it is shown that the facts were not reasonably consistent with any explanation other than an intention to reserve the right contended for. See *Peckham* v *Ellison* [1998] EGCS 174. The facts of the present case were not comparable with the exceptional circumstances found in *Peckham*, and *Re Webb's Lease* was followed.

In *Sweet* v *Sommer* [2004] EWHC 1504 (Ch), Hart J had to consider a dispute concerning a right of way and whether a plot of land which had been retained by T, the transferor, on transfer by him of the adjacent plot, could be regarded as landlocked, when it had been theoretically possible, at the time of the transfer, for T to gain access to his retained land by demolishing part of a workshop which formed the physical boundary between the retained land and a third plot owned by T. As Hart J said, 'There is no direct authority on the point of which I am aware'. However, while the doctrine of implied reservation of necessity

> may not rest at all firmly on the presumed intentions of the parties, or on their actual intentions, [it] must be sensitive to physical as well as legal facts existing at the date of the relevant grant. Where access to the property retained is only available either over the property granted or by destruction of a physical barrier the continued existence of which was obviously contemplated by the parties, it is consistent with the doctrine (and not contradicted by authority) to say that a way over the property is impliedly reserved as a matter of necessity.

The case went to appeal – [2005] 2 All ER 64 – and it may yet go to the House of Lords. In an excellent commentary on the case – 'Land Registration, Easements and Overriding Interests' [2005] Conv 545 – the Precedents Editor rightly describes this case as 'an argument that should never have found its way into court, let alone the Court of Appeal . . . [concerning] a "classic neighbour dispute, involving certain rights of way arising from defective conveyancing and one which, in all probability, has brought nothing but grief to the litigants, even the victors". With errors in conveyancing and (at both first instance and on appeal) in regard to registration, it is an interesting and instructive case.'

(b) Common intention. Again, cases of common intention are rare, but the reservation of an easement may be implied into a conveyance in order to give effect to

some common, though unexpressed, intention of the parties. 'The law will readily imply the grant or reservation of such easements as may be necessary to give effect to the common intention of the parties to a grant of real property, with reference to the manner or purposes in and for which the land granted ... is to be used' – Lord Parker of Waddington in *Pwllbach Colliery Co Ltd* v *Woodman* [1915] AC 634. However, his Lordship went on to stress that the intended manner of user must be definite and particular; it is not enough that the land 'should be intended to be used in a manner which may or may not involve this definite and particular use'.

The burden of proof, which is very heavy, lies with the vendor, because he is, of course, the one who is seeking to reserve the benefit. Easements of support are the most common example, for instance between adjoining houses.

Stafford v *Lee* (1992) The Times, 16 November

It was held here that the common intention could be proved 'on the balance of probabilities'. We saw earlier that this case concerned an area of woodland, granted by deed of gift, but making no mention of any right of way over Marley Drive, which it fronted. When Mr and Mrs Stafford, the current owners of the woodland, obtained planning permission to build a house on it the owners of Marley Drive objected, arguing that any right of way which existed did not extend to use by construction lorries and would not extend to occupiers of the house when it was built. Nourse LJ stated that common intention depended on the parties having intended that the land 'should be used in some definite and particular manner' and that the grantee must, therefore, 'show a common intention as to some definite and particular use'. In addition, he must show 'that the easements he claims are necessary to give effect to it'. Although the defendants felt that any right was limited to use for purposes necessary for reasonable enjoyment of the land as woodland, the court held it was not a question of how the land was used at the date of grant, but whether the parties had at that time intended that it should be used in some definite and particular manner and, if so, what: the answer to be arrived at on the balance of probabilities. By reference to the plan in the conveyance of the woodland it was held that the parties could only have intended that a dwelling for residential use would be constructed and the easement would be so limited. This case shows the importance not only of good drafting, but also of accurate plans.

The Court of Appeal, in *Chaffe* v *Kingsley* (2000) 79 P&CR 404, held that where it was clearly established that the circumstances of any particular case raised a necessary inference that the common intention of the parties must have been to reserve some easement to the grantor, or such as to preclude the grantee from denying the right consistently with good faith, the court would imply the appropriate reservation. However, the 'appropriate reservation' must be that which the parties intended to be reserved. Only a common intention to reserve a right specific as to its precise nature and extent could found a case for an implied reservation. On the facts, this was not so.

Easements other than reservations may be implied in one of three ways: by way of grant, by statute or under the rule in *Wheeldon* v *Burrows*.

By grant

(a) Necessity. In cases of grant it is, of course, the purchaser who needs the easement in order to reach land which he has purchased but which is totally surrounded by land retained by his vendor. Here the courts are much more willing to imply a grant of an easement and, ironically, for exactly the same reason that they are unwilling to imply a reservation – derogation from grant. Whereas with reservation the vendor is attempting to keep something back for himself, by not granting the right of way to his purchaser he is depriving him of access to the land. (However, note *Hillman* v *Rodgers*, above.)

The Court of Appeal in *Nickerson* v *Barraclough* [1981] 2 WLR 773 held that a right of necessity can only arise upon the grant – that is, sale – of land. It has also been held that it cannot arise where the land only became landlocked upon a subsequent grant but was not locked at the date of the conveyance in question – *Midland Railway Co* v *Miles* (1886) 33 Ch D 632. In *Corporation of London* v *Riggs* (1880) 13 Ch D 798, Lord Jessel MR had to consider:

> whether, on a grant of land wholly surrounding a close, the implied grant, or re-grant, of a right of way by the grantee to the grantor to enable him to get to the reserved, or excepted, or inclosed close, is a grant of a general right of way for all purposes, or only a grant of a right of way for the purpose of the enjoyment of the reserved or excepted close in its then state.

He held that the extent of a reserved right of necessity:

> must be limited to that which is necessary at the time of grant,

admitting, in so doing, that:

> I am afraid . . . laying down the law for the first time – that I am for the first time declaring the law; but it is a matter of necessity from which I cannot escape[!]

Necessity is limited to cases where the land has become landlocked following the grant of the surrounding land. However, land may become landlocked in other ways. *Crabb* v *Arun DC* [1976] Ch 179 provides an example. In that case there had been between the parties an 'agreement in principle' under which Crabb was to have a right of access to and egress over adjacent land belonging to the Council. In reliance upon this agreement, Crabb had landlocked himself. He was held to have acquired an equity by way of estoppel.

As we have already seen, an easement of necessity is strictly limited in extent to the circumstances which gave rise to it.

(b) Common intention. According to Megarry VC in *Nickerson* v *Barraclough*, 'a way of necessity' should be 'more accurately referred to as a way implied from the common intention of the parties, based on a necessity apparent from the deeds', and, in fact, an implied grant of an easement to give effect to the common intention of the parties will usually only arise in cases of necessity.

Wong v Beaumont Property Trust Ltd [1965] 1 QB 173

In an assignment of a lease of premises which were intended to be used as a Chinese restaurant, the assignee covenanted to eliminate all noxious smells and odours and to comply with public health regulations. Unbeknownst to the parties at the date of the assignment, it would be necessary for a new ventilation system to be installed if the assignee were to be able to comply with the covenant and the regulations. Such a system would have to lead into the premises belonging to the landlord. The Court of Appeal held that, as the assignee could not comply with the terms of the lease, nor with the public health regulations, without the ventilation duct, an easement of necessity would be implied to give effect to the common intention of the parties, namely that the assignee run a Chinese restaurant.

By statute

The relevant statutory provision here is the Law of Property Act 1925, s 62(1), which provides that every conveyance of land:

> shall be deemed to include and shall by virtue of this Act operate to convey, with the land, all buildings, erections, fixtures, commons, hedges, ditches, fences, ways, waters, watercourses, liberties, privileges, easements, rights, and advantages whatsoever, appertaining or reputed to appertain to the land, or any part thereof, or, at the time of conveyance, demised, occupied, or enjoyed with or reputed or known as part or parcel of or appurtenant to the land or any part thereof ...

The effect of s 62 is, therefore, that unless express provision to the contrary is made in the conveyance, the conveyance will pass not only the legal estate but also the benefit of any existing easements automatically. However, for s 62 to apply certain requirements must be satisfied:

(a) Diversity of ownership or occupation.

> ... it is difficult to see how, when there is a common ownership of both [tenements], there can be any such relationship between the two [tenements] as (apart from the case of continuous and apparent easements or that of a way of necessity) would be necessary to create a 'privilege, easement, right or advantage within the words of [s 62] ... For this purpose, it would seem that there must be some diversity of ownership or occupation of the two [tenements] sufficient to refer the act or acts relied on not to mere occupying ownership, but to some advantage or privilege (however far short of a legal right) attaching to the owner or occupier of [one tenement] as such and de facto exercised over [the other] – Sargant J in *Long* v *Gowlett* [1923] 2 Ch 177.

Sovmots Investments Ltd v *Secretary of State for the Environment* [1979] AC 144

There must, then, have been some 'diversity of ownership or occupation of the quasi-dominant and servient tenements prior to the conveyance' – Lord Edmund-Davies. Therefore, there must be no 'unity of seisin' immediately prior to the conveyance: the two properties must have been owned or occupied by different persons. As Lord Wilberforce stated in *Sovmots*:

> – when land is under one ownership, one cannot speak in any intelligible sense of rights, or privileges, or easements being exercised over one part for the benefit of another. Whatever the owner does, he does as owner and, until a separation occurs, of ownership or at least of occupation, the condition for the existence of rights, etc does not exist.

Sovmots was adopted as the authority on this point (though it was not universally accepted, see eg P Smith in [1978] Conv 449 at 454–5), but the point has now been revisited by the Court of Appeal in *P & S Platt* v *Crouch* [2004] 1 P&CR 18, and it may well set the cat among the pigeons, for their Lordships held that the benefit of an easement could pass under s 62 – even though there was unity of seisin, ie no diversity of ownership or occupation, immediately prior to the conveyance! Peter Gibson LJ explained that,

> ... the rights in question did appertain to and were reputed to appertain to and were enjoyed with [the land in question]... The rights were continuous and apparent, and so it matters not that prior to the sale of the hotel there was no prior diversity of occupation of the dominant and servient tenements ... Accordingly s 62 operated to convert the rights into full easements ... – p 254.

This reopens *Sovmots*, and should lead to some lively academic debate – we shall, of course, have to wait and see how the courts react.

(b) There must be a deed of conveyance. Section 62 is a word-saving provision and there must, therefore, be a deed out of which to save them! Thus, notwithstanding that a lease for less than three years can be legal even if created orally, it cannot activate s 62 unless by deed. Similarly, a contract for a lease cannot give the tenant the benefit of s 62 – and this is one of the reasons why an equitable lease is not as good as a legal lease. See *Borman* v *Griffith* [1930] 1 Ch 493.

(c) The right must be capable of being an easement. Because s 62 implies 'all ... easements, rights and advantages whatsoever', it can have the magical effect of transforming a mere licence into an easement. However, the right **must be capable of being an easement** – it must, therefore, comply with all the requirements of *Re Ellenborough Park*. Section 62 cannot turn into an easement something which is not capable of being one.

> ### Example
> Say, Linda, the fee simple owner of a house and a lodge cottage, allows Brian, the tenant of the cottage, to cross over her garden in order to reach the cottage more easily. This would be a mere licence. However, if Linda renews Brian's lease, the licence will become an easement by operation of s 62 – provided, of course, that the lease was by deed. As this example shows, the deed must be between the parties to the licence.

The magic of s 62 was held to have turned a licence into an easement in *Hain* v *Gillman & Inskip* (2000) 80 P&CR 108. The Court of Appeal held that notwithstanding that the permission was not itself an easement or the grant of an easement; that it was never made with the necessary formality to satisfy the Law of Property Act; that it could not take effect in equity under an enforceable agreement (rule in *Walsh* v *Lonsdale)* because there was no consideration, and that the permission was at all times precarious in that it could be withdrawn at any time (being a bare licence), it had been converted into a legal easement on the conveyance of the legal estate to the person enjoying the permission.

> **Example**
>
> If on the other hand, L frequently allows N to cross over Blackacre in order to visit his friend on Blueacre, this could not be an easement. It is a purely personal advantage to N. It does not accommodate the dominant land. It can only be a bare licence.

(It must be understood that 'allowing' someone to do something on your land does not give him an easement, even if the right satisfies *Re Ellenborough Park*. There must be an intention to grant an interest in the land, not merely to allow someone a privilege over it.)

Section 62 cannot, however, have the effect of granting an easement over someone else's land,

> **Example**
>
> If Brian had owned a cottage next door to Linda's, and she had allowed him to cross over her garden as a short cut to the village, if Brian later sold his cottage, that conveyance would not imply an easement over Linda's land in favour of Brian's purchaser.

Section 62 operates to pass the benefit, not the burden!

Nor can s 62 operate to create new rights where there has been no actual enjoyment by the owner of the dominant tenement over the servient tenement. There must be a pre-existing right which can, by a combination of the conveyance and s 62, be turned into an easement. Needless to say, the right claimed must satisfy the requirements of *Re Ellenborough Park* if it is to become an easement (see *Payne v Inwood* (1996) 74 P&CR 42). As the Court of Appeal explained in *Nickerson v Barraclough* [1981] 2 WLR 773, s 62 is not concerned with the future, but only with an advantage that could properly be regarded as appertaining to the land granted **at the time of grant**. In *Mulvaney v Gough* [2002] EWCA Civ 1078, it was pointed out, in regard to the need under *Ellenborough Park* for the right to be capable of forming the subject matter of a grant, that 'the court has the more difficult task of assessing the evidence as to alleged use in order to determine whether the claimed right has been established' in claims under s 62 and prescription than in cases of express grant, where 'the issue is simply one of construction of the grant' – Latham LJ.

Section 62 applies only 'if and so far as a contrary intention is not expressed in the conveyance' – s 62(4). It was held in *Hansford v Jago* [1921] 1 Ch 322 that the inclusion of an express grant in a conveyance did not amount to an expressed contrary intention for the purposes of s 62(4).

An easement acquired by virtue of s 62 is legal.

The rule in *Wheeldon v Burrows*

Though narrower in scope than s 62, the rule in *Wheeldon v Burrows* (1879) 12 Ch D 31 may enable a purchaser to acquire an easement where s 62 does not apply. For example, the rule only applies where there is unity of seisin, that is, where the same person, immediately prior to the conveyance, owned or occupied both pieces of land, a situation in which s 62 cannot apply. The rule is another application of the principle that a vendor or grantor may not derogate from his grant, in that: 'He cannot grant or agree to grant land and at the same time deny to the grantee what is at the time of the grant obviously necessary for its reasonable enjoyment' – Lord Wilberforce in *Sovmots Investments Ltd*.

Thesiger LJ, in *Wheeldon* v *Burrows*, stated the rule to be:

> On the grant by the owner of a tenement of part of that tenement as it is then used and enjoyed, there will pass to the grantee all those continuous and apparent easements (by which, of course, I mean *quasi* easements), or, in other words, all those easements which are necessary to the reasonable enjoyment of the property granted, and which have been and are at the time of the grant used by the owners of the entirety for the benefit of the part granted.

As pointed out by Cheshire and Burn (*Modern Law of Real Property*, 2000, p 592): 'The two words "continuous" and "apparent" must be read together and understood as pointing to an easement which is accompanied by some obvious and permanent mark on the land itself, or at least by some mark which will be disclosed by a careful inspection of the premises'. Whether or not the right must be 'continuous and apparent' and 'necessary to the reasonable enjoyment of the property granted' is uncertain, but from Thesiger J's words it would seem that they are alternatives, and Ungoed-Thomas J, addressing the point in *Ward* v *Kirkland* [1967] Ch 194, said:

> Reading that passage on its own, on first impression, it would appear that the 'easements which are necessary to the reasonable enjoyment of the property conveyed' might be a separate class from 'continuous and apparent easements' . . . It has been suggested that perhaps the 'easements necessary to the reasonable enjoyment of the property conveyed' might refer to negative easements . . . I understand that there is no case in which positive easements which are not 'continuous and apparent' have been held to come within the doctrine of *Wheeldon* v *Burrows*.

'Necessary to the reasonable enjoyment' is nowhere near as strict a requirement as necessity, but what is certain is that there must be an element of user of the claimed right right up to the date of the grant – *Ward* v *Kirkland*.

Wheeler v *J J Saunders Ltd* [1995] 2 All ER 97

This case concerned a farmhouse, owned by the Wheelers, on land adjacent to a pig farm owned by the defendant company. Both properties had previously been owned by one person. There were two means of access to the Wheelers' property, one of which could only be reached by crossing the defendants' land. There was no express grant of a right of way over their land, and the defendants blocked it off by building a wall. The Wheelers claimed an easement of necessity, but the Court of Appeal held that as the blocked entrance to their property was not the only one, there could be no necessity. At first instance the judge had held that the Wheelers obtained a right of way under the rule in *Wheeldon* v *Burrows*, but the Court of Appeal held that the blocked entrance was not necessary for the reasonable enjoyment of the land, since the alternative entrance would do just as well.

As to whether the right must be continuous and apparent and necessary for the reasonable enjoyment of the land, Peter Gibson LJ stated:

> to my mind it is tolerably clear from Thesiger LJ's introduction of the test of necessity by the words 'or, in other words' that he was treating the first requirement as synonymous with the second. It is plain that the test of what is necessary for the reasonable enjoyment of land is not the same as the test for a way of necessity.

An easement of necessity is a right without which the dominant land cannot be enjoyed at all. Under *Wheeldon* v *Burrows* the test is whether or not reasonable or convenient enjoyment of the land can only be had with the easement (see *Goldberg* v *Edwards* [1950] Ch 247).

In *Sovmots Investments Ltd* v *Secretary of State* for the Environment Lord Wilberforce explained that:

> The rule is a rule of intention, based on the proposition that a man may not derogate from his grant. He cannot grant or agree to grant land and at the same time deny to his grantee what is at the time of the grant obviously necessary for its reasonable enjoyment. Morever . . . for the rule to apply there must be actual and apparent use and enjoyment at the time of the grant.

The rule in *Wheeldon* v *Burrows* is not limited to situations where the owner of two quasi-tenements conveys one to someone else.

Schwann v Cotton [1916] 2 Ch 120

It was held here that the rule also applies where the owner of land, instead of selling only one part of it and retaining the rest for himself, makes several simultaneous sales or grants to different persons by way of contemporaneous conveyances, retaining none of the land for himself. All grantees of the common vendor acquire all the quasi-easements which satisfy the requirements of the rule. In *Schwann* v *Cotton*, a testator, the owner of Blackacre and Whiteacre, devised Blackacre to X and Whiteacre to Y. It was held that a right of free passage of water that flowed across Blackacre to Whiteacre through an underground pipe passed by implication to Y. (However, the rule can only be applied in this way where all the sales or grants are made at the same time by the common owner.)

Wheeldon v Burrows	LPA 1925, s 62
Unity of seisin immediately before grant	Diversity of ownership or occupation immediately before grant
The right must be continuous, apparent from careful inspection of the servient tenement and necessary for *the reasonable enjoyment* of the dominant tenement	The right must be potentially a proprietary right and capable of being classified as an easement under *Re Ellenborough Park*
The right must have been enjoyed by the servient owner right up to the date of grant and must not be inconsistent with any intention of the parties to be inferred from the circumstances	There must be a conveyence in which there is no contrary intention
Applies to grants only	Applies to grants only
Passes the benefit	Passes the benefit
Creates a legal easement	Creates a legal easement
Applies to easements only	Applies to all 'privileges, easements, rights, and advantages whatsoever, appertaining or reputed to appertain to the land, or any part thereof, at the time of the conveyance'. Therefore, profits *à prendre* can pass too.

Once acquired by virtue of the rule, the easement shares the legal nature of the estate granted.

Whereas s 62 can only operate by virtue of a conveyance of a legal estate, the rule in *Wheeldon* v *Burrows* can also operate upon grants in equity – *Borman* v *Griffith*.

It was held in *Millman* v *Ellis* (1996) 71 P&CR 158, that even if there is an express grant of an easement, a more extensive right can be acquired under the rule in *Wheeldon* v *Burrows*. On the facts, however, the claimant could not show that the use of the additional land was necessary for the reasonable enjoyment of the dominant land, even though this meant that his property could be approached with safety from one direction only due to a concealed entrance. The Court of Appeal, in 1997, in *Hillman* v *Rodgers* (1997) (unreported) confirmed *Millman*.

The rule in *Wheeldon* v *Burrows* only operates to the extent that it is not inconsistent with any intention of the parties which might be inferred from the circumstances – see *Selby District Council* v *Samuel Smith Old Brewery (Tadcaster)* (2000) 80 P&CR 466, CA.

Finally, the rule has no application on a conveyance by a landlord to his tenant of the freehold so as to convert into an easement a right enjoyed by that tenant over the land of *another* tenant (unless there was evidence that the landlord had consented to the exercise of that right, or that the right was being exercised at the time when the relevant transfer was made) – *Kent* v *Kavanagh* [2000] 2 All ER 645.

An easement acquired under the rule is legal.

Presumed easements

Presumed easements, also known as prescriptive easements, are often referred to as 'easements of long user' because:

> [t]he basis of prescription is that if long enjoyment of a lawful right is shown, the court will uphold the right by presuming that it had a lawful origin, ie that there once was an actual grant of the right, even though it is impossible to produce any evidence of such a grant. However, it is not enough to show long user by itself; user of a particular kind is required. There are three types of prescription, namely, prescription at common law, prescription under the doctrine of lost modern grant, and prescription under the Prescription Act 1832 – Megarry (2002, p 430).

All three types operate on grants in fee simple only, and in practice all three are claimed. Therefore, an easement for life or for a term of years cannot be prescriptive. Although a tenant can claim an easement on behalf of his landlord if he is the fee simple owner, one tenant cannot claim an easement by prescription against another tenant of the same landlord. *Simmons* v *Dobson* [1991] 4 All ER 25 provides an illustration of this. The freeholder of two adjoining properties leased both to separate tenants. One tenant blocked a passageway on his land, which prevented the other tenant, the plaintiff, from reaching the road from the rear of his garden. He claimed a right of way over the passage, but failed on this ground.

With the exception of s 3, the Prescription Act 1832 is only supplementary to the common-law rules; it does not supplant them, so that if a claim under the Act fails, one can be made either at common law or under the doctrine of lost modern grant. It is usual for claimants to make their claims in that order of preference but, as a plaintiff can succeed on one ground only, it is always advisable to plead the three as alternative claims. However, failure in one can often mean failure in all, as in *Simmons* v *Dobson* where it was held that as prescription was not available at either common law or under the Prescription Act 1832, the doctrine of lost modern grant was not applicable.

Though a claimant will begin with the Act, it is easier for us to begin with the common law because, unless the Act provides otherwise, the following requirements must be satisfied.

(a) User must be as of right. This means that the claimed easement must have been enjoyed without force, without secrecy and without permission – *nec vi, nec clam, nec precario*. In other words, the claimant, that is, the dominant tenement owner, must have used the right he is claiming as an owner, as if he were entitled to do so 'as of right'. Therefore, there must be no permission, for that would be use by permission and not as of right.

'Without force' is not limited only to physical force, but includes continued user in the face of clear and continuous protests by the servient owner.

'Without secrecy' means that the servient owner must be in a position to protest against the dominant owner's user. Therefore, the servient owner must know of the dominant owner's activities and this incorporates a requirement of some acquiescence on the part of the servient owner. Indeed:

> the whole law of prescription and the whole law which governs the presumption or inference of a grant or covenant rests upon acquiescence ... I cannot imagine any case of acquiescence in which there is not shown to be in the servient owner:
>
> (1) a knowledge of the acts done;
> (2) a power in him to stop the acts or to sue in respect of them; and
> (3) an abstinence on his part from the exercise of such power – Fry J in *Dalton* v *Angus* (1881) 6 App Cas 740.

Thus, '[t]he whole of prescription rests upon acquiescence; and mere toleration is enough' Megarry, (2002, p 431). Thesiger LJ in *Sturgess* v *Bridgman* (1879) 11 Ch D 852 provided the following explanation:

> ... the laws governing the acquisition of easements by user stands thus: consent or acquiescence of the owner of the servient tenement lies at the root of prescription, and of the fiction of the lost modern grant, and hence the acts or user, which go to the proof of either the one or the other, must be ... *nec vi, nec clam, nec precario*; for a man cannot, as a general rule, be said to consent to or acquiesce in the acquisition by his neighbour of an easement through an enjoyment of which he has no knowledge, actual or constructive, or which he contests and endeavours to interrupt, or which he temporarily licenses.

However, *Diment* v *NH Foot Ltd* [1974] 2 All ER 785 shows that knowledge of the servient owner is essential. Because the plaintiff, the claimed servient owner, had no knowledge or means of knowledge, either by herself or through her agents, of the user of a right of way over one of her fields, the defendant's claim to a prescriptive easement failed. See *Mills* v *Silver* [1991] 1 All ER 449 – an excellent case on all aspects of prescription.

'Without permission' is self-explanatory. However, user which originated by permission was held in *Healey* v *Hawkins* [1968] 1 WLR 1967 to have become prescriptive after the term to which the permission related came to an end. (Had the servient owner demanded even a nominal annual payment, this would have evidenced a continuation of reliance by the dominant owner on the original consent.) If the dominant owner asks the servient owner for permission, such request will defeat user as of right as it acknowledges that no right exists. It must be noted that if at any time the claimant was in possession of both the dominant and the servient tenements, he could not, during such joint possession, have exercised user 'as of right'.

A mistaken belief that the claimant was entitled to the servient tenement does not amount to user as of right, though the mistaken belief that an easement had been legally acquired was held not to prevent user being as of right in *Bridle* v *Ruby* [1988] 3 All ER 64.

(b) User must be continuous. This requirement is in addition to the user being as of right. To satisfy it a claimant must show a continuity of enjoyment, though this need not necessarily have been exercised by himself alone, as exercise of the right by successive owners of the fee simple estate in the dominant tenement can also be relied upon.

'Continuous' does not mean incessant, so that it is not necessary to use a right of way 24 hours a day for the entirety of the relevant period! It is usually sufficient to show that user was exercised whenever circumstances required it, but there must not be any excessive intervals of non-user. Thus, a claim to a right to go on to land to remove cut timber once every 12 years failed in *Hollins* v *Verney* (1884) 13 QBD 304. However, if user is varied by agreement between the parties, continuity is not broken – *Davis* v *Whitby* [1974] Ch 186.

We now need to look at the three types of prescription.

Prescription at common law

At common law user has to be continuous since time immemorial, that is, since 1189. As this is virtually impossible to prove the courts came to accept 20 years' user or more, presuming that such user had been continuous since 1189. However, proof that it could not have been so would rebut the presumption. This happened in *Bryant* v *Foot* (1867) LR 2 QB 161 where a rector tried to establish a claim to a fee of 13 shillings (65p), based on long user, for marriages performed in his parish church. User since 1808 was proved, but not for any time earlier than that. It was held that the fee of 13 shillings could not have been so high in 1189 and therefore the right could not possibly have existed since time immemorial.

A claim would also fail if it could be shown that at any time since 1189 the dominant and servient tenements had been owned or occupied by the same person, as in *Hulbert* v *Dale* [1909] 2 Ch 570, where, for a period of six years, the same person occupied both the dominant and servient tenements, thus defeating a claim to a right of way since 1804.

In *Duke of Norfolk* v *Arbuthnot* (1880) 5 CPD 390 a claim to prescription failed upon proof that the church in question had been built around 1380 and therefore, though the right had existed for centuries, it had not existed since 1189.

Lost modern grant

In an attempt to save claims such as that in the *Duke of Norfolk*'s case, the legal (or 'revolting' according to Lush J) fiction of the lost modern grant was created. This was based upon the presumption that an actual grant of the right had been made some time after 1189 but prior to the actual user, but that it had been lost. As Cockburn CJ explained in *Bryant* v *Foot* (1867) LR 2 QB 161:

> Juries were first told that from user, during living memory, or even during twenty years, they might presume a lost grant or deed; next they were recommended to make such presumption; and lastly. . . it was held that a jury should be told, not only that they might, but also that they were bound to presume the existence of such a lost grant, although neither judge nor jury nor anyone else, had the shadow of a belief that any such instrument had ever really existed.

In fact, it was held in *Dalton* v *Angus* (a case 'which in the course of its history enjoyed the attention of no less than 18 judges and members of the House of Lords, perhaps embodying a greater variety of judicial opinion than any other leading case' – Buckley LJ in *Tehidy Minerals Ltd* v *Norman* [1971] 2 QB 528) – that the legal fiction would be adopted 'where there has been upwards of 20 years' uninterrupted enjoyment of an easement, such enjoyment having the necessary qualities to fulfil the requirements of prescription, then unless, for some reason such as legal incapacity on the part of the person or persons who might at some time before the commencement of the 20-year period have made a grant, the existence of such a grant is impossible, the law will adopt a legal fiction that such a grant was made, in spite of any direct evidence that no such grant was in fact made'.

However, evidence that there was no person capable of making the grant would rebut the presumption, as in *Roberts* v *James* (1903) 89 LT 282 where land had been held by way of a strict settlement under which there was no power in the tenant for life to make a grant of an easement (prior to the Act) from the time when the use began to the time of the action. The presumption would also be rebutted by a grant made in contravention of a statute; but the presumption cannot be rebutted by evidence that no grant was ever made.

Evidence to raise the presumption must be stronger than that required for prescription at common law, and the fiction can only be relied upon if a claim fails at common law. However 'in virtually every case, the claim founded on prescription at common law . . . adds nothing to the claim of presumed lost grant; they stand or fall together' – Dillon LJ in *Mills & Another* v *Silver & Another* [1991] 1 All ER 449. Once a claim has succeeded by way of lost modern grant, subsequent cesser of user has no effect.

The subject matter of a presumed lost modern grant has to be a right capable of existing as an easement, that is a right to do or enjoy doing something, in relation to the grantee's land which affects the unfettered use of the grantor's land. A benefit which is an essential incident of the ownership of the land, without need for a grant by another landowner (here, the natural drainage of rainwater from higher land into ditches on lower ground), could not create a presumed lost modern grant – Court of Appeal in *Palmer* v *Bowman* [2000] 1 All ER 22.

The Prescription Act 1832

Thus, whilst the fiction of a lost modern grant could save a claim, it was not free from difficulties, not least of which was the problem of trying to persuade juries to make the presumption, especially where there was evidence to show that no grant had been made.

The Prescription Act, which has been nominated one of the worst drafted Acts on the statute books, was passed in order to remedy the situation: it was 'an Act for shortening the time of prescription in certain cases. And, really, it did nothing more' – Lord Macnaghten in *Gardner* v *Hodgson's Kingston Brewery Co Ltd* [1903] AC 229. As Thesiger J explained in *Sturges* v *Bridgman* (1879) 11 Ch D 852, the Act 'fixes periods for the acquisition of easements, but, except in regard to the particular easement of light . . . it does not alter the character of easements, or of the user or enjoyment by which they are acquired'. If we take first easements other than easements of light, no claim to an easement which could be lawfully made at common law shall be defeasible upon proof only that it commenced after 1189 if 20 years' uninterrupted enjoyment as of right is shown. However, it is defeasible in any other way unless it has been exercised for 40 years, after which time it becomes 'absolute and indefeasible' unless a deed or written agreement giving consent can be produced (which would, of course, mean it could not have been user as of right) – s 2 of the Act. However, user still has to be as of right, and even then,

> . . . no actual user can be sufficient to satisfy the statute, unless during the whole of the statutory term (whether acts of user be proved in each year or not) the user is enough at any rate to carry to the mind of a reasonable person who is in possession of the servient tenement, the fact that a continuous right to enjoyment is being asserted, and ought to be resisted if such right is not recognised, and if resistance to it is intended – Lindley LJ in *Hollins* v *Verney* (1884) 13 QBD 304.

The period laid down by the Prescription Act must be 'next before action', in other words, 'As to the claim under the 1832 Act, the period of 20 years to found a prescriptive right under the Act has to be the 20 years next before action brought – that is, up to the issue of the writ' – Dillon LJ in *Mills* v *Silver*. Therefore, the period must be calculated back from 'some suit or action wherein the claim or matter to which such right may relate shall have been or shall be brought into question . . .' – s 4. This means that, even though user has been enjoyed over, say, 80 years, unless the last 20 (at least) immediately before the action have been 'without interruption', the claim will fail. If both tenements have been owned or occupied by the same person for any time immediately before action, that too will defeat a claim, because the user would not have been user as an easement during the full period. However, it may be possible successfully to claim an easement under the Act after any period longer than 19 years and one day (though of no lesser period – the one day is crucial!) where there has been a recent interruption. Because the minimum period of 20 years has to be 'next before action' and without interruption, if the interruption originated 19 years and one day prior to the action (that is, the legal action taken to prove or establish the easement), the year's interruption would not be completed until one day after the 20 years had been clocked up. Of course, the 'dominant' owner would have no time to lose – if he did not make his claim on the last day of the year he would be too late – for on the next day the fatal period of one year's interruption would be complete. Thus, he has but one day only in which to make his claim.

In *Reilly* v *Orange* [1955] 2 QB 112, the defendant argued that the commencement of the action was itself an 'interruption' under s 4. However Jenkins LJ did not agree: 'The commencement of the suit or action . . . is clearly not an interruption within the meaning of s 4 but is the event marking the date down to which the requisite period of user must be shown. What must be shown is a full 20 years reckoned down to the date of action brought that must be an uninterrupted period'.

'Interruption' has a special meaning for the purposes of the Prescription Act. It was held in *Smith v Baxter* [1900] 2 Ch 138 that there must be some hostile obstruction – mere non-user will not suffice. Even where there is some hostile obstruction, such as a barbed wire fence erected across a right of way, it will still not amount to an interruption unless and until the claimant has acquiesced in the obstruction for one year after becoming aware of it and knowing who was responsible for it: '. . . interruptions not acquiesced in for at least a year are not to be counted as interruptions' – Jenkins LJ in *Reilly v Orange*. A complaint or protest against the interruption made by the dominant owner to the servient owner will usually be sufficient to negative acquiescence, provided it is communicated to the servient owner. The burden of proving that he has not acquiesced in the obstruction for more than a year rests with the dominant owner. Glidewell LJ stated in *Dance v Triplow* (1992) 64 P&CR 1 that:

> if the interruption has in fact lasted for more than a year, the onus is on the plaintiff to prove that he did not submit to or acquiesce in it . . . in my view the difference between acquiescence and submission is that a person acquiesces where he is eventually satisfied to submit to the interruption. Submission occurs when the plaintiff is not content to submit, but does not make his opposition to the interruption apparent directly. In other words, in order to disprove 'submission', a plaintiff must prove both unwillingness on his part to accept the interruption and some words or act by which his opposition is made clear to the person who is responsible for the interruption.

According to Birkett LJ in *Davies v Du Paver* [1952] 2 All ER 1991:

> Submission to, or acquiescence in, is a state of mind evidenced by the conduct of the parties, and . . . it was a question of fact for the judge to decide on all the facts of the case, and that it was not to be decided merely by saying that there was in fact a period of a year in which nothing was done, without considering all the surrounding circumstances . . . it is a question of fact whether these circumstances show a submission to, or acquiescence in, the interruption for one year, despite the fact that one year had admittedly gone by during which no outward protest was made or any other action taken. The fact that there was a complete year in which the plaintiff did nothing is some evidence that he had submitted to, or acquiesced in, the interruption: but the fact also that he protested most strongly up to August 1950, and then actually took proceedings in September 1951 is some evidence that he did not. It is a question of fact for the judge.

Thus, a protest can last for some time after it has been made, even for a year. As Morris LJ explained in the *Du Paver* case:

> The parties were breathing fury on each side of the newly painted fence. Could it be said that the challenging protests of the plaintiff must, as the August days passed, be deemed to have signified nothing, and that his former claims and assertions should be regarded as supplanted by submission and acquiescence? As time went by, it might well be that silence and inaction could be interpreted as submission or acquiescence. But the date when submission or acquiescence begins must be determined as a question of fact, having regard to all the circumstances.

Although an interruption of more than one year will defeat a claim under the Act, it will not necessarily prevent a claim by way of lost modern grant, however – see *Smith v Brudenell-Bruce* [2002] 2 P&CR 4.

As well as interruptions, certain deductions may defeat a claim. However, whereas an interruption means that the time will start to run afresh, a deduction allows any time before it to be added to any time after it which is still next before action.

> **Example**
>
> D enjoyed a right of way over S's land from 1930 until 1990 but in 1974 S built a wall across the way and D did nothing about it until 1976, these two years would amount to an interruption and then D would only have 16 years next before an action in 1992. However, had the two years been deducted, D would still have 60 years next before action - 44 before the deduction and 16 after.

Section 7 of the Prescription Act, which applies only to the shorter of the statutory periods, provides that deductions should be made for any period during which the servient owner was a minor, a tenant for life or a patient under the Mental Health Act 1983. Section 8, on the other hand, provides for deductions from the longer periods where the servient land has been held by a tenant for life or for a term of years greater than three. Here the servient owner must resist the claim within three years of the ending of the life interest or lease.

> **Example**
>
> If D started to use the footpath over S's land in 1930, but S leased the land to T from 1974 to 1978, D could still claim a prescriptive easement because he has 44 years before the lease and 14 years after it ends, that is, 58 years in all - more than sufficient for a claim to an absolute and indefeasible easement.

As we know, any permission will usually defeat a claim to prescription, because a right enjoyed by permission cannot be one enjoyed 'as of right'. However, Goff J in *Healey* v *Hawkins* (1968) 1 WLR 1967, whilst agreeing that, 'In principle ... once permission has been given the user must remain permissive and not be capable of ripening into a right', stated that under the provisions of the Prescription Act:

> where the permission is oral and the user has continued for 40 or 60 years, unless and until, having been given for a limited period only, it expires, or, being general, it is revoked, or there is a change in circumstances from which revocation may fairly be implied ... when the user has continued for 40 or 60 years a prior consent affords no answer, because it is excluded by the express terms of section 2 of the Prescription Act, but, even so, permission given during the period will defeat the claimant because it negatives user as of right.

This is because s 1 of the Act provides that '... when such right, profit, or benefit shall have been so taken and enjoyed as aforesaid for the full period ... the right shall be deemed absolute and indefeasible, unless it shall appear that the same was taken and enjoyed by some consent or, agreement expressly made or given for that purpose **by deed or writing** [my emphasis].

However, written permission given at the start of the statutory period will defeat either the 20- or 40-year period, but an oral permission will defeat only a claim for 20 years – s 2.

Continuity of user is not broken by an agreed variation in the user: *Davis* v *Whitby* [1974] Ch 186.

We have already seen that where an easement is acquired by prescription (as opposed to necessity), provided that its user and nature remain the same, there is no objection to an increase in that user (see, for example, *British Rail* v *Glass*).

Easements of light

As already stated, the Prescription Act treats easements of light differently from all other easements. Section 3 provides that:

> when the access and use of light to and for any dwellinghouse, workshop or other building shall have been actually enjoyed therewith for a full period of 20 years without interruption, the right thereto shall be deemed absolute and indefeasible ... unless it appears that the same was enjoyed by some consent or agreement expressly made or given for that purpose by deed or writing.

Thus, there is only one statutory period for light – 20 years. The Act requires only that the light be 'actually enjoyed': user as of right is not required, though written, but not oral, consent will defeat it, as will unity of possession of the dominant and servient tenements. As it is the 20 years' actual enjoyment of light by the dominant tenement which confers the right, there is no need to show user in fee simple; therefore one tenant can claim an easement of light under the Act against another tenant of the same landlord, or against the landlord himself. In *Paragon Finance plc* v *City of London Real Property Company Ltd* [2002] 1 P&CR 36, the inclusion in a lease of a clause permitting the landlord to infringe any rights which it had covenanted not to interrupt was construed as the granting to the tenant of the right to light attached to the buildings, and that was a consent within the meaning of s 3. Therefore, the tenant had no easement. Sections 7 and 8 do not apply to easements of light. However, the Act only affects the periods during which enjoyment of the light must be proved: it cannot increase the possible amount of light, which is the same as we saw earlier.

Easements acquired by prescription are legal.

Illegality and prescription

We have seen that s 62 cannot turn a right into an easement unless the right is capable of being an easement, but can prescription convert an illegal act into a right protected at law?

Hanning v Top Deck Travel Group Ltd (1993) NPC 73

The defendants, a bus company, repaired and maintained their vehicles at a farm, gaining access thereto and egress therefrom along a track crossing a common. Under the Law of Property Act 1925, s 193, persons driving vehicles across a common without lawful authority are liable on summary conviction to a fine: in other words, such an act is unlawful. The Court of Appeal held that whilst prescription had long validated acts which are contrary to the law of tort, this is a far cry from allowing acts which are contrary to public statute.

Thus, although a right which amounted to a private nuisance was upheld in *Pwllbach Colliery Co Ltd* v *Woodman* [1915] AC 634, acts which amount to a public nuisance will not be upheld – *Butterworth* v *West Riding Rivers Board* [1909] AC 45 and

Hanning. Note also that there will be no presumption of a lost modern grant where the grant would have been in contravention of a statute – *Hulley* v *Silversprings Bleaching & Dyeing Co* [1992] 2 Ch 268.

Bakewell Management Ltd v *Brandwood* [2004] 2 AC 519

The House of Lords revisited this issue and held that an easement over land could be acquired either by prescription or by the fiction of lost modern grant, if the easement could have been lawfully granted by the landowner, whether the use relied on in the acquisition was illegal in the sense of being 'criminal or tortious'. Public policy did not prevent tortious conduct from leading to the acquisition of property rights by long user – that was how prescription operated. Where the conduct in question was criminal, but criminal only because it was user of the land for which the landowner had given no lawful authority, not a criminal use of the land against which the public law set its face in all cases, there was no public policy reason to bar that acquisition. Thus *Hanning* was overruled. On the facts, as the easement could have been lawfully granted by the claimant, it was valid.

The Court of Appeal held in *Hayling* v *Harper* [2004] 1 P&CR 35 that driving a vehicle on a footpath without lawful authority is unlawful and an easement cannot be acquired by conduct which, at the time, is prohibited by statute (ie public law). However, on the facts, there had been over 20 years, user prior to the Act in question (the Road Traffic Act 1988), and thus the right of way had already been acquired under the doctrine of lost modern grant based on the period before the action had become illegal.

Access to Neighbouring Land Act 1992

Under this Act 'being good neighbours becomes good law' – Terence Shaw [1993] *Daily Telegraph*, 30 January. As the Press Notice of 28 January 1993 from the Lord Chancellor's Department explains:

The Act enables people who need access to their neighbour's land to get a court order authorising entry to do remedial work on their own land or property.

Under the present law a person who needs access to his neighbour's land cannot get it without the neighbour's permission. The Act seeks to remedy the problems that can be caused if the neighbour withholds agreement.

The Act will enable a person to obtain, on application to a county court, a right of access to neighbouring land for the purpose of carrying out certain types of repair and maintenance work to his own land and property if the neighbour has refused to give consent to the access. The Act does not apply to the construction of new buildings or improvements to existing buildings unless they are incidental to remedial work.

The Act does not apply if either the dominant or servient land is a highway. The Act came into force on 31 January 1993 and its provisions cannot be avoided, any such attempt being itself void.

The Act does not create an easement, of course, for it does not create an interest in land. However, it does provide for a licence. Thus, in the absence of an easement or ancillary right of repair or maintenance, and in the face of a neighbour's refusal to grant access, application can be made to the court for an order enabling the repair

PRESCRIPTION

COMMON LAW	LOST MODERN GRANT	PRESCRIPTION ACT 1832
Continuous user since 1189 (rebuttable presumption after 20 years)	Continuous user during living memory or for at least 20 years	Uninterrupted user during statutory periods next before action
User as of right: no permission, no force, no secrecy, no protest by servient owner	User as of right as for common law	User as of right as for common law except for easements of light (20 years' actual enjoyment without written permission or interruption)
Some element of acquiescence on part of servient owner	Some element of acquiescence on part of servient owner	Some element of acquiescence on part of servient owner (except for light)
User in fee simple: by a FS owner, against a FS owner	User in fee simple: by a FS owner, against a FS owner	User in fee simple, on behalf of a FS owner, not necessarily against a FS owner
Rebuttable on proof right could not have existed at 1189 or that both tenements owned by same person in 1189, etc	Rebuttable only on proof that there was no person legally capable of making the grant	Shorter periods not defeasible on proof did not go back to 1189. Longer period defeasible only by written permission. For light, only defeasible by written permission or unity of seisin during period.
Easements are legal	Easements are legal	Easements are legal

Figure 12.2

work to be carried out where it would be impossible so to do without gaining such access.

Any damage caused to the neighbour's land (or, indeed, building, for the dominant and servient land may be flats within a block) in the exercise of such an order must be made good, and the neighbour whose land is being made available must be indemnified against any loss or damage to his land caused by the entry upon it.

Under s 1(1):

A person –

(a) who, for the purpose of carrying out works to any land (the 'dominant land'), desires to enter upon any adjoining or adjacent land (the 'servient land'); and

(b) who needs, but does not have, the consent of some other person to that entry,

may make application to the court for an order . . . against that other person; but

(2) . . . the court shall make an access order, if and only if, it is satisfied –

(a) that the works are reasonably necessary for the preservation of the whole or any part of the dominant land; and

(b) that they cannot be carried out, or would be substantially more difficult to carry out, without entry upon the servient land;

and

(3) The court shall not make an access order in any case where it is satisfied that, were it to make such an order –

(a) the respondent or any other person would suffer interference with, or disturbance of, his use or enjoyment of the servient land; or

(b) the respondent, or any other person (whether of full age or capacity or not) in occupation of the whole or any part of the servient land, would suffer hardship,

to such a degree by reason of the entry . . . that it would be unreasonable to make the order.

Thus it is not merely the owner of the dominant land who can apply; his agent, for example his architect, surveyor or builder, could seek the order. (Obviously, if your neighbour is quite prepared to allow you access, you would not need an order! However, it is not always known who owns the servient land, but if this is the case, a search of the Index Map at HM Land Registry should clear up the problem. Of course, if the land is unregistered it will be more difficult to trace the owner.)

The applicant must identify the land to which he wishes to gain access, detail the work he wishes to carry out, state why such access is required, specify by reference to a plan the precise area to which access is required, state who will be carrying out the work, state the proposed dates on or period during which the work will be carried out, state the approximate duration of the works, and state what, if any, insurance provision has been made in regard to injury to persons or damage to property which may arise out of the proposed works.

Applications can be made to both County and High Court, but should be commenced in the County Court. The court is not bound to grant the order, but if it does, the person against whom it is sought must allow entry to the persons authorised by the order to carry out the specified works authorised thereby. Failure to comply with the order may render the servient owner liable to pay damages to anyone affected who applies to the court for relief, for example the contractor for loss of work.

Once granted, access orders should be entered on the title of the servient land as minor interests by way of notice or caution. They cannot be converted into an overriding interest, but the order is binding upon any successor in title of the servient owner. (Application for an order can be protected as a pending land action.)

Following exercise of the order, the servient land should be left as it was found.

Needless to say, application should only be made as a last resort – try to settle the matter amicably with your neighbour first!

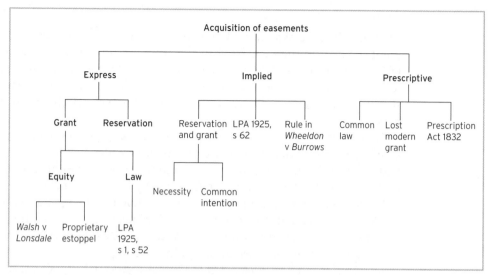

Figure 12.3

In *Dean* v *Walker* (1996) 73 P&CR 366, the neighbouring parties had been unable to agree over a right of access for the repair of a party wall. The appellant argued that he owned the wall, but even if it were held to be a party wall it would be deemed to be divided vertically (by virtue of the Law of Property Act 1925, s 38), which would mean that the respondent was seeking an order to repair the appellant's land! The Court of Appeal held that 'land' for the purposes of the Access to Neighbouring Land Act 1992 was as defined in the Interpretation Act 1978 and was, therefore, wide enough to include a party wall deemed to be divided vertically.

Under the Party Wall, etc Act 1996, where there is no party wall between properties, either landowner may serve upon the other notice of intention to build one – s 1. If the adjoining owner agrees, the wall is built on the boundary and expenses are shared in proportion to use. If there is no such agreement, the wall must be built upon the landowner's own land at his own expense, but he may have the foundations or footings of the wall projecting onto the adjoining property. If there is already a party wall, a landowner may demolish and rebuild, strengthen or underpin it, even if it is a dividing wall of a building – s 2. He must give the adjoining owner two months' notice, safeguard the adjoining land and, if necessary, pay compensation.

When and for how long?

Duration of easements

While time can be crucial to the acquisition of an easement by way of prescription, it can also mark the limit of an easement's existence, for an easement created for a specified term will end on the designated date. Likewise, an (equitable) easement for life will terminate upon the relevant death.

Extinguishment

Additionally, an easement will be extinguished if the dominant and servient tenements come into the ownership of the same person, for there can be no easement
where there is unity of seisin, unless, of course, the tenements are occupied by different persons. The acquisition by the servient owner of a lease will merely
suspend, rather than extinguish, the easement, which will revive at the end of the
lease.

Easements can also be extinguished by statute, particularly under the Town and
Country Planning Act 1971, s 127(1), which provides that all private rights of way
and rights of laying down, erecting, continuing or maintaining any apparatus on,
under or over the land can be extinguished by local authorities.

If the dominant tenement becomes so altered as to substantially increase the
burden of the servient tenement, to the detriment of its owner, the easement may
be extinguished – see *Attwood* v *Bovis Homes Ltd* [2000]4 All ER 948, which provides
a very useful review of cases on this point.

In *Huckvale* v *Aegean Hotels Ltd* (1989) 58 P&CR 163, the Court of Appeal had a
novel question to consider: could an easement be extinguished because it no longer
was capable of accommodating the dominant tenement? Although all three judges
accepted that circumstances might arise where an easement could be extinguished
in that way, on the facts the question was left unanswered.

Release

Obviously, a dominant owner can release the servient owner from the burden of an
easement. Such release should be granted by way of deed, though it may succeed
notwithstanding failure to comply with this formal requirement under the rule in
Walsh v *Lonsdale*, or by estoppel.

Abandonment

In rare cases, release from the burden of an easement may be implied where the
dominant owner is deemed to have abandoned his right, but mere non-user will not
constitute abandonment; in every case it will depend upon all the circumstances.
Buckley LJ in *Tehidy Minerals Ltd* v *Norman* [1971] 2 QB 528 stated that only 'where
the person entitled to it has demonstrated a fixed intention never at any time thereafter to assert the right himself or to attempt to transmit it to anyone else' would
abandonment of an easement or profit occur. However, if the non-user can only be
explained by being held to be an abandonment of the right, it may be held to be an
implied release. Thus it was held in *Ward* v *Ward* (1852) 7 Exch 838 that, where a
right of way had not been used for many years, the dominant owner having a more
convenient way across his own land, such non-user, being adequately explained,
was not an abandonment, for:

> Non-user is not by itself conclusive evidence that a private right of easement is abandoned.
> The non-user must be considered with, and may be explained by, the surrounding circum-
> stances. If those circumstances clearly indicate an intention of not resuming the user then
> a presumption of a release of the easements will, in general, be implied and the easement
> will be lost – Pollock MR in *Swan* v *Sinclair* [1924] 1 Ch 254.

Thus, in *Benn v Hardinge* (1992) 66 P&CR 246, the Court of Appeal held that the failure to use a right of way for 175 years was not abandonment, non-user in itself not being sufficient: there must be a clear intention to abandon.

Moore v *Rawson* (1824) 3 B&C 332

Such an intention was found when an easement of light to windows was held to have been abandoned when the dominant owner rebuilt the building without windows. Here, the plaintiff had had a wall, in which there were several windows, pulled down and rebuilt as a stable-wall with no windows; it was held that he could not succeed in his claim, some 14 years later, that he had not abandoned his right to light to the now non-existent windows. Thus, when his neighbour erected a building which would have blocked the light from the windows, had they still been there, the plaintiff was not entitled to claim a right of light for a new window which he made in the exact place where one of the older ones had been. However, had the plaintiff 'done some act to show that he intended to build another in its place, then the new house, when built, would in effect have been a continuation of the old house, and the rights attached to the old house would have continued' – Holroyd J. (Indeed, after the Second World War, it became customary to paint 'ancient lights' on blank walls in order to establish a right to unobstructed daylight.)

CDC2020 Plc v *George Ferreira* [2005] EWCA Civ 611

The Court of Appeal held that a dominant owner must manifest an intention to abandon the right, making it clear that his intention is that neither he nor his successors in title should thereafter make any use of the right. Their lordships also confirmed that the question of abandonment has to be tested at the time of the acts relied upon as showing abandonment, without reference to later events.

On the facts, demolition, substantial and reinstatement works did not justify an inference that the then owner intended to abandon the right of way forever so that neither he nor his successors could ever resume its exercise. The fact that the right of way had continued to be used unlawfully did not prevent the respondent's right to retain the easement.

Variation of easements

We saw earlier that increased user of the same kind will not generally extinguish an easement, and this would seem to be so (except for rights acquired by prescription) even when the dominant tenement has changed. In *Graham v Philcox* [1984] QB 747 the dominant owner acquired neighbouring land and incorporated this into his own land. This, of course, increased the user of the right of way, but it was held not to have extinguished the easement. However, if the change in the dominant tenement creates a burden greater than that which would reasonably have been contemplated at the time of the grant, the right will be limited to the original extent of the user. Thus, in *Jelbert v Davis* [1968] 1 WLR 589 where the dominant tenement was originally agricultural land but later turned into a caravan park, thereby greatly increasing user over the dominant tenement, an injunction was granted. (Contrast this case with *British Railways Board v Glass*. See also 'Accommodating the dominant tenement'.)

However, if the dominant owner wishes to extend the right for a different purpose, he must renegotiate this with the servient owner.

How can you protect them?

Ensuring rights against third parties

In unregistered land, an easement, if legal, will bind the world. If it is only equitable, then the date of its creation will determine the relevant mode of protection. If created before 1926, it is subject to the doctrine of notice; if created after 1925, it is registrable as a Class D(iii) land charge. It is only void for non-registration against a purchaser for value.

In registered land, though they do not have their own separate titles, express legal easements and profits are registrable dispositions and may be registered on the dominant tenement title (a notice will be entered on the servient tenement title). LRA 2002, Sched 3, para 3(1) provides that:

> A legal easement or profit *à prendre*, except for an easement, or a profit *à prendre* which is not registered under the Commons Registration Act 1965, which at the time of the disposition –
>
> (a) is not within the actual knowledge of the person to whom the disposition is made, and
> (b) would not have been obvious on a reasonably careful inspection of the land over which the easement or profit is exercisable,

shall be overriding. Both (a) and (b) must be satisfied. However, if the right has not actually been exercised within one year ending with the day of the disposition, the interest will not be overriding – para 3(2). Proof lies on the person with the benefit of the easement.

Schedule 12, para 9 provides that easements and profits which were overriding under s 70(1)(a) of the 1925 Act immediately before Sched 3 came into force are to be treated as if they were included in Sched 3. (In regard to a profit which is not registered under the Commons Registration Act 1965 and which is an exception to

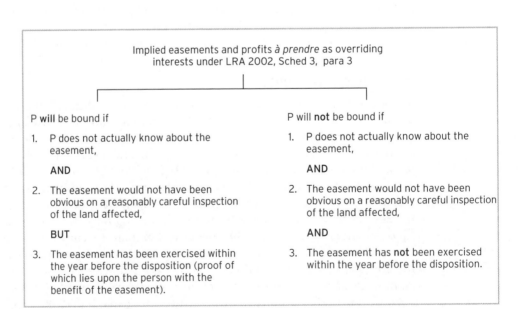

Figure 12.4

Sched 3, para 1, this exception does not apply until three years after Sched 3 comes into force – Sched 12, para 10.)

It was held in *Celsteel Ltd* v *Alton House Holdings* [1925] 1 WLR 204, that an *equitable* easement could fall within s 70(1)(a), provided that the right was being openly exercised and enjoyed at the time the servient land was transferred. The decision was upheld by the Court of Appeal in *Thatcher* v *Douglas* [1996] NLJ 1. However, under Sched 3 only legal easements can override (and only then if they fulfil the requirements of para 3(i)). Yet, it may be that, like other minor interests, an equitable easement which satisfies the requirements of Sched 3, para 2, can become overriding (though satisfying all the conditions could prove difficult, if not impossible).

Equitable easements will be minor interests under the 2002 Act.

So, express legal easements and profits, including profits in gross, will be registrable; implied legal easements and profits generally will be overriding; all equitable easements and profits will be minor.

Reform

The Law Commission, in its Consultation Document, *Land Registration for the Twenty-First Century* (Law Com No 254), recommended that, 'In anticipation of the introduction of electronic conveyancing it should not be possible to claim an easement or profit *à prendre* by prescription except under the provisions of the Prescriptions Act 1832'.

This recommendation is in direct opposition to that made by the Law Reform Committee in 1996 (Cm 3100), which was in favour of abolishing prescriptive easements (but, if they were to be retained, the prescriptive period should be reduced to 12 years in gross, with no need for it to be 'next before action').

In the same report, the Law Reform Committee also recommended that the Lands Tribunal should have the power to discharge easements or to substitute more convenient ones: where appropriate, compensation would be payable (this would, presumably, be similar to the Lands Tribunal's current powers in regard to Restrictive Covenants).

The Law Commission intends to set up a project to examine easements and publish a Consultation Paper with the aim of producing 'a more coherent scheme of easements and covenants which is compatible with both the commonhold system and the system of registration introduced by the Land Registration Act 2002' – www.lawcom.gov.uk/easements.htm.

Summary

In this chapter the following matters have been considered:

- The nature and characteristics of easements –
  - The need for a dominant and a servient tenement, owned or occupied by different persons
  - The need to accommodate the dominant tenement

- The right claimed must be capable of grant –
  - capable grantor and grantee
  - scope and extent of the right
- Repairs and maintenance.
- Rules, principles and formalities for acquisition –
  - Express easements –
    - By statute, grant or reservation;
  - Implied easements –
    - By reservation –
      - necessity
      - common intention
    - By grant –
    - necessity
    - common intention
    - statute – LPA, s 62
    - the rule in *Wheeldon* v *Burrows*
  - Prescription –
    - At common law –
    - continuous user as of right
    - Lost modern grant
    - Statutory –
  - easements of light
  - Illegality and prescription
  - Access to neighbouring land.
- Duration of easements –
  - Extinguishment
  - Release
  - Abandonment
  - Variation.
- Protection –
  - Unregistered land
  - Registered land.

References

Burn, E H, *Cheshire and Burn's Modern Law of Real Property*, 16th edition, London: Butterworths, 2000.

Gray, K.J. and Symes, P.D., *Real Property and Real People*, London: Butterworths, 1981.

Law Commission, *Land Registration for the Twenty-First Century* (Law Com No 254, 1998).

Maurice, S.G., *Gale on Easements*, 14th edition, London: Sweet & Maxwell, 1972.

Maurice, S.G., *Gale on Easements*, 15th edition, London: Sweet & Maxwell, 1986.

Oakley, J.A., *Megarry's Manual of the Law of Real Property*, 8th edition, London: Sweet and Maxwell, 2002.

Further reading

Nature and characteristics

Dawson, I and Dunn, A, 'Negative Easements - a crumb of analysis' (1998) 18(4) *Legal Studies* 510.

Luther, P, 'Easements and exclusive possession' (1996) 16(1) *Legal Studies* 51.

Acquisition - prescription

Barnsley, D G, 'Equitable Easements - Sixty Years On' (1999) 115 LQR 89.

Bridle v *Ruby* [1988] 3 All ER 64.

Harpum, C, 'The Acquisition of Easements' (1992) CLJ 220.

Mills v *Silver* [1991] 1 All ER 449.

Sara, C, 'Prescription - What is it for?' [2004] Conv 13.

Duration - abandonment

Davis, C J, 'Abandonment of an Easement: is it a question of intention only?' [1995] Conv 291.

Protection - registered land

Precedents Editor, 'Land Registration, Easements and overriding interests' [2005] Conv 545.

13 Profits *À prendre*

What's the problem?
Profits à prendre in context

What a lovely name. It rolls off the tongue! Often treated as the poor relation to easements, profits *à prendre* (or profits) are very important rights in land: though very similar to their cousins, profits must be distinguished from easements.

Farmer Brown grants Mr Blue the right to catch rabbits on his land for one year for a fee of £100 and then sets snares; the local squire lets you pasture your sheep or graze your cattle on his land and then erects a fence which excludes your animals; your neighbour says you may pick as many mushrooms as you like from her grounds and then sprays the land with fungicide; the owner of a nearby stretch of river grants you the right to take fish from the river for a fee of £1,000 per year and later bars your access.

Who cares?
Those who will be affected

The grantees: the persons to whom the right or permission was given. All of these 'rights' have value in that they provide the owner of them with, at the very least, a hobby or sport in the case of the rabbits and fish: they could have a monetary value, as could the picking of mushrooms and the grazing of stock.

The grantor: the person who gave the right or permission. The grants may provide a source of income, as with the rabbits and fish. On the other hand, the grants may prove to be a disadvantage if the grantor wishes to sell his land: prospective purchasers may wish to keep all the rabbits, fish, mushrooms and pasturing for themselves.

Purchasers from the grantor or grantees. Just as a purchaser from the grantor may wish to deny any of these rights, so too the purchaser from the grantees will probably wish to enforce them, against either the grantor or any purchaser from him.

What are they?

The nature and characteristics of profits à prendre

If any of these 'rights' are to be enforceable by or against a purchaser from one of the original parties, it must be an interest in land. The interest in each case would be a profit *à prendre*. The original grantees would also wish their right to be a profit, rather than a licence: an interest in land is far superior to a mere personal one.

As has already been mentioned, profits, though similar in many respects to easements, have to be distinguished from them.

Profits *à prendre* differ from easements in that an easement is a right over the land of another, whilst a profit is the right to take something from the land of another. Whereas an easement cannot exist *in gross*, a profit can – there is no need for a dominant tenement. However, a profit may benefit a piece of land and where it does it is called a profit *appurtenant*. A profit *appurtenant* must satisfy all four requirements of an easement, but for a profit *in gross*, only the fourth requirement need be satisfied, that is, the right claimed must be capable of forming the subject matter of a grant. In order to satisfy this latter requirement the thing taken must be either the soil or something produced by and taken out of it, or some wild animal living on it. Also, the thing taken must be capable of ownership. Rights to pick mushrooms, graze animals, take turf or peat, wood or sand, game or fish are all capable of being owned, but water from a spring or pump is not, nor is it part of the soil. Therefore, you cannot have a profit of such water, either for yourself or for your cattle (though you could have an easement in respect of it). However, you can have a profit of ice, and where water is stored in a cistern or some other artificial vessel it may possibly be a profit, though more likely it will be a mere licence, but never could it be an easement. Buckley J in *White* v *Taylor (No 2)* [1969] 1 Ch 160 held that the plaintiffs, who had a profit of grazing sheep on the defendant's down, were entitled to water their sheep on the down, by means of suitably located troughs, as an ancillary right under an implied grant.

The extent of the profit, that is the amount of the thing which you can take, differs depending upon whether the profit is *appurtenant* or *in gross*. If *in gross*, then there is no limit, but if *appurtenant* the requirements of the dominant tenement will define the amount required to accommodate it. Thus a profit to take fish (a profit of piscary), if *appurtenant*, will be limited to the number of fish required to satisfy the needs of the dominant tenement, and cannot be extended to commercial exploitation – *Harris* v *Earl of Chesterfield* [1911] AC 623. In *Lewis, Brain & Mitchell* v *Cavaciuti* (1993) NLJ 4 June 813, the question arose whether a profit *à prendre* of fishing appurtenant extends to a right to fish for all species of fish, or should a distinction be drawn between different species where there is evidence of a justifiable distinction? Judge Moseley QC held that as a matter of law a distinction can and should be made between different species of fish: a grantor can grant a profit limited to a particular species of fish. The House of Lords held, in *Bettison* v *Langton* [2001] 2 WLR 1605, that a profit of grazing appurtenant to a particular property, if limited to a fixed number of animals, could be severed from the dominant tenement so as to convert it from an appurtenant profit to a profit in gross.

A profit, then, is the right to take something from the servient tenement, but what right does the owner of the profit have to go on to the servient land in order to take the thing? A licence will always be implied in favour of a valid profit owner in order to give effect to the profit: this is an example of a licence coupled with a grant or interest.

We saw, in Chapter 12, Easements, that the public may enjoy certain rights – public rights. In regard to rights similar to profits, there is a natural right to fish (and navigate) on the foreshore (but not to engage in beachcombing) – *Alfred F Beckett Ltd v Lyons* [1967] Ch 449.

A right to take things from land cannot be acquired by custom – *Beckett*. However, in its reluctance to strike down rights that have been exercised for centuries, the courts have developed two ways (both of which depend upon the fact that a profit, which can exist in gross, can be owned by a company) of giving effect to them. They are both legal fictions. The first assumes that the Crown incorporated the 'fluctuating body', for example the inhabitants of a village, and then granted it the profit; the second works a bit like the lost modern grant, in that it assumes there was a grant to an existing corporation (usually a local authority) by way of a charitable trust for the fluctuating body. Clearly, these are of limited application.

How can they exist?

Classification: legal or equitable?

A profit *à prendre* falls within the Law of Property Act 1925, s 1(2)(a), being a 'right, or privilege in or over land'. Therefore, if it is equivalent to an estate in fee simple absolute in possession or a term of years absolute, and created by deed, it will be legal. It will also be legal if acquired by prescription or under the Law of Property Act 1925, s 62. Otherwise, it can only be equitable.

How can you acquire them?

Rules, principles and formalities

The rules for the acquisition of profits are, for the most part, the same as those for easements. This being so, we shall simply note the differences.

We spent much time in the last chapter looking at easements of necessity. There is no such thing as a profit of necessity – at least, not in land law! Similarly, a profit to give effect to a common intention of the parties will not be implied.

The rule in *Wheeldon* v *Burrows* (1879) 12 Ch D 31 applies to easements only.

Upon conveyance of the dominant tenement, any profit attached to it will automatically pass if the profit is appurtenant; if in gross, the benefit of it must be assigned specifically, that is expressly – see *Lovett* v *Fairclough* (1990) 61 P&CR 385.

The periods for a prescriptive profit under the Prescription Act are 30 years and 60 years. In all other respects, the Act applies to profits in the same way as it does to easements other than easements of light, with the exception that, though s 7 applies to profits, s 8 does not.

When and for how long?
Duration of profits à prendre

Profits can be extinguished and released in the same way as easements.

How can you protect them?
Ensuring rights against third parties

In both registered and unregistered land, profits *à prendre* are protected in the same way as easements, unless, in registered land, it has been registered under the Commons Registration Act 1965.

In addition, in registered land, under LRA 2002, 'a disposition ... of a legal profit *à prendre in gross,* other than one created for, or for an interest equivalent to, a term of years absolute not exceeding seven years from the date of creation' must be entered by way of a notice, and the grantee, or his successor in title, must be registered as proprietor of the profit – LRA 2002, Sched 2, para 6. Legal profits *appurtenant* are protected in the same way as easements under LRA 2002.

Fishing rights have been recognised as falling within the protection of Article 1, Protocol 1 of the European Convention on Human Rights – *Banner* v *Sweden* [1989] 60 DR 128, EctHR.

Reform

Proposals for reform are the same as for easements, except that in regard to the acquisition of profits by prescription, the Law Reform Committee, in its 1966 Report, recommended unanimously that prescriptive profits be abolished: 1966 Cmnd 3100.

Summary

In this chapter we have seen that although profits *à prendre* are very similar to easements, there are some important differences, all of which have been discussed.

14 Restrictive covenants

What's the problem?

Restrictive covenants in context

Have you been to Leicester Square in London? If not, perhaps you have seen one of the Royal film galas on television – these usually take place at The Odeon, Leicester Square. Either way, you would probably have noticed an open square of land opposite the cinema. This plot is like an oasis of well cultivated and maintained greenery and is now surrounded by a low wall with entrances flanked by imposing pillars adorned by busts of famous people.

How did this small emerald jewel survive any building development? The answer is to be found in the leading case on restrictive – or freehold – covenants: *Tulk* v *Moxhay* (1848) 2 Ph 774. Mr Tulk had sold the vacant piece of land in Leicester Square to Mr Elms. Elms covenanted (promised), on behalf of himself and his heirs and assigns, that he would at all times, at his own cost, keep and maintain the land, 'in its then form and in sufficient and proper repair, as a square garden and pleasure ground, in an open state and uncovered with any buildings, in a neat and ornamental order'. Notwithstanding several conveyances of the land, the covenant held good, until, that is, Mr Moxhay bought it. His conveyance, for some reason, did not contain the covenant. However, Moxhay admitted that he had notice of the original covenant in the conveyance to Elms. Moxhay proposed to erect buildings on the land. Tulk, who still owned several of the houses which surrounded the 'garden', sought to enforce the covenant against him. Did he succeed?

Who cares?

Those who will be affected

Mr Tulk, the original owner and vendor. Why? Ask yourself why he included the original covenant in the conveyance: to maintain an attractive open space for the benefit of the land he was retaining. Such a pleasant aspect as the 'garden' would, especially in the heart of London, greatly enhance not only the enjoyment of those houses surrounding the garden, but also their value. (Here, then, is a way in which the right to a view may be secured, unlike easements.)

Mr Elms, the original purchaser of the burdened (servient) land. One wonders why Mr Elms bought the land on the condition he did. Perhaps he wanted a 'garden' for his own house. Whatever, should he change his mind and wish to build on the land, he had hamstrung himself by the covenant. Not only that: Elms had covenanted also for his heirs and assigns who, if the covenant held, would also be bound by it.

Mr Moxhay, a successor in title (assignee) of the servient land. He wants the land, but wants it to build upon. Can he do so? Is he bound by the original promise made by Mr Elms, even though he was not a party to it?

A successor in title (assignee) of the benefited, or dominant, land. Can he, who was not a party to the original promise either, benefit from it?

What are they?

The nature and characteristics of restrictive covenants

If the covenant is binding on Mr Moxhay, a third party, it will be a proprietary right, not merely a personal one, and will impose upon him an obligation in regard to the land which he did not himself undertake.

We already have a good idea of what a covenant is, having seen those in leases and, just as with leasehold covenants, freehold covenants can be positive or negative; the positive requiring something to be done, the negative prohibiting the doing of something. However, leasehold covenants are concerned with a landlord and his tenant, freehold covenants are concerned with the different owners of two pieces of land. Thus, as with easements, we require a dominant and a servient tenement, with the dominant enjoying the benefit, the servient the burden of the covenant. Again, as with easements, you cannot have a covenant against yourself, so there must be separate owners of the two freehold tenements.

The most common freehold covenants are those which prohibit the building of more than a specified number of houses on the servient tenement, and those which restrict the use of the property to that of a dwellinghouse only. (In *Roberts* v *Howlett* [2002] 1 P&CR 19, a covenant 'not to use the property or permit the same to be used for any purpose other than as a single private dwellinghouse ...' had to be considered when the house in question was let to a group of four students, under a single tenancy, the students being jointly and severally liable for payment of the rent. Was this letting a breach of the covenant, in that the way in which the students used the house was not as a single private dwellinghouse? Did the fact that the house was being let to them for profit breach the requirement that the house remain a *private* dwelling? The court held a covenant to use property as a private dwellinghouse is distinct from a covenant to reside personally in a property, and is not broken by a covenantor who lets his house to another person who then lives in it as his home. The way in which the students used the house was as a single private dwellinghouse and there was, therefore, no breach. The words 'a private dwellinghouse' in a covenant were considered by the Court of Appeal in *Martin* v *David Wilson Homes Ltd* [2004] EWCA Civ 1027, where it held that the indefinite article 'a' restricted the manner of use, but not the number of buildings that could be built on the servient land. Covenants limiting the height of any buildings on the servient tenement to, say, two floors only are not uncommon. In the 1960s, 'open plan' housing estates were popular and the conveyance of each house on such estates contained a covenant against the erection of any fence, wall or hedge above a certain height, usually 12 inches. These are all examples of negative, or restrictive, covenants, preventing, as they do, the owner of the servient land from doing something upon it.

An example of a positive covenant, one which requires the servient owner to do, rather than to refrain from doing, something for the benefit of the dominant land, would be one to maintain his own property in good repair. In almost every case, a positive covenant will involve the covenantor in expenditure. We shall see shortly that, unlike leasehold covenants, in freehold land, a positive covenant cannot bind anyone other than the original covenantor – it cannot 'run with the land': the burden cannot pass to a successor in title to the servient land. (As we saw in leases, many of the most important covenants in a lease are positive, such as the covenant to pay rent and, in regard to flats, where the common parts such as stairs and landings need to be maintained, a covenant to contribute to such maintenance is included in the lease of each flat. If the burden of such covenants could not pass to an assignee of the tenant, there would be difficulties; so much so that no one would be willing to grant a lease for fear of any assignment of it to someone who would not be bound by these obligations. This is why the vast majority of flats in this country are leasehold, not freehold.) So, whilst the 1960s style of covenant for retaining an open plan is restrictive or negative, one to maintain a fence, wall or hedge would be positive: the burden of the latter can not 'run' with the land and thereby bind a third party.

However, just as you may be able to maintain a view by way of a restrictive covenant, though not with an easement, so, in *Crow* v *Wood* [1971] 1 QB 77 it was held that the right to have a fence or wall kept in repair by a neighbouring farmer was a right in the nature of an easement – albeit a 'spurious' one. Whether a covenant is positive or negative is a matter of substance, not form: a covenant not to let your property fall into disrepair is still a positive one, notwithstanding it is couched in negative terms – you still have to maintain the property in order to comply with the covenant.

The reason for covenants is to protect the dominant tenement, its enjoyment and value, often by retaining the character of the neighbourhood. Thus, restrictive covenants provide a way in which private individuals can control the use of land, not only their own land but also that which they sell. As Gray (1993) says:

> In an age of increasing intensification of land use, covenants also provide a means for resolving in advance the problems thrown up by potentially incompatible forms of user in adjacent land areas ... the law relating to covenants provides a highly convenient means of adjusting neighbourhood relationships in such a way as to enhance the optimal utilisation of land ... The device of the covenant thus facilitates entire regimes of private ordering between neighbouring landowners with the result that covenants operate effectively as a form of private legislation affecting a succession of future owners – p 1123.

A covenant is, then, an agreement contained in a deed in which one party promises the other that he will do or not do certain things on or in relation to certain land. The person making the promise is the covenantor, and the person to whom he makes it, the covenantee. Thus, the covenantor has the burden of the covenant, and his land is the servient tenement, whilst the covenantee has the benefit and his land is the dominant tenement.

We have seen that easements must 'accommodate' the land, and the equivalent requirement for covenants is that they 'touch and concern' the land. In freeholds this means that the covenant was entered into for the benefit of the land of the covenantee, not just the covenantee personally. Thus, a covenant, in order to touch and concern the land, 'must either affect the land as regards mode of occupation, or it must be such as *per se*, and not merely from collateral circumstances, affects the value of the land' – Tucker LJ in *Smith and Snipes Hall Farm Ltd* v *River Douglas Catchment Board* [1949] 2 KB 500. As we have just seen, freehold covenants must be restrictive, or negative, if they are to bind a subsequent owner of the servient tenement, that is they must not involve the servient owner in any positive action and expense.

How can they exist?

Classification: legal or equitable?

Covenants are not included in the Law of Property Act 1925, s 1(1) or (2), and can, therefore, only be equitable, even though created by deed.

In freehold land, positive covenants cannot 'run with the burdened land'. This means that, though such covenants will bind the original parties to the promise, they cannot bind later purchasers of the servient land. Therefore, only negative – restrictive – covenants can run with the burdened land.

Notwithstanding that the desired result, that is making the burden of the covenant enforceable against a purchaser of the servient land, can sometimes be achieved by other means, such as the creation of an estates rentcharge, the Law Commission, as we shall see shortly, has proposed that freehold covenants be replaced by land obligations.

How can you acquire them?

Rules, principles and formalities

There are different rules for the acquisition of covenants depending upon whether they are freehold or leasehold. Needless to say, there is no problem of enforcement of any covenant whilst the original parties retain their land. This is because of the existence of privity of contract, under which each can sue the other for damages or seek either an order of specific performance or an injunction. However, what happens when either or both of the original covenanting parties conveys his land to another? Can that person – a stranger to the original covenant – take the benefit of, or be burdened with, the terms of the covenant? This was Mr Tulk's and Mr Moxhay's question.

If the original covenantee assigns his interest in the dominant land, he can still sue the original covenantor upon his promise. However, having suffered no actual loss, he will only be able to claim nominal damages, if any. The real difficulty arises when a subsequent owner of the dominant land wishes to enforce the covenant against the owner of the servient land – whether he be the original covenantor or a successor in title. At common law the successor of the covenantee cannot sue because he was not a party to the original agreement. The Law of Property Act 1925, s 56(1), went some way to modifying this situation by providing that 'a person may take ... the benefit of any ... covenant over or respecting land ... although he may not be named as a party to the conveyance or other instrument'. However, this provision is not as all-embracing as it may seem, for all it does is remove the necessity for a party to be named expressly. In fact s 56 can only be of benefit to persons who are both in existence and identifiable at the date of the covenant. Thus, a covenant in a conveyance of Blackacre purporting to be for the benefit not only of P but also of 'the owners for the time being of Redacre and Whiteacre, their heirs and assigns' will only extend the benefit to the current owners of Redacre and Whiteacre, their 'heirs and assigns' being unidentifiable at the date of the covenant. As stated by Cheshire and Burn (2000, p 690):

> It is important to notice that this section is not concerned with the *passing* of the benefit of a covenant. It is concerned with the *giving* of the benefit of a covenant, at the time when the covenant is created, to a person other than the covenantee.

However, a person who acquires the benefit under s 56(1) can pass it to his successors in title by annexation or assignment: it is simply that s 56(1) **will not have the effect of running the benefit beyond him**, though, as Maudsley and Burn explain (2004, p 991) it does 'make into a covenantee a person claiming the benefit of the covenant, even though he was not a party to the instrument in which the covenant was contained'. It is quite different, therefore, from the situations which we shall be looking at next where the question is whether successors in title from the original covenantor and covenantee are bound or benefited.

Re Shaw's Application (1995) 68 P&CR 591

An original owner, O, converted a large house into two flats in 1961; later, he converted an adjacent building into a third flat. Flat 1 was sold in 1961 subject to covenants for the benefit of the owners of flat 2 and their successors. Flat 2 was sold in 1962 subject to the same covenants in favour of the owners of flat 1 and their successors. No mention was made of flat 3. In 1962, flat 3 was sold subject to a covenant made with the original owner that alterations to the flat could only be made after submitting the plans to 'the vendor or its successors in title the owners and occupiers of adjoining property' and consent obtained from the relevant persons. In 1993 the owner of flat 3 proposed to demolish the flat and build a bungalow. The owners of flats 1 and 2 objected relying upon the covenant. The owner of flat 3 claimed that the covenant could not be relied upon because: (a) there was no assignment of the benefit of the covenant to the objectors; (b) the covenant had not been expressly annexed to the land; and (c) the objectors were not successors in title to the original owner because he did not own flats 1 and 2 at the time of the conveyance of flat 3. *Held* that the objectors could rely upon the covenant because they were referred to generically in the conveyance. Flats 1 and 2 were the only properties adjoining flat 3 and, therefore, they must be the properties referred to for the purposes of s 56(1).

Re Shaw followed *Re Ecclesiastical Commissioners for England's Conveyance* [1936] Ch 430, where Luxmore J stated, that what is necessary to consider is, 'the true construction of the conveyance ... in order to ascertain whether any persons, not parties thereto, are described therein as covenantees, and whether any such covenants are expressed to affect any and what hereditaments'.

White v Bijou Mansions Ltd [1937] Ch 610

Here Simonds J explained that:

> ... under section 56 ... only that person can call it in aid who, although not named as a party to the conveyance or other instrument is yet a person to whom that conveyance or other instrument purports to grant something or with whom some agreement or covenant is purported to be made ... I interpret [s 56] as a section which can be called in aid only by a person in whose favour the grant purports to be made or with whom the covenant or agreement purports to be made.

Simonds J's decision was upheld in the Court of Appeal, where Sir Wilfred Greene MR expressed the view that:

> Whatever else section 56 may mean, it is, I think, confined to cases where the person seeking to take advantage of it is a person within the benefit of the covenant in question ... The mere fact that somebody comes along and says: 'It would be useful to me if I could enforce that covenant' does not make him a person entitled to enforce it under section 56. Before he can enforce it he must be a person who falls within the scope and benefit of the covenant according to the true construction of the document in question.

In *Drive Yourself Hire Co (London) Ltd* v *Strutt* [1954] 1 QB 250, Denning LJ said, *obiter*, that too narrow an interpretation must not be placed upon Simonds J's words in *Bijou*, and went on to state that, 'Enforceability does not depend on the form of the obligation, but on the substance of it. A covenant is, for this purpose, sufficiently made "with" a person if it is, on the face of it, made directly for his benefit in such circumstances that it was intended to be enforceable by him'.

Amstrop Trading Ltd v Harris Distribution Ltd [1997] 2 All ER 990

A sub-tenant, H, covenanted with the tenant that 'it shall be lawful for the superior landlords and the landlords ... to enter and to repair at the cost of the sub-tenant'. H refused to pay for repairs which the superior landlord, A, had undertaken. As neither privity of contract nor privity of estate existed between A and H, A sought to enforce the covenant by way of s 56, claiming that it was obvious that A was intended to benefit from the covenant. Neuberger J held that it was not enough that the covenant was made for A's benefit: the covenant must purport to be made with A. On this construction, A failed.

Once one or both of the original parties to the covenant parts with his interest in the land, whether or not his successor in title can enforce the benefit, or be bound by the burden of the covenant, depends upon whether it 'runs with the land'. In order to run with the land, both the burden and the benefit of the covenant must run, and there are different rules for each both at law and in equity.

As 'equity follows the law', it is necessary to start with the common-law rules, turning to equity where they fail.

Running the benefit

At common law

It has for centuries been the rule that the benefit of covenants, whether positive or negative, runs with the land of the original covenantee. The liability of the covenantor arises from his promise, and therefore he remains liable on it to the original covenantee and to his successors in title even when he, the original covenantor, no longer owns any land. Indeed, the rule is the same where the covenantor never owned any land which could carry the burden of the covenant. In *The Prior's Case* (1368) YB 42 Edw III, a positive covenant that a prior and his convent would sing all week in the covenantee's chapel was upheld, notwithstanding the fact that there was no servient tenement to carry the burden and in *Smith & Snipes Hall Farm Ltd* v *River Douglas Catchment Board* [1949] 2 KB 500, it was stated that though there must be a covenantee with land capable of benefiting, the covenantor need not have any land capable of bearing the burden.

If the benefit of a covenant is to run at law, four requirements must be satisfied:

1 *The covenant must touch and concern the land*: 'that is, it must either affect the land as regards mode of occupation, or it must be such as per se, and not merely from collateral circumstances, affects the value of the land' – Tucker LJ in *Snipes Hall Farm*. 'Touch and concern the land' is, therefore, analogous with the need for an easement to 'accommodate the land'.

2 *There must have been, at the date of the covenant, an intention that the benefit of it should run with the land of the covenantee*: words to this effect incorporated in the original conveyance will prove the necessary intention. In *Snipes Hall Farm* this condition was satisfied by the inclusion in the deed of conveyance of an explanation of the purpose of the covenant, which was 'to improve the drainage of land liable to flooding and prevent future flooding'. It was also held in that case that the effect of the Law of Property Act 1925, s 78 is that the benefit of a covenant can be enforced, not only by the original covenantee but also by a purchaser of the dominant land from him. Section 78(1) provides that: 'A covenant relating to any land of the covenantee shall be deemed to be made with the covenantee and his successors in title and the persons deriving title under him or them, and shall have effect as if such successors and other persons were expressed'.

3 *The covenantee must have had, at the date of the covenant, a legal estate in the land to be benefited*: thus, at common law, no benefit can pass unless the original covenantee had a legal estate, and not merely an equitable interest, in the land.

4 *The assignee of the covenantee must have a legal estate in the land*: it used to be that if the original covenantee was an owner in fee simple, his assignee had also to be an owner in fee simple – the benefit could not pass from a fee simple owner to a leasehold owner. This harsh rule was modified by *Snipes Hall Farm*, where a lessee was held to be entitled to the benefit of a covenant notwithstanding the fact that he had a lesser estate than the original covenantor who was a fee simple owner. The court held that the effect of s 78 is that a covenant is enforceable on behalf of not only the original covenantee, but all successors in title and all persons deriving title from such successors.

In addition to these common law rules for running the benefit of a covenant, the LPA 1925, s 136 provides that the benefit of a covenant may be transferred by assignment, provided the assignment is in writing and express notice in writing is given to the covenantor. Another statutory method has been provided by the Contracts (Rights of Third Parties) Act 1999. This applies only to contracts (including leases and contracts for land) and covenants therein entered into on or after 11 May 2000.

Section 1 provides that:

(1) ... a person who is not a party to a contract (a 'third party') may in his own right enforce a term of the contract if –
(a) the contract expressly provides that he may, or
(b) subject to subsection (2), the term purports to confer a benefit on him.
(2) Subsection (1)(b) does not apply if on a proper construction of the contract it appears that the parties did not intend the term to be enforceable by the third party.
(3) The third party must be expressly identified in the contract by name, as a member of a class or as answering a particular description but need not be in existence when the contract is entered into.
(4) This section does not confer a right on a third party to enforce a term of the contract otherwise than subject to and in accordance with any other relevant terms of the contract.

Thus,

in so far as this Act applies to the enforcement of a freehold covenant at common law, we can make these observations. First, such phrases as successors in title bring the covenant within s 1(3), enabling them to sue directly the original covenantor on the covenant. Secondly, being a contractual and not a land law right, there is no need to satisfy the common law requirements of touching and concerning the land and of a legal estate to be benefited. And, thirdly, it will only be rarely necessary to invoke the Act, since in most cases the width of s 178(1) of the Law of Property Act 1925 will suffice – Cheshire and Burn (2000, p 666).

Four further points need to be noted:

1 it is possible for covenants which do not touch and concern the land to be enforced by a third party under the Act, but such a claim is likely to be defeated by the need to show that such a covenant was intended to benefit the third party – s 1(2) and (4);

2 the Act does not affect the running of the burden of a covenant;

3 the Act protects the covenantee against double liability, so that if the covenantee has recovered his losses from the covenantor, any award to a third party claiming under s 1 will be reduced 'to such extent as [the court or arbitral tribunal] thinks appropriate to take account of the sum recovered' by the covenantee – s 5. In addition, s 1(2) may well defeat a third party's claim;

4 the Act can be expressly excluded.

We saw earlier the effect of LPA 1925, s 56(1) and its limitations – the fact that the third party must be 'alive and identifiable' at the creation of the covenant; and that there can be no 'running of the benefit of the covenant' beyond such person. The 1999 Act is different in both cases – s 1(3) provides that the third party 'need not be in existence when the contract is entered into'; and, provided they satisfy s 1(3), 'successors' can gain the benefit (subject, of course, to s 1(2) and (4)).

In equity

If the benefit of a covenant cannot run at law – say for instance if the covenantee, or his successor, has only an equitable interest in the land – then it may run in equity. If it is to do so, it must not only touch and concern the land, but it must also run by virtue of one of the methods laid down by equity. There are three:

1 by annexation;

2 by assignment;

3 by a building scheme.

Annexation

Annexation has been described by Gray and Symes (1981, p 622) as 'the metaphorical "nailing" of the benefit of a restrictive covenant to a clearly defined area of land belonging to the covenantee, in such a way that the benefit passes with any subsequent transfer of the covenantee's interest in that land ... the benefit of the covenant is notionally fastened upon, or annexed to, the covenantee's land, with the result that the benefit passes to all successive owners, tenants and occupiers of the land'.

There are three types of annexation: express, implied and statutory, the latter by virtue of s 78 as interpreted first in *Snipes Hall Farm* and later in *Federated Homes* v *Mill Lodge Properties*.

Federated Homes Ltd v *Mill Lodge Properties Ltd* [1980] 1 WLR 594

If as the language of s 78 implies, a covenant relating to land which is restrictive of the user thereof is enforceable at the suit of (1) a successor in title of the covenantee; (2) a person deriving title under the covenantee or his successors in title; and (3) the owner or occupier of the land intended to be benefited by the covenant, it must, in my view, follow that the covenant runs with the land because ex hypothesi every successor in title to the land, every derivative proprietor of the land and every other owner and occupier has a right by statute to the covenant. In other words, if the condition precedent of s 78 is satisfied, that is to say there exists a covenant which touches and concerns the land of the covenantee, that covenant runs with the land for the benefit of his successors in title, persons deriving title under him or them and other owners and occupiers - Brightman LJ.

The decision in *Federated Homes* was not universally welcomed, and indeed it has been distinguished in two later cases. The first is *Roake* v *Chadha* [1984] 1 WLR 40 where Judge Paul Baker QC held that in spite of the words of s 78(1), which is not expressly made subject to any contrary intention, the covenant had to be construed as a whole to see whether the benefit was annexed. Holding that the express provision in the covenant that it was not to enure for the benefit of any owner or subsequent purchaser 'unless the benefit of [it] shall be expressly assigned' could not be ignored, the judge decided that there had been no annexation.

Crest Nicholson Residential (South) Ltd v McAllister [2004] 1 WLR 2409

The Court of Appeal confirmed the approach taken in *Roake*, stating that it provides the answer to the question why, if the legislature did not intend to distinguish between the effect of s 78 (mandatory) and the effect of s 79 (subject to contrary intention), it did not include the words 'unless a contrary intention is expressed' in the first of those sections. The answer is that it did not need to. The qualification 'subject to contrary intention' is implicit in the definition of 'successors in title' which appears in s 78 (1); that is the effect of the words 'the land of the covenantee intended to be benefited'. If the terms in which the covenant is imposed show – as they did in … *Roake v Chadha* – that the land of the covenantee intended to be benefited does not include land which may subsequently be sold off by the original covenantee in circumstances where (at the time of that subsequent sale) there is no express assignment of the benefit of the covenant, then the owners and occupiers of the land sold off in those circumstances are not 'owners and occupiers for the time being of the land of the covenantee intended to be benefited'; and so are not 'successors in title' of the original covenantee for the purposes of s 78(1) in its application to covenants restrictive of the user of land. By contrast, the definition 'successors in title' for the purposes of s 79(1) appears in subs.(2) of that section: 'the owners and occupiers for the time being of *such* land'. In that context, 'such land' means 'any land of the covenantor or capable of being bound by him [to which the covenant relates]'. The counterpart in s 79 of 'land of the covenantee intended to be benefited' (in s 78(1)) is 'such land'.' – Chadwick LJ at p 2426 (original emphasis).

In the second case, *Sainsbury (J) v Enfield London Borough Council* [1989] 1 WLR 590, it was held that the conveyance had to be construed in the light of all the circumstances, including any necessary implication raised thereby. However, *Federated Homes*, though heavily criticised by those who consider s 78 to be no more than a word-saving provision, still stands and it creates an almost automatic annexation which renders express and implied annexation redundant. However, as it is still controversial, the older methods may still need to be considered. *Crest Nicholson* was applied in *University of East London Higher Education Corp v Barking and Dagenham LBC* (2005) *The Times*, 3 January and in *Sugarman v Porter* [2006] 2 P&CR 14, and considered in *Mohammadzadeh v Joseph* [2006] EWHC 1040 (Ch) (which applied *Federated Homes*).

Equity laid down harsher rules for express annexation than those required by the common law for the running of the benefit, requiring that the covenant be taken for the benefit of certain land or by the covenantee in his capacity as owner of the dominant land, the latter being clearly identified in the deed or identifiable from the terms of it. Thus in *Newton Abbot Co-operative Society Ltd v Williamson & Treadgold Ltd* [1952] Ch 286, there was no annexation where there was nothing in the conveyance which identified the land for the benefit of which the covenant was alleged to be taken. This is because, as Collins LJ had explained in *Rogers v Hosegood* [1900] 2 Ch 388, annexation makes the benefit run 'not because the conscience of either party is affected, but because the purchaser has bought something which inhered in or was annexed to the land bought'.

An intention to annex also has to be shown in the original deed containing the covenant, and this can be inferred from the language used. Greene LJ in *Drake v Gray* [1936] Ch 451 provided the example of a covenant made 'with so and so, owners or owner for the time being of whatever the land may be'. Another method is to state by means of an appropriate declaration that the covenant is taken 'for the benefit of' whatever the lands may be. Thus a provision made 'with the intent that the covenants might so far as possible bind the premises thereby conveyed and every part thereof and might enure to the benefit of the vendors ... their heirs and assigns and others claiming under them to all or any of their lands adjoining or near to the said premises' was held to annex the covenant to the land in *Rogers* v *Hosegood*, whereas a covenant with the vendors, 'their heirs, executors, administrators and assigns' was held in *Renals* v *Cowlishaw* (1878) 9 Ch D 125 not to annex, the word 'assigns' implying merely assignees of the covenant rather than the land, and no dominant land being specified.

It was held in *Re Ballards Conveyance* [1937] Ch 473 that there would be no annexation of a covenant which purportedly benefited the whole of an estate of 17,000 acres. However, this strict approach was relaxed by Brightman J in *Wrotham Park Estates Co Ltd* v *Parkside Homes Ltd* [1974] 1 WLR 798, where he held that if the covenant benefits a substantial part of the dominant tenement, it is capable of annexation. This was modified still further by Brightman LJ in *Federated Homes* where he stated that 'if the benefit of the covenant is, on a proper construction of a document, annexed to the land, prima facie it is annexed to every part thereof, unless the contrary clearly appears'. See also *Newton Abbot* v *Williamson & Treadgold*.

It has been held in two cases – *Marten* v *Flight Refuelling Ltd* [1962] Ch 115 and *Rogers* v *Hosegood* [1900] 2 Ch 388 – that annexation can be implied from circumstances. In *Marten* v *Flight*, Wilberforce J felt that, although annexation was not expressed in the deed containing the original conveyance, annexation was so obviously intended by the covenanting parties that to ignore it would be 'not only an injustice but a departure from common sense'; and in *Rogers* v *Hosegood* the Court of Appeal implied the annexation of a covenant, Collins LJ stating that it required merely an 'indication in the original conveyance, or something in the circumstances surrounding it, that the burden of the restrictive covenant is imposed for the benefit of the land reserved'.

As with express annexation, the benefit of the covenant must be clearly referable to a defined piece of land and the parties must have intended that the benefit attach to the land, not merely to the covenantee personally.

Assignment

Assignment differs from annexation in that the two are 'directed at quite different targets. Annexation involves the attachment of the benefit to *land*; assignment involves the conferment of benefit upon a *person*' – Gray, (1993, p 1157). As Gray also points out, the timing is different, too: '[a]nnexation is effected at the date of the making of the restrictive covenant. Assignment is effected, perhaps many years later, on subsequent transfers of the covenantee's title to later purchasers of the dominant land'. Just as the relevance of express and implied annexation has been diminished by the decision in *Federated Homes*, so too has the scope for assignment been reduced. However, in cases like *Roake* v *Chadha* and *Sainsbury* v *Enfield LBC*, where s 78 does not have the same effect, assignment may be relevant.

Miles v Easter [1933] Ch 611

Here Romer LJ laid down the five requirements that must be satisfied:

> (i) The covenant must have been taken for the benefit of the land of the covenantee and (ii) that land must be indicated with reasonable certainty. This indication need not appear in the conveyance creating the covenant. It is sufficient if in the light of the attending circumstances the identity of the dominant land is in some other way ascertainable with reasonable certainty. (iii) It must also be retained in whole or part by the plaintiff and (iv) be capable of benefiting from the covenant. (v) The assignment of the covenant and the conveyance of the land to which it relates must be contemporaneous.

Requirement (i) means that the covenant must touch and concern the dominant land; thus equity requires a dominant tenement. With regard to (ii), it was stated by Upjohn J in *Newton Abbot Co-operative Society Ltd* v *Williamson & Treadgold Ltd* that the court can look at the attendant circumstances to see if the land to be benefited is shown 'in some other way with reasonable certainty'. With regard to requirement (iv), the current view is that there must be an unbroken chain of assignments, created by each conveyance of the benefited land, as it passes the benefit of the covenant to each new owner down to the person seeking to enforce it – *Re Pinewood Estate, Farnborough* [1958] Ch 280.

An attempted assignment by declaring the benefit of a covenant for the 'heirs and assigns' of the covenantee, with no express mention of any land (or dominant tenement) to be benefited, will not suffice for express assignment – *Renals* v *Cowlishaw* (1878) 9 Ch D 125.

A building scheme

The circumstances which will give rise to a building scheme were laid down in *Elliston* v *Reacher* (below), and the effect of such a scheme was explained by Halsbury: 'A building scheme constitutes a local law for the area over which it extends and has the practical effect of rendering each purchaser and his successors in title subject to the restrictions and of conferring upon them the benefits of the scheme, as between themselves and all other purchasers and their respective successors in title'. Thus it enables the owners of houses within the scheme to enforce covenants which were created in order to maintain the character of the estate and the value of the properties thereof, even after the developer, that is, the original covenantee, has parted with all interest in the estate. In such cases, the builder was the only covenantee, the dominant tenement being the land he retains: thus, the dominant tenement shrinks with each sale of a plot until, eventually, there is no dominant tenement left. This leaves merely servient land occupied by covenantors! Once a building scheme has been upheld, however, all the plot owners become both covenantee and covenantor, each being able to enforce the benefit of the covenants against all the others, but, also being liable to them for the burden.

Elliston v Reacher [1908] 2 Ch 374

Here Parker J laid down the four essential requirements for a building scheme:

1 both the plaintiff and the defendant must have derived title from a common owner;

2 the common vendor must, prior to the sale of the plots now owned by the plaintiff and defendant, have laid out a definite scheme of development;

3 there must have been an intention to impose upon not only purchasers of land within the development, but also their successors in title, a scheme of mutually enforceable restrictions;

4 every purchaser must have bought his land in full knowledge of the scheme, and with an intention to be bound by its mutually enforceable restrictions.

To these, a fifth requirement was added by *Reid* v *Bickerstaff* [1909] 2 Ch 305 – the area affected by the scheme must be clearly defined. *Elliston* v *Reacher* and *Reid* v *Bickerstaff* were applied more recently by the Privy Council in *Emile Elias & Co Ltd* v *Pine Groves* [1993] 1 WLR 305. As Lord Browne-Wilkinson explained:

> In this case, the plaintiff seeks to enforce against the defendant restrictive covenants affecting a parcel of land which formerly formed part of a small development which took place in 1938 when the then common owner ... ('the company'), sold five parcels of land to four different purchasers, each of the purchasers entering into restrictive covenants affecting the land bought by them.

One of the covenants was not to erect any building other than one dwellinghouse and the purchasers of lots 1, 4 and 5 entered into this. A similar restriction was imposed on lots 2 and 3, but they also entered into substantially different covenants from those relating to lots 1, 4 and 5. In 1948 the company and all four owners executed a deed in which the owner of lots 4 and 5, who had built a house on lot 4, was released from the restriction so that he could build a house on lot 5. The subsequent owner of lot 1 began construction of another house on his plot; the subsequent owner of lot 3 sought to enforce the covenant against him. At first instance, the judge held no building scheme had been created in 1938 and thus the covenant was unenforceable. The Privy Council dismissed the appeal; the lack of uniformity in the covenants imposed on lots of a similar nature indicated that there had been no intention to create reciprocally enforceable rights, and, in any event, the intention of the company and the purchasers in 1938 was inconsistent with an intention to create a building scheme, the 1948 deed being too equivocal to prove the requisite intention.

These strict requirements were later modified in two respects. Requirement (b) had not been complied with in *Baxter* v *Four Oaks Properties Ltd* [1965] Ch 816 but a scheme was upheld upon evidence being brought to show that the intention of the parties was that purchasers would be able to choose lots of varying sizes, such lots to form a scheme. In *Re Dolphin's Conveyance* [1970] Ch 654 requirement (a) was modified. The purchasers had not acquired their plots from a common vendor – later purchasers of plots taking from the nephew of the original vendors. However, the nephew continued to sell plots subject to the same restrictions as his aunts, the clear intention being that a local law be created. Megarry J laid stress on intention. On this basis, a building scheme was upheld:

> To hold that only where you find the necessary concomitants of a building scheme or a deed of mutual covenant can you give effect to the common intention found in the conveyances themselves, would, in my judgment, be to ignore the wider principle on which

the building scheme cases are founded and to fly in the face of other authority of which the clearest and most recent is *Baxter* v *Four Oaks Properties Ltd* ... .The building scheme cases stem, as I understand the law, from the wider rule that if there be found the common intention and the common interest ... the court will give effect to it, and are but an extension and example of that rule – Stamp J in *Dolphin*.

Furthermore,

[t]his right exists not only where the several parties execute a mutual deed of covenant, but wherever a mutual contract can be sufficiently established – Hall VC in *Renals* v *Cowlishaw*.

This is because:

[h]ere the equity, in my judgment, arises not by the effect of an implication derived from the existence of the four points specified by Parker J in *Elliston* v *Reacher*, or by the implication derived from the existence of a deed of mutual covenant, but by the existence of the common interest and the common intention actually expressed in the conveyances themselves – Stamp J.

According to the Law Commission in its report *Transfer of Land: Obsolete Restrictive Covenants* (Law Com No 201):

Over the years, however, and particularly in comparatively recent times, decided cases have shown that several of these conditions are not in fact necessary. As matters stand at present it seems that only two requirements are essential – namely, that the area of the scheme be defined; and that those who purchase from the creator of the scheme do so on the footing that all purchasers shall be mutually bound by, and mutually entitled to enforce, a defined set of restrictions (which may nonetheless vary to some extent between the lots). It remains to add that building schemes are not confined to cases where the units are sold freehold.

In *Small* v *Oliver and Saunders (Developments) Ltd* [2006] EWHC 1293 (Ch), a claim to a building scheme was not upheld, because the claimant failed to provide direct evidence that the several purchasers of properties on an estate had been aware of the reciprocal nature of the obligations contained in the several covenants. (However, the benefit of a restrictive covenant had been annexed and the dominant tenement owner was awarded £3,270 damages in lieu of an injunction for breach of it by the servient tenement owner.)

The establishment of a building scheme, because it creates a local law, enables the benefit of restrictive covenants to run which would otherwise be defeated – either because one of the essential requirements of running the burden cannot be satisfied when the developer sells the last plot, or, having sold the last plot, he has no interest in enforcing the covenants.

It was stated in *Re Wembley Park Estate Co Ltd's Transfer* [1968] Ch 491 that, although the courts are wary of finding in favour of a building scheme, if all the circumstances suggest one such an inference will readily be drawn. Indeed, in later cases the courts have been willing to modify the general law on restrictive covenants in order to uphold a building scheme. In *Brunner* v *Greenslade* [1971] Ch 993 it was held that, in a building scheme, both the benefit and the burden of covenants will run to a purchaser of part only of his vendor's original plot; and in *Texaco Antilles Ltd* v *Kernochan* [1973] AC 609, where two plots had, for a time, been held by a common owner (which would normally extinguish the covenant), it was held that, upon the plots again being owned by different persons, the covenant revived automatically. In *Re Spike & Rocca Group Ltd* (1980) 107 DLR (3d) 62 it was held that the principles of a building scheme apply not only to housing developments, but also to units in a shopping precinct.

One wonders if (quite apart from the positive 'covenants') the latest housing communities in America, comprising houses modelled on those of 'domestic goddess' Martha Stewart – both inside and out – would be upheld as building schemes here. 'Stringent rules protect the exterior look of the community: gardens must be maintained "in a neat and attractive condition", garage doors must be closed when not in use, "outside clothes-hanging devices are not permitted" and any fence must be pre-approved and "must be scalloped or have some other ornamental design (plain fences will not be permitted)". The chairman of the development company explained that a team will "help owners keep the houses the way Martha envisaged, but we're not the Martha Police [though] we'll be visiting regularly to help them"!' – source: *The Week*, 25 November 2006.

However, the latest suggestion with regard to the introduction of land obligations is that building schemes ought to be phased out by rendering them inoperative after a specified period, say 60 years. This would mean, of course, that the covenants could no longer be enforced, but this problem, it is suggested, could be solved by turning the area covered by the scheme into a commonhold. However, given that in commonholds you can only sell or mortgage the whole of your unit, and not part of it, and that it is extremely doubtful whether you will be able to grant a lease of it for more than 21 years, such a move would leave the properties subject to some of the harshest restrictions imaginable.

(Although not common, it is possible to have 'a letting scheme' in leasehold property, and this is similar to a building scheme. Apparently for the first time, such a scheme was upheld where it related to commercial property – shops – in *Williams* v *Kiley* [2002] EWCA Civ 1645.)

Running the burden

At common law

It was held in *Austerberry* v *Corporation of Oldham* (1885) 29 Ch D 750 that the burden of a positive covenant cannot run with the fee simple, that is, it cannot travel beyond the original covenantor. The reason for this was explained by Templeman LJ in *Rhone* v *Stephens* [1994] 2 All ER 65:

> For over 100 years it has been clear and accepted law that equity will enforce negative covenants against freehold land but has no power to enforce positive covenants against successors in title of the land. To enforce positive covenants would be to enforce a personal obligation against a person who has not covenanted. To enforce negative covenants is only to treat the land as subject to a restriction.

As we have seen, a positive covenant is one which involves the covenantor in expenditure.

E & G C Ltd v Bate (1935) 79 L J News 203

It was held that a covenant to construct a road upon the land of the covenantee when required so to do could not run so as to bind a successor in title of the covenantor.

It is the **effect** of the covenant which makes it positive or negative, not the words used, so that a covenant 'not to allow premises to fall into disrepair', although worded negatively, is, in fact, a positive covenant to repair.

Rhone v Stephens [1994] 2 All ER 65

The rule in *Austerberry* was reaffirmed by the House of Lords in *Rhone v Stephens*. The covenant required the covenantor to 'maintain to the reasonable satisfaction of the purchasers and their successors in title such part of the roof ... as lies above the property conveyed in wind and water tight condition'. The benefit of this covenant had been expressly assigned and the subsequent purchaser of the servient tenement had bought with notice of it. Nevertheless, the burden of the covenant was held to be unenforceable when severe leaks in the roof appeared.

This case highlights yet again the problems with positive covenants in freehold land; it does not seem fair or equitable that a person taking the servient land with full knowledge of the covenant should not be bound by it. The proposed land obligation would solve this problem. However, it is not only the burden of positive covenants which cannot run at law: the general rule is that the burden of any covenant affecting freehold land does not run with the land at common law. 'The rule is one of the many results of the wider principle of privity of contract' (Burn, 2004, p 934). Therefore, in order to truly 'run' the burden of a covenant we shall have to turn to equity.

However, given that covenants are usually created in order to retain the character, and therefore the value, of property, it is not surprising that several methods evolved by which this rule could be circumvented.

(a) Chains of covenants. The chain is forged, link by link, as each successive purchaser from the covenantor undertakes to indemnify his immediate predecessor in title, that is, his vendor. Of course, the original covenantor will always remain liable under his original covenant but, so long as the chain remains intact, each covenantor, including the original covenantor, can sue his successor in title, that is, his purchaser, for damages. While there is no break in the chain it can continue indefinitely, but any break in it (which could be caused by the failure of a covenantor-vendor to acquire an indemnity from his purchaser) would destroy the protection, rendering the original covenantor the only person liable for any breaches caused by the non-indemnifying purchaser or any assignee from him. Naturally, the protection would also be lost if the original covenantor were to die or disappear. (However, the original covenantee may be able to sue the present owner of the servient tenement under the Contracts (Rights of Third Parties) Act 1999, provided he can show the intention that the term be enforceable by the original covenantee – s 1(2).)

(b) Estate rentcharges. One of only two kinds of rentcharge which can still be created is an estate rentcharge – Rentcharges Act 1977, s 2(1) (the other being the family rentcharge – see Chapter 7).

As provided in s 2(1), estate rentcharges are those created for the purpose of:

(a) making covenants to be performed by the owner of the land affected by the rentcharge enforceable by the rent owner against the owner for the time being of the land; or

(b) meeting, or contributing towards, the cost of the performance by the rent owner of covenants for the provision of services, the carrying out of maintenance or repairs, the effecting of insurance or the making of any payment by him for the benefit of the land affected by the rentcharge or for the benefit of that and other land.

A rentcharge 'in possession issuing out of or charged on land being either perpetual or for a term of years absolute' is capable of being legal – Law of Property Act 1925, s 1(2)(b) – as is any right of entry attached to it.

In unregistered land, a legal rentcharge binds the world; an equitable one must be registered as a C(iii) land charge – Land Charges Act 1972, s 2(4). In registered land, a legal rentcharge is a registrable interest and must be substantively registered; an equitable one is a minor interest. Any right of entry attached to the rentcharge requires the same method of protection.

An estate rentcharge can be used to render the owner of servient land liable for the payment of money, or some other contribution, towards the maintenance of the dominant land and thereby make the covenant – even (and usually) a positive covenant – enforceable against him. Thus, estate rentcharges are commonly created in order to enforce covenants for repair, maintenance, services and insurance within a block of freehold flats. The sum fixed under the rentcharge must be reasonable having regard to the obligation imposed upon the servient owner.

(c) Rights of entry. The dominant owner can reserve a right of entry which will become exercisable upon the breach of a positive covenant.

(d) The rule in Halsall v Brizell [1957] Ch 169. This is also known as the doctrine of mutual benefit and burden, under which:

> In some cases a positive covenant can be enforced in practice by the operation of the maxim … This obliges a person who wishes to take advantage of a service or facility (eg a road or drains) to comply with any corresponding obligation to contribute to the cost of providing and maintaining it. The maxim cannot, however, be invoked where the burdened owner does not enjoy any service or facility to which his obligations attach or has no sufficient interest in the continuance of these benefits – Upjohn J in *Halsall v Brizell*.

Therefore, if a purchaser takes with the benefit of the use of a private road, he cannot enjoy that benefit without accepting a corresponding burden to contribute to its upkeep. (However, if his property is well served by a public highway, so that he does not use the private road, he will not be liable.) There are, however, several conditions that must be satisfied before the burden can be enforced under the rule: the benefit relied upon must arise out of the same subject matter as the burden, or be granted or reserved in exchange for, or in consideration of, the assumption of the burden (see *Four Oaks Estate Ltd* v *Hadley* (1986) 83 Law Soc Gaz 2326); the benefit must be real and substantial and not technical and minimal (*Tito* v *Waddell (No 2)* [1977] Ch 106); the benefit must be specifically granted or reserved. All three were accepted by Nourse LJ in the Court of Appeal in *Rhone* v *Stephens*.

In addition, per Lord Templeman in the House of Lords in *Rhone* v *Stephens*, the rule is limited to cases where the burden is 'relevant' to the enjoyment of the benefit; where the successor in title to the original covenantor has the opportunity to renounce the benefit of the transaction, and thus avoid the burden, and where the successor in title can be deprived of the benefit if he fails to assume the corresponding burden.

In *Thameside Town Ltd* v *Allotey* (1998) 76 P&CR D20, the Court of Appeal considered the scope and application of the rule. Peter Gibson LJ reiterated the view of the House of Lords in *Rhone* v *Stevens*, that a successor in title must have a choice whether to exercise the right or, having taken the right, whether to renounce the benefit. Peter Gibson LJ criticised the existing law and called for reform (which he felt was for Parliament to provide).

(e) The Law of Property Act 1925, s 79. It has been argued that if s 79 were given an interpretation similar to that given to s 78 in *Federated Homes*, it would have the effect of enabling a positive covenant to run with the land. However, any such argument is unlikely to succeed, given the view of the House of Lords in *Tophams Ltd* v *Earl of Sefton* [1967] 1 AC 50, where Upjohn LJ was emphatic that s 79 'does no more than render it unnecessary in the description of the parties to the conveyance to add after [the covenantor's] name "his executors, administrators and assigns"'. Thus Upjohn LJ believed that s 79 was no more than 'a form of statutory shorthand', and Wilberforce LJ agreed with him, saying that 'surely s 78 has no larger effect'. Therefore, any call for an interpretation of s 79 similar to that of s 78 in *Federated Homes* may well result in the overruling of *Federated Homes* itself! More recently, in *Rhone* v *Stephens* the House of Lords' view in *Tophams* was reaffirmed:

> [Section 79] has always been regarded as intended to remove conveyancing difficulties with regard to the form of covenants and to make it unnecessary to refer to successors in title. A similar provision relating to the benefit of covenants is to be found in section 78 of the Act of 1925. In *Smith and Snipes Hall Farm Ltd* v *River Douglas Catchment Board* [1949] ... it was held by the Court of Appeal that section 78 of the Act of 1925 had the effect of making the benefit of positive covenants run with the land. Without casting any doubt on those long-standing decisions I do not consider that it follows that section 79 of the Act of 1925 had the corresponding effect of making the burden of positive covenants run with the land ...

In *Tophams*, Lord Upjohn and Lord Wilberforce stated that s 79 of the Act of 1925 does not have the effect of causing covenents to run with the land. Finally, in *Federated Homes* Brightman J referred to the authorities on s 78 of the Act of 1925 and said that: 'section 79, in my view, involves quite different considerations and I do not think that it provides a helpful analogy'.

It seems clear, then, that **s 79 will not have the effect of running the burden of covenants – positive or negative – with the land.**

(f) The enlargement of a long leasehold into a freehold. The Law of Property Act 1925, s 153, enables a long lease to be enlarged into a freehold, whereupon the freehold

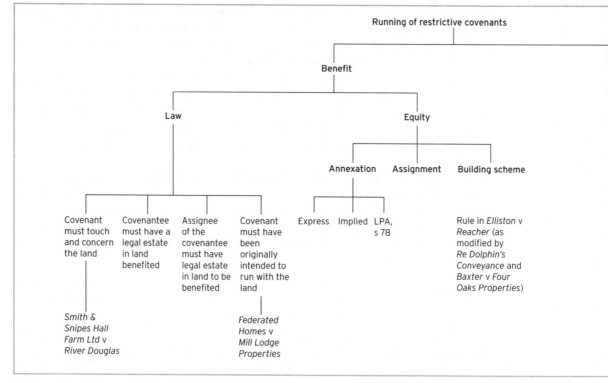

Figure 14.1

thus created is subject 'to all the same covenants … as the tenant would have been subject to if it had not been so enlarged'. For the purposes of s 153 a 'long lease' is one which was originally granted for more than 300 years with no rent or money value payable, and which has more than 200 years still to run. Therefore, this exception rarely, if ever, arises. The Leasehold Reform Act 1967 provides much the same effect upon the enfranchisement of a long lease.

(g) Granting a lease. The servient land can always be leased, rather than sold, in which case, as we saw in Chapter 8, there is no difficulty in running the covenants so long as there is privity of estate between the parties. It is for this reason that most flats are held on lease.

It is crucial to understand that these methods, though they may well enable an obligation to be enforced, do not have the effect of running the burden of a covenant.

In equity

Various though the exceptions to the rule in *Austerberry* v *Corporation of Oldham* may be, it remains the case that the burden of covenants – whether positive or negative – will never run with the land at common law. However, equity did step in, in the case of negative, that is, restrictive, covenants, the burden of which can now run with the land, provided that the requirements of the rule in *Tulk* v *Moxhay* are satisfied.

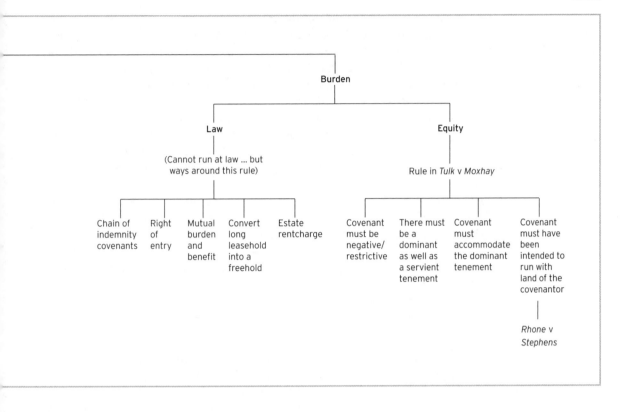

Tulk v *Moxhay* (1848) 2 Ph 774

The decision in this case itself was really no more than an application of the doctrine of notice in that Moxhay, a subsequent purchaser of land in Leicester Square which was subject to a covenant to keep, repair and maintain it as a 'square garden and pleasure ground . . . uncovered with any buildings' was held to be bound by the covenant having admittedly purchased the land with notice of it. The House of Lords granted Tulk an injunction against Moxhay building on the land.

However, what has become known as 'the rule in *Tulk* v *Moxhay*' lays down four essential requirements, all of which must be satisfied if the burden is to run in equity.

(a) *The covenant must be negative in nature.* Therefore, the burden of a positive covenant can never run – neither at law nor in equity. However, care must be taken to ensure that it is the substance of the covenant which is negative, not merely the words used. Thus, a covenant 'not to allow Blackacre to fall into disrepair', though couched in negative words, is in fact a positive covenant because it will involve the covenantor in expense.

(b) *The covenant must accommodate the dominant tenement.* Thus, there must be a dominant, as well as a servient, tenement, and both covenantor and covenantee must own an estate in his tenement. In addition, the covenant must have been made for the benefit of the dominant tenement – it must 'accommodate', or touch and concern, it. It is usual for courts today to presume that a covenant benefits, that is, accommodates, the dominant tenement unless it can be shown that this cannot reasonably be the case.

(c) *The covenantee must, at the date of the covenant, have owned land benefited by the covenant.* Thus, in *London County Council* v *Allen* [1914] 3 KB 642, where a builder covenanted with the Council as covenantee not to build on a certain plot of land, it was held that the benefit of the covenant did not bind a subsequent purchaser of that plot – Mrs Allen – because the Council had never owned the dominant tenement.

This requirement could cause difficulties for building schemes. However, so long as all the requirements of *Elliston* v *Reacher* and the remaining three under *Tulk* v *Moxhay* are satisfied, the burden of restrictive covenants can be imposed by subsequent purchasers of each dominant tenement even though, upon sale of the final plot, the original covenantee, that is, the builder, parts with all his estate and interest in the land.

(d) *The covenant must have been intended to run with the servient tenement.* This intention is usually presumed in the absence of anything to the contrary in the conveyance. In *Re Royal Victoria Pavilion, Ramsgate* [1961] Ch 581, Pennycuick J held that a covenant which began, 'The vendors hereby covenant with the purchasers that they the vendors will ...' was sufficient indication of a contrary intention, even though, 'the covenant contains no express provision to the effect that it is not made on behalf of successors in title'. As confirmed in *Rhone* v *Stephens*, s 79 will not satisfy this requirement.

If all four requirements of the rule are satisfied, **and the purchaser has notice of it** – for 'if an equity is attached to the property by the owner, no one purchasing with notice of that equity can stand in a different position from the party from whom he purchased', Lord Cottenham LC in *Tulk* v *Moxhay* – the burden of the covenant runs with the land. As we know, whether or not a purchaser has 'notice' depends, generally, upon the registration or not of the interest: Law of Property Act 1925, s 198.

It **does not matter that the benefit passed at common law and the burden in equity**, so long as both pass – *Rogers* v *Hosegood* [1900] Ch 388, where Farwell J stated:

> there can be no difference between law and equity in construing such covenants with a view to seeing whether they do or do not run with the land ... in many cases decided by the Court of Chancery expressions are found to the effect that the defendants are bound in equity, whether the covenants in strictness run with the land at law or not.

As Lord Templeman said, quite rightly, in *Rhone* v *Stephens* 'Equity supplements but does not contradict the common law'. This being so, would equity refuse to pass the benefit of a covenant which has passed at common law? In any case:

> the rules applicable to the benefit running are ... the same in law and in equity, except that equity, unlike law, does not require that the assumption of the benefit of the covenant be limited to an assignment of the whole of the covenantee's relevant land but permits separate assignments to assignees of parts of that land ... – Ungoed-Thomas J in *Stilwell* v *Blackman* [1967] 3 WLR 1408.

So, if anything, equity is even more generous than the common law!
Thus:

> The benefit of a restrictive covenant can pass at *law* (if the common law conditions for transmission are fulfilled), even though successful enforcement of the covenant depends

ultimately on the transmission of the burden in accordance with *equitable* principles. (The doubt introduced on this point by Romer LJ in *Miles* v *Easter* [1933] Ch 611 at 630 has now been submerged by *Federated Homes Ltd* v *Mill Lodge Properties Ltd* [1980] 1 WLR 594.) – Gray and Gray (2000, p 1163).

This echoes R E Megarry and H W R Wade (2005, p 1024), who said:

> Since 1875 it ought to make no practical difference whether the benefit passes under the rules of law or of equity, since the same court can enforce both ... Equity merely follows the law. But more complicated rules have developed which are now assumed to apply in all actions ... so making the law follow equity.

Ironically, a building has, in fact, recently been allowed upon the garden in Leicester Square. In *R* v *Westminster City Council, ex parte Leicester Square Coventry Street Association* (1989) 87 LGR 675, Simon Brown J held that the City Council had the power to dispose of the land to the London Electricity Board for the purpose of building a substation thereon. However, the substation is small and the only building.

When and for how long?

Duration of restrictive covenants

A restrictive covenant can only be enforced if and when both the burden and the benefit of it run with the servient and dominant tenements, and, prima facie, it remains enforceable indefinitely. However, if the dominant owner acquiesces in any open breach by the servient owner for such a period and in such circumstances that a reasonable person would believe the covenant had been abandoned, the court will not enforce it. The court will also refuse to enforce a covenant where it can no longer be of value to the dominant tenement because of the changed character of the surrounding neighbourhood.

Even if a covenant is enforceable, the court may, instead, award damages to the dominant owner if it considers that this would compensate him sufficiently. This is rarely likely to be the case, and more often a mandatory injunction preventing the servient owner from breach would be the most suitable remedy, though if such an order would be oppressive to the defendant, the court would award damages in lieu.

Wakeham v Wood (1981) 43 P&CR 40

The servient owner, in breach of covenant, constructed a building which obstructed the dominant owner's sea view. The court held that such a 'flagrant disregard' of the dominant owner's rights could not be compensated by money – indeed, merely to award damages against the defendant would allow him to 'buy his way out of his wrong'. Accordingly the court ordered a mandatory injunction under the terms of which the defendant had to demolish the obstruction.

Jacob LJ warned in *Bailey* v *Mortimer* [2004] EWCA Civ 1514 that 'where there is doubt as to whether a restrictive covenant applies or whether consent under a restrictive covenant is being unreasonably withheld, the prudent party will get the matter sorted out before starting buildings, as could have been done in this case. If he takes a chance, then it will require very strong circumstances where, if the chance having been taken and lost, an injunction will be withheld'. On the facts, an injunction to remove an extension was granted.

Unity of seisin

As with easements and profits, unity of seisin will extinguish a restrictive covenant, though not necessarily in the case of a building scheme. In *Texaco Antilles Ltd* v *Kernochan* [1973] AC 609, where two plots were owned between 1942 and 1951 by the same company, Lord Cross of Chelsea explained that:

> As soon as the two sets of lots came into the same hands it became impossible for any action to enforce the covenants to be brought by the owner of one set against the owner of the other since he was the same person.
>
> The point of law which arises for consideration is therefore whether in a case where there is nothing in the conveyancing putting an end to the unity of seisin or in the surrounding circumstances to indicate that the restrictions in the scheme are no longer to apply as between the owners of the lots previously in common ownership the fact that they have been in common ownership puts an end to the restrictions so far as concerns the relations of subsequent owners for the time being of that part of the estate inter se so that if the common owner of those lots wished them to apply after the severance he would have to reimpose them as fresh restrictions under a sub-scheme relating to them. It would their Lordships think be somewhat unfortunate if this was the law . . . It is no doubt true that if the restrictions in question exist simply for the mutual benefit of two adjoining properties and both those properties are bought by one man the restrictions will automatically come to an end and will not revive on a subsequent severance unless the common owner then recreates them. But their Lordships cannot see that it follows from this that if a number of people agree that the area covered by all their properties shall be subject to a 'local law' the provisions of which shall be enforceable by any owner for the time being of any part against any other owner and the whole area has never at any time come into common ownership an action by one owner of a part against another owner of a part must fail if it can be shown that both parts were either at the inception of the scheme or at any time subsequently in common ownership.

However, the High Court made it clear in *University of East London Higher Education Corp* v *Barking and Dagenham LBC* [2004] EWHC 2710, (Ch), that there is no extinguishment of restrictive covenants when dominant and servient properties are held by the same trustee of distinct trusts, nor when both properties are held by a public authority for different statutory purposes.

Release

It is also possible for a servient owner to be released from the burden of a restrictive covenant. In *Chatsworth Estates Co* v *Fewell* [1931] 1 Ch 224, Farwell J stated that it is possible for release to be implied from the acts and omissions of the covenantee or his assignees: where the covenantee acquiesces in past breaches of the covenant, he thought the situation to be 'analogous to the doctrine of estoppel' and that 'it is a fair test to treat it in that way and ask, "Have the plaintiffs by their acts and omissions represented to the defendant that the covenants are no longer to be enforceable . . . ?"' Obviously, the parties to, or those bound by, a covenant can agree a release expressly between them.

Lands Tribunal

The major means of extinguishing or modifying a restrictive covenant, however, is by an application under the Law of Property Act 1925, s 84, which provides that:

(1) The Lands Tribunal shall . . . have power . . . on the application of any person interested in any freehold land affected by any restriction arising under covenant or otherwise as to the user thereof or the building thereon, by order wholly or partially to discharge or modify any such restriction on being satisfied –

    (a)   that by reason of changes in the character of the property or the neighbourhood or other circumstances of the case which the Lands Tribunal may deem material, the restriction ought to be deemed obsolete; or

    (aa)   that . . . the continued existence thereof would impede some reasonable user of the land for public or private purposes or, as the case may be, would unless modified so impede such user; or

    (b)   that the persons of full age and capacity . . . entitled to the benefit of the restriction . . . have agreed, either expressly or by implication, by their acts or omissions, to the same being discharged or modified; or

    (c)   that the proposed discharge or modification will not injure the persons entitled to the benefit of the restriction.

(2) The courts shall have power on the application of any person interested –

    (a)   to declare whether or not in any particular case any freehold land is, or would in any given event be, affected by a restriction imposed by any instrument; or

    (b)   to declare what, upon the true construction of any instrument purporting to impose a restriction, is the nature and extent of the restriction thereby imposed and whether the same is, or would in any given event be, enforceable and if so by whom.

In deciding whether or not to modify or discharge a restrictive covenant, the tribunal ought, according to *Re Bass Ltd's Application* (1973) 26 P&CR 156, to ask the following questions:

1 Is the proposed user reasonable?

2 Do the covenants impede that user?

3 Does impeding the proposed user secure practical benefits to the objectors?

4 If so, are those benefits of substantial value or advantage?

5 Is impeding the proposed user contrary to the public interest?

6 Would money be an adequate compensation?

It was stated in *Robins v Berkeley Homes (Kent) Ltd* [1996] EGCS 75 that where application is made on the basis of s 84(1)(a), the burden of showing that a change in neighbourhood had occurred is a heavy one.

It was said in *Gilbert v Spoor* [1983] Ch 27 that discharge or modification should be refused so long as the benefit is reasonable, and in *Haliday v Burford* (1982) (unreported) that a covenant will not be obsolete so long as someone still wants to enforce it.

Re Edward's Application (1983) 47 P&CR 458

Notwithstanding *Spoor* and *Burford*, a covenant restricting the use of the servient land to that of a private dwellinghouse was modified in order to allow the owner to use it as a general store, as well as a dwellinghouse, notwithstanding that such modification was opposed by and adversely affected the objector. The Lands Tribunal felt that the injury, such as it was, was minor and the restriction secured no practical benefit of substantial advantage. Therefore, the modification was compensatable by money – £500 to be exact!

Readers are recommended to see the comprehensive discussion on the way in which the Lands Tribunal exercises its powers under s 84 in Maudsley and Burn (2004, pp 1001–1012).

Re Beech's Application (1990) 59 P&CR 502

The Lands Tribunal can, if it sees fit, refuse to discharge or modify a covenant even though planning permission has been granted. The covenant in *Beech* again restricted use of a house to that of a dwellinghouse. The house was a council house which had been sold by the local authority under the 'right to buy' legislation. Subsequently, the purchaser decided to sell the house to a firm of solicitors which wanted to use it as one of their offices. Planning permission had been obtained by the solicitors for the proposed change of user and an application was made to the Lands Tribunal under s 84(1) for the discharge of the covenant. The local authority opposed the application. The Lands Tribunal rejected the application and the Court of Appeal upheld that decision, their Lordships making it clear that the tribunal's powers under s 84 operate within a separate system from that applicable to authorities under planning law, and though the tribunal is required to take any grant of planning permission into account as a relevant consideration, it is not bound to modify or discharge a covenant simply because such permission has been granted. The court also accepted the local authority's 'thin end of the wedge' argument – defined in Maudsley and Burn (6th edition, 1992, p 827) as 'a relevant consideration that the proposal, though not particularly harmful in itself, must be rejected in case it gives rise to similar proposals which would succeed because the first had done so, and which would cumulatively be disadvantageous' – that modification or discharge would make it more difficult for the council to resist any similar application in the future 'whether as covenantee or as planning authority'.

See also *Re Azfar's Application* [2002] 1 P&CR 215.

In *Re Hopcraft's Application* (1993) 66 P&CR 475 the Lands Tribunal held that the fact that a local authority grants planning permission for use of land for a particular purpose does not mean that the authority should no longer be entitled to the benefit of the covenant. The tribunal's task is to examine the facts of each application and reach its own conclusion as to whether the applicant has established one or more of the statutory grounds upon which the tribunal is bound to discharge or modify the covenant. On the facts, no statutory ground was made out. However, where a statutory body has statutory functions to be discharged in the public interest, and has power to acquire and hold land for the purpose of discharging that function, private rights will not be enforced by the courts. Thus, the benefit of a restrictive covenant cannot stand in the way of property acquired by a statutory body for a statutory purpose being used for that purpose – *Brown* v *Heathlands Mental National Health Service Trust* [1996] 1 All ER 133. However, in *Re Hextall's Application* (2000) 79 P&CR 382, the fact that a council had resolved to grant planning permission was held to be strongly persuasive that the council's proposal would be a reasonable user and the application was rejected under s 84(1)(a) but allowed under s 84(1)(aa), subject to payments of compensation to five of the objectors.

Two cases concerned the government's 'Care in the Community' policy. In the first, *C & G Homes* v *Secretary of State for Health* [1991] 2 All ER 841, the Secretary of State's use of two dwellinghouses on a residential estate as homes for former hospital patients who had suffered from mental disability and who were to be returned to the community was held to be in breach of a covenant which restricted user of the houses to that of a private dwelling only. Ferris J, in granting the plaintiff a declaration that the use was in breach of the covenant, ordered an inquiry as to damages, the difficulty being that though the purpose of the covenant was to protect enjoyment of the dominant tenement, it did not cover financial loss suffered by the impaired marketability of the dominant tenements. In contrast, in the second case, *National Schizophrenia Fellowship* v *Ribble Estates SA* (1993) 25 HLR 476, the planned use of houses to provide accommodation for persons who had been receiving treatment in mental hospitals and who were ready to be discharged back into the community, was held to be merely residential. The words of the covenant were held not to be wide enough to restrict or control the owners of the property as to the identity and personal characteristics of the individuals they chose to permit to occupy it.

In *Re Lloyd's & Lloyd's Application* (1993) 66 P&CR 112, the applicants wanted to use a house for the care of ten psychiatric patients. The property was subject to a covenant restricting its use to that of a dwellinghouse, school or boarding house. The application was based on the fact that the character of the neighbourhood had changed – another house in the area was being used as an old people's home. It was also contended that the proposed user was no more detrimental to the area than a boarding school, which user was allowed under the covenant. The application was granted, notwithstanding objectors argued that the proposed use would adversely affect the area and the value of neighbouring properties.

It may seem that most applications succeed; however, if the tribunal is not satisfied that the application falls within one of the grounds provided in s 84(1), it will dismiss the application. Thus in *Re Beechwood Homes' Application* (1992) 64 P&CR 535, the application was dismissed because the restriction ought not to be deemed obsolete and to modify it would result in substantial harm to the objectors. In addition, although the restriction did impede a reasonable user, it also secured for the dominant tenement practical benefits of substantial advantage. In *Re Hunt's Application* (1996) 73 P&CR 126, although none of the objectors would suffer any loss of view, and their fears as to increased traffic were unfounded, the application would be refused since the house, which the applicant had already built in breach of a covenant under a building scheme, which was well in advance of the building line, presented a generally cramped appearance which was obtrusive in relation to the remainder of the building scheme area: the relaxation of the scheme of covenants would, in this case, create an undesirable and dangerous precedent for the further subdivision of plots. Finally, the tribunal held that it was not contrary to the public interest to order the demolition of the house. A final example is provided by *Re North's Application* (1998) 75 P&CR 117, where the tribunal held that although there had been changes in the character of the neighbourhood since the covenant was created, they were not material as the neighbourhood had retained its 'attractive semi-rural character'. Also, the original purpose of the restriction could still be achieved in respect of the house in question, which meant that the covenant was not obsolete. Although the proposed development was a reasonable user of the servient land, the restriction secured practical benefits of substantial advantage to the dominant owner in that it prevented deterioration of the view from the house and the obstruction of light from and to the windows in the living room wall. In any event, even if the benefit did not attach to a house built some 40 years after the restriction was imposed, it did attach to the garden of that house and still secured substantial practical benefits to the objector, as it would greatly affect the enjoyment of that garden. Not surprisingly, for all these reasons the application was refused. However, in so doing the tribunal stated that power granted under s 84 did not extend to the insertion by the tribunal of additional words in a restrictive covenant, which would rewrite the original contract, where such words were wholly unrelated to the requirements of the section.

It can be seen, then, that each application is considered on its own facts. Further, in *Re University of Westminster* v *President of the Lands Tribunal* [1998] 3 All ER 1014 the Court of Appeal held that the tribunal was under a duty to exercise its discretion judicially in the light of known relevant circumstances, but there was nothing in s 84 to indicate that the tribunal's discretion was limited or abrogated by reason of the fact that the application was unopposed: the tribunal must have regard to the applicant's proposals for the user of the property and to the interests of those whom the restrictions may have been intended to protect.

In making its decisions, the Lands Tribunal has a wide range of possible 'remedies' for objectors. In *Re Fisher & Gimson (Builders) Ltd's Application* (1992) 65 P&CR 312, a covenant restricted the use of land to that of a garden. The applicant built a house on the land. Objectors applied to have it demolished. It was held that although the covenant was not obsolete, the detriment to the objectors was not substantial and could be overcome by compensation of £6,000 each. The applicants were lucky for, as we saw in *Re Hunt*, demolition could have been ordered by the tribunal, had it seen fit.

The findings of fact by the Lands Tribunal are not open to challenge – Court of Appeal in *University of Westminster's Application* (1999) 78 P&CR 82.

Can the exact meaning of a covenant change with the passage of time, so that it has become extinguished? This question was addressed in *Dano Ltd* v *Earl Cadogan* [2003] 2 P&CR 10. The covenant in question restricted the use of the premises to 'housing of the working classes'. Did this phrase have the same meaning as it had when created in 1930, or indeed, any meaning capable of precise definition today? The court accepted that nowadays the term 'working classes' means those who, due to their low income, require inexpensive accommodation. The wording of the covenant was changed to 'affordable housing'. This is an interesting and important point, given the phenomenal rise in house prices and rents and the resultant inability of people in essential jobs – nurses, teachers, firefighters, police, etc – to be able to afford accommodation in certain areas, especially London, leaving such areas under resourced. (However, government plans to build tens of thousands of 'low cost' houses are being met by strong objections from the environmental lobby.)

Dano came before the Court of Appeal a year later – [2004] 1 P&CR 169 – on a different issue and it held that where,

> the benefit of a covenant is annexed to land described by reference to a named 'estate', it will be a matter of construction of the particular covenant whether it continues to apply to a land originally within it once the named estate has ceased to exist in any recognisable form – Carnwath LJ at p 174.

On the facts, the original intention (as gleaned from the document as a whole) was that the covenant would last only so long as the dominant tenement remained settled land. As this was no longer the case, the covenant was no longer enforceable.

These two hearings show how important restrictive covenants are – both to the holder of the benefit, and to the party seeking to avoid the burden.

As can be seen from the references to many of the cases, the *Property and Conveyancing Reports* are a fertile source of s 84(1) applications.

How can you protect them?

Ensuring rights against third parties

In unregistered land, as restrictive covenants can only ever be equitable, they must be protected. The form of protection depends upon the date of creation – if before 1926, the covenant is subject to the doctrine of notice; if after 1925 it is registrable as a Class D(ii) land charge, being void for non-registration only against a purchaser for value.

The Law of Property Act 1925, s 198(1) provides that:

> The registration of any instrument or matter under the Land Charges Act 1972 ... shall be deemed to constitute actual notice of such instrument or matter, and of the fact of registration, to all persons and for all purposes connected with the land affected, as from the date of registration ...

In registered land, restrictive covenants are minor interests and should be entered by way of notice. Of course, 'the fact that an interest is the subject of a notice does not necessarily mean that the interest is valid, but does mean that the priority of the interest, if valid, is protected for the purposes of sections 29 and 30' – LRA 2002, s 32(3). Section 30(2) provides that 'the priority of an interest is protected in any case, if the interest is ... the subject of a notice in the register'.

As already noted, the effectiveness of the rule in *Tulk* v *Moxhay* in running the burden of restrictive covenants depends upon the servient owner having notice of the covenant.

Reform

The area of restrictive covenants has so vexed the Law Commission that it has published several reports on it (as well as those of the Wilberforce Committee (1965), the Royal Commission on Legal Services (1979), the Standing Committee on Conveyancing Revision (1986) and the Nugee Committee (1986)). The most recent

Law Commission report is *Transfer of Land: Obsolete Restrictive Covenants* (Law Com No 201, 1991)). The main problem is seen to be the rule that the burden of positive covenants cannot run with freehold land (which results in most flats being leasehold). It seems a pity that the recommendation of 1965, that the burden of positive covenants should be able to run, was never acted on. Now we are faced with the proposed 'land obligation' which has already been mentioned at various points in this book. The land obligation will take the form either of a 'neighbour obligation' in the case of existing positive and negative covenants, or a 'development obligation' in the case of common rights and duties between owners of units in integrated developments (Law Com No 127, 1984).

Positive as well as negative obligations would be enforceable only as between current owners of the dominant and servient tenements.

From the above, and particularly the difficulties in running the burden of covenants with freehold land, it will be appreciated that reform is long overdue. Indeed, restrictive covenants have been the subject of some eight Law Commission reports and working parties. It is, perhaps, a pity that the recommendation of the first of these – the Wilberforce Committee on Positive Covenants Affecting Land (which was set up in 1963 and reported in 1965) – that positive covenants should be made to run with the land, was not implemented. However, the Law Commission in its Report No 127, *Transfer of Land – The Law of Positive and Restrictive Covenants*, in 1984, the mainspring of which was 'the need to deal with the unsatisfactory state of the present law about positive obligations imposed upon one piece of land for the benefit of another', pointed out that:

> great problems would be encountered, and an unsatisfactory result produced, if reform of the law relating to positive obligations were carried out in isolation and without any associated reform of the law of restrictive covenants ... the latter is itself in many ways imperfect and uncertain ... To build a new law of positive obligations upon these unsatisfactory foundations would therefore serve only to exacerbate the difficulties ... This difficulty could be solved only in one way, by extending the process of law reform to include both positive and restrictive obligations and welding the two into a system which was both unified and satisfactory.

The Commission's solution is 'land obligations'. This new interest in land will:

> lean heavily ... on analogies with the existing law of easements ... The highly technical rules determining whether the benefit and the burden of restrictive covenants may pass to new owners of the land affected will ... disappear; and any doubt which might otherwise arise as to whether an obligation was intended to run with the land or operate only between the parties will be removed by requiring the parties who intend to create an obligation running with the land to label it by express words as a 'land obligation' ... Finally, since the interest is essentially an interest attaching to the ownership of particular parcels of land, it will only be enforceable by and against the current owners of those parcels of land. Unlike a restrictive covenant it will not remain enforceable between the original parties after they have parted with the land.

When land obligations come into being, it is proposed by the Law Commission that:

> after a fixed period of eighty years from the original creation of a restrictive covenant, it is to be considered obsolete unless there is proof that it is not ... this involves a rule that all restrictive covenants should lapse at the end of that time ... We consider that dealing with

all pre-1926 covenants ... by the end of the year 2005 is an acceptable target – Law Com No 201, 1991.

The burden of proving a covenant is not obsolete lies with the covenantee. Even covenants which are not obsolete by the end of this period are to lapse, but the covenantee/dominant owner will be able to apply for it to be replaced by a land obligation.

In its September 2006 update the Law Commission announced 'a project to examine easements, covenants and similar land law rights with a view to their reform and rationalisation' and went on to state, 'we intend to tie this work in with a reconsideration of the Law Commission's earlier work [in LC127]' – www.lawcom.gov.uk/easements.htm.

In unregistered land, land obligations will be either legal by virtue of an amendment to the Law of Property Act 1925, s 1(2)(a), or equitable. The Law Commission recommends that 'whether legal or equitable' they 'should be added to the list of things which are registrable under the Land Charges Act 1972, taking their place amongst those now registrable as charges of Class C'.

In registered land, 'Land obligations shall not be capable of being overriding interests for the purposes of the Land Registration Act 1925' – presumably the same will be the case for LRA 2002.

Summary

In this final chapter we have considered the following in regard to restrictive covenants of freehold land:

■ Their nature and classification.

■ The rules, principles and formalities of acquisition:

- Running the benefit –
  - At common law – covenants must touch and concern the land; there must have been an intention that the benefit run with the land; the original covenantee must have had a legal estate in the dominant land; the assignee of the covenantee must have a legal estate in the dominant land; Contracts (Rights of Third Parties) Act 1999.

- In equity – annexation; assignment; building schemes.

- Running the burden –
  - At common law – chains of covenants; estate rentcharges; rights of entry; rule in *Halsall* v *Brizell*; creation by lease; LPA 1925, s 79 (non-effect of).

  - In equity –
    - Rule in *Tulk* v *Moxhay* –
      - Covenant must be negative;
      - Covenant must accommodate the dominant tenement;
      - Covenantee must have owned the dominant tenement;

  – Covenant must have been intended to run with the servient tenement;

  – Servient owner must have had notice.

- Duration of restrictive covenants – unity of seisin; release; application to the Lands Tribunal under LPA 1925, s 84(1).
- Protection – unregistered land; registered land.
- Reform.

References

Burn, E H, *Cheshire and Burn's Modern Law of Real Property*, 16th edition, London: Butterworths, 2000.

Burn, E H, *Maudsley & Burn's Land Law Cases and Materials*, 8th edition, London: Oxford University Press, 2004.

Gray, K, *Elements of Land Law*, 2nd edition, London: Butterworths, 1993.

Gray, K and Gray, S F, *Elements of Land Law*, 3rd edition, London: Butterworths, 2000.

Gray, K.J. and Symes, P.D., *Real Property and Real People*, London: Butterworths, 1981.

Harpum, C, Megarry and Wade, *The Law of Real Property*, 6th edition, London: Sweet and Maxwell, 2000.

Law Commission, *Transfer of Land - The Law of Positive and Restrictive Covenants* (Law Com No 127, 1984).

Law Commission, *Transfer of Land: Obsolete Restrictive Covenants* (Law Com No 201, 1991).

Further reading

Running the benefit
At common law

Stevens , R, 'The Contracts (Rights of Third Parties) Act 1999' (2004) 14 LQR 292.

Building schemes

George, S (2000) *Liverpool Park Estates*, Liverpool University Press, 2000.

Running the burden
At common law

Davis, CJ, "The Principle of Benefit and Burden', 57 CLJ 522.

Rhone v *Stephens* [1994] 2 All ER 65

In equity

Chappelle, D, 'Looking at covenants positively, for a change', in *New Perspectives on Property Law, Human Rights and the Home*, ed. Alistair Hudson, Cavendish, 2003.

George, S I, '*Tulk* v *Moxhay* Restored - to its Historical Context' (1990) *Liverpool Law Review* 173.

Gravells, N, 'Enforcement of Positive Covenants Affecting Freehold Land' (1994) 110 LQR 346.

Remedies

Martin, J, 'Remedies for Breach of Restrictive Covenants' [1996] Conv 329.

Reform

George, S I, 'The Tail on the Kite of Commonholds' [1992] *Liverpool Law Review* 83.

Gravells, N P, 'Enforcement of Positive Covenants Affecting Freehold Land' (1994) 110 LQR 346.

Wilkinson, H W, 'Nothing to Lose but your Fetters: Obsolete Restrictive Covenants' [1992] Conv 2.

Glossary

Land law has a language of its own which frequently creates difficulty for students. Not only are many of the expressions technical, but also even apparently familiar words are given a different meaning. Obviously, if you cannot understand its language, you cannot hope to understand land law. Therefore, this glossary aims to explain the meanings of words and phrases which commonly arise in land law. As well as the technical terms appearing in this book, those which you may encounter in your lectures and in your other reading are also included. Although the most frequently used expressions are explained here, this glossary does not provide an exhaustive list and you should, whenever you come across a term which is not contained in it, immediately ascertain its meaning, noting also the context in which it is used, and add it to the glossary.

abatement the removal of an obstruction to the exercise of an easement by the dominant tenement owner.

absolute an interest which is neither conditional nor determinable by some specified event.

abstract of title a summary of all matters which affect the title offered by the vendor, including the various dispositions, eg sales of the property and deaths of interest holders.

acquiescence failure to take steps to prevent some act, such as the exercise of a right which has not been granted, or an obstruction to the exercise of a right which is in the course of being acquired.

administrators persons appointed by the court to administer the estate of a person who died intestate, ie without leaving a will.

adverse possession a means by which an adverse possessor can acquire the title to land, thus dispossessing the previous 'paper-title' owner.

alienation the transfer of interests in property from one owner to another. This can be by way of sale, gift or some other transaction.

animus possidendi the intention to (adversely) possess the land of another.

annexation the attaching of the benefit of a restrictive covenant to the dominant tenement so that it will run with the land.

ante-nuptial prior to marriage.

appendant a right which is attached to the land by operation of law.

appurtenant (1) a right which is attached to the land by agreement between the parties. (2) A profit à prendre which benefits a piece of land, and not merely the owner of it.

assent the means by which personal representatives vest the deceased's property in those entitled under his will or intestacy. An assent need not be by deed.

assignment the transfer of property, usually a lease.

barring the entail the means by which an entailed interest can be disentailed and converted into a fee simple.

base fee arises where an entail has been incompletely barred.

beneficial owner a person entitled to an interest for his own benefit and not, for example, as trustee.

beneficiaries those entitled under a trust.

bequest gift of personalty made by will.

bona vacantia property which reverts to the Crown for lack of any other owner.

caution a method of protecting minor interests in registered land.

cestui que trust another name for a beneficiary under a trust.

cesser on redemption the automatic ending of a mortgage upon the mortgagor complying with all his obligations to the mortgagee, eg paying off the monies lent and interest thereon as agreed.

charge an incumbrance upon the land – either legal or equitable – by which a debt or other obligation is secured, eg a mortgage.

chattel any property other than freehold land.

chattels real leasehold land.

choses in action intangible rights in property other than land, eg copyrights, debts.

choses in possession tangible property other than land, eg cars, jewellery.

clog some restriction placed by the mortgagee upon the mortgagor's right to redeem.

commonhold a method by which flats can be held as freeholds and under which obligations – either positive or negative – can be enforced.

conditional interest an interest which is subject to some conditioning event – either a condition precedent or subsequent. Until a condition precedent is satisfied, the holder of it has merely a hope of attaining the interest. Upon the happening of a stipulated subsequent event, the grantor has a right of re-entry.

consolidation the means by which a mortgagee can require a mortgagor to redeem more than one mortgage at the same time.

constructive notice *see* **notice**

constructive trust a trust imposed by equity in order to give effect to some common intention between the parties.

contingent a future interest which is uncertain, eg an interest subject to a condition precedent. Contingent interests are subject to the rule against perpetuities.

conversion equitable doctrine under which the interests of beneficiaries behind a trust for sale are treated as interests in the proceeds of sale, not in the land.

conveyance any instrument, other than a will, which transfers property from one owner to another.

co-ownership ownership which is shared by two or more persons at the same time holding as joint tenants (legal estate and/or equitable interests) or tenant in common (equitable interests only).

corporeal capable of being physically possessed, eg soil, bricks.

covenant a promise made by deed.

covenantee the person who has the benefit of a covenant.

covenantor the person who has the burden of a covenant.

deed (1) before 1 August 1991 – a document which has been signed, sealed and delivered. (2) After 31 July 1991 – a document which has been executed and signed as a deed in the presence of witnesses, and then delivered.

deed of discharge a document which brings a strict settlement to an end.

defeasance the determination of an interest upon a specified event.

demise the grant of a lease.

determinable interest one which will determine automatically upon the happening of some specified event.

determine come to an end.

devise gift of realty made by will.

disentail convert an entailed interest into a fee simple.

distrain, distress the legal right to seize chattels, without a court order, in order to satisfy some debt or claim. Usually exercised by a landlord against his tenant by way of compensation for unpaid rent.

dominant tenement land which enjoys the benefit of some right, eg an easement or restrictive covenant.

easement a right enjoyed over the servient tenement for the benefit of the dominant tenement, eg a right of way.

encumbrance a liability attached to a piece of land, eg the burden of a restrictive covenant.

entail an interest in land which lasts only as long as there is issue of the relevant gender of the original grantor.

en ventre sa mère in the mother's womb; conceived but not born.

equity of redemption the sum total of a mortgagor's rights in property during the continuance of a mortgage thereon.

equity's darling a bona fide purchaser for value of the legal estate without notice.

estate (1) an interest in land for a prescribed period. (2) The whole of property left by a deceased person.

estate contract a contract to create or convey an estate or interest in land.

estate rentcharge a means by which a positive covenant can be made to run with freehold land.

estoppel equitable doctrine under which any person who makes a promise or representation to another and allows the other person to act to his detriment in reliance thereon, will be precluded from denying that promise or representation.

execute complete a conveyance.

executors persons appointed by will to administer the deceased's estate.

executory not yet executed.

fee simple absolute in possession a legal estate in land which lasts indefinitely whilst there are persons entitled under the prior owner's will or intestacy. The first legal estate in land provided for by LPA 1925, s 1(1).

fee tail an entailed interest (abolished as from 1 January 1997).

fine payment of a capital sum. Also called 'premium'.

fittings personal property which has not become a fixture and which can, therefore, be removed by a vendor (subject to any contrary agreement in the contract).

fixed-term tenancy one of specified length, not periodic.

fixtures items which have become attached to the land and are, therefore, realty. Fixtures can only be removed by a vendor if the contract specifically so provides.

flying freehold a freehold of a flat above ground level.

foreclosure method by which a mortgagee acquires the whole of the mortgagor's equity of redemption in order to satisfy the mortgage debt or other obligation.

freehold the fee simple absolute in possession.

gazumping where a would-be purchaser of land is defeated by another who offers a higher price after the vendor has agreed to sell at the lower price, but before contracts have been exchanged.

gazundering where a vendor of land is forced to accept an unreasonably low offer from a purchaser who reduces his previous higher offer at the last minute. The opposite, in fact, of gazumping.

hereditaments inheritable rights in land. Hereditaments may be (a) corporeal, ie tangible, physical, such as the soil, or any physical structure attached thereto; or (b) incorporeal, ie intangible rights over land, such as easements, profits and rentcharges.

incumbrance a burden attached to land.

indenture outmoded term for a deed.

infant anyone under 18 years of age. Also called a 'minor'.

in gross existing without a dominant tenement. Easements cannot exist in gross, though profits *à prendre* can.

inhibition a method of protecting minor interests in registered land.

in possession method of holding an interest in land, whereby the holder has immediate enjoyment of it.

instrument any legal document.

intestacy state of dying without leaving a valid will, so that the deceased's estate is subject to intestacy rules. Even where a person has left a will, any property for which he does not provide therein will be subject to intestacy.

inter vivos during one's lifetime.

issue descendants of any generation.

joint tenancy a form of co-ownership under which all the joint tenants own the whole property without individually owning any separate share in it. (Hence the expression, 'joint tenants own everything and yet own nothing'.) As between the joint tenants, the right of survivorship, or *jus accrescendi*, applies. Contrast joint tenancy with tenancy in common.

jus accrescendi the right of survivorship whereby, upon the death of a joint tenant, the whole of his interest devolves upon the surviving joint tenants.

laches the equitable doctrine of delay.

land obligation proposed new interest in land to replace restrictive covenants.

lapse the failure of a gift, eg where a beneficiary dies before the testator.

lease also known as a 'term of years absolute' and a 'tenancy'. Can only exist where one party (the lessee or tenant) is granted exclusive possession of land for a fixed term, usually (though not necessarily – *see* LPA 1925, s 205(xxvii)) at a rent, by the other party (the lessor or landlord). The second legal estate in land provided for by LPA 1925, s 1(1). Also the document which creates same.

lease of the reversion also known as a concurrent lease. Arises where a fee simple owner (lessor or landlord) grants a second lease of property which is already subject to a subsisting lease. Not to be confused with a reversionary lease – *see* below.

lessee tenant.

lessor landlord.

letters of administration granted to personal representatives in order that they may administer the estate of a deceased person.

licence permission, eg to do on another's land something which would otherwise amount to a trespass.

lien a form of security over land for unpaid money.

limitation **(1)** of actions. The barring of a right of action after a specified period, currently governed by the Limitation Act 1980. *See* adverse possession. **(2)** Words of. Words which delimit the estate granted – *see* LPA 1925, s 60.

limited owner one who holds an estate less than a fee simple absolute in possession.

matrimonial home right right of occupation of a non-owning spouse as against the other spouse.

merger where two or more estates or interests are fused together. To be distinguished from surrender.

mesne intermediate.

minor infant.

minor interest category of interest in registered land. Must be protected by an entry on the register by way of notice, caution, restriction or inhibition.

minority during infancy.

mortgage grant of an interest in property as security for a loan or other obligation.

mortgagee the person who lends the money and to whom the mortgage is granted.

mortgagor the person who borrows the money and the one who grants the mortgage.

nec vi, nec clam, nec precario 'without force, without secrecy, without permission' – the way in which a person must act if he or she is to be able to claim an easement or profit by prescription.

notice **(1)** a method of protecting minor interests in registered land. **(2)** Knowledge which a person has or which is attributed to him under the doctrine of notice, ie (a) actual notice – actual knowledge; (b) constructive notice – knowledge which a person would have had, had he made all necessary enquiries; (c) imputed notice – the actual and constructive notice of a person's agent, eg his solicitor. **(3)** Notice attributed to a person by virtue of the registration of a land charge in accordance with the Land Charges Act 1972. All three forms of notice to be distinguished.

notice to quit method by which a landlord or tenant may terminate a periodic tenancy.

option to purchase a right whereby the holder can require an estate owner to convey that estate to the option holder. A form of estate contract.

oral by word of mouth, not written. To be distinguished from 'verbal' (which can be either oral or written).

overreaching method by which interests in land are shifted from the land into the proceeds of sale, thereby enabling a purchaser to take the legal estate free of any equitable interests existing behind a trust of land or strict settlement, provided he pays the capital (purchase) monies to at least two trustees or a trust corporation.

overriding interest category of interest in registered land. Such interests need not be protected by registration or entry on the register (indeed, any such entry would convert them into minor interests). They are binding upon the registered proprietor and all who acquire later interests in the land. *See* LRA 2002, Scheds 1 & 3 for a complete list of overriding interests.

parcel a piece of land.

parol by word of mouth, oral.

partition method by which a piece of land is physically divided so that what was previously a single plot held by several co-owners becomes several plots, each held by a sole owner.

periodic tenancy form of tenancy whereby the tenant is in possession of the land and paying rent calculated on a periodic basis, eg weekly, monthly, quarterly, annually, to the landlord.

perpetually renewable lease one which contains a covenant by the landlord that he will from time to time renew the lease (ie grant a new one to the tenant) at the termination of the current lease. Such leases are automatically converted into a term of 2,000 years – *see* LPA 1922, s 145.

personal property property other than freehold land.

personal representatives persons authorised to administer the estate of a dead person.

(a) Executors – appointed by will. (b) *Administrators* – appointed by the court where the deceased died intestate (or where an executor is unwilling or unable to act).

personal rights those which attach only to the person, and not to the land, eg licences (other than estoppel licences).

personalty personal property.

plot piece of land.

possession the immediate right to occupation of land or receipt of rents and profits therefrom.

post-nuptial after marriage.

pre-emption, right of a right whereby the holder is entitled to first refusal of property should the owner decide to sell. A form of estate contract.

prescription method of acquiring an easement or profit *à prendre* by long user.

privity of contract the relationship between contracting parties, especially between the original landlord and tenant.

privity of estate the relationship existing between landlord and tenant, or current lessor and lessee.

probate the granting by the court of approval of a will.

profit *à prendre* the right to take something from the land of another, eg grass by grazing cattle. Can be (a) in gross – benefiting the holder of the profit only, there being no dominant tenement; or (b) appurtenant – benefiting a piece of land, a dominant tenement.

proprietary rights those which attach to the land and are thus capable of binding third parties.

puisne mortgage a legal mortgage which is not protected by a deposit of the title deeds.

pur autre vie for the life of another.

purchaser a person who acquires an estate or interest by act of the parties, though not necessarily a 'buyer', eg a person who takes under a deed of gift (a 'donee'). However, see the definition section in each statute for particular meaning, eg LPA 1925, s 205(1)(xxi).

purchaser for value one who buys.

quasi-easement a right enjoyed by the owner of land which has the potential to be an easement, if enjoyed by someone else.

realty, real property freehold land.

registered proprietor in registered land, the person registered as legal estate owner.

remainder an interest which is subject to a prior interest, eg 'to Deirdre for life, remainder to Tracy absolutely'. Interests in remainder can only exist in equity (although they can become legal when they fall into possession) – LPA 1925, s 1(3).

rentcharge the right of the holder to receive a periodic sum of money from the current owner of the land charged with it. To be distinguished from rent service, ie payments made by a tenant to his landlord under a lease.

reservation method whereby a grantor of land retains for himself an easement or profit *à prendre*.

residual interests those interests in unregistered land which, being neither registrable as land charges nor overreachable, remain subject to the doctrine of notice.

restriction method of protecting minor interests in registered land, especially beneficial interests behind a trust.

restrictive covenant a covenant which restricts the use of land in a specified way.

resulting returning to the grantor.

reversion the right remaining in a grantor who has not parted with the whole of his interest. Usually used with reference to the remaining estate of a landlord and his right, during the continuance of the lease, to receive rents and profits and to regain possession of the land at the end of the term granted. Also applies to settlements under which the fee simple owner grants an interest less than he has – for example a life interest – at the end of which the land will revert to him.

reversionary lease a lease the term of which is to begin in the future. *See* LPA 1925, s 149. To be distinguished from a lease of the reversion – see above.

rights *in personam* rights enforceable against the person only.

rights in rem rights enforceable against the land.

root of title the earliest document upon which clear title can be proved. The root must be traced back at least 15 years – LPA 1969, s 23 – unless a contrary intention appears in the contract.

seisin possession of land by a freeholder.

servient tenement land which carries the burden of some right, eg an easement or restrictive covenant.

settlement method of creating a series of successive interests. *See* SLA 1925.

severance **(1)** method of converting a joint tenancy, or the interest of a joint tenant, into a tenancy in common. Operates upon the equitable interests only – *see* LPA 1925, s 1(6). **(2)** Words of severance – express words which show an intention to create a tenancy in common, and not a joint tenancy, of the equitable interests.

socage the last surviving tenure, known today as 'freehold'.

specialty a contract by deed.

squatter a trespasser, a person wrongfully occupying land.

strict settlement method of holding successive interests prior to 1 January 1997.

sublease a lease granted by a tenant to a subtenant (the tenant becoming the subtenant's landlord).

sui juris not subject to any legal disability, eg not a minor.

surrender the transfer of an interest to the person next entitled, eg surrender of the remainder of a term by a tenant to his landlord. To be distinguished from merger.

survivorship *see jus accrescendi.*

tacking method by which a mortgagee can extend his security by adding a later loan (a further advance) to an earlier one secured by mortgage. In this way, the mortgagee can defeat later mortgagees by increasing his priority to cover the later loan.

tenancy a lease.

tenancy at sufferance where a tenant remains in possession following the termination of his lease.

tenancy at will where a tenant enjoys possession of the land with the landlord's consent, it being agreed that the tenancy can be terminated by either party giving notice to the other.

tenancy by estoppel where a landlord has, in fact, no legal title, the parties will be estopped from denying their obligations under the lease. When the landlord's title is perfected, the estoppel is 'fed' and the lease becomes a full legal lease.

tenancy in common a form of co-ownership under which each tenant in common has an identifiable (an undivided) share. The right of survivorship does not operate upon tenancies in common, therefore each tenant's share will pass, on his death, by his will or intestacy. Can only exist in regard to the equitable interests – LPA 1925, s 1(6). To be contrasted with a joint tenancy.

tenant for life the person who, in a strict settlement, holds the legal estate and enjoys all the powers of management and disposition over the settled land provided for by SLA 1925.

tenure the conditions upon which a tenant held land from his lord in the feudal system. Today only the tenure of socage remains.

term of years absolute a lease.

time immemorial beyond legal memory. Fixed as the first year of the reign of Richard I (1189).

title a person's right to property. Also evidence of such right.

transfer in registered land, the deed used to pass the legal estate from one owner to another.

trust for sale method of holding concurrent interests, prior to 1 January 1997, by which a duty to sell was imposed.

trust instrument document setting out a settlor's wishes – the terms of the trust/settlement.

trust of land method of holding successive and concurrent interests in land subject to any trust of property which consists of or includes land, by which a power to sell is vested in the trustees (who have all the powers of an absolute owner).

undivided shares in land the interests of tenants in common. Also a tenancy in common. Can only exist in equity – LPA 1925, s 1(6).

unity of seisin where the same person owns both the dominant and servient tenement.

value **(1)** at common law – money, money's worth, or a valid deed. **(2)** In equity – money, money's worth, or marriage consideration. **(3)** For the purposes of the Land Registration Act 2002, 'valuable consideration' does not include marriage consideration or a nominal consideration in money – s 132.

vested owned unconditionally, not contingent (a) in possession – with immediate right to possession, eg 'to Barry for life . . . .'; (b) in interest – with future right to possession, eg '. . . and then to Katrina absolutely'.

voluntary conveyance one granted for no valuable consideration.

volunteer one who gives no value upon taking property.

waiver abandonment of a legal right.

waste an act or omission committed by a limited owner, eg a tenant for life, which alters the land for better or for worse: (a) voluntary waste – a positive act of injury to the land; (b) ameliorating waste – a positive act which enhances the land; (c) permissive waste – an act of omission which results in injury to the land; (d) equitable waste – acts or omissions which a reasonable man would not commit in the management of his own property.

Index